CU01561784

PUBLICATIONS OF THE

ARMY RECORDS SOCIETY

VOL. 40

THE MILITARY PAPERS OF FIELD MARSHAL SIR CLAUDE AUCHINLECK, VOLUME I: 1940–42

'Lieutenant General C. J. E. Auchinleck (1884–1981), CB, CSI, DSO, OBE' by
Cyril Mount (1920–2013), based on sketches Mount made in June 1942 while
serving in the Royal Artillery, 4th Indian Division © Imperial War Museum
(Art.IWM ART LD 6056)

The Military Papers of Field Marshal Sir Claude Auchinleck, Volume I: 1940–42

edited by

Timothy Bowman

Published by

THE BOYDELL PRESS
for the
ARMY RECORDS SOCIETY
2021

© Army Records Society 2021

All Rights Reserved. Except as permitted under current legislation
no part of this work may be photocopied, stored in a retrieval system,
published, performed in public, adapted, broadcast,
transmitted, recorded or reproduced in any form or by any means,
without the prior permission of the copyright owner

First published 2021

An Army Records Society publication
published by The Boydell Press
an imprint of Boydell & Brewer Ltd
PO Box 9, Woodbridge, Suffolk IP12 3DF, UK
and of Boydell & Brewer Inc.
668 Mt Hope Avenue, Rochester, NY 14620–2731, USA
website: www.boydellandbrewer.com

ISBN 978 1 83838 770 9

A CIP catalogue record for this book is available
from the British Library

The publisher has no responsibility for the continued existence or accuracy of URLs for
external or third-party internet websites referred to in this book, and does not guarantee
that any content on such websites is, or will remain, accurate or appropriate

This publication is printed on acid-free paper

Typeset by BBR Design, Sheffield

Printed and bound in Great Britain by
TJ Books Limited, Padstow, Cornwall

MIX
Paper from
responsible sources
FSC® C013056
www.fsc.org

The Army Records Society was founded in 1984 in order to publish original records describing the development, organisation, administration and activities of the British Army from early times.

Any person wishing to become a Member of the Society should consult our website for details of the procedure. Members receive at least one volume per annum and are entitled to purchase back volumes at reduced prices.

The Council of the Army Records Society wish it to be clearly understood that they are not answerable for opinions or observations that may appear in the Society's publications. For these the responsibility rests entirely with the Editors of the several works.

The Society's website can be found at
www.armyrecordssociety.org.uk

ARMY RECORDS SOCIETY
COUNCIL FOR 2019–20

PRESIDENT
Professor Sir Michael Howard OM CH CBE MC DLitt FBA

VICE-PRESIDENTS
Field Marshal Sir John Chapple GCB CBE DL MA FSA FRSA
Professor David French BA PhD FRHistS
Professor John Gooch BA PhD FRHistS
Professor Ian Beckett BA PhD FRHistS
Lieutenant General Sir Alistair Irwin KCB CBE MA

HONORARY SECRETARY
George Hay BA PhD FRHistS

HONORARY TREASURER
Derek Blair BA MA ACMA

MEMBERSHIP SECRETARY
William Butler BA MA PhD

COUNCILLORS
Huw Bennett BSc MSc PhD FRHistS
Timothy Bowman BA PhD FRHistS (Chairman)
Colonel Patrick Crowley DL BA MA
Aimée Fox BA MA PhD
Alan Jeffreys BA MPhil
Peter Johnston BA MA PhD
Kevin Linch BA MA PhD FRHistS
Helen Parr BA MA PhD
Ismini Pells MA MPhil PhD
Nicholas Perry BA
Major General John Sutherell CB CBE DL BA
Erica Wald BA MSc PhD FRHistS
Daniel Whittingham BA MA PhD
Colonel Ray Wilkinson DMS MBA QVRM TD VR
Alexander Wilson BA MA PhD

Contents

Acknowledgements

I cannot quite remember when I was first made aware of the military career of Field Marshal Sir Claude Auchinleck. It may have been seeing his portrait in the Royal Inniskilling Fusiliers Museum in Enniskillen as a young teenager, or more probably, through hearing a Radio Ulster programme about him in a series which Richard Doherty scripted and presented in 1992 or reading Tom Fraser's piece on him in an edited collection *Nine Ulster Lives* in the Carnegie Library in Bangor, Co. Down one wet afternoon.[1] Certainly by the time I was an undergraduate at Queen's University, Belfast, I was conscious of the widespread feeling in Northern Ireland that Auchinleck was an Ulsterman who had been in some sense 'done down' by the military establishment.

This memory remained with me as I developed my academic career as a specialist on the British Army in the First World War and paramilitarism in early twentieth-century Ireland. In 2008 I was invited to become the External Examiner for the BA in Contemporary Military and International History at the University of Salford and took the opportunity of visiting Greater Manchester over the following three years to pay a number of visits to the John Rylands Library. The staff there immediately introduced me to the detailed catalogue of Auchinleck's papers and dealt with my requests over the subsequent years with unfailing courtesy and professionalism.

Finally, in 2018 I felt able to bring a full proposal to the Council of the Army Records Society, then for a volume covering 1940–45 and this was quickly accepted. I appreciate the support of the Council as this book has come to fruition. I would particularly like to thank Ian Beckett, Jonathan Fennell, David French and John Sutherell who, as Councillors

---

1   The book of the BBC Radio Ulster series was: Richard Doherty, *Irish Generals in the Second World War* (Belfast, 1993). T. G. Fraser, 'Claude Auchinleck 1884–1981: Military Leader', in Gerald O'Brien and Peter Roebuck, eds, *Nine Ulster Lives* (Belfast, 1992).

of the Society, were particularly supportive of the project and George Hay who, as Secretary, saw the book through the publication process with his customary efficiency and good humour. Initially it was hoped that a single volume covering 1940–47 would be produced. However, with the large amount of material available it has been felt appropriate to cover 1940–42 in this volume, with another volume covering Auchinleck's period as Commander in Chief, India, 1943–47 to follow in due course.

The University of Kent was a supportive environment in which to work on this project. My colleagues, especially Barbara Bombi, Philip Boobbyer, William Butler (who has since moved to The National Archives), Mark Connelly, Peter Donaldson, Mario Draper, Ben Marsh and Juliette Pattinson were particularly supportive of the project. The University was good enough to grant me research leave in the Autumn Term of 2019–20 which allowed me an extended period of time to finish selecting and photographing the documents I wanted to include. The University also paid for the support of three students under one of its 'Employability Schemes' to help with the transcription. Cameron Kemp, Charles Taylor and Adam Whitehead carried out the bulk of the work on transcribing these documents and, without them, I would have struggled to complete this book. The undergraduates on our BA Military History programme who have studied my 'Churchill's Army: The British Army in the Second World War' module provided various useful insights and questions, as did those who attended a talk on Auchinleck's military career which I presented to the student Military History Society.

The 'War, Society and Culture' seminar group at the Institute of Historical Research were kind enough to invite me to present a paper to them (as it turned out, online due to COVID restrictions) which helped me to develop some of my thoughts on Auchinleck's initial period as Commander in Chief of the Indian Army.

For the maps, I have to thank Barbara Taylor, who completed them with her customary efficiency. Gillian Northcott Liles undertook the copy-editing of the manuscript and saved me from a number of errors.

The publication of this work marks something of a new departure for the Army Records Society in that this and all future works published by the Society will be published with The Boydell Press. I would like to thank all at The Boydell Press, especially Peter Sowden, for their help in seeing this work through the production process.

Finally, as always, I'd like to thank my parents who indulged my interests in military history from an early age and provided a comfortable writing retreat at their home in rural Ulster.

Curiously, when the Auchinleck papers were deposited at the John Rylands Library, no arrangements were made about copyright and it is now unclear who the copyright holder is. The Society is, of course, prepared to make reasonable renumeration to the copyright holder if they make themselves known.

The Imperial War Museum kindly allowed the use of two portraits of Auchinleck held in their collections. R. G. Eves's posed portrait of Auchinleck in 1940, as reproduced on the front cover and Cyril Mount's portrait as reproduced in the frontispiece. Mount's portrait is based on sketches which he made in June 1942 while serving in the 4th Indian Division. I think Cyril Mount's portrait captures, very well, the pressures Auchinleck was experiencing at this critical moment in the Desert War and I am very grateful to the Estate of Cyril Mount for permission to reproduce it in this volume.

Abbreviations

AA	Anti-Aircraft [gun]
AAG	Assistant Adjutant General
ADC	Aide-de-camp
AFV	Armoured Fighting Vehicle
AG	Adjutant General
AOC	Air Office Commanding
AOC in C	Air Officer Commanding in Chief
Armd	Armoured
Arty	Artillery
AT/ATk	Anti-Tank [gun]
Bde	Brigade
BEF	British Expeditionary Force
BGS	Brigadier General Staff
Bn	Battalion
BOAC	British Overseas Airways Corporation
BSA	British Small Arms
CAS	Chief of Air Staff
CCS	Casualty Clearing Station
CGS	Chief of General Staff
CIGS	Chief of the Imperial General Staff
C in C	Commander in Chief
COS	Chiefs of Staff
CRA	Commander Royal Artillery
DAG	Deputy Adjutant General
DCGS	Deputy Chief of General Staff
DCIGS	Deputy Chief of the Imperial General Staff

Div	Division
DMI	Director of Military Intelligence
DMO	Director of Military Operations
DMOI	Director of Military Operations and Intelligence
DMT	Director of Military Training
DQMG	Deputy Quartermaster General
fd	field [guns]
FSR	Field Service Regulations
GOC	General Officer Commanding
GOC in C	General Officer Commanding in Chief
Gp	Group
GSO1	General Staff Officer, Grade 1
HMG	His Majesty's Government
IA	Indian Army
IAF	Indian Air Force
i/c	in charge of
IDC	Imperial Defence College
IMC	Indian Military College
Ind	Independent
IND/Ind	Indian
Inf	Infantry
ISF	Indian States Forces
L of C	Lines of Communication
LDV	Local Defence Volunteers
LMG	Light Machine Gun
LRDG	Long Range Desert Group
ME	Middle East
MGA	Major General Administration
MT	Motor Transport
NWF	North Western Frontier
NZ	New Zealand
pdr	pounder
PSO	Personnel Selection Officer

QMG	Quartermaster General
RA	Royal Artillery
RAC	Royal Armoured Corps
RAOC	Royal Army Ordnance Corps
RE	Royal Engineers
Regt	Regiment
RFA	Royal Field Artillery
RHA	Royal Horse Artillery
RMA	Royal Military Academy, Woolwich
RMC	Royal Military College, Sandhurst
rpt	repeat
RTR	Royal Tank Regiment
SA	South African
SHAEF	Supreme Headquarters Allied Expeditionary Force
Sigint	Signals Intelligence
TLC	Tank Landing Craft
ULTRA	Code name applied to high level intelligence based on decrypting Axis signals
VCIGS	Vice Chief of the Imperial General Staff

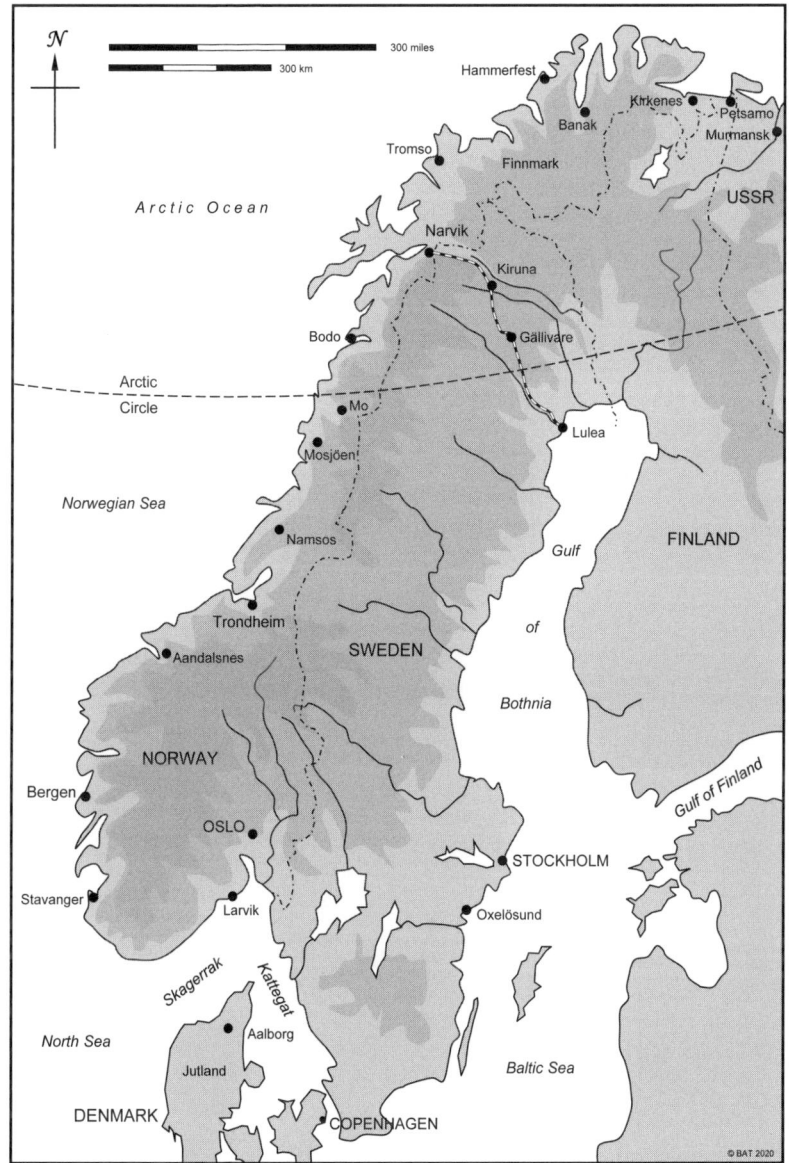

Map 1. Norway, 1940

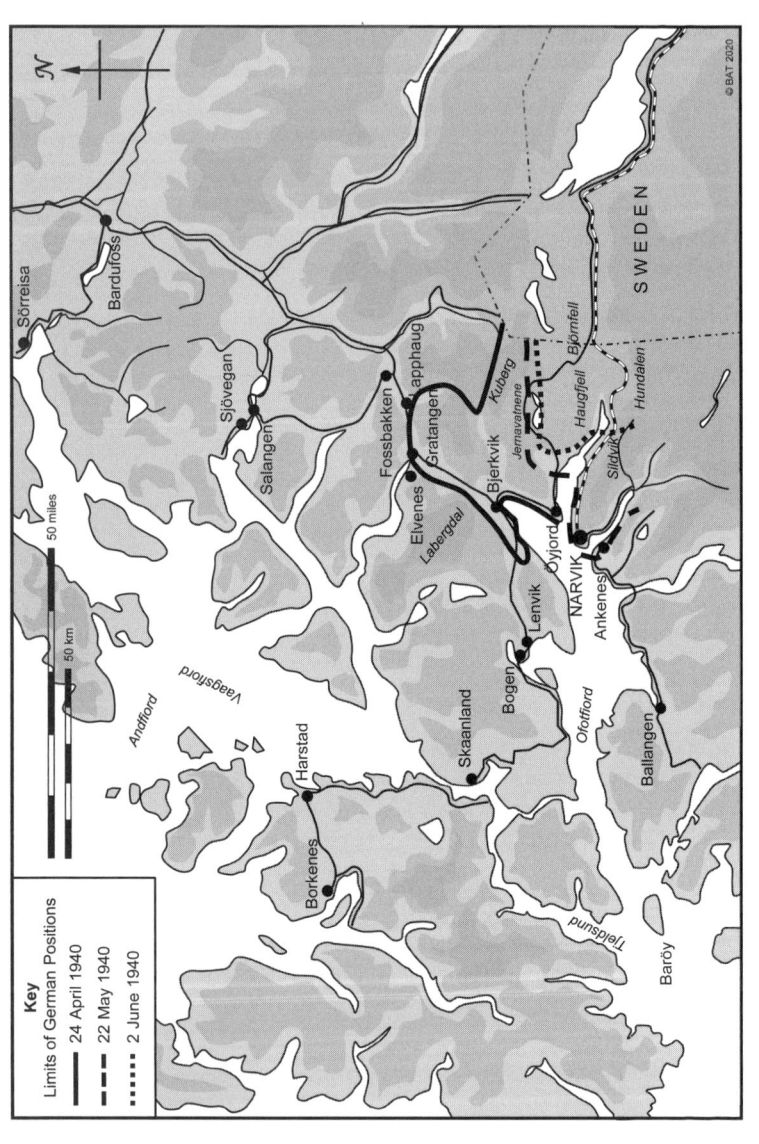

Map 2. Narvik, 1940

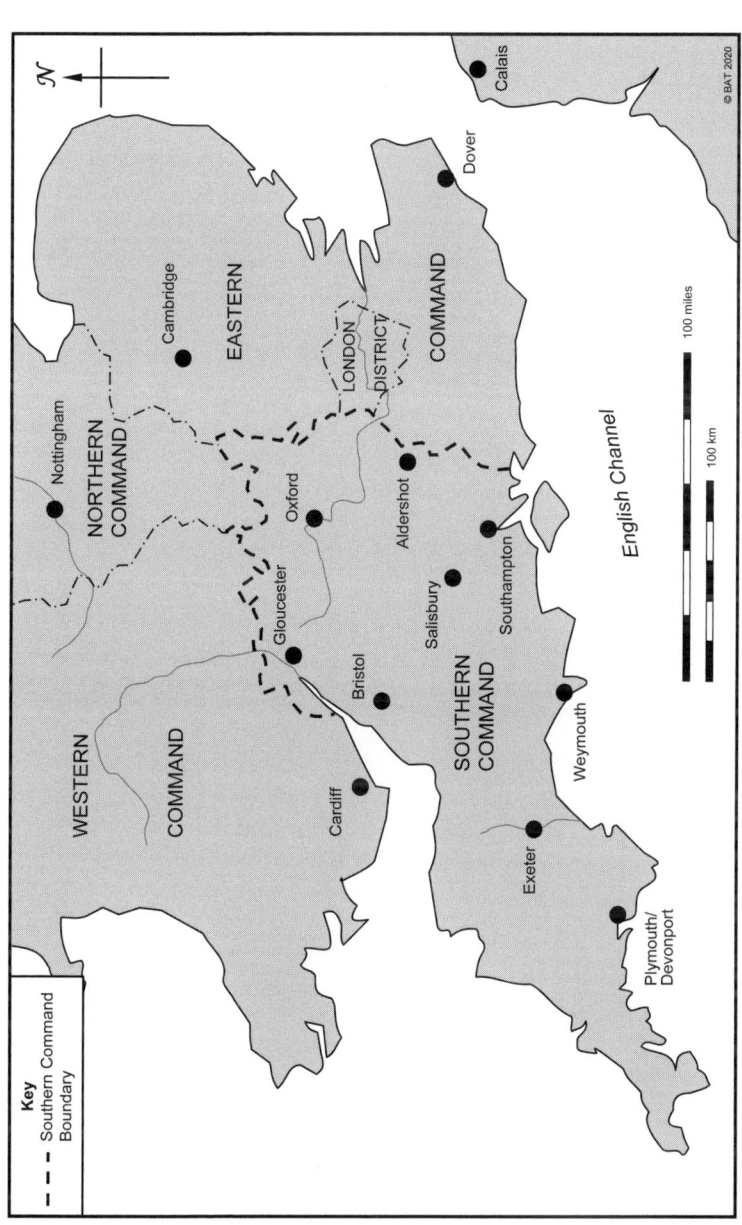

Map 3. Army Command Areas, England, 1940

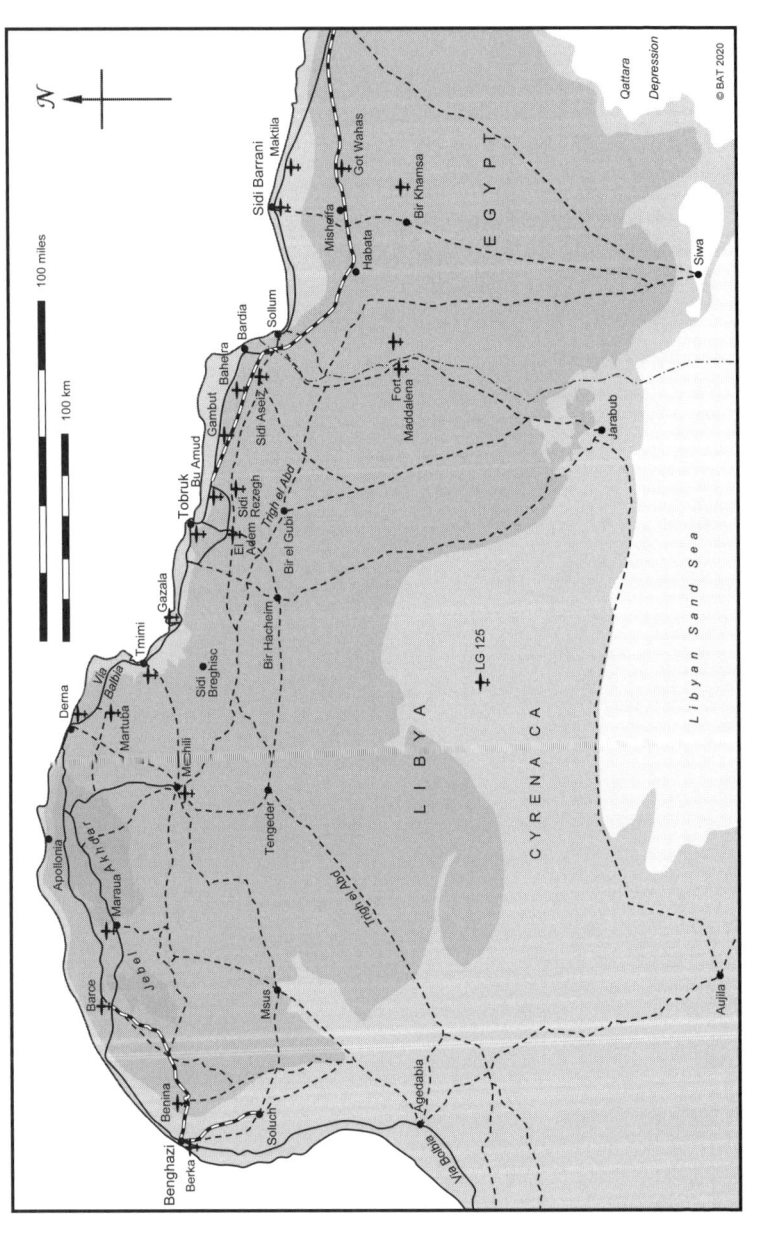

Map 4. The Western Desert (west), 1941

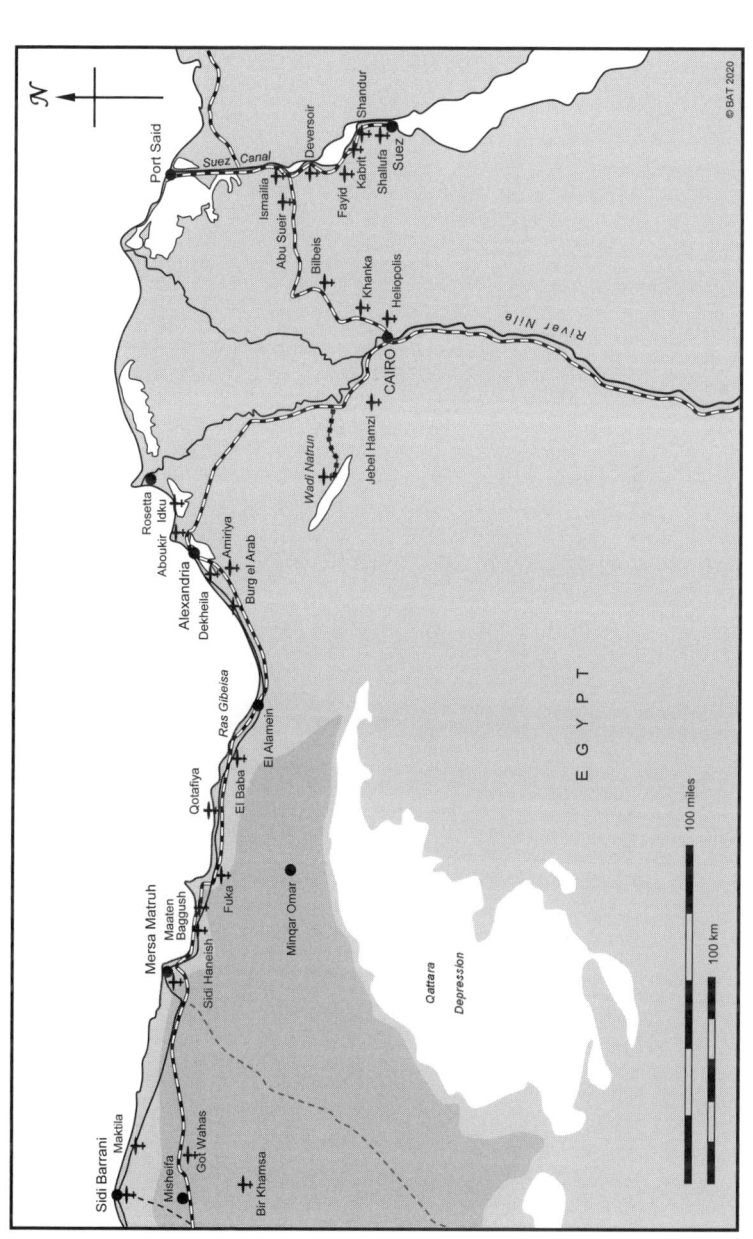

Map 5. The Western Desert (east), 1941

Introduction

Claude John Eyre Auchinleck was born in Aldershot on 21 June 1884.[1] He was the eldest son of Colonel John Claude Alexander Auchinleck, Royal Horse Artillery and Mary Eleanor, daughter of John Eyre. Claude Auchinleck, like many of the senior officers in the British army in the Second World War, most notably, Field Marshals Harold Alexander, Alan Brooke, John Dill and Bernard Montgomery, was from an Anglo-Irish gentry background, though the family's origins were in the village of Auchinleck in Ayrshire. Given the number of Anglo-Irish officers who reached high rank in the British army, there is a tendency to see the Anglo-Irish officer as over-represented. H. J. Hanham noted that, 'In terms of officers per head the Church of Ireland … was presumably the most army-orientated denomination in the British Isles.'[2] Correlli Barnett believed that the Anglo-Irish were a British version of the 'Prussian Junker class'.[3] However, Nick Perry's careful study of this issue suggests that the Anglo-Irish gentry were as likely to be commissioned into the army as Scots gentry (40 per cent of male gentry of military age), whereas the English and Welsh figure stood at 30 per cent.[4]

---

1   Auchinleck is the subject of five biographies and, unless otherwise noted, these have been drawn on in writing this introduction: John Connell, *Auchinleck: A Biography of Field Marshal Sir Claude Auchinleck* (London, 1959), Alexander Greenwood, *Field Marshal Auchinleck* (Brockerscliffe, 1990), Evan McGilvray, *Field Marshal Claude Auchinleck* (Barnsley, 2020), Roger Parkinson, *The Auk: Auchinleck, Victor at Alamein* (London, 1977) and Philip Warner, *Auchinleck: The Lonely Soldier* (London, 1981).

2   H. J. Hanham, 'Religion and Nationality in the Mid-Victorian Army' in *War and Society: Historical essays in honour and memory of J. R. Western 1928–1971*, ed. M. R. D. Foot (London, 1973), p. 162.

3   Correlli Barnett, *Britain and Her Army, 1509–1970: A Military, Political and Social Survey* (London, 1970), pp. 314–15.

4   Nicholas Perry, 'The Irish Landed Class and the British Army, 1850–1950', *War in History*, 18: 3 (2011), 304–32 and *Major General Oliver Nugent and the Ulster Division 1915–1918* (Stroud, 2007), pp. 1–4. Nicholas Perry is currently

Claude Auchinleck himself, when relinquishing the colonelcy of the Royal Inniskilling Fusiliers, which he held between 1941 and 1947, identified his Irish origins by stating, 'My forefathers lived in Enniskillen and Fermanagh for very many years and this makes me all the prouder to have belonged to the regiment.'[5] In fact Auchinleck's father had equally firm roots in Counties Tyrone and Wexford and his mother's family came from Galway.[6] Auchinleck's 'Irishness' can be questioned by the fact that the *Irish Times*, which had been the newspaper of the Anglo-Irish establishment, though it had moved far away from these origins by 1981, did not carry a full length obituary of him and the recently published *Dictionary of Irish Biography* does not devote an entry to him. T. G. Fraser's overstates the contrary interpretation by noting that, 'Two things stand out from Auchinleck's background and early life: his sense of identity as an Ulsterman and his commitment to India.'[7] However, it is clear that Auchinleck spent most of his school holidays at Crevenagh House, near Omagh, Co. Tyrone and visiting the house in August 1946 his private secretary, Shahid Hamid, remembered Auchinleck saying, 'This is where I belong and that is why I am glad to be back here again to see you all.'[8]

Claude Auchinleck's father, John, had a distinguished military career, serving in the Indian Mutiny, Second Afghan War and Third Burma War, and reaching the rank of Colonel. Claude Auchinleck was, therefore born into what could be identified as a 'military family' and was expected to follow in its traditions, which he did willingly; his younger brother, Armar Leslie, also became a soldier.[9] Claude Auchinleck spent his

---

undertaking research for a PhD thesis at the University of Kent entitled, 'The Irish landed class and the regular officer corps of the British army, 1775–1903: a distinctive Irish contribution?'

5 Frank Fox, *The Royal Inniskilling Fusiliers in the Second World War, 1939–45* (Aldershot, 1951), p. 143. The Regimental Recruiting District of the Royal Inniskilling Fusiliers had, historically, consisted of the Counties of Donegal, Fermanagh, Londonderry and Tyrone. The partition of Ireland in 1920 meant that the recruiting district was then Counties Fermanagh, Londonderry and Tyrone, all part of Northern Ireland, while Donegal was one of the historic Ulster counties situated in the Irish Free State.

6 Connell, *Auchinleck*, pp. 5–6.

7 Fraser, 'Claude Auchinleck 1884–1981: Military Leader' in *Nine Ulster Lives*, ed. O'Brien and Roebuck, p. 36.

8 Shahid Hamid, *Disastrous Twilight: A personal record of the partition of India* (London, 1986), p. 96.

9 Armar Leslie Auchinleck joined the 4th Cameronians (Scottish Rifles) in 1908 as a second lieutenant with the intention of obtaining a regular commission. However, he lost the sight in his right eye in a sporting injury, which prevented

early years in Cheshunt in Hertfordshire and, when his father retired from the army in 1890, the family moved to Langstone near Havant in Hampshire. In December 1892 Colonel John Auchinleck died from the effects of pernicious anaemia contracted in Burma.

Mary Auchinleck and her young family were left in genteel poverty by the death of her husband. She quickly moved to a smaller house in Warblington, Hampshire, in an attempt to economise. Claude Auchinleck was then sent to a Dame-school in Southsea and then Crowthorne, a preparatory school, in 1894. He entered Wellington College in 1896 as a Foundationer. Wellington College, established in memory of the First Duke in 1859, had a scheme for the sons of officers who had died within five years of being on full or half pay, and whose family could prove financial hardship, which meant that they could be educated at a much-reduced fee of £10 p.a. which included all school fees, food and board. It was only because of this scheme that Claude Auchinleck could enjoy a public school education and he remained grateful to his old school in later years, opening the War Memorial reading room and heading up an appeal launched in 1949 so that the number of Foundationers could be increased allowing for the sons of deceased officers of the Royal Navy, Royal Marines and RAF to take advantage of the scheme.[10]

Auchinleck was not seen as an outstanding pupil at Wellington, but he was above average in history, English, geography and divinity, and was given some responsibility by being appointed a Dormitory Prefect. His weakness in mathematics meant that he could not think of following his father into the Royal Artillery, through the very competitive examination for the Royal Military Academy, Woolwich. In any case, family finances, meant that Auchinleck's only route to a military career as a commissioned officer would be in the Indian Army, where officers could live on their pay. Even in an unfashionable county regiment of the British army, young officers would be expected to have a private income of at least £100 p.a. to cover mess bills, uniforms, horses, band subscriptions, etc.[11]

---

him transferring to the regular army. He entered the Colonial Civil Service and was posted to Northern Nigeria. On leave on the outbreak of war he was recalled to his battalion and killed in action on the Somme on 17 September 1916, as a Captain, attached to 123rd Company, Machine Gun Corps.

10 David Newsome, *A History of Wellington College, 1859–1959* (London, 1959), pp. 30–32 and 376–80.

11 Timothy Bowman and Mark Connelly, *The Edwardian Army: Recruiting, training and deploying the British Army, 1902–1914* (Oxford, 2012), pp. 10–12.

In the entrance examination for the Royal Military College, Sandhurst, John Connell suggested that Auchinleck was placed 45th, which would then have meant that he took the last competitive place available for a commission in the Indian Army; contributing to a rather romantic tale of a cadet just scraping into the Indian Army but rising to become its Commander in Chief.[12] Oddly, when Auchinleck entered the RMC, candidates for the Indian Army were selected based on where they were placed in the entrance examination, rather than on their final marks at the College; a system which was to change shortly after he left. Therefore his placing in *The London Gazette*, announcing his appointment to the Unattached List, Indian Army, along with those of the other Gentleman Cadets from his cohort at Sandhurst, which placed him thirty-three out of forty-seven officers is an accurate statement of where he was placed in the entrance examination.[13] Auchinleck's performance in the entrance examination may not seem very impressive, but it should be remembered that he was at almost the youngest age possible to sit the entrance examination when he took it and that he managed to reach this position without relying on the expensive crammers which many Sandhurst and Woolwich cadets employed. Auchinleck entered the RMC in January 1902, five months short of his eighteenth birthday.

The Sandhurst course then lasted for only a year and Auchinleck does not seem to have enjoyed his time there. He appears to have passed out 82nd and seems to have regarded Sandhurst merely as a rite of passage.[14] Of course, with limited private means, many of the activities indulged in by gentlemen cadets at the RMC must have been closed to him. But 1902 was an unfortunate year in the history of the College with a number of cases of incendiarism and the rustication of a large number of blameless cadets, which led to questions in parliament. Following a public campaign led by Winston Churchill and Lord Hugh Cecil, most of the cadets were reinstated, without any loss of seniority, following an enquiry by Field Marshal Lord Roberts, the Commander in Chief.[15] It is unclear if Auchinleck was one of those rusticated or not; if he was, the

---

12 Connell, *Auchinleck*, p. 11; this was followed by Parkinson, *The Auk*, p. 12.

13 *The London Gazette*, 20 January 1903, p. 390. *The Times*, 4 January 1902, p. 10 noted Auchinleck as placed 40 out of 125 RMC cadets destined for the infantry.

14 Connell merely notes that Auchinleck, 'was dismayed when he saw how many places he had dropped in the passing out list', Connell, *Auchinleck*, p. 12.

15 *The Times*, 5 July 1902, p. 9; 7 July 1902, p. 12; 8 July 1902, pp. 6 and 11 and 26 July 1902, p. 8.

threatened additional expense of an extra term's fees would have been a major problem for him.

In March 1903 the eighteen-year-old Second Lieutenant Claude Auchinleck boarded the P&O liner, *Britannia*, at Tilbury en route for India. On arrival in India, Auchinleck, as was normal for officers destined for the Indian Army who were initially commissioned on to the unattached list, was sent to a British army battalion, the 2nd King's Shropshire Light Infantry, for further training before joining the Indian Army proper. While with 2nd King's Shropshire Light Infantry Auchinleck was careful with his finances, but the lavish mess dinners and extensive guest lists meant that Auchinleck was living beyond his means. Indeed, he was to write to his mother to ask her for £10 to settle his outstanding mess bills, noting that, 'Mess-bills are high, and this is an expensive regiment ... The messing alone comes to Rs90 odd, and everyone has to pay that. Then if you only drink sodas and lemonades, the drink bill comes to about Rs10 more and guests and Club Bill, subscriptions, etc. bring it up to Rs150 to Rs180, and pay is Rs215, so it does not leave much, but once I am square I can manage.' This financial embarrassment remained a painful memory for Auchinleck over sixty years later.[16]

Auchinleck appears to have had a choice of regiments. Captain W. D. Villiers-Stuart, the adjutant of the 1/5th Gurkha Rifles (Frontier Force), who had been told by Lieutenant Colonel James Stewart CO of the 2/5th Gurkha Rifles (Frontier Force) to look out for Auchinleck, met him on board the *Britannia* and, on the long voyage to India, formed a very favourable opinion.[17] Stewart certainly seems to have applied for Auchinleck to be posted to his regiment, though a vacancy there may not have been immediately available, so, for reasons which are unclear, Auchinleck opted for the 62nd Punjabis.[18] The commanding officer of this regiment was then Colonel Rainey Robinson, an Ulsterman from Co. Down, who had just transferred from the 12th Burma Infantry, so Anglo-Irish networks may have been important. It may, again, have been a matter of finance, with Gurkha uniforms, designed in the style of the British rifle regiments, being more expensive than the standard uniform worn by other Indian Army infantry regiments.

---

16 Connell, *Auchinleck*, pp. 19–20 citing a letter sent from Auchinleck to his mother on 16 September 1903 and Parkinson, *The Auk*, p. 14 citing an interview with Auchinleck.

17 Connell, *Auchinleck*, p. 16, citing a letter he had received from the then Brigadier General W. D. Villiers-Stuart.

18 Connell, *Auchinleck*, pp. 24–25.

Auchinleck joined the 62nd Punjabis in April 1904. This regiment had originally been formed in 1759 as the 2nd Madras Infantry and was reorganised in October 1903, as part of Lord Kitchener's reorganisation of the Indian Army.[19] Only three British officers transferred from the old 2nd Madras Infantry to the new regiment and men were absorbed from a number of other units, including the recently disbanded Hong Kong Regiment of Punjabi Musulmans.[20] Following the martial races theories, evident in the Indian Army then, the 62nd Punjabis recruited amongst Sikh, Punjabi and Rajput communities.[21]

When Auchinleck joined the 62nd Punjabis they were based in Fyzabad. This was a 'regulation pattern' station, of brigade strength, where the 62nd Punjabis were in garrison with an Indian cavalry regiment, a British infantry battalion, another Indian infantry battalion and a battery of the RFA. In the winter months the brigade attended training camps. In 1906 the regiment, now deemed to be reformed and properly trained, was ordered up to the frontier, with half based in the Tibet–Sikkim area and half in Assam. The 62nd Punjabi, like most Indian Army regiments, had no more than ten British officers serving with it at any one time, which meant that junior officers were given considerably more responsibility than their counterparts in the British army. Auchinleck was in command of a detachment of about 100 men located in the isolated region of Gyantse, about 200 miles inside Tibet, with only a single telegraph wire connecting him to regimental headquarters; his first independent command and at the age of 23. The frontier was quiet during this posting but Auchinleck became accustomed to acting on his own authority and seems to have impressed his superiors as in 1907 he was transferred to command a larger detachment in Sikkim.

---

19 A further major reorganisation of the Indian Army in 1922 saw this regiment retitled as the 1st/1st Punjab Regiment, with the 66th, 76th and 82nd Punjabis becoming the 2nd/1st, 3rd/1st and 4th/1st respectively.

20 Connell, *Auchinleck*, p. 24.

21 On the concept and development of 'martial races' recruitment in the Indian Army see Tarak Barkawi, *Soldiers of Empire: Indian and British Armies in World War II* (Cambridge, 2017), pp. 17–48; David Omissi, *The Sepoy and the Raj: The Indian Army, 1860–1940* (Basingstoke, 1994), pp. 1–76; Gavin Rand and K. A. Wagner, 'Recruiting the "martial races": identities and military service in colonial India', *Patterns of Prejudice*, 46: 3–4 (2012), pp. 232–54; Kaushik Roy, *Brown Warriors of the Raj: Recruitment & the Mechanics of Command in the Sepoy Army, 1859–1913* (New Delhi, 2008), pp. 80–144 and Heather Streets, *Martial races: The military, race and masculinity in British imperial culture, 1857–1914* (Manchester, 2004), pp. 87–190.

In 1908 the regiment was withdrawn from the frontier and sent to Benares, where it would remain until the outbreak of the First World War. Auchinleck suffered severely from diphtheria in 1908, as a result of which he went on his first home leave in six years. When he returned to India he had three uneventful years as adjutant of his regiment. In the Indian Army of that time recruits were sent directly to their regiments, and Auchinleck had particular charge of them, overseeing both recruiting and training. He had another home leave in 1912 when he failed in an attempt to get seconded to the Spanish Army, then engaged in operations in Morocco, but was seconded to the 2nd Royal Inniskilling Fusiliers, in which his cousin, Daniel Auchinleck, was then serving as a captain. Auchinleck witnessed the large-scale manoeuvres held in East Anglia but was not that impressed with what he saw of the British army, believing the manoeuvres to have been almost useless as the units taking part were at less than half their war strength. When he returned to India, Auchinleck was employed as an assistant recruiting officer in the Northern Punjab, a post which appears to have given him a real insight into the lives of Indian soldiers and the army pensioners who helped to identify potential recruits from their local communities.

On 28 October 1914 the 62nd Punjabis, as part of the third Indian Army contingent earmarked for France and Belgium, sailed from Bombay on board SS *Glen Etive* and SS *Elysia* destined for France to reinforce the Indian Corps. While the 62nd Punjabis were at sea, the Ottoman Empire entered the war, on 29 October, by bombarding the Russian ports of Odessa, Sevastopol and Theodosia on the Black Sea Coast. The Bombay troop convoy was therefore diverted to Port Said, anchoring there on the 16 November 1914 and the 62nd Punjabis moved to Ismailia to defend the Timsah–Bitter Lake section of the Suez Canal, against an expected Turkish advance.

The 62nd Punjabis came under attack from Turkish forces at 3.30am on 3 February 1915, as a Turkish force of about 22,000 men, under the command of Djemal Pasha, tried to capture the Suez Canal. At this time Auchinleck was commanding the battalion machine guns: two Maxim guns, placed in a forward redoubt on the eastern side of the Canal. Bitter fighting continued through 3 February and into the morning of 4 February, at which stage the Turkish forces withdrew. Enemy casualties totalled about 2,000 along the Canal front; British and Indian casualties were much less; the 62nd Punjabis suffered nine dead and eighteen wounded.[22]

---

22 Parkinson, *The Auk*, p. 18.

After this attempt to force a crossing over the Canal, the Turks made no new effort to invade metropolitan Egypt and the 62nd Punjabis were involved in patrol activity for the next five months.

At short notice, on 12 July 1915, the 62nd Punjabis were moved to Aden, along with the 28th (Punjab Frontier Force) Brigade, with the intention of forcing Turkish troops to leave Sheikh Othman. This task was successfully completed on the 21 July, with the regiment spending the rest of 1915 in Aden; regarded as one of the worst postings in the British Empire due to the searing heat and lack of fresh water.

In late December 1915 the 62nd Punjabis were sent to Basra, to join the relief force, assembled under the command of Lieutenant General Sir Fenton Aylmer, to relieve Kut, where 10,000 British and Indian troops under the command of Major General Charles Townshend had been besieged since 7 December.[23] Auchinleck and his regiment were embarked on paddle steamers for the journey up the Tigris in the first week of 1916. However, the attempt to break through to Kut failed dismally on 6 January, while the 62nd Punjabis were still downstream. On 7 January the regiment arrived at Hissah and were immediately ordered to join the force attacking Sheikh Saad, five miles south of Kut. Sheikh Saad was captured on 8 January, with the Turks falling back to stronger positions, following this the 62nd Punjabis were moved to the left bank of the Tigris to join the 35th Infantry Brigade.

A renewed advance was ordered by Lieutenant General Aylmer for the night of 12–13 January 1916 with the 62nd Punjabis, still part of 35th Brigade, acting as part of the reserve. However, by the afternoon of 13 January the British forces had been checked, with over 1,100 British and Indian troops killed. Immediately following this, the 62nd Punjabis were moved to the 9th Brigade, part of the newly arrived 3rd Indian Division. On 15 January Lieutenant General Sir Percy Lake replaced General Sir John Nixon as Army Commander in Mesopotamia and ordered a breakthrough to Kut, at all costs. Aylmer's latest plan to relieve Kut relied on the 9th Brigade moving across the Tigris to join a renewed offensive on the right bank. However, when the 62nd Punjabis reached the crossing point on 17 January, they found that the pontoon bridge had been washed away in floods. The decision was then made to use the battalion in an attack on Hanna.

---

23 A fine modern study of the Mesopotamian campaigns is Charles Townshend, *When God made hell: the British invasion of Mesopotamia and the creation of Iraq, 1914–1921* (London, 2010).

Bad weather had prevented an aerial reconnaissance of the enemy positions at Hanna and these proved to be much stronger than had been expected. The 62nd Punjabis attacked at 7.45am on 21 January 1916, with the rest of their brigade, and immediately met sustained Turkish fire. At 7.55am the British artillery which, in any case, had no heavy guns, lifted to the Turkish second line, before it had made much impression on the Turkish front line. Heavy rain, turning the ground into a quagmire, made it even more difficult for the battalion to advance. By mid-afternoon the 62nd Punjabis had advanced to within about 250 yards of the Turkish line, but a further advance was impossible, given both fierce Turkish fire and the danger that the battalion would become cut off from its brigade. Major General G. J. Younghusband issued orders for a withdrawal at 3.30pm, but the 62nd Punjabis did not receive these until after nightfall. Auchinleck, in command of a Double Company did not receive the order to withdrawal until about 3am on 22 January. Later that morning, the 62nd Punjabis was reorganised with the senior surviving officer, Major C. H. B. Wright, taking command and Auchinleck appointed as acting adjutant. Casualties in the regiment totalled 372 men; 30 killed, 327 wounded and 15 missing and the losses were so heavy that it was reorganised into just two companies, rather than the normal four. Auchinleck was to remember, 'This costly frontal attack was a fatal mistake. Instead of trying to outflank, the infantry was pushed in under what was called an artillery barrage, and of course the Turks were heavily entrenched, machine guns and all that sort of thing, and we were just murdered … Absolute murder. Just stupidity on the part of the GOC-in-C.'[24]

Following this engagement, Aylmer claimed that his relief force, having taken heavy casualties in action and through disease, could not manage to reach Kut, unless reinforced. The 62nd Punjabis therefore remained on entrenching and outpost duties until 14 February, when they were attached to the 36th Brigade, in reserve. A renewed attempt was made to relieve Kut in March 1916 and on the night of 7–8 March the 62nd Punjabis, now under the command of Lieutenant Colonel H. H. Harrington (recently transferred from the 84th Punjabis) prepared, with the rest of the 36th Brigade, to attack trenches about two and a half miles south-east of the main Dujaila redoubt. Delays caused during the night led to the attack being delayed; originally planned as a dawn attack, British artillery did not open fire on Turkish positions until 8.45am

---

24 Parkinson, *The Auk*, p. 22, citing an interview with Auchinleck.

with a frontal attack by the infantry commencing at 9.45am. The 62nd Punjabis managed to seize their initial objective by 11.30am; another attack began at 2pm when the regiment advanced to within two hundred yards of the main Turkish fortifications. In this action the 62nd Punjabis was reduced to just 12 officers and 235 other ranks. Captain Auchinleck took temporary command when Lieutenant Colonel Harrington was severely wounded, rallying the regiment to the rear of the firing line. Auchinleck later reflected on this action, 'It was absolutely flat and the battalions which were advancing were just mowed down. I was only a regimental officer but it was quite obvious that this frontal attack business, under what was supposed to be an artillery barrage but which was nothing like heavy enough – there weren't enough guns – was quite hopeless. Very bad generalship. Terrible.'[25]

Following this action, Aylmer ordered a general withdrawal to Hanna and the 62nd Punjabis arrived at their bivouacs at 11am on the 9 March. Shortly after this Lieutenant General Sir George Gorringe replaced Aylmer and a series of fruitless attacks were launched by British and Indian troops; though not the 62nd Punjabis, over the following six weeks. On 29 April 1916, the garrison at Kut surrendered to the Turks; the siege and attempted relief having caused 30,000 British and Indian casualties. Over the course of the relief operations, the 62nd Punjabis alone lost 560 men, dead and wounded. The infamous death march, forced upon the POWs captured at Kut, saw the deaths of 4,250 of the 11,800 men taken prisoner.

The 62nd Punjabis were left to absorb reinforcements during the rest of the spring and summer of 1916. Conditions were poor, with high temperatures, little water, as the Tigris was then heavily polluted with decomposing bodies, and dense clouds of flies infecting all available food stocks. Disease was rife amongst the troops with cholera, dysentery and scurvy; in August 1916 alone the 62nd Punjabis had a sick roll of 194 men. During this period Auchinleck was allowed two periods of leave. First, for ten days in June at Amara a hundred miles downstream, where rations were more plentiful and more varied than at the front. Then for a month's leave in India, starting in August. Auchinleck visited Karachi and Simla, but his respite was marred by news of the death of his younger brother, killed in action on the Somme.

Auchinleck returned to Mesopotamia to find many changes. The 62nd Punjabis had been brought back up to strength with fresh recruits and

---

25 Parkinson, *The Auk*, pp. 24–25, citing an interview with Auchinleck.

a new commanding officer, Lieutenant Colonel G. M. Morris had been appointed. The 62nd Punjabis were still in the 36th Brigade, but this had now been incorporated into the 14th Division. General Sir Frederick Maude had arrived as the new operational commander and had brought renewed dynamism to the campaign, centred on reorganising the logistical support available.[26] Auchinleck was clearly impressed by the rapid progress made by Maude and later commented, 'The army was alive again.'[27]

Maude, having taken time to establish proper logistics, planned a new offensive, to recapture Kut, which commenced on 13 December 1916. The 14th Division, of which the 62nd Punjabis were a part, was held in reserve in the initial phases of this campaign. The 62nd Punjabis went into action on 1 February 1917, attacking Turkish forces in a narrow area where the Shatt el Hai joined the Tigris. The Turks maintained a strong defence and in three days the 62nd Punjabis lost 193 men, including two British officers killed and three wounded. The commanding officer, Lieutenant Colonel Morris, protested at orders for the regiment to be removed from the frontline and, in response, Maude sent him a message on 4 February, 'How much I admire not only your excellent work yesterday but also the splendid spirit which has prompted you to ask to be allowed the carry on instead of being relieved.'[28] Four days later, Auchinleck took command of the 62nd Punjabis, when Colonel Morris assumed command of 36th Brigade. On 10 February the regiment took the last remaining Turkish position on the south bank of the Tigris.

An advance guard, the 1/9th Gurkha Rifles, was ferried across the Tigris on the morning of 23 February 1917 and succeeded in holding off a Turkish counter-attack while a pontoon bridge was constructed. Auchinleck led the 62nd Punjabis across at nightfall and they relieved the Gurkhas. On the night of 23–24 February the 62nd Punjabis occupied and extended hastily constructed trenches. On the morning of 24 February they, with other battalions of the 36th Brigade (the 1/4th Hampshire Regiment and 82nd Punjabis), were committed to a frontal assault. However, Auchinleck, as acting CO, had given considerable thought to this problem and ordered the battalion to advance in sections to avoid casualties. He later explained, 'The ordinary old advance was a sort of extended order, a long line of men. We advanced that day in sections in

---

26 Andrew Syk, ed., The military papers of Lieutenant General Frederick Stanley Maude, 1914–17 (Stroud, 2012).

27 Parkinson, *The Auk*, p. 26, apparently from an interview with Auchinleck.

28 Connell, *Auchinleck*, pp. 44–45.

single file, five men one behind the other, leaving plenty of gaps ... A formation like that, with the section commander leading, ensured much more control than if the men were extended.' Auchinleck remembered that his men, 'were very steady' in the successful advance and the 62nd Punjabis reached their objective with eight killed and fifty-eight wounded, as opposed to the 82nd Punjabis who had a casualty rate of 50 per cent.[29] By 25 February Turkish forces had abandoned Kut and were in full retreat, with Maude's force now advancing on Baghdad. Baghdad was captured, with little opposition, on 11 March 1917, marking the end of Maude's campaign.

On 13 March, Auchinleck relinquished his temporary command of the 62nd Punjabis to Colonel Morris. In the summer of 1917 Auchinleck moved to 52nd Brigade, Indian Army, to take up the post of Brigade Major and early in 1918 he moved with them to the Daur-Tikrit district, north of Baghdad. John Connell believed that this posting signified that Auchinleck 'had been noticed as an officer of promise and meritorious achievement, to be singled out for promotion'.[30] However, the move from Acting CO to Brigade Major (a post normally filled by a substantive captain in the British army) can hardly be seen as a promotion. Auchinleck spent a leave period in Ceylon staying with his sister, Cherry, who now married to a tea planter living in the hill country below Nuwara Eliya, over the summer of 1918 and returned for the final stages of the Mesopotamian campaign in the Kurdistan mountains.

During his service in the First World War, Auchinleck had gained some experience of command, as an acting battalion CO and of staff work, as a Brigade Major. He had also developed his own thoughts about minor tactics. During the Mesopotamian campaign he had seen the importance of developing good logistics and the need for a commander to look after the needs of the men under his command. He had also seen some of the problems with divided command, with Aylmer, as operational commander, being overruled by Lake, the theatre commander which had caused confusion.[31]

At the end of the First World War, Auchinleck remained in the Middle East. He was appointed GSO2 with the division garrisoning Mosul and in August 1919 he was promoted to GSO1 and transferred to a division

---

29 Parkinson, *The Auk*, p. 27 based on an interview with Auchinleck.
30 Connell, *Auchinleck*, p. 47.
31 On Auchinleck's experiences in the First World War see TNA, WO95/5178/1 and 2, war diary of the 62nd Punjabis 1915–18.

pacifying the mountains of Kurdistan. When he left the Middle East, at the end of 1919, he received a glowing recommendation from his GOC, General 'Snowball' Fraser, 'I wish to mention specially Major Auchinleck, DSO, OBE, my Chief Staff Officer, who has borne the whole burden of "G" work on his own back, and has proved himself a tower of strength. He has been most helpful to all my units as well as to myself, and the success of the operations is largely due to his vigorous personality, to his suggestive mind and to his professional ability.'[32]

Auchinleck sailed for India as a newly promoted brevet Lieutenant Colonel to take up a place at the Staff College in Quetta. This establishment had been created by Lord Kitchener, when C in C India, as an equivalent to the Staff College at Camberley. Auchinleck always viewed his education at Quetta as the equal of that at Camberley. However, had he attended Camberley he would have mixed with many of those who were later to become senior officers in the Second World War and this would have given him a greater insight into the subordinates available when he was in command in the Middle East in 1941–42.

In late 1920 Auchinleck enjoyed his first home leave since 1912. He had saved a lot of his pay during the war and decided to take his mother and unmarried sister, Ruth, for a holiday at Hyères in the south of France. There he met Jessie Stewart, fifteen years his junior. They were married in 1921 and sailed together for India at the end of Auchinleck's leave. It was, unfortunately, not to be a happy marriage, ending in divorce in December 1945.

Auchinleck's next posting was to Simla, the Indian Army HQ 150 miles north of Delhi, almost in the Kashmir foothills. There Auchinleck spent four years as Deputy Assistant Quartermaster General, working directly under General Sir George MacMunn, the Quartermaster General. Auchinleck quickly established a good working relationship with both MacMunn and with Hastings 'Pug' Ismay, who arrived in early 1923 as another Deputy Assistant Quartermaster General, working alongside Auchinleck. This relationship was to become very important when Ismay became Chief of Staff to Winston Churchill, in his capacity as Minister of Defence, between 1940 and 1945. Ismay was later to write of Auchinleck that he was 'a most impressive figure: dignified, commanding, and apparently self-confident. Only those who knew him

---

32   Connell, *Auchinleck*, p. 48.

well realized that he was shy and sensitive'.[33] Auchinleck was later to say that he regarded Ismay as, 'a very great friend of mine'.[34]

Auchinleck returned to his regiment, which under the army reforms of 1922 had been redesignated as the 1st/1st Punjab Regiment in 1923, as second in command. The 1st/1st Punjab Regiment was then based in Peshawar, only thirty miles from the Khyber Pass. The North-West Frontier was quiet during this period, though in March 1926 the regiment had to travel 180 miles through the mountains to settle a boundary dispute between the Wazirs and Mahsuds. During his period as second in command, Auchinleck was seconded to act as GSO2 to the district commander, General Sir Robert Cassels, who he had first met in 1917 when Cassels was GSOI of 14th Division. In this role Auchinleck was on the directing staff of a major exercise held around Attock on the Indus. Again, Auchinleck seemed to establish a very good working relationship with a superior and he was, ultimately, to succeed Cassels as C in C India in 1941.

The Auchinlecks went on home leave in 1926, holidaying in Scotland and Devonshire, though, interestingly it seems, making no visit to Ireland. This period of leave continued into 1927 and ended with Auchinleck becoming a student at the newly opened Imperial Defence College. The IDC had just opened and offered a one-year higher course to officers from all three services, preparing them for the highest military commands. It is unclear why Auchinleck was selected for this course. In later life, and perhaps with customary modesty, he reflected, 'There were two vacancies for the Indian Army. I was given one of them and another friend [Colonel, later General Sir, Eric de Burgh] also home on leave, got the other. We always thought we got the two vacancies because they didn't want to have to pay the fares for two other officers from India.'[35] Attendance at the IDC was clearly of professional benefit to Auchinleck as that was where he met John Dill, who was then Chief Instructor, and Alan Brooke, a fellow student. Both became Chiefs of the Imperial General Staff and certainly one could portray Auchinleck as a protégé of Dill.

Auchinleck returned to India to rejoin his regiment, now at Jhelum close to the Kashmir mountains. In late 1928 he became the CO of the 1st/1st Punjab Regiment. This appointment, which lasted for two years,

33 Hastings Ismay, *The Memoirs of General the Lord Ismay* (London, 1960), p. 269.
34 Parkinson, *The Auk*, p. 31, citing an interview with Auchinleck.
35 Parkinson, *The Auk*, p. 33 citing interview with Auchinleck.

perhaps gave Auchinleck the greatest pleasures of his service life. Roger Parkinson noted, 'Long afterwards he talked about these exhilarating months with more enthusiasm than perhaps any other stage of his career.'[36]

In 1930 Auchinleck was posted to the Staff College at Quetta as Chief Instructor of the Junior Division, as a full colonel and GSO1. This meant that he was responsible for the instruction of the thirty officers who were in the first year of the two year course. Auchinleck later remembered his time as Chief Instructor:

> You had to study very hard again what you had already learnt at the Staff College, what you had learnt from your experience after you'd left Staff College, and what you'd read, and you had to be able to spread this knowledge among the students. I enjoyed it very much, because I liked acquiring the necessary knowledge. And of course it was a very good experience of making up one's mind about the problems which you'd set yourself.[37]

Auchinleck left Quetta in late 1932, taking his wife on a home leave. He returned to take command of the Brigade in Peshawar. This was seen as a prize posting in the Indian Army as, while a brigade command, this consisted of five infantry battalions, one of them British, a cavalry regiment and three Royal Artillery batteries plus engineer and signals detachments, so in many respects, it was closer to divisional strength. Soon after his arrival, the Peshawar Brigade was involved in actions against the Mohmand tribesmen in the mountains to the north of Peshawar. The actions were short lived and successful in 1933, which saw Auchinleck awarded the Companion of the Bath. In 1935 trouble again erupted with the Mohmand tribesmen, this time on a wider scale. Major General Sir Sydney Muspratt, GOC Peshawar District, was absent on leave at the time, so Auchinleck as senior brigadier was ordered to lead his own brigade and the neighbouring Nowshera Brigade, supported by tanks, into the mountains. The Nowshera Brigade was then commanded by Harold Alexander, to be Auchinleck's replacement as C in C Middle East in 1942, and the men soon became firm friends.

The parameters of the campaign against the Mohmand tribesmen had been set by Sir Ralph Griffith, Governor of the North-West Frontier Province. He had proclaimed that British and Indian troops would

---

36 Parkinson, *The Auk*, p. 34.
37 Parkinson, *The Auk*, p. 35 citing an interview with Auchinleck.

continue their march until they reached Kamalai, the heartland of Mohmand territory, and would do this even if the tribesmen abandoned their defences. Auchinleck opened his operations with the first operational use of tanks in India. Vickers Mark IIB tanks were sent forward in pairs to batter through roadblocks and, by the end of the first day of operations they had cleared the road enabling the two brigades to advance into the mountains. The road ended soon after the ascent into the mountains and Auchinleck then spent six weeks with his troops in a defended camp, while engineers extended the road network, allowing for a further advance. By mid-September operations could be reopened and Auchinleck sent forward three columns, in a night operation, to seize the heights on either side of Nahakki gorge, allowed cavalry and tanks to advance into the Kamalai Plain the following morning. Auchinleck reverted to the command of his own brigade when Muspratt returned but he had broken the back of Mohmand resistance and the tribesmen submitted on 1 October. This was viewed as a highly successful campaign and both Auchinleck and Alexander were created Commanders of the Star of India. Among visitors to their camp during the operation were Field Marshal Chetwode, C in C India and Sir James Grigg, who was then Finance Member of the Government of India and was the become Secretary of State for War from 1942 to 1945.

Auchinleck had a home leave in the Summer of 1936 and he returned to India in the Autumn as Deputy Chief of the General Staff, based in Simla. The C in C was then General Sir Robert Cassels and the Chief of the General Staff, General Eric de Burgh; two officers already well known to Auchinleck. It was while he was Deputy Chief of the General Staff that Auchinleck met Lieutenant Colonel Eric Dorman-Smith, who arrived in Simla in early 1938 as Director of Military Training. Auchinleck quickly got to know Dorman-Smith well and later reflected:

We used to go for long walks together in the morning before breakfast in the Simla hills, 8,000 feet up. We discussed war and training, training mostly, and I found him very intelligent and very valuable to talk to. I got a lot out of him. Very valuable indeed. Very imaginative. Not popular because he was a little bit inclined to state his opnions very openly, and the less intelligent didn't like him very much. But I had a very great opinion of him – he proved it afterwards.[38]

---

38 Parkinson, *The Auk*, pp. 38–39 citing an interview with Auchinleck.

Auchinleck was later to choose Dorman-Smith to accompany him, effectively as his army Chief of Staff, when he took personal control of Eighth Army in 1942, in what proved to be an ill-judged decision.

During Auchinleck's time as Deputy Chief of Staff the Indian Army was undergoing some modest reform. While recruitment of the rank and file remained tied to the 'martial races', the officer corps was being slowly 'Indianised', that is, opened to educated Indians through competitive examinations. From 1918 small numbers of Indian officers had been trained at the RMC. However, the numbers only became significant when the Indian Military Academy opened in October 1932 at Dehra Dun. By May 1941, just 535 cadets had been commissioned. To put this in context, the pre-war Indian Army had approximately 2,500 officers. Of equal concern to many Indians was the fact that Indian officers were often replacing Viceroys' Commissioned Officers, effectively a variety of Warrant Officer, rather than white officers holding the King's commission and the plan to Indianise only one division meant that Indian officers would not have the same promotion opportunities as their British counterparts.[39]

The other major issue being debated in the late 1930s was the modernisation of the Indian Army and its capacity to provide an 'Imperial Reserve' as it had during the First World War. During the summer of 1938 the C in C India created a Modernisation Committee at Simla, which was chaired by Auchinleck as de Burgh, the Chief of General Staff, was away on home leave. Other members were Lieutenant General G. N. Molesworth, Director of Military Operations and Intelligence and Lieutenant Colonel Eric Dorman-Smith as Director of Military Training. As laid down by the 1937 Imperial Conference, the primary role of the Indian Army was for home defence. Within a month the Modernisation Committee had assembled much evidence and prepared its report. Five specific functions were outlined for the Indian Army: frontier defence, internal security, coastal defence, external defence and the creation of a general reserve. The British Government's contribution to the Indian Army was a mere £1,500,000 p.a., which meant that the reforms proposed had to be modest and designed to take place over a four-year period. Indeed, the Modernisation Committee recommended

---

39 P. P. Barua, *Gentlemen of the Raj: The Indian Army Officer Corps, 1817–1949* (Westport, 2003), pp. 14–87 and P. S. Gupta, 'The Debate on Indianization 1918–39', in *The British Raj and its Indian Armed Forces 1857–1939*, ed. P. S. Gupta and Anirudh Deshpande (New Delhi, 2002), pp. 228–70.

the disbandment of three Indian cavalry regiments, fourteen Indian infantry battalions and four companies of sappers and miners to help meet the costs of mechanisation and motorisation. Within these limitations, the Committee recommended that the General Reserve should consist of three brigade groups and the equipping of these formations, along with mechanisation, should have the highest priority.

The C in C, General Sir Robert Cassels, accepted the report of the Modernisation Committee completely. It is worth noting that a sub-committee of the CID, under Major General H. R. Pownall had made similar recommendations and, indeed, estimated that the British government needed to provide a minimum of £2,285,000 p.a. if modernisation was to progress properly. These reports were to prove timely as, with the situation deteriorating in Europe, Admiral of the Fleet Lord Chatfield had been appointed to chair a committee which was to enquire into how best India's military resources could be used, in the event of war. On 24 October 1938 Auchinleck received a letter from Lord Zetland, Secretary of State for India, in which he was invited to serve as a member of the Chatfield Committee. Auchinleck flew to Port Said to meet Lord Chatfield and his other colleagues and on the sea voyage to India was able to present his existing report, which was, ultimately, to be incorporated in the conclusions of the Chatfield Committee. The Chatfield Committee worked throughout November and December, based in Delhi but visiting a number of military establishments throughout India. By the end of January 1939 the preliminary conclusions had been reached, covering all three services in India. Lord Chatfield and his other committee members, including Auchinleck, flew from Delhi to London in late January 1939 to complete their report there.

Recommendations were presented to the British Government in early spring. As a result, the Government decided to increase its expenditure on the Indian Army by 25 per cent, bringing this up to £2,000,000 p.a. and the Government also pledged a capital sum of £5,000,000 to be put at the disposal of the Government of India to help implement modernisation. By Spring 1940 there were three Indian Army divisions either serving overseas or available for such duty and another three divisions in preparation for overseas deployment. This owed something to the foundations laid by the Chatfield report.[40]

---

40 On the planned reforms of the Modernisation, CID and Chatfield Committees, see Pradeep Barua, 'Strategies and doctrines of imperial defence: Britain and India, 1919–45', *Journal of Imperial and Commonwealth History*, 25: 2 (1997),

Auchinleck stayed in England after the completion of the Chatfield report. He participated in a Higher Commanders' Course at Aldershot, where Lord Mountbatten, with whom he was to work closely during 1943 to 1947 when Mountbatten was C in C, South East Asia Command and then Viceroy of India, was a member of his syndicate. Following this he took leave and spent holidays with his wife in England and in the United States of America, where his wife had spent her childhood. They returned to Scotland in August 1939 and late in that month Auchinleck received orders to report at Edinburgh on 3 September. When he arrived there, on 2 September, he found his hotel crowded with Indian Army officers, who had all been recalled to their regiments and, like him, were to sail on the Canadian Pacific liner *Duchess of Bedford*.

Auchinleck reached Bombay at the beginning of October and immediately moved to Dehra Dun to take command of the Meerut District. He began to make arrangements to prepare the 3rd Indian Division for war but within three months he was ordered to return with all possible haste to England. On arrival in England, in January 1940 at the height of the 'Phoney War', Auchinleck was ordered to raise, train and command the 4 Corps. This corps was to be formed in an area to the south-west of London and the intention was that Auchinleck would take it to France in June. This was an odd posting for an Indian Army officer and later Auchinleck was to reflect, 'I don't know why they chose me. Most Indian Army officers had commands in India rather than in England – it was most unusual as a matter of fact.'[41] Auchinleck faced many problems with his new command. Of his two divisions, the 52nd Lowland Division was based in Peeblesshire and the Border country, while his other was in Dorset, whereas his HQ, initially to have been at Camberley was moved to Alresford in Hampshire, remote from both divisions. Both were Territorial Army formations, with many raw recruits, and training facilities were sparse. Whilst preparing 4 Corps for its final training and

240–66; Barua, *Gentlemen of the Raj*, pp. 89–106; Brian Bond, *British Military Policy between the Two World Wars* (Oxford, 1980), pp. 121–24; Anirudh Deshpande, *British Military Policy in India, 1900–1945: Colonial Constraints and Declining Power* (New Delhi, 2005), pp. 135–39; D. P. Marston, *Phoenix from the Ashes: The Indian Army in the Burma Campaign* (London, 2003), pp. 28–30 and S. N. Prasad, *Official History of the Indian Army in the Second World War 1939–45: Expansion of the Armed Forces and Defence Organisation 1939–45* (Calcutta, 1956), pp. 434–38.

41 Parkinson, *The Auk*, p. 43, citing an interview with Auchinleck.

deployment to France, Auchinleck was called to the War Office to be given his first independent command in Norway.

Norway first came to the attention of British military planners in January 1940 when consideration was given to seizing Narvik, in Northern Norway to prevent the port being used to ship Swedish iron ore to Germany.[42] In February, when a force was being organised to support Finland against the USSR, consideration was again given to seizing the ports of Trondheim and Narvik to support that operation. Finland capitulated on 12 March 1940, which removed one reason for intervention, but the Chamberlain government decided to authorise mine-laying operations to block the passage of German ships carrying iron ore on 8 April. On this same day German forces invaded Denmark and Norway, occupying most of the major cities by 10 April. As a result of the German invasion, it was decided that a force, consisting of troops initially earmarked for Finland, would be sent to Norway and this force sailed on 11 April 1940. Initially, the naval elements were commanded by Admiral of the Fleet Lord Cork, with Major General P. J. Mackesy in command of troops. Mackesy's initial task was to establish his force at Harstad on Hinnoy Island, opposite Narvik. In mid-April British and French troops also gained footholds at Namsos and Aalsund, immediately to the north and south of Trondheim. By late April the situation had deteriorated badly as German reinforcements arrived. It was decided that the Trondheim area would be evacuated, though renewed efforts would be made to capture Narvik, more for political, than strategic reasons.

It was against this background that Auchinleck was selected to command troops in Northern Norway on 28 April. It is unclear why Auchinleck was chosen for this operation; he had never been to Norway and knew little of the country, he had never worked closely with the Royal Navy and he didn't speak French. It may well have been that his long-standing patron, Sir John Dill, recently appointed as VCIGS, recommended him and his experience in mountain warfare in India may have been deemed useful, though given that none of the British troops under his command had been trained or equipped for mountain warfare, this is questionable. On 29 April Auchinleck assembled a staff and obtained what material he could about Norway. On the same day Major General Mackesy was

---

42 The best modern study of the Norway campaign is John Kiszely, *Anatomy of a campaign: The British Fiasco in Norway, 1940* (Cambridge, 2017). The official history, T. K. Derry, *The Campaign in Norway* (London, 1952), still contains much of value.

ordered to send a small unit to seize Bodo, South of Narvik, to prevent German troops reinforcing the town by road.

Auchinleck questioned the wisdom of an attack on Narvik, but Winston Churchill, as First Lord of the Admiralty, and the Chamberlain government as a whole, maintained that such an attack was needed to restore British and, indeed, Allied prestige, given the decision to evacuate forces from Southern Norway. Auchinleck had to wait until 5 May until he received his official orders to depart for Norway as GOC in C designate of Anglo-French military forces and the RAF in Northern Norway, with instructions to act in close co-operation with the Senior Naval Officer. This created a confused command situation, where Auchinleck would immediately supersede Mackesy as commander of British troops, but Mackesy would remain under his command. Auchinleck left for Scotland on 6 May and on the morning of 7 May boarded the Polish liner *Chrobry* at Leith, which under destroyer escort, took him and his staff to Norway. While he was still at sea the German blitzkrieg swept forward in the Low Countries and France.

When he heard the news of the German advance, Auchinleck wondered what his force could now achieve. He believed that at least twelve infantry battalions were needed for the defence of the Narvik area and reinforcements would be impossible in the changing circumstances. In reality the British forces under his command were to consist of 24th Guards Brigade, three Independent Companies which had been specially recruited from the Territorial Army and supporting RA and RE units. The RA available consisted of the 55th and 56th Light Anti-Aircraft Regiments and the 51st and 82nd Heavy Anti-Aircraft Regiments; this was below the level of anti-aircraft support which Auchinleck viewed as a minimum and, in any case, ammunition supplies were very limited. Not only was this British force as, a whole, insufficient to capture and secure Narvik in Auchinleck's view, but it meant that the French contingent, four battalions of Chasseurs Alpins and two battalions of the French Foreign Legion, outnumbered British troops, while a Polish brigade of four battalions, which had been raised in France, was almost equal to it. This made Auchinleck's job as the commander of an Allied force difficult and its polyglot nature was further reinforced by the addition of two Norwegian battalions.[43] When he arrived at Harstad he met with Mackesy and Lord Cork, quickly forming the impression that there

---

43 Derry, *The Campaign in Norway*, pp. 266–67; Kiszely, *Anatomy of a campaign*, p. 252 and Parkinson, *The Auk*, p. 48 citing an interview with Auchinleck.

was not a good working relationship between the two senior officers.[44] Auchinleck arranged to have Mackesy recalled to London, though had to move decisively to remove him on 13 May before authorisation came through from the VCIGS. On 12 May, Auchinleck observed French troops capture Bjervik, following a bombardment by the Royal Navy.

Over the next nine days the situation deteriorated further. A small British force had to be withdrawn from Mo and Luftwaffe attacks became very heavy, sinking amongst other ships, the *Chrobry*. With the deteriorating situation in France and Belgium, the Chiefs of Staff made it clear to Auchinleck that he could not expect any reinforcements and on 21 May the War Cabinet discussed withdrawing British troops from the Narvik area. Auchinleck was ordered to evacuate the whole of northern Norway by an order sent in the early hours of 25 May, but the Chiefs of Staff left it to Auchinleck and Lord Cork to decide whether the long-planned assault on Narvik itself should take place before withdrawal. Cork and Auchinleck consulted with the senior French officer, Brigadier General Antoine Béthouart, and all agreed to carry out the assault as planned. Auchinleck later explained, 'We simply had to make a plan to get the troops out without letting the Germans know that we were doing it to begin with. So we went ahead and captured Narvik – I think that foxed the Germans. I don't think they expected us to retire immediately after we'd taken Narvik.'[45] Over the night of 27–28 May Allied forces captured Narvik. The bombardment by the Royal Navy commenced at midnight and by 4am the assault troops, drawn from the Norwegian Army, French Foreign Legion and Free Polish forces were advancing on the town. Luftwaffe attacks on the attacking force remained fierce throughout 28 May, with HMS *Cairo*, on which Auchinleck had established his Headquarters, being struck by two bombs, causing heavy casualties. RAF support from Hurricane fighters was essential and by 5pm Allied troops had occupied Narvik. To be welcomed as liberators by the Norwegian inhabitants of Norway was difficult for Auchinleck and other senior officers who knew of the plans for evacuation. The evacuation of the 25,000 Allied troops began on the night of 3 June and was completed on the evening of 7 June with Auchinleck himself leaving on HMS *Southampton*; completely deceiving German forces. The Allied troops sailed for the Clyde in two convoys, Auchinleck embarking on HMS *Southampton*. On 8 June the *Gneisenau*

---

44 Kiszely, *Anatomy of a campaign*, pp. 251–52 and 257–59.
45 Parkinson, *The Auk*, p. 51, citing an interview with Auchinleck.

and *Scharnhorst* made contact with the convoy sinking the tanker, *Oil Pioneer*, the aircraft carrier, HMS *Glorious* and two destroyers, HMS *Acasta* and HMS *Arden*.

On his return from Norway, Auchinleck was informed on 14 June that he was to take command of the 5 Corps, in Southern Command, the only operational military formation then in the south and west of England. His new command consisted of the 4th Division, a regular formation and the 50th (Northumbrian) Division, composed of TA units, who Auchinleck felt were only partially trained; the 48th (South Midland) Division was, on paper, part of 5 Corps but did not come under Auchinleck's direct command. He was ordered to defend the coastline between Bognor and Bristol against the threatened German invasion. On 19 July 1940, when Alan Brooke was promoted from GOC Southern Command to become Commander of Home Forces, replacing General Sir Edmund Ironside, who was promoted to Field Marshal; Auchinleck was given Southern Command.

In defence planning there were serious discussions amongst senior generals and politicians about how a German invasion might best be resisted. Some felt that British forces should be concentrated inland, allowing them to counter-attack a German landing quickly, with others believing that the strongest defence should come on the coast itself. Both Ironside and Brooke as C in C Home Forces stressed the need for mobility and the need to prevent a 'Maginot Line' complex amongst British troops.[46] Auchinleck did not fundamentally disagree with his superiors but, particularly in the immediate aftermath of Dunkirk, he feared that with vehicles in very short supply he could not rely on reserve troops being moved quickly to invasion beaches. Auchinleck also believed that the key element in British defence was to prevent the Germans establishing a beach head through which they could land armoured units and artillery.

The Local Defence Volunteers (LDV), renamed the Home Guard on 31 July 1940, provided additional reinforcements to the troops under Auchinleck's command. Auchinleck seems to have seen them as of some use, but clearly understood their limitations. Reflecting on the LDV many years later he commented, 'The Home Guard were excellent,

---

46 Basil Collier, *The Defence of the United Kingdom* (London, 1957), pp. 129–34; Jonathan Fennell, *Fighting the People's War: The British and Commonwealth Armies and the Second World War* (Cambridge, 2019), pp. 115–16 and David French, *Raising Churchill's Army: The British Army and the War against Germany 1919–45* (Oxford, 2000), pp. 184–92.

excellent, and would have been very useful. I liked them very much. They wouldn't have stopped the Germans of course – just shot them up and that sort of thing. They weren't really tactical.'[47] The Home Guard gave Auchinleck more than a few headaches, with Home Guard officers in Southern Command as likely as those elsewhere to raise their grievances with senior officers, ignoring the chain of command.[48] Auchinleck clearly had problems with officers in the Hampshire Home Guard where, it appears that Viscount Lymington, who had been Conservative MP for Basingstoke, 1929–34, had encouraged some platoon commanders to argue for his promotion within the Home Guard, while other platoon commanders seem to have threatened to resign if he was promoted, citing his supposed Fascist sympathies.[49]

When Auchinleck was promoted to GOC Southern Command, Lieutenant General B. L. Montgomery took over command of 5 Corps. Montgomery's approach was very different to Auchinleck's as he introduced a more demanding training regime and seems to have suggested that any time spent on building fixed defences was time wasted. Montgomery reported unfavourably on commanders and units who Auchinleck had, presumably, found quite satisfactory. Things came to a head between them over Montgomery's 'poaching' of officers from other formations and his dealing directly with the War Office, ignoring Auchinleck, his superior officer. Nigel Hamilton, Montgomery's biographer, in this case, as all others, defended his subject to the extreme, portraying Auchinleck as a Blimpish figure, obsessed with static defence and neglecting proper training.[50] This was a crude caricature of Auchinleck's position.

In November 1940 Auchinleck was appointed C in C India, taking up the post in January 1941 having discussed the situation in the Middle East with General Archibald Wavell, en route. The Indian Army which he took command of was in the process of transformation from what was, essentially a lightly armed constabulary force, into a modern army, with considerable expeditionary capabilities. Indeed, it was only in May 1940 that major expansion of the Indian Army had begun. In the brief period in which he was first C in C India (Auchinleck took up the position of C in C Middle East in June 1941; he returned as C in C India in June

---

47 Parkinson, *The Auk*, p. 57 citing an interview with Auchinleck.
48 S. P. Mackenzie, *The Home Guard* (Oxford, 1995), p. 186.
49 JRL, AUC 95, letter Major General G. J. St Clair to Auchinleck, 18 October 1940, not reproduced below.
50 Nigel Hamilton, *The Full Monty: Montgomery of Alamein 1887–1942* (London, 2001), pp. 377–81.

1943) Auchinleck appears to have accomplished a lot, although it must be acknowledged that major decisions about expansion and resources had been taken before he took command. Auchinleck firmly supported the commissioning of large numbers of Indian Officers for the expanding army, whereas his predecessor, General Sir Robert Cassells had tried to relegate Indian officers to garrison or administrative posts.[51] While recruitment for new classes and in new areas had started in October 1939, Auchinleck did much to develop this, identifying areas where new regiments should be formed and making use of old regimental traditions and the Indian Territorial Force in expanding the recruiting base.[52] In terms of training, Alan Jeffreys has given his opinion that Auchinleck, 'provided a new stimulus to the transformation of the Indian Army', introducing effective training pamphlets in 1941.[53]

While in 1943–47 Auchinleck was to experience no operational command as C in C India, in 1941, briefly, he became responsible for the campaign in Iraq while holding this post. A pro-German coup in April 1941 saw the major RAF base at Habbaniya besieged. While Wavell as C in C Middle East made it clear that he could offer few forces to relieve the situation, and, indeed, he seems to have believed that diplomatic rather than military measures would suffice, Auchinleck was able to send troops from India, including a small detachment sent by air, which did much to retrieve the situation.[54]

Auchinleck was appointed C in C Middle East in June 1941 to take over command from General Archibald Wavell. Churchill had been key in this appointment, while General Sir John Dill, CIGS, otherwise a patron of Auchinleck, did not think he was the right appointment for the Middle East. On arrival Auchinleck quickly came under pressure from Churchill to launch a new offensive against the Axis forces. Auchinleck insisted on taking time to build up troop levels, tank strength and training, with the result that the 'Crusader' offensive did not start until November 1941. This offensive initially faltered under the command of Lieutenant General Alan Cunningham, the newly appointed commander of Eighth

---

51 Srinath Raghavan, 'Building the sinews of power: India in the Second World War', *Journal of Strategic Studies*, 42: 5 (2019), 586–87.
52 Marston, *Phoenix from the Ashes*, pp. 49–50 and Prasad, *Expansion of the armed forces*, pp. 79–93.
53 Alan Jeffreys, *Approach to Battle: Training the Indian Army during the Second World War* (Solihull, 2017), pp. 71–72.
54 Ashley Jackson, *Persian Gulf Command: A History of the Second World War in Iran and Iraq* (London, 2018), pp. 54–59.

Army, who was quickly replaced by Lieutenant General Neil Ritchie. Up to January 1942 the 'Crusader' offensive had achieved most of its aims, having relieved the siege of Tobruk and cleared Cyrenaica of Axis forces. However, Erwin Rommel's offensive, launched on 29 January 1942, quickly recaptured Benghazi and the Eighth Army fell back on the Gazala line. On 26 May, Axis forces attacked the Gazala line which then saw confused fighting in the 'Cauldron' and 'Knightsbridge' box battles into mid-June 1942. On 20 June Ritchie decided to fall back to Mersa Matruh and on 21 June Tobruk fell to Axis forces with 33,000 Allied troops captured. At this critical point, Auchinleck took personal command of the Eighth Army on 25 June. He then fought what many historians refer to as the First Battle of El Alamein between 1 July and 27 July; though these encounters are referred to as 'The Fighting in the El Alamein Line' in the official history.[55] In these actions Auchinleck at least stabilised the British position, and arguably came close to inflicting a major defeat on the Axis forces. Nevertheless, Churchill, having visited the Middle East with General Sir Alan Brooke, the CIGS, decided that Auchinleck had to be replaced as C in C Middle East with General Sir Harold Alexander. Initially Lieutenant General William Gott was to be put in command of Eighth Army, but his death saw Lieutenant General Bernard Montgomery selected for this role.

Auchinleck's time as C in C Middle East has been the subject of many studies.[56] His controversial sacking by Winston Churchill in August 1942 has led his biographers to adopt the approach of defence counsel in their works and Correlli Barnett has added a particularly strong argument in favour of Auchinleck's generalship, describing him as 'The Victor of Alamein'.[57] Those critical of Auchinleck suggest that he was not a good judge of character and made a number of mistaken appointments. They also suggest that Auchinleck did not understand armoured warfare and broke up established British divisions into ineffective Brigade Groups.

---

55 I. S. O. Playfair, ed., *The Mediterranean and Middle East: Vol. III: British Fortunes reach their Lowest Ebb* (London, 1960), pp. 331–60.

56 Important recent works include: Niall Barr, *Pendulum of War: The Three Battles of El Alamein* (London, 2004), pp. 11–217; Jonathan Fennell, *Combat and Morale in the North African Campaign: The Eighth Army and the Path to El Alamein* (Cambridge, 2011), pp. 119–287; Martin Kitchen, *Rommel's Desert War: Waging World War II in North Africa, 1941–1943* (Cambridge, 2009), pp. 107–308 and Douglas Porch, *Hitler's Mediterranean gamble: The North African and Mediterranean campaigns in World War II* (London, 2004), pp. 235–99.

57 Correlli Barnett, *The Desert Generals* (London, 2nd edition, 1983), pp. 7–9 and 88–248.

One of the most damning criticisms of Auchinleck is that he was preparing the Eighth Army for further retreat in July 1942; an accusation based on a misreading of some 'worst case' contingency planning.[58] The gap between Auchinleck's supporters and detractors is neatly demonstrated over the use that he made of ULTRA. Nigel Hamilton suggests that Auchinleck made very little effective use of this, whereas Martin Kitchen notes that with excellent Sigint and aerial reconnaissance Auchinleck was able to anticipate every German move in the El Alamein fighting of June and July 1942.[59] Bringing much needed balance and a new focus to this acrimonious debate between what could, crudely, be termed the Auchinleck and Montgomery schools of thought, Jonathan Fennell demonstrates that there was clearly a morale crisis in the Eighth Army in the summer of 1942 and, whatever Auchinleck's talents in the area of operational command, he was clearly not the man to resolve this crisis; Montgomery was.[60] Niall Barr's considered conclusion is that, 'There is no question that Auchinleck could identify what needed to be done but encountered real difficulty in translating those ideas into practice.'[61]

Criticisms of Auchinleck as a judge of character focus particularly on his choice of Lieutenant General Neil Ritchie as C in C Eighth Army and Major General Eric Dorman-Smith as Chief of Staff 'in the field' when Auchinleck took direct command of Eighth Army after sacking Ritchie. Each of these appointments has found historians to justify them. Ritchie was put in a difficult position by Auchinleck as an acting Lieutenant General over two more senior corps commanders. There was some wisdom in Auchinleck's choice of Ritchie for this role, in that Ritchie, having been DCGS in Cairo, knew the plans and intelligence summaries well and promoting either of the existing Corps commanders would have led to other command problems. Auchinleck, having seen an experienced commander, Lieutenant General Sir Alan Cunningham, fail as C in C Eighth Army probably thought that mentoring a younger general was a more promising approach. Michael Carver, who ended

---

58 The most damning critique of Auchinleck is Hamilton, *Monty: The Making of a General*, pp. 508–11. On Auchinleck's choice of subordinates see, for example, David Belchem, *All in the day's march* (London, 1978), p. 101. Belchem was GSO I (Staff Duties) in Eighth Army and Duff Hart-Davis, ed., *King's Counsellor: Abdication and War: The diaries of Sir Alan Lascelles* (London, 2006), p. 41.
59 Hamilton, *Monty: The Making of a General*, p. 653 and Kitchen, *Rommel's Desert War*, p. 261.
60 Fennell, *Combat and Morale in the North African campaign*, pp. 188–218.
61 Barr, *Pendulum of War*, p. 216.

his own military career as a Field Marshal and served under Ritchie in North West Europe in 1944–45, formed a very high opinion of him. He thought that Ritchie's problems stemmed from his being appointed as a chargé d'affaires, rather than a plenipotentiary; that is, that Auchinleck did not allow him the full authority that he should have possessed as an Army Commander and the lack of support he received from his Corps Commanders.[62]

Major General Eric 'Chink' Dorman-Smith was a man who was seen as deeply problematic by many of his contemporaries; undoubtedly intelligent but a dangerous eminence gris whose various plans distracted Auchinleck and other planning staff from more essential tasks. Montgomery was brief in his analysis, describing Dorman-Smith as a 'menace'.[63] Charles Richardson, who was appointed GSO1 (Plans) at Eighth Army HQ in June 1942 already knew Dorman-Smith well and noted, 'His vigorous, restless and inventive mind was continually looking for clever, unconventional and daring solutions to the dire battlefield problems with which Rommel confronted us. Few if any of these solutions were attuned to the capabilities of Eighth Army, which had recently been disastrously defeated. Moreover, Chink was seldom content with pursuing only one solution … it was not possible to arrange the removal of this dangerous supernumerary adviser.'[64] Francis De Guingand, recently appointed as BGS Eighth Army noted of Dorman-Smith in his role as 'DCGS in the Field':

> His quick brain and fertile mind produced appreciations and plans at a quicker rate than anyone I have ever met; he was perhaps too clever to be wise. The usual procedure was for these papers to be marked by the C.-in-C.: 'B.G.S., please examine this idea.' At first I sat up all night conscientiously working on these projects, but soon I found they took up too much of my time and, I regret to say, wasted a lot of it as well. Some had merit and might have been of use when we became strong enough but a lot were somewhat impracticable.[65]

---

62 Michael Carver, *Dilemmas of the Desert War: The Libyan Campaign 1940–1942* (Staplehurst, 2002), pp. 145–46.

63 Stephen Brooks, ed., *Montgomery and the Eighth Army* (London, 1991), p. 20 citing IWM, Montgomery Papers, BLM 27/1, 'Review of the Situation in Eighth Army from 12 August to 23 October 1942'.

64 Charles Richardson, *Flashback: A Soldier's Story* (London, 1985), p. 103.

65 Francis De Guingand, *Operation Victory* (London, 1947), pp. 132–33.

While one might regard this litany of complaints about Dorman-Smith, by men who were later to rise to the very top of their profession, as conclusive, Dorman-Smith has found his defenders, notably Correlli Barnett and Lavinia Greacen. They portray Dorman-Smith as an original thinker who didn't suffer fools gladly and who provided the careful reading of German intentions which allowed Auchinleck to halt the German advance at El Alamein.[66] Whatever his merits, Dorman-Smith had a nasty habit of alienating those with whom he had to work and his subsequent career ended in abject failure when he was put in command of an infantry brigade in Italy. It should also be added that at Eighth Army HQ Auchinleck had a group of particularly talented and capable staff officers and more delegation to them could have proved much more effective than imposing Dorman-Smith on a functioning staff system.

One of the many criticisms of Auchinleck is that he broke up established divisions into brigade groups and Jock columns, which prevented the Eighth Army from concentrating firepower at a decisive point.[67] However, if, as David French suggests, the main problem suffered by the British forces in the Western Desert was their inability to practice combined arms tactics, then the development of these formations could be seen as an attempt to integrate armour, infantry and artillery; the problem then being that they did not have enough armour, infantry or artillery to take on an entire Axis division unaided.[68] While German tanks did not completely outclass British tanks and British tanks were more than a match for most Italian models, it would be wrong to downplay problems with British tank production. British tanks in 1941 to 1942 suffered from inadequate firepower, insufficient armour and slow speeds; these were particularly problems with the Valentine tank. The Crusader tank was an improvement, but its performance was hampered by poor build quality.[69] It should also be noted that much later in the war, armoured doctrine remained confused and co-operation between armour and infantry patchy.[70]

---

66 Barnett, *The Desert Generals*, pp. 181–99 and Lavinia Greacen, *Chink: A Biography* (London, 1989), pp. 172–294. Lavinia Greacen is currently working on an edited collection of Dorman-Smith's papers held in the JRL.
67 Fennell, *Combat and Morale in the North African campaign*, p. 284.
68 French, *Raising Churchill's Army*, pp. 220–26.
69 Benjamin Coombs, *British Tank Production and the War Economy, 1934–1945* (London, 2013), pp. 89–91.
70 John Buckley, *Monty's Men: The British Army and the Liberation of Europe* (London, 2013), pp. 129–35.

The Auchinleck papers reveal, in detail, his problems in dealing with Winston Churchill. Churchill's role as a Generalissimo or, indeed, warlord, has been the focus of a number of important studies.[71] Churchill certainly took a keen interest in military affairs and Geoffrey Best notes, 'Churchill may not have been misguided in thinking that his generals and the War Office performed the better for his prodding and probing. He actually thought the generals would appreciate the interest he showed in them. On the whole they didn't.'[72] In May 1942 General Sir Alan Brooke, as CIGS, was candid about the problems apparent in Churchill's relationship with Auchinleck:

> I can so very well imagine what your feelings must have been lately with the decisions you have had to make on your Western Front. I do hope you have not felt that I did not realize what the conditions are that you are facing, and I can assure you that I have done what I could to ensure that your situation was fully appreciated and realized by the Cabinet. Some of your arguments have made it difficult to support your case, and arguments based on mathematical calculations of ratios of tank strengths to the exclusion of the main strategical arguments of the situation as a whole produced reactions on the part of the P.M. which were very hard to counter. It was only with considerable difficulties that we induced him to accept your date.
>
> I still feel that it would have been of great assistance if you had been able to come home when originally suggested; he has not taken it well and repeatedly harps back to this fact. Another advice I would give is when possible to send telegrams in your own capacity instead of coming from the Defence Council. The latter procedure annoys him and I think gives him the wrong impression that you are taking cover behind the cloak of the Defence Council! I can assure you that I do all I can from this end to make your path as easy as possible, but I am afraid that you do not always realize what a difficult matter this is when having to handle the Defence Committee, War Cabinet and a personality such as the P.M.![73]

---

71 Carlo D'Este, *Warlord: A Life of Churchill at War, 1874–1945* (London, 2008), pp. 443–689 and Max Hastings, *Finest Years: Churchill as Warlord 1940–45* (London, 2009), pp. 139–343.

72 Geoffrey Best, *Churchill and War* (London, 2005), p. 171.

73 JRL, AUC 852, Letter from General Sir Alan Brooke, CIGS to Auchinleck, 16 May 1942, not reproduced below.

Auchinleck did not see himself as a diplomat and it is fair to conclude that he did not always appreciate the pressures under which Churchill was working. The vision of Churchill as a great war leader can, all too easily, ignore the practical problems he faced in needing to show the Americans and Soviets that the British army could develop a successful 'second front' and the problems faced from both backbench MPs and by-election defeats. It says something for Churchill's management of military affairs and respect for Auchinleck that he personally notified Auchinleck of his replacement as C in C Middle East in August 1942, rather than leaving that task to Brooke, and offered Auchinleck the newly created post of C in C Iraq and Persia, which Auchinleck declined.

Having been removed from command in the Middle East, Auchinleck returned to India. There he wrote his official reports and then was unemployed for a lengthy period. In June 1943 he was reappointed as C in C India, a post he continued to hold until the end of the British Raj in August 1947. This period as C in C India is the focus of another volume of Auchinleck's military papers, due to be published by the Army Records Society in the near future.

Sources and Editorial Method

This volume of Field Marshal Sir Claude Auchinleck's papers reproduces only a selection from those held in the Auchinleck papers at the John Rylands Library, University of Manchester. The collection there consists of 1,353 individual documents; in total around 1,500,000 words, and it was felt that in producing this volume, these papers alone should be used, rather than including official papers held in the War Office files at The National Archives (TNA), Kew or in the Indian Office collections held at the British Library. As it transpired the closure of archives and libraries due to the COVID 19 emergency prevented much use being made of these additional sources in any case.

These papers were deposited in the John Rylands Library (then an independent institution, which merged with the University of Manchester in 1972) by the wish of Auchinleck himself in 1967. Michael Elliott-Bateman, a lecturer in military studies at the University of Manchester had visited Eric Dorman O'Gowan (formerly Dorman-Smith), Auchinleck's erstwhile chief of staff, at his home in Ireland to discuss the deposit of Dorman O'Gowan's papers. After some discussion, Dorman O'Gowan had agreed to the deposit of his own papers with the John Rylands Library and had suggested to Auchinleck that he might do the same. Auchinleck was, at this stage, preparing to emigrate to Marrakech, where he took up permanent residence in January 1968 and wanted to safely deposit his papers before he left the UK. Writing in 1967, Auchinleck noted that the papers, 'fill a medium sized suitcase' and that the Department of War Studies at King's College London was interested in having them. The papers had already been, 'roughly classified and filed according to subject and period' by John Connell, when he was working on his biography.[74] Indeed, Connell's work, which consists of 952 substantive pages makes considerable use of these papers, many of which are quoted at length.

The acquisition of Auchinleck's papers occurred at a time when the Department of Military Studies was being revitalised at the University of Manchester, and when Professor M. R. D. Foot, one of the official historians of the Second World War, held the post of Professor of Modern History.[75] Foot seems to have been excited by the acquisition of Auchinleck's papers, commenting, 'this really puts us on the map in military studies and as a result of this gift we could easily become a focal point for such collections of military history'. Writing to Auchinleck himself, Foot remarked, 'They quite clearly constitute a source of the first importance, for the military historian, for the historian of government and war, and for the tale of the end of British rule in India.'[76] Auchinleck was assured that the papers had been catalogued and indexed by October 1968, though these were not made generally available as Brian Chapman, the Professor of Government at the University of Manchester, along with M. R. D. Foot and Michael Elliott-Bateman, were supposedly preparing them for publication by Manchester University Press. Indeed, Auchinleck's second biographer, Roger Parkinson, appears to have made no use of the papers themselves, relying on Connell's earlier quotations, as he believed that the publication of an edited collection of the papers was imminent when he published his book in 1977.[77]

---

74   JRL, Auchinleck papers, uncatalogued papers relating to deposit and access, letter Auchinleck to Dr F. W. Ratcliffe, 15 August 1967.

75   Obituary of M. R. D. Foot, *The Guardian*, 21 February 2012. Foot's best-known publications include, *S. O. E. In France: An account of the British Special Operations Executive in France 1940–44* (London, 1966) and *Resistance: European resistance to the Nazis, 1940–45* (London, 1978).

76   JRL, Auchinleck papers, uncatalogued papers relating to deposit and access, letter Ratcliffe to the Vice Chancellor of the University of Manchester, 21 November 1967 and letter, Foot to Auchinleck, 22 November 1967.

77   Parkinson, *The Auk*, p. 8.

Auchinleck was continually assured from 1968 to 1978 that work on this publication, which never appeared, was ongoing.[78] M. R. D. Foot left the University of Manchester in 1973 to take up a post as director of the European Discussion Centre, which may explain this, while Michael Elliott-Bateman's publications had little real focus on British, or, indeed, Indian, military history and Chapman's published work had no real military focus at all.[79] While the academic staff at the University of Manchester conspicuously failed to produce an edited collection of Auchinleck's papers, Dr Margaret M. Wright, the Keeper of Printed Books at the John Rylands Library, produced a very detailed and comprehensive catalogue. This was originally published in the *Bulletin of the John Rylands University Library of Manchester* and is now available, in its entirety online.[80] Unfortunately, Dr Wright suffered from ill-health over a long period and she died in late 1989, which meant that Dr C. D. Field, Head of Publications at the John Rylands Library completed the final editing of this work, before it was published.[81]

It should be noted here that the biographies of Auchinleck produced by Philip Warner, a Senior Lecturer at the Royal Military Academy Sandhurst and Alexander Greenwood, who had been one of Auchinleck's ADCs 1943–44 and remained a lifelong friend, made very limited use of the Auchinleck papers. Warner's book on Auchinleck seems to have relied heavily on O'Connell's quotations from the Auchinleck papers, rather than the papers themselves, though the lack of proper footnotes does not make this clear. Warner's research consisting primarily of hundreds

---

78 JRL, Auchinleck papers, uncatalogued papers relating to deposit and access, letter Ratcliffe to Auchinleck, 26 May 1970, 12 June 1970, 11 April 1974, 16 December 1975 and 15 June 1978.

79 Michael Elliott Bateman, ed., *The fourth dimension of warfare. Vol. I, Intelligence, subversion, resistance* (Manchester, 1970) and *Vol. II, Revolt to revolution: studies in the 19th and 20th Century European experience* (Manchester, 1974) and *Defeat in the East: The work of Mao Tse-tung on war* (Oxford, 1967). Brian Chapman, *Introduction to French local government* (London, 1953), *The profession of government: the public service in Europe* (London, 1959) and *British government observed: some European reflections* (London, 1963).

80 Margaret M. Wright, 'The Military Papers, 1940–48, of Field-Marshal Sir Claude Auchinleck: A Calendar and Index', *Bulletin of the John Rylands University Library of Manchester*, 70: 2 (1988), 146–393 and: http:// www.library.manchester.ac.uk/search-resources/special-collections/ guide-to-special-collections/atoz/auchinleck-papers/.

81 JRL, Auchinleck papers, uncatalogued papers relating to deposit and access, letter, Dr C. D. Field to Alexander Greenwood, 4 January 1990.

of hours spent interviewing those who worked with Auchinleck. Indeed, the origins of this book lie in interviews which David Dimbleby recorded with Auchinleck between 1974 and 1976, some of which were broadcast as a BBC programme, *The Auk at 90*. David Dimbleby had planned to develop these interviews into a book but with other commitments, he passed this opportunity on to Philip Warner.[82] Alexander Greenwood's biography of Auchinleck was written without proper footnotes, so it is not always clear where he was drawing from the Auchinleck papers. Certainly, he had asked for copies of some of the papers, regarding Auchinleck's period as Commander in Chief, India 1944–47. Curiously, though, Greenwood devoted only 53 pages of his 320-page book to this period.[83] Evan McGilvray in his recent biography has made use of the Auchinleck papers but has provided very limited quotation from them.

The Auchinleck papers, as they survive, contain nothing before 1940: 67 documents concern the Norway campaign, 50 Southern Command in 1940, 153 Auchinleck's first period as Commander in Chief, India in 1941, 749 the Middle East 1941–43 and 288 Auchinleck's second period as Commander in Chief, India, 1943–47. The Middle East collection probably dominates as the letters and telegrams Auchinleck received and sent in this period could be argued to be 'personal' in a way that the official paperwork which he generated as Commander in Chief, India could not.

None of Dorman O'Gowan's papers have been reproduced in this collection as they do not directly correspond with the Auchinleck papers being, in very large part, memoirs written after the war and post-war correspondence. Lavinia Greacen published a very readable biography of Dorman O'Gowan in 1989 and is now working on an edited collection of his papers.[84]

There have been some difficult decisions to make in editing these military papers for the period 1940–42 to remain within a reasonable word count. Many of the after-action reports have been omitted, especially concerning those at the start of the 'Crusader' offensive, as they are summarised in other documents and more readily available in war

---

82   Warner, *Lonely Soldier*, pp. 2–3 and 237.

83   Greenwood, *Auchinleck*, pp. 233–86 and JRL, Auchinleck papers, uncatalogued papers relating to deposit and access, letter Alexander Greenwood to C. D. Field, 11 January 1990.

84   Greacen, Chink. A catalogue of Dorman O'Gowan's papers is available at: https://archiveshub.jisc.ac.uk/manchesteruniversity/archives/a3ebb59b-e147 -351f-a8d4-7b1119e66190?component=571c7d09-5399-3fde-b68c-0ef1098b00f2.

diaries held at TNA. The 'top' and 'tail' of letters and messages have been omitted. Documents have been reproduced as per the originals, so any spelling variants are true to the source material. Where numbered paragraphs commence with number 2, number 1 has not been omitted, this is simply the style used in these documents. Where (.) and (,) appear in the text of military ciphers and telegrams these are reproduced as in the original documents, when this punctuation was inserted by cipher clerks or telegraphists. The vast majority of the documents reproduced in this volume were typescript; a small number were holograph [6, 7, 36, 42, 75, 82, 230, 231], a few printed [30, 37, 67, 121] and the others were a mixture of typescript and holograph [61, 107, 109, 112, 152, 181, 182, 189, 199, 204]. The overall introduction has sought to provide an outline of Auchinleck's military career to August 1942, with a brief discussion of the main publications concerning this, while the individual section introductions have focused on the documents themselves.

Norway, 1940

The campaign in Norway was beset with many problems from the outset and these are neatly revealed in the Auchinleck papers. Auchinleck's position was, of course, a rather usual one, in that he was appointed to take command of an ongoing operation and, rather than being flown immediately to northern Norway, he was given time to make his own appreciation of the situation. Auchinleck's concerns about the attempt to capture Narvik and the military resources required to do this are clear; in particular he was clearly concerned about German air superiority and asked for a very large number of anti-aircraft guns, clearly believing that RAF support was inadequate [1, 2, 5, 6, 8, 16]. It is also clear that the decision to capture and occupy Narvik was a political, rather than military one, with Narvik harbour having very limited strategic value [4, 5].

The confused system of command, which meant that there was no overall theatre commander, and the inability of Admiral Lord Cork and Major General Mackesy to work effectively together is very clear [6, 11, 12]. Similarly, Auchinleck was concerned at how he could establish his authority as an Allied commander, given the small number of British forces at his disposal [2, 5].

The forces, under Auchinleck's command, were a very mixed bag. He seems to have been impressed by the French troops and the 24th Guards Brigade contained some of the best units in the British army. However, he was less than impressed by the Independent Companies, which can be seen as the precursors of the Commandos. They were designed as specialist irregular units, able to engage in irregular warfare; though the fact that the area around Narvik was sparsely populated made any efforts to develop a guerrilla campaign, with local support, doomed to failure. These companies, each consisting of 20 officers and 270 other ranks, were recruited from throughout the TA in the UK; one company raised from each of the ten TA divisions (only five of these companies saw service in Norway). They had a high allocation of officers and each company included a doctor, demolition experts, a Norwegian interpreter and a mountain warfare officer from the Indian Army. They were well-equipped, with a higher than normal allocation of light machine guns, mortars and radios, and with specialist winter clothing, Alpine rucksacks and snow shoes. However, Auchinleck did not think this experiment was particularly useful and he did what he could to form the companies under his command into a standard infantry battalion [2, 5].[1]

There was remarkably little co-operation with the Norwegian government over the operations in the Narvik area. It seems that the British government was concerned that information shared with Norwegian forces, would quickly leak to German forces; though there is little evidence of this [15, 16].

The need to abandon the campaign to bolster the defences of France and the UK is evident amongst these papers [8, 13]. There was some concern that while the troops were evacuated with few casualties, many of the anti-aircraft guns were left behind, when some Royal Artillery and merchant marine officers felt that more could have been done to save them [13, 16].

---

1   Derry, *The Campaign in Norway*, pp. 168–69 and Kiszely, *Anatomy of a Campaign*, pp. 260–61.

I

'Narvik: appreciation of the situation' by Auchinleck, with marginal comments by Sir John Dill, VCIGS[2] [the latter noted in italics], 3 May 1940

MOST SECRET

The Object

1. Object, as provisionally stated, is to develop NARVIK area to provide:-
   (a) defended naval anchorage.
   (b) secure base for land and air operations in or against Northern SWEDEN.

Considerations.

Defended Anchorage

2. (a) Understood that defended anchorage needed as base for naval operations in NORTHERN waters and to counter GERMAN naval operations on NORWEGIAN coast from bases such as TRONDHEIM, NAMSOS, etc., and to prevent establishment of similar bases further NORTH as at BODO, MOSJOEN, etc.? *Yes*
   (b) Understand that purpose of anchorage is not merely to defend port and potential army base at NARVIK? *No*
   (c) It is to be taken, therefore, that a defended anchorage at NARVIK (or elsewhere) is essential irrespective of its relation to any other purpose for which NARVIK may be used? *Yes*
   (d) If this is so, is NARVIK best site for naval anchorage?
   (e) Would a more SOUTHERN site be suitable for the purely naval aspect?
   (f) If so, where?

---

2   Dill was appointed VCIGS on 22 April 1940; relinquishing command of 1 Corps of the BEF to take up this appointment.

Army Base

3. (a) Assumed that when we get NARVIK, port and railway facilities will be so destroyed as to render them incapable of being used for at least six months or more, dependent on the possibility of work from October onwards. *Agree* Understand that therefore NARVIK as an ORE PORT unlikely to be of real use to us or Germans before 1st December, 1940, assuming restoration work starts 1st June.

    (b) With railway destroyed and (b) no road, operations on sufficient scale to capture ore areas KIRUNA (100 miles) or GALLIVARE (160 miles) against GERMAN ground and air opposition based on LULEA and BODO, are not a practicable proposition unless overwhelming air superiority has been obtained? *Agree*

    (c) If this is so, only chance of operating with an organized force in NORTHERN SWEDEN is with full SWEDISH co-operation especially in so far as use of air bases is concerned? *Yes*

    (d) Unless such co-operation is forthcoming, is there any object in developing army base for future offensive eastwards?

    (e) If, in future, efforts should be made by combined operations on coast to recover footing in SOUTHERN NORWAY, it would not be essential to hold NARVIK or the railway solely for this purpose? *Yes, because we can't be in a position to help Sweden should opportunities occur.*

    (f) Should GERMANS try to retake NARVIK (unlikely if reports that they are now busy destroying it are true) via LULEA and the railway, it should be possible to provide adequate landward defence for defended anchorage without holding NARVIK itself, and, at the same time, to deny exit by sea from NARVIK to GERMANS?

Air Bases

4. Assumed that unless bases for operation adequate fighter and bomber aircraft are provided, GERMANS will soon make defended anchorage and/or army base untenable or virtually useless. *Yes we know that.*

    (a) GERMAN air attack most likely to come NORTHWARD from TRONDHEIM, NAMSOS, and such other landing grounds as they can get NORTH of NAMSOS. *I agree.*

(b) To meet this attack our air bases should be SOUTH of NARVIK, otherwise defence will lose much power?

See in consultation with RAF.

(c) GERMAN air attack may come from SWEDISH bases. To get air bases in SWEDEN for our aircraft means SWEDISH co-operation. Only alternative seems air base or bases NORTH or N.E. of NARVIK?

(d) Essential requirements seem therefore at least one air base SOUTH of NARVIK, one to NORTH and another centrally situated?

Three bases is the minimum?

(e) Defence of air bases SOUTH of NARVIK implies defended naval anchorage and small land garrison in vicinity to repel seaborne raids?

(f) Air base or bases NORTH of NARVIK probably need small land garrison only?

(g) All air bases and defended anchorages need anti-aircraft ground defences?

(h) Unless fighter and ground defences for all bases large and small can be established <u>before</u> bases are put to use, probability is bases will never be established at all?

SUMMARY

5. (a) NARVIK port and the railway may not be available for the transport of ore, troops or supplies for six months or more?

(b) Unless NARVIK is essential from an ore point of view, is it necessary to go there at all?

(c) If not, cannot a better defended anchorage be found further SOUTH?

(d) If so, should not every effort be made now to obtain such an anchorage obtained with an air and army base?

JRL, AUC 6

2

'Defence of Narvik: note on requirements' by Auchinleck, 4 May 1940

MOST SECRET.

Assumptions.

1.   I understand

(a)   That the force of infantry which it is proposed eventually to send to NARVIK and its vicinity may comprise:-

One British Infantry Brigade	(three battalions)
Two French Light Divisions	(twelve battalions)
Foreign Legion	(two battalions)
Polish Contingent	(four battalions).

Should this be the eventual [size] of the force, I wish to emphasise that only one seventh of it will be British and this fact may very possibly make it extremely difficult for me to exercise command as freely as may be required. I strongly advocate the proportion of British troops be increased at an early date.

(b)   That the independent companies, which may eventually number ten, operating at the SOUTH of BODO will eventually come under my command, as their operations must be considered as being an essential part of the general plan for the defence of the NARVIK area.

(c)   144 heavy anti-aircraft guns)
144 light anti-aircraft guns   )   will be provided.[3]

Land Forces.

2.   I have made a provisional estimate of the land forces which I think may be needed for the defence of the NARVIK area. These forces

---

3   It seems unlikely that Auchinleck had access to so much AA support and this comment probably reflects Auchinleck's concern at the lack of RAF support for the forces in Norway. Auchinleck never had more than five AA Regiments under his command in Norway, which suggests a total of 120 AA guns of both types.

are exclusive of any that might at some future date be needed for an offensive into SWEDEN.

Exclusive of the independent companies, these requirements are:-

(a) One divisional cavalry or light tank regiment,

(b) One or two squadrons of armoured cars,

(c) Three or four companies of mounted infantry (e.g. Lovats Scouts)[4]

(d) Five batteries of field or mountain artillery

(e) One or two medium howitzer batteries

(f) Four field companies of engineers (exclusive of engineers for construction work)

(g) Twelve infantry battalions (four brigade commands)

(h) One machine gun battalion (might have to be increased to two later).

I understand that these troops may be British or French, or even Norwegian, should these be found suitable.

I wish to stress the fact that this estimate is extremely theoretical.

As regards (b), (c) and (d) I consider it essential that some mounted units should be included in the force in order to ensure the efficient patrolling of roads and coasts and the rapid reinforcement of outlying detachments, of which there will be many.

---

4   Lovat's Scouts had been formed in January 1900 as a specialist unit of mounted infantry, recruiting amongst gamekeepers, ghillies and stalkers in the Highlands of Scotland for service in the South African War. In 1903 the force was re-established as two regiments of Yeomanry, becoming part of the Territorial Force in 1908. During the First World War Lovat's Scouts saw action in Gallipoli, Egypt, Salonika and on the Western Front. Following the establishment of the Territorial Army in 1920 and conversion of many Yeomanry regiments to an artillery or armoured car role, the renamed Lovat Scouts were reformed in 1922 as a three squadron TA regiment, 400 strong, with one-quarter of the men equipped with ponies and the rest with bicycles. In 1935–36 the regiment was reformed, with the aim of having most men mounted on horses, with motorised transport and an above average allocation of BREN light machine guns. Then it was stated that the regiment's role would be, 'to provide mobile troops for duties of reconnaissance and protection, probably in a minor theatre of war'. Thus, in asking for Lovat Scouts, Auchinleck was demonstrating a familiarity with one of the specialist units of the TA and seeking a unit which would be fully mobile in the difficult Norwegian terrain. M. L. Melville, *The Story of the Lovat Scouts, 1900–1980* (Edinburgh: St Andrew Press, 1981).

As regards (d) and (e) some form of artillery support for troops operating inland must be provided, and that asked for is, I consider, the minimum.

As regards (h) the numerous landing places, dumps and detached posts which will require continuous protection, make it most desirable that a reasonable quota of medium machine guns should be provided, so that the maximum number of infantry can be kept mobile.

AIR FORCES.

3.   It is the intention to establish and protect at least three landing grounds from which fighting and bomber aircraft can co-operate in the defence of the occupied area.

It is intended to have one of these at BARDU FOSS N.E. of Narvik.

It is hoped to put another near HARSTAD or in the area HARSTAD – NARVIK.

I am convinced that the air defence of NARVIK will not be adequate unless a landing ground can be established and maintained south of NARVIK.

In my opinion it is essential to make every effort now to establish such a landing ground at or near BODO, where I understand a landing ground already exists.

BARDU FOSS should be established first and then under cover of fighters from BARDU FOSS, the BODO landing ground should be established <u>at once.</u>

In my opinion this is the only way the bases of the independent companies operating SOUTH of BODO can be secured from capture by German forces, operating by sea under cover of bomber aircraft; and the maintenance in being of these independent companies is, in my opinion, essential to the eventual security of NARVIK.

This may entail the installation of seaward defences for the protection of the BODO landing ground but this must be faced.

Anti-Aircraft artillery will necessarily be required and have been included in the provisional estimate of requirements.

JRL, AUC 8

3

Personal instructions from the CIGS to Auchinleck, appointing him commander of the Anglo-French forces when it has been decided that the system of unified command should cease. Signed by Sir John Dill, VCIGS, 5 May 1940

<u>MOST SECRET.</u>

With reference to paragraphs 3 and 4 of your instructions.

It is the intention that you should take over command of the Anglo-French forces at the same time that His Majesty's Government decides that the system of unified command is to cease.

If, however, when you arrive in the NARVIK area you consider that local conditions necessitate, you may assume command of the Anglo-French troops, thus placing yourself under Admiral of the Fleet Lord Cork and Orrery for as long as His Majesty's Government decide that a single commander is necessary.

JRL, AUC 9

4

Note by Admiral of the Fleet Lord Cork and Orrery to Auchinleck, given on board HMS *Effingham*, off Skaanland, expressing his views on the proposed attempt to capture Narvik, 11 May 1940

The position as I see it in the light of recent events is:-

The forces in the NARVIK area are sufficient for the moment. With what is now here the frontier could well be established at the VEST, OFOT, and ROMBAK Fiords, leaving only some 20 miles of land frontier to the Swedish frontier.

The position at BODO could be held to deny enemy possible aerodrome sites, but by gaining NAMSOS a nearly completed aerodrome has been acquired.

With the development of aerodromes at BARDUFOSS, SKAANLAND and BANAK (PORSANGER) however, the situation could no doubt be kept in hand and the frontier stabilised from the SOUTH.

An additional force, however, will be required to watch the approaches from MURMANSK and, if the neutrality of SWEDEN is violated, the frontier of that country.

The actual town of NARVIK is of no material value, everything of potential use has been destroyed, the harbour is blocked with wrecks which would take some months to clear.

Nor if HUNDALEN is in our hands can the railway be used by the enemy.

The value of NARVIK from a political point of view is high, in the opinion of H.M. Government, and the desire to occupy it great. I should like to make a determined attempt to bring this about.

My views on the subject are known. It could, in my opinion, be carried out with some loss.

The contrary opinion, however, is very strong, so much so that I feel it would be hopeless to attempt it with the British troops.

However devotedly the duty might be carried out, the necessary optimism to ensure success would be lacking.

This is not meant as a reflection on anybody; to go into any trial of strength believing you are foredoomed to failure is half way to that result.

The development of the enemy's air power, which will increase considerably in a few weeks as a result of the enemy's gain of the NAMSOS area does introduce an additional difficulty which cannot be ignored.

My recommendation is that the present military movements continue, and by them, in time NARVIK will be neutralised if not evacuated, and the line HUNDALEN – Swedish frontier established.

That the Navy should guarantee the safety of the water frontier – NARVIK to the extreme Western entrance to the VESTFIORD, and the Army assisted by some Naval units maintain an advanced position in the BODO area.

JRL, AUC 12

5

Report by Auchinleck addressed to Sir John Dill, VCIGS, describing the first meeting with Lord Cork, from HMS *Effingham*, 13 May 1940

<u>MOST SECRET AND PERSONAL.</u>

1. I hope to send you at the same time as this the report called for in my Instructions. I am afraid that it is rather long, but the subject is a wide one and I trust that I have covered all the ground and given you the information you need.

2. I disembarked at Harstad, which is Force H.Q. and the general base area, on the morning of the 11th, apparently rather unexpectedly. Lord Cork was away in his flagship, and Mackesy[5] was also out. I had a talk with Mackesy later in the morning. He looks well and seems in good heart, though I suspect that he is sore inwardly. He seemed to have a good grip on the situation, and was particularly firm on the need for retaining BODO at all costs. Here I am in entire agreement with him; it is essential to the continued security of NARVIK and TROMSO.

3. He explained a proposed operation by the French which has since taken place and his reasons for it which were to enable him eventually to establish artillery on the OIJORD POINT opposite NARVIK town to support a landing on the opposite shore. As you will see from my report I consider NARVIK in its present condition to be of NO <u>military</u> value. However, his plan and reasons were sound and good in their way and I saw no reason to interfere with them, particularly as the impending operation had been approved and ordered by Lord Cork.

4. Mackesy explained his ideas on BODO which he is reinforcing at once with the 24th Infantry Brigade, less the [2nd] S[outh].W[ales]. B[orderers]., who are at ANKENES. This also I agreed with, and with Mackesy's order to the Brigade Commander that BODO was to be held at all costs. Later Lord Cork asked if he should cancel

---

5   Major General P. J. Mackesy was the original commander of land forces in the Narvik area.

this reinforcement order in view of the probability of my assuming command from Mackesy. I said that I agreed with it, and asked him to let it stand. It may yet be necessary further to reinforce BODO unless we can get some land based aircraft quickly.

5. After lunch I and Gammell[6] motored to SKAANLAND anchorage and went on board EFFINGHAM; Lord Cork's flagship. He was charming and most forthcoming, and acceded at once to my suggestion that I should stay on board and witness the impeding operation which was fixed for the following night. I may say here that I think it odd that neither Mackesy nor any member of his staff was present on the flagship, although General Bethouard,[7] to whom Mackesy had entrusted with execution of the operation, was on board with his staff in close liaison with Lord Cork. However, both Mackesy and Cork assured me that relations were most cordial and co-operation good; the latter is certainly true, and I have no reason to doubt the former.

6. I showed Lord Cork my Instructions and explained the situation to him. He, on his part, told me what had happened. He is I think disappointed and surprised that any project for a landing at NARVIK itself should have been so definitely and unanimously negatived by the British soldiers. Yesterday I sailed past NARVIK at one thousand yards range and had a good look at it while the ship's guns did some field firing at motor lorries, possible machine gun posts and the like. I admit at once that, if the enemy has as many machine guns as he is reliably reported to have, the houses of the town and the ground generally provide all that can be needed in the way of cover for them, and that a landing there in the face of strong opposition is bound to be costly and might end in failure. The trouble is that information as to the enemy strength and dispositions is practically non-existant and appears unobtainable. However, the enemy cannot be strong everywhere.

7. I then asked Lord Cork directly whether he thought I should take over from Mackesy as soon as the impending operation was over. He answered "Yes" without hesitation. As there was no immediate urgency I sent you a telegram asking you to recall Mackesy for

---

6   Brigadier James Andrew Harcourt Gammell, Auchinleck's BGS.
7   Brigadier General Antoine Béthouart, commander of French forces in Narvik area.

consultation. I did this because I feel that there appear to be no obvious grounds for imputing blame to Mackesy, who may have done all or more than anyone else might have done. In fact, if Lord Cork's reply had not been so unhesitating I might very well have recommended to you that Mackesy should remain in command. Even now I am a little doubtful about it, but I think I am right. I want to keep Dowler[8] and others of Mackey's staff for the present at any rate.

8.   Last night and in the early hours of this morning the French landed two battalions of the [French Foreign] Legion at the head of the HERJANG FJORD after a preliminary bombardment by the Fleet. Though no previous practice had taken place, and though landing craft of the right type were few and far between, the operation appears to have been completely successful.

(I am writing at 7.a.m., the operation having been started at midnight and been carried out in broad daylight throughout – there is no night here now).

Luckily, the opposition appears to have been slight, though there may have been half a dozen enemy machine guns in action. The French landed four tanks, and I thought their infantry worked very well indeed. I watched the whole operation from the ship, half a mile from the shore. I like General Bethouard, who knows what he wants, and the French officers seem most capable. The Navy did their part very well indeed. The only pity is that no <u>British</u> units participated. The success represents a definite advance, and I hope that prisoners may have been taken. It will I hope be good for morale and show the troops that such things can be done. Needless to say, it was a most interesting experience.

9.   I have a feeling that the Navy dislike these operations as at present prosecuted. They are being subjected daily to a lot of bombing and have had losses and casualties on an appreciable scale. They do not like being bombed in these narrow waters, which is natural as they have no really effective reply. They would not mind if they could see some result in the shape of a definite and quick decision, but they do not like the rather objectless work which they perforce have to do day after day. They are also anxious as to the feasibility of discharging efficiently and quickly the shipping which will be

---

8   Colonel Arthur Dowler who was then GSO1.

needed to maintain the forces as a whole. Here again, it is the bombing which worries them. I do not mean that they are faint-hearted – far from it – but there is no doubt that the advent of land based fighter aircraft would make them much happier. Incidentally, I have yet to meet a sailor who thinks that a defended anchorage at NARVIK is a necessity to the Navy, so it is NOT a question of the Army protecting the anchorage for the use of the Navy on the high seas, but of the Navy using the anchorage for the protection of the Army in the coastal waters of Norway. I rather thought that this would prove to be the true situation, and I am laying my plans accordingly.

10. I am a little anxious about the situation at MO and as to the chance of stabilization at BODO. There is no doubt whatever that the enemy bombers, if unmolested, can offset the value of sea power in these narrow waters, and that they can make the maintenance of small forces almost impossible unless we can provide an adequate counter in the air and on the ground. I know that you know this well enough, and I hope that the War Cabinet realise it too. I hope to have fighter aircraft in the air on or about 20th May. I did not expect much from the "independent" companies. To be a successful guerrilla you must, I think, be a guerrilla in your own country, not in someone else's. I now propose to coalesce them into a unit of light infantry under Gubbins and to put them under the Commander, 24th Infantry Brigade. I notice that in one or two recent War Office messages they speak of the "desirability" of holding BODO. In my humble opinion it is not a question of "desirability", but of sheer necessity. I hope you will agree, for if BODO goes I can not long be responsible for NARVIK.

11. I know how hard pressed you must be to find men for all require-ments, but I would like to remind you that with the departure of the 24th Brigade to BODO my <u>British</u> troops in NARVIK will be reduced to one battalion, exclusive of artillery, sappers, etc. I do feel it most desirable that I should be given another British brigade if it can possibly be made available.

12. In every campaign there is a certain minimum of force which must, in my opinion, be provided in fairness to the responsible Commander and to the troops under him. This applies at present particularly to air forces and anti-aircraft artillery, but also in the long run to all the other forces specified. I have done my best to reduce my

estimate to the great extent compatible with security, but it would be criminal to pretend that one can make bricks without straw. If H.M.G. think that the commitment involved in the preservation of Northern Norway is worth adding to their other commitments, I trust that they will set aside <u>definitely</u> the forces required for the purpose. I feel very strongly that if they are not prepared to do this it would be better to come away now than to risk throwing good money after bad by failing to provide the necessary forces. I would like to point out also that even if the forces required can be provided the difficulty of finding an adequate number of suitable landing grounds in this very broken terrain might still prove to be the deciding factor, though I hope that things may possibly be better in this respect than they appear at present. I cannot say yet. If there is any chance of it being decided to evacuate Norway the sooner the decision is taken the better, as every day's delay must increase the difficulty of the operation of withdrawal. In any event, land based aircraft and anti-aircraft artillery will be needed to cover the evacuation, so the development of landing grounds and the installation of artillery must continue.

13. I do not wish to appear pessimistic, and I am not pessimistic, but I feel that I must say what I think without fear or favour. That is what I have tried to do in this letter, and what I shall continue to do.

14. One thing more I would like to add, and that is if we do hold Northern Norway, and I hope we will, our defence should be active and not passive. As soon as we are in position to do so we should give the German a taste of his own medicine. This can be done, I think, without seriously increasing our commitments in the country, and I am already looking ahead with this in view.

JRL, AUC 14

6

Personal letter from Auchinleck to Sir John Dill, VCIGS, 14–15 May 1940

<u>Private & Personal</u>

Since writing my letter yesterday, things have happened. I got back to Harstad in [HMS] Effingham after lunch and at once Fraser[9] (24th Guards Brigade) and Dowler[10] (G.S.O.I.) came onboard to discuss with Lord Cork plans for the reinforcement of the Scots Guards at Mo, at which place the situation, owing to the rapid German advance has become unpleasant and may become critical. I listened in and soon realised that all was not well. The fact that Mackesy was not there to discuss what might easily become a serious commitment (it has since become so) made me suspicious at once. As this matter was bound to concern me vitally in a few hours time I confirmed my suspicious by a few words aside with Maund[11] the Admiral's Chief of Staff and with Dowler. I then spoke to the Admiral and with his concurrence, announced that I have assumed command via Mackesy (your telegram had not then arrived).

2.   I then, with the Admiral's agreement issued orders for Fraser and the Scots Guards to go to Bodo instead of Mo. Mo is at the end of a long and narrow fjord in which ships are and have been very exposed to bombing attacks, so much so that the Admiral is very averse from having to maintain it by sea. The road north from Mo to Bodo is reported still unusable because of snow so the detachment there is in an unpleasant position. It was no use, however, putting more troops into the same bag, so I plumbed for Bodo and told Fraser to work South as fast as possible and get touch with Mo if he could, but in any way, to hold Bodo. The transport which put the Scots Guards ashore at Mo was very heavily bombed all day and only escaped being sunk by a miracle it seems! The Germans are advancing by road from the South and put almost a battalion ashore at Hemnesberget 20 miles SW of Mo. The Navy missed

---

9   Brigadier William Fraser.
10   Colonel Arthur Dowler.
11   Captain, L. E. H. Maund.

this lot by 40 minutes but sank their ship after they landed and with it, we hope their equipment and stores.

3.   I am reinforcing Bodo at once with the third battalion of the 24th Bde – ([2nd] S[outh].W[ales].B[orderers].) and am also going to send a whole 25 pdr battery and some Bofors.[12] I hope these will be in time to take the Mo chestnut out of the fire but it is a tedious business – Anyway, we must keep Bodo.

   If I have to let go at Mo, I will have a shot a[t] getting it back as soon as I can, but you will see that this Southern front is becoming a relatively serious commitment. I have put Gubbins[13] and his companies under Fraser.

4.   I saw Mackesy again yesterday evening and tackled him about his curious aloofness when major matters were being decided. His answers were most unconvincing and I am sure he is unfitted to command anything. He is, I think a complete megalomaniac, more concerned, in fact alone concerned with what the world will think of Mackesy, the War office scapegoat than with getting on with the war. He has allowed his cleverness and cynicism completely to outweigh his reason and <u>I honestly think he is unbalanced.</u> Sorry to have to say this, but I am sure I am right. <u>He is of no use to anyone in his present condition and I hope he will not be allowed to command any troops anywhere.</u> He is also in a nervous state and suffering from insomnia. He told me with pride he had dictated a long screed at 2:30am in the morning for no valid reason whatever. I know you think highly of him but I must tell you what I think. He has been charming to me and helpful, but his whole mental outlook is warped. The clash between him and Cork was not all his fault. I am sure of that. They were quite impossible bedfellows from the start, entirely incompatible temperaments. Nothing would make them work together, I thought at first that nothing was seriously wrong but I was wrong in this – quite wrong. I am thankful I found out in time, though the legacy I inherit is not altogether pleasant.

5.   The combined operation by the French was a complete success and a very good show indeed. The French have exploited well and are all for going on. They have got 60 prisoners and some

---

12   The Bofors 40 mm anti-aircraft gun.
13   Brigadier Colin McVean Gubbins, an expert in irregular warfare, who had been instrumental in the formation of the Independent Companies.

material. Casualties were few. I have now put Bethouard who I like very much indeed, in charge of the whole centre sector – Narvik-Bardu Foss and this should work well. I have had a long talk with him to day and been very full and frank with him. He is a most refreshing person to work with. They are getting on with Bardu Foss aerodrome and we <u>hope</u> to use it on the 20th but meanwhile the German bombers are a damned nuisance even though we have some AA artillery in position. They bomb us every day more or less and usually make a dead set at the warships. We have been lucky to have so few casualties as they make good practice at 15,000 feet, being almost uninterrupted.

If only we could get something into the air we could hit back and give him some of his own medicine, and also I am sure bite him in his hinder parts, instead of letting him always bite us.

There is a hell of a lot to do here especially on the administrative side and I shall shortly have to have a wholescale clearing out of the inhabitants from the occupied areas. The place is riddled, I am convinced, with spies.

I apologise for the writing but bits of this letter are too private to have typed. I hope you are very well.

<u>P.S.</u>   15th May

Last night as you know, the ship taking the Irish Guards and 24th Bde HQ to Bodo was bombed and set on fire. It was bad luck and all due to <u>one</u> lucky bomb.

Unfortunately, the bomb hit the officers' cabins and killed the C.O. and several others. Very few men were hurt but the ship and all in her, including three light tanks is lost. We had the battalion back here by 9 this morning thanks to the Navy who did splendidly – they are grand.

The Battalion is now in rest billets and will be refitted. They have no rifles, machine guns or anything. I saw them came ashore and was much impressed by their bearing – a fine crowd. I have been all day arranging to set the S[outh].W[ales].B[orders]. off in their place and the Admiral is taking them down in his flagship. We must get them there somehow. Fraser who had gone ahead to Mo & Bodo in a destroyer – Somali – is also away, as Somali was badly damaged by a separate attack on the same night and is now on her way to Scapa. I have put Gubbins in command at Bodo-Mo and am sending him with the 24th Bde staff. I can not say I am happy about the situation down there but, if we can hang on till we get our aeroplanes functioning, we ought to be all right.

It is our turn to have a bit of luck!

I am just off to say a few words to the Irish Guards.

Mackesy sails tonight, the best thing I think.

These fleet air arm fighters do their very best but they have not got the performance to keep off the Hun and he does not seem to think much of our AA fire!!! However, our tails are up!

JRL, AUC 20

7

Note by Major General P. J. Mackesy, written just before his departure for England, restating his view that Mo should be held at all costs. With marginal comments by Auchinleck [the latter noted in italics], 15 May 1940

Excuse manuscript but my typewriter has been taken from me.

1.   I have always been very puzzled as to what the Boche has been doing here. The word NARVIK has always meant very little to me. I have always tried to study the map, and to understand what the Boche is after in order to check it.

2.   I think for some reason, which we can imagine but cannot be sure of, the Boche, in addition to destroying NARVIK as a source of ore supply to us, has been endeavouring to maintain a sort of bridgehead in the area GRATANGEN–BJERVIK–OIJORD–NARVIK–ANKENES, for future operations. *Yes* Movements South from this area by land seem to me to be nonsense. Movement North on TROMSO seems to be possible. It may of course be neither, and the intention may be to maintain a base for operations from which it may in time seem to him profitable to undertake operations form land, sea or air.   *Yes*

3.   Whatever the answer, I feel that our right procedure is to destroy the Boche forces wherever they are. That, while holding the OIJORD peninsular against possibility of counter attack, and establishing upon it artillery to command NARVIK itself and the approach South of ROMBAK FJORD, the French should endeavour, if it

is a reasonable military operation, to operate against the right flank of the Germans in the HUNDALEN area. *Yes*

4. It has always been my intention to occupy BEISFJORD area from the south, but the urgent need of sending troops to the BODO-MO area has held this up for the time being.

5. In short I believe our right strategy is, if physical conditions make it possible, to destroy German concentrations East of NARVIK and establish troops in the mountains which will definitely prevent any incursion of German forces along the midway from SWEDEN. *Yes*

6. Either after this, or at any time during this operation, I am sure that NARVIK itself will fall into our hands like a ripe plum, the moment it is considered right to bother about it. On the whole I would be inclined to take up the operation as soon as possible and I think carry it out soon because if the Germans manage to bring guns down the midway, our shipping position in the WEST FJORD might become serious. The railway must be kept cut, and the Germans and the big viaduct at HUNDALEN should be constantly bombed.

7. I should like to warn against a direct attack on NARVIK until:-

   (a) It is worth it
   (b) We can defend it against concentrated air attack
   (c) It is quite clear that machine guns on those steep slopes East of NARVIK itself, can be effectively dealt with by artillery fire and tanks. *A different time?*

   I see no difficulty in getting ashore, it is subsequent operations which matter.

8. As regards what has now become the Southern front, I personally regard the definite holding of MO as being vital. The instructions given by me were that MO was to be held at all costs. These instructions were altered on the night of May 13th.
   Yes they were and for good reasons.
   I am very much afraid that if we do not hold MO and its aerodrome, our ships will be bombed out of this area, and our position here will become impossible.

JRL, AUC 21

8

Letter from Auchinleck to Colonel Colin Gubbins, commanding troops in the Bodo-Mo area, 16 May 1940[14]

<u>SECRET.</u>

You will have had my telegram telling you that I wish the detachment at Mo to hold on to its position, and not withdraw.

I think it most important that we should give up no more ground. I know the detachment is somewhat isolated at present, and I know the Germans may be in superior force to the south of you, but I am pretty sure that they are groping in the dark very much as we are, and I hope that when they come up against really determined opposition that they will sit back and think about it.

Reinforcements for you should arrive with this letter, and I hope that their arrival will enable you, in your turn, to reinforce Trappes-Lomax[15] at Mo.

He is very anxious to get back Fotheringham's Company to his own Battalion. However, I leave all this to you.

Gammell is going down with this letter, and I want you to tell him exactly what you think about the situation, and what your requirements are to enable you to hold on in the Bodo – Mo area. I will do my utmost to send you whatever you may want.

It will not be long now, I hope, before we have our own aircraft in the air, and that ought to make a lot of difference.

Things are going well here, and the French are pushing on towards Narvik.

Thank you very much for all you have done so far. I wish you good luck. I have the greatest confidence in you. I hope to get down before long to see you.

JRL, AUC 25

---

14 Note by Auchinleck, 'Sent by hand of Brigadier Gammell in HMS Effingham but never received as ship struck a rock'. HMS *Effingham* ran aground and was lost on the 17 May. S. W. Roskill, *The War at Sea 1939–1945* (London, 1954), Vol. I, p. 192.
15 Lieutenant Colonel Thomas Trappes-Lomax, commanding 1st Scots Guards.

9

Order of the Day, issued by Auchinleck on re-embarkation for the UK, 8 June 1940

Now that the North-Western Expeditionary Force has re-embarked for the United Kingdom I wish to express my sincere thanks to Commanders, Staffs and All Ranks of the Force for their loyal and willing co-operation on all occasions, and to express my admiration for your unfailing determination and good-cheer.

Some of you have fought under adverse conditions against the enemy in the face of strong hostile air attack. Others have worked hard at the Base to produce all that was necessary to enable the campaign to be conducted to a successful conclusion.

Thanks to the excellent work of the Air Component, the splendid co-operation of the Royal Navy and the magnificent achievements of our French Allies on the NARVIK PENINSULA, we were well on the way to meeting the enemy on equal terms.

But Great Britain and France are now in danger and it is for this reason that our Governments have ordered us home to help in the defence of our own countries.

Therefore, to my great regret, we have had to relinquish our task but other and more urgent ones lie ahead.

I wish you all success, and rely upon you all to play your full part in re-building our Armies and so achieving final victory.

JRL, AUC 67

10

Draft report, Auchinleck to the Secretary of State for War on the operations in Northern Norway, 14 May–7 June

I have the honour to inform you that in accordance with your Instructions the Forces under my command:-

(a)   Have captured NARVIK.
(b)   Have evacuated Northern Norway.

Landing at Bjerkvik.

The landing round BJERKVIK, at the head of the HERJANGS FJORD, was carried out with the object of attacking from the rear the enemy forces which were holding up the advance of the French and Norwegian forces pushing South [South – repeated] from GRATANGEN towards NARVIK.

These enemy forces were holding a very strong position at the head of the pass astride the road which leads from GRATANGEN to BJERKVIK and ELVEGAARDE. The flanks of the position rested on high mountains deeply covered with snow, and the Germans, who were mainly supplied by air, were well equipped with machine guns and ammunition.

It was anticipated that a successful landing in the HERJANGS FJORD would have the effect of cutting the normal road communications between NARVIK and the German detachment further North, and force that detachment either to surrender or fall back along the road past Lake HARTVIG and thence along the difficult track leading to the Eastern end of the ROMBAKS FJORD and the railway at HUNDALEN.

A landing was therefore planned and carried out by General Bethouart with two Battalions of the Foreign Legion on 13 May. The launching craft available for the operations were three M.L.C.s and four A.L.C.'s.[16] Troops were transported in the cruisers Effingham and Aurora, the repair ship Vindictive, and the net layer Protector, while the battleship Resolution had, in addition, the task of transferring the French tanks, which were to lead the assault, into M.L.C.'s.

The first flight of the infantry were carried in four A.L.C.'s, the second in tow of ships' boats further reinforced by the A.L.C.'s when they were available after their first trip.

The force collected gradually in OFOT FJORD on 13 May, but, thanks to low cloud and mist, there was no interference from hostile aircraft throughout the whole operation.

Late in the evening the force moved up to the head of Herjangs Fjord, preceded by five destroyers which opened fire on all the houses which fringed the head of the Bay round the selected landing places. This bombardment was very effective and within a few minutes the houses were ablaze. The cruisers then got into position, joined in the bombardment with their six inch guns and pom poms, and the M.L.C.'s,

---

16   Motor Landing Craft and Assault Landing Craft.

carrying the tanks, moved forward to the beaches followed by the four A.L.C.'s carrying 120 men.

The advance was met by machine gun fire from the right flank and the A.L.C.'s sheered off from the original landing place selected. The infantry managed, however, to effect a landing further to the West, and quickly secured, without serious opposition, some high ground in this area which overlooked the beaches further East. The bombardment in this Western sector had proved effective since no machine gun fire was experienced and from prisoners' statements it was learned that about 100 Germans were killed in one group of buildings and some 20 in another. An ammunition dump was set on fire and at least one German machine gun position was destroyed. One tank, later followed by a second, landed close to the landing place originally selected.

The successful advance inland of the tanks and infantry on the left enabled further landings to be made at the head of the bay near the quay, and soon the whole of this areas as far East as the road landing northwards towards GRATANGEN was in French hands.

Although one or two machine guns which could not be located continued to fire, two more tanks were landed on the East shore of the bay. Concurrently, further detachments of infantry were landed from A.L.C.'s and ships' boats still further to the East, close to the road running South towards OYORD along the Eastern shore of the FJORD. These landings were covered by heavy fire from the six inch guns and pom poms of H.M.S. Effingham and a destroyer, and were effected without loss.

Once ashore the tanks and infantry, working in excellent co-operation, rapidly overcame such enemy opposition as still remained and advanced [deleted – rapidly] along the road leading to Lake HARTVIG. The enemy retreated into the hills to the Eastwards leaving some 60 prisoners in French hands.

General Bethouart's next concern was the security of his left flank, and he organised a force of one company of the Foreign Legion, supported by a destroyer, to move along the West bank of the HERJANGS FJORD towards BOGEN. Before this movement materialised, however, the Polish battalion which was advancing from BOGEN arrived in the area, having succeeded in traversing a road which had been considered impassable owing to snow.

His left flank now being secure, General Bethouart organised immediately a party of some thirty motor cyclists to move along the coast road towards OYORD and arranged to support them from the sea with a destroyer.

This mobile detachment met with no opposition, and at OYORD was met by a landing party put ashore from the destroyer. By this rapid movement the control of the North shore at the entrance of ROMBAKS FJORD passed into French hands, and the enemy's line of retreat was restricted to the difficult road through the hills to HUNDALEN.

By these successful operations, carried out with the loss of less than twenty casualties, General Bethouart prepared the ground for the eventual capture of NARVIK. The way was cleared for the advance of the French forces from GRATANGEN, and the Germans were gradually forced Eastwards through the difficult country North of the ROMBAKS FJORD until sufficient room was available to launch an attack on NARVIK across the ROMBAKS FJORD without risk of enemy interference.

The success of the operation was due, in my opinion, first to the fact that the enemy appeared to be taken by surprise and had not organised his defences against a landing in BJERVIK as thoroughly as might have been expected. Secondly, it was due to the skill and thoroughness with which the operation was prepared and carried out both by General Bethouart and his troops, and all ranks of the Royal Navy. Thirdly, it was due to the favourable weather conditions – complete calm with low clouds and mist. This facilitated the movement of landing craft and ships' boats, and, most important of all, prevented any interference at all from hostile aircraft throughout the operation.

JRL, AUC 68

11

Letter from R. H. Dewing, Director of Military Operations and Plans at the War Office to Auchinleck, 21 June 1940

I am directed to request that you will forward, for the information of the Chief of the Imperial General Staff, a report on the reasons which led you to consider it advisable to exercise the authority given by him in his personal instructions to you, and to assume command of the Anglo-French troops and air components in Northern Norway on 13th May, 1940.

JRL, AUC 70

12

Auchinleck's report in reply to the above, addressed to the Undersecretary of State, War Office, 24 June 1940

1. In reply to your letter 0157/1089 (M.o.1) of 21st June 1940, I have the honour to inform you that the reasons which led me to consider it advisable to exercise the authority, given by the Chief of the Imperial General Staff in his personal instructions to me, to assume command of the Anglo–French troops and air components in Northern Norway on 13th May 1940, are stated briefly in paragraph 12 of the "Report on the Operations in Northern Norway" submitted by me to you on the 19th June 1940.

2. Should this explanation not suffice, I give the following details in amplification. I may mention here that before I left London, I had been given to believe by the Chief of the Imperial General Staff that relations between Major-General Mackesy and Lord Cork were not cordial.

3. (i)   I disembarked at HARSTAD in the forenoon of the 11th May 1940 and met Major-General Mackesy at his quarters and learned the general tactical situation from him and his senior general staff officer, Colonel Dowler. My original intention had been first to see Lord Cork, the Commander-in-Chief and then General Mackesy, but Lord Cork was away in his flagship at SKAANLAND, about two hour's journey from HARSTAD by car and boat.

    (ii)   General Mackesy had apparently been unwell and suffering from insomnia, but so far as I could judge from what he said, the relations between him and Lord Cork seemed to be then satisfactory, whatever they might have been in the past.

    (iii) I then visited Lord Cork and explained my position to him and said that, in accordance with my instructions and in view of the fact that an operation for landing French troops at BJERVIK had been fully planned and was to take place the following day, I had set aside any idea of taking over command at once.

    I asked Lord Cork directly whether he thought I should take over command as soon as the present operations were over and he replied unhesitatingly in the affirmative. I then sent a personal telegram to the Vice-C.I.G.S., General Sir John Dill, asking him to recall Major-General Mackesy "for consultation".

I did this as, at that time, I did not think that the need for a change in command was urgent, and because I did not wish it to be publicly apparent that Major-General Mackesy had been superseded.

(iv) I then obtained permission from Lord Cork to stay in the flagship and watch the forthcoming operation as a spectator. I may mention that though General Bethouart, in actual command of the troops who were to carry out the operation, and his staff were on board, neither Major-General Mackesy or any of his staff were present. This struck me as unusual and gave me cause to doubt whether relations between Lord Cork and Major-General Mackesy were in fact satisfactory. Major-General Mackesy told me afterwards that he thought that the presence in the flagship of himself or his staff might have embarrassed General Bethouart.

(v) After the operation had successfully concluded, I returned to HARSTAD in the flagship, which on arrival was boarded by Brigadier Fraser, Commanding 24th Guards Brigade and Colonel Dowler, G.S.O.I to General Mackesy.

These two officers came to discuss with Lord Cork, the Commander-in-Chief, whether certain reinforcements, destined for the Southern front and already embarked, should be sent to MO, where a detachment had recently landed under heavy air attack, or to BODO, with a view to disembarkation there and subsequent movement by land to reinforce MO. Again I was disquieted by the absence of Major-General Mackesy but was later informed that it was due to his state of health. The decision to be taken was a most important one, and as I listened to the discussion, it became quite apparent to me that all was not as it should be. As, in any event, I expected to succeed Major-General Mackesy in a few days time, I hastily consulted Lord Cork's Chief of Staff and was confirmed in my opinion that Lord Cork and Major-General Mackesy were so antipathetic to each other as to make it impossible for them to work together in complete accord. I then consulted Lord Cork privately and told him that I considered that I should at once take over command instead of waiting for the result of my telegram to General Sir John Dill. With his concurrence I then announced my decision to the conference and issued orders on the spot for the despatch of the reinforcements to BODO. I then disembarked and informed Major-General Mackesy of the action I had taken and my reasons for taking it.

4. I hope I have made it clear that in acting as I did, I was moved solely by what seemed to me the urgent need for ensuring that the commander of the army should be able to co-operate fully and willingly with the Commander-in-Chief.

I came to the conclusion that, for personal reasons, which I thought irremediable, relations between Lord Cork and Major-General Mackesy were such as to make it impossible for them to co-operate whole-heartedly one with the other, and I acted accordingly.

I am not in a position to impute the blame for what appeared to me to be an impossible situation, either to Lord Cork or to Major-General Mackesy.

JRL, AUC 70

13

Copy of a letter from Sir J. S. Barnes, Secretary, Admiralty, to Admiral of the Fleet, the Earl of Cork and Orrery, 3 July 1940

MOST SECRET

I am to refer to Admiralty telegram 2005/24th May [see document 14 below] in which you were informed of the decision of His Majesty's Government that the forces under your command were to evacuate Northern Norway and that the reason for this decision was that the troops, ships, guns and certain equipment were urgently required for the defence of the United Kingdom. That telegram stated that the evacuation of all equipment, vehicles and stores would clearly take too long and that the following were required to be evacuated in order of importance from the point of view of the defence of this country:-

(a)   Personnel.
(b)   Light Anti-Aircraft guns and ammunition.

(c) 25 Pounders.
(d) Heavy Anti-Aircraft guns and ammunition.

These instructions were supplemented by Admiralty Telegram 1637/6th June which stated that in addition to the items of equipment mentioned in Admiralty Telegram 2005/24th May, great importance was attached to removing as many rifles and as much small arms ammunition as possible.

Exact information of the numbers of Anti-Aircraft guns brought away from Northern Norway is not yet available. According to present information, the numbers are as follows:-

Light Anti-Aircraft guns: 16 out of 60.
Heavy Anti-Aircraft guns: 6 out of 48.

I am to request that you will report on the small proportion that was brought away.

JRL, AUC 74

14

Copy of Admiralty Telegram to Flag Officer, Narvik, 24 May 1940

Following from Chiefs of Staff:

H.M. Government has decided your forces are to evacuate Northern Norway at earliest moment. Reason for this is that the Troops, Ships, Guns and certain equipment are urgently required for the defence of the U.K.

We understand from Military point of view operations of evacuation will be facilitated if enemy forces are largely destroyed or captured. Moreover, destruction of railways and Narvik Port facilities make its capture highly desirable.

Nevertheless, speed of evacuation once begun should be of primary consideration in order to limit duration of maximum naval effort.

Two Officers will be sent at once from U.K. to concert evacuation plans with you and General Auchinleck.

Evacuation of all equipment, vehicles and stores will clearly take too long. Following are required to be evacuated in order of importance from point of view of defence of U.K. (a) personnel (b) light A/A guns and ammunition (c) 25-pounders (d) Heavy A/A Guns and ammunition.

Tactical conditions must rule but so far as they permit plans should be framed accordingly.

Norwegian Government have not, repetition not, been informed and greatest secrecy should be observed.

JRL, AUC 74

15

Copy of message to Flag Officer, Narvik, from Admiralty, undated [24 May 1940?]

Following from Chiefs of Staff.

Since Admiralty Telegram 1637/6 was despatched, Norwegian Authorities here have made urgent requests for supply to Norwegian Forces of a minimum 4500 rifles together with not more than 2 million rounds of ammunition. If any way possible to meet this request you should do so.

JRL, AUC 74

16

Report from Lord Cork to Sir J. S. Barnes, the Secretary of the Admiralty, 4 July 1940

1. In reply to Admiralty letter N. 012261/4 of the 3rd July, 1940, be pleased to inform Their Lordships that action on the Admiralty Telegram 2005/24th May was based upon –

   (1) Tactical considerations.
   (2) The necessity for secrecy.
   (3) Paucity of resources.

   In forwarding the report called for upon what I regret to note is considered the "small proportion" of A/A guns saved, the following remarks are submitted.

2. (1) The directions contained in the Telegram referred to (a complete copy of which is attached) were studied and discussed and it was decided that, for tactical reasons (mentioned in (d) of the message quoted), –

(i)   The A/A defences must be kept efficient and in action to protect the embarkation and to cover the final retirement.

(ii)   That a limited amount of thinning out of guns could be done – but that it was essential that aerodromes and points of embarkation should be adequately protected up to the end.

(2)   The necessity for secrecy was great – and, in fact, the "greatest secrecy" was enjoined in the final paragraph of the message quoted. There was every reason to believe that what happened in the HARSTAD area was soon known to the enemy, in addition to which, enemy aerial reconnaissance was a daily occurrence. How would it have been possible to have started the dismantling and embarkation of A/A guns in the fourth week of May, after all efforts had been devoted to mounting them in the third week, without arousing suspicion? It was not until June 2nd that, on my initiative, the Norwegian Government was informed of impending evacuation. June 2nd was the original date fixed for the start.

(3)   Apart from all other considerations, in order to remove any large proportion of the guns, time was essential – owing to the wide dispersion, water distances to be covered, and almost negligible means of transport and facilities existing. Time was not available.

3.   The distribution of the guns was approximately as follows:-

	Heavy	*Light*
BARDUFOSS Aerodrome	12	12
SORREISA	–	2
ELVENES	–	4
TROMSO	4	4
HARSTAD	16	8
SKAANLAND	15	10
BALLANGEN	–	4
ANKENES	–	4
BJERVIK	–	4
BODO	–	2

4. BARDU FOSS:

The guns were required to protect the aerodrome. Communication with BARDU FOSS was by 20 odd miles of indifferent road (on which much labour had been expended to get guns up) from SORREISA, at which place everything of any weight had to be embarked or disembarked on an open beach.

5. At TROMSO, the guns had only recently been sent there. Under the circumstances prevailing prior to the evacuation – at first secrecy from latterly somewhat delicate relations with the Norwegian Government – it was not in my view advisable to attempt their withdrawal but instructions were sent for the control instruments to be embarked in DEVONSHIRE.

6. At HARSTAD, it was essential to retain defence against aerial attack – which, in suitable weather, had become heavy and frequent – for these were the only wharves available that allowed vessels of any size coming alongside and loading up – and which were in use until midnight June 7th both for loading stores and troops into destroyers. We had no steamers or destroyers to spare.

7. SKAANLAND was one of the four main areas of embarkation and was in use on the final night. The Batteries here had been established by the use of M.L.Cs. and their movement across the water was only possible by means of M.L.Cs. There was only one M.L.C. available and this formed an essential item in the re-embarkation of French and Polish Troops at ANKENES, NARVIK and ROMBAKS. It was by means of this M.L.C. that two Bofors Guns were embarked in the Trawler "Man o' War" at SKJOMEN FIORD on the 6th. It is important to bear in mind that the distance from HARSTAD to SKAANLAND by water is just 14 miles and from SKAANLAND to NARVIK 50 miles.

8. BALLENGEN, ANKENES and BJERVIK were the embarking places of French and Polish troops actually in touch with the enemy, and where the troops had to be ferried to the waiting destroyers in fishing boats from the open beaches. Aerial attacks were actually delivered in this area during the afternoon of the day of departure.

9. Owing to the weather conditions prevailing during the last few days of embarkation, heavy low clouds and rain, German air activity was small. Immunity could not be counted on – attacks could

and, in fact, were renewed as soon as conditions improved – and subsequent events seem to have shown German efforts to interfere with the departure were maturing, and that the departure was just in time.

10. No doubt, some artillery officers thought they could save more of their guns, some mercantile officers considered their ships might have remained rather longer alongside. Such sentiments may be laudable, but are the product of a restricted view of the general position.

11. A timetable was being worked to and my object was to get the ships away and into convoy under cover of the final withdrawal of the men-of-war without delay.

   To retain a ship, already well loaded because another gun or two might have been got onboard would have been either to delay the last convoy or cause the ship to miss it and, in my view, neither would be justifiable.

   It was the ships out of convoy that were sunk, e.g., VANDYCK; none of those that took part in the evacuation were lost. This alone might be held to justify the arrangements made; arrangements which, I suggest, merit praise, rather than blame, to the officers who were directly responsible for the details of their execution.

12. In conclusion, I am not quite clear as to the reason of the introduction of the subject of rifles in this letter, in view of the message 1625/7 (copy attached), upon which, however, I took no action.

My interest in this Message was that it seemed to justify my judgement as to the inadvisability of taking any action as regards the withdrawal of A/A guns from TROMSO.

13. I regret if the efforts made by the Senior and Staff Officers on the occasion under discussion do not meet with the approval of His Majesty's Government – I can only state my personal opinion that praise not blame, is due – and, finally, I would emphasise that the retirement was carried out in a perfectly orderly manner in every respect and that freedom from heavy attack on the last days was due to an act of Providence and could not possibly have been foreseen or counted upon when the final orders for evacuation were put into execution.

JRL, AUC 75

17

Letter from Lord Cork to Auchinleck, 4 July 1940

<u>Personal</u>

I was glad to get your letter and copy of your report. I wish I could think mine would be as concise & interesting. Mine hangs fire because all ships scattered at once, many going direct to the French Coast, and their letters are only now arriving.

The enclosed will interest you and hope the answer will suffice – Mr Sandys[17] is at the bottom of it, he & some naval or mercantile marine officers he has got to agree they could have stayed longer.

I find a general & fairly free criticism went on in this building about the delay in capturing Narvik & on receipt of this letter on the subject of the saving of guns, I went and saw the 1st Lord and said that if they were not satisfied with me would they have an enquiry & allow my side of the matter to be heard.

He himself had nothing to do with it, & was sympathetic.

Yesterday afternoon I had a talk with the C.I.G.S. who mentioned a possible Court of Enquiry upon the abandonment of guns, he had been approached on the subject & declined to have anything to do with it – but named me. On my return to Adray. [Admiralty] the letter of which I send you a copy awaited me.

One would think they had plenty to occupy themselves without taking up each matters on which they form a judgement never having troubled to learn the conditions.

My hope is to be employed somewhere shortly which will remove me from this atmosphere.

I hope all goes well – in fact am sure it does – with your new command.

There is far too much talk about how we are going to repulse the enemy not enough as how to down him.

---

17 Presumably (Edwin) Duncan Sandys, Conservative MP for Norwood and son-in-law of Winston Churchill, having married his eldest daughter, Diana. Sandys had been a prominent opponent of appeasement and in 1938 had been threatened with a court martial for revealing classified material, which he had obtained as an officer in the Territorial Army, in a parliamentary debate. Sandys had been in command of an AA Regiment during the Norway campaign.

I hope to be in your vicinity soon on a few days leave and if I am will try a run over to see you – but who knows where anyone will be in a few days ahead.

My best wishes to you however for all good fortune and great success.

JRL, AUC 76

18

Letter from Auchinleck to Lord Cork, 7 July 1940

Thank you very much for your letter of the 4th July. I was very surprised and disappointed to read the letter which you received. It can, I suppose, be justified on the grounds of ignorance of the facts, but not on any grounds in my opinion. I think your own letter is a complete answer. Should, however, more reasons be needed, which I hope will not happen, then these can be adduced.

As you know on the 24th May, the Bodo situation was critical and unless Gubbins could have been reinforced, he would probably have been pushed into the sea, as happened at Namsos and Andalsnes, or been surrounded. As you know also, we had reinforcements actually embarked and ready to go down; if the order for evacuation had not come, these reinforcements would have had to be sent. Similarly, if the general evacuation had been appreciably delayed or postponed, these reinforcements would have had to go, as Bodo could not be evacuated too far in advance of the evacuation of Harstad, for the reason that the enemy pushing up the coast (as they did do) would have seriously compromised the latter operation. In actual fact, the period between the evacuation of Bodo and the final evacuation of Harstad – Narvik was only just long enough as you will remember.

If Bodo had had to be reinforced and a delaying action fought around it, the withdrawal from that area would have been infinitely more complicated and difficult and might well have become another Andalsnes or minor Dunkirk. As it was, owing to lack of suitable ships and port facilities, the four field guns and two Bofors had to be abandoned there (the other two Bofors were left at Mo as you will remember).

I heartily agree with you that all things considered, we ought to be very grateful that we got all the men away, which is what we were primarily asked to do. I think it was a fine feat. I take full responsibility for any orders issued about the A.A. artillery.

If you are in this neighbourhood I would be delighted to see you.

I am living at Clive House, Tidworth – it is near the big club – Tidworth House and is occupied by O.C. Troops at Tidworth, Brigadier Hawtrey. Telephone number is Tidworth 197.

JRL, AUC 77

Southern Command
and the Defence of the
United Kingdom, 1940

Auchinleck, in command of 5 Corps and then Southern Command, was keen to instil in the troops under his command the idea that they were on active service and in the front line, defending, as they were, a long and vulnerable section of the South Coast of England [20, 27, 30]. Auchinleck summed up his own ideas on defence as the 'offensive defensive', which meant both that he wanted to fight a mobile war, but did not have enough transport to ensure mobility, and that he believed that the Germans would be considerably more difficult to defeat if they were allowed to establish a beach head and land heavy equipment [21, 22, 30].

Auchinleck was concerned at the disparities between the regular and Territorial troops under his command. These were seen throughout the army with some TA officers complaining that they were patronised by regulars to a much greater extent than that seen during the First World War.[1] Auchinleck was not convinced that the standard of training of British regular troops was much better than that of the TA, but he did wonder why, if it was believed to be the case, the regulars were not broken up and dispersed amongst TA formations to provide a solid cadre [21, 23, 24]. By mid-August 1940 Auchinleck was developing interesting ideas about how officer–man relations could best be fostered in the new citizen army [26].

Auchinleck clearly felt that LDV and Home Guard units would be useful in defence, particularly in scouting and reconnaissance duties and

---

1   Peter Dennis, *The Territorial Army 1907–1940* (Woodbridge, 1987), pp. 251–58.

in guarding lines of communication [22, 29]. However, he was concerned that if anti-tank emplacements were built incorrectly, they would serve to prevent the rapid movement of British reinforcements to launch a counter-attack [22]. Auchinleck was clearly drawn into some acrimonious correspondence regarding the appointment of senior officers in the Home Guard. This was seen most clearly in the appointment of Lieutenant Colonel C. E. Turner as a Zone Commander in the Gloucestershire Home Guard [28]. Defending his decision over this appointment, Auchinleck was to explain, 'I selected him after full consultation with, and with the concurrence of, the Duke of Beaufort, who is Lord Lieutenant of the County and the Area Commander, in whose good sense and sound judgement I have full confidence. I also took special care to ascertain whether he was likely to prove physically capable of doing the job. The fact that he is a M.F.H., and a Chairman of the Conservative party does not interest me in the slightest. I don't hunt the fox and I have no politics!'[2]

Auchinleck's difficulties with the then Lieutenant General B. L. Montgomery over Montgomery's dismissal of officers who Auchinleck had felt were perfectly satisfactory, revised training regime and, most problematically, Montgomery's attempts to bypass Auchinleck, his superior officer and deal directly with the War Office to obtain certain officers and equipment, are well covered in the letters below [23, 24, 25]. The fact that Auchinleck wrote initially to 'My Dear Monty', with this subsequently as, 'My Dear Montgomery' [24, 25] is telling.

Otherwise, Auchinleck's correspondence for this period is useful in demonstrating his concerns about troops being regarded as available to help with all sorts of civil defence work [31] and the establishment of the separate Anti-Aircraft Command [34].

---

2   JRL, AUC 90, Letter Auchinleck to Lieutenant General B. C. T. Paget, CGS, Home Forces, 1 September 1940. See also JRL, AUC 89, Report defending the appointment of Colonel C. Turner, Gloucestershire Home Guard.

19

Memorandum from
Sir John Dill, CIGS,[3] 21 June 1940

PERSONAL AND CONFIDENTIAL

The operations which the British Army has been called upon to undertake have involved many withdrawals in the face of superior numbers and often with open flanks threatened by armoured formations. Formations and units have fought most gallantly under these adverse conditions, and have inflicted heavy losses upon the enemy. Having constantly to withdraw is not, however, good for any Army and it is important to take drastic measures to counteract its evil effect. The first requirement is a vigorous discipline combined with a spirit of self-sacrifice. The second is an offensive spirit which can primarily be developed by training.

All experience goes to show that the Germans do not withstand determined counter-attacks. It is essential, therefore, to get back to a realization of the fact that attack is the best defence.

The enemy must be struck many blows before we gain the victory. To strike him and strike him hard not counting the cost must be the aim of every commander. And when a blow cannot be struck there must on no account be any withdrawal. To withdraw in order to maintain continuous lines of defence is not the way in which to beat the German. The German is not over-anxious about his flanks. Nor must we be. If any enemy does not penetrate between defended localities he automatically exposes his own flanks, and at those flanks we must strike.

To strike effectively there must be the closest possible co-operation between all arms. Something much closer than we have ever known before. Brigade Groups must be as one unit. Initiative and energy, combined with aggressive spirit and selfless determination to destroy the enemy, must be the keynote of our action in defence of our country.

JRL, AUC 71

---

3   Dill was appointed CIGS on 27 May 1940.

20

Special Order of the Day, issued by Auchinleck as Commander, 5 Corps,[4] 25 June 1940

1. All troops in the 5 Corps Area whether mobile or static or whether they belong to field units or instructional or other establishments are now in a forward area of a theatre of war and will act accordingly.

2. There is now no question of being on or off "duty". All ranks are permanently on duty and will be ready to act against the enemy at a moment's notice.

3. Commanders will impose the necessary restrictions so as to ensure that in an emergency all available personnel will be at their posts at the shortest notice fully armed, equipped and rationed for 24 hours.

    All commanders will exercise the strictest supervision over the movement of personnel under their command and permission to leave the immediate vicinity of quarters, except on duty, will be granted only in exceptional cases – this applies particularly to officers.

4. All parties and detachments which leave their quarters for whatever purposes on duty which entails them being unable to return to quarters within ten minutes will be fully armed and in "fighting order".

    Working parties while at work will have their weapons under armed guard (at least two sentries) placed ready for instant use in their immediate vicinity. No civilian or unauthorised person will be allowed to approach within ten yards of such arms.

5. All despatch riders, orderlies, messengers and other individual soldiers on duty whose work takes them more than ten minutes distance from their quarters will be fully armed and in fighting order.

6. Soldiers granted permission to be away from quarters for purposes of recreation such as attendance at or participation in games, entertainment etc., will proceed in organized parties with their arms and sufficient equipment and ammunition to ensure that they can defend themselves if suddenly attacked and regain their

---

4   Auchinleck took over command of 5 Corps on 14 June 1940.

quarters without delay. When necessary these parties will be under command of officers of suitable rank.

7. The orders regarding the carrying of arms will be strictly enforced. Officers are personally responsible for the safe custody of their individual weapons.

8. (a) The posting of "ceremonial" or "peace time" guards and sentries throughout the Corps Area will cease herewith. The Corps Area is now a "war zone" and all guards and sentries will be posted solely for security purposes as dictated by war needs.

   (b) Guards and sentries will be tactically sited and protected wherever they may be. Every guard or piquet will have an alarm post which it will man in emergency. If it is necessary to make use of private or civilian public property for this purpose it will be done through the appropriate civil authority.

   Instances of lack of co-operation by the civil authorities will be reported at once to Corps H.Q.

   (c) No compliments will be paid to anyone by guards and sentries. Sentries, who will invariably be posted in pairs, will make themselves as inconspicuous as possible and will not slope arms but will carry them ready for instant use. They will not march up and down on a fixed beat. The fixing of bayonets by sentries is left to the discretion of commanders concerned. The two sentries of a pair will always be disposed so as to cover each other and never so that both can be disposed of at once by an enemy.

   (d) Sentries whose duties demand that they shall move about will do so as if on patrol making intelligent use of cover. Flying Sentries or patrols must at all costs avoid following the same track or doing the same thing in the same way twice running.

   (e) Guards and piquets must be ready instantly to support their sentries or to man their alarm posts and will sleep in fighting order with their arms at their sides protected by sentries to prevent them being surprised.

   (f) No civilian or unauthorised person is to be permitted to loiter in the immediate vicinity of guards or sentries or to enter into conversation with them on any pretext whatever. When necessary the aid of the local civil authorities is to be invoked to enforce this order.

9. All troops will always carry Eyeshields, anti-gas. On receipt of an Air Raid Warning eyeshields will be adjusted by all personnel in the open.

10. It is the duty of every commander down to platoon and equivalent commanders to impress on all under their command that they are now in a forward area which may at any moment become a battle zone without notice and that their duty as soldiers comes before any other consideration and must always be in their thoughts.

To be distributed down to Coys. and equivalent sub-units.

JRL, AUC 72

21

Letter from Auchinleck to Lieutenant General Sir Robert Haining, VCIGS, 30 June 1940

URGENT AND SECRET

Sorry I could not hear more of your thoughts the other day. I know you are full of work, but I would value a good talk with you. I am pretty busy here making bricks without much straw. Two Divisions on a 100 mile front! However, we are getting on with it and every day makes things better, but the lack of mobile reserves is serious. At the moment we have all our goods in the front window which, in my opinion, is the right policy, as our lack of equipment and transport does not make it possible for us to fight a mobile battle in the interior. I hope we will be in a position to do so before long as equipment seems to be coming along well, though the distribution of it seems patchy and incoherent. But this may be justified by reasons beyond my ken.

Anyway, I am sure that we should make every effort to prevent the enemy landing on the beach. I still believe that this is the most difficult task, and my recent small experience confirms me in this opinion. After all, the holding of a "line" such as the coast line cannot be likened to the holding of a "line or the attempt to hold a line" in France, which some say was the cause of our downfall.

Until he can get his heavy stuff <u>ashore</u> the enemy cannot do much. Therefore he must be prevented by all possible means from getting it ashore. At least, that is how I see it. Once he does establish himself at all securely it won't be so easy to get him out, if experience goes for anything. Anyway, he'd be a damn nuisance if nothing worse!

I have been thinking a lot about the Army of Tomorrow – the Army of the offensive which is to come! I have a lot of half-baked ideas, but I suppose you have a gang of capable people who are thinking of nothing else. I hope you have!

By the way, there is some bizarre "guff" about a "Dunkirk Medal": which is causing some alarm amongst level-headed people. I hope it isn't true, and I can't believe it is. We do not want to perpetuate the memory of that episode, surely?

What might be appreciated, so I gather, is a "1940 Star" (France and Norway), if anything is contemplated at all, which seems to me to be unlikely. However, the gossip may interest you.

Another thing – people are still persisting in perpetuating and stressing the difference between Regular and Territorial Divisions. This, to my mind, is lamentable. If the Regulars are so much better than the Territorials (which is not <u>generally</u> true, in my opinion) then they should be used to leaven the Territorials, and not be kept as a corps d'elite in separate Divisions. We shall not win this war so long as we cling to worn out shibboleths and snobberies. I am sure of this. Cobwebs want removing at once.

JRL, AUC 73

22

5 Corps, Conference minutes, 9 July 1940

SECRET

1. ## ARMY COM[MAN]D[ER]'S POLICY.

    Corps Com[man]d[er] outlined policy as laid down by Army Com[man]d[er]:

    (a) General lines similar to those already adopted. Enemy to be stopped on beaches; but maximum possible reserve to be made available for hitting enemy. Briefly – an offensive defensive.

    (b) A formation to be organized as mobile striking forces for immediate counter-attacks against landings. Defence would NOT be passive.

(c)   War mentality must be cultivated; i.e. phrase "IF we are attacked" should never be used; the phrase should be "WHEN we are attacked." Attitude of mind to be cultivated was that attack was not improbable but practically certain.

(d)   All resources, civil and military to be co-ordinated, Army, L[ocal].D[efence].V[olunteers]., Police, A[ir].R[aid]. P[recautions]., etc. Corps Com[man]d[er] stressed there must be give and take.

(e)   Army Com[man]d[er] had stressed necessity for countering defeatism and fostering offensive spirit. On this point Corps Com[man]d[er] added that it was easy to talk in a defeatist manner without being defeatist minded. All ranks must think before they speak. Offenders, if necessary, should be arrested and even court martialled. Any officer who failed to behave himself as an officer must be dealt with very firmly. Offences should NOT be condoned.

(f)   L[ocal].D[efence].V[olunteer].s to be issued with Ross rifles[5] and ammunition to release army equipment.

(g)   First reinforcements would remain with units unless formation moved considerable distance for tactical reasons.

(h)   S[mall].A[rms].A[mmunition]. economy, even in action, would be necessary.

(i)   Statements had been issued on the power of military authorities to deal with:-
(i)   Civilians
(ii)   Requisitioning of lands and buildings.
Statements cleared up many doubts.

---

5   75,000 Ross rifles were ordered from Canada in May 1940 and they arrived in the United Kingdom during July and August 1940. The Ross rifle had been designed and manufactured in Canada between 1903 and 1918 and was used to equip the initial Canadian Expeditionary Force in 1914–15. However, it was not a successful battlefield weapon, being prone to jamming and, indeed, had been withdrawn from Canadian units during the First World War, seeing them re-equipped with British Short Magazine Lee Enfield rifles. Those Ross rifles ordered in 1940 were of 1903–18 vintage and arrived coated in thick grease, which it took a considerable effort to clean off; another reason for their unpopularity with Home Guard units.

2.   ## DISPOSAL OF ALIENS.[6]

G.2 (I) explained regulations with regard to aliens in defence areas. Latter were divided into two classes:-

(i)   <u>Class A Area</u>. (at present extending West to BEXHILL) from which Chief Constables were instructed to remove all aliens forthwith.

(ii) <u>Class B Area</u>. Only enemy aliens to be removed.

Chief Constables had power to arrest and intern aliens between the ages of 16 and 70. Military powers limited to detention for 24 hours, after which, civil police would deal with case.

3.   ## COMBINED HEADQUARTERS.

B[rigadier].G[eneral].S[taff]. raised the necessity for combining headquarters in PORTSMOUTH and SOUTHAMPTON Areas, quoting need for such organization to deal with petrol demolitions.

After discussion, Corps Commander directed:-

Com[man]der 4 Div[ision] to go into the question of setting up combined H.Q.s in the PORTSMOUTH and SOUTHAMPTON Areas; suggesting PORTSMOUTH Area Commander to establish these with C-in-C., PORTSMOUTH or representative. Headquarters should be located at FAREHAM.

Com[man]d[er] 50 Div[ision] to explore the necessity for combined headquarters in PORTLAND; or to ensure that liaison between R.N. and military was sound.

---

6   Upon the declaration of war on 3 September 1939, some 70,000 Germans and Austrians resident in the UK were designated as enemy aliens. By 28 September, the Aliens Department of the Home Office had established internment tribunals which classified enemy aliens into three categories: Category A, to be interned; Category B, to be exempt from internment but subject to the restrictions decreed by the Special Order; and Category C, to be exempt from both internment and restrictions. By February 1940 some 73,000 cases had been investigated by the tribunals. The vast majority of enemy aliens (about 66,000) were then classed as Category C. In May 1940, with the invasion threat at its height, 8,000 of these enemy aliens, living in Southern England, were interned and, with Italy's entry to the war 4,000 Italians, mostly known members of Fascist organisations, were also interned. The Home Office remained convinced that this widespread internment would prevent the 'Fifth Column' activities supposedly seen in France and the Low Countries in May 1940.

4. ROAD BLOCKS STOP POLICY.

(a) Corps Com[man]d[er] outlined plans for the stop lines A[nti]. T[an]k islands; latter selected, some by G.H.Q., some by div[ision]s. In 50 Div[ision] area also, L[ocal].D[efence]. V[olunteer]s. independently making own village into A[nti]. T[an]k islands. Corps Com[man]d[er] stressed that NO permanent road blocks should be placed on roadways.

Army Com[man]d[er] was very anxious that military traffic should not be obstructed as it had been in France. Road blocks should therefore be of a moveable type.

Important points to decide were:-
(i) When should these moveable road blocks be erected?
(ii) Who should be responsible?

(b) During discussion, following points were decided:-
(i) All road blocks must be easily removable; Various types, including rails, wire hawser, loaded lorries, tetrahedra were approved with foregoing proviso.
(ii) Columns on the move must have advanced guards well ahead, with role NOT only of dealing with enemy but of removing road blocks where necessary.
(iii) Reference military A[nti]. T[an]k islands, decisions as to time of erection of road blocks to be decentralized down to b[attalio]n areas.

Corps Com[man]d[er] directed draft to be prepared and sent out on this basis.
(iv) Reference A[nti]. T[an]k islands manned by L[ocal]. D[efence].V[olunteer]s.,

Corps Com[man]d[er] stated this needed further thought to avoid danger of every village being an obstacle to troop movements.

5. DEFENSIVE FIRE.

C[orps].C[ommander].R[oyal].A[rtillery]. raised question of policy for defensive fire plan. Necessity for system of signals and numbered targets on beaches where landings likely.

Com[man]d[er] 4 Div[ision] asked for defensive fire to be brought down on water and guns to be kept off beaches until enemy definitely ashore.

Com[man]d[er] 50 Div[ision] suggested observed fire while boats coming in and concentrations to be called for on points affected by successful landing.

C[orps].C[ommander].R[oyal].A[rtillery]. said at present guns were prepared to bring down fire on the water; and to take on the beaches by observed and predicted fire is landing affected.

Corps Com[man]d[er] directed C[orps].C[ommander].R[oyal]. A[rtillery]. to issue defensive fire plans in writing. Army H.Q. to be informed.

6. ADDITIONAL GUNS.

C[orps].C[ommander].R[oyal].A[rtillery]. notified two new btys [batteries]:-
    (i)   Mob[ile] A[nti]. T[an]k guns (3-pdr and 12-pdr)
    (ii)   Four 4-inch guns.
Corps Com[man]d[er] directed both to be allotted to 50 Div[ision].

7. MOB[ILE] COL[UM]NS IN DIV[ISIONAL] RES[ERVE].

Present position:-

4 Div. Res[erve] B[riga]des Mobile; each b[attalio]n capable of moving independently.

50 Div. Res[erve] b[riga]de mobile.
Buses allotted to each b[attalio]n.

Corps Com[man]d[er] laid down policy that Res[erve] B[riga]de Groups should be organized with b[attalio]ns as separate col[um]ns. Guns and A[nti]. T[an]k guns to be sub-allocated to b[attalio]n groups.

Training of Res[erve] B[riga]des to be carried out in these roles.

8. DEFENCE OF TOWNS AND VILLAGES.

Corps Com[man]d[er] drew attention to question of defending blocks inside towns. Directed that officers concerned should consider feasibility of placing defensive posts in the upper floors or roofs of houses rather than ground floors.

9. ## 4 CORPS.

Corps Com[man]d[er] stated that, in event of necessity, Com[man]d[er] 4 Corps had already discussed with him possible moves to support 5 Corps. Concentration areas had been agreed to deal with threats on either right or left flanks or from air-borne troops on Salisbury Plain.

10. ## MEDICAL.

Question of evacuating casualties was being considered at Army H.Q. (S[outher]n. Com[man]d).

11. ## ACCOMMODATION 4 DIV[ISION].

Com[man]d[er] 4 Div[ision] asked for additional R[oyal].E[ngineer]. facilities for men under canvas.

C[ommander].E[ngineers]. asked for forecast of moves and probable B[riga]de areas; facilities would then be arranged.

Corps Com[man]d[er] directed 4 Div[ision] to give forecast.

12. ## WARRANT TO CONVENE GENERAL COURTS MARTIAL.

D[eputy].A[ssistant]. & Q[uarter].M[aster].G[eneral]. to arrange necessary warrant for Com[man]d[er] 4 Div[ision].

13. ## TROOP MOVEMENT 50 DIV[ISION].

(a) If 2 Corps Art[iller]y move away, 50 Div[isional] reserve would be reduced to 2 b[attalio]ns.
Corps Com[man]d[er] promised to help ease this position if possible.

(b) Com[man]d[er] 50 Div[ision] asked if 11 S[outh]. Staff[ord]s[hire] [Regiment] would remain in his area; at present working on RINGWOOD Line. Definite answer not possible at this stage.

14. ## DEMOLITIONS.

Com[man]d[er] 4 Div[ision] asked for clarification on policy for demolitions.

Present position:-

(a) On certain roads no demolitions carried out.

(b) On other roads demolitions which would take more than 7 days to repair not to be carried out.

Result that main road and railway bridges could not be demolished.

Corps Com[man]d[er] raised question of demolitions on stop lines.

Under present policy, was informed by C[ommander].E[ngineers]. that only subsidiary bridges could be blown, others must be held. Corps Com[man]d[er] stressed need for more clear-cut policy to be obtained.

15. VISIT OF SECRETARY OF STATE FOR WAR.

Arrangements for the visit of Secretary of State for War to 5 Corps Area, 10 July, were discussed.

JRL, AUC 78

23

Letter from Auchinleck to Major General Giffard Le Quesne Martel, Commander, 50th Division, 15 July 1940

My dear Q

Thank you very much for yesterday which I thoroughly enjoyed.

I was very pleased indeed with all I saw from Lyme Regis to Abbotsbury.

Great progress has been and is being made, and I thought the whole sector was being run in a very thorough and businesslike way. More power to you and those under you. Will you tell them from me.

JRL, AUC 80

24

Letter from Auchinleck to Lieutenant General B. L. Montgomery, commanding 5 Corps, 29 July 1940

<u>Confidential</u>

My dear Monty

Thank you very much for your notes on the 50th Division

1. I agree with much of what you say and I see you realise the reasons for the present state of affairs. I think you have perhaps overstated the situation in one or two respects. For instance, to my knowledge, P.T. and drill has not been by any means entirely neglected, though the time allotted to it has had perforce to be restricted. The remedy is, of course, to relieve the forward units periodically and they have already been told to do this, as you are aware.

2. As regards morale, I thought it was good and I still think so. No doubt a good deal remains to be done in the instilling of the offensive spirit and this can be done as training becomes more intense, consequent on cessation of work on the beaches. I want to make it quite clear, however, that I wish the instructions as to the urgent need for the completion of the defences so as to admit of the withdrawal of men for training, which I issued to the Corps just before I left, (Operation Instruction No. 14), carried out. I intend to issue a Command Instruction to the same effect.

3. My own estimate of the time required to get Divisions ready for a major offensive overseas is about 6 months, assuming the necessary equipment to be forthcoming.

4. We have already discussed the "drain" on manpower from Divisions and I am doing all I can to stop it but orders are orders and will, of course, be obeyed. I am returning to the charge at G.H.Q. tomorrow.

5. The organization of the Divisional front is your affair. I have asked for the adjustment with Eastern Command on the Hants/Sussex boundary, and will find out about it tomorrow, I hope.

6. I entirely agree with your estimate of the contentment and will to co-operate of the Division as a whole. It is remarkable and reflects

great credit on the Commander. I think in our Army there can be no true and lasting efficiency without contentment!

I am a firm believer in that saying, but this does not mean that we would tolerate inefficiency!

JRL, AUC 83

25

Letter from Auchinleck to Lieutenant General B. L. Montgomery, 15 August 1940

My dear Montgomery

I want to draw your attention to your 84/A of the 7th August. In this it is stated that you interviewed the Adjutant-General on the transfer of personnel with B.E.F. experience.

There are two points with regard to this minute. I am quite aware that it is a common practice in the Army for officers of all ranks to visit the War Office, but in this case it appears that you interviewed the Adjutant-General on a matter which directly concerned my Headquarters, in that they had issued orders for certain transfers to take place. I do not consider this the proper manner in which this, or any other matter of this nature, should be handled. When orders are issued from these Headquarters, whether they come from the War Office or direct from these Headquarters, and you wish to make a protest, from whatever point of view, against orders, I wish such protests to be made to these Headquarters and not to the War Office officials over my head.

The second point is that I think it is unfortunate that, having interviewed the Adjutant-General, special reference should have been made in the memo to which I have referred above to this fact, thereby indicating to your subordinates that you had gone over the head of my Headquarters to deal with the problem direct with the War Office.

I would like to add that the subject of transfer of personnel with B.E.F. experience from your formations to others in England had actually been the subject of protest both by my predecessor and myself to the War Office, in order to save formations under your command from being depleted of their trained personnel, and moreover these protests were made as the result of representations made by the 5th Corps. These protests having been turned down by the War Office, there was no alternative but to issue orders for the transfers to take place, and these should have been obeyed without any further reference to anybody.

I am afraid I must ask you to cancel the memorandum in question. You will, I am sure, understand that my sympathies are entirely with you in this matter and that my object in writing to you as I have is to ensure that our common object shall not be defeated by the "short cut" method of conducting business, which in my experience, nearly always ends in confusion, however efficient it may appear at the time.

Please show me the cancellation.

JRL, AUC 85

26

Letter from Auchinleck to Sir Robert Haining, VCIGS, 19 August 1940

Very many thanks for your long and most interesting letter of the 14th August. I quite see the value of getting early information as to the general state of feeling in the Army, particularly at the present time when as you say, it is living cheek by jowl with the ordinary public and, moreover, contains a very large number of men of considerable intelligence and experience, competent and quick to criticise any stupidities or lapses on the part of their officers.

So long as this information is got by discreet methods and not mixed up with a petty inquisition into minor disciplinary failures, I am sure no one can have any objection. I certainly have not.

I am uneasy about the disparity of wages earned by the civilian and the soldier. It may not matter how much now, but thinking ahead in terms of years, not months, it seems to me that it has in it the germs of really serious trouble – possibly mutiny on the largest scale!! I cannot help feeling that something drastic should be done in the very near future to equalize conditions. I know it bristles with difficulties.

I am sure that the more that can be done to impress on the officer class as a whole, and particularly on the less imaginative and more rigid type of regular officer, the fact that the rank and file of the army of today need quite different treatment to that which suited the regular soldier of the old army, the better.

There is no doubt that the man-mastership and force of example to be displayed by all officers must be of the very highest standard, and that it will be necessary for officers to be more self sacrificing and spartan in their habits than many of them are today. The critical faculties of a great majority of the modern soldier in the ranks are very keen and we can no longer afford to gloss over or hide away failure in their leaders. Dirty linen may <u>have</u> to be washed in public, but that cannot be helped.

We should take to heart Kipling's "Song of the Old Guard",[7] even though it was written forty years ago!

JLR, AUC 86

27

Memorandum from Auchinleck addressed to Lt. Gen. H. E. Franklyn,[8] Lt. Gen. B. L. Montgomery and Maj. Gen. J. A. H. Gammell,[9] 27 August 1940

<u>PERSONAL & CONFIDENTIAL</u>

As a result of our conference on Saturday the 24th August, I am seriously perturbed as to the possible effects on our war efficiency and training of the restrictions which are apparently to be imposed on the use of transport etc., in the interests of the economy.

2. I am fully alive to the need for economy and so, I am sure, are you, but to my mind we have only one task at the moment and that is to win the war. To do this we must first prevent an enemy occupation of this country and, secondly, prepare an army fit to invade his country at the first favourable opportunity.

3. The prevention of invasion is so essential that nothing can be allowed to lessen the efficiency of the troops entrusted with this task. The training of the army for this counter-offensive which must come is

---

7   This poem reflects on the hidebound nature of the British army at the time of the South African War (1899–1902).
8   GOC 8 Corps.
9   GOC 3rd Division.

so urgent that it too should not be hampered by purely peace-time conceptions of administration.

4.   I feel quite sure that if the matter is put fairly and squarely to the troops, the instances of wilful extravagance and misuce of our resources will be so few and far between as to be negligible.

In order to assure myself that the restrictions now being imposed will not in any way affect our efforts to achieve our objects, I shall be grateful if you will let me have your considered opinion on the whole subject, as soon as you conveniently can, bearing in mind that in this, as in most matters, <u>some</u> degree of compromise will probably be necessary.

JRL, AUC 88

28

Report from Auchinleck, defending the appointment of Lieutenant Colonel C. E. Turner[10] as Zone Commander, Gloucestershire Home Guard, *c.* 28 August 1940

In reply to your memo in regard to the appointment of Col. C. Turner, D.S.O. as Zone Commander Gloucestershire.

When the choice of a successor to General Sir R. Stephens had to be made, four names were submitted to me by the Area Commander.

The Lord Lieutenant was consulted and had no hesitation in picking Col. Turner, who was duly appointed by the Area Commander with my approval, though according to A.C.I. 924 of 15th August, 1940 this was not necessary.

I admit that the battalion commander was not consulted, but the procedure adopted had the full approval of the Area Commander.

---

10   Lieutenant Colonel Charles Edward Turner had served in Lumsden's Horse in the South African War and in the Royal Gloucestershire Hussars during the First World War. He commanded the Royal Gloucestershire Hussars when they were reformed as an Armoured Car Company between 1923 and 1926. He was to command the Gloucestershire Home Guard from August 1940 to November 1944. He was Joint Master of the Berkeley Hounds, 1928–41.

Col. Turner had a good war record, was awarded the D.S.O., commanded the Royal Gloucestershire Hussars, is a D.L., also a member of the T.A. Association, which fact alone will be of great help to the H.G. organization.

He is at present High Sheriff of the county.

It is true that he is a Master of Hounds, but as on account of local conditions his pack is not going to hunt this season, he will be able to give all his time to Home Guard affairs.

He is well known throughout the county and in my opinion eminently suitable for Zone Commander.

JRL, AUC 89

29

Southern Command Operation Instruction no. 27, 7 September 1940

<u>The Home Guard</u>

1. The Home Guard is capable of playing a great part in the defence of the country against attack from the air or from the sea. This instruction shall be used to the best advantage.

<u>ROLE.</u>

2. The Home Guard forms a most important part of the land forces but it is essentially a voluntary and localized force. Home Guards are not meant to be far away from their homes and will not be so used.

    Home Guards are not designed or armed to attack considerable bodies of highly trained and powerfully equipped enemy troops, but they are well adapted to carry our surprise attacks and ambushes against small parties of enemy, and in properly sited and prepared positions should be able to repulse attacks by enemy troops even when these are helped by armoured cars, light tanks or light artillery.

    Home Guards, by their local knowledge, are also admirably fitted to act with other troops as observers, guides, scouts and messengers.

TASKS.

3. It follows then that Home Guards can best be used:-

   (a) To make and man defence works of all kinds for the local protection of their own towns and villages with or without the help of other troops.

   (b) Wherever possible, to hold defences on "Stop Lines" and in "Anti-Tank Islands" either with or without the help of other troops.

   (c) To patrol beaches, possible air landing grounds, and roads near their homes on which an enemy might land or advance.

   (d) To guide troops arriving from a distance to prepare positions already prepared on "stop lines" or in "anti-tank islands".

   (e) To act as scouts, observers and messengers within the limits of their own local knowledge for troops preparing in these areas and to provide the commanders [directing troops?] with detailed information about local conditions.

   (f) To round up and [destroy?] quickly enemy patrols or parties of parachutists [unreadable].

   These activities [unreadable] will thoroughly dishearten the enemy.

4. To make up for their relative weakness in arms and equipment it is essential that all defence works to be manned by the Home Guard shall be sited with the greatest care [unreadable] An enemy is most unlikely to hit works which he cannot see however powerfully [unreadable] and it is vitally important that every possible artifice and trick should be used to hide any defences wherever they may be made. In the circumstances in which the Home Guard will move to fight, concealment is ninety per cent of the battle. No defence work should be recognisable for what it is at over fifty yards range. Much well-intentioned work which was done in the earlier stages of the battle for this country suffers from being too obvious and it is necessary now to put this right without delay. The mere sight of a sandbag is enough to put an enemy on his guard. A good deal of the earlier work is not proof against rifle fire, and is therefore an actual danger rather than a safeguard.

PATROLS.

5. The efficient patrolling of wide open tracts calls for training and practice especially at night. The way to avoid the ambushing of a

whole patrol by the enemy and the methods of moving from cover to cover are simple and easy to learn, but if neglected will lead to casualties. It should be the constant aim of every Home Guard to avoid being killed himself so that he can kill as many of the enemy as possible. To do this he must be cunning and skilled in scoutcraft and this entails steady practice by day and night. The use of patrols mounted on horses and ponies for the patrolling of downland and common land is to be encouraged wherever possible.

6. The patrolling of roads and beaches calls for different methods but the principles are the same and only common sense is needed to apply them. Here again the object is to see the enemy before he sees you and to kill him before he kills you.

GUIDES.

7. The guiding of troops to chosen positions needs first class knowledge of tracks and roads and a quick brain so as to admit of alternative routes being used should the direct road be blocked for any reason. The way to approach each position without being seen by an enemy needs study and practice. When the time comes, every minute may count.

MOBILITY.

8. The training of men to act as scouts and messengers needs careful attention, as unless these can get about the country quickly and cunningly they are likely to lose a lot of their value. If messengers and scouts can be provided with motor cycles or ordinary bicycles their value is likely to be much greater.

SKIRMISHING

9. The rounding up of enemy patrols, tanks, armoured cars and stray vehicles of all sorts is a task particularly suitable for Home Guards and one in which they should be [unreadable]. For this work men should be organized in special parties trained to [unreadable].

DRILL

10. Drill and smartness of turnout are as good for discipline in the Home Guard as in any other kind of troops, but time should not be wasted in teaching men useless movements merely for the sake of doing them. All forms of drill should be of the simplest kind

and such as are needed as for the work in hand. For instance Rifle Exercises might well be confined to the following movements:-

> The Order.
> The Trail.
> The Shoulder (as in Rifle Regiments)
> The Port Arms.
> The Examine Arms.

While the following drill movements should meet all ordinary needs:-

> Platoon in Line (3 ranks).
> Column of Route (threes).

The usual formation for Home Guards on the move in action should be in single file following the section leader, until it is necessary for them to shake out into open order. Home Guards should be "Skirmishers" in the proper sense of the term and should not be tempted to become rigid and set in their methods. Their methods should be those of the "light companies" of Wellington's day. Instructors lent to the Home Guards from other units should bear these facts in mind and not waste their own and other's time by trying to teach all the movements and exercises set out in the drill books. Simplicity, utility and speed should be the watchwords in all forms of instruction. Home Guards should be trained to shoot to kill at short ranges, that is not exceeding 200 yards. At this distance every shot should tell.

WINTER.

11. The enemy may not try to invade us this autumn. No one can tell how the war may go elsewhere in the world in the near future. If it goes well for us, we may early in the New Year need to send large forces of our field army abroad to carry the war into his country. Should the tide be slower to turn in our favour, Hitler may still have a fling at invasion next Spring. Whichever way things go, there is no doubt at all that the Home Guards' part in the defence of this country will become more and not less important, and that they will be called on to an ever growing degree to relieve other more mobile troops of this duty. It is most important, therefore, that their training should continue all through the winter and that their strength should be maintained at the highest possible level.

WORK WITH FIELD ARMY.

12. Commanders of formations and units of the Field Army and Area Commanders will do all they can to help Home Guard commanders to train their men and will share their training facilities with them to the greatest extent possible in the circumstances. The Home Guard should be invited to take part in exercises and schemes whenever this can be arranged and soldiers and Home Guards should be accustomed to working together as part of one common army.

JRL, AUC 91

30

Southern Command Order
no. 78, 20 September 1940

FOR OFFICIAL USE ONLY

Not to be published

1. The enemy is said to be ready to invade this country. He seems to have enough aircraft, ships and troops to attack in strength on a wide front should he care risk it.

2. To invade us he has first to cross the Channel in the face of continuous attack by the Navy and the R.A.F. He has then to land on open beaches well covered by the fire of weapons of all sorts and exposed to the attack of our bombers. His is one of the hardest tasks an army can be asked to do and he knows it. He knows, therefore, that to have any chance of success at all he must surprise us in one way or another.

3. In his efforts to surprise us:-
    (a) He may choose rough weather in which to cross the Channel, hoping that we will have relaxed our guard.
    (b) He may try to cross by day under cover of his fighter and bomber aircraft, or under cover of fog and mist, hoping we expect him only to cross at night and attack in traditional fashion at dawn.
    (c) He may pass by the obvious beaches and try to land on the more difficult places, hoping that we may think them impossible

for boats or that the cliffs behind them are unscalable (Wolfe at Quebec.)

(d) He may very likely use smoke and gas, or both, in the hope of blinding and confusing our forward troops and thus making their fire useless.

(e) He may use gas spray against our reserves in the hope of disorganising them and preventing them from carrying out their task.

(f) He is likely to use his dive bombers against our positions in the hope of paralysing us, as he did the Norwegians, Danes, Dutch, Belgians and others.

(g) He is likely to use every device to get his tanks and light artillery and mortars ashore quickly, and we must expect to see large ships run aground so that he can disembark directly from them.

(h) He is likely to land troops by parachute and from troop carriers in rear of our forward troops with the object of diverting them from their proper task of preventing landings on the beaches.

(i) He will try to land advanced detachments from the air or from the sea dressed in our uniforms which he has thousands of suits, in the hope of disorganising our defence and defeating us by treachery.

(j) He will try spreading lies, rumours and false orders, to break up our defence and shake our confidence in ourselves.

4. We, knowing what to expect, will not be surprised. If the enemy cannot surprise us, he is beaten before he starts.

To avoid any chance of being surprised:-

(a) We must be on our toes at all times, in clear weather or fog, wet or fine, rough or smooth, dark or light. We must never relax our watch at any point from Bognor to Bristol.

(b) We must give the enemy full credit and expect him to do the desperate and dangerous thing. He is a desperate man.

(c) We must keep our powder dry, our weapons bright and our equipment, especially our anti-gas equipment, in tip-top condition and ready at all times for instant use.

(d) We must meet his air attacks without a moment's hesitation by the heaviest possible fire from all available weapons, and confuse the aim of his airmen by using every trick to conceal our positions from them.

(e) We must never take anything, or anyone, for granted, but must at all times take every possible step to make sure that friends are friends and not enemies disguised as friends. Strangers in or out of uniform must be looked on as possible enemies until they have been proved to be friends.

(f) We must at all times be ready to defend every post and every position from attack from <u>any</u> direction, and must always be on the watch against attacks from the flanks or rear.

5. We must remember:-

(a) That the experiences of the B.E.F. in France showed that the bark of the dive bomber is much worse than its bite.

(b) That gas is a feeble weapon against vigilant troops who know how to protect themselves against it.

(c) That an enemy trying to invade this country starts under a tremendous handicap and has to face unknown dangers and hazards. He has every reason to have doubts and fears. We have none.

6. Forewarned is forearmed, and no trick or ruse will avail the enemy if we remember that there are only two orders which really matter and from which nothing should distract us:-

For those in front line positions	"Hang on."
For those in reserve	"Push on."

JRL, AUC 92

31

Letter from Auchinleck to General Sir Alan Brooke, C-in-C, Home Forces, 2 October 1940

<u>PERSONAL & CONFIDENTIAL</u>

I am loath to bother you, but I think the enclosed copy of a paragraph in the "Spectator" of last week needs attention.

I suggest that it is a most dangerous statement which should be refuted as soon as possible by the highest authority. It is also grossly unfair to the troops, who, for the most part, have really been working, and still are working, pretty hard. I have told my Commanders that whenever they can, they are to give all possible help to the civil authorities in salvage work such as the clearing of debris etc., but any large scale use of soldiers to take the place of the civil defence services can hardly fail to have a most serious adverse effect on training.

You may know that the "Spectator" recently violently repudiated the idea that there could be any need for a large scale offensive by the Army in this war. This new effort on its part may be connected with this theory.

Extract from "A Spectator's Notebook"

The Spectator, September 27th 1940.
Page 309.

"Support, I see, is being given in other quarters to the suggestion I made a fortnight ago that soldiers should be called in where desirable to reinforce the civilian defence services. The reasons for this are obvious. Some of the services concerned, the air-raid wardens in particular, are working under an immense strain. They are in perpetual danger, their hours are too long and their numbers in some localities too few. At the same time there are tens of thousands of soldiers all over the country doing nothing but standing by, pending the development of more active military operations."

JRL, AUC 93

32

Letter from Auchinleck to Lieutenant General B. L. Montgomery, 19 October 1940

PERSONAL & CONFIDENTIAL

It has come to my notice that in your understandable desire to get the best officers available in your Corps, you have been dealing direct with the branches of the A.G.'s department at the War Office, and asking them to post officers to specific appointments in your Corps from units and headquarters of other formations in this Command. You will, no doubt, recollect one or two incidents.

I want you to realise that this procedure, however justifiable it may seem to you, is likely to cause extreme annoyance to the commanders of the formations and units concerned, more particularly where, in their opinion, your selections do not tally with their ideas as to who is the best man in the unit concerned for the job for which you want him. I am sure that you do not mean to cause friction or to give offence, but I am afraid that, unless you first consult the commander, you will do so and I do not want friction!

I shall be grateful, therefore, if in future when you want a particular officer for a particular appointment from another formation in this Command, you will either approach me or the formation (Corps) commander first. I am sure that generally your wishes can be met.

JRL, AUC 97

33

Letter from Auchinleck to Lieutenant General H. C. B. Wemyss, Adjutant General, 19 October 1940

PERSONAL

You probably know that Monty, commanding the 5th Corps, is in the habit of going direct to branches of your department in order to work transfers of officers from other formations to his own Corps. He has done this recently more than once I think.

I sympathise with his desire to get the best and his energy (binge, he would call it!) in making personally sure that he gets what he wants. Heaven helps those who help themselves! However, this practice tends to cause friction and I have had complaints from Commanders of formations from which Monty has kidnapped officers, to the effect that his selections do not always coincide with their own ideas as to the relative efficiency of officers in the units concerned, and that, consequently, the officers passed over by these personal selections become disgruntled. I know the whole subject is a very difficult one, but I daresay you will agree that it is undesirable that this practice should become prevalent.

I have written to Monty telling him my views on the subject. I shall be grateful if you will treat this letter as private between ourselves.

JRL, AUC 98

34

Letter from Auchinleck to General Sir Alan Brooke, C-in-C, Home Forces, *c.* 25–26 October 1940

Forgive me for returning to the charge.

Sometime ago I wrote pointing out the apparent dangers involved in the further separation of the A.A. formations from the rest of the Army, and suggesting that they should be administered in the same way as any other troops. I know that higher authority has decided otherwise, but I still feel so strongly that a big mistake is being made that I venture to raise the subject again.

I have just seen a copy of the "Report of the Committee Reorganization of the Anti-Aircraft Command". It has been compiled apparently by a committee of four A.A. Commanders sitting in judgement on themselves, and is a voluminous affair which I would not dream of suggesting you should read in full. But, if you have time I think you should look at Appendix "D" to the Report, which shows how absolutely and completely they propose to cut themselves adrift from the Army. So much so that it really seems as it might be better to put them in to Air Force uniform at once! You will see that, although A.A. personnel are to be dispersed in large numbers in every army command, ordinary commanders are to have no say in their discipline or administration. Items 1, 6, 9, 10, 11, 27 (vi), 29 (Note), 46, 51, 53, 61, 62, and 63, are illuminating.

While not wishing to make more work for myself or my staff, I cannot really see how this system is going to work economically and smoothly. It has been difficult up to date. Now it looks likely to become worse. Perhaps I am unduly pessimistic and I dare say there are factors of which I know nothing, but I thought I had better tell you how the business struck me.

I hope you will have a very good leave.

JRL, AUC 100

35

Letter from Auchinleck to General Sir Sydney Muspratt, India Office, 5 November 1940

I am sorry to bother you but I have just had a pitiful letter from "Taffy" Davies who is, as you know, marooned in Iceland.

He considers that India has treated him very shabbily and I am bound to say that, on the face of it, it looks as if she had. He is a Major (Bt. Lt.-Colonel) who was temporary Lt.-Colonel in command of his battalion in India. On my application he was sent home to be G.S.O.1. on the H.Q. of the N.W.E.F. He never got there through no fault of his own and then became G.S.O.1. of a division as you know.

He has lost command of his battalion, also his temporary rank in the I.A. (He is, or was, really permanent Commandant of his battalion) and is being paid as G.S.O.1. (Major and Temporary Lt.-Colonel in the British Service). If I had known that this was likely to happen to him, I would certainly never have asked for him. I thought that I.A. officers brought home for duty were paid at Indian rates, but I am afraid I have not had the time or opportunity to make myself au fait with the rules. I do feel, however, that it is wrong at this juncture that an officer should be penalised financially because he has been specially chosen to fill an important post.

I am sure you will sympathise and I do hope you may be able to help to get things put right.

JRL, AUC 102

36

Letter from General Sir Alan Brooke, C-in-C, Home Forces, to Auchinleck, 22 November 1940

My dear Auchinleck

I was longing to congratulate you yesterday morning but felt a must wait till you have seen Dill.

I am delighted about your appointment, but very sad that it entails losing you from Southern Command.

We shall miss you badly in "Home Forces" but shall have to comfort ourselves with the thought that though our loss India gains the best possible selection for the appointment.

I do hope I shall see you before you leave to thank you for all your help and assistance.

With heartiest congratulations, and with best of luck.

JRL, AUC 104

37

Southern Command Special Order of the Day no. 103, 12 December 1940

On leaving Southern Command I wish to thank all ranks of the staffs, units, services and departments for their unfailing help during the last four months.

It has not been an easy time for any of us, but, looking back, it is a good record. A great stretch of coast line has been fortified and made secure.

At the same time, formations and units have been completely re-organized and re-equipped, and have started training intensively to fit themselves to take the offensive against the Germans overseas.

Much help and support has also been given to the Home Guard, the results of which are becoming more and more apparent every day.

It has been mainly due to your determination and good cheer on all occasions and in all conditions of weather that the work has been well done. I know that the even more strenuous task which lies before you will be done well and truly, too.

I am very sorry to leave you and wish you all the very best of luck in the future.

JRL, AUC 119

3

Commander in Chief,
India, 1940–41

Auchinleck as C in C India was anxious to develop a programme which would modernise and expand the Indian Army. On his return to India, he was impressed by what had been achieved in his absence and believed that within seven months armoured units would be sufficiently developed to take the field [40]. The development of armoured forces was something Auchinleck was to return to [50, 57]. Auchinleck's desire to develop the Indian Army's AA capabilities, when the number of guns was limited is also evident [41]. Most surprising, in terms of modernisation, was Auchinleck's desire to develop a parachute brigade within the Indian Army. A lesser general might have concluded that the lack of aircraft, gliders or parachutes made this a pointless task [65, 66].

Auchinleck was keen to expand the recruiting base of the Indian Army far beyond that of the traditional martial races by resurrecting old regiments and forming new ones. In doing this he promoted the development of modern recruiting campaigns [43, 67]. He believed that expansion should go ahead, even if the British contingents normally supplied to each Indian Division were not forthcoming [68]. With regard to the martial races, Auchinleck also outlined the problems seen in the rapid expansion of the number of Gurkha battalions within the Indian Army, which led to serious shortages of officers and NCOs [41].

Auchinleck maintained his belief in the need to Indianise the officer corps of the Indian Army, but at the same time he was keen to obtain as many trained officers as possible from the UK and from British families living in India. Perhaps with memories of his own early career he did not want cadets coming from Britain to be put to the expense of equipping themselves with civilian clothes and he was concerned at the pay disparity between British and Indian officers serving in the Indian Army [40, 43]. He was particularly concerned at the lack of middle-ranking officers in the expanded Indian Army and resisted attempts to obtain such regular officers for irregular units being formed in Singapore [43]. Auchinleck also believed that a wartime spirit should be adopted by officers in India, insisting that all officers should wear uniform, and he was also keen to centralise all headquarters staff in Delhi [40, 59].

Of course, while Auchinleck was C in C India in 1941 it was amongst much else an operational command, with oversight over the campaign in Iraq. This was not the case in 1943–47 when the Indian Command was shorn of operational responsibilities and, of course, memories of the poorly managed Mesopotamia campaign of the First World War cast a long shadow over Indian involvement in British strategic planning at the start of the war. From March 1941 Auchinleck was organising Indian Army units to send to Iraq, and the CIGS agreed that Auchinleck should be in charge of this theatre [42]. This was originally unproblematic as Wavell, C in C Middle East, made it clear that he could spare no troops for Iraq [45]. However, Iraq was soon put back under Middle East Command, at least temporarily [52, 53]. Auchinleck's dispatch of troops, including by air, and obvious interest in the Iraq theatre impressed Churchill and the War Cabinet [48, 49, 50, 55, 56, 61, 62].

It is important to note the lack of correspondence here on the growing Japanese threat in the Far East [39, 41, 43, 61]. In Auchinleck's defence it might be noted that the pressure from the British government was for Indian troops to be sent primarily to the Middle East in this period.

38

Letter from Auchinleck to
General Sir Archibald Wavell,[1] 8 February 1941

1. Since I arrived here I have been considering the question of SYBIL [?] and SABINE[2] and the implications entailed by their move on the dates arranged to the theatre for which they are intended. I am not at all happy in my mind regarding the progress which has been made in the planning for this force either operationally or administratively. I feel that time is getting short and also that the situation in Iraq looks none too pleasant. I am therefore most anxious to clear the air on major problems as soon as possible so that we can then get down to detailed planning here in India.

2. We have revised the Order of Battle on the lines of a completely Indian force and we understand that you are shortly sending your own comments. There is, however, much more in it than that: the only War Office instructions on the subject date, I believe, to the days when France was still our Ally. All they have done is to say that you are still to be responsible and that "a Corps Commander will be appointed soon." On this latter point I should be glad if you would send a reminder as I have several senior appointments to fill and I must know whether to nominate somebody for this role or not. Furthermore, the Commander elect should obviously come in now on the planning.

3. I know well that you and your staff have many pre-occupations in Africa and to the North and I therefore think that my staff here can make a useful contribution to solving the problems involved. I am therefore having an appreciation made now from which I will send you as early as possible by air mail for your consideration. In addition to the appreciation, I will also send you a draft directive to the Force Commander based on it. If we can come to an early agreement on this I think we shall be able to get down straight away,

---

1 Wavell took up his post as General Officer Commanding in Chief, Middle East on 2 August 1939.

2 SABINE was the codename for an operation which envisaged the occupation of Basra by British or Indian troops to hold the oilfields and installations of South-West Persia and the Gulf.

with nucleus Force and Base Staffs in India, to detailed planning. The sooner we can do this the better as we shall have to have our plans cut and dried well in advance if the shipping problem is to be dealt with satisfactorily. To put you into the preliminary picture of the lines on which we are thinking I attach a copy of the minutes held here recently at which Armstrong was present. I would however like you to await the appreciation I have promised before you come to any definite conclusions.

4.   In addition I am also examining the possibility of sending a force – even if only partially trained and equipped – to Iraq in a sudden emergency should the situation there deteriorate seriously in the intervening period before SABINE and SYBIL are ready. This examination has not yet been completed but my present feeling is that if troops are required suddenly as a stabilising element in the Baghdad Habbaniyah area it would be simpler and quicker to employ LOBSTER (or some force of that nature)[3] from Palestine, if necessary replacing it from here.

JRL, AUC 123

39

Letter from L. S. Amery, Secretary of State for India, to Auchinleck, 19 February 1941

By the time you get this you will have had the best part of a couple of months in which to feel your feet and size up things and I should be very glad to have your impressions of how the present first stage of the expansion of the Indian Army is getting on and what you feel about the possibilities of the next stage, what you have in mind to do and whether I can help you if help is required from this end.

I think I was not far wrong when I suggested to you before you left that you might find yourself quite as much in the thick of things in India as here. I think the Japanese definitely mean mischief and while I doubt if they will act precipitately, but rather move by stages into Indo-China and Thailand, I have a feeling that things may well come to a head

---

3   This, presumably, refers to the forces which were to be assembled in Palestine as Habforce to relieve RAF Habbaniyah in May 1941.

between them and us by May. If so, you will no doubt have to make a big immediate effort to help Brooke-Popham[4] and your whole problem will in every way become more difficult and more urgent. However weak our position, I am sure it would be a mistake now to show any signs of hesitation in face of Japanese action. As long as a cat arches her back, spits and faces the dog in front of her, he will hesitate and sometimes go away: the moment she turns tail she is done for. Similarly, if once war becomes inevitable, I believe we shall be wise either to attack, i.e. seize or torpedo all Japanese ships we can everywhere, or at any rate take up advance defensive positions, e.g. by seizing the Isthmus of Kra and so having a narrower front to defend on land against any movement through Thailand.[5]

On the West[6] I hope Wavell will have cleared out the Wops[7] from North Africa before the German push against Greece through Bulgaria becomes effective. If only the Yugoslavs and the Turks had had the courage to coerce Bulgaria and present a solid Balkan front, we could have steadily reinforced it.[8] It will be much more difficult to reinforce the Greeks at Salonika and the Turks, especially if the Turks simply stay on the defensive and refuse to join in the war till they are invaded.[9] It is difficult to see what is going to happen in that part of the world, but it may well be that sooner or later you may have to face the necessity of sending troops to Basra.

Altogether, the next six months promise to be exciting, if anxious. If we can hold our ground well during those months it will bring the end

---

4   Air Chief Marshal Sir Robert Brooke-Popham was appointed Commander in Chief, Far East in October 1940. Prior to this, he had retired from active service with the RAF and was Governor of Kenya.

5   It was only on the 5 December 1941 that the British Cabinet authorised Brooke-Popham to take up defensive positions in Thailand, breaching Thai neutrality.

6   A reference to the Western Desert campaign.

7   A demeaning phrase, referring to Italians.

8   Initially neutral, Bulgaria became allied to the Axis powers when it became a signatory to the Tripartite Pact on 1 March 1941 under pressure from Germany who wanted to move troops, unopposed, through Bulgaria to attack Greece.

9   There was an Anglo-Turkish declaration of martial co-operation and assistance signed in May 1939 and a tripartite agreement between Britain, France and Turkey signed in October 1939. Crucially these agreements only committed Turkey to action at such time as Britain and France had delivered sufficient quantities of war materials; something which was never achieved. The Turco-German neutrality pact of June 1941 saw Turkey move away from its earlier alliances.

of the war much nearer. If not, we and the Americans may have a long uphill road before us.

However, I didn't mean to take up your time with these generalisations, which will be out of date by the time you get this, but just to say that I hope that when the spirit moves you you will write and tell me about things as they strike you.

JRL, AUC 125

40

Letter from Auchinleck to
Field Marshal Sir John Dill, CIGS,
20 February 1941

Thank you very much for arranging to have the verdict of the Chiefs of Staff regarding the air threat to Eastern India altered. It has made things very much easier for us here. It is not that we are experiencing any obstruction from the Finance people – quite the reverse; they are extremely helpful and most reasonable. All the same they have to carry out their job of doing watch-dog over Defence expenditure and they are very loath to take action against professional advice, especially the advice of the Chiefs of Staff, which, quite rightly, in their minds overrides the opinion of the local military experts.

2. I am beginning at last to be able to get some kind of general idea of what is going on out here and of what has been done in the last year. Knowing what India was like a year ago, I am quite frankly astonished at what has been done out here and also at what is being done now. There is a tremendous lot still to do of course, but I think we really are getting on with the job. I need not tell you – you know it only too well – that the limiting factor is equipment, as it is everywhere else. However, things have improved a lot in this respect since you gave us our quota of 10%, and we have also had several other unexpected windfalls lately, such as the 3″ mortars from South Africa.

   Our vehicles too look like materialising at last and when we get them I think we ought to have some pretty useful armoured units, which we may be able to offer you towards the beginning of the autumn should you have need of them. Strictly speaking, as you know, these armoured formations are designed for the defence of India, but if there is no threat to our Western Frontier I personally would have no hesitation in offering them to you. What the Government of India would say is another matter, but I don't think it is any use trying to gauge their attitude so far in advance.

As I said before, I think things really are moving in this country and there is any amount of enthusiasm and keenness. The army is training hard and so far as I can see on sound and up to date lines.

3. I am sorry I was not able to meet you in the matter of Norton for the Western (Ind.) District,[10] but I hope you understand how matters lie. As a matter of fact, since I sent you my telegram about him the position has changed and now there seem to be possibilities of securing two or three other vacancies for Lieut.-Generals. However, between ourselves, I have heard recently, from what I think is a reliable source, that Reuben [?] has got very old lately and that he is not really fit for an important and active command. I don't know what truth there is in this, and as he is a very old friend of mine, I only mention it to you for your personal information.

4. Bill Holden[11] arrived here the day before yesterday and has been staying with me for a couple of nights before going on to take up his abode with Clement Armitage.[12] He has got by no means an easy job in front of him and I think he has realised that already. However, he ought to do it very well and I am sure he will.

5. Carter [?] has also arrived but I have not had an opportunity of talking to him yet.

6. I have put all the army out here into uniform in the same way as they are at home and although this met with a certain amount of grousing from some quarters I am sure it is a good thing and that

---

10 Lieutenant General E. F. Norton, who was Acting Governor of Hong Kong, 1940–41 and Commanded Western (Independent) District, India 1941–42 after which he retired.

11 Major General W. C. Holden was, at this time, Military Member of the Eastern Group Supply Council (Delhi–Simla) in which capacity he visited Australia, New Zealand, South Africa, Malaya, Burma, Rhodesia, Kenya, Uganda and the Netherlands East Indies to investigate munitions output.

12 General Sir (Charles) Clement Armitage, Master General of the Ordnance, India, 1938–42.

it will do nobody any harm. If it does nothing else it will stop this ridiculous nonsense of cadets and young officers coming out to this country with a complete civilian outfit which they may never use.

7. By sending our only two bomber squadrons to the Far East we have left ourselves very naked indeed as regards aircraft – dangerously so in fact. I know you realise this and I am sure the C.A.S. realises it too, as he has just encouraged us all tremendously by sending us a telegram to the effect that he is speeding up the delivery of Lysanders[13] and Glen Martin bombers[14] to us.

I am not really worried about having a lot of aircraft on the Frontier so long as it is only the tribes whom we have to face. I would be quite prepared to take the tribes on with troops alone with no aircraft at all. On the other hand our ports, Calcutta, Bombay, etc., are really extremely ill defended. Coast defence guns are either obsolete or too few to be any good. As you know, we have no A.A. at all except for one miserable battery of eight guns, and we are still short of craft for local naval defence. The adverse moral effect on public opinion generally in this country of an uninterrupted bombardment by enemy ships of any of our ports might be very serious, much more serious than it would be at home. At the moment, to assist in the defence of these ports, all we have are a few old aircraft, Wapiti,[15] Audax[16] and the like, which really are not reliable enough to be sent to sea at all and would not, I am afraid, make much impression against a modern

---

13 The Westland Lysander had been introduced into the RAF in 1936 as an Army Co-operation Aircraft. Losses were heavy, against modern fighter aircraft, in France in 1940 and during the rest of the Second World War most were employed on duties with Special Operations Executive, landing agents, munitions and radios behind enemy lines.

14 Presumably Martin Maryland Bombers, which entered RAF service in June 1940. These aircraft were manufactured in the USA and had originally been adapted for service with the French Air Force. By the standards of the time these were fast and effective aircraft, faster than the Bristol Blenheim.

15 The Westland Wapiti was a single engine biplane. It entered service with the RAF in 1928 and remained in production until 1932. It was withdrawn from RAF service in 1940.

16 The Hawker Audax was developed from the Hawker Hart, for service in India and Singapore. It was a single engine biplane and entered service with the RAF in 1932. A considerable number remained in service in 1940, seeing active service in Iraq in 1941 and, elsewhere, were used for training purposes until 1944.

cruiser. However, we will carry on as best we can until you can help us out with some modern aircraft.

8.   I see that Far East have recommended to you the formation of a Corps in Northern Malaya. If you agree to this I presume we shall be called upon to provide a Commander and most of the staff. I have got this in hand already and have asked Wavell if he can spare Heath[17] for the job should the proposal materialise. He has proved himself a good divisional commander in the Sudan and his experience of modern fighting, even though the country may be different, would be invaluable in a new formation. Wavell may, of course, have ideas of forming an Indian Corps of his own in Egypt out of the 4th and 5th Divisions and might want to keep Heath for this. However, he has not said anything about this yet.

9.   Some time ago we had a telegram from you saying that a Commander for Sabine would be nominated shortly, but we have heard no more about this. I am a little worried about Sabine generally, because up to date no reasoned plan for its possible employment seems to have been worked out. There are so many permutations and combinations which might affect operations in Iraq should it ever become necessary to send troops to that country that we have tried our hand at making an appreciation of the situation in respect of the possible employment of Sabine. I am sending this to Wavell and am sending a copy to you personally in a separate letter. I feel that if there is any chance of troops going in that direction in the near future, detailed planning should start at once, particularly on the administrative side. I feel, also, that a draft directive for the Commander should be agreed upon and put on record.

JRL, AUC 126

---

17   Lieutenant General Sir Lewis Heath who commanded 3 Indian Corps in Malaya, 1941–42.

41

Letter from Auchinleck to
General Sir Archibald Wavell, 13 March 1941

Thank you very much for your letter of the 5th March, which I received today.

1. With regard to the brigade of Gurkhas which you say might be of use to you, I will be only too glad to let you have it as soon as I can get it ready for you, if you feel you want it. There is, however, a difficulty. When I mentioned the matter to you in Cairo I did not know what the situation regarding the Gurkhas as a whole was. The older battalions which were in existence when the war broke out have been very severely drained of officers and n.c.os. in order to form new battalions of Gurkhas as for each old battalion one new battalion is being formed. This, in addition to the peculiar conditions attaching to Gurkha recruitment, has resulted in all Gurkha battalions being not only under strength for the time being, but also in rather a backward state of training. This condition will not last long, of course, but it might be two or three months before I could produce for you a properly trained and efficient brigade of three Gurkha battalions. However, if you think you are likely to want such a brigade some time during the summer, I will work to that end. Meanwhile, should you want a brigade of infantry accustomed to and trained in hill warfare I could probably find you one made up of battalions of the ordinary Line, that is to say, Frontier Force, Punjabi or Baluch battalions, as these units are not suffering under the same handicap as the Gurkhas are at the moment. It would of course be of great advantage in a detached brigade of this sort if all three battalions were of the same class so that the brigade could be homogeneous, but if your need is urgent I think I would have to send you the ordinary infantry battalions instead of Gurkhas.

   As for political reactions, I do not see why there should be any, but I will make discreet enquiries in the right quarter and find out whether there would be any objection to the use of Indian troops in the theatres which you have in mind.

   Perhaps you will let me know what you think about the situation as explained by me above.

2. Thank you very much for promising to look after the Nawab of Bhopal.[18] I hope he won't be a nuisance.

    If it is really no trouble to you and your staff, I should very much like to continue to send you visitors of this type, that is to say, ruling Princes, prominent politicians and other public men. Their visits do a tremendous lot of good in the education of public opinion in this country and make our task of pulling our weight in the war correspondingly easier. But if they are a nuisance I hope you will say so at once and I will try to discourage the idea of sending any more of them, though I should be very sorry to have to do this.

3. Thank you very much for your remarks about the Sabine plan and for getting things on the move so quickly. I shall feel much easier in my mind when we really have got something concrete on which we can work at short notice, because I feel myself that, with events moving at the pace they are, the notice we shall get may be very short.

    I have nominated Quinan as Commander of the Force and have sent his name home to the War Office. I propose to give him Slim as his B.G.S. and I think the combination should be a good one. Quinan is an educated soldier, i.d.c. and all the rest of it, and has had considerable experience in command on service lately, even if only on the Frontier. Beresford,[19] whom you may know, has been nominated for some time as the Commander of the Base and I do not propose to change this selection. Quinan and Beresford, with Slim[20] and one or two other senior nominees for the staff of the Force, are coming here on the 17th to be put into the picture and to rough out the first outline plans. As soon as they have done that, I

---

18 Sir Hamidullah Khan Sikandar Saulat (1894–1960) became ruler of the independent state of Bhopal in March 1926. Bhopal, with a population of more than 800,000 people and occupying 7,000 square miles, was a Muslim ruled state amongst the many Hindu principalities in Central India. Auchinleck's fears of the Begum being a nuisance were misplaced; indeed, he was seen to be a strong supporter of the British war effort and as Chancellor of the Chamber of Princes from 1944 he was important in maintaining the loyalty of this body to the King Emperor.

19 Major General George de la Poer Beresford.

20 Brigadier W. J. Slim, the future Field Marshal. Slim had been wounded serving against the Italians in East Africa and when Auchinleck was considering potential staff officers for service in Iraq, Slim was employed in Army Headquarters, India, working on contingency plans considering a German breakthrough in the Caucasus or the defection of the Iraqis to the Axis.

propose to send them straight off to Cairo if that will be convenient to you. I will, of course, send you an official telegram asking for your agreement. With them I propose to send a representative of the A.O.C.-in-C. in India or possibly the A.O.C.-in-C. himself, to discuss the question of the air component with you and the A.O.C.-in-C. Middle East. I take it that we shall only be concerned with the air forces actually required for close co-operation with the Force itself and that the bigger strategical question connected with air offensives at a distance will continue to be dealt with by the A.O.C.-in-C., Middle East.

4.   Thornhill,[21] your propaganda merchant, has been staying with me for the last week or so and has been of very great help to us in connection with the handling of the Italian prisoners of war in this country. He has given me some very valuable notes and advice, of which I hope to be able to make the fullest use.

5.   I wonder if you could possibly manage to spare us any of your captured Italian A.A. artillery, heavy or light, or both. We are frightfully short of anything of the kind in this country, in fact we really have none at all as the only 3 guns we have (3″) are all being used to train the personnel of the A.A. regiments which we are raising in anticipation of receiving equipments from home. The result is that at the ports and in our vulnerable areas where our big factories are we have no A.A. protection at all other than light machine guns. India being what she is, it is most important that we should have something to make a noise and to show that action is being taken against attacking aircraft in order to keep the morale of the people, and especially the factory workers and workers in the dock areas, as high as possible. So long as we could get some guns it would not matter very much to us whether they had only got a little ammunition; some guns with a few rounds which they could fire should an attack take place would be quite invaluable to us. I know that you must have demands on you for these guns, but perhaps you might be able to spare us a few.

6.   I have not yet had a firm reply from the War Office about the formation of the Indian Corps in Malaya, but so far as I know the

---

21   Colonel Cudbert Thornhill had been sent to Cairo by Department E H, the predecessor of SOE and the Political Warfare Executive, to draft and disseminate Allied propaganda amongst Italian soldiers and POWs in North Africa.

project has been, for all practical purposes, approved; perhaps they are waiting for the C.I.G.S. to get home before they finally decide. I mention this because I think you must be wondering why I have not given you a definite reply about Heath and Mayne.[22]

7.   I won't take up any more of your time as I am sure you are very busy and have very many more important things to think about. I will write again before long.

JRL, AUC 130

42

Letter from Field Marshal Sir John Dill to Auchinleck, 13 March 1941[23]

As I seem to be a little nearer to you than usual I feel that I must write you a line. Archie Wavell & I have discussed 'Sabine' as fully as we could and are agreed, as I think he has told you, that you should do the planning and that, in the early stages at any rate, you should control. My own feeling is that the necessity for 'Sabine' will arise sooner or later – & probably sooner than later.

Conditions in Iraq are, as you know, bad & show little sign of improving. We have had that nasty little red fox Tewfiq Suwaidi, the Foreign Minister, over here. He has been all honeyed words but is obviously quite unrealistic. The Regent, they tell me is good, but can he control or deal with the soldiers who have gone political?

In all these plans and preparations it is a race against time. The Foreign Secretary & I have had a not too easy time and it is impossible to say yet whether or not we have done any good.

The Turks are sound at heart – the Foreign Secretary had a wonderful reception from them – but will do all in their power to postpone the day they must fight. They are woefully short of modern equipment and are, I should say, quite incapable of any offensive action. The great danger is that they will try to fight it out in Thrace, where they would be destroyed by German armoured divisions, rather than fight back to the Bosporus where they really could hold a German advance.

---

22   Major General Mosley Mayne.
23   At the time he sent this letter, Dill was visiting H.Q. Middle East in Cairo.

Cakmak[24] is old & none too fit, but I fancy he is pretty wise. He and the rest of them are much more inclined to accept British advice since Archie Wavell's victories – & that is all to the good.

The Greeks are fighting & are quite determined to continue to fight even if – or I should say when – the Germans come in. Their moral is high at present but is apt to go up and down with incredible velocity!

The question is, what are the Yugo-slavs going to do? I expect you will know by the time you get this letter.

By the way, to return to 'Sabine'. I will take up the question of your dealing direct with me, & cutting out the India Office, when I return to London. Knowing the India Office and the present S. of S. as I do, I may have some difficulty.

I will, of course, promise to keep the India Office fully in touch [missing section of document].

I hope that all [illegible] well with you and your lady. Please give her my best.

I am delighted to know that you hold your great appointment in these difficult days.

JRL, AUC 131

43

Letter from Auchinleck to L. S. Amery, Secretary of State for India, 17 March 1941

Thank you very much for your letter of the 19th February which reached me on the 14th of this month. I must apologise for not having written to you sooner, but it has taken me all my time since I arrived at the end of January to get a grasp of what has been done in the last year and of proposals for the future. I am still in the process of learning what the situation really is and I am afraid I am likely to stay in that state for some little time to come.

I am amazed at what has been done in so short a time, and at the ingenuity, flexibility and energy which has been shown, particularly in the production of munitions. Things are being done which two

---

24   General Fevzi Cakmak (1876–1950) was Chief of the General Staff of the Turkish Army from 1922 to 1944.

years ago would not have been considered possible in India. This is all very good I think and augurs well for the future. There is a colossal amount still to be done of course, but this is likely always to be so, I suppose.

2. The expansion of the army has gone very well and wonderfully smoothly all things considered. Here again, I am very much impressed with the results achieved and I am deeply grateful to those, including my predecessor, who are responsible for this state of affairs. I think that the moment has now come to review the position generally and make certain modifications in the original proposals. These modifications which I am now thinking over, will be aimed at simplification of the organisation generally and the prevention of the springing up of new corps and units which have no very definite purpose or firm foundation.

Generally speaking, I have found very little to quarrel with in the actual composition, organisation or equipment of the new formations we are raising. Such alterations, and they are of minor character, as I am making are again aimed at simplification. You ask for my ideas on the next stage. I do not myself think that for the moment we can look further ahead than we are doing at the moment. You know what present plans are. The production of formations for H.M.G. as they say they need them, and then replacement by similar formations to be kept in India for its own immediate defence. We can get the men without difficulty, I think, but one can not go beyond a certain limit in the raising of new formations unless there is a prospect of being able to equip them within a reasonable time.

It is possible to do a lot in the training line with dummy weapons and the like, but I do not think one can keep troops in an unequipped state indefinitely.

3. Equipment and officers are the two bottlenecks and likely to remain as such, I think, till the end.

4. Equipment is coming in, steadily if slowly and the progress made in manufacture in this country is most encouraging. I recently visited the ordnance and other factories at Calcutta and Tatanagar and was very favourably impressed. Much more can and, I hope will be done. The Roger Mission[25] has done most valuable work out here

---

25 This was a group of technical experts, assembled under the leadership of Sir Alexander Roger, Chairman of the Automatic Telephone Company and a

and has presented, as you know, a remarkable series of reports. All the same, equipment is short – very short – and it disturbs me to think that I shall not have a single division in the country equipped for modern war once "Capable"[26] has departed for Singapore, until next July. We have certainly got troops and plenty of them which could be sent, say to Iraq to restore the internal situation in that country, and if necessary deal with the Iraq army, but they would not be fit, from the equipment point of view, to go to Anatolia to fight the Germans! I feel more and more certain that it will not be long before we shall have to send troops to Iraq, and that this alternative L[ines] of C[ommunication] via Basra, Baghdad, Mosul and Aleppo may become really important strategically before the war is much older. However, as you know, we are preparing for that contingency and planning has now started in earnest.

5. The supply of suitable "middle-piece" officers is getting more difficult every day and I have had, much against my will, to refuse demands from Singapore for regular officers for various irregular units that they propose raising. I have always been rather sceptical (hidebound – I suppose!) of the value of these specialized small units. I feel that the officers and N.C.Os. they absorb could be much greater value training and leading regular units on which we must rely on to win the battle finally.

I am not too happy about our system for the recruitment of Indians for emergency commissions. We are getting some quite good stuff, but I feel we are losing many of the best of them. I have this in hand. Of one thing I am quite sure – we can no longer afford to differentiate between Englishman and Indians in the matter of pay etc. when both are doing the same job side by side. There are many anomalies which need adjusting and I am hoping to be able to do this.

The Indian Office have been very good in sending us out so many good cadets from Home and we are correspondingly grateful. All the same, we must at our end see that we get an adequate supply

---

former Chairman of B.S.A. This group had been formed in August 1940 and was charged by Herbert Morrison, the Minister of Supply, with advising the British and Indian Governments on the possibility of expanding munitions production in India.

26 15th Indian Brigade was sent to Singapore in March 1941, followed by the 22nd Indian Brigade and the headquarters of 9th Indian Division in April.

of Indians, both as regards quantity and quality. I am sure we shall want them all before we have done.

The cadet colleges are working well and turning out good material. I hope to visit most of them during the next month. The "middle-piece" officers simply are not there, so we must do the best we can without them, I suppose.

6. As regards recruitment for the rank and file, I have no doubt at all that, apart from any political considerations, we must broaden our basis and this was already in hand before I arrived. I propose to continue and hasten the process. There is plenty of good untouched material which we can and should use. Politically too it is, I think, essential to meet to an appreciable extent the almost universal demand for general recruitment and to give the process proper publicity.

This I hope to be able to do by reviving old units, such as the Madras Regiment and raising new regular (as opposed to Territorial Force)[27] units to represent provinces hitherto unrepresented, such as Bengal, Assam and Bihar. This can easily be done as in some cases territorial units, which can be converted to regular units, already exist.[28]

These units will by no means be "for show" only. They can be made and will be made, to take their share of the work. Generally speaking, I am opposed to any further expansion of the Territorial Force as such. It is an anomaly in war time and a great complication in many ways. I hope in fact to be able to regularize most of the existing T.F. provincial units.

I don't think it will be difficult, and it will help greatly in meeting the political demand for wider representation in the Army.

---

27 The Indian Territorial Force had been raised in 1920 and was largely composed of Indian personnel; the Auxiliary Force recruited amongst Europeans and Anglo-Indians. Members of the Indian Territorial Force were only liable for service within their own districts and these units were used for internal security duties during the Second World War, to relieve regular units for active service. The Territorial Force was approximately 20,000 strong in 1938.

28 By June 1941 six new Indian Army Regiments had been created; the Bengal Regiment, Assam Regiment, Bihar Regiment and Madras Regiment, which relied on voluntary recruitment amongst specific Indian Territorial Force regiments, effectively seeing some 'regularised'; and the Mahar Regiment and Mazbhi Sikh Regiment.

7. The Air Force is desperately weak and worries me greatly. I hear that the Air Ministry will not agree our fifteen squadron expansion scheme for the Indian Air Force. This is a disappointment to all of us but I realize that they can not help themselves. We are now busy on a new scheme based on such aircraft as are actually in sight, and there are quite a number of them, though most of them are obsolescent. I feel we must expand the I.A.F. by hook or by crook as it is becoming more and more evident that we have very little hope getting anything from outside. Even if we do not need our expanded I.A.F. in India, they may be able to lend a hand outside India and I hope they will.

8. The Navy is going on well and expanding with great energy. I like the looks of what I have seen of the personnel very much (the ratings) and I hope to see a good deal of them next week at Bombay and Karachi. I am off tomorrow by air to Secunderabad, Madras, Bangalore, Bombay and Karachi. I hope to do the N.W.F. and the Punjab in April.

9. Wilson has just handed over Adjutant-General to Haig,[29] whose place as Q.M.G. has been taken by Noyes.[30] De Burgh[31] gave place some weeks ago to Hutton. I think the new team is a good one and should do well. The Wilson change was difficult to make and distressing to me, but it necessary for the good of the whole.

10. This letter already is inordinately long and I will finish.

As I indicated earlier, I am anxious that the machinery of expansion shall not get out of control and over-run itself. Some consolidation and reconsideration is wanted, I think, but this need have no deterrent effect on eventual progress. I think probably it will have the reverse effect.

May I thank you for your generous help in arranging that in operational matters affecting Force Sabine the War Office should deal direct with us.

JRL, AUC 132

---

29 General Sir Arthur Brodie Haig.
30 Lieutenant General Sir Cyril Noyes.
31 General Sir Eric De Burgh, Chief of the General Staff, India, 1939–41.

44

Auchinleck to General Sir Archibald Wavell, 10 April 1941

Certain personal telegrams have passed between S. of S. India and Viceroy regarding despatch of (a) a force immediately to Basra and (b) a battalion by air to SHAIBA (.) Action being taken to make this correspondence official but in meantime regard it as private and personal (.) Gist of Viceroy's reply as follows (.) Begins (.) First (.) Proposes to divert to Basra one infantry brigade and one field regiment with ancillary troops now in ships at Karachi and destined for Malaya (.) This force not (repeat not) tactically loaded so naval and air support will be necessary if landing likely to be opposed (.)

Second (.)   Between 13/4 and 22/4 we will despatch one C.G Hospital and base stores (.)

Third (.)   We are convinced that force in and around Basra should be brought up as soon as possible to equivalent of at least one division (.) We should follow first brigade group by two further brigade groups and base units for SYBIL (.) Second echelon could probably be embarked after twenty-one days.

Fourth (.)   We can send approximately 400 British infantry with twelve L.M.Gs and six Vickers guns[32] by air to SHAIBA starting move 13/4 and completing in seven to eleven days (.)

Fifth (.)   We are examining possibility of sending infantry brigade groups later to Palestine but unless it is to have priority over troops for Basrah or special shipping can be provided it will have to sail after division is established at Basrah (.) End (.) I understand H.M.G. would consider these proposals on 9/4 (.) We have asked for urgent decisions (.)

JRL, AUC 137

---

32   Heavy, water-cooled .303″ machine guns, based on the Maxim pattern.

45

Cipher message from
General Sir Archibald Wavell to
Auchinleck, 10 April 1941

This proposal involves critical decisions. It is just possible that this Force might suffice to swing the scale in Iraq. I am fully committed in Cyrenaica and can spare nothing for Iraq. Longmore[33] could spare squadron Wellington's temporarily r[e]p[ea]t. temporarily to support landing at Basra in addition to Air Force already in Iraq.

JRL, AUC 138

46

Letter from Auchinleck to Sir Gilbert Laithwaite,
Private Secretary to the Viceroy, 12 April 1941

My Dear Laithwaite,

I attach a copy of a telegram from the India Office which we have just received (No 4030 of 12/4). You will have a copy of telegram No. 314 of 11/4 from Cornwallis, Baghdad to F.O. London rep[ea]t[e]d Cairo and G[overnment]. of I[ndia].

2.   My own opinion is that the acceptance of the Ambassador's advice to defer action for the securing of Basrah may very well result in our never getting Basrah at all.

3.   I have already informed His Excellency of my considered opinion that it is essential for us to establish ourselves in Basrah so as to secure its use for us as a base as soon as we possibly can. I am convinced myself that the possession of base at Basrah may be the difference between success and failure to us in the Near and Middle East during the next six months. This being so, I view with the greatest anxiety the decision of H.M.G. to postpone the immediate action proposed by us to secure it.

---

33   Air Chief Marshal Sir Arthur Longmore.

In my opinion, the time for diplomatic parleying has past. I think there is a very definite danger that Rashid[34] will use the breathing space Cornwallis[35] proposes to give him to consolidate his position and, probably, to invoke German aid, which might even take the form of air borne troops and aircraft.

I am convinced that, if we are to prevent a general deterioration of the situation in Asia generally, and especially in Turkey, Iran, Iraq and Arabia, we must show now that we are prepared to maintain our position by force.

I view this with the gravest misgiving the proposal of H.M.G. to temporise and compromise, and I shall be grateful if you will ask His Excellency whether he is prepared to represent these views to the Secretary of State. I regard the matter as one of extreme urgency.

JRL, AUC 139

47

Auchinleck to Sir Gilbert Laithwaite, Private Secretary to the Viceroy, 17 April 1941

Your letter of the 17th just received.

I have sent a telegram to London regarding the importance of not disclosing the fact that the force was originally intended for another destination. The telegram has been repeated to other authorities concerned.

2. I will send the C.-in-C., East Indies, a message regarding the development of the port and the arrangement to be made for its defence against attack from the sea.

3. Our suggestion that a portion of the British battalion might in emergency be sent on from Shaiba to Habbaniyeh was made so as to give the A.O.C., Iraq, the chance of availing himself of this potential reinforcement should the situation at the latter place become really critical. In view of the latest development in the situation, I propose

---

34 Rashid Ali el Gailani, a leading Iraqi nationalist politician who was in close touch with the Axis powers.
35 Sir Kinahan Cornwallis, recently appointed as British Ambassador to Iraq.

not to despatch the remainder of this battalion from Karachi unless I hear from Fraser,[36] after he has arrived, that it is really required. If he does not want it I shall not send it at all and, as soon as he can relieve the advance guard that has already been despatched, I will get that back to India. It does not look at the moment as if the A.O.C., Iraq, is likely to require aid at Habbaniyeh, although of course the situation is liable to change rapidly.

4. So far as I know, complete secrecy is being maintained as heretofore and there is no intention of breaking it so far as we are concerned.

5. I think it is too early yet to consider whether the force shall remain at Basra or whether a part of it can move up-country soon after it arrives. Details of such moves will have to be decided by Fraser and later, when he arrives, by Quinan. My own opinion is that, to begin with, it would be wise to concentrate on consolidating our position in Basra; when we are sure of our footing there we can then begin to think about extending ourselves. This process will include, probably, the establishing or the opening of a rest camp at Baghdad, the stationing of troops at Habbaniyeh and, in order to give force to our reasons for exerting our rights under the treaty, the actual despatch of troops or transport through from Basra to Palestine. We are now drafting a telegram to the Secretary of State suggesting a course of action on these lines; a copy of the draft will be sent to you for His Excellency's information and concurrence before it is despatched.

6. As regards the billeting of troops in Basra or elsewhere, I do not anticipate any immediate difficulties as the number of troops is very small at present and I am told that the whole contingent is well off for tentage and other camp equipment. If we can not get permanent accommodation for them, temporary hutting should present no difficulties; we had plenty of experience of it in the last war. His Excellency may rest assured that I shall do everything in my power to see that the troops are as well found as possible; this is already under the active consideration of P.S.Os.

7. I have already given you my comments and those of the F.A.,M.F. [Financial Authority, Military Finance?] on the draft of the telegram which His Excellency has since sent to the Secretary of State.

JRL, AUC 141

---

36   Major General W. A. K. Fraser.

48

Cipher message from Field Marshal Sir John Dill, to Auchinleck, 25 April 1941

Since War Office Telegram 62661 21/4 was despatched War Cabinet have been told of the programme outlined in your 4265/G 21/4 and have expressed anxiety at the prospect of no reinforcements for Force Converse reaching Iraq before the middle of May. They feel that the sooner we can increase our forces in Basra the less the risk of losing our initial advantage. War Cabinet are most grateful for the speed with which you have helped us and I am very reluctant to press you further especially as my request may be impracticable. Would it however be in any way possible to expedite the despatch of the whole or a portion of Force Cling. Alternatively or even perhaps additionally could the third brigade be despatched simultaneously with Cling or immediately afterwards.

JRL, AUC 143

49

Paraphrase of cipher message no. 412 from HQ, RAF, Middle East to Auchinleck, 1 May 1941

Following is the text of leaflets headed in each case to people of Iraq from British Government:-

(1) Your Government have sent military forces to Habbaniya and informed A.O.C that normal training can no longer be permitted that any aircraft or troops leaving enemy camp will be fired on. British Government do not understand reason for this action which is not in keeping with Treaty between our two nations. They have no quarrel with their friends the people of Iraq, and have told your government that British Forces at Habbaniya will continue their training, and that if any hostile act is committed against the British Forces the British Government will retaliate at once by bombing headquarters of the Government in Baghdad and the army.

(2) Your government have been informed by British Government that if Iraq Armed Forces, which in opposition to Treaty between

us, have surrounded British camp at Habbaniya are not ordered to return to Bagdad within four hours, strong air action will be taken against Government in Bagdad and Iraq Army and Air Force wherever they may be. The British Government have no quarrel with the Iraqi people, but merely with their misguided Government and few senior Officers who are wilfully misleading them.

JRL, AUC 151

50

Draft appreciation: India and the situation in the ME by Auchinleck, 2 May 1941 [Working copy]

India and the situation in the Middle East

1. The enemy's recovery of CYRENAICA gives him bases from which the German and Italian Air Forces may be able to deny:-

    (a)   the use of ALEXANDRIA to our fleet
    (b)   the use of SUEZ, PORT SAID and the Canal to our shipping.

2. The enemy's conquest of GREECE gives him bases from which the German Air Force can threaten TURKEY and the communications from that country to EGYPT through SYRIA and PALESTINE. The possession of these bases also lays open ALEXANDRIA and the Canal to air attack from the NORTH as well as from the WEST, thereby increasing the risk of their usefulness to us being reduced or nullified by enemy action.

    The Italian air bases in the DODECANESE will be of material aid to the enemy in these operations.

3. Should the fleet be forced to leave ALEXANDRIA owing to enemy attacks from the air or on land, there is no other base in the Eastern Mediterranean from which it can operate. In this event the enemy may be able to transport troops and stores freely in these waters.

    The French in SYRIA are most unlikely to be able to offer any effective resistance to a German attack on the country and it is highly probable therefore that the enemy, making full use of his superiority in the air, will try to obtain a footing in that country with the objects:-

(a) of encircling TURKEY and forcing her to submit to his dictates.

(b) of striking at EGYPT and the Canal from the NORTH as well as from the WEST.

(c) of moving against IRAQ so as to deny to us the use of BASRA and the lines of communication thence to TURKEY and EGYPT, and also to secure the IRAQ oil fields.

(d) of setting all the Middle Eastern Muslim countries against us and of causing serious disaffection in India.

(e) of cutting off our supply of oil from South-Western Iran, and also, possibly, from Bolivia and the Persian Gulf generally.

4. The effect on our position in the East generally of the loss of control at sea in the Eastern Mediterranean, and of the total or partial denial to us of the use of the Canal and its ports would be most serious but not necessarily disastrous.

We shall doubtless make every effort to retain our hold on EGYPT, but even the loss of it, once we had ceased to be able to make use of ALEXANDRIA and the Canal, need not be decisive.

Even if the enemy secured LOWER EGYPT it should still be possible for us to retain our hold on UPPER EGYPT and the SUDAN using PORT SUDAN as a base, and we should be able also to prevent the enemy using the Canal to pass his war ships into the RED SEA and INDIAN OCEAN. It is most important that he should not be able to do this, as by doing so, he begins at once to turn our flank in the PERSIAN GULF.

The loss of LOWER EGYPT would however give the enemy a good sea base in ALEXANDRIA and a land line of advance thence against PALESTINE, SYRIA and IRAQ. The advantages of maintaining our position in EGYPT for as long as possible with a view to our ultimate resumption of the offensive are too obvious to need definition and this must, for the present, remain our main object in this theatre.

5. On the other hand if we are to prevent TURKEY joining the Axis, actively or passively, and to deny our enemies access to IRAQ, the PERSIAN GULF, IRAN and eventually INDIA, it is essential for us to retain our hold on PALESTINE and to prevent the enemy establishing himself firmly in SYRIA.

It seems then that our primary object in the Middle East may soon become the retention of our hold on PALESTINE, SYRIA and IRAQ.

6. It is apparent that, should the use of ALEXANDRIA, SUEZ and PORT SAID as bases for our armies and air forces in the Middle East be denied to us, BASRA and PORT SUDAN are the only possible substitutes. Of these two ports BASRA is by far the most useful as it can be used to maintain not only forces in EGYPT but also forces in ANATOLIA, SYRIA, PALESTINE and IRAQ, as well as in IRAN, should it be necessary to send troops into that country. Before next autumn BASRA may well become the principal port of disembarkation for personnel and munitions for the Middle East not only from INDIA but also from AUSTRALASIA and the U.S.A.

In short, BASRA and the various lines of communication leading thence, have now assumed a major strategic importance.

7. BASRA is of no use in itself except as a fortified port of entry at which troops could be landed to restore the situation in the Middle East should IRAQ, PALESTINE and SYRIA fall into enemy hands. Such a contingency is by no means impossible but it is supremely important to prevent its arising. This can only be done by consolidating our hold in IRAQ, and developing the communications leading through it NORTH and NORTH WEST from BASRA to their utmost capacity as soon as possible, so that we can use them to forestall the enemy in SYRIA and to help TURKEY to resist enemy pressure in ANATOLIA. It is quite likely that the alternative line of aid to TURKEY through SYRIA may not be available, either because of French action, or on account of enemy air attack. Hence the whole of IRAQ becomes just as strategically important to us as BASRA.

8. At the moment INDIA seems to be the only part of the Empire capable of producing even the minimum number of troops necessary to consolidate our position in IRAQ. At a later date help might be forthcoming from AUSTRALIA and NEW ZEALAND.

9. Ever-increasing calls are being made on INDIA for help in personnel and material for the Middle East and FAR EAST Commands and these demands are not likely to diminish.

Meanwhile, INDIA herself, no doubt for very good strategic reasons, has up to date been denied any appreciable share of modern equipment, particularly tanks, anti-aircraft artillery and aircraft, which are being produced in the Empire and the U.S.A.

The result is that though INDIA can produce considerable force measured in terms of men, she cannot equip this force to fit it to meet an enemy provided with modern weapons.

The responsibility for securing IRAQ to our use has been placed on INDIA and to enable her to carry out this task, she must be given her proper share of such modern equipment as she can not produce herself. Otherwise, we run the risk of incurring in IRAQ yet another disaster similar to those which we have experienced in NORWAY, FRANCE and GREECE.

10. We entered IRAQ on the pretext of availing ourselves of our rights under the treaty, that is, of our rights to open a line of communication from BASRA to HAIFA. It is imperative now that we should as soon as possible make it clear to IRAQ and the World that we are compelled to occupy IRAQ and that we intend to do so by force if necessary.

11. The conclusions are:-

(i) If we can no longer use ALEXANDRIA and the Canal because of enemy air action, the loss of EGYPT though serious need not be a major strategic disaster, though the importance of continuing to hold it can not be minimised.

(ii) Even if we lose EGYPT we should be able to hold the SUDAN, and control the RED SEA.

(iii) To support TURKEY and to stop he enemy penetrating into ASIA, it is essential for us to deny him SYRIA, PALESTINE and IRAQ, and this may soon become our strategic object in this theatre.

(iv) BASRA and IRAQ are assuming a major strategic importance as a base and line of communication area for operations in the Middle East.

(v) The development of BASRA and the communications leading thence NORTH and NORTH WEST is an exceedingly urgent necessity.

(vi) The consolidation, by force if necessary, of our position in IRAQ is an urgent necessity and diplomatic considerations must not stand in its way.

(vii) At the moment INDIA alone can produce troops for the occupation of IRAQ, but these troops will be inadequate for the task unless they are provided with the modern weapons and aircraft which INDIA can not give them.

JRL, AUC 159

51

Memorandum from Auchinleck to Lieutenant General E. P. Quinan, 2 May 1941

1. You will command all British Empire land forces in IRAQ from the time of your arrival at BASRA.

2. You will be under my orders.

3. It is the intention of His Majesty's Government:-

    (a) To develop and organise the port of BASRA to any extent necessary to enable it to maintain such forces, our own or allied, as may be required to operate in the Middle East, including EGYPT, TURKEY, IRAQ and IRAN.

    (b) To secure control of all means of communication including all aerodromes and landing grounds in IRAQ and to develop these to the extent requisite to enable the port of BASRA to function to its fullest capacity.

4. You will be responsible for carrying out these intentions, and may find it convenient to do so in the following stages:-

    (a) Occupation and development of BASRA as a base for the maintenance of at least three divisions. The base must be capable of expansion to serve at least six divisions.

    (b) Occupation of BAGHDAD and the development of L. of C. installations there.

    (c) Development and protection of the L. of C. from BAGHDAD westwards to the frontier of TRANS JORDAN.

    (d) Development and protection of the L. of C. from BAGHDAD northward to MOSUL.

Notes

(i)   Middle East Command have been asked to assume responsibility for the development and protection of the L. of C. westwards beyond the Trans Jordian frontier.

(ii)   The order of priority as between (c) and (d) above may have to be altered at your discretion in accordance with circumstances existing at the time.

5.   You will at once begin to plan a system of defence to protect the BASRA base against attack by armoured forces supported by strong air forces.

An estimate of the equipment, stores and material required should be sent to me as soon as possible.

Note:

The Commander-in-Chief, East Indies is already considering the defence of BASRA against attack from the sea and your plan should be made in consultation with him or his representative and with the A.O.C. IRAQ.

6.   You will examine without delay in conjunction with the naval authorities and the Port Authority BASRA the possibility of establishing an alternative port to BASRA at KOWEIT [Kuwait], UMM KASR or elsewhere and consider the measures necessary for its protection from attack by land, sea and air.

7.   You will be ready if necessary to take special measures to protect:-

(a)   Royal Air Force installations and personnel at HABBANIYEH and SHAIBA.

(b)   The lives of British subjects in BAGHDAD and elsewhere in IRAQ.

(c)   The KIRKUK oilfields and the pipeline to HAIFA. You will be prepared on the orders of H.Q. M.E. to carry out the demolition of the KIRKUK oil field installations.

8.   (i)   You may be called upon to protect the Anglo-Iranian Oil Company's installations and its British employees in S.W. IRAN, and plans should be laid accordingly.

(ii)   Meanwhile, you will take great care to ensure the strictest observance by all under your command of IRANIAN neutrality, which presents particularly difficult problems on the SHATT-EL-ARAB below BASRA.

(iii) Any hostile act on the part of IRAN is to be reported at once to me. Reprisals for such acts except in self defence are not to be undertaken except on my orders.

9. You may have to resist enemy attempts to invade IRAQ with air or ground forces from SYRIA, and you may be called on to co-operate with TURKISH forces in ANATOLIA or the CAUCASUS.

10. (i) It is the desire of His Majesty's Government to act throughout in friendly co-operation with the IRAQ authorities and people, so long as such co-operation is forthcoming. If it is withheld you will take such forcible measures as you think fit to achieve your object, after consultation with H.M. Minister in BAGHDAD so long as he is available for the purpose.

(ii) To enable you to carry out your task you have been given certain financial powers and you are to take any steps you consider essential to ensure the safety of your force at all times. Such steps may if necessary include the assumption of control over the civil population, the occupation or destruction of buildings, the impressment of transport of all kinds and of labour, the taking over of public utility services, the confiscation of weapons and the taking of hostages etc.

(iii) You will make special efforts to establish and maintain friendly relations between your troops and the local inhabitants. Special Service officers will be attached to your headquarters to assist you in this task.

11. It is my present intention to increase your force by two more divisions, making three in all, and, possibly, by an armoured division, as soon as these troops can be despatched from INDIA.

12. Demands for air action in all forms in Iraq will be addressed by you to A.O.C. Iraq who, under the A.O.C.-in-C. Middle East, is responsible for meeting your requirements.

13. Should the British Military Mission in Iraq cease to operate as such in the normal way under the Iraq Government its personnel will come under your command.

14. You will maintain the closest possible touch with H.M. Minister in BAGHDAD and whenever possible, obtain his concurrence to any military dispositions you wish to make. In the event of a difference of opinion, military considerations affecting the attainment of your object and the security of your forces will be paramount.

15. You will work in the closest co-operation with the G.O.C.-in-C Middle East, to whose headquarters you will depute a liaison officer of suitable standing.

16. You will work in close co-operation with the Senior Naval Officer Persian Gulf and keep in touch with the Resident in the Persian Gulf.

17. You will report to me periodically and you will receive further instructions from me from time to time. Copies of your situation reports to me will be sent by you to:-

    (a)   The War Office.

    (b)   G.H.Q. Middle East.

    (c)   A.O.C. IRAQ.

    (d)   C.-in-C. East Indies, so far as co-operation with the Navy is concerned, through the Senior Naval Officer Persian Gulf.

JRL, AUC 160

52

Cipher message from the Chiefs of Staff to Auchinleck, 2 May 1941[37]

Part one.   In view of situation in Iraq which is not that which was visualised when India took responsibility it seems that operational command should now pass temporarily to Middle East whence alone immediate assistance can be given. This will take place forthwith unless you see strong objections.

Part two.   Reference Air Officer Commanding Iraq telegrams No. SA 433 of May 1st and AW 502 of May 2nd hope Commander-in-Chief Middle East will send all assistance possible to Air Officer Commanding Iraq. Troop carrying aircraft from India now believed at Shaibah or Habbaniya might be used.

Middle East please pass to A.O.C. in Chief.

JRL, AUC 162

---

37 A duplicate of this message was sent to General Sir Archibald Wavell, as C in C Middle East.

53

Cipher message from Auchinleck to Field Marshal Sir John Dill, CIGS, 3 May 1941

In consultation with my Chief of Staff have appreciated India's situation relative to Middle East and my conclusions are:-

First (.) If ALEXANDRIA and the Canal should be closed to us by enemy air action, loss of EGYPT would not be major disaster, though importance of continuing to hold it can not be minimised (.)

Second (.) Even if we lose EGYPT we should be able to hold SUDAN and deny use of RED SEA to enemy (.)

Third (.) To support TURKEY and to stop enemy penetrating ASIA, it is essential to deny to him SYRIA, PALESTINE and IRAQ, and this may soon become our primary strategic object in this theatre (.)

Fourth (.) BASRA and IRAQ are assuming major strategic importance as a base and line of communications area for operations in Middle East (.)

Fifth (.) Development of BASRA and communications leading thence NORTH and NORTH WEST is urgent necessity (.)

Sixth (.) Consolidation, by force if necessary, of our position in IRAQ is urgent need (.)

Seventh (.) At present India alone can produce troops for occupation of IRAQ but these troops can not perform task unless provided with modern weapons and aircraft which INDIA can not give them (.) Provisions of these exceedingly urgent (.)

JRL, AUC 164

54

Letter from Auchinleck to
Lord Linlithgow, 3 May 1941

Yesterday evening Your Excellency mentioned the question of providing money for propaganda purposes in Iraq.

I have been thinking over the whole situation in that country and I have come to the firm conclusion that we must establish ourselves in Baghdad at the earliest possible moment. If the country as a whole is against us, and this is now a possible contingency in view of recent happenings, we are unlikely to be able to get to Baghdad by force except after considerable delay owing to our present weakness in troops and aircraft. There is the possibility of forcing our way to Baghdad by river up the Tigris, using gunboats and river steamers, and I have pointed this out to Quinan. In any event, we can not afford to be delayed and I think we should begin to spend money at once with the object of establishing ourselves in Baghdad as soon as possible. If we do not get to Baghdad soon, the Germans will.

I know the control of operations has passed to the Middle East temporarily, but I do not think this should preclude us from urging on H.M.G. the immediate need for spending money on a large scale.

The people on whom it should be spent in the first instance are, I consider, the Euphrates tribes who can cut the Basra–Baghdad railway at any time. I think that Quinan and his political officers may very well be the best agents for this purpose. The whole of this affair concerns India and her future in this war so closely that I feel we can not leave this important factor to be dealt with by the Ambassador of the Middle East Command which has so many other things to think about and has not so far, in my opinion, shown a real grasp of the Iraq problem as a whole. It is because I hold these views strongly that I venture to write to you.

JRL, AUC 168

55

Letter from Auchinleck to Lord Linlithgow, 3 May 1941

We are using all our serviceable troop carrying aircraft (including one civil B.O.A.C. flying boat) to take more of the King's Own Royal Regiment to Basra. They are under orders to start tomorrow morning, probably about 120 men, with some anti-tank rifles and extra light machine guns. It is not a large number but we can not transport any more and every little helps.

Where this party will eventually arrive I can not say.

We propose to leave the aircraft (about nine of them altogether) in Iraq temporarily to help in ferrying troops about that country.

I have asked A.O.C.-in-C. to go into the matter of trying to get back our Blenheim squadrons from Malaya.

JRL, AUC 169

56

Letter from Auchinleck to Sir Gilbert Laithwaite, Private Secretary to the Viceroy, 4 May 1941

Reference my conversation with His Excellency last night. We are proposing to take the following steps.

(a)   We are sending a telegram at once to Troopers [War Office] telling them in general terms that, if they can provide us with shipping, we may be able to accelerate the despatch of the reinforcements to Basra to a considerable extent. This is the nature of a warning message.

(b)   We are following this up this afternoon by a more detailed telegram giving, so far as we can foresee them at the moment, our actual requirements in shipping for the troops which we think we may be able to send.

2.   We have already arranged for the despatch about the 23rd of this month of another infantry brigade, a field artillery regiment and various odds and ends of the 10th Division, the leading two brigades of which have already been dispatched.

In addition, we now hope to despatch in our own shipping a fourth infantry brigade, which up to date has been destined for Malaya to complete the 9th Division with its 3 infantry brigades. This we hope to get off somewhere towards the beginning of June, if all goes well.

3.   We have already asked the War Office whether we can re-allot to Iraq the 2 I.S.F. battalions which are due to sail for Mideast on the 6th of May. The arrival of these battalions at Basra would release the infantry brigade already there for a more mobile role.

4.   We are taking immediate steps to prepare the following units for despatch overseas as soon as possible. The 3rd Cavalry Brigade H.Q. (Meerut); the 13th Lancers (Armoured Car regiment, from the N.-W. Frontier); the 14/20th Hussars (Meerut, and to be equipped through with Mark VI light tanks); one field artillery regiment belonging to the 1st Armoured Division; one battery of 6″ How[itzer]s and an infantry brigade of the 8th Division.

We are also investigating the possibility of sending one of the motorised infantry battalions which belong to the Support Group of the Armoured Division.

In addition to the above, there would be of course administrative and base units.

It is for the transport of these troops that we propose to ask H.M.G. to allot shipping from other sources for our use.

5.   I enclose a note from Air H.Q. India which contains what I think is a useful propaganda suggestion. His Excellency may care to make use of it.

JRL, AUC 172

57

Cipher message from Auchinleck to War Office, 5 May 1941

Part I.

First (.)   In view of the present critical situation in IRAQ we have examined the question of what is the maximum force with which we can reinforce BASRA in the immediate future (.)

Second (.)   Decisive factor is shipping and if additional personnel and M[ilitary].T[ransport]. ships can be made available in time we may be able to bring force up to five inf Brigades and ancillary troops by 10 June (.) Details follow but we must emphasise that we shall still be deficient of A.A. A/Tk. and AFVs and that we shall have to take risks in India to make troops available (.) We are wiring separately about shipping (.)

Part II.

Third (.)   In addition to SYBIL we can if you agree divert to BASRA

(a)   Following earmarked to replace BASIN in Malaya (.) Inf Bde (.) Field Regt (.) Bde Transport Coy (.) G.P. Transport Coy (.) Field Ambulance (.) M.A. Section (.) Necessary Workshops (.)

(b)   Two of remaining four I.S.F. battalions instead of the two I.S.F battalions referred to your 64035 of 29/4 (not to MIDEAST) which we are sending to Port Sudan (.)

Fourth (.)

(a)   We are sending following also additional to SYBIL (.) Inf Bde less one battalion (.) Frontier armoured regiment (withdrawn from frontier equipped with frontier pattern armoured cars only (Crossley body conventional Chevrolet chassis) no (repeat no) tanks) (.) Field Ambulance (.) Inf Bde Transport Coy (.) C.G. Hospital (.) Necessary workshops (.)

Above will be ready embark 2 June and will be at expense postponement which we can accept certain non-divisional units SYBIL unless extra shipping for which we are asking separately provided (.)

(b)   Following also ready embark 2 June if additional shipping available (.) One 6-inch how[itzer] battery (.) One section 3-inch A.A. guns (.)

Fifth (.)   Following armoured component (additional to SYBIL – SILAS) will be ready embark 25 June (.) Armoured Bde Headquarters and Signal Section (.) 14/20th Hussars (41 (41) Mark VI light tanks and we hope some armoured carriers) (.) Field regiment (.) Field squadron (.) Light Field Ambulance (.) Bde Transport Coy. (.) Necessary workshops (.)

Sixth (.)   Balance SYBIL will follow above as shipping becomes available (.)

Part III.

Seventh (.)   Equipment of armoured units is very poor and seriously denudes India (.) Moreover maintenance of Mark VI Tanks and Mk VII Vickers will be difficult owing shortage components (.) Lt Tanks and Armoured cars have no repeat no A/Tk weapons (.) Both vehicles are being fitted with Boys rifle,[38] but as we have no stocks available can you send 100 (100) Boys rifles and repeat and ammunition quickest possible means (.) In any case request you despatch armoured cars and tanks fitted with A/Tk weapons in replacement our vehicles as early as possible (.)

JRL, AUC 176

58

Cipher message from Auchinleck to Field Marshal Sir John Dill, CIGS, 9 May 1941

One.   Although control of forces in IRAQ now rests with Mideast it is impossible for India to disassociate herself from the formulation of policy in that area. Not only is success or failure in IRAQ vital to the safety of India but most of the forces and material employed in that theatre must come from India. I gather also that it is intention that control of operations will eventually revert to India.

Two.   We are prepared to make great efforts and to take great risks to support a sound policy which in our opinion has some prospect of success and also will continue as in the past to give all help possible to Mideast. The opportunity for controlling the situation in IRAQ by means of force stationed in N. Palestine is however passed and the main advantage of that proposal is now nullified by the fact that we are firmly established at BASRA. In our opinion there is now only one policy which will call a definite halt to German penetration into IRAQ IRAN and possibly TURKEY and SYRIA. As you are aware German influence is already firmly established in IRAN and failing some positive action on our part will no doubt greatly influence the situation both in IRAN and elsewhere.

Three.   This policy is to establish ourselves with the minimum delay in sufficient force at Baghdad and other key points such as MOSUL

---

38   The Boys .55″ anti-tank rifle.

and KIRKUK so as to be able to resist any attack internal or external by the Axis. These forces must have a secure L of C and this must in our opinion load from BASRA. Except as very temporary alternative the BAGHDAD – MAIFA L of C is too difficult and too vulnerable to Axis forces based on SYRIA.

Four.   The present time when (vide AOC IRAQ a 518 date 7/5) IRAQ forces have suffered a serious set back, are short of ammunition and indecisive of purpose is ideal for obtaining our objective with the minimum effort and if we act boldly and employ suitable personnel methods we may do it with the support rather than the opposition of the tribes.

Five.   The forces we can make available were shown in our signal of May 5th and it is only lack of equipment that prevents them from being augmented. Provided no time is lost there is in our opinion a very good prospect that they will be sufficient to ensure success. If they are not we should at any rate be in a better position to re-establish our position than if we restrict ourselves to passive defence attitude at BASRA.

JRL, AUC 191

59

Letter from Auchinleck to Lord Linlithgow, 9 May 1941

At my request the P.S.Os., F.O.C. [?], A.O.C.-in-C. and Financial Adviser considered recently the circumstance which would arise should it appear necessary for the Government to move to Delhi before the end of the summer. They reached the conclusion that no attempt should be made to move to Delhi before the beginning of the cold weather, unless a situation arose in which there was a real risk of communications to Simla being cut.

2.   The reasons which influenced them in coming to this decision were, briefly –

(a)   The first effect of a sudden move down to Delhi would be completely to dislocate the working of the Supply Department, which is now housed in the Secretariat at Delhi.

(b)   An immediate move following upon a sudden emergency would not be possible because the organisation of the various

H.Q. of the Defence Forces would be entirely upset, so that in any event the move would probably have to be postponed for some weeks after the initial emergency.

(c) So far as I know, no really adequate arrangements have been made in Delhi to ensure suitable accommodation for officers and to those who would have to work for long hours in the heat. As a result efficiency would be bound to suffer. It would be essential to grant leave at regular intervals and this would probably entail an increase in establishments.

(d) Except for wireless facilities, communications from Simla are practically as good as they are from Delhi.

(e) Operations could be conducted more efficiently from Simla than from Delhi in the hot season, unless India herself invaded.

The chief advantage of the move to Delhi would be that all the Defence Services could be housed under one roof.

3. I agree generally with the conclusions reached by the P.S.Os. and I don't think that a sudden move from Simla to Delhi is practicable in the circumstances. I must add, however, that I feel most strongly that steps to make Delhi habitable in the hot weather should be pushed forward in accordance with instructions already given by Your Excellency. We may easily be faced next year with a war situation in which a move from Delhi to Simla would be most imprudent.

JRL, AUC 193

60

Letter from Auchinleck to
Lord Linlithgow, 11 May 1941

I heard today from General Quinan that Major-General W.A.K. Fraser, the Commander of the 10th Division, who went with the first contingent of troops to Basra, had asked to be relieved of his command on the grounds that he had no longer the confidence of his subordinate commanders. General Quinan recommended the immediate acceptance of his request and added that the strain of the past few weeks had undoubtedly adversely affected General Fraser's power of command.

I have cabled General Wavell asking his concurrence to the replacement of General Fraser in command of the 10th Division by Brigadier Slim, who is Brigadier, General Staff, to General Quinan. I have every reason to expect that Slim's energy, determination and force of character generally will prove equal to the task. I propose to replace Slim by Colonel Boucher, whom I know very well personally and consider to be admirably suited to the appointment. I know he will be acceptable to Quinan, as rather fearing that this situation might arise, I mentioned the matter to Quinan before he left.

I am sorry about Fraser but, as you know, I have not been easy in my mind since he first reached Basra. He was appointed by my predecessor on, I imagine, his past record, which is very good. I have asked for him to be returned to India at once.

I have troubled you with this letter as I did not wish you to hear of the affair, which will soon get out, at second hand.

JRL, AUC 199

61

Letter from Auchinleck to
Lord Linlithgow, 11 May 1941

As you know I am most uneasy about the situation in Iraq in particular and about the views of G.H.Q., Middle East, on the strategic situation in Western Asia generally. The telegrams we have received today have not allayed my anxiety.

2. As I see it, "Mideast" are looking at the Asiatic strategic situation from a parochial angle and visualise North Africa and the Levant as one fortress, India as another and Malaya–Burma–Hong Kong as a third.

3. I would prefer to look at this situation as being one continuous and united front divided into three sectors, each interlocking with and interdependent on the other. The right sector is Far East Command, the centre sector the India Command and the left sector the Mideast Command.

The annexure explains my meaning in diagrammatic form.[39]

I feel that until all concerned are prepared to accept this view and work to it to a common end, we shall waste much of our effort in voicing our divergent views one against the other.

I had considered cabling General Dill on these lines, but I feel I have done a lot of cabling lately and I wondered whether Your Excellency thinks it worth while trying to press this point of view any further at the moment.

JRL, AUC 200

62

Telegram from Winston Churchill to Auchinleck, 14 May 1941

I am very glad you are going to meet Wavell at Basra. He will tell you about Tiger[40] and Scorcher.[41] A victory in Libya would alter all values in Iraq both in German and Iraqi minds.

2. We are most grateful to you for the energetic efforts you have made about Basra the stronger the forces India can assemble the better. But we have not rep[ea]t not yet felt able to commit ourselves yet to any advance (except with small parties when the going is good) northward towards Baghdad and still less to occupation in force of Kirkuk and or Mosul. This cannot rep[ea]t not be contemplated until we see what happens about Tiger and Scorcher. We are therefore confined at the moment to trying to get a friendly Government installed in Baghdad and building up the largest possible bridgehead at Basra. Even less can we attempt to dominate Syria at the present

---

39 No attempt has been made to reproduce this diagram here.

40 Operation Tiger involved five fast merchant ships, capable of 15 knots: *Clan Chattan, Clan Lamont, Clan Campbell, Empire Song* and *New Zealand Star*, which were loaded with 295 tanks and 53 Hurricane aircraft. They were brought under Royal Navy escort to Alexandria through the Western Mediterranean, which had, effectively, been closed to British convoys since January 1941. The convoy passed through the Straits of Gibraltar during the night of the 5/6 May, and arrived in Alexandria on the 12 May. En route the *Empire Song* was sunk by enemy action, and while her crew were saved, 57 tanks and 10 Hurricanes were lost.

41 The code name for the defence of Crete.

time though the Free French may be allowed to do their best there the defeat of the Germans in Libya is the commanding event and larger and longer views cannot rep[ea]t not be taken till that is achieved and everything will be much easier then. Ends.

JRL, AUC 211

63

Telegram from Auchinleck to Lieutenant General E. P. Quinan, 4 June 1941

<u>One</u> (.)   It is essential to clarify as early as possible your position vis-à-vis Cornwallis the new Iraqi Government and the Iraqi Army (.) Following is a draft telegram which subject to consideration of any comments you wish to make will be sent to H.M.G. (.)

<u>Two</u> (.)   Draft begins (.)

> <u>First</u> (.)   On the taking over of military control in Iraq by INDIA we consider we should simultaneously regularize the position of the Force Commander in the political field vis-à-vis the Ambassador the Iraqi Government and the loyal elements of the Iraqi defences forces (.) We consider that the present lull presents an opportunity to provide and install adequate machinery for future developments in the situation which may later deteriorate either as the result of direct Axis attack or internal disorders (.)

> <u>Second</u> (.)   In our judgement primary consideration is that Iraq is now a war zone, that our forces are in Iraq to aid the Iraqi Government and people against external aggression and internal disorder, and military considerations must be paramount (.) Force Commander must therefore be empowered to override political considerations or objections from any source if military situation necessitates this (.)

> <u>Third</u> (.)   We therefore ask your early approval to the following proposals (.)

> (a)   H.M.G. should deal direct with Governor General (Defence) on all matters of policy (.)

> (b)   Governor General (Defence) should communicate all orders and decisions on policy to Force Commander repeating to

Ambassador if necessary (.) Ambassador should continue to address H.M.G. direct on matters not affecting major policy sending copies to Force Commander and Governor General (Defence) (.)

(c) Ambassador should act as Chief Political Adviser to Force Commander and his intermediary with the Regent and the Iraqi Government on all questions affecting policy except as regards purely military matters affecting the carrying out of his role (.)

(d) The Force Commander should deal with matters affecting the Iraqi defence forces through the Military Mission (.)

(e) Contact between local military commanders and local civil officials should be by liaison officers on staff of local commanders (.) A Chief Liaison Officer on staff of Force Commander will control local liaison officers (.)

Fourth (.)   These arrangements should not (repeat not) be communicated to Iraq Government between whom H.M.G. Ambassador should maintain façade of normal diplomatic relations (.) Draft ends (.)

Three (.)   Submit your comments immediately (.)

JRL, AUC 255

64

Letter from Lieutenant General E. P. Quinan to Auchinleck, 13 June 1941

Dear Chief

This is to acknowledge receipt of your D/O Q-1/? Of 29 May 41 for which I thank you.

I am very clear as to what you expect from us: the various problems are being solved as time and our resources permit.

2.   The chief problem is the development of the TIGRIS L of C. By pushing and pulling I have managed to get Weld's HQ[42] and

---

42   Brigadier C. J. Weld, who commanded the 21st Indian Brigade Group.

a battalion with a lot of supplies started off to KUT en route to BAGHDAD. The fact is now clear that there is very little craft on the TIGRIS that is suitable for our purposes. Those that took Weld's party were functioning here in the last war. We shall not be able to get hold of mahailas in time: for the present their owners will not co–operate, nor will they run up the river on their own business. I am sure that half their show of reluctance is designed to squeeze higher rates out of our transportation people. The latter have been reinforced so I expect great improvements in performance.

3. The problem next in importance is the stocking of HABBANIYA and BAGHDAD.

    This implies the retention here of SLIM's third Bde (MOUNTAIN's) which however can put in some very necessary collective training in the SHAIBA – ZUBAIR area.

4. The arrival of a Labour Bn here will help matters here considerably.

    The 17 Bde (GRACEY) is in the BASRA area and is already settling down to work and training.

5. The Mutassarif[43] has taken over the administration and this has reduced the number of Det[achment?]s very considerably. He is 100% more efficient than MADFAI.[44]

6. We are still awaiting sanction to begin expending money on the QASI [?] project.

    I have seen the site and the day before yesterday examined charts at FAO and saw some of the gear there that WARD has stored for it. It is essential that we should have a sea survey of the KHOR from the ROOKA float. I sent the C[hief].E[ngineer]. and my Survey man today to see if we can help until the R.N. produce the men for whom BERESFORD[45] has cabled you. The weather at present permits of some survey work being done, next month it becomes worse and worse. The survey has to be hydrographic and a survey ship is needed for 3 months.

---

43 Nuri Pasha al–Said.
44 Jamal Madfai, a pro–British former Prime Minister of Iraq and leading supporter of the Regent.
45 Presumably Major General George de la Poer Beresford.

7. SLIM has gone up to BAGHDAD to ensure that POWELL[46] pushes on at once to MOSUL and KIRKUK. I joined him on the 16th for the best part of a week in order to become au fait with the local difficulties. I know the Ambassador and by means of letters and liaison visits on my behalf SLIM, BOUCHER[47] and others am well acquainted with his policy, and personal views.

8. As for MIDEAST and HABFORCE, their only thought as regards IRAQ has been to get shot of the country and have HABFORCE back in PALESTINE.

    It was to help them in this direction that I have remained here to push things along and to overrule the Jeremiahs that abound in the railway and other administrations.

9. The health of the troops is much better, but with the advent of melon and other fruit I expect the figures for dysentery to rise.

JRL, AUC 259

65

Letter from Auchinleck to
Lord Linlithgow, 17 June 1941

Secret.

Thank you very much for your letter of the 16th June enclosing a letter from the Secretary of State, dated the 28th May, concerning air borne troops.

We are, as you know, already considering this matter in India, though so far on a very small scale only. A couple of days ago I actually issued instructions for the preliminary arrangements to be made for the formation of an air borne brigade at Delhi.

This particular project was referred by us some time ago to the Chiefs of Staff at home for a statement of policy by them. A considerable time has elapsed since this reference was made but we have had no answer as yet.

The aircraft, parachutes, and the other special equipment required for this brigade are not, of course, in sight, but I think that we should get

---

46 Brigadier Donald Powell, commanding 20th Indian Brigade Group.
47 Major C. H. Boucher.

on with its formation and start its training, of which a very considerable amount can be done on the ground, even though it may be months before we can begin to equip it for its special task.

I shall be very glad to discuss the Secretary of State's letter with you at your convenience.

JRL, AUC 260

66

Extract of letter from Lord Linlithgow to L. S. Amery, 17 June 1941

2.   On the matter of finance I indicated some of my hesitations to you in my letters of 3/4th June, paragraph 10, and 6th June, paragraph 5, and I do not propose to develop the matter further now. I would only add to what I have said in my earlier letter on this matter of India and her financial contribution, direct or indirect, to the war, that, as I know you realise, we cannot escape from the consequences of our constitutional position. The first thing I think is to get the answer (so far as air-borne warfare is concerned) to the problems of manufacture in this country of gliders and of parachutes, and when I know where we stand about that it will be easier to see the problem in its true perspective. Auchinleck has already been active on the <u>general</u> issue of air-borne warfare, and a few days ago issued instructions for the preliminary arrangements to be made for the formation of an air-borne Brigade at Delhi. He tells me that this particular project was referred home by us some time ago to the Chiefs of Staff for a statement of policy by them, but that though a considerable time has elapsed since that reference was made, there has been no answer yet. Clearly the issue is one of the first importance and urgency; and I should be grateful for your help over it, and for a telegraphic indication of how things stand. Meanwhile, though the aircraft, parachutes, and other special equipment required for the Brigade I have just mentioned are not yet in sight, Auchinleck feels, and I entirely agree, that we should get on with its formation and start on its training, of which a very considerable amount can be done on the ground and before planes or gliders become available. I propose to discuss further with Auchinleck the general issue and will let you know the result. But

as you will see, we are held up both over gliders and over air-borne troops by delays at home, and I am sure I can rely on your personal interest and assistance to overcome these.

JRL, AUC 261

67

Letter from Lord Linlithgow to the Governors of Madras, Bengal, the Punjab, Bihar, the Central Provinces and Berar, Assam, the North-West Frontier Province, Orissa and Sind, 18 June 1941

It is matter, as I know you appreciate, of very great importance, from the point of view of countering enemy propaganda and anti-war sentiment, in this country, to stimulate and maintain the interests of the public in the war, and particularly in India's war effort.

This can be, and is being done by means of speeches and the encouragement of subscriptions to war funds and war loans, but the extent to which these can maintain interest in India's war effort for any length of time is limited.

I was much impressed by the reports of the recently completed War Week in Bombay City and by the extraordinary enthusiasm aroused by the displays given on that occasion by the Royal Indian Navy and by the sight of a few armoured vehicles. I am sure that displays of this kind are the quickest way to appeal to the imagination of the masses, and the best possible corrective to any defeatist tendency in public opinion generally.

The Commander-in-Chief, who is fully alive to the importance of this matter, and also to the difficulties of lending troops at all frequently for such displays (as training is likely to suffer), proposes to start travelling "circuses" which would visit various big cities and cantonments, with a nucleus of tanks and other modern vehicles and equipment, round which the local Commander can build an expanded exhibit from his local resources. He also proposes to collect teams of lecturers who would go to schools, universities, public gatherings, &c., and talk on the war situation and matters affecting the Defence Services on a good deal larger scale than is being done at present.

I should be very grateful for any suggestions you may have to make on these proposals, as well as for other means of simulating and maintaining public interest in the war.

JRL, AUC 262

68

Letter from L. S. Amery, Secretary of State for India, to Auchinleck, 14 August 1941

You may be interested to hear that just after you left I managed to get the Defence Committee to allow me to authorise India to go ahead with your 1942 expansion programme without waiting for the War Office to make up their minds whether they could find the necessary European complement or not. You will remember you asked for sanction to this expansion at the beginning of May. Three months later the War Office were no nearer making up their minds, and would be no nearer three months hence, if I had not insisted that they should be brushed aside.

2.   What frightens me is that a minute's reflexion should have made it clear from the outset that such an offer could not be refused, seeing that it gave the War Office five divisions in the field next year at the cost of one division's worth of British personnel. Somehow or other the men obviously must and will be found, even if it meant breaking up a British division. Even if they were only found in part and the Indian force proportionately reduced, the surplus of Indian personnel would be worth something, as drafts if for no other purpose. Besides it is absurd to think that the total man power figure here cannot be stretched when it comes to the pinch, whether by raising the age or by internal economies.

3.   What appals me is this awful obsession with fixed figures laid down and with fixed programmes and formations which cannot be sanctioned unless and until every item is definitely provided for in advance. War is a business above all of time and of improvisation in which regular schemes and formations are quite secondary. The first thing is to begin at once to make all the weapons you can. The second is to begin at once to raise and train all the men you can. The third is to match the two in such units and formations

as circumstances allow and, if necessary, make your tactics and even your strategy conform to the kind of units you can provide. The weapons and formations that are most suitable for the dense network of European communications are not necessarily the best for deserts or mountains, and, if we can't make our production fit our strategy we can adapt our strategy to our production.

4. Similarly I am always rather alarmed by the unquestioning acceptance of the principle that whatever weapon or formation the enemy adopt we should follow. Nobody argues that the best way of dealing with a rhinocerous is to fix a horn on your own nose. But everybody assumes that if the Germans have done well with tanks our answer is more and heavier tanks of our own. Is it possible that the same effort might not be better put into more and heavier anti-tank guns, mounted on high speed lightly armoured vehicles, or heavily armed low flying aeroplanes? I don't know, but I have an uncomfortable feeling that the question has never been faced.

5. The Boers put up a wonderful fight just because they had a tactical system fitted to their way of life and their country. They had only two weapons, the rifle and the pony. If they tried to build up an army on British lines, they couldn't have raised and equipped two brigades and the war would have lasted a month at most. The Germans have built up a wonderful tactical system based on their industries and on the dense communications and comparatively level ground of Europe. Is there no tactical system of our own which we can build up to beat theirs, at any rate in Africa, Asia and Eastern Europe and perhaps even in Western Europe as well? We once had such a system in the use of the long bow, and for a century 5,000 English could walk all over Europe. The Macedonian phalanx – the ancient Panzer division – was irresistible against all similar shock tactics. It broke down against the loose open order and short range throwing spear of the Roman legion.

6. But I fear I have strayed all over the place with these reflexions of mine, which have probably very little bearing on your problem, which is to make what use you can of the troops and weapons that we send you. I can only hope that they will enable you to put together a besom with which to sweep Africa clean from Sollum to Casablanca. One of Mahomed's generals – I've forgotten his name at the moment – did just that, and only stopped when he had

ridden his horse breasthigh into the Atlantic. There is, of course, the alternative of following the old Ottoman trail through Belgrade to Budapest and Vienna. Not being Defence Minister, I have no instructions to give you, but leave the choice to you!

JRL, AUC 293

4

Commander in Chief, Middle East, 1941–42

A consideration of Auchinleck's time as C in C Middle East must consider four aspects of his command, which are, of course, inter-related. The first concerns Auchinleck's relationship with Winston Churchill; this is difficult as Churchill communicated to Auchinleck as Churchill often failing to make it clear if he was acting solely as Prime Minister, as Prime Minster with the authority of the Cabinet and/or Chiefs of Staff behind him, as Minister of Defence or as trusted confidant. The second aspect of Auchinleck's command concerns his relationship with the CIGS, Field Marshal Sir John Dill and General Sir Alan Brooke. This, of course, is difficult to divide from Auchinleck's relationship with Churchill as, often, Auchinleck looked to Dill or Brooke to defend his position. Indeed, Auchinleck's problems in dealing with Churchill may, partly have stemmed from the fact that Auchinleck expected the CIGS to back him and defend his position as theatre and army commander, while the CIGS sometimes took on this role and sometimes tried to act as honest brokers between Churchill and Auchinleck. Auchinleck's relationship with Dill was closer than that with Brooke, but this, of course, was problematic in itself as Dill was not always well placed on how best to advise Auchinleck on how to deal with Churchill's demands, given his own difficult relationship with the Prime Minister. The third aspect of Auchinleck's command which comes through in these papers is concerned with the military appointments Auchinleck made, especially with regard to the command of Eighth Army. Auchinleck picked his own commanders, but sacking Lieutenant General Sir Alan Cunningham was no easy task and Lieutenant General Neil Ritchie was probably not the right man for the job in that Auchinleck did not have complete confidence in him and

Ritchie's subordinates did not easily accept his authority. More broadly, the papers show Auchinleck's wider decisions about staff and command appointments to have been, at times, less than inspired, particularly with respect to Major General Eric 'Chink' Dorman-Smith. Finally, the papers are revealing about the problems Auchinleck confronted as, effectively, a coalition commander, commanding British Dominion and Indian Army troops, Free French and Free Poles as well as British troops.

Underlying all of these discussions were considerations of how effective British armour and equipment was compared to their German equivalents, leading to lengthy discussions about the quality and quantity of tanks sent to British forces in the Middle East, many, of course, manufactured in the USA. Allied to this were discussions concerning the organisation of British forces in the Middle East, especially concerning how armour could be integrated with infantry and the possibilities and difficulties associated with the development of the so-called 'Jock' columns.

Churchill's initial communication with Auchinleck, when he took up the position as C in C Middle East, in July 1941, suggested that he would have considerable latitude in deciding how to balance his forces amongst the competing demands placed on them and over when to renew the offensive in the Western Desert [71]. Auchinleck clearly believed that his first duty was to secure his base and to defeat Vichy French forces in Syria [72]. A matter of days after suggesting that Auchinleck would be left to decide on priorities, Churchill then urged a rapid resumption of the offensive in the Western Desert, supposedly to assist the Royal Navy and RAF operating in the Western Mediterranean [73]. Churchill was then confronted with a closely argued response from Auchinleck, who had consulted with his counterparts in the Royal Navy and RAF and gave his considered opinion that resources, especially in terms of tanks and trained personnel, were insufficient to launch a new offensive in the Western Desert and, indeed, that the Northern front of Middle Eastern Command could become active in the very near future [74]. Churchill retorted, in late July, with the authority of the Chiefs of Staff behind him, again urging a renewed offensive in the Western Desert and noting that Auchinleck would receive a considerable armoured reinforcement in September [76]. Intervention by Field Marshal Sir John Dill, CIGS, as discussed below, along with the briefings Auchinleck gave to the War Cabinet and Churchill personally on 31 July and 2 August seem to have decided Churchill to leave the decision over a renewed offensive to Auchinleck. By August Churchill was promising major reinforcements to assist a renewed offensive, which was envisaged for November 1941

[83]. In October Churchill seemed in a much more supportive mood and was reminding Auchinleck that success in the Western Desert would provide Britain with valuable military credit in dealing with the USA and USSR [87].

A further short delay to what was by then the Crusader offensive, was explained in some detail by Auchinleck to Churchill, where problems in the training of South African troops and in the mechanical reliability of certain tanks were explained [89]. This seems to have been appreciated by Churchill, who regarded Auchinleck's explanation as useful and he shared in Auchinleck's optimism for the success of the offensive [91]. Churchill was then treated to regular, and rather optimistic reports about the Crusader offensive in November and December 1941 [98, 99, 114]. Churchill himself, reviewing the deteriorating situation in the Far East, had to order some forces, notably 18th Division and squadrons of Hurricane aircraft, to be diverted to the Far East, but he clearly felt that Auchinleck would be able to maintain momentum in the Crusader offensive without these [125, 133]. On 24 January 1942 the Prime Minister was treated to a summary of the Crusader offensive, which noted considerable successes [138].

Churchill was then deeply shocked, as was Auchinleck himself, by the counter-offensive launched by Axis forces in the Western Desert. Having recently congratulated Auchinleck on the recapture of Benghazi, Churchill was very concerned at its loss in late January 1942 [139]. At the same time Churchill was expressing particular concern that British armour had been defeated by 'inferior enemy numbers'.[1] The deteriorating situation meant that Churchill asked Auchinleck to journey to London for consultation with him in mid-March, which Auchinleck refused to do [170, 171]. At the same time Churchill wrote of the 'special sources' he had which informed him of exact German tank strength, which was at variance with the figures Auchinleck had quoted. This was Churchill acknowledging that he had access to ULTRA sources which Auchinleck either did not have access to at all, or received only many hours after Churchill had seen them [173]. Auchinleck queried the German tank strength quoted by Churchill in a later communication [183]. By mid-May Auchinleck was telling Churchill what he really didn't want to hear, which was that Allied and Axis forces were so evenly matched that a future Allied offensive in the Western Desert was, 'NOT likely

---

1   JRL, AUC 662, Cipher message from Churchill to Auchinleck, 28 January 1942. Not reproduced in edited papers.

to be rapid or spectacular' [194]. Churchill responded by calling for a renewed offensive in the Western Desert and urged Auchinleck to take personal command of the Eighth Army [196]. In urging new offensive action, Churchill promised major reinforcements to Auchinleck, though noting that some formations in the Middle East would also have to be transferred to the Far East [208]. Auchinleck kept Churchill informed of his plans for new defensive positions, crucially over plans to hold Tobruk in the face of Rommel's latest offensive in June 1942 [213, 214]. Churchill cautioned about fighting the war as a defensive war in the model of the First World War noting that 'Armoured Warfare seems to favour the offensive' [215]. On a visit to Washington, Churchill again referred to his 'special Intelligence' (i.e. ULTRA) which showed that Axis forces had suffered serious losses and urged Auchinleck to stage a stubborn defensive. Churchill was concerned about the plans to defend the Nile Delta and also that there was a real danger that British Imperial forces would be pushed back to the position they had held eighteen months previously [219]. In response, Auchinleck reassured Churchill that the position had been stabilised and a new offensive was planned as soon as armoured formations were regrouped. He sadly reflected that the situation was no better than it had been a year ago, when he took command in the Middle East, and possibly worse as the Axis forces had now captured Tobruk [222]. As the situation worsened in June and July 1942, Churchill raised concerns about the speed with which Auchinleck was receiving ULTRA intelligence [226].

One of Churchill's favourite topics was to discuss tank strengths in the Middle East and Auchinleck's concerns about the poor quality of Valentine Tanks, which arrived in the Middle East in June 1942, must have been unsettling [232]. As late as 27 July 1942 communications from Churchill suggested confidence in Auchinleck's ability to manage both the Eighth Army and Middle East Command [236]. However, Churchill's letter, effectively relieving Auchinleck of command, was sent from Cairo on 8 August 1942 following the visit of Churchill and Brooke to the Middle East and their series of meetings with senior commanders. This, of course, was not a brutal sacking, offering Auchinleck command of the newly planned Iraq and Persia theatre and noting both that Auchinleck himself had suggested a change of command in late June [221] and that the decision to remove him was a collective one by the War Cabinet [237].

Churchill showed considerable naïveté over the complexities of desert warfare. As the Desert War reached a critical phase in June 1942, Churchill was urging that, 'every fit male should be made to fight and die for victory', suggesting that the situation was essentially similar to that if German troops invaded the UK. This showed incomprehension of the complicated logistics of desert warfare and the large numbers of troops needed to maintain supply lines [223]. In November 1941 Churchill had shown little consideration of the need to train and acclimatise troops for desert warfare, stating, 'You have no doubt had my message about the rest of the 1st. Armd. Div. landing SUEZ today. Ram it in if useful at earliest without regard for future. Close grip upon the enemy by all Units will choke the life out of him.'[2]

Auchinleck can be seen, very much, as a protégé of Dill. It was therefore very unfortunate that Dill's letter to Auchinleck, giving him some advice on how to deal with political pressure from London and outlining the problems which Wavell had experienced as GOC in C Middle East was sent with no priority and did not reach Auchinleck until he had already come under pressure from Churchill to renew the offensive [70]. Further useful advice on how to handle Churchill's requests was provided by General Hastings Ismay, who was Chief of Staff to the Minister of Defence [82]. Auchinleck appears to have followed Pug Ismay's advice for a time as in October 1941 Churchill was reflecting on three letters he had recently received from him [87].

In total Dill sent Auchinleck thirty-one direct communications while Auchinleck was GOC in C Middle East and Dill was CIGS, but many of these were brief and Auchinleck received little sense from these either of Dill's own deteriorating relationship with Churchill, or that Auchinleck's own communications with Churchill were not always well received. Dill also gave a rather misleading impression on the extent to which the newly appointed Minister of State, resident in the Middle East, would be able to relieve Auchinleck of political pressure from London [75]. Auchinleck, in his communications with Dill, made it clear that he believed that a theatre commander should have considerable latitude over the decision to renew an offensive and should also have his own choice of subordinates [77, 79, 85]. A more lengthy communication to Dill, written at a time when Auchinleck was ill with a cold, perhaps demonstrates Auchinleck's desire to keep Dill more fully informed of his decisions [88].

Alan Brooke was not as close a confidant of Auchinleck as Dill; however, Auchinleck seems to have quickly built up a very good working relationship with him and Auchinleck's outline of the problems facing

---

2   JRL, AUC 462, Cipher message from Churchill to Auchinleck, 25 November 1941. Not reproduced in edited papers.

him and the decisions he had made, expressed to Brooke in late December 1941 [131] bears comparison to the earlier communications with Dill [88]. Brooke had initial concerns about the way in which Auchinleck was communicating directly with Churchill and some of his earliest correspondence with Auchinleck was to restore the proper channels of communication through the CIGS [119, 120]. Managing Churchill's expectations of what Auchinleck could achieve in the Middle East was then a major problem for Alan Brooke, and Auchinleck voiced concerns that his position was not being made clear to the Prime Minister by Brooke and other senior officers in London [164, 188]. For his part, Alan Brooke noted that work by the Chiefs of Staff had meant that some of Churchill's more intemperate telegrams to Auchinleck had been modified [165, 178, 179]. Auchinleck was also concerned at the paucity of senior officer training for command and staff positions in the Middle East. He advocated the establishment of a Higher War Course and this was approved by Alan Brooke [167, 186, 211].

In writing to Alan Brooke about the fall of Tobruk, Auchinleck was clear that he felt able to carry on and retrieve the situation, but, interestingly, he suggested Harold Alexander as his possible successor [221]. It is telling that when Auchinleck was removed as GOC in C Middle East the news came directly from Churchill, though the earlier exchange with the CIGS was noted, rather than from Alan Brooke [237].

One of the major charges levelled against Auchinleck is that he was poor at selecting subordinates. The Auchinleck papers demonstrate that Auchinleck was both aware of the criticisms and shortcomings of some of his senior subordinates and dogged in his defence of those who he had selected for senior command or staff posts. Major General Eric Dorman-Smith was possibly the most controversial of Auchinleck's senior appointments. In seeking, unsuccessfully, Dorman-Smith's appointment to direct a Higher War Course for senior officers in the Middle East in May 1942, Auchinleck revealed some of the problems facing him; finding senior officers with sufficient staff and command experience at that stage in the war was difficult and the senior officer who he would have preferred for the appointment, rather than Dorman-Smith, was commanding a division [186]. In June 1942, when taking direct personal command of Eighth Army, Auchinleck blithely informed Alan Brooke that he was taking Dorman-Smith with him as Chief of Staff [224]. Not only did this action seem to ignore the reservations which Alan Brooke had previously shared about Dorman-Smith, but it created an unorthodox new senior staff role without reference to the CIGS.

Alan Brooke's concerns were not alleviated by other news in this communication [224] which informed him that Lieutenant General Thomas Corbett, CGS, Middle East, another officer who Brooke did not rate, would effectively be left with wider executive powers in Cairo in Auchinleck's absence. It is unclear why Alan Brooke had taken against Corbett, it may have simply been that Alan Brooke's preferred candidate for the position was Lieutenant General Sir Henry Pownall [119, 125]. When Corbett communicated directly with Churchill, in Auchinleck's absence from Cairo, his telegram demonstrated sound staff work and a good grasp of the realities of the situation [227]. Corbett was clearly a trusted confidant of Auchinleck [169, 191, 197, 200] and in communications with Alan Brooke, Auchinleck praised Corbett's abilities [168, 188]. If, in the crisis of June 1942, the Eighth Army had been forced to abandon the El Alamein position, Corbett was designated by Auchinleck to take command of the Eighth Army, while shortly before his removal, Auchinleck was planning to put Corbett in charge of Tenth Army [225, 235].

Auchinleck inherited Brigadier Eric James 'John' Shearer as his DMI. Shearer's appointment was a rather odd one in that he had left the regular army in 1929 to pursue a career in business and only returned to the army on the outbreak of war. He was initially put in charge of a Military Intelligence training establishment in England and later sent to the Middle East when Wavell was appointed C in C. When Auchinleck took command in the Middle East he kept Shearer on as DMI, possibly on Dill's or Wavell's recommendation. Certainly, in the early months of Auchinleck's command Shearer seemed to be a perfectly capable officer, impressing Churchill and Ismay [82, 83]. However, Brooke was far from impressed by Shearer, complaining of his highly optimistic intelligence reports and how these severely under-estimated Axis capabilities [137, 152]. Characteristically, Auchinleck supported Shearer and noted that as C in C he was ultimately responsible for reports on German intentions [157].

When selecting Lieutenant General Sir Alan Cunningham to command Western Desert Force (renamed Eighth Army on 26 September 1941), Auchinleck resisted pressure from Churchill who wanted Henry Maitland Wilson in this role. Auchinleck was selecting Cunningham based on his successful war record, not on personal knowledge, and he clearly thought that Cunningham's Corps and Divisional commanders would provide the experience of using armoured formations which Cunningham himself lacked [79, 89]. Auchinleck's papers show something of the role of Brigadier Alexander Galloway, BGS, Eighth Army in having Cunningham removed from this command [92, 93]. Sacking Cunningham was clearly a difficult task for Auchinleck, made rather more difficult by an attempt to suggest that Cunningham was medically unfit to continue in command [94, 95, 98, 100, 105]. Auchinleck removed Cunningham as he felt that he was lacking in offensive spirit [97, 98]. Initially it seemed that Cunningham would quietly accept Auchinleck's decision but soon he raised the issue of an appeal to the Army Council [100, 103, 112, 122]. There were also questions as to how to explain Cunningham's supersession to the public [106, 116].

In November 1941, when Auchinleck removed Cunningham as commander of Eighth Army, he decided to replace him with Major General Neil Ritchie, who was DCGS in Cairo. Churchill thought that Auchinleck should assume direct command of Eighth Army after removing Cunningham, 'C.I.G.S. and I both wonder whether as you saved battle once you should not go up again and win it now. Your presence on spot will be an inspiration to all. However this is of course entirely for you to judge.'[3] Auchinleck responded in detail to this suggestion [102]. Dill agreed with Churchill writing, 'What I had in mind was that moment will come in fact may already have come when your drive and personality will be essential to reap full fruits of victory. Troops will be dog tired vehicles badly needing overhaul and petrol and water short. Every one will say they cannot press on and with your drive will find they can go another hundred miles at least.'[4] In March 1942 Churchill again wanted Auchinleck to take command of Eighth Army. Auchinleck asked Alan Brooke to use his influence against the idea.[5]

Auchinleck's relationship with Ritchie was a complex one and the lengthy correspondence between them is illuminating on this. Auchinleck probably saw his role as a 'mentor', conscious of Ritchie's lack of seniority and, indeed, of command experience. Indeed, in some communications Auchinleck stated that he did not want to interfere in what was, properly, the business of the GOC Eighth Army [154, 191]. Auchinleck was also fully supportive of Ritchie when he had trouble with one of his Corps Commanders [140, 148]. For his part, Ritchie provided detailed

3   JRL, AUC 477, Cipher message from Churchill to Auchinleck, 27 November 1941. Not reproduced in edited papers.
4   JRL, AUC 483, Cipher message from Field Marshal Sir John Dill to Auchinleck, 28 November 1941. Not reproduced in edited papers.
5   JRL, AUC 747, Cipher message from Auchinleck to General Sir Alan Brooke, 8 March 1942. Not reproduced in edited papers.

appreciations of the situation which, at least up to May 1942 seemed to be well-considered [see, for example, 104, 124, 149, 182]. In May 1942 Ritchie was confused about whether he should be preparing to attack German positions or await a German offensive [187, 189], though it must be noted that he had concerns about the ability of Eighth Army to hold Tobruk [192]. However, it must be acknowledged that Auchinleck was also uncertain about a German offensive and did not read German intentions accurately [202]. It is worth noting that Ritchie claimed that he modelled his command style and relationship with Corps commanders on the relationship set up between General Sir Henry Maitland Wilson and Lieutenant General Richard O'Connor in the early stages of the Desert War [195].

With regard to the Axis offensive, which commenced on 26 May 1942 it is clear that, had he been in direct command of Eighth Army, Auchinleck would have reacted differently, launching a counter-attack [203, 204, 205]. One can then note Auchinleck's confidence in Ritchie ebbing. Ritchie's appreciation of 11 June, with annotation by Auchinleck, shows the disagreements between them [210]. This was not resolved by a personal visit by Auchinleck to Eighth Army HQ on 12 June. Auchinleck then noted that he had issued, 'very definite orders' to Ritchie on 16 June [214] before removing him from command on 25 June [224]. Unlike Cunningham, Ritchie went quietly, apparently glad to escape, 'the greatest hell' which he had experienced in commanding Eighth Army [231]. Unlike Cunningham, Ritchie retained the confidence of Alan Brooke and it is interesting to note that, shortly after being removed from his command, Brooke was holding lengthy discussions with Ritchie about future equipment and, presumably, what exactly had gone wrong in the Western Desert [233].

Those minded to criticise Auchinleck's ability to judge subordinates and commanders properly might note how the career of Brigadier Frederick de Guingand, later to become a highly effective Chief of Staff under Bernard Law Montgomery, prospered under Auchinleck's patronage, with promotion to DMI, Middle East and then BGS Eighth Army [168, 235]. Auchinleck was also a dogged defender of Air Chief Marshal Arthur Tedder, AOC in C, Middle East, when Churchill wanted to relieve him of his command [96, 123].

Commanding a multi-national force created various problems for Auchinleck. Some of these were alleviated by the appointment of a British Minister of State resident in Cairo, who was a member of the War Cabinet. This role was originally held by Oliver Lyttleton from June 1941 to February 1942 and then by Richard Casey, though Walter Monckton held the post as, effectively, Acting Minister, for two months in 1942 as Casey was not immediately able to take up the appointment [75, 98, 109, 180, 188, 214]. It is notable though that, as late as June 1942 the role of the Minister of State was still being clarified [207]. The post of Intendant General, Middle East, meant to relieve the C in C of responsibility for administrative affairs was a less happy experiment [75, 77].

Of the Dominion Forces, Auchinleck was most impressed by the New Zealand Division. He found the division to be well-trained and with its own integrated forced of heavy tanks [88]. Auchinleck also found Major General Bernard Freyberg to be a very effective divisional commander, despite some early reservations by the New Zealand Government [80, 88]. Auchinleck found the New Zealand Government themselves very accommodating, commenting, in February 1942 that they had been, 'so wonderfully good all through' [157].

Auchinleck's relationship with the Australian Government was more strained. It is, indeed, noticeable how little his supposed Deputy C in C Middle East, General Sir Thomas Blamey, appointed to this post in April 1941 when the Australian Government insisted on a share of senior command positions for their officers, features in these papers [134, 152]. The insistence by the Australian Government that their forces should be removed from Tobruk in July 1941 caused serious problems and Auchinleck was also concerned at the role of Blamey in this [77]. The decision of the Australian Government to remove most of their troops from the Middle East to face the Japanese threat to Australia caused Auchinleck further anguish [137]. Of course, this removal of Australian troops was a particular problem given how highly he rated their abilities [84].

Field Marshal Smuts, Prime Minister of South Africa was in regular contact with Auchinleck. South African troops presented a particular challenge to the British military establishment as they could not serve outside Africa [77], and given the South African Government's desire to recruit only white soldiers it was clear that maintaining two South African Divisions with a 20 per cent reinforcement was impossible [159]. What the South African Government sought were assurances that the South African Divisions would be quickly mechanised, allowing armour to be substituted for manpower [86, 88]. The training of South African troops was seen as deficient, which led to a postponement of the Crusader offensive [89, 109]. One of the bleakest communications Auchinleck had to send was that informing Smuts that Tobruk had fallen to the enemy, with the loss of the 2nd South African Division [220].

Auchinleck's appointment to be C in C Middle East was only ever meant to be temporary, with the role of C in C India kept open for him [69]. With that in mind, Auchinleck, quite properly, remained very interested in Indian Army matters while in the Middle East. He noted the importance of the Indian Army in the Middle East noting that 216,270 Indian soldiers were serving in this theatre by May 1942 [163, 185]. He remained concerned about officer supply for the Indian Army and thought that battle experienced British, Australian and New Zealand soldiers should be considered for commissions [128 and 156]. Not surprisingly, Auchinleck rated highly the abilities of Indian soldiers, especially in 4th Indian Division [89, 113, 150] and was concerned at the demands of the Far Eastern Theatre removing experienced Indian soldiers from his command [137, 209]. The strategic responsibilities and demarcation between the C in Cs Middle East and India continued to exercise Auchinleck [86, 88, 119].

Commanding the Free French Brigade proved to be demanding of Auchinleck's time. It was regarded as under-strength and, as late as January 1942, was still seen as an unknown quantity. However, General de Gaulle was concerned that it should not be relegated to rear areas as a 'guard and duty' force [88, 116, 131, 135, 176]. Of course, once the Free French Brigade went into action it was seen to do well [177, 212]. Dealing with the diplomatic aspects of Free French forces proved more problematic and Auchinleck found it particularly difficult to deal with Major General Edward Spears who had a liaison role with the Free French; it seems that the Minister of State removed some of these pressures from Auchinleck [77, 180].

Many of the problems which Auchinleck encountered in the Middle East came from the lack of a proper armoured doctrine within the British army. Major General Vyvyan Pope's untimely death robbed Auchinleck of an armoured expert and commander who he seems to have valued [78]. Auchinleck regarded other RAC senior officers as purely interested in developing their own arm as a corps d'elite rather than considering how armour should operate in an all arms approach to modern warfare [131, 134, 147, 152]. Auchinleck was concerned about the standards of training and leadership in the RAC [174]. He was also critical of the quality of British tanks, suggesting that he needed a 50 per cent superiority over German armour for a reasonable chance of success [146, 175]. Auchinleck's solution to the problem of integrating armour with infantry and artillery saw the formation of 'Jock' Columns and then more formal Brigade Groups. Initially these seemed to perform well [113, 115, 117] but by February 1942 this was being questioned by Ritchie, who had his own ideas on the use of armour [153, 184, 210].

With regard to the other services, Auchinleck had limited contact with the Royal Navy; not surprising given that he had sacked Alan Cunningham, the brother of Admiral Sir Andrew Cunningham, the C in C Mediterranean. Co-operation with the RAF was well developed though. Auchinleck clearly built up a very good working relationship with Air Vice Marshal Arthur 'Mary' Coningham, who commanded the Desert Air Force, and felt that the support which he provided to the army was of a very high standard [131, 147, 216]. Auchinleck also worked closely with Air Chief Marshal Arthur Tedder, AOC in C, Middle East and was, it appears, instrumental in retaining his services in the Middle East when Churchill thought he should be removed from command [74, 96, 123].

Finally, given the comments made by some historians regarding the collapse of morale in Eighth Army, it is worth considering the Orders of the Day issued by Auchinleck in December 1941 and July 1942 [121, 234]. These seemed to be well-written and inspirational but are clearly harking back to the methods of the First World War rather than the methods introduced by Field Marshals Bernard Montgomery and William Slim.

69

Telegram from L. S. Amery, Secretary of State for India to Lord Linlithgow, Viceroy of India, 25 June 1941

Losing Auchinleck is a great blow but you were clearly right in appreciating without demur or qualification in view of supreme issues at stake. I have however strongly urged Prime Minister to make the change over an avowedly temporary one (a) in Auchinleck's own interest to enable him to complete his appointment; (b) in India's interest for the organisation of defence at the end of the war; (c) because German advance through TRANSCAUSASIA into Iran may before many months are out make Iraq, Iran and Afghanistan the main theatre. Meanwhile please convey following message from me to Auchinleck. (Begins.) Warmest congratulations on great opportunity. I know you will fully justify Prime Minister's confidence. Deeply as I regret your loss for India at this creative moment I look forward to you coming back with even greater authority and experience to complete work you have so well begun. (Ends.)

JRL, AUC 271

70

Letter from Sir John Dill to Auchinleck, 26 June 1941[6]

On your taking over command in the Middle East, may I add to my congratulations, which I have sent to you by telegram, a few words on the situation and perhaps of advice.

After Wavell had captured Benghazi, there was a possibility that he might have pressed on to Tripoli. He could only have done this with very small forces (as the so-called 7th Armoured Division was worn out) in the hope that the Italians were so demoralised that they could

---

6 This letter was sent to Auchinleck marked 'c/o Commander-in-Chief, Middle East'; however, misdirected, misplaced in the postal system or delayed by enemy action, it was not received by Auchinleck until 21 July 1941. See document 77 below.

offer no effective resistance. But any hope there was of such a venture was ruled out by the decision of H.M.G. to support the Greeks. It then became a case of sending the maximum strength to Greece and leaving the minimum to hold Cyrenaica.

The result you know. We did not leave enough to secure Cyrenaica and the forces we sent to Greece and subsequently to Crete suffered heavily and lost much precious material – material which, as you will realise from your experience in England, is desperately difficult to replace. To right the situation, we did our best to send equipment at express rate and some 295 tanks were sent through the Mediterranean at great risk, and with great luck and good management on the part of the Navy, 238 arrived, only one ship containing 57 was sunk. Then came a difficult period. It was most desirable to clear the Germans back in Libya at the earliest possible moment, so that the Navy might be able to get the air protection necessary to enable it to attack the enemy's communications with Tripoli and also maintain Malta.

It was also highly desirable to act rapidly in Syria to forestall the Germans.

From Whitehall, great pressure was applied to Wavell to induce him to act rapidly, and, under this pressure, he advanced into Syria with much less strength than was desirable and in the Western Desert, he attacked before in fact he was fully prepared. The fault was not Wavell's, except in so far as he did not resist the pressure from Whitehall with sufficient vigour.

You may say that I should have minimised this pressure or, better still, that I should have seen that, having been given his task in broad outline, he was left to carry it out in his own way and in his own time. I might possibly have done more to help Wavell than I did, but I doubt it. The fact is that the Commander in the field will always be subject to great and often undue pressure from his Government. Wellington suffered from it: Haig suffered from it: Wavell suffered from it. Nothing will stop it. In fact, pressure from those who alone see the picture as a whole and carry the main responsibility may be necessary. It was, I think, right to press Wavell against his will to send a force to Baghdad, but in other directions he was, I feel, over-pressed.

It is about this question of pressure which I particularly want to speak. You may be quite sure that I will back your military opinion in your local problems, but here the pressure often comes from very broad political considerations; these are sometimes so powerful as to make it necessary to take risks which, from the purely military point of view, may seem inadvisable. The main point is that you should make it quite clear what risks are involved if a course of action is forced upon you which, from the military point of view, is undesirable. You may even find it necessary, in the extreme case, to disassociate yourself from the consequences.

Further, it is necessary that such a Commander should not wait for pressure and suggestions or even orders. He should anticipate these things and put clearly before his Government in the most secret manner how he views the situation and the action he proposes to meet it. He should point clearly to the risks he is prepared to accept and those which he considers too great. He should demand the resources he considers strictly necessary to carry out any project and he should make it clear what he can and cannot do in their absence.

You, in your responsible Command, will never have in the near future all the resources which you would like to have to carry out your great task. You, having served here, know something of the situation and the immediate paucity of our resources. You know too what the essentials are in our great picture – to hold England, retain a position in the Middle East, maintain a firm hold in Malaya and keep open our sea communications, which last-named involves such things as continuing to be able to use West Africa. The time will come when we can strike out with effect and there is hardly a soul in the world outside Germany who will not rejoice at our success and join in our final victory. But in the meantime we have a grim fight to fight and we cannot afford hazardous adventures. So do not be afraid to state boldly the facts as you see them.

The second and last point upon which I would like to touch concerns 'air co-operation'. Nowhere is it good. Nowhere have we had sufficient training. You will find the 'Air' out to help, but they have no complete understanding of what is required of them from the purely Army point of view and how necessary training is. Also, to ensure that our military and air strategy works in complete harmony is uncommonly difficult. It is quite clear that Tedder[7] has to serve the Navy as well as the Army, but his main mission in life is to support the Army to the nth degree in any operation it has to undertake and to support it in the manner most acceptable to the Army Commander concerned. When you have had time to look round, you may be able to let me know how you view the problem and whether I can do anything to help.

7   Air Chief Marshal Arthur Tedder, AOC in C, Middle East.

I would add that telegrams marked 'Private from General Auchinleck to C.I.G.S.' are in fact private, whereas 'Personal' telegrams have a certain limited distribution. I may have told you this before.

God bless you.

JRL, AUC 274

71

Cipher message from Winston Churchill to Auchinleck, 1 July 1941

You take up your great command at a period of crisis. After all the facts have been laid before you it will be for you to decide whether to renew the offensive in the WESTERN DESERT and if so when. You should have regard especially to the situation at TOBRUK area and the process of enemy reinforcement in LIBYA and temporary German preoccupation in their invasion of RUSSIA. You would also consider vexatious dangers of operation in SYRIA flagging and need for a decision on one or both these fronts. You will decide whether and how these operations can be fitted in together. The urgency of these issues will naturally impress itself upon you. We shall be glad to hear from you at your earliest convenience.

JRL, AUC 275

72

Cipher message from Auchinleck to Winston Churchill, 4 July 1941

Thank you again for your telegram 0.61 (0.61) (.) Fully realize critical nature situation (.) Subject to further investigation and consideration my views are as follows (.)

1 (.) No further offensive Western Desert should be contemplated until base is secure (.)

2 (.) Security of base implies completion occupation and consolidation SYRIA (.)

3 (.) Consolidation SYRIA includes making CYPRUS secure against attack (.)

4 (.) Immediate action required is therefore elimination Vichy French from SYRIA earliest possible moment and completion defence measures in CYPRUS (.)

5 (.) Offensive in SYRIA being prosecuted already with all vigour but hampered by shortage mechanical transport (.) IRAQ force is giving all possible aid (.)

6 (.) Reconnaissance shows at least one division required ensure reasonable possibility successful defence CYPRUS and plans are being made accordingly (.)

7 (.) Once SYRIA is secure (,) and this implies consolidation of our position in IRAQ (,) offensive in Western Desert can be considered but for this adequate and properly trained armoured forces say at least two and preferably three armoured divisions with a motor division will be required to ensure success (,) this is first essential (.)

8 (.) Final object should be complete elimination enemy from Northern AFRICA but administrative considerations would entail advance by stages so that first objective would probably be re-occupation CYRENAICA which itself would have to be effected by stages for same reason (.)

9 (.) It is quite clear to me that infantry divisions however well trained and equipped are no good for offensive operations in this terrain against enemy armoured forces (.) Infantry divisions are and will be needed to hold defenced localities and to capture enemy defended localities after repeat after enemy armoured forces gave been neutralized or destroyed but the main offensive must be carried out by armoured formations supported by motorized formations (.)

10 (.) Second essential to successful offensive is adequate and suitably trained air component at disposal Army for all its needs including fighters medium bombers tactical reconnaissance and close support on the battlefield (.) This is non-existent at present (.)

11 (.) In my opinion there can be no question of carrying out simultaneously offensive operations in Western Desert and SYRIA (.) To do so is to invite failure on both fronts (.)

12 (.) Third essential to success in any offensive operation in this theatre is close and constant co-operation of Fleet both in close support of Army and in harrying enemy sea communications (.) This co-operation is taken for granted but itself entails constant close support by air forces which must be at the disposal of the Navy and additional to those required for close support of Army and for long-range strategic air operations.

JRL, AUC 280

73

Cipher message from Winston Churchill to Auchinleck, 6 July 1941

MOST IMMEDIATE CLEAR THE LINE

1. Your telegram No, 1527 of 4th July. I agree about finishing off SYRIA and here [we?] always thought holding SYRIA is necessary foundation for holding or re-taking CYPRUS. One hopes that SYRIA may not be long now and that you will not be forestalled in CYPRUS. This priority of both these operations over offensive action to complete WESTERN DESERT after what has happened is fully recognised.

2. Nevertheless WESTERN DESERT remains decisive theatre this autumn for defence of NILE VALLEY. Only by reconquering the lost airfields of Eastern CYRENAICA can Fleet and Air Force resume effective action against the enemy's seaborne supplies.

3. In General Wavell's No. SD/57777 of 18th April he stated he had six regiments of trained armoured personnel awaiting tanks. This was a main element in decision to send 'TIGER'.[8] Besides this,

---

8   The 'Tiger' convoy was made up of five fast merchant ships which, under RN escort, were to risk the hazardous route through the Western Mediterranean to bring urgently requested reinforcements of tanks and aircraft to Egypt. Since January all reinforcements to Egypt had been sent via the Cape of Good Hope as the Luftwaffe had taken a heavy toll of Allied shipping. 295 tanks and 53 Hurricane aircraft were sent; one ship, the *Empire Song* was lost due to enemy action, with the loss of 57 tanks and 10 Hurricanes; her crew were all saved by a RN destroyer. The convoy arrived in Alexandria Harbour on 12 May 1941.

personnel for three additional tank regiments are now approaching round the CAPE. Your need for armoured vehicles is therefore fully realised in spite of stress which WAVELL and you both lay upon further training for these fully-trained armoured units. We make out that you should have by the end of July 500 cruiser, infantry and American cruiser tanks workshops are properly organised, beside a large number of ill-conceived light tanks and armoured cars.

4. This cannot be improved upon in months of July and August except by certain American arrivals and a few replacements from Home. Even thereafter remember we have to be at concert pitch to resist invasion from September 1st and General Staff are naturally reluctant to send another substantial instalment of tanks around the CAPE (now the only way) thus putting them out of action till early October at either end. After October American supplies should grow and our position here be easier but much will have happened before then.

5. At present Intelligence shows considerable Italian (reinforcements) of LIBYA but little [?] German. However, a Russian collapse might soon alter this to your detriment without diminishing invasion menace here.

6. Scale of our air reinforcements had been laid before you. Air Staff are becoming anxious about our heavy struggle and are disinclined to repeat RAILWAY.[9] Even so it seems probable during July, August and part of September you should have decided air superiority but then again a Russian collapse would liberate considerable German air reinforcements for AFRICA and if enemy do not attempt invasion but merely pretend, they can obtain air superiority on your Western Front during September.

7. On top of this comes the question of TOBRUK. We cannot judge from here what offensive value TOBRUK will be in two months' time or what may happen meanwhile. It would seem reduction or complete panning of TOBRUK by enemy is indispensable preliminary to serious invasion of EGYPT.

---

9   It is unclear what operation this referred to and, indeed, this is queried in the original.

8. From all these points of view it is difficult to see how your situation goes to be better after middle of September than it is now and it may well be worsened. I have no doubt you will maturely but swiftly consider whole problem.

9. In light of your decision and as a part of it please tell us if you desire any alteration of composition convoys W.S.10 and W.S.11 bearing in mind reinforcements in man power from AUSTRALIA and facts which are already on their way. When I queried as I have during the last six months the immense proportion of rearwards services and non-combatant troops included in our convoys I recognised the fact that we have to supply these services for Australian and New Zealand man-power fighting units. Nevertheless when I am told that you have 33 Field Artillery Regiments and three on way apart from A.A. Regiments surely wonder in what battle circumstances this mass of artillery can be deployed. There is hardly time to alter composition of W.S.10 which leaves at the end of this month but I should like to know that it is what you want.

10. Convoy W.S.11 is still however in hand. Over 75,000 men are earmarked for this convoy although at present there I only shipping for under 30,000. It would be possible by making costly sacrifices here like bringing home ships from SOUTH AFRICA without cargoes though circuitous and dangerous routes which alone are open some other measures to make efforts to carry a much larger reinforcement in W.S.11 than is now planned. On present showing Defence Committee does not think these sacrifices justifiable. But if you have plans which require special implementing you should ask us wants and we will do our best.

11. About air. I feel for all major operational purposes your plans must govern employment of whole Air Forces throughout MIDDLE EAST bearing in mind of course that Air Force has its own dominant strategical role to play and must not be frittered away in providing small umbrellas for Army as it seems to have been in SOLLUM battle. In your telegram No. 1527 you speak of aircraft supporting the Army and aircraft supporting the Navy and aircraft employed on independent strategical tasks. The question is what are the proportions? This will have to be arranged from time to time by C. in C. in consultation. But nothing in these arrangements should mar the integrity of Air Force contribution to any major scheme you have in hand. One cannot help feeling in SOLLUM fight our

air superiority was wasted and that our forces in TOBRUK stood idle whilst all available enemy tanks were sent to defeat our desert offensive.

12. I shall be obliged if you will consider foregoing points, consulting so far as necessary with Mr. LYTTELTON and General HAINING and thereafter let me know how we can best help you.

JRL, AUC 281

74

Cipher message from Auchinleck to Winston Churchill, 15 July 1941

A (.) I have carefully considered your telegram 0.64 (0.64) of 6 (6) July and have consulted with Minister of State[10] and the Intendant General[11] (.)

B (.) Your para. one (.) After consultation with C.-in-C. Med[iterranean] and A.O.C.-in-C. I have decided to adhere my predecessor's plan to re-inforce CYPRUS as soon as possible by one division (.)

C (.) Your para. two (.) I fully appreciate need for reconquering CYRENAICA but see para. II below (.)

D (.) Your para. three (.) Personnel of six regts referred to in our telegram SD 57777 (57777) of 18 April were fully trained with their own type of tanks but lacked individual and collective training for the different types of tank many of them had to man (.) Characteristics and armament of American tanks introduce certain modifications in tactical handling and a certain time must be allowed for these lessons to be studied and absorbed (.)

E (.) While I agree I shall have here end of July about 500 (500) Cruisers (,) Infantry and American tanks (,) past experience has

---

10 Oliver Lyttleton, Minister of State and Member of the War Cabinet, resident in Cairo.
11 The post of Intendant General, Middle East was a short lived one, established in June 1941 it was abolished in January 1942 with General Sir Robert Haining as the only incumbent.

clearly demonstrated that for any given operation we need 50 (50) per cent reserve of tanks (.) This permits 25 (25) per cent in workshops and 25 (25) per cent available for immediate replacement of battle casualties (.) Allowing for 50 (50) tanks in TOBRUK and requisite reserves I shall not have more than 350 (350) available for active operations (.)

F (.) Owing to casualties to tanks and number in workshops units have had little opportunity for training (.) Would stress importance of time being allowed for both individual and collective training (.) BATTLEAXE showed that present standards of training is not repeat not enough (,) and we must secure that team spirit which is essential for efficiency (.)

G (.) Your para. six (.) This is understood and agreed to by TEDDER and self provided enemy offensive does not develop from North against SYRIA and/or Iraq (.)

H (.) Your para. seven (.) Consider there is every indication that enemy would like to be free of commitment of containing TOBRUK and while I do not intend to alter our present policy of holding TOBRUK (,) I cannot be confident that TOBRUK can be maintained after September (.) Everything possible is being done but enemy air action against ships at sea and in harbour is taking its toll (.) Furthermore should enemy secure SIDI BARRANI (which he could do at any time) it will not be possible to provide the present scale of fighter protection for supply ships to and from TOBRUK (.)

J (.) Your para. eight (.) I agree that with possible threat from the North our situation may well be worsened (.) North repeat North may become the decisive front (.)

K (.) Your para. nine (.) I wish no change in composition W.S.10 (.) Regarding artillery I have twenty-seven field and five R.H.A. regts here including those of 50 (50) Division (.) Further five field regts belonging to South African Divisions are due to arrive from EAST and SOUTH AFRICA as operations and shipping permit (.) This total of artillery represents about the correct allotment for the number of divisions in my Command (,) but allows nothing for Corps or Army artillery (.) It will be divided according to circumstances between the two fronts (,) Northern and Western (,) the bulk being concentrated on the decisive front for the time being which may be West or repeat or North (.) Our shortage of armoured formations and absence of adequate close support artillery makes it essential that we should man as many of the artillery pieces as are available in the country for use in an emergency anti-tank role (.) With the guns here and those reported en route we should be able to equip all regts with 25-pdrs on a 24 gun basis by about end of September (,) but owing to shortage of personnel for manning (,) five British regts could not be increased above a 16 gun basis (.) It is essential that we should obtain the necessary personnel for transfer to the artillery to enable us to provide for manning the additional 8 (8) guns in each of these regts (.) With forecasts of reinforcements en route I see no alternatives but to obtain this additional personnel by the disbandment of certain British units in this country and the matter is now being investigated here (.) The position is further complicated by the fact that I am short of a number of anti-tank regts which should be allotted to Middle East forces (.) The eight which I will be equipped only with 36 (36) 2-pdrs the remaining guns being completed by using 18-pdrs and captured weapons (.)

L (.) Your para. ten (.) I have just received some details regarding composition W.S. 11 (.) I will have its composition considered and forward priorities (.) In meantime it would greatly help if I could be given some idea as to what units and drafts are likely to be available (.) Would stress urgent need for draft of at least 750 (750) R.A. F[iel]d personnel to be included in W.S. 11 (.) I would draw your attention to cable to TROOPERS A1/72585 (72585) of 12 June giving full particulars of manpower situation mid June on assumption that W.S.10 contained drafts of 26,600 (26,600) (.) Casualties SYRIA and BATTLEAXE have made the position worse (.)

M (.) Your para. eleven (.) Have discussed with TEDDER (.) We both agreed that principles enunciated by you for use of Royal Air Force are correct (,) but C.-in-C. MED[ITERANNEAN] suggests that employment of R.A.F. cannot be subordinated exclusively to implementing Army plans since there may well be an urgent operational requirement for co-operation with Navy (.) This aspect applies with particular force while the Fleet is without a carrier (.)

N (.) Your para. twelve (.) Have consulted Mr. LYTTELTON (,) General HAINING and CUNNINGHAM[12] as well as TEDDER (.) All agree (.)

O (.) Above answers seriatim questions of detail raised in your cable (.) Cs.-in-C. are preparing strategical appreciation dealing with major issues involved (.)

P (.) Minister of State is also cabling you on this subject.

JRL, AUC 282

75

Letter from Sir John Dill to Auchinleck, 16 July 1941

I hope that you are settling down to your general problems all right. And I hope very much that the Minister of State is going to be a help to you. I was always anxious to have a representative of the War Cabinet in Egypt since I saw the situation out there myself. Archie Wavell too was anxious to have one there & said so on paper, but the P.M. would have none of it till quite recently. I am not so happy about the Intendant General. I feel that he should be under you with direct authority to deal direct with the War Office on certain subjects – much as the M.G.As in Commands do at home. Also I hope that Haining will play the game. He has plenty of ability & experience but is inclined to think too much about himself.

Russia has done much better than I expected & I hope that she will go on doing so. But now that the Germans have reached the open country I would fear that the superiority in material, training & command would tell.

I watch the situation very closely because if I were sure that the Germans were [bogged?] in Russia & England were safe from invasion this year I could give you much more help. But, as you know, we are none too thick on the ground in men & material in this island. Don't over-load yourself & let me know in what direction you want help & I will do all I can.

Good luck & God bless you.

JRL, AUC 283

---

12 Admiral Sir Andrew Cunningham, C in C Mediterranean.

76

Cipher message from Winston Churchill to Auchinleck, 20 July 1941

<u>MOST SECRET</u>

1. Prolonged consideration has been given by both Chiefs of Staff and Defence Committee of War Cabinet to your telegram number 1533 of 15th July in reply to my 064 of 6th July. Chiefs of Staff now send you their number 148 of today with which we are in full agreement.

2. It would seem if you had a substantial further consignment of tanks from here and U.S.A. approaching during middle of September together with other large reinforcements, this might act as a reserve on which you could count either to press your offensive if successful or to defend EGYPT if it failed.

3. Defence Committee were concerned to see 50th Division, your one complete BRITISH Division, locked up in CYPRUS in what appeared to be a purely defensive role, and wonder whether other troops might not have been found.

4. It did not see how a GERMAN offensive could develop upon SYRIA, PALESTINE and IRAQ from North before end of September at earliest. Defence Committee felt PERSIA was in far greater danger of GERMAN infiltration and intrigue and that strong action may have to be taken there. This however is in General WAVELL's sphere, and he wishes evidently to act [?] telegram 9392/G of 17th July is receiving urgent and earnest attention here.

5. If we do NOT use the lull accorded us by GERMAN entanglement in RUSSIA to restore situation in CYRENAICA, opportunity may never recur. A month has passed since failure at SOLLUM, and presumably another month may have to pass before a renewed effort is possible. This interval should certainly give plenty of time for training. It would seem justifiable to fight a hard and decisive battle in WESTERN DESERT before situation changes to our detriment, and to run those major risks without which victory has rarely been gained.

6. It is difficult to understand on information we have at present the reason underlying the plan of offensive of June 15th. Our forces were defeated in detail by (1 group) @ [see note at end of document] on 3rd morning (1 group) the enemy's tanks from TOBRUK, whose garrison meanwhile stood idle. It would have seemed more consistent (have) accepted principle strategy and common sense to have engaged the TOBRUK garrison in heavy and continuous action before or during climax attack upon SOLLUM.[13] There may of course be reason which we are NOT aware which rendered these well worn principles of war inapplicable. Neither can we judge from here on our present information whether it was right to break off battle on 3rd day. There are always excellent reasons in favour [of] retirements. Victory (rewards) those whose will-power overcomes those reasons.

7. Thirdly, it seems Air Force was used as a more series small UMBRELLAS spread over our march (?columns), and that its large superiority was frittered away in passive defence by standing patrols, instead of being used in offensive strategic combination with Army for general purposes of battle. No doubt this arose from earnest desire of Air Force to protect Army. This however does NOT alter facts of what happened.

8. Before battle I expressed to your predecessor my doubt whether General WILSON,[14] with his vast experience WESTERN DESERT, would NOT have been a better choice than General BERESFORD-PIERSE[15] whose standing in Army was so much less. We still think WILSON should have the Command next offensive if there is to be one unless of course you propose to take personal command yourself.

9. I should be very much obliged if you will let us know waht your general intentions are for immediate future; and you may be assured that our only desire is to sustain you and furnish you with means success.

@ (Group omitted in vicinity of this stage of message. This message delayed – one group was missing from cryptogram)

JRL, AUC 288

---

13 This garbled sentence is reproduced exactly as in the original document.

14 General Henry Maitland Wilson, then GOC of British troops in Palestine and Trans-Jordan. He had commanded British troops in Egypt 1939–41.

15 Lieutenant General Noel Beresford-Peirse, who had been appointed Commander, Western Desert Force.

77

Letter from Auchinleck to
Sir John Dill, 21 July 1941

I apologise for not having written to you before this, But I have really hardly had time to turn round, and I am afraid I am still very much a "new boy" here. I think I have grasped the broad outline of the situation, but there are many essential matters about which I have still to gain a more complete knowledge. It is a most complex problem and is not made any easier by the disorganisation and improvisation resulting from GREECE, CRETE, TOBRUK and the recent SOLLUM fighting.

However, things will straighten themselves out gradually, but there is a lot of mixing of formations and even units which, though unavoidable in the circumstances, does not make for increased efficiency.

2. I have two letters from you:

(i)   Dated 26th June which arrived some days ago and was written in answer to my D/5 of 3rd May and mainly concerns INDIA. Thank you very much for it and the information it contains. I am passing it on to Wavell.

(ii) Also dated 26th June which has just arrived. This deals with recent events here and how they came about, and goes on to explain my position vis-à-vis Whitehall and the pressure which I may expect to be put on me from there. I am most grateful to you for this letter, which puts the whole matter very clearly, and also for your promise of support, of which I have never been in doubt. I quite understand the position and am prepared for it. I had, if you remember, a minor experience in these matters at Narvik!

The pressure has already begun as you know. The Prime Minister's telegram No. 069 of 20th July is an instance.

You may be quite sure that I shall give my opinion firmly and without reservation and that if I think a risk is unjustifiable I shall say so. I am a little disturbed by the implications of paragraphs 3 and 8 of the telegram I have just mentioned, as I feel that these are matters in which I alone can be the deciding authority, and I intend to be that authority. I fully realise the burden that rests on the Prime Minister and the supreme need for not increasing it, by seeming to run counter in any way to his wishes, and I shall not forget this. All the same there are matters such as these I have indicated, which can not be settled by any one except myself, I think you will agree with me in this.

3.   I have not much time as the liaison officer who takes this to you leaves early tomorrow, but I will try very briefly to give you my ideas on the main issues current at the moment.

4.   <u>TOBRUK</u>

    (i)   I feel that we must do all we can to hold TOBRUK. At present we are managing to make supply keep abreast of expenditure and we have reserves in the place – about 50 days. Maintenance is however, a difficult problem and may become more difficult, if, for instance, the enemy deny the use of SIDI BARRANI to our air force.

           All the same, I am not going to abandon the place except in the last resort. It is most valuable as a thorn in the enemy's side and if he could get it and use it as a base, it would be most damaging to our position.

    (ii)   Blamey (pressed by his Government, I imagine) is pressing me to relieve the 9 Australian Division and the 26 Australian Infantry Brigade, which form the major part of the garrison. The morale of the garrison is high and they have been doing some excellent offensive patrolling, but their health and stamina is said to be beginning to suffer.

           In any event, it would be a good thing to get them out for a change but it is going to be a difficult and perhaps an impossible business. The Joint Planning Staffs are working on it now. If I <u>can</u> carry out the relief I shall put the 6 Division (British) into the place. Blamey is also insistent on the need for concentrating all the Australian troops under one command and wants them put into Syria and Palestine. This would suit me all right and I propose to work to this end, but it will take time. Blamey's idea is that he should then take command, under Wilson of course, of this Corps himself (see note enclosed).

5. CYPRUS

Having decided to hold CYPRUS I am determined to make a job of it. Putting in scratch units and formations with improvised staffs is no good, and hence my decision to put in the 50th Division. I took this decision after the most careful consideration and in face of some opposition from my staff and I am not prepared to go back on it. Some relevant considerations are:

(a) Decision had to be taken <u>before</u> I knew whether Syrian operations were going to end soon or not. Hence 6th Division (British) was not available for an immediate move, and speed was, and is, essential in my opinion.

(b) I am sure that we cannot afford to use any more Dominion formations in these "detached post" and "forlorn hope" operations. British troops must take their share.

(c) In any event, the South Africans cannot be used outside Africa, the 4th Indian Division is in BAGUSH, the 5th Indian Division is not yet concentrating or re-equipped, the New Zealanders are reorganising and re-equipping as are the 6th Australian Division.

So you see I had not much choice if my decision to use a homogeneous formation was the right one, as I am sure it is. If the Defence Council really want to know the reasons there they are!

Of course I realise that the force in CYPRUS suffers from all the disadvantages of a detachment and that it has little offensive value, though it has some as providing air and sea bases. In any event, I am sure that it is a necessary outpost of the defence of SYRIA and must be held. If it is to be held it must be held properly. We have had our lessons.

6. SYRIA:

(i) This is going ahead and you will have had our joint appreciation on the subject. It is most important that we should, by some means or other, be enabled to go forward on to the line KHARPUT–MALATIA–TAURUS, which would make it possible to oppose an advance by superior enemy armoured forces with a reasonable hope of success. Once the enemy can deploy armoured divisions in the open, relatively flat country South of the Turkish Frontier, our positions round ALEPPO, in the LEBANON or round MOSUL will always be liable to be turned unless we can oppose him with armoured forces more or less equal to his.

It would be a tremendous thing, therefore, if we could reach agreement with TURKEY to allow us to prepare and hold these positions before the enemy moves against ANATOLIA. I know the difficulties, but I would urge that every effort should be made to reach such agreement.

As regards the command in SYRIA, I have already told you that I do not wish to move Wilson who is, I think, admirably suited for it (see enclosed notes).

My ideas for the defence of SYRIA and PALESTINE are roughly not lines but a series of localities capable of all round defence blocking the defiles and approaches. I am elaborating this now. The localities may hold anything from a Brigade Group to a Division but this requires further examination.

(ii)   We are going to have trouble, I fear, and plenty of it from De Gaulle over the Free French position in SYRIA. It has already started as you will have heard. It is absolutely essential that they should not be allowed to do anything to prejudice the security of our position in SYRIA so far as its defence against the enemy is concerned. If they refuse to see reason and persist in their present illogical and unrealistic attitude, I am afraid they will have to be dealt with firmly and drastically. After all, we are paying the piper and must call the tune. I realize the delicate political issues involved, but to win the war is our primary object I imagine.

7.   <u>The Intendant General:</u>

This is going well in spite of the anomalous nature of the situation created by his appointment. Bob Haining and I know and understand each other well and there will be no trouble, but I am sure you will realize that the system is not too easy to run, as it cuts across all established ideas as to organization and responsibility. Many officers will to a large degree be serving two masters, and Hutchinson's[16] position is not too easy. However, as I have said, it will be worked all right. This leads me to another matter.

---

16   Lieutenant General Balfour Hutchinson, Deputy QMG, Middle East.

8.   The High Command:

I feel myself that the administrative control in this command is too highly centralized and too concentrated altogether. I have not had time to get down to detail yet, but I am pretty sure in my own mind that what is wanted is an operational staff here at G.H.Q., with directors or advisers dealing with the broad administrative policy required to give effect to my operational decisions, and that all or nearly all administrative detail can be decentralized to the Army Commanders, leaving the really big administrative problems of bases, base depots, railways, major repairs, etc., to be dealt with by the Intendant General, who becomes a sort of super-Inspector General of Communications. After all a G.O.C.-in-C. should be capable of dealing with nearly all administrative matters, including discipline, awards, promotions, etc. within his own command – we did it at Home. I have given my ideas to Bob Haining and we are both working on them, but I am anxious not to make them public until they are more definite. There are vested interests involved! One thing I am very anxious to do and that is to get G.H.Q. out of CAIRO if I can. There are far too many distractions here, social and otherwise, and the climate is enervating. This too I do not want to say too much about at the moment.

9.   Central and East AFRICA:

I can see no advantage and many disadvantages in retaining Central and East AFRICA in this command now that they have ceased, or practically ceased, to be theatres of active operations. I would like to be rid as soon as possible of all of that area, including ERITREA, ABYSSINIA and all three SOMALILANDS. We must, I am sure, keep the SUDAN for military as well as political reasons. I hope that nothing will arise to prevent this shedding of unwanted territories! I am anxious to concentrate all of our energies to the North.

10.   The Western Desert:

You will have had our applications and reviews, so I need not go into the factors and considerations again here.

What I would like to repeat is that it is not sound to take unreasonable risk (I am quite ready to take a reasonable risk) as I think you know, but to attack with patently inadequate means is to take an unreasonable risk in the present circumstances, and is almost certain to result in a much greater delay eventually than if we wait until the odds are reasonable. I am afraid I shall be quite firm on this point and all the more so because I feel you will agree with me. As to what constitutes a reasonable risk, I think that I alone can be the judge. You may be assured that no-one is more anxious than I to get going.

In our recent papers sent to you we have tried to balance the needs of our two fronts and I am sure that this is essential. Neither front can be viewed in isolation, and it perturbs me a little to see that in the recent telegrams received from Home, this balance between the two fronts is not always maintained. As I see it, there is now one continuous front in ASIA and North AFRICA stretching from AFGHANISTAN through IRAN, IRAQ, SYRIA and PALESTINE to CYRENICA, and action on it must be co-ordinated throughout. You know all this of course far better than I do, and it is presumptious of me to talk to you like this, but I am not sure that others are equally alive to it. INDIA and the Viceroy certainly understand it.

11. Communications:

Assuming that this War is going to last a good deal longer and that eventually we may find ourselves taking an offensive into Southern and South-Eastern EUROPE from bases in the MIDDLE EAST, I am impressed by the need of a really far-seeing policy for the development of communications in this part of the world. Much, as you know, is already being done, and in outlining further suggestions, I am speaking without data and in comparative ignorance. Taking the long view, I look on the following as important –

(a) The putting through of the standard gauge from HAIFA to RAYAK thus obviating the need for breaking gauge;
(b) The connecting of BAGHDAD or KARBALA with HAIFA by rail;
(c) The connecting of MARDIN and DIARBEKR by rail;
(d) The joining up of WADI HALFA and ASWAN by rail.

These are all big projects and if they are to be done, need the greatest impulse and co-ordination from the centre, that is from Whitehall. They entail the provision of a tremendous amount of labour and material, which can only be provided by centralized co-ordination. As you know, these are all under consideration, but I feel only tentatively because the subordinate authorities who are considering them don't really feel that the highest command is in earnest or that it will see things through urgently and consistently. I may be wrong, but that's how I feel. As you are probably aware, there is a school which says "Don't build these railways – they will help the enemy IF he comes on". I think this is rank heresy to say the least of it. We must make up our minds that it is we who are going to use them not the enemy!

12. By the way, the Prime Minister suggested in his 0.69 that I might possibly take command in the Western Desert myself. This is a possibility, but would not be sound if there were any chance of our being attacked in SYRIA and IRAQ at the same time. In this event, I feel I must remain detached and able to take an unbiassed view of the whole situation, but please see my note enclosed.

I do not think I can usefully add anything to this letter, which will I hope give you some idea of what I have in my head at the moment. If it is not the sort of letter you want, will you please tell me so and say what you would like.

I hope you are very well.

JRL, AUC 289

78

Letter from Auchinleck to Sir John Dill, CIGS, 5 August 1941

As you know, the question of the desirability of having a major-general at G.H.Q., Middle East has been considered for some time. In view of the large increase in A.F.V.'s in Middle East and the probability that in the near future there may be two or more armoured divisions fully equipped in the Western Desert, I am convinced that it is desirable to have a senior officer of the R.A.C. at my Headquarters to supervise and co-ordinate training and be prepared, if required, to command an armoured corps in the field. If you agree to this in principle, I should like Major-General Pope[17] appointed both on account of his seniority and

---

17 Major General Vyvyan Pope was then Director of AFV at the War Office and was sent to the Middle East at Auchinleck's request. He was to briefly command the newly formed 30 Corps before being killed in an air accident on 5 October 1941.

experience and because he is an officer who came from the Royal Tank Regiment. I would like him to come out as soon as possible to Egypt, where he can study his requirements as to staff and signal communications. I think that his responsibilities and staff should be on the lines outlined in a letter addressed to G(S.D.) by the Commander, Home Forces (HF/6086/R.A.C.).

With regard to the command of 7th Armd. Division., I feel that General Creagh has had a long time in the desert and in some ways will need a change. His experience as the Commander of the only armoured division that has seen considerable active service should be of great value in England, and I would like to recommend that General McCreery[18] and General Creagh change places. I particularly suggest General McCreery because he has knowledge of conditions in the Western Desert.

With regard to the H.Q. 1st Armoured Division, I understand that the remainder of 1st Armd. Division will probably leave England in October, arriving in Egypt in December. I would be very grateful if the Commander, Staff and Signal of 1 Armd. Div. could be sent out to arrive in Egypt not later than the first week in October. I have no means of improvising a commander and staff for a second Armd. Division out of my resources in Middle East and feel that a second divisional H.Q. might be required before the arrival of the remainder of the 1st Armd. Division.

I would be most grateful if you could see your way to agreeing to these requests.

I would like to make it quite clear that I am not trying to oust Creagh against whom I have nothing whatever. Should you agree to exchange him, I think it must be made very clear that he is being sent home because you wish to make use of his unrivalled experience to train your new tank formations.

Thank you very much for all your kindness.

JRL, AUC 292

---

18   Major General Richard McCreery, Major General AFV, Middle East.

79

Letter from Auchinleck to
Sir John Dill, CIGS, 16 August 1941

I hope you had a pleasant trip with no alarms or excursions and that you were able to get a rest. I want to thank you most sincerely for all your kindness and help, and for your hospitality to Phillpotts[19] and myself. It made a lot of difference being so well looked after and so comfortable. I would not have missed those ten days for anything in spite of the rushing about and talking! We had a very good journey back and no mishaps, though we were delayed for a night at Plymouth.

2. I am sending you today a wire about command in the Western Desert and I hope you will approve of my proposals. I realise very well that I am taking a risk in removing commanders who have fought in the desert, and that my suggested replacements, except McCreery, are new to that part of the world. In spite of this drawback I think the changes should be carried out. I feel in my bones that the windows and doors need opening very wide so that fresh air and new ideas can enter, and I believe that this would more than offset any initial and temporary lack of local knowledge in the new men.

3. Beresford-Peirse should I think be moved, partly because I do not think he is really suited to that kind of fighting and partly because I feel that his prestige has suffered as a result of the last battle. All the same he has many good points and would I think be a useful commander in the Sudan, which is not yet by any means a backwater; he is quite young still and has a reputation from Sidi Barrani and Keren. I hope, therefore, that you will be able to agree to his going to Khartoum. On the whole I'd rather have him there than Nosworthy[20] I think, and his local knowledge will be valuable.

4. Creagh should have a change, I am now quite sure of this. He has been at one job and in one atmosphere for too long. Here again I think that we must avoid any suspicion of "stellenbosching", as he has a great record and vast experience. I hope you will be able to

---

19 Captain A. B. Philpotts, Auchinleck's aide-de-camp.
20 Lieutenant General Sir Francis Nosworthy.

give him a division at Home. I am not prepared to recommend him for a Corps at present. I hope you will be able to spare McCreery, but if you cannot, I will think again. As you know he has been in the Desert and knows the conditions. He would be welcomed here with open arms.

5. Cunningham I have now met as he came up here with Smuts, and from what I have seen of him and heard of him, I feel that he ought to fill the bill very well as G.O.C.-in-C Western Desert. The South Africans who will be under him, know him well and think a lot of him, which cannot fail to help. He will bring a fresh brain to old problems which I feel are getting a bit stale and fishlike. In view of the Prime Minister's strong advocacy of Wilson for the Western Desert, I have sent him a private wire today telling him that my final choice is Cunningham, I hope he will understand. I am quite sure that Jumbo[21] is better where he is and I have a very strong feeling that Lyttelton agrees with me. I want you to know that I have been thinking very hard over this problem as I realise how essential it is to have the right man in the right place. It means everything. I am handicapped by my lack of personal knowledge of most of those concerned, but I am convinced that I am right, and have now no further doubts in the matter. My mind cleared today and I came out of the fog into clear weather! I now want to go straight ahead and get the new men into their stride as soon as I can.

6. Holmes[22] should, I think, be all right in charge of the "Coast Corps" whose job it will be to mop up and break down the resistance of enemy strong places. We will give him his own Corps Staff and make a new staff for Cunningham out of Beresford-Peirse's present staff.

7. We have occupied Jiarabub and our Long Range Desert Patrols have been putting in some really good work forward of El Agheila.

Tobruk too has its tail well up, and I hear that the 18th Cavalry (Indian Army) have been doing particularly well against the Italians on their front. This goes home to you by Shearer,[23] who is due to

---

21 General Henry Maitland Wilson.
22 Lieutenant General William Holmes.
23 Brigadier Eric James 'John' Shearer, DMI, Middle East.

leave tomorrow evening for a short visit. If you can spare the time, I think a few minutes with him would interest you.

I will write again very soon on more general topics.

JRL, AUC 295

80

Cipher message from Field Marshal Sir John Dill, CIGS to Auchinleck, 20 August 1941

<u>MOST SECRET</u>

<u>MOST IMMEDIATE</u>

NEW ZEALAND PRIME MINISTER has had information from various sources which leads him to doubt if FREYBERG is right man to command NEW ZEALAND Division. While Mr. FRASER likes FREYBERG and is keeping an open mind this is causing him grave anxiety. It is clear that NEW ZEALAND's only Division of such splendid men must have a really good Commander. Could you let me have your opinions which I could communicate to Mr. FRASER and if Gen. AUCHINLECK is not (rept not) satisfied I will ask him to initiate a confidential report.

JRL, AUC 297

81

Cipher message from Auchinleck to Field Marshal Sir John Dill, CIGS, 23 August 1941

1 (.) Many thanks for your telegram 85411 (85411) 85500 (85500) 85583 (85583) 85614 (85614)[24] (.)

2 (.) Agree to PLATT[25] succeeding CUNNINGHAM would be grateful for immediate official telegram appointing him (.)

---

24 This suggests code that could not be properly deciphered.
25 Lieutenant General Sir William Platt, GOC in C East Africa, 1941–45.

3 (.) Also request at the same time official appointment BERESFORD PEIRSE to SUDAN where he should remain Lieut. General (.) Will help me if notification these appointments is made in press at same time (.)

4 (.) GODWIN AUSTIN[26] will command EAST AFRICA temporarily and sequence of relief will be GODWIN AUSTIN relieves CUNNINGHAM who relieves BERESFORD PEIRSE who relieves PLATT who takes holiday in EAST AFRICA or U.K. and then relieves GODWIN AUSTIN (.)

5 (.) About GOTT (.) Have been very seriously considering him for command 7 (7) Armd Div but most anxious there shall be no repeat no suspicion that CREAGH is being displaced hence my desire to represent change as transfer of commanders between home and this theatre (.) Am very willing to appoint GOTT but would beg that CREAGH be given new equivalent or better appointment and that this be announced first or at least simultaneously with GOTT's appointment (.) Consider it most important from point of view my personal influence I should not be regarded as firer of tried commanders on large scale (.) Would help me tremendously if you would ask for CREAGH at once and then I will ask for GOTT as successor.

JRL, AUC 299

82

Letter from Major General Hastings Ismay, Chief of Staff to Minister of Defence[27] to Auchinleck, 28 August 1941

My dear Claude,

I am taking the opportunity of John Shearer's return to send you a line. It has been valuable to have him here; and he had a long and useful talk with the P.M., which he will of course tell you about.

---

26 Lieutenant General Alfred Godwin-Austen, then commanding 13 Corps.
27 Winston Churchill combined the roles of Prime Minister and Minister of Defence, 1940–45. The post of Minister of Defence gave him an overview of the

The P.M. thoroughly enjoyed his visit to the President, and has returned full of health and energy. He was, on the whole, pleased with the results, and is particularly delighted at having established such an intimate personal contact with Roosevelt. I dare swear that they admire each other immensely. Personally, I cannot help being a little disappointed. It is true that the Joint Declaration, if read carefully, is a very weighty document, but I had hoped that America would take a more definite and more dramatic step towards full participation. We'll never get a third of the production for which they have the potential until they are in the fight.

I shall be very interested to hear about your impressions of Smuts. Everything that he has said and done since the war started seems to stamp him as a very wise old bird. Incidentally – and this is, I think, a justifiable breach of confidence – he was loud in your praises in his private wire to the P.M.

Your telegraphic appreciation met with a mixed reception. The C.O.S. entirely agreed with it, and said so emphatically; but the P.M. went all over the ground that he traversed during that stormy meeting before our visit to Chequers, and marshalled exactly the same arguments. At the end of it all he seemed – temporarily – resigned, but, like Rachel, refused to be comforted. You needn't worry at all that his confidence in you has been impaired. I know it hasn't; but I do advise you most earnestly to write him a long private letter, telling him your hopes and fears more fully and freely than is possible in a telegram or even in an official letter.

The point that you want to get over above all others is that a tank force, which has not got superiority, cannot take as much or as little as it likes of a fight: and that if it starts off with the idea of making the enemy use up his substance, it may quite easily get knocked out. Isn't a tank battle in these days quite like a naval battle, than a land battle of the last war? If so you might paint your picture in those colours. I've tried to, but failed!

Another point is this. He was quite hurt that you applied epithet 'appreciable' to the reinforcements of the M.T. that you have recently had from the U.S.A. If you had said 'M.T. from the U.S.A. is coming along splendidly; but the demands of modern armies in desert warfare are so insatiable that we are still short', you would have made your point and he would have been perfectly happy. As it is, he regards the epithet

work of the service ministries: Admiralty, War Office and Ministry of Air, which continued to function, under their own cabinet ministers.

'appreciable' as a reflection on or at least a grudging acknowledgement of the efforts and sacrifices made at Home to keep you well supplied!

But the main point is – do write him long personal chatty letters occasionally. I know that normally you would recoil in your modesty from doing so. But he isn't a normal person (Thank God), and these aren't normal times.

I'm so sleepy Claude; and brain and hand are very tired. So forgive this very disjointed and illegible scrawl.

I think of you a lot in your immensely responsible job; and like all your friends, I'm supremely confident of your success.

JRL, AUC 303

83

Letter from Winston Churchill to Auchinleck [n.d., but August 1941]

I was depressed by receiving your Telegram No. 1549, in which you spoke about no action before November and advocated patience. It is not a question of 'impatience' or 'patience' but of balancing risks, which are grievous either way.

I was also chilled by your remark that M.T. was now arriving in "appreciable quantities"; because my figures show me you have received in June, July and August over 18,000 trucks, while in the same time the enemy have not received above 1,700.

However, I have had the advantage of several long talks with General Shearer, and he has explained to me for my most secret information something of what you have in mind, the look of which I like very much. I agree that it would be worth waiting for something like that, providing the enemy and the general march of events allow it. It looks much more likely than it did when you first took over the Command in M.E., or even when you were here a month ago to-day, that the necessary time for thorough preparation and massing will be given us. The Russian resistance is impressive, and it seems almost certain that Hitler will be entangled in the Russian miscalculation and morass during the whole winter. This will be hard for him on account of our bombing in the West and of the difficulties supplying his vast army in the East, which will, I am assured from Russian sources, be subjected to strenuous counter-attack. All reports tend to show no increase in the German Africa Corps, and that their health and conditions are far from good. The maintenance of this force by Germany and Italy in Africa is costly, and as we sink 25 per cent. of their convoy shipping and damage another 10 per cent., I agree that it is doubtful whether they will be able to maintain a substantially larger force than they have now got upon the ground. There remains the serious danger of their rapid reinforcement by Air, tending to deprive us of our Air superiority, so painfully acquired. However, here again the Russian prolongation and the German Air Force losses of that campaign give further reassurance. It may therefore be possible that you will have the time you need or demand. General Smuts, with whom I have been in correspondence, was favourably impressed by all you told him in Cairo.

You are I am sure aware of the dangers of delay, and the very high price which may have to be paid for it. It is inexplicable to the general public that we should remain absolutely inert during these months when the enemy is involved in Russia; but I can assure you I am only looking at the merits of the Middle Eastern problem, and not worrying about public opinion here, which I believe I can guide. It is on those merits that I am sure you will feel that every day that could be saved would be a diminution of risks of the situation altering to your detriment. However, I say no more on the point, as I am sure you must after all our talks see the case in all its bearings.

Meanwhile, I have set in motion a good many things which should help you. First, the whole of the 1st Armoured Division will be sent, and should be with you by mid-November.

The fact that this powerful reserve will be approaching should make you more free to throw all in when the time comes, because even in the event of failure (and no one can guarantee success in a great battle) you would have additional means of defending Egypt against counter-stroke by a damaged and weakened enemy. Secondly, the 250 Bofors guns are on their way, so that you should be able to have a proper moving 'flak' for your columns and assembly points. As this consignment is additional to the regular supplies, I trust it will not be inroaded upon for the static defence of ports, but will be used to liberate the Air Force for its main strategic and tactical contribution to the battle. [annotation?] Thirdly, in order to hamper the enemy's accumulation of supplies, I have arranged to send our last four suitable submarines from the Bay of Biscay to the Mediterranean and for two additional Blenheim Squadrons to operate from Malta. This should greatly increase the stringency of the enemy's supplies.

While, however, we thus try to turn off the tap by which the enemy's barrel is filled, can you not make it leak more freely by boring holes in its bottom? Tobruk should surely be the scene of ceaseless wearing down action, our troops being relieved in a manner not open to the enemy. I still feel that here is a place where the I. Tank with its short range might play an important part. It is not a question of moving far out into the Desert, or capturing El Adem at this stage, but simply of forcing the enemy to fire off his scanty ammunition and use up the life strength of his troops, cumbering himself also with wounded. An endless gnawing action developed from Tobruk would seem to be in harmony with all your larger conceptions. Now we can see how foolish were those who thought Tobruk should have been given up, and what a decisive strategic part is played in the defence of the Nile Valley.

I hope you are reconstituting the Commandos as we agreed, and will make them and their landing vessels play their part.

Persia has gone extremely well, and you must now feel very great reassurance for your Eastern flank. I find it difficult to believe that Turkey will be attacked by Germany while the Russian situation is so tense and heavy. Nor can I feel that the Turks will allow Germans to walk about their country or through it. The renewal of the Staff conversations is important, and we must do all we can to magnify their scope. I am trying very hard to obtain shipping from here and the United States to send two more division from here to the Middle East, arriving in December or early January. Whether I shall succeed is not yet known.

I am also considering an additional reinforcement of the Middle East Air, having regard to Persia and the Caspian, by drawing on the fighter strength available for home defence (now 100 Squadrons) after the invasion season has passed. It is of the utmost importance to gain Turkey at any rate so far as is necessary to make her maintain a forbidding and resolute neutrality against German passage or intrusion. If we can be sure of her as a solid oblong pad impassable by the enemy in the North, that is almost as good as if she were fighting and drawing heavily upon us.

Arrangements must be made at once to improve the railway from the Persian Gulf to the Caspian. General Wavell, who will be with you as soon as this letter, I hope, has a plan for doubling the metre-gauge railway by the Spring. I am having the whole problem examined here with extreme priority, and hope to telegraph fully about it next week.

You are no doubt apprised of the remarkable strength of the Russian naval force in the Caspian Sea, and of the reports we have had that they are gathering a very large reserve army behind the Volga. Our endeavour must be to give them a good through railway route to the warm water of the Persian Gulf, along which United States supplies can flow in an ever-broadening stream during 1942 and 1943. The great half-circle from the mouth of the Volga to the Western Desert with Turkey as a dull, stubborn bastion of its centre, should prove a barrier to the Nazi conquest dreams in the East. It is the shield of India, for which her troops may rightly be used to keep war from the Indian peoples and their homes.

All this brings me back to the Western Desert. The destruction of Rommel's army and Italian auxiliaries is by far the greatest military event open to the British arms in 1941. It justifies the greatest sacrifices and hazards. The defeat of a German corps by the British will have resounding effects in every land. Indeed, no one can measure the benefits that might flow therefrom. Once you have settled your Western flank satisfactorily by destroying the armed force of the enemy, it seems unlikely they would try the same game again. All your armies would therefore be free in conjunction with Wavell's to give their right hand to the Russians, and to animate or even draw in the Turks. Nothing can compare with this, and you may be sure that we shall back you to the utmost, well knowing the hazards and disappointments of war.

You are I am sure as you told me always reviewing the position of the 50th Division in Cyprus, which is clearly affected by any improved attitude in Turkey and any reinforcement of our Air Force in Syria.

I am very glad you sent General Shearer home at this time, and the talks I have had with him have added to my confidence in you and all your plans.

With every good wish

Believe me

P.S.   Perhaps you will show this letter to the Minister of State to whom I have mentioned it.

JRL, AUC 305

84

Letter from Auchinleck to Winston Churchill, 23 October 1941

Thank you very much for your letter of 16 October, which I have shown to the Minister of State.

I am not and have not been unduly anxious about the air situation in spite of the way in which the relative strength of ourselves and the enemy may have been displayed from time to time. Unless there is a tremendous disparity one way or another, which does not seem likely in this particular case, I feel that the gaining of a reasonable degree of superiority, which I feel is the most one can legitimately expect in the circumstance, is more a matter of leadership, skill and general efficiency than of numbers.

I have confidence in the ability of Tedder and his subordinate commanders to do what we require of them, and I am glad to be able to think that the confidence of the Army generally in the R.A.F. in this theatre, which was somewhat shaken after the campaigns in Greece and Crete, is now restored. The co-operation between the two Services is very good and I hope that they understand each other's capabilities and the limitations much better than has sometimes been the case in the past.

As regards estimates of opposing strengths, I feel that one must always consider the worst possible case and state it, though one need not necessarily be overawed by it when making plans for future operations. Figures can be made to prove anything, but I do not think we have allowed ourselves to be governed by them.

I have sent you a telegram replying to the observations on the second page of your letter, and I now confirm what I said in it.

Air Chief Marshal Freeman's[28] visit has been of the greatest value to us, especially in connection with WHIPCORD.[29] I will not conceal from you that I view this project with a certain amount of misgiving, because of the timing of it. I would feel much happier if I knew that I could complete the task you have given me first, before having to divert energy and resources in another direction.

I fully realise the need for speed in this new project and the magnitude of the prize to be gained, should it be successful. Nevertheless, an operation of this kind demands the most careful planning and preparation and the possession of really accurate information.

So far as we are concerned, I shall find great difficulty in finding sufficient troops adequately trained for the purpose. As you know I have devoted all my available resources in men and weapons to give Cunningham all he wants for CRUSADER and I have little left except the Australians who cannot be made available, even if they were trained for the business, which they are not. I am not making difficulties, but you know I have stripped everything else for CRUSADER and to provide a

---

28 Air Chief Marshal Sir Wilfrid Freeman, Vice Chief of the Air Staff.
29 A planned invasion of Sicily.

division without weakening CRUSADER is going to be a tricky problem. The use of troops without special training for an operation of this kind is, in my opinion, out of the question. A brigade is just starting training at our instructional establishment. The course lasts from two to three weeks, and there is only sufficient equipment to train one brigade at a time. Other brigades have been through this course before but they are now irretrievably committed elsewhere and cannot be extricated without seriously dislocating CRUSADER.

With regard to the sequel to CRUSADER, now called ACROBAT, I fully realise the need for speed and the avoidance of delay, and I assure you again that there will be no avoidance delay. All the same, no advance can take place until adequate supplies of petrol, ammunition and other supplies can be accumulated and carried forward, and this must take time. The distances to be covered are great and the means of transportation scanty. General Cunningham and all others concerned have been firmly impressed with the imperative necessity for haste and for improvisation to overcome the very real difficulties of maintenance.

I hope that Brigadier Whiteley has been able to give you the information you desire.

This morning I saw the first Medium American tank to reach this country. It had just reached our tank testing establishment at Abbassia, having come from Suez by road under its own "steam", a good distance of about 80 miles, in 4 or 5 hours, which is very good going for a monster of this kind.

It is a most formidable looking affair – very high when compared with our Infantry and Cruiser tanks which as you know, are rather squat. Its height may be held by some to be a disadvantage but I do not attach any real importance to this myself. I spent an hour or so crawling about it and having its parts explained to me by Major Colby, the U.S. Army expert who is helping us here. He had a major part in the designing of this tank and was very interesting and instructive to listen to.

Its armament is most impressive and looked to me to be exceptionally well arranged for ease of control and use generally. This tank is what we have been waiting for to enable us to "see off" the German tank which mounts a field gun, as so far we have nothing comparable to this. This medium machine with its .75 mm field gun .37 mm anti-tank gun in the turret, and its three .30 machine-guns, to say nothing of its anti-aircraft machine gun, looks to me to be a first class answer to anything the Germans have so far produced, and its speed on the road and across country is remarkable for its weight and size. It has, of course, the rubber tracks and these may need watching, in the light of our recent experience with the tracks of the American light tank in a certain type of stony ground. However, forewarned is forearmed and on most types of ordinary ground, the rubber tracks have proved an outstanding success. The engine is similar to that of the light tank whose reliability and ability to keep itself out of the shops are still the wonder of our tank units.

We want as many of these medium tanks as we can get and I wish we had some for CRUSADER. However, they will be all the more valuable later on and I grudge our having to surrender some of our allotment to the Russians, but we all realise the necessity for this. What we need are units containing a judicious mixture of American light and medium tanks in a proportion of about two to one.

The complete relief of the Australians in Tobruk is reaching its final stages and so far, I am glad to say, has been carried out without casualties. The Navy have been magnificent in the way they carried out this difficult and hazardous operation. General Morshead of the Australian Forces who has conducted the defence from the beginning, hands over his charge to General Scobie, the commander of the 70th Division, which has relieved the Australians, tomorrow.

I am sure you would like to express your appreciation of General Morshead's fine work, but for the time being, we must not, for reasons of secrecy which will be obvious to you, make any public announcement concerning the change over of the troops composing the garrison.

I shall in due course recomment General Morshead for an appropriate reward.

The final withdrawal of the Australians from Tobruk will enable me virtually to complete the concentration of the Australian Imperial Force in Syria and Palestine. There may be a few odd and unimportant units remaining in Egypt, but that is all. This should please the Australian Government, though I have reason to believe that the Australians themselves view the Tobruk affair with mixed feelings. We have sent the Czech battalion to join the Poles in Tobruk – this meets the wishes of both parties and will provide a valuable reinforcement to the garrison.

JRL, AUC 403

85

Letter from Auchinleck to Field Marshal Sir John Dill, CIGS, 24 October 1941

You will have had the cabled views of the Commanders-in-Chief on WHIPCORD, to which I naturally have subscribed. All the same, these communications are necessarily always in the nature of a compromise and I would like to give you my views in my own words.

I am of the opinion that the conception of this operation is sound and the advantages likely to accrue from its successful execution are great. I do not, however, agree that the conditions laid down as requisite for its success are in any way likely to be fulfilled before the date suggested for its execution. Moreover I consider that it would be wrong to attempt this operation before we have cleared the enemy out of NORTH AFRICA and stabilised the situation in ANATOLIA and the CAUCASUS. I consider these objects vital to the future successful prosecution of the war and that any diversion of effort from them would be most unsound. Once these objects have been achieved we may be able to consider the undertaking of an offensive against the enemy in Europe, but even then not until he is so seriously embarrassed and committed elsewhere as to make it impossible for him to use his interior lines to concentrate greatly superior forces, and especially air forces, against our attack.

We are now at last coming within sight of the time when we may expect to have air and land forces of a quality and quantity which hold out a reasonable hope of our being able to strike a really hard blow at some vital but weak joint in the enemy's armour but these forces are NOT yet ready neither can we be sure that our bases in the Middle East are reasonably secure from enemy attack. The strategic situation in this theatre must, I feel, be viewed as a whole and a premature offensive in SICILY is sure to affect adversely not only North Africa but also the entire Asian front. I consider therefore that to attempt this operation in the immediate future would be strategically most unwise and likely to undo the steady progress recently made towards the building up of forces adequate for the carrying out of long term plans scientifically conceived.

JRL, AUC 406

86

Letter from Auchinleck to
Field Marshal J. C. Smuts, 27 October 1941

Very many thanks for your letter of 17 October which reached me on the 24th. I am most grateful to you for your explanation of your wishes in regard to the allotment of the new eight-wheeler heavy armoured cars and I will see that they are observed.

Thank you too for your remarks about the future employment of South African forces. I understand the position and I will not let any consideration of this nature stand in the way of their training and eventual equipment as armoured units: I do not think that any impression to the contrary has gained credence and we will be careful to see that it does not.

Moscow still holds out I am glad to say and the news if anything has been better from that part of the front for the last few days. I agree with you that the steady and rapid German advance towards the Caucasus is a matter for grave concern on our part. We are watching this development very carefully, and General Wavell recently flew to Tiflis to consult with the Russian commander in that region. On his way back to India, he came to Cairo to give the Defence Committee here the result of his enquiries. I cannot say that they were reassuring. So far as he could judge, the Russian forces in the Caucasus are not strong, neither are they properly organised for defence. In fact there seems to be a lack of organisation and planning. This is a serious state of affairs which was reported at once to the Chiefs of Staff.

The Caucasus is not in my sphere of control but in that of Commander-in-Chief India, as it is inseparable from control in Persia, and Wavell is sending his C.G.S. at once to continue conversations with the Russians and to try to produce a co-ordinated plan. I on my part, am considering ways and means of sending help to the Caucasus. As you so rightly point out, the Caucasus front is of supreme importance to us. It is of little use holding our ground in Egypt and Syria if we are to be outflanked by a movement through Iraq and Persia, which I am convinced is what the Germans will try to accomplish. I am fully alive to the danger and always have been once I took over the command in India last January. You will realise of course the effect on our Western front in Libya of our having to detach any substantial forces, air or land, to the east, before the next phase is completed. I hope this will not be necessary, for if it does happen, our position will be difficult as you point out.

I am thoroughly impressed with the value of the time factor and am working to pretty narrow margins, I assure you, so as to avoid any semblance of avoidable delay. I too trust with you that the authorities in London realise how much depends on this front, and also that they thoroughly understand that it cannot be treated except as one indivisible whole, of which all parts are interdependent. There are occasions when I wonder if this aspect is always kept in view, and I am very sure that anything which you can do to stress the paramount importance of it, will be of the utmost value. I am continually stressing it myself.

Theron[30] leaves tomorrow for a visit to you and I hope he will take this letter with him if I can get it ready in time. He has just come back from the Desert and brings a very good account of your divisions. They have made a great name for themselves here already, although they have had little fighting in this part of the world as yet. Their bearing, behaviour and general attitude are most praiseworthy and have created a great impression on all those who have come into contact with them. I need not tell you how proud I am to have them under my command.

I have it in mind to ask you to send up a senior staff officer, your Chief of Staff if you can spare him, and if not, perhaps his deputy, so that I can inform him personally concerning future policy and the probable course of events. I would have given this information to Theron, but the moment has not yet I think arrived. I would like the information I wish to give you to be as up to date as possible, so that you can yourself have the fullest possible grasp of the situation and be able to read between the lines of the official summaries which I know you receive but which are necessarily brief and deal with past happenings only. If you could hold a responsible officer in readiness to leave at short notice on receipt of a private telegram from me, I would keep him here for a day or two only.

Alternatively, if this arrangements is not convenient to you, I will send one of my own staff officers down to you. If you would prefer this will you please let me know.

Every one is in good heart, and, I feel, quietly confident about the future. The American tanks are coming in well, and we are overcoming the usual crop of obstacles, which never cease to spring up like weeds in our path.

---

30 Major General Frank Theron, the South African senior liaison officer to GHQ, Middle East.

Your letters are a great inspiration and encouragement to me and I hope you will find the leisure to continue to write to me from time to time.

JRL, AUC 410

87

Letter from Winston Churchill to Auchinleck, 30 October 1941

Brigadier Whiteley has been a great help over here and will be able to give you a full account of our affairs. I have also to thank you for your three interesting letters which were a real pleasure to read and to receive.

Everything seems perfect now and I can only hope and pray that the weather will not change in the interval. For us that interval is trying as we have nothing to say to Russia, to the United States or to many enquirers here. However, it may be that the luck will hold and certainly the destruction of the enemy armour will open the door to many possibilities.

At present we have scarcely any military credit and it is little use talking to the United States, to Russia, to Spain, to Turkey or to Weygand. Should success attend your efforts, I shall try my utmost to win the last-named factor by the offer of a substantial force and I am not without hopes of obtaining American support. I fully agree with Middle East that the acquisition of Bizerta, and all that would imply, would be the best of all. But we have no right to count upon it.

I was very sorry to give up WHIPCORD. The Chiefs of Staff were so keen upon it and so were the appointed Commanders. It was, however, perhaps "a task beyond the compass of our stride". For the reasons I gave in my telegram to you, I do not think the opportunity will remain open.

Whiteley will tell you of my talk with him. You need not worry about the last 1,000 Australians in Tobruk or let their relief complicate your future plans. They can come out by the front door instead of the back. I also think that you ought to make sure of having some refreshment from Malta during ACROBAT.[31] Whiteley is going into this with Dobbie on his return. Even if you look at it as no more than an extra insurance, it would be prudent.

---

31 Acrobat was the codename for an operation designed to exploit 'Crusader' by an advance into Tripolitania.

I am going to have an enquiry for my personal information into the tragical lack of contact between the War Office and the Ministry of Supply on the one hand and Middle East reception on the other about the front axles of the 22nd Armoured Brigade. This is not so much for the purpose of fixing responsibility as for avoiding a recurrence of such break-downs. Considering the many months over which tanks have been passing from us to you, it is astonishing that no one at your end thought of saying "We distrust all your axles and are fitting our slabs to strengthen them thus taking (so many) days"; or that no one from our end arrived with the tanks able to answer all your questions and to give a good warrant. On such mishaps the fates of battles and of empires turn.

I am greatly cheered by what the Brigadier has told me of the way in which you are concentrating all your power upon the destruction of the enemy's armour and of his armed force generally. Here is the true principle. "…… seek ye the kingdom of God; and all these things shall be added unto you", or, as Napoleon put it, "Frappez la masse et tout le reste vient par surcroit".

JRL, AUC 415

88

Letter from Auchinleck to Field Marshal Sir John Dill, CIGS, 8 November 1941

1. I am afraid I have not written to you for some time, but things have been a bit hectic and I have been going about a good deal. Besides, Jock Whiteley will have told you all the news worth hearing!

2. I have just got back from a three days tour in the Western Desert, where I found everyone in very good heart. No undue exuberance or optimism, but a very cheerful and happy atmosphere, and an air of quiet confidence which I found most inspiring. Moreover, the general standard of physical fitness is truly remarkable. Everybody looks so well and feels so well, quite different to this sink of a city, where the air is always dead and the smells are always with one! I went forward to the 4th Indian Division which is, as you know, in the front line opposite Sollum, and met Frank Messervy and some of his commanders and staff officers – also a few of the men

of various units. In the forward area, it is virtually impossible to see anything of the men, as the distances are so vast and dispersion so tremendous. It has to be seen to be believed. In the armoured units, it is usual to find the men messing by tank crews, each little party cooking their own grub and living always beside their vehicle. It is no exaggeration to say that the curve of the Earth's surface prevents you seeing from one edge of a battalion area to another! It makes discipline a little hard to maintain sometimes, but it certainly develops imitative and self-reliance.

I had a day with Godwin-Austin and spent the night at his headquarters in the desert. He is in good form and quite sure of himself. I like him and think he is good and sound in his views. I also met Gott, who seems quite happy and confident in his brigadiers and troops – he gives me tremendous confidence.

3.   The next day I had a good look at the railway which really has made and is making the most remarkable progress. They are laying well over two miles a day, and aiming at three! They can't go much further, however, or they will be through the outposts. It is being done by the New Zealand construction companies, very ably helped by three Indian labour companies, about whose keenness and efficiency the New Zealanders, who are super-efficient themselves, cannot say too much. A very happy combination, all working like a piece of clockwork. The organisation of the work is really very good indeed, and they deserve a great deal of credit. It is extraordinary that the enemy air has never tried to interfere with the work, as railhead is always a good target, with its construction train, strings of lorries and great gangs of labourers. Thank goodness they have been left alone. When I was there the rails had reached a point due south of Sidi Barrani, and they had only a few miles left to do, before beginning to form the railhead lay out.

4.   I also on the same morning had the pleasure of turning on the water at the head of the pipeline, which is another very creditable achievement and one which has had to overcome many obstacles. There have been attempts to sabotage it by putting obstructions in the newly-laid pipes at night. We suspect Libyan labout gangs, but have not caught anyone yet. However, not that it is all joined up, it ought to be all right. Everyone in the Desert is down to a ration of ¾ gallons of water a day, which isn't very much. No baths or anything of that sort! However, they seem to get along all right,

though washing clothes is a difficult problem. They <u>look</u> clean enough anyway, and those near the sea can always get a bathe as the water is still fairly warm.

5.   I lunched with Brink[32] and his staff in their dugout at Matruh, and it was then that I heard for the first time of his training difficulty. As you will realise, I was most upset and my first reaction was a flat negative. However, after hearing what Willoughby Norrie and Alan Cunningham had to say, I realised that it would not do to give Brink a direct order to work to the original date, although he, of course, said he would do this if I ordered it. I sensed very strongly the psychological side of the matter, which is particularly important when dealing with that particular formation, and I became quite convinced that that course of action would be unsound, having in mind the tremendous issue that hang on the success or failure of the 30th Corps in what may be one short battle. So I then told Cunningham to explore at once the possibility of substituting the 4th Indian Division or the New Zealand Division for the South Africans. The 8th Army Staff worked all night at this, and said that the substitution of the 4th Division was a possibility. I rejected the idea of the New Zealanders, as they are all trained and set with the "I" tanks for their own particular job. Substituting the Indians had many disadvantages, apart from the inevitable dislocation it would cause in arrangements already made. Chief of them would have been the loss of extra fire power and, particularly, of the armoured cars which are such a striking feature of the South Africans' organisation. It was for these very characteristics that I originally cast them for the role they are to play.

    After much and very anxious thought I agreed to let Brink have three days extra in which to carry out divisional exercises in desert movement. There is no doubt that this is a most complicated business for large formations over long distances, and he, like everyone else, has been working against time. The trouble is that these movements cannot be practised seriously unless all vehicles are at full strength, and may of his, through no fault of anyone's, were late in reaching him. I told Cunningham to find out if he was prepared to give an assurance that the extra days would allay his doubts, and he has said in writing that they would. I know that

---

32   Major General G. L. Brink, GOC 1st South African Division.

the first criticism that springs to one's mind is why was not this discovered earlier. The only reason I can give is that with an ordinary formation it certainly would have been, but these South Africans are curiously reticent and secretive. I gather they work very much by committees and everything is turned over and discussed at length before being brought into the open. It is a most disconcerting trait, but I do not see what can be done about it. I know from experience of trying to get down to hard facts on their future organisation and man-power potentialities, how difficult it is to get anything definite out of them. Don't think I am decrying them, for they are grand chaps and all out to co-operate, but their ways are not our ways. However, both Alan Cunningham and Norrie both wanted to keep the South Africans where they are, even at the expense of the extra time, and I agreed, after explaining the matter fully to the Defence Committee on my return to Cairo. I know how distasteful my decision will be to Whitehall generally and to the Prime Minister in particular, but I weighed all these things before making it, and am sure that I was right, <u>all</u> things considered.

6. During my stay in the Desert, I saw a lot of the New Zealanders and Freyberg. They and he are in tremendous form, and extraordinarily fit. Freyberg has taken an immense amount of trouble with their training, and his methods are very thorough – safety precautions do not deter him from realism in training and he is quite right. One or two men blown up during training may save the loss of hundreds later on. The whole formation is most throoughly organised and prepared, and I doubt if you could find a better trained or finer division anywhere. They have masses of reinforcements too. The other day at Maadi, their base camp, I inspected 5,000 men on parade, all reinforcements. I wish I could say the same for our own units!

7. The rubber tracks of the American tanks are not so bad as we thought they were going to be. When they first began to go, they looked awful, and I was very anxious about them. Since then, however, we have found that they have a tremendous lot of life left in them, even though great chunks of rubber have come off them. I gather that you have found the same at home.

   The axle arm controversy still rages, and I still think that we were right to take no chances, particularly as we did not really get a clear line from the Ministry of Supply people at home. We have not got so many tanks that we can take chances on <u>some</u> of them being all right while others may not. I hope it will be possible to clear the matter up now once and for all. The Prime Minister seems to think that we were slow in getting them off the ships, but I have been into this and it is not so. I was rubbing it in to all concerned for weeks before they arrived that everything must be done to get them on shore quickly. Tanks stowed with all sorts of other cargo above and around them must wait their turn before they can even be got at.

By the way, these new little cars – "Bantams" I think they call them – are absolutely first-class: they are exactly what we want and have the motor cycle beaten into a frazzle! We can do with as many as you can give us.

8.   I am sending home Macleod[33] from our Combined Training Centre to explain our urgent requirements in craft and equipment. I know we shall want all we can get some time, and I hope, next year. We have not got nearly enough yet, not enough for really thorough training. I have, I hope, at last put a stopper on the use of landing craft as lighters for taking stores to Tobruk, or unloading ships, and our new Directorate of Opposed Landings will, I trust, see that our equipment is not misused in future. An Admiral – Baillie-Grohman[34] – is chairman of the Directorate, and Macleod is on it. They are a strong combination. If you can find time to see Macleod I would be grateful, as he knows the business from A to Z – no one better.

9.   Marshall-Cornwall[35] is not too pleased, I fear, at his translation from here. I shall be sorry to lose him in many ways, and he certainly knows all about Egypt. I sent you a wire suggesting that Holmes[36] might replace him. Riddell-Webster, who would have to work very closely with him, would like Holmes, and I would welcome him too. I cannot see much prospect of his having a corps to command in the near future, though he is doing useful work at present, planning

---

33   Probably Colonel Roderick MacLeod.
34   Vice Admiral Harold Baillie-Grohman who was attached to the Staff of GOC Middle East, 1941.
35   Lieutenant General J. H. Marshal-Cornwall was removed as GOC in C Egypt on 12 November 1941.
36   Lieutenant General William Holmes, then commanding 10 Corps. He replaced Marshall-Cornwall as GOC British Troops, Egypt on 13 November 1941.

defences in Syria. I realise there may be reasons for not appointing him, but it would suit if you could see your way to letting me have him.

10. I shall be sorry to lose the 50th Division, but realise that it is badly needed where it is going. I hope you will bear in mind the replacement of it before the Spring, because in certain eventualities, such as the non-completion of "Acrobat", I may find myself a bit short, should Anatolia come into the picture, as it very well may. It does not look to me as if the Free French "divisions", which are really only brigade groups, are going to be of very great value.

The Navy and our "Q" people did very well, I think, to effect the change over of the 50th and 5th Indian Divisions so rapidly. The onward move of the 50th depends entirely on the availability of mechanical transport, which you will realise is not too easy to provide, having in mind the needs of "Crusader". We will do our level best, however, to accelerate the movement.

11. Some people are making what I think is heavy weather over the question of command on the northern front. I can not see myself that there is likely to be any difficulty, if the proposals put forward in our J.P.S. paper are accepted. There must be an inter-command boundary somewhere. The more I study it the more convinced I am that it would be wrong to try and make this headquarters control operations in Iraq, Persia and Caucasia. The converse also holds good – that is, India cannot control operations in Syria and Anatolia. I know that there are quite a number who think otherwise, but I have thought a lot about this matter as you know, even so long ago as March when I was in India, and I feel that I am right. Given commonsense and the will to co-operate, I can see no difficulty about it. Troops can be moved quite freely from one command to the other on your instructions, as been been proved several times already. The move of the 5th Division to Persia, and now of the 50th Division are good enough examples. I do not think there was any stickiness about them – nor will there be in the future, provided your operations staff at Home are completely in the picture and can balance the essential needs of each front.

12. I am glad you are sending Watson out to look into staffs out here. We haven't really got the time to do it ourselves.

13. I must stop now, and I don't think I've got very much more of interest to tell you. I have had a foul cold for the last four or five days but it is going now I hope. Sikorski[37] has arrived; I didn't go to meet him because of my cold, and haven't seen him yet, but he is dining with me tonight. I don't think we shall be able to put him into Tobruk unless he prolongs his stay. He has arrived here at just the wrong phase of the moon, and our services are suspended for the time being!

P.S.   I enclose a statement which I think will interest you. It shows conclusively that, so far as actual numbers are concerned, "British" troops, i.e. troops from the U.K., exceeded troops from the Dominions in Greece and Crete, and suffered much more heavily than they did. I realise that a good many of these "British troops" may have belonged to administrative units, but I do not think that is really material. In view of the ideas so often expressed about the "sacrifice" of Dominion troops in these operations, you may like to use these figures.

While I am on this subject, I saw a criticism in the Press recently regarding our use of the term "British" troops. The argument was that all our troops are drawn from the <u>British</u> Empire or Commonwealth, whichever you prefer, and that the proper term to denote what we have always called "British" troops is "United Kingdom troops", or, if you prefer, Scots, Irish, English or Welsh troops! I think there is something in it!

JRL, AUC 427

89

Letter from Auchinleck to Winston Churchill, 8 November 1941

Very many thanks for your letter of the 30th October, which reached me by the hand of Brigadier Whiteley when he arrived here on the 5th of this month. I am indeed glad that he was able to be of some help to you; I look on him as a most able officer.

---

37   General Władysław Sikorski, Prime Minister of the Polish Government in Exile and C in C of the Free Polish Forces.

I am afraid that this further postponement of Crusader must have been a blow to you, and I can only say that I am deeply grieved to have had to add this further anxiety to your already heavy burden. I ask you to believe me when I say that I do realise what this delay of three days means to you, and that I would not have inflicted it on you had I not been certain in my own mind that it was necessary and, in the circumstances, unavoidable. I am very much upset myself, chiefly because I feel that I must have caused you bitter disappointment.

I became aware of General Brink's doubt as to the readiness of his division – the 1st. South African – for its task on Monday, when I was visiting the troops in the Western Desert. His fears were based on what he considered to be the insufficient training of the division, and one of its brigades in particular, in mechanised movement in open formation in the desert. This insufficiency of training was said to be due to the fact the the full scale of vehicles for the division had not been issued to it by the date on which they had been promised. He was quite honest about it, and said that he was prepared to go into battle on the assigned date if I ordered him to do so, but that he would not feel confident in himself or his division.

The first question I asked myself was why was this lack of confidence [was] not disclosed before, and the only answer I can find is that General Brink, in common with many of his fellow countrymen, is secretive and reserved by nature. Their disinclination to commit themselves to a definite statement is very marked, as I have found out for myself in my dealings with them on other matters. They are magnificent men, but they have their own peculiar traits. The Corps Commander, General Willoughby Norrie, might have found out the state of affairs, but, as you know, he has only recently been appointed and has been very fully occupied in organising his headquarters and in supervising the training of the armoured brigades of his division, with the result that the South Africans have been left rather to themselves.

As you may imagine, this disclosure of unreadiness or alleged unreadiness gave me a great shock, and I investigated [it] at once on the spot with Generals Cunningham, Brink and Willoughby Norrie. I came to the conclusion that the psychological effect of forcing General Brink to go into battle without his having full confidence in himself or his division might be disastrous. As you know, everything hangs on the action of the Armoured Corps, of which the 1st. South African Division is an integral and important part with a difficult role to play. So much depends on the result of this action, which may be decided one way or another in the course of a few hours, that I felt could not risk any grave weakness in the machinery. I told General Cunningham, therefore, to investigate at once the possibility of substituting the 4th Indian Division, which is in the front line facing the enemy at Halfaya and Sollum, for the South Africans. His staff worked all night at this and reported next morning that it was possible, at the cost of much dislocation of existing plans and arrangements. The 4th Indian Division is very well trained and ably commanded, and I considered this alternative very carefully, but eventually discarded it.

My reasons for discarding it were chiefly because the 1st South African Division has always been a fully motorised division with its own armoured car regiment and a quota of armoured cars in each individual battalion as well. It is also much more heavily armed with mortars and machine guns than the Indian Division. Generals Cunningham and Norrie both pressed for the retention of the South Africans in their original role for the reasons I have given.

I also considered the substitution of the New Zealand Division for the South Africans, but rejected this because the New Zealanders have an important role of their own to play, for which they, and the heavy tanks which are to work with them, have been very well and intensively trained by General Freyberg.

In the end, with the greatest reluctance and with bitter feelings, I agreed to a three days' postponement, which General Brink assured General Cunningham would just give him time to carry out the extra full scale exercise he wished to do to complete his training. He originally wanted six days. That is the whole story, a most unsatisfactory one I feel, and one that has affected me deeply.

As soon as I got back to Cairo – the next day – I explained the whole affair to the Minister of State, who was most helpful, though I failed to convince him that I had done the right thing. However, the responsibility was mine and no one else's, though I naturally had to obtain the concurrence of the Admiral[38] and Air Marshal[39] before giving the final order.

I fear you had another disappointment over Whipcord. We here gave the project our most careful consideration, although we were only junior partners, so to speak, in the enterprise. I am quite sure myself that the scheme is a perfectly sound one, and I have had it in mind as a future possibility for some time. I am distressed to see that in your opinion the

---

38   Admiral Sir Andrew Cunningham, C in C, Mediterranean.
39   Air Chief Marshal Sir Arthur Tedder, AOC in C, Middle East.

opportunity is not likely to remain open. I venture to hope that it will. We are continuing to plan for it at any rate, as we feel that it might have great possibility in certain eventualities. We understand that Bizerta can not be counted upon.

We are going thoroughly into the matter of refreshment from Malta during Acrobat, but it looks to us at the moment as if we can do anything which Malta might be able to do rather better than they can. We are not being ungrateful or conceited, but the factors affecting such an operation seem to favour it being done by us. We are examining all the possibilities – the unreliability of the weather in that region at this season is the most disturbing feature, but we will leave no avenue unexplored.

General Sikorski has arrived. I am much taken with him, and we have had an interesting talk. We will help him as much as we can. He is anxious to visit his Poles in Tobruk, but this is a bright half of the moon, and we are not running any ships into Tobruk at present. I think it will be possible to get the remaining Australians out of Tobruk without prejud[g]ing Crusader in any way. In fact it might be a valuable piece of "cover".

I have had a cordial telegram from the Prime Minister of New Zealand thanking me for some information I was able to send him.

The controversy about the axle arms of the Cruiser tanks of the 22nd Armoured Brigade is a most unsatisfactory one, and I am glad you are going to hold an enquiry into the affair. I have made all the enquiries I can here, and, though we may not be altogether free from blame in that we did not represent the matter as urgently as we might have done perhaps, I am satisfied that our people here acted in good faith and were genuinely convinced that the strengthening was necessary. We have not so many tanks as yet that we can afford to take risks with them. As I have mentioned before, the matter was represented from here some months ago, but possibly through the wrong channel. However, they are all done now and in service.

I spent three days with Cunningham and his Eighth Army and saw a great deal. I am glad to be able to report to you that everywhere I went I found an excellent spirit and no sign of doubt. Commanders and men were alike in their cheerfulness and quiet confidence. The vast majority, of course, do not know when or where they will be required to fight, but, unless my knowledge of men is very much at fault, they are ready to go anywhere and do anything. I feel great confidence too in the Commanders – Generals Cunningham, Godwin Austen, Freyberg, Brink, Messervy, Willoughby Norrie and Gott, who leads the 7th Armoured Division. It is on these last two, and their tactical ability on the day of battle, that everything hangs. It is a solemn thought, which is always with me, that this should be so. It is, I think, a unique condition which could only obtain, to a such preponderating degree, in this particular theatre. It is much more a condition of pertaining to sea warfare than to land warfare as known to us hitherto. It is, I suppose, a revival of the days when the issue was decided by the clash of the armoured knights, but it is very much a matter of all the eggs being in one basket! However, as I have said, I have full confidence in the commanders and their troops.

While in the Desert I had the good fortune to be able to see seven battalions of the New Zealand Division, as they are still in the rearward area. They are a magnificent lot of men and I was much impressed by them and their officers. They have been finely trained and organised by General Freyberg. It gave me great pleasure to present the ribbon of the Victoria Cross to one of their officers who gained it in Crete. We have now had a stock of ribboned brooches made up, and as soon after an award is made possible, the recipient is presented with the ribbon on parade. The moral effect of this ought to be good for every one.

In the forward area I was immensely struck by the very high standard of concealment and camouflage generally – the 4th Indian Division are particularly good in this respect. The degree of dispersion of men and vehicles is really astonishing: one never sees more than two vehicles together and the next pair will be hundreds of yards away. A group of more than six men is a rarity. These results betoken a high standard of intelligence, discipline and training, which is most gratifying.

I saw the railway being pushed forward at a great pace – two and a half miles a day, which is, I understand, a remarkable performance. The work was being done by New Zealand engineers and Indian Labour Companies, commanded for the most part by old Indian officers and non-commissioned officers, brought back to service from pension. The whole outfit were working together in the most perfect harmony and in the most cheerful spirits. The organisation of the work was remarkable, and most inspiring.

I also had the privilege of turning on the tap at the head of the pipeline which stretches back for over 300 miles. They are severely rationed for water in the Desert, the daily allowance being three-quarters of a gallon a man a day for everything. Those who live by the sea are lucky as they get a bathe now and again. Those inland have to very careful in their ablutions! However, they are all of them in excellent health and wonderful spirits. To meet them is a tonic in itself.

The organisation of the staffs and headquarters is, so far as I could judge in a brief visit, very good, and the liaison between the Army and the Air Force is excellent. The Intelligence Service is, I think, most efficient, and, I believe, considerably superior to the enemy's, judging by what we can deduce from the results of his efforts.

We believe that the main part of his armoured force, the two German divisions, is still between Tobruk and Bardia, but we have had no positive information of them for some little time now. He is lying very close. We think we know pretty accurately the dispositions of the Italian troops, including their one armoured and two motorised divisions.

Our air force has been doing excellent work lately, not only at sea and in Italy against his ships and harbours, but also against the enemy depots and ports in Cyrenaica. I am quite sure that every available aircraft is being employed to the best advantage.

The weather has been extremely warm for the time of year, quite unpleasantly so, but this can not last long.

JRL, AUC 428

90

Cipher message from Winston Churchill to Auchinleck, 16 November 1941

I have it in command from the King to express to all ranks of the Army and R.A.F. in WESTERN DESERT, and to the MEDITERRANEAN Fleet, His Majesty's confidence that they will do their duty with exemplary devotion in the supremely important battle which lies before them.

For the first time British and Empire troops will meet the Germans with an ample equipment in modern weapons of all kinds. The battle itself will affect the whole course of the war. Now is the time to strik[e] the hardest blow yet for final victory, Home and Freedom. The Desert Army may add a page to history which will rank with BLENHEIM and with WATERLOO.

The eyes of all Nations are upon you. All our hearts are with you. May God uphold the right.

Ends.

You should use this message [if and] when and as you think fit.

I gave a copy to AOC in C who will take to Coningham + inform him a message has gone to 8 army on which he must act as far as RAF are concerned.

JRL, AUC 436

91

Cipher message from Winston Churchill to Auchinleck, 23 November 1941

MOST IMMEDIATE.

One.   Most grateful for your appreciation which I realise is given under necessary reserve. Personally I like the look of things and share your confidence. Prolongation of battle must wear down enemy with his limited resources. I shall not broadcast Sunday night as decision is not immediately in sight. I have sent an epitome of your last message to President.[40] Remember I am waiting moment to appeal to President to tell VICHY FRANCE it is now or never and to make boldest offer for aid in FRENCH NORTH AFRICA from U.S.A. and BRITAIN. I hope this moment may come within next week.

Two.   [I?] think [I will?] tell troops "Enthusiasm for magnificent fighting and manoeuvres of Desert Army rising high here at home and throughout Empire. Your Countrymen and comrades in British Army, R.A.F. and Royal Navy are watching from hour to hour. We are sure you will shake the life out of the enemy in this famous battle!"

JRL, AUC 449

---

40   F. D. Roosevelt, President of the USA.

92

Gist of Conversation between C-in-C [Auchinleck] and GOC-in-C Eighth Army [Lieutenant General Sir Alan Cunningham] on evening 23 November 1941 (Brigadier Galloway, BGS Eighth Army, also present)

G.O.C.-in-C. 8th Army told C-in-C that as a result of our losses in Cruisers and American tanks during the past five days, the enemy was now probably superior to us in fast tanks which enabled him to attack and over-run our infantry without interference from our tanks.

This gave rise to a situation in which it might be possible to turn the southern flank of our forces in the SIDI REZEGH area and cut them off from their base. As the Army Comdr had by this time practically nothing in reserve, this meant that there might be nothing to oppose an enemy advance into EGYPT.

In these circumstances General CUNNINGHAM had thought it his duty to ask the C-in-C to visit his H.Q. so that he might learn the situation at first hand, and decide whether it was necessary to break off the battle and adopt a defensive attitude or continue the offensive with the object of destroying the German armoured forces. The Army Commander pointed out that a continuation of the offensive might result in our having no fast tanks left at all.

The C-in-C replied that he had no doubt whatever that our only course was to continue our offensive with every means at our disposal and that he wished the Army Commander to act accordingly.

JRL, AUC 454

93

Auchinleck to Lieutenant General Sir Alan Cunningham, 24 November 1941

1. Having discussed the situation with you and learned from you the weak state to which 7 Armd Div has been reduced by the past five days fighting, I fully realise that to continue our offensive may result in the immobilisation, temporarily at any rate, of all our Cruiser and American M.3 tanks.

2.   I realise also that should as a result of our continued offensive, the enemy be left with a superiority of fast moving tanks, there is a risk that he may try to outflank our advanced formations in the SIDI REZEGH – GAMBUT area and cut them off from their bases in EGYPT. I realise also that in this event, there would remain only very weak forces to oppose an enemy advance into EGYPT. On the other hand, it is clear to me that after the fighting of the last few days, it is most improbably that the enemy will be able to stage a major advance for some time to come.

3.   There are only two courses open to us:

(ii)   To break off the battle and stand on the defensive either on the line GAMBUT, GABR – SALEM or on the frontier. This is a possible solution as it is unlikely that the enemy would be able to mount a strong offensive against us for many weeks and would enable us to retain much of the ground we have gained, including valuable forward landing grounds. On the other hand it would be counted as an Axis triumph and would entail abandoning for an indefinite time the relief of TOBRUK.

(ii)   The second course is to continue to press our offensive with every means in our power.

There is no possible doubt that the second is the right and only course. The risks involved in it must be accepted.

4.   You will therefore:-

(i)   Continue to attack the enemy relentlessly using all your resources even to the last tank.

(ii)   Your main immediate object will be as always to destroy the enemy tank forces.

(iii)   Your ultimate object remains the conquest of CYRENAICA and then an advance on TRIPOLI.

5.   To achieve the objects set out in para 4 it seems essential that you should:-

(i)   Recapture the SIDI REZEGH – LUDA ridge at the earliest possible moment and join hands with TOBRUK garrison. It is to my mind essential that the TOBRUK garrison should co-operate to the utmost limit of their resources in this operation.

(ii) Direct the OASIS Force at the <u>earliest possible moment</u> against the coast road to stop all traffic on it and if possible capture JEDBAYA or BENINA neither of which are strongly held apparently.

(iii) Use the Long Range Desert Group patrols offensively to the limit of their endurance against every possible objective on the enemy lines of communication from MIDOHILI to BENGHASI, JEDBAYA and beyond to the WEST. All available Armd cars should be used with the utmost boldness to take part in this offensive. The advantage to be gained by a determined effort against the enemy lines of communication are worth immense risks which will be taken.

JRL, AUC 456

94

Letter from Auchinleck to Lieutenant General Sir Alan Cunningham, 25 November 1941

1. With the greatest regret I have to tell you that, after the most anxious consideration, I have decided that I must relieve you of the command of the 8th Army.

2. During my recent visit to your Advanced Headquarters, you asked me to give a decision as to whether we should continue an offensive against the enemy in Libya, or abandon it. After due consideration of the reasons for and against each course, I gave my decision that an offensive must be pressed relentlessly, regardless of loss.

3. You loyally accepted this decision and at once gave orders to give effect to it.

4. I have formed the opinion, however, that you are now thinking in terms of defence rather than of offence, and I have lost confidence in your ability to press to the bitter end the offensive which I have ordered to continue.

5. I have decided, therefore, to replace you as Commander of the 8th Army by Acting/Lieut. General N. M. Ritchie. I request you to hand over your command to him on receipt of this letter.

6.   You will realise, I hope, that this is an extremely painful decision for me to make. It is all the more painful because I realise that I owe you a deep debt of gratitude for your conduct of the battle up to this moment.

JRL, AUC 458

95

Letter from Auchinleck to Lieutenant General Sir Alan Cunningham, 25 November 1941

My dear Alan,

This letter accompanies my official letter to you telling you that I have decided to relieve you of your command.

It is no use, I am afraid, my telling you how I hate to have had to do this thing, but I must act according to my belief and I have done so. It is most painful to me because I like and respect you a very great deal, and I never thought that I should have to act in this way towards you. I can only assure you that I do so because I honestly feel that it is necessary to ensure the total defeat of the enemy in the shortest possible time.

As I have said in my official letter, I have nothing but admiration and gratitude for the way in which you have planned and conducted the operations up to date.

You will realise, I am sure, that it is most important for the success of the campaign in Libya and for the winning of the war as a whole, that it should not become public property that you have superseded in your command. I realise that this is supersession must be a most bitter blow to you, and that I am not entitled to ask favours of you. In the public interest, however, I do ask you to agree to being placed on the sick list and go into hospital for a period. I know that this will be against all your instincts, and that you will hate doing it. All the same, I think you should agree to this suggestion of mine, and if I may say so, I think the strain under which you have been working for the last three months, and the last few days in particular, does provide justification for a rest.

You may not believe me when I tell you that I have nothing but sympathy for you, but it is true all the same. I feel my responsibility very deeply.

JRL, AUC 459

96

Letter from Air Chief Marshal
Sir Charles Portal, CAS to Auchinleck,
25 November 1941

I am writing this for your eye alone in the hope that by the time you get it the troops will have won the victory they so well deserve and you will have the time to consider a problem that affects all of us very closely.

It is about Tedder.[41] First of all I would like to thank you very much for the support you gave Freeman[42] and me in our efforts to avoid Tedder's supersession last month. Your help was decisive and prevented a really dreadful mistake being made.

The question is whether, after the battle, we should make a change, and I feel that your advice on this will be valuable even if other influences prevent my following it.

The first reason in favour of a change is that, as you know, the P.M. does not think Tedder is a big enough man for the job. However much one disagrees, one must concede that the Prime Minister, with all his tremendous cares, ought not to be pressed to retain in a key position someone in whom he has not full confidence. This is quite apart from the desirability of reducing avoidable friction here which is inevitability generated every time the question of Tedder's "adequacy" comes up.

The second reason in favour of a change is that by sending out Peirse[43] I believe we could affect several improvements in our higher posts. In case you do not know Peirse, he is very steady and sound, has much experience, both of Command also of the Whitehall machinery in war, knows the Prime Minister well and is very good in Council. I could replace him in Bomber Command by an even better man for that job and this would leave an opening for yet another very advantageous change, and so on!

The only reason I know against a change is that it would be a change that might affect you, as I believe you think a lot of Tedder and get on well with him. I know he reciprocates such a feeling.

---

41 Air Chief Marshal Arthur Tedder, AOC in C, Middle East. Winston Churchill had been keen to have Tedder removed as AOC in C, Middle East due to a dispute about air strength on the eve of Operation Crusader.

42 Air Chief Marshal Sir Wilfrid Freeman, Vice Chief of the Air Staff.

43 Air Chief Marshal Sir Richard Peirse, who was then AOC in C, Bomber Command. Auchinleck's wife, Jessie, was to leave him to marry Peirse.

If he were to be relieved by Peirse, Tedder would get an Air Council post (Training) in which he could use his recent experience to very great advantage.

I hope he will get a "K" in the new year, which would also help to soften the blow that he would fell on leaving his Command, with however much glory and for however good a post.

I should like to take action as soon as possible after Crusader because of the large number of moves involved and the time they would take to affect. I hope you will give me your candid opinion, though as I said before, I cannot promise to do what you would like.

Finally, I think Tedder realises that he does not really enjoy the P.M's confidence and he might secretly welcome a change "with full honours".

If you think that there would be great advantage in your discussing this subject with the Minister of State I would have no objection, but I am sure you will understand that it would be better that Tedder himself should not know that I have written to you about it.

JRL, AUC 460

97

Cipher message from Auchinleck to Field Marshal Sir John Dill, CIGS, 25 November 1941

I got back this afternoon from Advanced HQ 8th Army (.) As result my two days visit am convinced CUNNINGHAM no longer fit to conduct intensive offensive required (.) In consequence after exhaustive consideration have ordered him hand over command to RITCHIE from 26 Nov (.) Am making RITCHIE LOCAL LIEUT.GENERAL for this purpose (.) Request your approval (.) This decision does not r[e]p[ea]t not mean that operations have been mishandled up to date or that their successful issue has been in any way prejudiced (.) CUNNINGHAM most loyal but in my opinion has lost spirit of offensive and consequently I have lost confidence in him (.) Would have referred matter to you first but every hour counts at the moment.

JRL, AUC 463

98

Cipher message from Auchinleck to
Winston Churchill, 25 November 1941

1 (.) Thank you most sincerely for your telegram 132 (132) which I appreciate greatly (.)

2 (.) Have just returned from HQ 8th Army (.) Issue of battle is still in balance but I am convinced that we have only to persist to win (.) Enemy is thrusting here there and everywhere in desperate attempt to throw us off our balance disorganise our command and cause chaos in our ranks (.) He is showing great skill and determination (.) All the same he has little behind his effort and so far from all I have seen and heard has failed completely to shake the morale of our commands and troops who are fighting magnificently (.)

3 (.) The enemy is trying desperately to regain the initiative (.) In this he has succeeded in part but locally and temporarily only (.) So long as we can maintain our pressure towards TOBRUK the real initiative is ours and we can disregard diversion towards SOLLUM or MADDALENA or even further east temporarily inconvenient and unpleasant as these may be (.) Every effort is being devoted to the forwarding of the offensive by the New Zealand Division and other troops of 13th Corps towards TOBRUK and I believe it is going well (.) While in the forward area I heard of no one who was not r[e]p[ea]t not sure that we are going to win (.) There may be disquieting episodes but the general situation should remain greatly in our favour (.)

4 (.) I have telegraphed to CIGS to say that I have decided to replace General CUNNINGHAM temporarily by General RITCHIE my present DCGS (.) This is not r[e]p[ea]t not on account of any misgiving as to present situation in my mind but because I have reluctantly concluded that CUNNINGHAM admirable as he has been up to date has now begun to think defensively instead of offensively mainly because of our large tank losses (.) Before taking this drastic step I gave matter prolonged and anxious consideration and consulted Minister of State on my return this afternoon (.) I am convinced I am right though I realise undesirability of such a step at present moment on general grounds (.) I will try and minimise publicity as much as possible (.)

5 (.) Meanwhile we are making every effort to replace losses of tanks and armoured cars and 8th Army are organising defences against enemy raids in our back areas such as SIDI OMAR MADDALENA and Railhead (.)

6 (.) At same time our light forces to southward have been ordered to press forward relentlessly towards enemy L of C MECHILI – BENGHAZI – EL AGHEILA and interrupt traffic thereon (.)

7 (.) Have made certain personally that every possible precaution is being taken in regard to your special stuff importance of which is fully realised by all concerned.

8 (.) Am very much alive to importance of early employment of 1st Armoured Division and this is receiving my urgent personal attention will cable details later (.)

9 (.) Everyone overjoyed by exploits of AURORA and PENELOPE (.)

JRL, AUC 464

99

Cipher message, Auchinleck to Winston Churchill, 25 November 1941

Before leaving 8th Army HQ I issued following message to General CUNNINGHAM (,) for wide distribution of troops (.) It may interest you (.) Begins (.) During three days at Advance HQ I have seen and heard enough to convince me though I did not need convincing that the determination to beat the enemy of your commanders and troops could NOT repeat NOT be greater and I have no doubt whatever that he will be beaten (.) His position is desperate and he is trying by lashing out in all directions to distract us from our object which is to destroy him utterly (.) You have got your teeth into him (.) Hang on and bite deeper and deeper and hang on till he is finished (.) Give him no rest (.) The general situation in NORTH AFRICA is excellent (.) There is only one order ATTACK AND PURSUE (.) All out everyone (.) Ends.

JRL, AUC 466

100

Cipher message, Auchinleck to Field Marshal Sir John Dill, CIGS, 27 November 1941

Cunningham took blow very well and consented to go to hospital ALEXANDRIA where he is now incognito (.) He is NOT repeat NOT really ill but his eyes have troubled him and he admits being tired (.) Because of eye trouble he recently suddenly gave up smoking which may have had something to do with it (.) He can NOT repeat NOT remain indefinitely in hospital incognito and I shall be grateful if you will order him home (.) Am asking him how he would like to travel (.) I hope he may be fit for further employment later.

JRL, AUC 476

101

Letter from Lieutenant General Neil Ritchie to Auchinleck, 25 November 1941

My Dear Chief,

1. Arthur Smith[44] will have told you of our safe arrival here[45] last night, and that he was able to get away fairly quickly. Since then I have heard that he got back to Alexandria without difficulty.

2. I wish I could discuss the situation with you because writing it is so much more difficult to explain ones feelings and repercussions. As I see it the major situation in CYRENAICA as a whole is excellent from our point of view and all indications are that the enemy is getting more and more hard put to it.

3. As regards the local battle field of the Eighth Army; this appears to me now to have developed itself into two battle areas:

---

44 Lieutenant General Arthur Smith, CGS, Middle East.
45 HQ Eighth Army.

a) South-East of TOBRUK, where we are effecting a junction with the Garrison.

b) The other is the area MENISTIR – HALFAYA – OMAR AZIZ.

Of these two, the former is the chief to us. We must get on there for it is essential that we should ease our administrative situation by starting to run supplies from TOBRUK. Progress appears to be slow but a junction has, I hear now (1000 hrs) been effected between the New Zealanders and the TOBRUK garrison at EL DUDA. This, I hope, is the beginning of our real success there. In the second area the situation is still very confused but I cannot afford to spend my time looking backwards towards there to the detriment of our operations forward, and this is the line I have decided to pursue.

4. To this end I am putting both the 5th Ind and 11th Ind Bdes under command of the 4th Ind Div once more, relieving them at once of their present roles by the 2 S.A. Div and any other oddments I can find. By thus strengthening up Frank Messervey and handing to him the complete responsibility for dealing with the enemy in the area MENISTER – HALFAYA – OMAR, I get on with the job ahead. (In this connection I send you a copy of a D.O. [Divisional Order?] from Frank Messervey which has reached me. Though confused, the situation seems to me thoroughly satisfactory.)

5. Godwin Austen is charged, as you know, with the operation to effect a junction with TOBRUK and roll up all enemy now facing the TOBRUK perimeter. At the moment I am concentrating the 7th Armd Div to his south flank to ensure that no action by the Germans from the East, the South or South-West can interfere with the operations to relieve TOBRUK. As soon as I see the situation sufficiently stabilised there I propose moving the 7th Armd Div wide round to the ACROMA area, where I do not think there is at present very much enemy armour; there to round up and disorganize and disrupt, so far as is possible, the Italian forces facing the South-West and Western faces of the perimeter.

6. Once this is accomplished, which I hope should not take more than 48 hours, I intend to form a mobile force of all the American tanks and the equivalent of a motorised Gp to move under Strafer Gott direct on BENGHASI straight across the desert. Coningham is playing on this and proposes to step up approximately five fighter

squadrons behind this force. This will then leave me with the N.Z. Div and one Armd Bde and one S.A. Bde to continue the advance towards DERNA, while Gott's force is moving on BENGHASI. If successful I feel that the enemy may then find himself without a base port and that such forces as he had left shut in amongst the GEBEL AKBAR.

7. Meanwhile I cannot help feeling that the enemy's effort in the MENISTER – HALFAYA – OMAR area can be successfully dealt with by Frank Messervey for the indications are that the enemy's radius of actions from that part of the world is very limited, and I feel that we must not allow our eyes to be tied down to this battle to the detriment of the major task of destroying the whole of the enemy's forces in CYRENAICA. I have just come back, by air, from H.Q. 30 Corps, who are with H.Q. 7 Armd Div near Pt. 172 (4534). Everyone in splendid fettle there and the strength of tanks in the Div improving hourly. The Div now consists in effect, of the 4th Armd Bde with 77 American Tanks, and the 22nd Armd Bde with 45 Cruisers, but as each hour passes this number of A.F.Vs increases. The Armd cars are doing very well and I do not think they have lost unduly heavy casualties. I send you copies of two messages given me by Willoughby Norrie[46] in which I think you will be interested.

8. Finally, everyone's spirits are at the top here, and I myself feel complete confidence in the ultimate issue. I am afraid this is somewhat confused as there is little time before the 'plane leaves for Cairo and I have had to dictate it straight off.

JRL, AUC 478

102

Cipher message Auchinleck to Winston Churchill, 28 November 1941

When I realised CUNNINGHAM was not fit I considered very carefully whether I myself should take his place in command Eighth Army (.) After much thought I decided against this and appointed RITCHIE (.)

---

46 Lieutenant General Willoughby Norrie, commanding 30 Corps. The messages mentioned here do not survive.

I realise well what hangs on this battle but concluded that I was more useful at GHQ where I could see whole picture and retain proper sense of proportion (.) RITCHIE is completely in my mind and his plans for future are exactly what I would do myself in his place (.) As you know I am at your service but my honest opinion is that for me to go now and supersede RITCHIE might have BAD not GOOD effect (.) I shall go forward to visit of course as required.

JRL, AUC 482

103

Letter from Auchinleck to Lieutenant General Sir Alan Cunningham, 29 November 1941

My dear Cunningham,

I have the longer of your two letters of 28 November which reached me this morning. I appreciate very much your desire not to embarrass me at this time. I hope you will believe me, however, when I say that I am most anxious to help you in any way I can, and to give you any information you may require. I will now try and answer your queries.

2. I must ask you to believe that in taking so drastic a step as removing an officer of your standing and reputation from his command in the middle of a most important battle, I did not act hastily or without the most prolonged and anxious consideration. The gravity of my action and its possible repercussions hereafter were and are fully realised by me.

3. As I told you when I was with you at your Advanced Headquarters, you did quite right to send for me to visit you, so that you might acquaint me with your apprehensions regarding the possible outcome of the battle, as a consequence of our heavy losses in tanks. Since you had this feeling, it was your duty to tell me of it, and you did.

4. I acknowledged in my letter (No. BM/GO/214/24) that you loyally accepted my decision to continue to prosecute the offensive with the utmost vigour, and at once gave orders to give effect to it. I do not wish to alter this acknowledgement in any way, and I am grateful to you for the loyal way in which you accepted my decision.

Nevertheless, the fact that you had even considered the possibility of breaking off the offensive and standing on the defensive seriously perturbed me.

5. I realise to the full the great responsibility imposed on you, and I hoped by talking personally to you, and by the issue to you of my directive of 24 November, to relieve you of part of the burden of that responsibility and to remove the fears you felt as to the results which might accrue from the continuation of the offensive.

6. I prolonged my stay at your headquarters in order to give myself an opportunity of seeing whether my hopes would be justified. As I have already told you, I gave the matter my deepest and most anxious consideration, and it was not until I had returned to Cairo on the evening of 25 November that I finally decided that I could no longer have confidence in you to prosecute the offensive as single-heartedly as I wished to see it prosecuted. Having reached this decision I had no alternative but to ask you to relinquish your command.

7. Whether I was right or wrong is, and must remain, a matter of opinion. If I had not been quite certain that I was right, I would never have taken so drastic a step, realising as I did all its implications and possible consequences.

8. As to the future, I can only say that I sincerely hope and desire that you will be re-employed in a position which will give the fullest scope for the development of your undoubted talents as a soldier.

9. You express some anxiety that if, unhappily, the battle inaugurated by you should not go well, your removal might indicate that the sole responsibility was of failure was yours. I can only tell you that I alone can bear that responsibility and I shall not hesitate to admit it. You may like to know that in my cable to the C.I.G.S. announcing my decision, I said "This decision does not mean that operations have been mishandled up to date, or that successful issue has been in any way prejudiced."

10. May I thank you once again for the loyal and uncomplaining way in which you accepted a decision which must have been a great shock to you, and also again express my gratitude for all you did to make this offensive of ours possible at all, and for your conduct of it in its initial stages.

JRL, AUC 493

104

Situation report by
Lieutenant General N. M. Ritchie,
09.30 hours,[47] 29 November 1941

1. ## GENERAL

The situation still seems somewhat confused but it appears to me quite definite from what happened yesterday that the enemy have concentrated all their Armd forces in a desperate effort to interfere with the TOBRUK battle and our operations there. So far we have successfully managed to frustrate this and inflicted considerable casualties on the enemy, though a final decision has not yet been reached.

2. ## TOBRUK BATTLE

This still remains the chief issue on the present battle field and we were much hampered yesterday from hereby failure to keep communications with 13 Corps and to find out what plan they had. It seems now that the N.Z. Div was very short of arty ammunition and water and that our attempt to drop arty ammunition from the air on the night 27th/28th failed. The reasons I do not yet know. As a result of this no major operation was undertaken, by the 13 Corps yesterday. The necessary convoy to get through water and ammunition was laid on in the F.S.D. area south of GABR SALEH but owing to the tank battle which continued practically all day without cessation in between this place and the 13 Corps it was not possible to attempt to run the gauntlet with this convoy until after dark. I have still not heard that it is safely through but believe that it must be. Early yesterday morning Godwin Austen asked for another Bde, and as I think I told you I decided to send up the 1st S.A. For the same reason that caused the delay in getting the convoy through this party did not leave until dark last night and it was halted on the way by order of Godwin, in the vicinity of HAGFET-EN-NADURA (4338). Why this halt was ordered I do not know, as I will explain to you later we were ourselves out of touch with 13 Corps H.Q. However, at about 2200 hrs

---

47   Times given are by Greenwich Mean Time.

last night I made the decision to order it on myself and I believe it has now joined hands with 13 Corps to the North. During the course of the night the corridor through to TOBRUK was enlarged sufficiently to allow of, anyhow, a portion of the 13 Corps being supplied from TOBRUK and I know for certain that this portion is not less than one Bde group. It was also sufficient to permit of the H.Q. 13 Corps moving through into the TOBRUK Fortress where it is now established and in touch with us once more. So this is good.

3. TANK BATTLE.

Continuing from where I left off yesterday. A further battle commenced somewhere about 3 o'clock in the afternoon when it was reported that 70 tanks were attacking the Armd Divv, then in position about BIR EL-HALEZIN (4439), while a further force of 37 enemy tanks was making North West from that place down the escarpment apparently with the object of taking the 13 Corps in rear. The battle continued in two portions:-

(a)   Our 7 Armd Div fighting a party of 70 tanks, against which they were successful and inflicted casualties.
(b)   A party of 37 tanks attacking the rear of 13 Corps, where they were held.

At nightfall the enemy tanks drew off again but I have just heard that a further attack was made on the 4th Armd Bde last night, when they held their ground successfully and knocked out, at any rate, 5 more German tanks. Personally I feel that the numbers of German tanks reported are exaggerated, for they are now obviously mixing up dummy tanks with the real ones. In my estimation there were probably not more than some 40 enemy A.F.Vs actually engaged in this battle yesterday evening. Last night the strength of running tanks in the 7 Armd Div was reported as 45. But I feel that more will have been collected in during the night, especially as I have just heard that the 4th Bde have 35 runners this morning. In addition I have 15 more American M3s on their way up to join this Bde. I have not yet been able to discover the fighting strength of the 22nd Armd Bde this morning. It is quite clear to me now that the whole of the maintenance and supply of the enemy Armd forces is now being carried out from BARDIA, and Frank Messervey's best contribution to the main TOBRUK battle will be to stop this supply. I issued him orders to this effect.

4. <u>MENISTER – SOLLUM – HALFAYA – OMAR, AREA.</u>

I have now got full details of Frank Messervey's dispositions here and this will be explained by the L.Q. by who this letter goes. The main point is, that contrary entirely to our previous supposition, the New Zealanders were not masking BARDIA at all. In the fact this enemy supply area is completely open and free for the supply of enemy armed forces operating further West. The next point is that I think Frank Messervey has successfully cleared up and opened the area SIDI SULEIMAN (5135) Conference (5233) BIR SHEFERZEN (4934), SIDI OMAR, with his mobile forces out of this area, and put it in the stop the process of supplying the Armd forces from BARDIA, and this I hope he has already done. The 5th Ind Inf Bde rejoined him yesterday and with those I feel that he should be able to cope with the situation. For, other than Armd forces of which his area is now apparently clear, the other Italian and German troops are to all intents and purposes static and can be left to be mopped up later. As I think I told you yesterday, I am taking his 11th Inf. Bde into Armd Reserve positioning it in the neighbourhood of L.G. 132 on the wire between SHEFERZEN and MADDALENA. I am making it one hundred per cent mobile as that it can be moved over to reinforce the TOBRUK battle concerned or to rejoin Frank Messervey quickly should necessity arise. On the whole I am pretty satisfied with the position in his area, but everything here really depends on his being able to stop the supplies reaching the Armd forces to the West.

5. FORCE "E"

A Liaison Officer arrived in from REID[48] yesterday. I send you on copies of the reports he brought me. What an excellent show. I find it will be of no value to pass his petrol by air because I will get it there just as quickly by the convoy which left here yesterday morning.

---

48 Brigadier D. W. Reid who commanded Oasis Force which captured Aujila on 22 November and Jalo on 24 November. Reid faced serious logistical problems as he found little at Jalo. His force remained at Jalo with little petrol and on half rations until the 20 December able only to send out light patrols towards Agedabia.

6.   I will be leaving for TOBRUK in about an hour's time and do not anticipate being back here until this evening. My chief trouble is communications which are far from right in this Army of ours, but once I have seen Godwin and got his plan and been able to co-ordinate this with 13 Corps I hope for great results. You will, of course realise that this armed battle is not yet over, but I have managed to send up a few extra tanks and I have great confidence in Strafer doing two things:-

(a)   Preventing the enemy getting out West.
(b)   Completely neutralising the usefulness of their armour to the enemy for the future.

JRL, AUC 494

105

Medical report on Lieutenant General Sir Alan Cunningham by Colonel W. D. D. Small, Consultant Physician, 30 November 1941

I examined General Cunningham on 29th November at No.64 General Hospital, and ascertained all medical facts relevant to his case.

I was informed that when he was admitted to hospital, on the evening of November 26th, he was exceedingly tired and showed signs of strain. His long and heavy responsibilities had culminated in a period of about a week with practically no sleep. His voice was weakened. When speaking he tended to break off in the middle of sentences. He showed a marked tremor of the hands.

It appears that about a month ago he consulted an ophthalmologist who found a scotoma affecting the right eye. He was advised to stop smoking, and did so. It is to be noted that sudden cessation of tobacco in a heavy smoker often produces marked irritability and unrest.

Since admission to hospital he has slept soundly each night. At the time of my examination, he looked rested, and all signs of strain had disappeared except a slight general increase of his deep reflexes. His general physical state is good. His voice is normal. The tremor has disappeared. He is composed, and very alert and mentally active. There is no evidence of any "nervous breakdown".

On admission to hospital, General Cunningham was suffering from severe physical exhaustion. Fortunately he is making a rapid recovery. I consider that he requires a further period of rest, of at least a month, before he returns to duty.

JRL, AUC 497

106

Cipher message, Winston Churchill to Auchinleck, 30 November 1941

1. Although I have no news from the Front later than your no.1626, I cannot help feeling that we are forging steadily ahead against a resourceful and determined foe. Thank you so much for your full accounts and for your kind good wishes.

2. I may have to make a statement to the House on Tuesday on information received to that date, especially if events continue to take a favourable turn.

I think it would then be proper, unless you object [?], to disclose the change in Command which will by then be more than a week old, and the reason.

Statement would be laconic and something like the following. "On November 23rd General AUCHINLECK repaired to General CUNNINGHAM Advance H.Qs where he remained for three days. On November 26th, he became convinced that General CUNNINGHAM's proposed dispositions were not in accord with the principle of relentless offensive at all risks and at all costs on which General AUCHINLECK's conception of the battle was founded. General AUCHINLECK therefore removed General CUNNINGHAM from the Command of 8th Army and replaced him by Major-General RITCHIE.

This decision was immediately approved and confirmed by the Minister of State and by me.

Since November 26th therefore, General RITCHIE has conducted the battle with skill and resolution under the general supervision of C in C."

Ends.

JRL, AUC 501

107

Situation report by
Lieutenant General N. M. Ritchie,
07.00 hours, 30 November 1941

1. I will not be writing you at great length today as Jock is up here and has full particulars of all details that have gone on since I wrote to you yesterday morning and he will be able to explain far better than I can on paper. Thank you very much for your wire telling me that you appreciate these letters and that they are of some use.

2. TOBRUK BATTLE

    At present it is difficult to divorce the Armd battle from the TOBRUK battle as all are one by virtue of the fact that the whole of the enemy's armour was, last night, thrown into the TOBRUK battle while ours naturally enough was there in attendance. I flew into TOBRUK yesterday morning where I saw Godwin Austen, all in great heart. The N.Z. Div has had a hardish time and suffered probably some 1500 casualties in all and as a result of this, it will be necessary to pass fresh troops through it to finish off TOBRUK and to carry on beyond. I have, therefore, decided to relieve the 4th Ind Div of its present role and move it forward preparatory to undertaking the relief of the N.Z. Div. I will return to this question later on. The German wireless was working in clear a good deal yesterday, and by virtue of this Godwin was able to get a clear picture of the German plan of attack on TOBRUK, which took the form of a concentrated offensive with all the armour he had in hand. Jock will explain this and how last night, at any rate, the 21st Armd Div and AERITE Div was squealing for help. Last night, as on the previous one, I did all I could to try and ensure that no supplies got through to the German armed forces but of course the results of this I have not yet been able to get this morning. I hope, however seriously to have disrupted his administrative arrangements. I think there little doubt now that he is maintaining himself from BARDIA as this has been borne out by statements of prisoners captured yesterday. It was the most tremendous relief to find that the convoy of ammunition, water and food had safely got through to TOBRUK, replenished the N.Z. Div and freshened them up for the battle they had yesterday. It was a great effort running the gauntlet in this way and the credit is due to Colonel CLIFTEN, late C.R.E. of the N.Z. Div who is now Deputy Chief Engineer of the 30 Corps. A first-class effort. I heard while in TOBRUK that the Commander of the 21st Armd Div had been captured and with his command car and documents. Before Jock leaves I hope I say get more details of the situation as it exists in the TOBRUK area this morning. In the night we heard that the New Zealanders had been attacked at EL DUDA, ostensibly by an enemy force reported at a strength of 55 tanks and one inf bn. Personally I consider that the tank strength is much exaggerated. However, the New Zealanders had, temporarily, to give up their position on EL DUDA but I understand that they retook it again later in the night.

3. BARDIA – HALFAYA – OMAR Area.

The situation here has remained quiet and yesterday, as far as I can gather it was clear of enemy A.F.Vs. The enemy troops remaining at the moment are static and consist of those in BARDIA, at HALFAYA, in the Couveau position and in a small keep about Pt.201 in square 4936. They have little t[rans]p[or]t so far as I can gather, and I do not think it will be a long time before we collect them in. In these circumstances I am taking the risk of moving up de Villers' 2 S.A. Div to relieve 4th Ind Div, thus releasing it to move forward to rejoin Godwin for the settlement of TOBRUK and the advance beyond. I know it is a risk but it had got to be taken as I must get more troops forward to the main battle.

JRL, AUC 503

108

Letter from Auchinleck at Advanced HQ, Eighth Army to Lieutenant General Arthur Smith, CGS, Middle East, 3 December 1941

Yesterday was uneventful, a bad day for the air; low cloud and heavy rain made reconnaissance very difficult so we had little or no news of the enemy. What news we had showed that he had possibly thrown out a screen of small columns – tanks, guns and M.T. – covering his troops round SIDI REZEGH from the EAST and N.E. – probably to let him clear the battlefield. There were also indications of a move by a strongish column on EL GUBI, but this was not confirmed by our Armd cars, which are supposed to be watching this place. I hope he does not succeed in re-establishing himself in a point d'appaui there as it would be a nuisance. We shall probably hear today.

Freyberg came in to lunch yesterday, looking exactly the same as ever. The N.Z. Div (less 5 Bde) fought magnificently, but were over-run by the enemy tanks in spite of the fact that they had their own "I" tanks. Truth is, I think, that they had become very weak in numbers after their own attacks on SIDI REZEGH etc., which were all done at night with the bayonet. Freyberg estimates their losses at 4,000 – 5,000, but there are no means whatever at present of confirming this – nor did he know, I think, how many he actually brought out with him. Quite a number are in TOBRUK, including most of the 2nd Line Transport. One battalion is still holding BEL HAMED and in touch with the TOBRUK garrison, which is holding fast.

The N.Z. M.DS [Medical Dressing Station?] with all their wounded was overrun and I suppose all in it (a lot) captured. The Div has lost 24 guns, but we can replace these at once I imagine? If the 1st S.A. Bde could have got to the N.Z. a bit quicker they might very well be there now, but this is another story, not to be told now. Neil [Ritchie] is sending Freyberg and his remnants back to BAGUSH to reform, and I expect A. is already arranging to send up drafts from MAADI. As you know, I hope eventually to send the Div to SYRIA, so it is not likely, I hope, to have to come back into the line here, but it may as well stay at BAGUSH for the time being until we can get the elements of it now in TOBRUK out and back. It can help to look after the L. of C.

I enclose a telegram drafted by Freyberg to be sent to New Zealand. I presume they have been prepared in some degree already by our omnibus telegrams to Dominions? Perhaps you had better show the draft to the Minister[49] in case he wants to send one to the N.Z. P.M. himself. I enclose a draft which I think we ought to send to Puttick[50] if you agree. It is a pity, but it can't be helped – its war.

They fought magnificently and inflicted heavy casualties on Germans, who Freyberg thinks have had their belly full. He says the carnage on SIDI REZEGH is worse than anything he has seen. The Germans

---

49 Oliver Lyttelton, Minister of State and Member of the War Cabinet, resident in Cairo, June 1941 to Feb 1942.

50 Lieutenant General Edward Pittick, Chief of General Staff, New Zealand, 1941–45.

turned their anti-tank guns on to our fellows and literally blew them to pieces, while the New Zealanders made a terrible mess of the Germans with the bayonet. Freyberg and the remnants of the Div – about 4,000 – spent the night on the wire some miles NORTH of here – all in good heart I believe. They made a most orderly and masterly withdrawal from the battle.

Neil [Ritchie] flew into TOBRUK yesterday and cleared up future plans with Godwin[51] very satisfactorily, I think; I do not want to discuss them, even with you, on paper. Godwin is quite confident he can hold the "appendix" without undue risk of its being pinched out, which is good news. He says it is very strongly held, and they have wire and mines, besides quite a number of "I" tanks. In fact, he is starting at once to work forward from its WESTERN face towards EL ADEM, which is good. He is relieving some of the more tried troops in the salient by the Poles. I hope he has sent back von Ravenstein[52] to you by this time. Guard him well! I gather he told Godwin that they had not been up against fighting of this kind before. They haven't done with it yet!

Neil is handling the affair very well indeed, I think. He is completely confident and knows exactly what he wants. I feel myself that the whole picture is much more purposeful and much tidier than it has ever been before. We have learned a lot and we are going to profit by it.

The situation round BARDIA and HALFAYA is not altogether satisfactory, but I am afraid we cannot yet afford the time or the troops to clear it up completely. 2 S.A. Div are taking over in this area with 5 N.Z. Inf Bde under command, and will gradually deal with the enemy here, who cannot be very comfortable. I am afraid the enemy still has dumps in BARDIA and GAMBUT area from which he can draw, but Neil hopes his "Jock" Columns, of which a lot are being organised, will deal with this nuisance pretty well, even if they cannot stop it altogether. A real cordon is impossible – distances are so vast.

Meanwhile 4 Ind Div, 22 Gds Bde, 1 S.A. Inf Bde, 7 Armd Div, plus Armd Cars etc. are concentrating under 30 Corps in area GABR SALEH, covered by "Jock" columns and Armd Cars with very definite orders to keep in close touch with the enemy all along the front. It looks as is the enemy had got all he has in the front window round TOBRUK. There is little or no movement in rear of ACROMA.

---

51 Lieutenant General Alfred Godwin-Austen, commanding 13 Corps.
52 Major General Johann von Ravenstein, commander of 21st Panzer Division, captured November 1941.

Force E (Oasis) should be making its presence felt again soon. I saw in the paper that the march of the German prisoners had proved a "flop". Was this so, and, if so, who gets the sack? If it was so, please make them do it again at once. I look on this as important as now the Egyptians will disbelieve that there ever were any prisoners!

I enclose a draft wire for the P.M., which you can edit or expand if you have later information. Please go on sending full telegrams to the Dominions.

The tank situation is improving rapidly – 100 with 4 Armd Bde and now I believe 50 cruisers with 22 Armd Bde. Trouble is enemy tanks won't close now, but try to draw us on their anti-tank guns.

I have decided, after hearing views of Neil [Ritchie], Willoughby Norrie, Gott, that 2 Armd Bde is to come up regiment by regiment as ready, manning their own tanks, and train in desert as directed by 8 Army. This is best, I think, as they could not be in time for the next push anyway, and may make all the difference in the following stage. So please keep them and all the other units hurrying. You have done wonders in sending troops up so quickly and I am most grateful – so is Neil.

Willoughby Norrie and Gott are said to be weary but full of spirit. They had a rest (?) yesterday, and may be refreshed now. Anyway, Neil wants to keep them and not send them away to rest.

Everybody is in fine heart, no sign of any despondency. I hear nothing but praise for 4 Ind Div, which is looked on as a really well-trained and experienced div. The S. Africans are not trained and are much too unwieldly. Neil has ordered them to reduce their sections and cut down their transport. For the present, they are to be used for semi-static duties. There is nothing wrong with their fighting qualities – they are magnificent in battle – and their armoured cars are first-class – but they don't know yet. They are learning fast.

I shall probably stay here till the 5th at any rate.

The protracted nature of the fighting is a nuisance, of course, but I am quite happy and so is Neil. We will get this stinker down where he belongs before long I hope.

JRL, AUC 509

109

Letter from Lieutenant General Arthur Smith, CGS, Middle East to Auchinleck, 3 December 1941

Thank you for your letter written this morning. I have sent off the various telegrams – yours to the Prime Minister and the C.G.S. New Zealand[53] and Bernard Freyberg's to the Prime Minister New Zealand. I showed these telegrams to the Minister of State[54] and he does not feel that he should cable the New Zealand Prime Minister himself as this might cut across a telegram from Winston. We had already told the New Zealand C.G.S. that the New Zealand Division had had big casualties, and I have kept in close touch with Stevens (the New Zealand Brigadier in charge of their Maadi Base) on the subject. I got him to go up to Bagush to-day to find out exactly what type of reinforcements they want. They are all teed up ready to go directly we get information as to units.

2.   Delighted to hear that New Zealanders fought so well and that their withdrawal was conducted in an orderly fashion. I am not surprised to hear this for they were indeed well trained.

3.   Twenty-eight guns are already on their way up to the forward area, and Maxwell[55] is collecting all he can and is in close touch with 8th Army regarding their reinforcements. I have impressed on the Staff here that we must try and anticipate demands for reinforcements and equipment and get them on the way up where possible before we get the official request.

4.   We have had a request for 2,300 reinforcements for TOBRUK and I have just discussed it with the D.A.G. The fact is that there are no reinforcements in the Infantry Base Depot for the 70th Division and I cannot see any way of producing them. They simply don't exist. You will remember that some 800 infantry soldiers had to be taken to drive lorries. If TOBRUK must be reinforced the only way would be to send up fresh units, but we are quite unable to say where these are to come from. The 2/5 Essex Regiment are at

---

53   Lieutenant General Edward Pittick.
54   Oliver Lyttleton, Minister of State and Member of the War Cabinet, resident in Cairo.
55   Major General Aymer Maxwell, CRA, Middle East.

SUEZ earmarked to go to IRAQ in the middle of this month. I feel it would be breaking faith with IRAQ if we did not send them as we have already had an Indian Battalion from IRAQ in their place. We have already had to keep the 150th Infantry Brigade from going to IRAQ.

5. Von Ravenstein[56] has not yet arrived from TOBRUK. I was interested to hear that he stated that he had not been up against fighting of this kind before.

6. Delighted to hear you are so pleased with Neil [Ritchie]. He is a grand fellow.

7. I am not surprised that the 1st South African Division proved to be untrained and inexperienced. I agree with you that they are learning fast, but it is rather an expensive lesson. I have had a feeling all along that the 1st South African Bde was a bit sticky in getting up to the support of the New Zealanders and I shall be interested to learn the reason why.

8. I am sorry there was a slip up about the German prisoners. Holmes[57] laid it all on and then one of his Staff officers rang up "A" Branch here and was told that marching German prisoners through CAIRO was not in accordance with your wishes. He did this on some previous ruling when the matter had been raised, and I am afraid "A" Branch had not been told what your real views were. I have seen Holmes and the D.A.G. and arrangements are being made for the next batch of German prisoners to be marched through CAIRO next Friday.

P.S.   Have just this minute sent a letter from Bill Ramsden.[58] He wrote from IRAQ –

"Now that you have pinched my 150 Bde Gp, my div[isiona]l recce B[attalio]n & long ago my 65 AT regt, I hope you will take the rest of us for 'The War in the West'.

---

56 Major General Johann von Ravenstein, commander of 21st Panzer Division, captured November 1941.
57 Lieutenant General William Holmes, GOC British Troops, Egypt.
58 Major General William Ramsden, GOC 50th Division, 1940–42. Commanded 30 Corps, July to September 1942.

"There appears to be no immediate need for us here ... I shall be most grateful for anything you can do to get this division a show. The prospects of a long winter in the plains of IRAQ with no real incentive is a dismal outlook".

JRL, AUC 510

110

Cipher message from Auchinleck to Field Marshal J. C. Smuts, 4 December 1941

1 (.) Experience in this battle shows that organization [of] your divisions is too overloaded with transport to make it possible for brigades adequately to protect themselves against A.F.V. attack at halt or on move in desert warfare (.) This leads to undue concentration of vehicles which affords favourable bombing target to enemy (.)

2 (.) Commander 8th Army has discussed this with divisional commander who agrees and has with my approval directed that both divisions shall be reduced as a temporary repeat temporary measure to British war establishments in respect of transport and number of men in the infantry section (.)

3 (.) Would not have taken this step even as temporary repeat temporary measure without asking you were I not repeat not convinced of urgent necessity (.) Hope you will agree (.)

4 (.) Your troops are fighting magnificently and your armoured cars in rear of enemy round ACROMA are doing most useful work (.) Saw DE VILLIERS[59] yesterday who is in great form (.) Enemy is still fighting but has suffered severely and situation is well in hand (.) Am confident of result.

JRL, AUC 513

---

59 Major General Issac de Villers, GOC 2nd South African Division.

III

Letter from Auchinleck to Lieutenant General Arthur Smith, CGS, Middle East, 4 December 1941

Many thanks yesterday for your letter of the 2nd, which reached me yesterday.

2. Am keeping John Shearer here for present to act "Rommel" for us.

3. You ask about the "I" tanks. They took part in all the SIDI REZEGH fighting, and suffered heavily though they did their job, except perhaps in the final show, but why is not apparent. Probably there were too few of them by then. They also suffered heavily in the attacks on the OMARS, being knocked out at close range by the German "88" guns. These are final dual (AA and A/Tk) weapons. I saw four of them at LIBYAN OMAR yesterday, captured by 4 Ind Div. 4 Ind Div took 59 guns of all calibres in the OMARS. I think this should be made known. At the moment the "I" tank position is said to be:-

In TOBRUK 30 odd
In the OMARS 30 odd with 2 S A Div.

Also 24 Valentines[60] with 30 Corps at GABR SALEH.

4. I am most grateful for the wonderful way in which you are hastening the sending up of reinforcements. Please thank all concerned. It is very much appreciated here.

5. I have decided after seeing Neil [Ritchie] and Lumsden[61] that 2 Armd Bde is to come up manning its own tanks. We are all agreed in this, and 8 Army are arranging details of move with Lumsden. I am sure this is the right course. Please keep P.M. informed of progress. Attachment of desert experienced officers and men is being arranged. As soon as this phase is over Neil has decided to put in Lumsden and 1 Armd Div HQ instead of 7 Armd Div HQ, who are getting a bit worn, though full of fight and vigour still. Thank you for sending up Lumsden and Lloyd [?]. Lumsden knows about Briggs coming up and is going back to Cairo today.

---

60   The Valentine Tank had armour up to 65 mm thick and a cross country speed of 8 mph. It carried a 2 pdr gun.

61   Major General Herbert Lumsden, commanding 1st Armoured Division.

6. Thank you for writing to Alan Cunningham.

7. I enclose a telegram for the P.M. and one for Smuts. I think your communique was admirable in view of the very difficult circumstances.

8. I saw Freyberg again yesterday at SIDI OMAR, where I went by car. He is all right and full of fight. I am hoping that his losses may prove less severe than first anticipated, but they are heavy I am afraid. Practically all the divisional medical equipment is lost, and will have to be replaced somehow. Maybe we will get some from the Bosche before long. The 5 N Z Inf Bde at MENASTIR is doing well and put it properly across a Bosche column yesterday, I am delighted to hear. Forty more Bosche dead! The N Z Div is moving back to BAGUSH (less 5 Inf Bde).

9. It is clear that Rommel is concentrating his forces between EL ADEM – SIDI REZEGH – ZAAFRAN between the two escarpments, both of which are strongly held and form good positions against tank attack. He can move along this corridor and come out either EAST or WEST. At same time he seems to be reopening a repair and, possibly, a supply area NORTH WEST of GAMBUT. Yesterday he pushed mixed columns, including tanks, towards SIDI AZEIZ and MENASTIR, but was roughly handled by our "Jock" columns and went back apparently.

My own opinion is that he may think we have shot our bolt. He has hammered the South Africans and hammered the New Zealanders, and cannot think we have much left. He may underestimate our tank strength (160 cruisers and M.3s this morning) as we have not done much for two days. If he does think this, I think he will go for BARDIA – CAPUZZO – SIDI OMAR with a view to joining up with the Germans in HALFAYA and establishing himself on the flank of the l of c of our main concentration at GABR SALEH. He may think that by doing this he can cause us to withdraw hurriedly to SIDI BARRANI – Railhead or administer the coup de grace. He can then turn and finish TOBRUK at his leisure. Against this is the fact that he must have suffered very heavily indeed – especially the German troops and Freyberg says they destroyed quantities of their equipment in the SIDI REZEGH battles. Also he can not have a great number of running tanks.

The R.E. (Kisch) have destroyed a total of 64 enemy tanks to date, and this excludes any round EL GUBI or SIDI REZEGH, where we know he had casualties. However, I still think he may have a crack at it as it must look most tempting to him IF he thinks we are down and out as he may well do. If he does this it should suit us very well, and I do not think he will get very far. At the moment, 2 S A Div is taking over from 4 Ind Div in the SIDI OMAR – CAPUZZO – SOLLUM area. Only one S A Bde (less one bn) has got up so far and the delay in getting the second Bde of this div is causing Neil (and me) a little anxiety, as it is most important that 5 Ind Bde should be released at once to join the remainder of the 4 Ind Div under 30 Corps at GABR SALEH. 7 Ind Bde was moving from SIDI OMAR yesterday while I was there.

Neil is withdrawing 5 N Z Bde from MENASTIR – BARDIA to CAPUZZO – SOLLUM, partly because, though it was in strong positions, he felt it was rather exposed and might be a nuisance if it had to divert troops to its support, and also in order to release 5 Ind Bde in view of late arrival of second Bde of 2 S A Div in that area.

His idea is to hold the CAPUZZO – SOLLUM – SIDI OMAR with 2 S A Div having its own two Bdes and 5 N Z Bde plus two sqns of "I" tanks. This div will organise as many "Jock" columns as possible with the view to maintaining control of country to NORTH and NORTH WEST. This strong pivot will remove anxiety as to security of L of C and NORTH flank of 30 Corps. If the enemy tries any nonsense in that direction, he should get a bloody nose. I sincerely hope he will.

Meanwhile 30 Corps is concentrating round GABR SALEH – 7 Armd Div, 22 Gds Bde (plus Worcesters from JALO), 4 Ind Div, 1 S A Inf Bde which is to be used in static role guarding concentration area and landing grounds, F.S.Ds [Fixed Static Defences?] etc., and to form "Jock" columns using all its armoured cars and some of its artillery. The Bde is not really sufficiently trained to undertake mobile operations as a formation on its present unwieldly organisation. It was a liability rather than an asset in the recent fighting. As you know, we are changing the organisation and it will rapidly find its feet in this "Jock" column fighting. It is full of guts and only needs to learn the job.

Our mixed columns on the whole front MENASTIR – EL GUBI are very offensive and will, I am sure, give the enemy no rest until we can have at him again.

10.   Tank futures: Within next few days we should have:-

Complete Armd Bde (4th) of Americans
"   Armd Regt (22 Bde) of A.13[62] and A.15[63]
1 ½ sqn of Valentines already in hand to be made up to complete regt.
1 complete regt Matildas[64] exclusive those in TOBRUK.

Not so dusty!?

11.   TOBRUK is in great form and worrying the enemy's rear.
      I feel we are a little short perhaps of good infantry on the ground
to confirm and exploit success, but I think we can make do.

12.   Last night air force fairly got into the enemy vehicle concentrations round SIDI REZEGH. The Abbacores came along, dropped
flares, found such wonderful targets that they went back on their
own and got more bombs! Great stuff! This morning they are at
it again, bombing and low flying attacks at SIDI REZEGH and
along the coastal area NORTH of the road BARDIA – TOBRUK.
They have just intercepted an enemy bomber attack on 1 S A Bde
and destroyed six Stukas and damaged six more. They really are
magnificent.

13.   I am staying on here for a bit. Its d—d cold but most refreshing
after Cairo.

14.   I enclose a note from Freyberg on the lessons of his battles. I think
they should go out at once – properly edited of course. Give my
love (or my respectful greetings) to the Minister.[65]

15.   Telegram for P.M. enclosed

It's a great life if you don't weaken!

JRL, AUC 516

---

62 The A 13 Cruiser Tank had a maximum of 30 mm of armour and a cross country
    speed of 12 mph. It was armed with a 2 pdr gun.
63 The A 15 Tank, more commonly known as the Crusader had a maximum of
    49 mm of armour and a cross country speed of 12 mph. It was armed with a 2
    pdr gun.
64 The Matilda Tank was comparatively heavily armoured, with up to 78 mm of
    armour. However, its slow speed of 6 mph cross country and 2-pdr gun soon saw
    it outclassed in the Western Desert campaigns.
65 Oliver Lyttleton, Minister of State and Member of the War Cabinet, resident in
    Cairo.

112

Letter from Lieutenant General Arthur Smith, CGS, Middle East, to Auchinleck, 4 December 1941

I have just come back from an extraordinarily awkward interview with Alan Cunningham. I think it best to record it at once.

Alan opened by saying "You know, I am not going to take this lying down. It may mean the end of my career but I don't care".

Thinking he might be going to tell me fully of his intentions I at once reminded him that I should have to report our conversation to yourself, but he replied that he had no objection.

He then added that he considered, after due reflection, that he had been very badly treated. He had never been given an adequate reason for his removal, except the state of his mind – "but I ought to know the state of my mind better than anyone". He was emphatic that he was not ill, and stated that he had discussed the matter with the doctors who he was sure in their heart of hearts knew he was not ill. He said that Small (I think he is the specialist) obviously realized he was not ill, but he had backed up the junior MOs and would not let them down after they had said he was ill.

He complained (perhaps that is too strong a word) that you had never given him an inkling that you doubted his ability to carry on efficiently in command when you were at Adv HQ 8 Army. He had shown the amber light, and in view of the subsequent events of the battle he had obviously been right. He had realized the importance of relieving Tobruk, but had urged the danger to his L of C etc.

He asked me strongly to represent the impossible position he was in while this secrecy about the change of command lasted. He asked the reason, and I explained it. He asked when the secrecy ban would be lifted, and I said that you would ask the PM to lift it at the earliest possible moment that you felt safe in the public interest. He asked the terms of the announcement and I told him that the PM had telegraphed to say he would consult you first. I added that in view of the difficulty of secrecy once he reached the War Office, I hope it would be soon be made public. He asked that the date of the change should be announced.

He remarked on more than once occasion that he was only too willing to play as regards a secrecy and anything in the "public interest" but from other remarks it is clear that he is going to appeal for the case to be investigated, presumably to the Army Council.

He also said that examination by a doctor was thrust upon him and had he refused to go to hospital he would never have been classified as sick. He went voluntarily at your request, but obviously feels that a medical overhaul was not part of the bargain.

So much for our talk.

Now my reactions. I suggest the first thing is to convince him that your decision was right. On this point (I forgot to mention it before) I told him that I myself could see he was suffering from strain, and that in my opinion there was ample reason for you to have had lack of confidence in his being able to carry out efficiently the duties of an Army Commander. He agreed that if you lacked confidence in him, you were right to remove him "but it was done in the wrong way".

I know you want no outside support to prove you were right, for the sole responsibility rests with you. On the other hand if Alan is not convinced, then he will talk and it must do harm. Therefore would it be wise to tell him that your misapprehensions were shared by five officers of the rank of Brigadier and upwards Conyngham,[66] Sandy,[67] Neil [Ritchie], Nares and myself – without mentioning names? Also John Shearer – six.

Next point is the announcement. Is it time to fix up with the PM the exact wording? I enclose your suggestion and the PM's. Also I remind you of your statement to the CIGS, for I feel it is important that the PM does not say anything contrary to this, of which Alan is aware.

I am sorry you should be bothered about all this just now, specially as I KNOW your decision was right.

P.S.   I am sending your letters & enclosures to CIGS about Alan back with him (by his hand) in flying boat today.

JRL, AUC 518

---

66   Air Vice Marshal Arthur 'Mary' Coningham, commanding Desert Air Force.
67   Brigadier Alexander Galloway, BGS, 8th Army, 1941–42.

113

Letter from Auchinleck to Lieutenant General Arthur Smith, CGS, Middle East, 5 December 1941

Your letter hasn't arrived yet, so I am starting this in anticipation.

I enclose draft telegram for P.M. which gives situation as known to me here, so I will not repeat in here. If you want to, you can use the telegram at your evening conference. You will have heard most of it from Sitreps already.

I do not to look too hopefully into the future, as you know, but there are signs that he is at least feeling the effect of our continual hammering, and as if our sudden and vigorous renewal of the offensive on the whole front from BARDIA to EL ADEM and beyond to ACROMA may have come as a bit of a shock to him. Anyway, his thrusts towards CAPUZZO seem to have been half-hearted and to have petered out under the attacks of our "Jock" columns. Of course they may never have been meant for anything more than feints. In any event, they represented energy and oil expended and he can't afford to waste these.

The fact that our columns were yesterday within a few miles of EL ADEM and SIDI REZEGH and shelling enemy on the roads to the NORTH is first-class news and must have made him think a lot. The 4 Ind Div (11 Ind Inf Bde) and the 4 Armd Bde seem to have done a first-class job with the remainds of ARIETE at BIR EL GUBI – a good bag. TOBRUK's repulse of the attack on the salient is great news too, particularly as they claim heavy enemy casualties – which are I hope mainly German. (Don't be too optimistic!) It looks as if Rommel <u>may</u> after all have thought we were down and out and incapable of further offensive action.

These "Jock" columns of which more and more are being organised are just what we want, they piquet his movements and give him no rest, and are I hope, giving us command of that enormous no man's land in the quadrilateral GAMBUT – BARDIA – OMAR – REZEGH. They seem to suit our peculiar genius for fighting, and are certainly going at the enemy with the greatest relish and vigour. I can quite understand why they suit our chaps. No red tabs! No written orders!! No ruddy principles of war!!! (Except hit and have after him). No generals!!!! (Except pretty far back). Of course they need close and careful co-ordination if the best is to be got out of them, and this means very good W/T communication.

This is all being organised and is, I hope, going well. If and when we really get the enemy on the run (Don't be too optimistic!) they will be invaluable biting him on his flanks and rear and cutting in in front of him. Some armoured cars, a few guns (field and A/Tk) and some lorried infantry. I think the Hun finds them somewhat unorthodox.

Neil [Ritchie] flew up to 30 Corps at 8 o'clock this morning, and is, I know, ready to take immediate advantage of any change in the situation in our favour. The JALO column still had not got its petrol yesterday – no one's fault, apparently, but the going is atrocious. I hope they get it today and get a move on. Neil does NOT want this drawn attention to just now. As you know he has other plans in hand for BENGHAZI.

I felt yesterday, for the first time since the end of the first abortive armoured battle, that the situation was really in hand. We know now more or less where we are, and have a very definitive offensive plan. Moreover, our reconnaissance and protective arrangements are, I feel, on a sound basis and should enable us to keep a proper tab on enemy movement.

As I said in my telegram to the Prime Minister, I am pretty sure Rommel will use the last of his armour in an attempt to throw us off our balance. He tried before, you remember, and very nearly succeeded. If he tries again he will find us very much on our toes I think, and not up against the ropes. Neil is very wisely keeping the bulk of our armour centrally placed ready to counter-attack NORTH, N.W., or N.E.. It is not being tied to the infantry.

I am very glad that the 4th Indian Div is now leading the offensive. Everyone seems to think that they are a most competent crowd, and yesterday's show seems to go to prove this.

I enclose a personal telegram to the Dominions which states the situation fairly, I think.

P.S.   You may expect me when you see me! Meanwhile, I am sure you are coping with the various Committees!

I sent you a wire about the Free French brigade. The sooner they can come up the better.

JRL, AUC 520

114

Cipher message from Auchinleck, at Advanced HQ, Eighth Army to Winston Churchill, 6 December 1941

1 (.) Most grateful for your 141 (141) 4/12 received here afternoon 5/12 (.) Am deeply touched and much encouraged by your continued confidence and unfailing support (.) I feel situation is well in hand and better than it has been for many days (.) We have always had strategical initiative and are now in fair way to regain permanently tactical initiative which we lost temporarily at SIDI REZEGH (.)

2 (.) Have discussed thoroughly with Gen RITCHIE question of further reinforcements (.) Am very grateful for your offer to get Australian Government to allow their troops to go to CYPRUS in relief 5 (5) Ind Div and for placing whole of 50 (50) Div unreservedly at my disposal (.)

3 (.) Reinforcement situation is as follows (.) One fresh Armd car regiment arrives at front today from SYRIA and second belonging 1st Armd Div expected in a few days (.) These should more than restore losses suffered in fighting so far and maintain our already great preponderance in this weapon (.)

4 (.) 150 (150) Infantry Bde and 50 (50) Divisional Recce Bn already concentrated at BAGUSH and at Gen RITCHIE's entire disposal (.) Nearly formed 138 (138) Ind Inf Bde at MATRUH also at Gen RITCHIE's disposal (.)

5 (.) NOT (R) NOT possible at the moment to maintain more infantry forward of railhead but this will change when TOBRUK is opened as advanced supply base (.) Stocking of TOBRUK by sea in progress now (.)

6 (.) Details regarding 1st Armd Div were sent in my SUSAN [cipher message] 1636 (1636) (.)

7 (.) Have arranged for Free French Bde from SYRIA to concentrate EGYPT soon as possible with view to being used in CYRENAICA (.)

8 (.) New Zealand Div less one inf Bde group in forward area is reforming at BAGUSH (.)

9 (.) 2 S A Div which is NOT (R) NOT fully mobile yet has relieved 4 Ind Div in area CAPUZZO SIDI OMAR thus releasing latter for offensive action further WEST (.)

10 (.) 22 Gds Bde is being strengthened by Worcester Regt brought up from SIWA (.)

11 (.) Am making available other odd units from CYPRUS and EGYPT to take over duties on lines of communication thus relieving mobile units for forward area (.) Am also trying to get Egyptian Army to take over protection of eastern portion of our lines of communication (.)

12 (.) Arrival of 18th Div will materially ease situation and give me something in GHQ reserve which I lack at present (.)

13 (.) 50 Div less the Bde and recce unit at BAGUSH is already in IRAQ and if brought back is unlikely to reach EGYPT much before 18th Div (.)

14 (.) As you realise maintenance capacity our lines of communication governs absolutely number of troops which can be employed forward but apart from this I am satisfied and Gen RITCHIE agrees that number of troops at his disposal should suffice for the achievement of the object which as always is the destruction of the German forces and then ACROBAT (.)

15 (.) Plans are laid ahead but would rather NOT (R) NOT discuss them on paper (.) I do not think therefore we need bring 50 (50) Div back from IRAQ or send Australians to CYPRUS particularly as I am most anxious NOT (R) NOT to retard defence work now in progress in SYRIA (.) If Germans are foiled or delayed in attempt to reach CAUCASUS they may be more likely to try ANATOLIA (.)

16 (.) Please do NOT (R) NOT think I am rejecting your advice or that I fail to appreciate your offers to help (.) Nothing could be further from my thoughts and I am most grateful for everything.

JRL, AUC 522

115

Letter from Auchinleck to Lieutenant General Arthur Smith, CGS, Middle East, 6 December 1941

I am afraid my letters and telegrams of yesterday only got off this morning which is a nuisance.

2. I enclose two telegrams for Prime Minister which please check and edit in light of later information if necessary. The reinforcement telegram may require amendment as I wrote it from memory, but the sense should not be altered. I shall be glad to know if you agree with it. I enclose also a telegram for Alan Brooke which I will be grateful if you will send for me.

3. I enclose a slip for my new temporary A.D.C. if Noel could give it to him for me and tell him to get the things sent up tomorrow.

4. My telegrams to the P.M. explains I think the battle situation as Neil [Ritchie] and I see it. We diagnosed Rommel's state of mind correctly I think. I believe he did think we had shot our bolt and that he had won the battle. Our renewed activity and our threat to El ADEM has, I feel, caused him to change his mind and take thought for his own future. Neil is very quick to diagnose the changing situations and he and I are very much in step. Having John[68] here as an independent interpreter of Von Rommel's mind helps a lot. I feel very confident that we have the situation very much in hand though he will do all he can to throw us out of step. In fact he is at it now with his armour. If by good luck Gatehouse[69] can give him a real smashing blow to-day and do in his remaining tanks we should have a clear run through. It is all teed up. But I am not hoping for too much and it may take a little time yet. However, the P.M. seems happy. Isn't he grand? A wonderful chap. All well here and everyone fighting like hell. The Air Force is magnificent and our Jock columns have been doing awfully well.

JRL, AUC 523

---

68 Brigadier John Harding.
69 Brigadier Alexander Gatehouse, commanding 4th Armoured Brigade.

116

Cipher message from Winston Churchill to Auchinleck, 7 December 1941

One. Your 1640. Glad indeed to receive all your news which certainly gives me impression we are wearing them down. Do whatever you please about reinforcements. Meanwhile I will not address Australian Government. I am telling DE GAULLE you will use the Free French Brigade which will relieve a somewhat tense situation.

Two. Your SUSAN [cipher message] 1636 puzzled us a good deal especially paragraph 5, but this is now explained. The War Office are replying about defective wireless sets and FORDSON trucks service contend their case is good.

Three. Please give me best estimate possible losses South African and New Zealand troops as if they are very heavy, I ought to send telegrams to their respective Governments.

Four. MOST SECRET for yourself alone. President has now definitely said U.S.A. will regard it as hostile act if Japanese invade SIAM, MALAYA, BURMA or EAST INDIES and he is warning JAPAN this week, probably Wednesday. We and Dutch are conforming. This is an immense relief as I had long dreaded being at war with JAPAN without or before U.S.A. Now I think it is all right.

Five. Also for yourself alone. Russian news continues to be good and a Russian success north of BLACK SEA will react favourably on TURKEY as will a victory in LIBYA. There is a good deal of evidence of rising anti-German feeling in FRENCH NORTH AFRICA resulting from WEYGAND's dismissal. So we may still have hope of GYMNAST which remains all set.

Six. Although General CUNNINGHAM is arriving home almost immediately and there will certainly be much talk behind the scenes I do NOT intend making any announcement until your news is decidedly good. Let me know the moment when you feel the tide has definitely turned. I should find it difficult to make out that he was superseded on health grounds because that was NOT the reason which you gave me in your original telegram which I imparted to Cabinet. I could however when time comes say something like this – begins "General AUCHINLECK proceeded to Battle H.Q. on November 24th and on

26th he decided to relieve General CUNNINGHAM and appointment Major General RITCHIE to command 8th Army in his place. This action was immediately endorsed by Minister of State[70] and by me. General CUNNINGHAM has rendered brilliant service in ABYSSINIA and is also responsible for planning and organisation of present offensive in LIBYA which began with surprise and success and is steadily progressing. He has since been reported by the medical authorities to be suffering from serious over-strain and has been granted sick leave." Ends.

SECRET No. 142 Folio No. 88766 Page 2.

The above seems to me wrong in interests of Army that classical severity of your action, which was greatly admired here, should be marred by explanations which many people knew would NOT square with actual facts.

Seven.   I hope progress of your operations will enable statement to be made some time this week. Let me know your views.

JRL, AUC 527

117

Letter from Auchinleck to Lieutenant General Arthur Smith, CGS, Middle East, 7 December 1941

I enclose a telegram for the Prime Minister which will give you the latest information available here, and my reading of the situation. You may use this for your evening meeting if you like.

As I have so often said, I am very much afraid of being too optimistic, but I do feel this morning as if the turning point may be near. I say "may", as the enemy has shown his wonderful powers of recovery more than once, and he may as well do so again before we finish him off.

As you will see, the news is encouraging. He has apparently withdrawn from the EAST of TOBRUK, except the pockets in the BARDIA – HALFAYA area, and the 2nd S A Div with the 5th New Zealand Brigade, I am told, patrols from TOBRUK, are combing the whole area GAMBUT – SIDI AZEIZ – SIDI REZEGH, and may, I think, pick

---

70   Oliver Lyttleton, Minister of State and Member of the War Cabinet.

up quite a lot one way and another. Once this area is clear, the air force will take the landing grounds in it into use, and the South Africans and New Zealanders will turn their attention to BARDIA, "COVO" and HALFAYA – at least, that is Neil Ritchie's present intention.

As for the southern flank, it remains to be seen what degree of resistance he will put up on the EL ADEM EL GUBI line, or whether he will attempt a desperate counter-stroke against our left or centre. It would be like him to stage a sudden transfer of what tanks he has lefy[71] from SOUTH to NORTH and erupt once more towards SIDI OMAR or GABR SALEH. If he does he will find these excellent "Jock" columns hanging on to his flanks and rear, giving him no rest. He isn't getting any rest and he must be damned tired. The Air Force are giving him a terrible pasting and our artillery is doing grand work.

I am not announcing the relief of TOBRUK yet, though it is possible that the P.M. may use the news. I do not mind if he does. When EL ADEM is securely in our hands then I will admit that TOBRUK is relieved – not before. Anyway, until we do get EL ADEM we can not really make full use of TOBRUK as an advanced base of supply, which it is most urgent that we should be able to do.

The Air Force last night had a most wonderful target and took full advantage of it. It is grand to see Neil [Ritchie] and "Mary"[72] working in the fullest possible accord, thinking out where the targets will be, and what is more wonderful – finding them!

It is great news about the New Zealand wounded having been recovered at SIDI REZEGH. I have no details yet, but we hope there are a lot of them. Neil has all his plans ready for immediate pursuit. In fact, pursuit has already started, not only in the air but on the ground, as our "Jock" columns and armoured cars are working well round behind him to the SOUTH. We must expect some setbacks yet, and may strike a major snag, but we are looking well ahead and I know very well that there will be no relaxation of the pressure while Neil – Conyingham are running this show. Everyone is in grand form – I have never met so few people with livers! I haven't met any!!

I can't come back yet, but I will as soon as I can. Meanwhile I know you are doing fine, as they say in the States!! I am very grateful to you.

Stop Press: Enemy 40 tanks and quantity M.T. on defensive WEST of EL GUBI being shelled by our artillery, on which M.T. or some of it

---

71 'left'.
72 Air Vice Marshal Arthur 'Mary' Coningham, commanding Desert Air Force.

went NORTH. Our Armd Bde standing off ready to go in if opportunity offers. "Jock" columns working round SOUTH flank.

P.P.S.   Just got your letter. By all means mention names British units such as 11th Hussars, Gds Bde, R. Sussex (SIDI OMAR).

2.   Not ready yet to dispense with a Corps HQ. Stop that gossip! Will write again tomorrow.

JRL, AUC 529

118

Letter from Lieutenant General Arthur Smith, CGS, Middle East, to Auchinleck, 8 December 1941

The Egyptian Minister of Defence has agreed to sending an Egyptian Light Car Regiment and one Egyptian Battalion to assist the defence of the L. of C. The Light Car Regiment should be in position to-day and the Egyptian Battalion moves up tomorrow: they are taking on duty between BAGUSH and HAMMAM.

2.   McCandlish[73] will be going back to the War Office in about a week's time. He will, of course, be primarily concerned with the reinforcement problem but he will also take other papers from the various Branches here.

3.   The Singapore cable has been cut from this morning – presumably as a result of the Japanese war – and that means practically all our telegrams to the War Office will now have to go by wireless. This will throw a terrific strain on our wireless, but I think we can cope with it. It does mean, however, that we must make a further effort to reduce the number of cables and their length. There is one cable route via South Africa but it is in rather a wonky condition and not to be relied on. [Annotation: 2000 hrs now mended.]

4.   I have seen Peter Drummond and emphasized that this break in communications once again shows the necessity for an improved air letter service to England.

---

73 Colonel J. E. C. McCandish, Assistant to Deputy Adjutant General.

5.   I forgot when I wrote yesterday to tell you that on the 6th December we despatched 17 "I" tanks to the forward area. We sent up 6 more yesterday.

6.   I enclose a note about Laycock[74] which is the latest information we have.

7.   I have now got the M.T. statement from D.Q.M.G. It wants some studying. I won't say more just now beyond the fact that I fear this Japanese war may interfere with shipping of vehicles from U.S.A. and therefore we must not be too confident that the inflow will be sufficient for our needs.

8.   1700 hrs, and your letter of this morning just received. Sorry that yesterday was rather a disappointment; although we apparently did not get a move on it is obvious that we have maintained pressure and been of considerable nuisance value to the enemy.

9.   I have had at the back of my mind the feeling that somewhere in the armoured corps there is a little lack of drive. This impression was confirmed by a talk I had with Bernard Freyberg. It may be that W.N.[75] has not quite got that Cavalry dash which should be, in my opinion, a characteristic of the R.A.C. But I agree that people like myself sitting comfortably back in G.H.Q. must not criticize, though it is sometimes our painful duty to apply whip and spurs.

10.   I enclose a telegram about the Free French and a note from me on the subject which I wrote before I got your letter. I will see that everything is teed up for the CHAD people to move when the word is given.

11.   No further news of VON RAVENSTEIN,[76] but we believed he was salvaged. Perhaps it would have been better if he had been drowned!

---

74   Lieutenant Colonel Robert Laycock, who was then hiding out in the Libyan Desert following a failed Commando raid against General Erwin Rommel's Headquarters.

75   Lieutenant General Willoughby Norrie, GOC 30 Corps. A strange comment given that Norrie's background was as a Cavalry officer; he had been first commissioned into the 11th (Prince Albert's Own) Hussars and had commanded the 10th Royal Hussars (Prince of Wales's Own), 1931–35 and 1st Cavalry Brigade, 1936–38.

76   Major General Johann von Ravenstein, commander of 21st Panzer Division, captured November 1941.

12. The M[inister] of S[tate][77] would be delighted to stay a night or two up at Advance HQ 8th Army, and will come directly you give the word. He has only one engagement this week, and that is on Thursday afternoon, so if other things are equal he proposes flying up on Friday. But he wants me to make it clear that he will certainly come before if that is more convenient, and will have no difficulty in putting off his engagement. He hopes you will be up forward when he pays his visit, and indeed rather stresses this point. [Annotation: Please cable date as soon as possible.].

13. I have told the A.D.C. to send up sweets and fruit, but apparently tomorrow he is sending up 500 eggs by L[iaison]. O[fficer]. He tells me you like fruit, especially oranges, so I have told him to send up one from me to you for which he – the A.D.C. – will pay.

14. I have had a letter from Chink[78] asking for a copy of any orders that you have been issued with regard to Crusader. I don't want to bother 8th Army, but if there are any operation orders or instructions or conference notes that would be of value for instructional purposes, the sooner we get them to the Staff School the better, so that Chink can make use of them before the present course disperses on 28 Dec.

15. Riddell is just back from SYRIA where he had quite a successful trip. The most important point is the question of the 60-day reserves that we have ordered to be put in the defended localities. After discussion with General Wilson he is convinced that these will lead to a great deal of waste if our instructions are carried out in the manner proposed by 9th Army. Riddell has got another plan with which Jumbo Wilson has agreed, and I will get on to it when I get details.

Has 8 Army sent the LRDG W/t set to CHAD. The F[ree]. F[rench]. will want this before they start.

JRL, AUC 531

---

77 Oliver Lyttleton, Minister of State and Member of the War Cabinet, resident in Cairo.
78 Brigadier Eric Dorman-Smith, who was then Commandant of the Staff College in Haifa.

119

Letter from General Sir Alan Brooke, CIGS, to Auchinleck, 10 December 1941

I am taking this opportunity of despatching you a line by Martel.[79]

It was very kind of you to send that telegram of congratulations, and I very much appreciated receiving it.

I am delighted that your operations are turning out so successfully and I feel certain that you must have had some anxious moments. I consider that at present, more than ever, successes in northern Africa are of primary importance. The more we can clear this northern coast the better from every point of view.

The turn of events in the Far East is bound to have fairly serious repercussions in most theatres and it is at present hard to estimate the full extent of our new commitments. At any rate America's entry into the war is certain to reduce the flow of equipment from that country, and make it harder than ever to complete new armoured formations and replace casualties in A.F.Vs.

I have told Martel to bring back from you your complete situation as regards armoured forces, what your deficiencies are, what your proposals are, and details of any difficulties you may be experiencing. I have also told him to ask you whether you would like to carry out any more exchanges with officers from Home Forces armoured formations or units.

Cunningham is expected home shortly, and I hope that the P.M. will have made the necessary announcement about him to-morrow.

I sent a telegram this morning to stop Pownall,[80] as, with the new situation in the Far East, a change of commander is no longer desirable. I am not certain at present where we may use him. Would he be any use to you to replace Jumbo Wilson if the latter is beginning to be a bit old? Or for any other purpose? Such as chief of your C.G.S. if necessary.

I do not like very much the present boundary between your Command and the Indian Command. In the event of a German advance through Turkey and the Caucasus it would mean divided control of the force opposed to the Germans. From my study of the problem up to date, I am inclined to think that your Command should extend to include Iraq and Western Persia. From an administrative point of view this sub-division

---

79 Lieutenant General Giffard Martel, Commander of the Royal Armoured Corps.
80 Lieutenant General Sir Henry Pownall.

certainly seems the best. What are your feelings about it, will your hands be too full? We should of course, visualise the possibility of operations in Tripoli being satisfactorily completed and a defensive front established. I should very much like to know what your feelings are on this point, as I believe you consider you might be over-loaded. On the other hand, Archie Wavell had the Western Desert, Abyssinia, and Greek fronts all at the same time; this may have been too much.

I sent you a wire as regards your private telegrams to the Prime Minister. It is, of course, very desirable that you should send private telegrams direct to the Prime Minister in reply to his and to keep him informed as to the general course of events, yet I do not think that this should in any way affect the normal channel which should exist between you and the War Office. The extensive use of private telegrams has caused confusion here at times owing to important messages never reaching either D.M.O., D.M.I., or myself. In addition, the flow of Military information and instructions connected with the use of reserves, etc. direct between you and the P.M. is apt to make my position difficult at times.

I therefore hope that whilst maintaining the necessary flow of information by direct messages to the P.M., you will ensure that such a procedure does not affect the normal channel of communication to me which should exist between us.

12.12.41.

Since writing above. Events have been moving and we have drafted another wire coming from P.M. with reference to withdrawal of 18th Bde for India. Also suggesting relief of Arthur Smith[81] by Pownall if you thought fit. There is still however just a possibility that Pownall might be required to go on to the Far East.

JRL, AUC 539

---

81 Lieutenant General Arthur Smith, CGS, Middle East.

120

Cipher message from Auchinleck to General Sir Alan Brooke, 10 December 1941

1 (.) Am most anxious to meet your wishes (.) Only difficulty is that Prime Minister sends me PRIVATE telegrams dealing with operations and presumably my replies should also be PRIVATE (.) Would it be possible for you to ask Prime Minister to allow me (a) either to address telegrams dealing with operations private to him repeated C.I.G.S. or (b) personal to him so that you at once get a copy (.)

2 (.) Meanwhile have tentatively adopted procedure suggested in your para three (.)

3 (.) You realise I am sure that my telegrams to Prime Minister are nearly always advanced copies of our sitreps but not detailed and differently worded (.)

4 (.) Reference your para four I hope that you have had all information in one form or another but if you are doubtful I can send you a personal telegram daily (.) Have so far refrained from this owing to enormous volume of traffic already existing.

JRL, AUC 540

121

Special Order of the Day by Auchinleck, 10 December 1941

To: Lieut.-General N.M. RITCHIE, C.B.E., D.S.O., M.C.
Commanding Eighth Army, M.E.F.

After ten days at your Advanced Headquarters, where I have been able closely to follow progress of operations directed by you, I wish to tell you how greatly impressed I am by the skill and vigour with which they have been conducted, and by the great success achieved by them. Such success would never have been achieved without the whole-hearted and unceasing co-operation of our Air Force, whose work has been magnificent throughout.

During this period the enemy has been out-manoeuvred and out-fought at all points, and has been driven back over sixty miles and forced to abandon the siege of TOBRUK.

I cannot tell you how much I admire the way in which your subordinate commanders, Lieut.-Generals NORRIE and GODWIN AUSTEN, commanding 30th and 13th Corps, and Major-General SCOBIE, commanding the TOBRUK garrison, have carried out your orders and maintained a relentless pressure on the enemy. As for the officers and men under these Commanders, whether British, New Zealand, Indian, South African, Australian, Polish or Czech, no praise can be too high for their splendid spirit and unshaken determination to win in the face of danger, hardship and more than one setback. They have shown that when it comes to sticking it they can outlast the Germans every time.

The enemy is not yet destroyed, and must be given no rest. I leave this task to you with the greatest confidence.

Good luck to the Eighth Army and all in it.

JRL, AUC 541

122

Cipher message from Auchinleck to General Sir Alan Brooke, 11 December 1941

You will have had papers connected with change of command 8th Army. The reason I gave CUNNINGHAM, namely, loss of confidence in him, is of course adequate and I did not enlarge on this because I wished to spare his feelings as much as possible.

Think you should know, however, that before making decision I made sure my conviction that he was taking counsel of his fears was shared by TEDDER and CONYNGHAM AOC Western Desert as well as by ARTHUR SMITH and others competent to observe.

Instead of concentrating on the prosecution of the offensive and nothing else he allowed himself to be distracted and perturbed by enemy threats against his rear areas, and lines of communication, and displayed considerable anxiety as to development of battle in light of these enemy activities. Am absolutely sure my decision was right and taken only just in time, but as CUNNINGHAM apparently intends to appeal to Army Council I send you this fuller information. Sorry to have landed you with this.

JRL, AUC 542

123

Letter from Auchinleck to Air Chief Marshal Sir Charles Portal, CAS, 11 December 1941

Your letter of the 25th November reached me yesterday. I am sorry we have not yet put paid to Rommel's account, but we are getting on with it and I think that at last we have him rattled. But he is a tough customer and full of resource. I feel we are tougher and can beat him at his own game.

I am glad to think that I was of some help to you last month when Tedder's fate was in the balance. As you say, it would have been a dreadful mistake. I am quite sure about that.

You ask me for my advice as to whether a change should be made after the battle. From my own point of view I can tell you at once that I should be very sorry indeed to see Tedder go. He has been absolutely splendid in this show, full of resolution and courage, and most helpful with suggestions. The co-operation has, I think, been almost perfect. Anyway, the Army thinks it has been wonderful and so do I.

In a very difficult moment when we had our first setback and I had to make a change in the Army Command, he was a real help in time of trouble, and it was largely due to his courageous outlook and complete straightforwardness that I was able to make the decision I did, which I am absolutely certain was the right one. I owe him a deep debt of gratitude for that.

As I say, I shall be most distressed if he does go, and I am left, and for my own selfish reasons I hope he will not. Also for the good of the Army I hope he will be left here. He knows the whole immense problem backwards, and that is saying a lot.

If it is necessary to change him for the reasons you mention, which are really beyond my ken, then it can't be helped I suppose.

I know Peirse quite well and I like him. We were at the I.D.C. together with Sholto Douglas,[82] and I am sure we could work together if it should be necessary to change Tedder. I feel that with the prospect of the war spreading to Anatolia and Syria and Iraq in the New Year, it would be a mistake to move a commander who has such a unique knowledge of the factors involved.

JRL, AUC 544

124

Letter from Lieutenant General N. M. Ritchie to Auchinleck, 11 December 1941

1.   We have arrived at the usual phase in the evening after dinner when we are waiting for situation reports to come in, when we lack information and are as usual anxious as to what the results of the day have really been. You will know what it means. On the whole I would say that today has been good but I have the feeling that the enemy's withdrawal is not over disorganized and that he succeeded in getting out a good deal; certainly more that I had hoped he might be able to do.

2.   EXPLOITATION WESTWARDS FROM TOBRUK AND THE SOUTH.

As I think you realised before leaving here today, the movement of the 30 corps round the South flank was developing well. It got on rapidly until the early afternoon, since when it has met with considerable opposition about 10 miles South of GAZALA. But despite this, Willoughby reports that they are getting on, have had good targets, have captured 12 guns at least and some 350 prisoners up to date. They have been up against, so far as I can make out, a mixture of German armour, some of ARIETE and some of TRIESTE as well. In addition there have been identifications of Brescia and Trento which to me implies either a considerable mix-up on the part of the Italian formations or possibly that all

---

82   Air Marshal (William) Sholto Douglas was then AOC in C, Fighter Command, UK. He was to replace Tedder as AOC in C, Middle East in December 1942.

formations left behind strong rear-parties, which are now somewhat mixed together. By noon TOBRUK had sallied forth and occupied ACROMA. Godwin[83] tells me that there was not a great deal of opposition nor does he think that a great many prisoners were taken. On the other hand, he believes that the Poles killed everything that they saw, which is a fact that may account for the lack of prisoners!! At 1600 hrs today 4 Ind Div came under command of 13 Corps who had orders from me then to push on, as hard as they could, astride the TOBRUK – GAZALA road and to the South of the escarpment at that place. My hope is that I might be able to mask GAZALA if serious opposition there is met and cut round in the first instance to TMIMI. So far as I have heard this is proceeding fairly well but there are signs that the enemy intend to dispute our occupation of GAZALA. From various sources we gather that much of the Italian fuel oil is stored in this neighbourhood which may give credence to the supposition that they will not give up the place while there is still any chance of evacuating any of it. The two Corps (13 and 30) have now converged and I am, therefore, transferring the command of 7 Armd Div to the 13 Corps and will, as opportunity offers, withdraw the 30 Corps to its new role of sorting up the rearward areas.

3. After much thought and examination of the problem I have come reluctantly to the conclusion that the time to use MARRIOTT[84] on the BENGHASI enterprise is passed. Things are going well in the northern battle, but I find I cannot maintain the impetus there and at the same time provide the necessary transport for MARRIOTT to proceed right across the desert. Furthermore, there are indications I think now, that the enemy has had sufficient time to provide a garrison in the BENGHASI area large enough to prevent a force of MARRIOTT's size being able, effectively, to take the place at the moment. Lastly, such as is left of the enemy's armour may well go round there. I do not feel that we would be justified in undertaking the operation planned for MARRIOTT unless I am reasonably certain that he can actually capture BENGHASI. In these circumstances, I am going to continue to use REID with "E" FORCE, strengthening it as I consider necessary for the role it has in hand. This role will continue the same as at present; to harass

83 Lieutenant General Alfred Godwin-Austen, commanding 13 Corps.
84 Brigadier J. C. O. Marriott, 22nd Guards Brigade.

the enemy's L of C between BENGHASI and AGHEILA. Later, when I see the enemy's future plans and when I have armour to spare, I hope to undertake a similar operation across the desert, starting from HACHEIM and moving via good going on the route EL AGENASC Z67 at DARAER BU IUEIGH Y87, ANTELAT X47. Meanwhile, I am going on hampering the enemy in the North.

4.   We were unfortunate in regard to air operations today for the weather has been much against us and there has been a great deal of enemy activity in the form of single fighters flying about low and attacking targets they may find. Today has been good for them for this, for they have been able to nip in and out of the low clouds with little chance of them themselves getting into trouble. In fact, they have been on the whole, rather impertinent but I doubt whether he will achieve much by this policy which savours very much of the disruptive tactics that he employed against us on the ground in the earlier phases of the battles. As a result of this we lost two Lysanders today at 30 Corps headquarters, both, I believe, shot up and demolished on the ground though in one case the pilot was killed. Both Packard and Bovill, who were the passengers, are safe. As a result of this, the A.O.C. asked me not to fly into TOBRUK today but I should go by road. This I found to be out of the question as it was not possible for me to be absent and out of touch with the Corps for some six hours which must have resulted had I gone by road. In these circumstances, I decided to remain here for today where at any rate I have been in good communication with both Corps.

5.   It is too early, I think, to try and forecast what the enemy is going to do but I think he will first try and hold us at GAZALA to gain time. He may then try and stand with his left flank south of TMIMI or just North of it while he holds his right flank out in the desert either at GADD EL AHAMAR U66 or MECHILI. When kicked or manoeuvred out of this he is likely to go and stand at DERNA.

6.   I leave here 0730 hrs tomorrow morning for TOBRUK to move to my new Headquarters so will not be able to write you tomorrow morning. This will go down by HUTCH or the GHQ Liaison Officer who proceeds to CAIRO tomorrow.

P.S.   Reports during the night confirm enemy holding positions covers GAZALA from the East.

JRL, AUC 545

125

Cipher message from Winston Churchill to Auchinleck, 12 December 1941

1. The great change in world situation during last four days requires a review of our affairs. I must ask you to spare 18th DIV now rounding the CAPE for diversion to BOMBAY. This seems justified by improved prospects of your battle and even more by the very decided RUSSIAN successes which relieve our immediate anxieties in CAUCASUS and South of CASPIAN. It is essential that we help grievous needs strengthening long starved INDIA and enabling a stronger resistance to be made to JAPANESE advance against BURMA and down MALAY PENINSULA. The easement in PERSIA and IRAQ makes you freer to use remainder 50 DIV from BAGHDAD or 5th IND DIV in CYPRUS if you need them. Nothing must of course prejudice CRUSADER and I hope even with this diversion you will be able to pursue ACROBAT and keep GYMNAST in mind dependent on VICHY FRENCH NORTH AFRICAN reaction to a LIBYAN victory.

2. It is proposed that your Command should be extended Eastwards to cover IRAQ and PERSIA thus giving local unity command in the event of TURKS and CAUCASUS danger reviving. The change will only be effected as convenient between you and WAVELL.

3. WAVELL must now look EAST. He will be given command of BURMA front. He will be reinforced by 18th DIV which he can work eastwards to best advantage as he chooses and will keep 17th IND DIV. Four aircraft squadrons now rounding CAPE for CAUCASUS will go INDIA. We are also sending WAVELL special hamper antiaircraft and A/tk guns some motor lorries 30cwt which are already en route.

4. JAPANESE war having broken out and AMERICAN and BRITISH battleship strength being so gravely reduced HONGKONG is isolated and must fight to the end. We cannot tell how AMERICA will fare at MANILA observing JAPANESE have battle fleet command these waters. BROOKE-POPHAM's command is therefore reduced to MALAY PENINSULA–SINGAPORE–BORNEO.

5.   POWNALL is with you in CAIRO. We think in view impending extension considered necessary command he may relieve Gen ARTHUR SMITH.[85]

6.   Disclosure of CUNNINGHAM's supercession passed off very well here in fact being submerged b[y] larger events. Please continue refer your (one group corrupt) appreciations which I greatly value. I am so glad things are going desirably in your campaign. Try increasingly to mention names of Regts about which enemy is already informed. It gives so much satisfaction here.

JRL, AUC 549

126

Letter from Lieutenant General N. M. Ritchie to Auchinleck, 13 December 1941

1.   Jock brought your letter with him today, since when I have gone once more most anxiously over the whole problem of John MARRIOTT's force.

2.   Since writing you on the night of the 10th things have, to some extent altered, chiefly I think in respect to the enemy's unenviable condition in CYRENAICA; special sources show this clearly.

3.   No-one realises better than I, unless it is you, that BENGHASI is the key to the whole of the enemy's power to resist. To him it is even more important than TOBRUK is to me. It is well worth taking great risk to capture the port, but such an operation, limited in size as it must be on account of maintenance can I believe only achieve the capture of BENGHASI itself if the enemy's fighting forces are very materially reduced in their fighting value. Since writing on the 10th I have had some chance of appreciating the extent of his losses, for having a look at the main battle fields gives one a pretty fair line on this matter. As a result I believe I can say that he has had a good deal harder knock than I previously thought possible. Yet he is still fighting a strong rear-guard action, and our advance in the past 24 hours has not been considerable. On the other hand,

---

85   Lieutenant General Arthur Smith, CGS, Middle East.

the whole of his remaining formations still retaining any semblance of fighting value are ranged opposite us now. Tonight we are pretty clear that 15 and 21 PANZER, ARIETE and TRIESTE Divisions are all concerned in the rearguard action he is fighting South and S.W. of GAZALA. Whatever he may have behind this is NOT, I believe, worth a great deal.

THIS all points towards making the risk of the BENGHASI enterprise worth the taking.

4. The administration aspect has been reviewed anew and by cutting down the size of the force of two Bns of infantry (REID can provide the third) and adding a squadron of M3 Tanks, I can just, with the additional Reserve M.T. Coy you generously promise, find the requisite lift for the force plus the needs of the R.A.F. The risk will be reasonable provided there is NOT serious interference with the working of TOBRUK harbour due to enemy interference.

But to provide for MARRIOTT's needs I must withdraw the troop carrying M.T. now allotted to 13 Corps, which must inevitably seriously affect the speed of advance on MACHILI – DERNA, and the close following up of the enemy should he withdraw on BENGHASI when MARRIOTT appears there. With various adjustments, calling on the late TOBRUK garrison resources and other economies, I think I may still be able to provide sufficient troop carrying vehicles to suffice for the "JOCK COLUMNS" of 4 Ind Div. In passing I might add that 11 Ind Inf Bde had pretty heavy casualties in personnel and vehicles in the GUBI affair and this formation have not been able to accompany 4 Ind Div in the advance Westwards from TOBRUK.

Everything is being done to get them ready.

5. I will not write at greater length for Jock was present at my conference and has heard the pros and cons at length.

You will not, I know, assume that BENGHASI can readily be captured by MARRIOTT's Force, nor, should it be captured, that he will be capable of holding it against a serious enemy concentration. But I believe, that he can undoubtedly do a lot of damage, materially and certainly mentally, to the enemy. So it is worth the risk and I have decided in view of all the facts to take it on.

6. Today has been disappointing for I feel we should have made more progress to the WEST. Tomorrow first thing I am off to see

GODWIN[86] for more risks MUST be taken in regard to moving wide and getting at the back-side of the enemy.

7. De Villiers[87] has done well and reduced CUVO, which is a great relief. Have not heard details yet, but he reports the capture of much enemy equipment. He says no opposition, which seems strange. The next thing is BARDIA. I believe strong fighting patrols could capture the place by night. I feel the enemy's main effort in the Frontier Area will be HALFAYAH. The Italian Div Comd removed itself from CUVO into HALFAYAH today!

8. We got about 500 prisoners yesterday – half and half Italian and German – in the GAZALA area, today at least 150 more there. East of TOBRUK today we must have got quite 100 excluding CUVO, including 1 German officer, 39 O.Rs and 1 Italian O.R. captured by Army Headquarters. We have the most bloodthirsty looking South African commanding our defence platoon. A combination of his looks, starvation and thirst, and no resistance was offered!

9. The move went pretty well on the whole, except for my staff car which was blown up on a land mine. Car smashed to pieces, but both ANGUS and the driver unscathed, which is a mercy.

JRL, AUC 551

127

Letter from Auchinleck to General Sir Alan Brooke, CIGS, 15 December 1941

As you know, Watson[88] has just left here after spending some time in examining our organisation of command, and enquiring into the size and composition of our staffs, about which he has produced a most valuable report, in my opinion.

While he was here I was able to discuss with him many matters, including the question of the status of the principal General Staff Officer

---

86 Lieutenant General Alfred Godwin-Austen, commanding 13 Corps.
87 Major General Issac de Villers, GOC 2nd South African Division.
88 Major General Daril Watson, Director of Staff Duties, War Office.

on the headquarters of an Army. Watson explained to me why your predecessor had decided against making this into a Major-General's appointment, and I quite appreciate his reasons. All the same, I still think that in the field, at any rate, whatever may be done at home, there is a very strong case for having a M.G.G.S. at the headquarters of an Army, and I am quite sure that, in the case of the 8th Army in Libya, it would have helped a good deal if Galloway had been a Major-General instead of a mere Brigadier!

I know the arguments, I think, and I agree that, in theory, it shouldn't matter whether a man is a major or a major-general, so long as he has the ability and personality to impress his will on those with whom he has to deal. Human nature being what it is, however, and unalterable, I feel that from the practical and human point of view it does matter a great deal.

In the absences of his commander, which nowadays are likely to be frequent and often prolonged, the senior General Staff officer of an Army has a very great responsibility to bear, and very senior commanders and staff officers to deal with. He becomes virtually second-in-command on many occasions. The labourer is worthy of his hire, and there is no doubt at all in my mind that the psychological effect of receiving a step in rank on promotion to such an important post is a very real one, and not to be lightly disregarded.

Many of our best men, being what they are, dislike instinctively these higher staff appointments, and much prefer to be in command of troops. I feel that some recompense is due to them. We are not all idealists!

I trust you will not mind my re-opening this matter, but I feel so strongly about it that I hope you may consent to reconsider it.

JRL, AUC 554

128

Letter from Auchinleck to L. S. Amery, Secretary of State for India, 15 December 1941

Thank you very much for your letter of the 1st November, which reached me on the 10th December.

I am very glad that the supply of cadets to India did not come to an untimely end, as that would have been a catastrophe. We will do all we can to help here, and I have said so officially in reply to an appeal from Wavell on the subject.

Australians and New Zealanders are perfectly all right and get on very well with Indians, generally speaking. So would South Africans, I think, so far as they individually are concerned, but the difficulty comes from India. The Government of India was, and I expect still is, loath to give commissions in the Indian Army to South Africans for very obvious reasons. However, there are not many South Africans to spare, as their military man-power (white) situation is most unsatisfactory.

I still think that the really important problem is how to get more senior and experienced officers to fill the middle-piece post in Indian units. I do not think that there is going to be much difficulty in finding subaltern officers – British or Indian – but they are not enough. I believe some scheme on the lines advocated by me in my letter of 17 September to you should be initiated. I am quite sure that before this war is over, we shall have to accept dilution of British units by Indians on a large scale – at any rate, in Eastern theatres.

The Libyan offensive is going well, but there are and must be pauses; these are inevitable for maintenance reasons. The distances covered in our advance, and the amount of transport needed to maintain our forward troops so far in advance of railhead, are fantastic when measured by pre-war standards. The enemy has fought very well, and is still fighting, but there is accumulative evidence (and it is still coming in) to show that he has had a series of really hard knocks, to which he is unaccustomed and doesn't like at all. We have counted over 7,000 prisoners through Alexandria to date, and there are many still to come from the forward areas. We have also captured a lot of equipment, as yet unlisted.

Prisoners are a nuisance really, as they greatly complicate the maintenance problem. However, we want all the Boxches we can get – the Italians don't matter so much. The troops have been magnificent, and the Air Force really superb. We have plenty of hard fighting still ahead of us, and we are not slackening our efforts in any way.

We are doing all we can to help the Yugo-Slav patriots, and have in fact done quite a lot, in view of the very restricted facilities at our disposal. It is as you say, entirely a matter of transportation, and we simply have not got the aircraft or the submarines to enable us to do anything on a big scale at present, but we are constantly reviewing the matter.

Julian[89] is looking very well and is absorbed in his job. He has decided not to go to the Staff School as he thinks he will be of more use where he is.

---

89 Captain Julian Amery, Leopold's son, then engaged in various special service work in the Eastern Mediterranean.

Quentin Hogg[90] has just taken up a new job with "Jumbo" Wilson, who had specially asked for him.

India is now right in the war zone, and I see that Burma has come under Wavell. I have always thought that this should be, but there was a very great reluctance, even up to months ago, to entrust India with any operational responsibility, as you know. This was, one can only suppose, a result of the Mesopotamian campaigns of 1914–1916.

The result of the Japanese attack on Malaya, and of the threat to Burma, must inevitably be to divert forces from Iraq and my command. This is not a serious matter at the moment, but is causing me some misgivings in relation to what may happen four or five months hence. We are therefore taking very careful stock of our future position.

JRL, AUC 555

129

Letter from Lieutenant General N. M. Ritchie to Auchinleck, 22 December 1941

I did not write yesterday; first because I hoped to get through by telephone, which failed and secondly because we were moving this H.Q. and I had to get up and get down to future plans with Godwin Austen.

2. GENERAL.

The main issue still remains the same, in my opinion to destroy everything of the Germans before they can escape into TRIPOLITANIA. I feel myself that with the forces he has available, he will do all he can today, as it appears to me he did yesterday, to cover the withdrawal Southwards of all he can save from the BENGHAZI area by holding us off on the general line of the escarpment from REGIMA to ANTELAT, X.74. It is extremely difficult, because of the long distances, to maintain communications with the forward troops and on this account I find myself often lacking in knowledge as to what exactly they are doing and where they have got to. I was able, however, yesterday, to get a very

---

90   Major Quentin Hogg, MP. Later to become Lord Chancellor as Lord Hailsham.

clear picture of what happened on the 20th, which clearly shows that the enemy retreat from MECHILI was in great disorder, and that he abandoned much material, much equipment, and that the 7 Armd Div over-ran many prisoners. We cannot be bothered with them just now. In general, therefore, the situation appears to be good so long as the Panzer Group carries out the orders that it has received to cover BENGHAZI and the Fleiderkorp, in which case I have great hopes of destroying the lot. So today seems to be a critical day once more; critical because it will produce either complete destruction of the Germans or will show me that they have succeeded once again in getting out of the box. I pray the latter may not occur again.

3.   GEBEL FRONT.

You will have heard that APOLLONIA and CIRENE were both occupied by us on the night 20/21, and yesterday's TAC/R indicated few enemy between those places and BARCE. So I hope that Frank[91] may have been able to get on a good bit yesterday with his columns. The main body of the Division can move by ferrying only as I have taken every bit of his transport possible to maintain troops for the main issue South of BENGHAZI. Frank Messervy is anxious for the 3/1st to be taken out for a while to reform and retrain and I have, therefore, ordered them to go to the 38th Ind Inf Bde and the 1/1/ Punjabs to replace them in the 5th Ind Brigade. I feel sure you will be glad of this. It is satisfactory that we got back a 100 or so of our wounded prisoners from DERNA. Also it was reported to me yesterday that the grave of NEUMAN, late commander of the 15th Panzer Div, who had been wounded, was discovered near DERNA. So we have captured one of their Panzer Div Commanders and killed the other.

4.   BENGHAZI – AGEDABIA.

The 7 Armd Div have made good progress as you will have seen from the Situation Reports. It is difficult exactly to find out what they have done, but so far as I can estimate, two columns, (CURRY and HUGO) with the 3rd RTR in support may get through the escarpment shortly and on to the BENGHAZI plain. The 12th Lancers operating from MSUS reported last

---

91   Major General Frank Messervy, commanding 4th Indian Division.

night that SCELEIDMA was clear and that they are making for SOLLUCH. This I hope is true, but I am inclined to doubt it from the intercepts we have had. Air recce yesterday showed that BENCOL was progressing well and I dropped on MARRIOTT yesterday afternoon about 3 o'clock, orders that he was to push on with the utmost speed for MAGRUM, from which place practically the whole of the G.A.F. [German Air Force?] are operating. At the same time I gave orders that he is to come under 13 Corps as the whole of this battle-front has now become one entity, and supplies for it will be reached by MECHILI–MSUS line.

5. ADVANCE INTO TRIPOLITANIA.

By tonight, Mary[92] and I will have our plans fixed for this. So far as I am concerned, the intention is to continue with the largest force possible in the circumstances, dictated by maintenance. In the first instance, this will not be much more than large columns operating as hard as one can against the enemy's retreating forces, their flanks and rear. Maintenance, of course, will be a difficulty, but I hope very much that we may be able to keep them going by running small vessels along the coast and add to this by the use of air transport. The next step in the advance will be by the 1 Armd Div, based on one Armd Bde and a motorised Bde (Gds Bde), but this cannot move far Westwards into TRIPOLITANIA until we can arrange supplies for it. On present calculations my "Q" think that this may mean a pause of 10 to 14 days, but I feel they may certainly have to think again!

6. The L.R.D.G. I am going to base on AGEDABIA, from which place they will operate wide Southwards in their minor offensive role that has been so successful up to date. Their operations will, generally speaking, be West of SIRTE and as far as TRIPOLI.

7. S.A. DIVISIONS

I think you might like to hear that BRINK tells me he is quite convinced that the man-power does not permit of maintaining two S.A. Divs in this theatre of war, and I was left with the impression that he feels the force here should be reduced to one. It surprises me somewhat as we have been saying this at G.H.Q., for the last five months!

---

92 Air Vice Marshal Arthur 'Mary' Coningham, commanding Desert Air Force.

8. Everybody is cursing everybody else at the moment, and I am doing so louder than anyone. These very big advances are the devil in respect of maintaining any communications. M.T. has made a withdrawal a great deal easier operation than it was in the past and the advance following up a retreat, a harder task than ever. F.S.R. will have to be revised considerably in regard to this!

JRL, AUC 570

130

Cipher message from Auchinleck to General Sir Alan Brooke, 25 December 1941

1 (.) Have refrained from comment hitherto in view of Gen WAVELL's 21059/G 16/12 to you giving you his views (.) When myself C in C INDIA I always urged that operational responsibility for IRAQ should rest with INDIA (.) RUSSIA and PERSIA had not then come into picture but I have always held that PERSIA too should be under INDIA's operational control as it is so closely connected with the immediate defence of the WESTERN frontiers of that country (.) I have little doubt that were I still C IN C INDIA I would have answered generally as Gen WAVELL has now (.)

2 (.) Although I have previously refused consistently to agree to recommendation that MIDEAST should take over IRAQ and PERSIA I think that with the inclusion of PERSIA in the war zone and the emergence of a definite threat of a German offensive through the CAUCASUS the strategic position has so changed as to make a unified command over the whole front desirable (.) The prospect of there being comparatively strong armoured forces available by next Spring which will be capable of being used in SYRIA IRAQ or PERSIA as circumstances may demand increases the desirability (.)

3 (.) From point of view of operational control there is NO (R) NO doubt that a unified higher command embracing SYRIA IRAQ and PERSIA would make for speedier planning for stronger and quicker direction of campaign in event of German offensive either through ANATOLIA or through CAUCASUS or both simultaneously (.) The fact that the Forces in IRAQ and SYRIA have

divergent lines of operations is inconvenient and if we should have to withdraw this divergence is likely in theory to nullify to some extent the advantages of a unified command whether exercised by INDIA or MIDEAST but I doubt whether this would be true in practice as the higher commander could still influence the campaign as a whole by using his reserves in the intervening area to the benefit of both fronts (.) In any event this disadvantage is outweighed operationally by the advantage likely to accrue from a unified command in the initial stages of the battle (.) Moreover the case for a unified control of the land forces is strengthened by the fact that the air forces in the whole area will and indeed must in any case be under a unified command (.) Operationally unification seems to have no disadvantage other than increasing the load on the higher commander (.)

4 (.) Administratively there could be no question of divorcing administrative from operational control in the theatre of war itself (.) SYRIA IRAQ and PERSIA would have to be completely under the administrative control of the unified command as are all the various fronts of MIDEAST now though the task would be heavy and one entailing a high degree of decentralisation in both fields (.)

5 (.) It seems clear that INDIA could not (R) NOT control SYRIA operationally or administratively unless she also controlled PALESTINE and EGYPT as the connection between the three is too intimate to be severed therefore a unified command could not be exercised by C IN C INDIA (.) On the other hand C IN C MIDEAST could control IRAQ and PERSIA operationally and administratively (.) In these circumstances INDIA while still remaining the main base and source of supply for IRAQ would no longer have a say in the disposal of reinforcements and material once these had reached BASRA (.) No other arrangement would work (.)

6 (.) Am fully aware of feeling in INDIA regarding need for IRAQ and PERSIA being under her control and that this has played no small part in making INDIA so generous with troops and materials for the defence of IRAQ (.) If IRAQ and PERSIA are removed from INDIA's control probability is that she will naturally tend to be less ready to use her resources there instead of devoting them to her own immediate defensive needs (.)

7 (.) Aid to RUSSIA via IRAQ and PERSIA (,) WHEELER Mission (,) and evacuation of POLES would all have to be taken over by MIDEAST but this would not be impossible (.) Divided control in these spheres would NOT (R) NOT be practicable (.) Change in financial control now exercised by INDIA might cause difficulty but presumably this would NOT be insuperable though likely to be most inconvenient (.)

8 (.) I disagree with Gen WAVELL that a temporary ad hoc unification to meet a particular situation would suffice and I am NOT (R) NOT prepared to accept such a proposition which is likely in my opinion to lead to confusion and improvisation when the time comes (.) If it is decided to make the change it should be made at once so that MIDEAST's responsibility for planning and arranging for the future may be clearly defined one way or the other (.) Otherwise uncertainty and delay which are already affecting thought and action will be intensified (.)

9 (.) To sum up (.) First I believe the operational reasons for placing IRAQ and PERSIA under MIDEAST are weighty and urgent (.) Second the difficulty and inconvenience of adjusting the administrative and financial complications caused by a transfer to MIDEAST will be great but NOT insuperable (.) Third the government of INDIA and INDIAN public opinion generally are likely to oppose the change strenuously and the feeling thus created may affect INDIA's willingness to provide troops and material not only for IRAQ and PERSIA (,) but also for the MIDDLE EAST on the same generous scale as heretofore (.)

10 (.) Present uncertainty is harmful and I shall be very grateful for an early decision (.)

11 (.) A telegram on this subject giving reasons for and against is also being sent to WAR CABINET by MIDEAST DEFENCE COMMITTEE.

JRL, AUC 580

131

Letter from Auchinleck to General Sir Alan Brooke, CIGS, 25 December 1941

Thank you very much for your letter of the 10th December which Martel brought with him. I am glad you are pleased with the result of our operations so far and I hope we shall be able to show further results before long. I entirely agree with you about the desirability of clearing as much of the North African coast as we possibly can. In this connection we are sending you by the hand of our delegation a paper expressing our considered opinion on the possible trend of future operations in this theatre. You may not agree with us regarding the possibility of carrying the war into GERMANY from AFRICA, but all three of us and Lyttelton feel that there is a good deal to be said for our proposals, great as the difficulties may seem to be at the moment. The Germans have more than once achieved the seemingly impossible and I, for one, feel that we can do at least as much, if not more, than they have done. I shall be very interested to hear what you think about it at home. I hope our paper will give you all the information you need about our present situation and future needs.

2. I realize very thoroughly that the Far Eastern situation is likely to affect us in this theatre to a considerable extent, and you can rely on us to help to the greatest extent possible. All the same, there is a minimum below which we should not go in view of the likelihood of our being heavily attacked through TURKEY in the Spring. We are even now working to narrow margins, particularly in respect of time for preparation, and equipment and transport for troops destined for the Northern Front. We are now definitely focussing our thoughts and energies on SYRIA and ANATOLIA, though we naturally still have to be able to send you my latest instruction regarding the conduct of the campaign on the Northern Front, and I hope it will meet with your approval. With the Turkish attitude still as uncertain as it is, it is not too easy to make very definite plans, but we are doing what we can.

It will be a great assistance to me and my Staff when we know definitely whether we are to take over IRAQ and PERSIA or not, and I hope it will be possible to let us know soon. As you will have seen from my telegrams to the Prime Minister which passed through you, I feel that from the operational point of view, it is desirable that we should control the whole front, because of the changed situation brought about by RUSSIA's entry into the War and events in PERSIA. On the other hand, the political, sentimental and administrative difficulties are considerable. I can not agree that any ad hoc change of control can be made on the spur of the moment as suggested by Wavell. This would be quite useless in my opinion and most difficult and dangerous to implement.

You will know, I am sure, that I am not out for aggrandisement! In fact I have up to now consistently opposed any proposal to amalgamate the commands, as John Kennedy[93] will tell you. If you decide to put IRAQ and PERSIA into this command, I shall probably have to ask for a second D.C.G.S. to help me to deal with the additional work on the operational side. I hope that you would see your way to agree to this.

The work on the Syrian defensive is going on steadily but not as quickly as I would wish. I am most anxious to get more troops up there to help in the work, and asked INDIA to let me have the 50th Division back, temporarily at any rate. Hutton,[94] in the absence of Wavell, demurred, not on very firm grounds I thought. However, I have returned to the charge. I gather from what I hear from IRAQ that the Division is not doing anything very particular at the moment.

3. Martel has been staying with me and is now on the Libyan front. I shall see him again when he gets back and before he leaves for ENGLAND. I hope he is not trying too hard to make the Royal Armoured Corps into a separate and private army. I admit to feeling a little uneasy about one or two of his ideas. Everything we have learned from our operations in LIBYA goes to show that the association between armoured units, infantry and artillery must be far closer than it has ever been before, and that any attempt at segregation is wrong and most dangerous. I have definitely come to the conclusion, and so has everyone else in a position of responsibility here, that the Armoured Brigade Group as a permanent organization is a necessity and I am not prepared to put armoured troops into battle in any other form. We are working hard at this now and will send you our considered opinion as soon as possible. I feel also that our divisional headquarters must not

---

93 Major General John Kennedy, Director of Military Operations.
94 Lieutenant General Thomas Hutton, Chief of General Staff, India.

be classified as "armoured" or "infantry", but must be prepared to control a collection of brigades of varying composition as the occasion demands. This is even more true of Corps Headquarters; for example our 13th (Infantry) Corps is now controlling the forward armoured formations, while the 30th (Armoured) Corps is controlling the operations for the reduction of BARDIA and HALFAYA. We have abolished the label "armoured" so far as 30th Corps Headquarters is concerned and will not resuscitate it.

4. I hope you are getting all you want in the way of telegraphic information from me. I realize very clearly the awkwardness of the present system, but it was not of my devising, and I can see no way of altering it. I daresay that, awkward as it may be at times, it has certain advantages when one considers the personalities involved. I send the periodical telegrams dealing with the progress of operations to the military heads of the various parts of the Empire which have troops in this Command. There are quite a lot of them! I am told we speak thirty-seven different languages or dialects!!

On all big questions of policy, we try to put matters on a local Defence Committee basis, or else on Cs.-in-C. basis, and this seems to me to be getting more and more necessary and desirable. It does not of course affect direct communication from G.H.Q. to the War Office on matters of purely Army concern, but the three Services out here tend to grow more and more interdependent which is all to the good I think.

5. As to the future, I hope that within the next few days Neil Ritchie will have cleared up the situation round AGEDABIA and AGHEILA one way or another. As you will realize without my having to tell you, his difficulties are 90% administrative. The distances are enormous and it is a physical impossibility to maintain more troops in contact with the enemy than he has at present. We both hope that we may be able to surround the remaining Germans and destroy them or capture them, but our troops are terribly thin on the ground and the German has not by any means thrown up the sponge, though we believe his losses to have been very heavy indeed. It looks at the moment as if Rommel (we think he is still with the remnants of his Panzer-Gruppe) really intends to make a stand at AGEDABIA and force us to attack him there with our relatively weak forces. He is, however, still very nervous of his Southern flank. He has all along, right from the start, been inclined to exaggerate the risk

from our JIALO force, which as you know is very small and devoid of hitting power. He must be getting very little information of our movements, and we think he was unaware of the move of 22nd Armoured Brigade round his Southern flank up to yesterday.

Anyway, whatever happens, plans are laid for the next stage, though I am afraid there is bound to be a pause for maintenance reasons. The problem really is tremendous, but everyone is doing their best to solve it, and we will solve it somehow. The enemy submarines are very active off TOBRUK and have seriously interfered with the supply of M.T. fuel into TOBRUK. This is causing me some anxiety as it is a long haul from railhead to AGEDABIA, and the first part of the journey is cross country, because the enemy hold HALFAYA still, and the wastage in petrol caused by jolting and bumping is very great. We are tightening up our measures for the reduction of BARDIA and HALFAYA, but I do not want to incur a lot of casualties in the process, particularly as the South Africans, who are somewhat casualty minded, are running that part of the show.

I had hoped to get up to the Front on Monday last, but there has been so much to do and think about on the higher strategic level that I could not manage it.

I hope to be able to go up about the 3rd. Neil has done magnificently; no one could have done better, and he started in none too easy circumstances either. "Mary" Coningham, the airman, too has been absolutely first-class.

6. We are now getting back the troops no longer required in the Western Desert as fast as we can. 70th Division are nearly concentrated in the Delta already and the New Zealanders are coming back to KABRIT on the Bitter Lakes to re-equip and start training again. I propose to keep them and the 4th Indian Division (which has been fighting continuously for a year almost) in G.H.Q. Reserve. I hope to fill up the 10th Corps with the 50th Division (if and when I get it!) and the 5th Indian from CYPRUS. I propose to put the 70th into CYPRUS for a spell to rest and train for mobile warfare again after TOBRUK. I would much rather have an "ad hoc" garrison for CYPRUS, but I can not find the troops, particularly the artillery, without breaking up divisions. However, I am going on exploring ways and means. I feel the threat of an attack on CYPRUS is becoming more likely, especially in view of the situation at sea, and I can not afford to take too many risks there. I'd like your opinion on this.

7. I have accepted a Free French Brigade for service in LIBYA and it is now arriving in EGYPT. The problem will be how to maintain it at the front. I feel that having accepted it I must try and give it a show.

8. As to the future of headquarters and commanders, my ideas are as follows. To give Neil Ritchie command of the G.H.Q. Reserve which I hope to form and which will contain one or more armoured divisions and two infantry divisions, plus perhaps an independent brigade group or two. I propose to give him a staff formed from the present 8th Army staff and to use the rest of this staff to fill up the 10th Corps staff which is now only skeleton as you know. I want to leave Godwin Austen with his 13th Corps H.Q. to run LIBYA which he ought to do very well. I must have a good man and a good staff there in case the Bosche tries to stage a come-back. Willoughby Norrie and the 30th Corps H.Q. I propose to keep on ice but to use them very actively as a training team to tour the command, set exercises and help generally. I feel there is plenty of room for this and it would be a pity to break up a team which has been trained under stress of battle. We may easily need another Corps H.Q. in IRAQ or elsewhere before long. I hope you will approve generally of these tentative ideas. General Reserve H.Q. would be of Corps status of course – not "Army".

9. I am anxious to put Holmes[95] back as 10th Corps Commander now that there is a chance of it becoming a "Corps in being" and not merely an Headquarters. He is very keen on this himself and Jumbo[96] would welcome him. I think he is good and takes a long, broad view. I am suggesting that Stone[97] should take his place in EGYPT. He should, I think, be very good at that, both the Egyptians, which is important, and on the Base of L. of C. side of it.

10. I must not write any more or this will never be typed in time! I will try and write more regularly in the future, but I really have not had much time this last month to think of anything else but LIBYA.

JRL, AUC 581

---

95 Lieutenant General William Holmes, GOC British Troops, Egypt, who was, indeed, to take command of 10th Corps in February 1942.
96 General Sir Henry Maitland Wilson, then commanding Ninth Army.
97 Lieutenant General R. G. W. H. Stone, who became GOC British Troops, Egypt, 1 February 1942.

132

Letter from Lieutenant General N. M. Ritchie
to Auchinleck, 25 December 1941

First of all, thank you for several things. Your wire of congratulations about BENGHAZI which we all appreciate very much, then the most welcome present of a bottle of Rum, which arrived safely tonight. It is very kind of you to have thought of this and the Mess will appreciate very much the Turkey and Lettuce. I will pass on your present to "Mary".[98]

I find now that the Liaison Officer departs for the DELTA usually in the middle of the night so in future I will try and dictate my daily letters to you in the evening. The arrangement is not very satisfactory because, as you know, the evening is the worst time for news before people collect themselves for the night and find out what their various elements have done during the previous day.

2. <u>WESTERN CYRENAICA.</u>

This has been to me the worst grievous disappointment, for the 22 Armd Bde, which was to have started last evening with the object of getting round the enemy's flank and rear was prevented from doing this and was still, at noon today, in the same position as yesterday. This is caused by the fact that their patrol echelons got completely bogged in the soft going while on the way to join them yesterday and did not reach them until this morning. It is a terribly bad business for I now feel that once more the enemy will have succeeded in extricating what remains of his Armd forces. A quite miserable business. But one never can be quite certain of these things and possibly the fact the enemy has not appreciated that there is any real threat to his Southern flank may entice him to hold on even long enough yet for us to get him in the bag.

The Gds Bde has continued operating against the enemy's armour today, but I feel that their progress has been somewhat slow. One of their columns, at any rate, with their Sqn of M3 tanks, was 21 miles South-West of ANTELAT at 1100 hrs this morning, on the road to AGEDABIA. The 12th Lancers have been given a wide mission of operating right through to MARADA, securing the road

---

98   Air Vice Marshal Arthur 'Mary' Coningham, commanding Desert Air Force.

centre there and discovering whether or not there is, in fact, any dangerous enemy force based on that place. There has been very little news of REID's movements, but I still hope that some of his force has succeeded in getting round the enemy's flank, for we got an intercept today in the morning in which GAK ordered the 15th PANZER DIV to clear the enemy off the escarpment. This, I feel, must be the escarpment South-West of AGEDABIA, and might possibly be REID's columns in that neighbourhood.

Tac/R and Stret/R this evening both report 5 merchant vessels, estimated at 4,000 tons each (an exaggeration I think), lying of the coast opposite RAZ EL-AALI, which is about 25 miles west of AGHEILA. If this report is correct, it is difficult to imagine what they are unless it is an attempt to provide more fuel oil by throwing it into the sea in order to enable them to get away their M.T., and possibly to operate more actively with their aircraft. Anyhow, MALTA have been asked to take this in hand, as I understand from "Mary"[99] that they have suitable torpedo-carrying aircraft for this purpose, and I have also asked C-in-C MED whether Naval action can be taken there too.

On the whole my information from this area today has been meagre.

There are undoubtedly indications from air reconnaissance that the enemy from the AGEDABIA area is making a move Westwards but so far this move has not been on any particularly large scale, as far as I can see.

3. GEBEL AREA.

TOCRA is reported clear of enemy today and the 4th Ind Div are pressing on with the object of taking over from the 7th Armd Div in BENINA and BENGHAZI. They found a considerable amount of abandoned M.T., in the BARCE area, 3 M.13 Italian tanks and some German light tanks. They are continuing mopping up operations in the GAZALA area.

4. BENGHAZI.

A first preliminary report has reached me about the harbour there. The north and centre Moles appear to be out of action for the moment. The former has been blown in many places and the latter is

---

99   Air Vice Marshal Arthur 'Mary' Coningham, commanding Desert Air Force.

blocked with a sunken ship alongside. The Southern Mole appears apparently intact, though the bridge between it and BENGHAZI itself has been destroyed. It is reported, however, that there are available at BENGHAZI, pontoons which should assist materially in rapidly bridging this gap.

5. I visited TOBRUK again today and find a decided improvement there since last I saw it over a week ago. There is still a lot to be done, but the Port is now able to deal with up to 900 tons a day, and by today week should be able to handle 1400 tons. The petrol situation, however, causes me considerable anxiety, as a petrol ship turned turtle yesterday. We can however, to some extent, bridge this gap by the use of road transport from R[ail].H[ead]., where our resources of P.O.L. [Petrol, Oil and Lubricants?] are reasonably satisfactory. But this is a very expensive matter of our slender M.T. resources. The hospital situation is far better. An Indian C.C.S. is established and working and we have been able to evacuate a large number of cases from the General Hospital there, which has much eased the situation. Recovery and salvage is going apace and on the whole is working quite well.

6. POLISH BRIGADE.

I visited the Polish Brigade today and thought theirs a good show. They have really done very well and, I am glad to say, have only suffered a little over 100 casualties. During the course of their operations they captured something in the region of 1,800 prisoners. KOPANSKI spoke to me about their future and feels that in view of the expected arrival of reinforcements from RUSSIA which would be available to complete a division, that it might be better for the Brigade Group to return to the DELTA Area in order to prepare for the reception and training of the reinforcements when they do get here. Personally, I do not see any urgent reason for keeping him here and I think it was your intention to get this Brigade into G.H.Q. reserve.

7. GENERAL.

From all we hear it seems that maintenance is still a very serious matter with the AXIS forces opposing us and this is chiefly due to fuel for aircraft and M.T. I still hope that this lack of fuel may yet delay the German armoured forces sufficiently for us to deal them a smashing blow, but this possibility, I fear, does not look half so good as it did 24 hours ago, when I thought the 22 Armd Bde would be well on the way to outflanking the enemy in the AGEDABIA neighbourhood.

JRL, AUC 583

133

Cipher message from Winston Churchill to Auchinleck, 27 December 1941

My heartiest congratulations to you RITCHIE and the Army and Air Force of the Nile on re-entry of BENGHAZI and on great victory won by so much hard fighting and skill chiefly now manifesting itself in CYRENAICA.

I have a hard request to make to you. We concentrated everything on your battle with results that we are now desperately short in new theatre which Japanese attack has opened. I think without compromising ACROBAT you should be able to spare at once for MALAYA and SINGAPORE:

(a)   A force of American tanks even if its full strength only amounted to 100.

(b)   Apart from Blenheims etc. already on way 4 squadrons of Hurricanes are needed urgently in SINGAPORE. Our ability to bring further reinforcements depends on our getting a sufficient air force there in good time to protect sea approaches. At present our old-quality aircraft are knocked about by Japanese sea-borne (fighters). Only air power at SINGAPORE and JOHORE can keep door open and if door is shut fortress will fall and this would take the bloom off our Libyan successes.

We are examining sending INDOMITABLE to pick up these 4 squadrons at KILINDINI by which means they could be flown off her deck to SINGAPORE before end of January. Pray ask Air Marshal TEDDER from me to study this most earnestly.

It has occurred to me that you might send some of your damaged tanks to INDIA for repair, thus relieving your workshops which must be congested and could not in any case cure these tanks for some months.

(In INDIA?) however when repaired they will form training nucleus for armoured units we are forming. Please explore this idea with General WAVELL.

JRL, AUC 591

134

Letter from Auchinleck to General Sir Alan Brooke, CIGS, 15 January 1942

1. I have just had your wire in answer to the one I sent you trying to explain why I want a Major-General for D.M.T., instead of a Major-General A.F.V.! You will have had by now my long letter, in which I give you, for what they are worth, my views on the future of the Royal Armoured Corps in general, and in this theatre of war in particular. I do not think I have anything to add to them, and I do hope I have convinced you of their soundness. The fact that they are supported by all my senior commanders and staff officers out here should, I think, count for something.

    We are very near realities here, and while I may not have had a tremendous amount of experience, those whom I have consulted have. Even I can claim to have been studying and considering these matters deeply and continuously, even before the war, and in a good many different sets of circumstances.

2. To put it briefly, I want a Major-General as D.M.T who will have as his main job the training of the three arms to work together in the closest possible association. It will be his chief concern to see that the infantry and the artillery, and especially their commanders, are trained to work with the R.A.C., so as to enable the latter to function to the best possible advantage. It will be his job to tie the infantry and gunners to the R.A.C., and not the converse. Equally he will have to teach the R.A.C. how to get the best value out of their equipment when properly supported by the infantry and artillery.

    He would have under him a Brigadier A.F.V., whose job it would be to advise him on technical matters, and to supervise the corps training of the R.A.C., that is, the training within armoured brigades and units.

Questions of promotion and appointment in the R.A.C. within the command would, as now, be dealt with by the advisory board of senior R.A.C. officers, which submits recommendation to my Selection Board, which then reports to me. This is working well in practice.

3.   I have discussed this question, as well as my reorganisation proposals, very fully with Martel, who has had every opportunity of meeting people and seeing all relevant documents while he has been here.

I have at times been a little perturbed by his outlook, and this feeling has been shared by my senior staff officers and others. He has been most helpful to us, and given us much food for thought by his constructive criticism. I do feel, however, that he may be a little over-impressed by the idea that the R.A.C. has to be a super-body on a plane above that of the rest of the army, and that no one who does not belong to it can understand the mysteries of handling armoured formations in battle. I am sure he would deny this, but all the same I think that his mind is working on these lines, quite unconsciously perhaps.

I think, too, he may be inclined to be a little complacent about the training and leadership of the armoured formations in the recent fighting out here. They fought magnificently, and their courage and endurance are worthy of the highest praise. All the same, it would be foolish to assume that the leadership was all that it might have been on every occasion. I have already mentioned to you the feeling that exists in the other arms on this point.

I hope, therefore, that you will believe me when I tell you, after very careful consideration and the fullest possible consultation with those who are in a position to know, having been in the closest touch with the recent fighting, that the R.A.C. has a lot to learn still, and that one of its most urgent problems is to find leaders of the highest standard – possessing originality and a very quick intelligence. As I said before, the material Is excellent, but it must have leaders capable of getting the best out of it.

4.   At the risk of boring you I would like to say once again that the R.A.C. must, in my opinion, be more and more closely associated with the other arms, and must not be allowed to grow in a Corps d'elite, with separatist tendencies. I do not say that it has done so, but there are disturbing indications that it might do so.

5.   I have not yet had an answer from you about the command of the
     10th Corps, and I am sure there are good reasons for this, but I
     must point out that it is a matter of some urgency, as there are
     plenty of jobs to be got on with, and a Corps Commander to replace
     Lavarack[100] in Syria is an urgent necessity.

6.   As you know, I am hoping to form a G.H.Q. Reserve before the end
     of the winter, and If I can get him back from Libya, I want Neil
     Ritchie to command, train and lead it. He would do this admirably,
     and I hope you will agree to this. I propose to leave Godwin Austen
     in Libya when the situation there stabilises. When this will be, it
     is at present impossible to foresee, but we are actively planning to
     bring it about.

7.   We have managed to get off some of the reinforcements for Malta,
     but shipping for the remainder can not be found, so the Admiral[101]
     tells me. As you know, the notice we were given was very short.
     I realise fully, of course, the value of Malta, and the need for
     maintaining it. Its fall would affect us vitally, apart from any other
     repercussions it might have, All the same, I was surprised to
     receive Dobbie's[102] appeal for aid, as when I was there in July he
     told me he was then perfectly happy, as he had received all he had
     asked for. I know that his need is more pressing than ours at the
     moment, but I confess I view with some alarm the way in which
     this command is being drained of troops and material. It is not as
     if we had inexhaustible supply of either, especially of things like
     anti-aircraft and anti-tank artillery.

     I am not grumbling, but there is, I feel, a limit beyond which is
     it not safe to go, and I shall have to say so if the need arises. I know
     understand this very well.

8.   The matter of Blamey's position here will need revising almost at
     once, in view of recent developments. The reasons which led to his
     present appointment will soon have largely ceased to exist, and he
     will not have a full time job to do.

     His position as Deputy C.-in-C is not too easy at any time, for,
     as you know, it is not by any means a military necessity, and I fancy

---

100 Lieutenant General J. D. Lavarack, commanding 1st Australian Corps.
101 Admiral Sir Andrew Cunningham, C in C, Mediterranean.
102 Lieutenant General Sir William Dobbie, Governor and C in C, Malta.

that Blamey feels this himself. I should have thought that better use could be of his [time] in the Far East, or, possibly, in Australia itself.

JRL, AUC 640

135

Letter from Lieutenant General Neil Ritchie to Auchinleck, 18 January 1942

I am just off to 30 Corps to fix up with them the necessary details for the re-adjustment of troops resulting from the Frontier Area now having been cleared up. The adjustments I propose I will explain when I come down on the 20th. What a nuisance these Germans are giving way like this and so interfering with our arrangements for the Free French and to test them out as a fighting formation!

2.   13 Corps.

I visited 13 Corps for two days and got back, as I told you, yesterday morning. They were all in very good form and I was able to see FRANK MESSERVY,[103] JOCK CAMPBELL[104] and JOHN MARRIOTT.[105] The trouble of course is the enormous area over which the Corps is spread and the extremely bad going which makes ones movement by car very slow. From Corps Headquarters it took me a day to visit JOHN MARRIOTT and a second one to visit FRANK MESSERVY. I discussed the plans for the future at great length with GODWIN,[106] and adjusted it where necessary to come within scope of our administrative resources. I think it is now a good one and, provided the enemy does not withdraw again, may, I sincerely hope, give us a reasonable chance of liquidating him altogether. I am very relieved to know that you were prepared for the dates I suggested. All details of it will bring with me on the 20th, and will of course be particularly anxious to discuss with JOHN the "cover" for it.

---

103 Major General Frank Messervy, in temporary command of 1st Armoured
    Division having given up command of 4th Indian Division on 2 January 1942.
104 Brigadier John 'Jock' Campbell, VC.
105 Brigadier J. C. O. Marriott, commanding 22nd Guards Brigade.
106 Lieutenant General Alfred Godwin-Austen, commanding 13 Corps.

3. ## MESSERVY.

I need hardly say that both GODWIN and I are most anxious that FRANK MESSERVY should stay in command of the 1st Armd Div for this operation. In view of the considerable re-organisation that you have decided upon I wonder whether you would permit this? One thing in particular makes it desirable that, if possible, he should stay. Ground is going to play a very important part in these operations and it is I suggest most important that the Commander of the Armour should know the ground and should have had a good chance of studying it beforehand. It is by far the most difficult country that we have so far experienced and everyone is hard at work carrying out the most careful reconnaissances.

4. ## DISPOSITIONS OF TROOPS.

In your letter of the 15th January you raise the question of a reserve brigade behind the 4th Div. I apologise. An alteration was made in my letter after I had signed it and after I had myself left here, and I was not available to be asked. It was my intention that a Reserve Brigade for the Corps should be stationed behind the 4th Ind. Div. In the initial stages this will provide the local security for the R.A.F. operation landing grounds in the area and for the safety of the L of C generally in that neighbourhood. It is my intention at the moment to move up the 1st S. A. Inf Bde Gp for this task, and in the circumstances I still feel that we would be justified in releasing for you the 150th Inf Bde Gp. now.

5. ## THE POLES

I have in mind to relieve the POLES as early as possible and make them available to return to the DELTA. Incidentally I see that General ZAJAC has written to you on this subject. The FREE FRENCH are a problem. I know nothing of their fighting value and I do not feel justified in maintaining them in the forward area for our next operation. In these circumstances, I [hope] you will agree to the FREE FRENCH reliving the POLES in the DERNA neighbourhood of the GEBEL. To complete the picture there I hope to move the 1st S.A. Div (less one Bde Gp) up in to the Western portion of the GEBEL to replace the 4th Ind Div there as the latter move down to assume their battle position in the AGEDABIA neighbourhood.

6.   7 SUPPORT GROUP.

I feel sure that this party should be relieved as early as possible and this is being done. They are weary and very thoroughly deserve a rest. Their relief by the 1st Support Group should be completed tomorrow and they will then start on their way back. to the DELTA.

7.   38 INDIAN INFANTRY BRIGADE.

I propose to put one Bde Group of the 2nd S.A. Div into the TOBRUK area to relieve the 38th Ind. Inf Bde there and this will be completed by the end of the month. They will then be released and return to EGYPT. I hope this will be suitable?

8.   JOHN MARRIOTT

I attach a letter from FRANK MESSERVY in reply to mine concerning the suitability of MARRIOTT as a Divisional Commander. This note of MESSERVY's is a result of a conversation we had on the matter. I have discussed it with GODWIN who agrees. There is nothing against JOHN MARRIOTT except, if one can put it like this, he is too nice to be really forceful and I think that FRANK MESSERVY sums up the situation very adequately. Quite decidedly I do not consider that he is fit for the command of an Armd Div.

9.   Thank you so much for your wire asking me stay on the 20th, which I will be delighted to do. ANGUS is coming with me and will send TONY a message later about the time of our arrival.

JRL, AUC 643

136

Letter from Auchinleck to Lieutenant General Charles Willoughby Norrie (Commander 30th Corps), 18 January 1942

Very many thanks for your letter of the 16th and the enclosures. I have had a talk with Pienaar[107] and realize the truth of your remarks. I agree that his military knowledge is good, and I think his ideas on

---

107 Major General D. H. Pienaar, GOC 1st South African Division.

organization and minor tactics are sound enough. For instance, his system of moving and leaguering a brigade group seems on the face of it sensible and effective. I wonder if you agree with me in this.

2.   I am going to ask you to come in here for a day or two next week as I want you and your staff to take on at once the job of organizing the SALUM–MADDALENA–GIARABUB line as a rear line of defence. This is an insurance which we must have, and I want plans made and work started at the earliest possible moment after you have been here and discussed it with Neil Ritchie and me.

3.   I am sending an official instruction to 8th Army.

4.   My best congratulations on HALFAYA. Taken with BARDIA it forms a great achievement at very small cost. More power to you!

JRL, AUC 644

137

Letter from General Sir Alan Brooke, CIGS to Auchinleck, 21 January 1942

Very many thanks for your letter of December 28th. I am taking the opportunity of Porter's return to answer it.

I was very interested in your paper on the future strategy of the war and your suggestion of carrying the war into Germany from Africa. There is a great deal to say for such a plan from many aspects, but I am afraid that it does not take into account the shipping situation. Shipping is exercising a stranglehold on strategy which is likely to be increased by recent events.

To attempt to supply large forces by sea to North Africa and from there through the Mediterranean may well present insoluble problems from a shipping point of view. There is, in addition, the exposure of sea communications through the Mediterranean, to air and under-water attack, which would require taking into account.

What I am certain of is that North Africa would provide an excellent base of attack on Italy through the action of air and naval forces.

At any rate, the first stage must be to secure North Africa, and we have got an awkward problem in front of us in the shape of Acrobat. The failure to destroy Rommel's force, the time gained by his rearguard actions, the unavoidable delays necessary to stage Acrobat, and the reduced strength of naval force in the Eastern Mediterranean, all affect the situation seriously.

The restrictions which the administrative situation imposes on the strength of the force which we can maintain for offensive operations in Tripoli is also a very serious handicap. Against Italians all would be well, but against Germans and with some 6 weeks to obtain reinforcements, the odds may well be heavily weighted against us when you are in a position to resume the offensive.

From the above I do not suggest that we should not carry out Acrobat as long as there is a reasonable chance of success. On the contrary, I attach the greatest importance to it and all it entails. We should, during the next few weeks, be able to form a fairly accurate estimate as to what reinforcements have got through and what the enemy forces opposed to us consist of.

The Far East is likely to exercise a very serious drain on our resources for some time to come. There is no idea of offensive action in the immediate future as one of your wires suggested we were contemplating; on the contrary, the difficulty is to find adequate resources to cork up the holes. I agree with you that there is a minimum below which we should not draw on the Middle East, owning to our North Eastern commitments; unfortunately we have already been forced to go below the minimum in my opinion. The withdrawals contemplated amount to some 5 Divisions, namely: two Australian, 18 Div., 17th and 14th Indian Divisions, and even the possibility of a third Australian Div! At present I do not see much hope, owing to shipping difficulties of replacing more than two of these Divisions from Home Forces before June! And even this programme may be upset owing to necessity for shipping reinforcements. And yet, if we don't withdraw from Middle East to reinforce Far East, we may well lose control of communications in the Indian Ocean to such an extent as to seriously endanger our communications with the Middle East, thus rendering it difficult to reinforce you at all. I can assure you that I have the security of your North Eastern Front at heart and shall do all I can to maintain and raise it to the required strength. Luckily, the Russian situation gives us a little more breathing space than we originally hoped for, and we should not have much to fear before July.

I am glad that we have now got Iraq and Persia definitely handed over to you; I did not like the other arrangement.

I entirely agree with you that Martel's tendency is to try and make a separate private Army of the Armoured Corps – I have spoken to him repeatedly about it, and am determined to have nothing of the kind. I had already given out at home that all Corps H.Q. must be capable of controlling either Armoured or Infantry Divisions, and that a Corps Commander incapable of handling Armoured Forces is not fit to hold his command. I had not yet gone as far as you suggest, namely that Div. H.Q. be regarded in the same way. You may be right, but I should like to consider this point further before expressing a definite opinion.

What is lamentable, and must be remedied, is the lack of knowledge in most senior officers of the handling of armoured forces.

I was interested to hear that you propose to return Holmes[108] to his Corps and to send him up to Jumbo Wilson. He is a rum bird and not one I have ever had a very high opinion of. He may be all right when it comes to fighting, but he is extraordinarily ignorant in the handling of the various arms other than infantry.

I see from one of your telegrams you think Holmes might eventually take over from Jumbo Wilson – I should have doubted it. The retention of Jumbo is, of course, producing a good deal of talk from those who have been moved on for age; it would therefore be inadvisable to retain him any longer if you feel that he is beginning to show signs of age.

Can we do more to help you from here by sending you out anybody? If you feel you want some fresh blood, let me know who you would like: we could work some exchanges. There is, unfortunately, not a great to deal to pick from here, but there are a few good young Div. Commanders coming on, and I feel certain exchanges are desirable. I was afraid that you might not have much use for Nosworthy,[109] but had to suggest him as he is at present spare and waiting for employment.

What I am worried about is that you have not got a first-class A.F.V. adviser on your staff. I do consider that you want someone on the same lines as your Chief Gunner, or Chief Sapper. There is a colossal amount of work for him in the re-equipping and re-forming of your Armoured Divisions and Army Tank Bde., and in the provision of general advice on Armoured matters.

As you express such a definite wish to raise your D.M.T. to the rank of Major-General I cannot but agree, and am getting Finance to accept. But I consider that an organization which retains the Brig. A.F.Vs. under the D.M.T. is definitely wrong. The Brig. A.F.Vs. must also deal with

---

108 Lieutenant General William Holmes, GOC British Troops, Egypt.
109 Lieutenant General Sir Francis Nosworthy. He was to be appointed C in C West Africa in 1943.

matters other than training, such as organization, equipment, personnel, etc. With a Force such as yours when the Chief Artillery representative is a Major-General, the Chief A.F.V. representative should be of similar rank. I attach a table of what I consider the organization should be. I feel that with such a system you would be in a much better position to tackle the large reorganization scheme which faces you.

It is essential that your four Armoured Divisions should be re-equipped and reorganised as quickly as possible to meet any threat that may develop through Turkey or Caucasus later on. I am examining the possibilities of sparing one more Armoured Division from Home Forces for you, which, together with the Indian one, would bring you up to 6. This could in any case only be done in lieu of an infantry div., owing to shipping restrictions.

I should very much have liked to be able to assist you by sending you Bond as you requested, but unfortunately he is one of the key men on the A.F.V. aide in the War Office whom I could not spare at present.

The telegrams are working better now, but I still feel that too free a use is made of "Private and Personal" ones to the P.M. For instance, the one concerning inadequate packing of Churchill tanks might well be in the first place have been sent personal to the Q.M.G.; as it was, it caused a good deal of unnecessary bad blood.

I also feel that it would be desirable to impress on Shearer that highly coloured optimistic reports which are not borne out by subsequent facts have been too frequent lately. There has been a continual tendency to over-estimate the destruction of the enemy's armoured forces and to convey a picture of completely surrounded hostile forces. These reports are apt to create a spirit of unwarranted optimism amongst politicians, which is followed by one of doubt as the veracity of our statements!

It has been very good value bringing Porter and the others back, they have been a great help to us. I have had a good talk with Porter so that he can let you know what is in my mind.

I have just received a letter from Dobbie[110] who is very grateful for the assistance which you so readily provided for him. I should not be surprised to see the Germans carry out some form of operation in that direction.

I am so sorry to be inflicting such a long letter on you, but miss the possibility of an occasional talk with you which would be so useful.

JRL, AUC 649

---

110 Lieutenant General Sir William Dobbie, Governor and C in C, Malta.

138

Cipher message from the Commanders-in-Chief Middle East to Churchill, 24 January 1942

1 (.) Army strengths at beginning CRUSADER (.) (A) German (,) two Armd Divs one Light Div (.) Italian (,) one Armd Div two Motorized Divs four Inf Divs (.) Total Axis divs ten (.) (B) Ours (,) equivalent two Armd Divs six Inf Divs (.) Total eight Divs (.)

2 (.) During period 18 Nov to 22 Jan the following losses were inflicted on the enemy by the Med Fleet and F.A.A. (.) One battleship damaged two cruisers sunk and two damaged one destroyer sunk and three damaged seven submarines sunk and one probably sunk (.) Twenty seven merchant ships totalling 92000 (92000) tons sunk and fourteen M/Vs damaged (.) Med Fleet and F.A.A. casualties during the same period were 2560 (2560) killed and 170 (170) wounded (.)

3 (.) Accurate figures are not yet available of enemy Army and Air losses in men and material (.) From visual observation captured documents and prisoners of war statements following estimate of losses are believed accurate (.) Enemy losses (.) Percentage figures represent loss in relation to original strength as now known from capture documents (.) (A) Personnel (.) Killed and wounded (.) German 11500 (11500) 27 per cent (,) Italian 13000 (13000) 23 per cent (.) Prisoners (.) German 10500 (10500) 25 per cent (,) Italian 26000 (26000) 46 per cent (.) Total Axis losses 61000 (61000) out of original strength 40000 (40000) Germans 60000 (60000) Italians (.) (B) Aircraft captured or destroyed (.) German 479 (479) Italian 373 (373) (.) (C) Equipment captured or destroyed (.) Medium tanks German 216 (216) 85 per cent (,) Italian 120 (120) 93 per cent (.) Field and medium guns German 125 (125) 82 per cent (,) Italian 290 (290) 69 per cent (.) A.Tk and other light guns (.) German 134 (134) 62 per cent (,) Italian 157 (157) 71 per cent (.) Heavy A.A, and dual purpose guns (.) German 40 (40) 33 per cent Italian 34 (34) 50 per cent (.) Ammunition 100,000 (100,000) tons (.)

4 (.) Our Army losses (,) 18,000 (18,000) men (.)

5 (.) Suggest following special points (.)

(a) As result of continuous pressure prior to land operations we started attack with marked degree of air superiority which was maintained and increased (.)

(b) Surprise of date/direction of attack due largely to our R.A.F. gaining before the battle air superiority which was never lost and also to good approach march by Army [.]

(c) Enemy shortage of supply due primarily to our continuous Naval and Air operations against his L of C prior to and during land operations (.)

(d) Co-operation of all three Services which was largely outcome of Army and Air H.Q. living and working together and to pressure at H.Q. of Naval Liaison Officer (.) Result was that Army and R.A.F. worked as one team (.)

(e) Assistance of land operations by Naval bombardment (.)

(f) Maintenance of TOBRUK by Navy for seven months (.)

(g) Offensive spirit of TOBRUK garrison and their command of No Man's Land (.)

(h) Morale of fighting services and determination has never been higher and has not been affected by sand storms and bad weather or desperate resistance by enemy (.)

(i) Excellent work by our Intelligence Staffs [.]

JRL, AUC 651

139

Cipher Message from Winston Churchill to Auchinleck, 25 January 1942

I am much disturbed my number 10005 B/23 from N[aval]. L[iaison]. O[fficer]. 8th Army which speaks of evacuation of BENGHAZI and DERNA. I had certainly never been led to believe that such a situation could arise. All this movement of non-fighting personnel EASTWARDS, and statement that demolition work at BENGHAZI has NOT (repeat NOT) been ordered yet, places the campaign on a very different level from any we had considered. Have you really been unable to compete with the RESUSCITATED GERMAN Tanks. It seems to me this is a serious crisis and one to me quite unexpected. Why should they all be off so quick, why should not the 4th INDIAN DIV hold out at BENGHAZI like the HUNS at HALFAYA. The kind of retirement now evidently envisaged by subordinate officers implies the failure of CRUSADER and the ruin of ACROBAT.

JRL, AUC 653

140

Letter from Auchinleck[111] to Lieutenant General Arthur Smith, CGS, Middle East, 26 January 1942

We had a good fly up yesterday, though we did not get here till 1 p.m., having had to come down at EL ADEM to get news of conditions forward. What with one thing and another, we did not get off from HELIOPOLIS till 9 a.m., so it was not too bad – no wind and no dust. Today is foul, easterly gale and clouds of dust.

2.   The situation is not satisfactory to my mind, chiefly because of the apparent inability of the 1st Armoured Division to hold the enemy for any length of time. I do not say they are not fighting hard, because they are, from all accounts, but the fact remains that they were pushed out of MSUS yesterday, though they had columns still East of that place engaged with the enemy yesterday evening. The latest reports are 1 Armd Div is South of CHARRUBA, on which place it is presumably concentrating. Some of the Guards Bde columns are said to be missing, "cut off" is one expression used, and it may be that some troops are short of petrol, which is, to my mind, the most serious possibility. However, we shall see, and I think the enemy must be pretty well stretched, though, true to form, he will push on to the utmost limit of his resources, even with the weakest forces, unless we can stabilise the situation.

Godwin Austen[112] had yesterday made up his mind that BENGASI could no longer be held, and that the 4th Indian Division must be withdrawn via DERNA. All heavy installations have been evacuated from BENGASI, and the Naval establishments should have got out last night. These are, I think, wise precautions, but I am very averse

---

111 Auchinleck was present at 8th Army HQ at this time.
112 Lieutenant General Alfred Godwin-Austen, commanding 13 Corps.

to abandoning the place unless it is absolutely necessary, as you know. I discussed the whole situation with Neil Ritchie yesterday evening, by which time 13th Corps HQ were on the move towards MECHILI from CHARRUBA and out of touch, and he has issued orders direct to Tuker[113] that the 4th Ind Div are to arrange to protect their own Eastward flank as far as EL ABIAR, and to push as strongly as possible with small mobile columns with artillery against the enemy's Western flank and communications in the direction of ANTELAT, while 1st Armd Div are to do all they can to prevent an enemy advance Northwards towards CHARRUBA and MECHILI. The Polish Bde Gp are moving on MECHILI, and should be concentrated there this afternoon – with luck. Some of them are there already. 150th Bde (Haydon[114] was here yesterday getting his orders) are to reach BIR HACEIM today, and to move on as quickly as possible to BUERAT – EL HALES and TENGEDER and secure the Southern approaches. They are to operate offensively Westwards with mobile columns.

3. Neil Ritchie spent a long time last night on the "Blower" talking to Godwin Austen and telling of this change of plan. G[odwin]-A[usten] is very much against any change and without hesitation dissociated himself from it, as he considered that to change now would be most difficult, and that the new plan was impracticable. Neil took full responsibility and ordered him to put it in effect at once. The necessary orders are being issued. Neil has taken 4th Ind Div under his direct command, as he has a better means of communication with it than 13th Corps, and is determined to stage this counter-offensive. So far there has been no sign of any enemy activity towards BENGASI, and we know that all his maintenance transport is strung out along the JEDABYA – ANTELAT track, and should be very sensitive to determined attack.

I realise that we are taking a big risk, but so is the enemy, and I think his risk is bigger than ours. We must recover the initiative as soon as we can, and it seems to me that this is the only immediately possible way of doing. I only wish it had been possible to it earlier. I gather that Tuker has been urging it for some time now, but I daresay Godwin Austen had good reasons for not resorting to it. It is difficult to say without knowing what the local situation is. It is possible that nothing may come of it, but I refuse to believe that

---

113 Major General Francis Tuker, GOC 4th Indian Division.
114 Brigadier C. W. Haydon.

the enemy's supply situation, or indeed his tactical situation, is all that he could wish it to be. I am ready to bet that he must be very surprised by the extent of the success he has achieved.

3.   I am staying up here today, and so is Tedder. Neil goes over to MECHILI this afternoon by air to meet G-A, who expects to arrive there by 4 p.m. Further action may be necessary in this direction, but I hope it will be necessary to do anything drastic, though I am quite ready for it.

4.   Neil intends to move this H.Q. to SIDI REZEIZ which will be much better in my opinion from every point of view. I have never really liked TMIMI as an 8th Army HQ. It was intended originally to be a temporary halt only, and is, to my mind, too much to one flank of the general axis of operations. His advanced parties are there already, and I think Neil will move as soon as communications are satisfactorily established, but his decision will of course be governed by the course of events.

Neil is laying plans for the future and the resumption of the offensive when the enemy has been held.

5.   I want the 3 Indian Motor Brigade placed at short notice to move in case it is needed here to replace losses in mobile troops. It would move by regiments if it does come, so one regiment with some fd guns and anti-tank guns should have first priority. Ninth Army will grumble probably about their internal security, but they will have to do the best they can.

6.   Also please find out the state of readiness of the New Zealanders, in case they too should be wanted again. Don't interrupt the KABRIT training in combined operations if it can be avoided, but it might be as well to warn Freyberg that it is just possible he may be called on to help if things go badly awry.

7.   I enclose a telegram for the Prime Minister. If you can, please repeat it to the Minister of State.[115] Keep the Ambassador as happy as you can!

P.S   I have asked John Shearer to stay here for tonight at any rate.

JRL, AUC 654

---

115 Oliver Lyttleton, Minister of State and Member of the War Cabinet, resident in Cairo.

141

Letter from Lieutenant General Arthur Smith, CGS, Middle East, to Auchinleck, 26 January 1942

I was very glad to get your telegram this afternoon, despatched this morning, giving the news. It did not quite agree with a situation report as sent shortly afterwards by 8th Army, but in order to avoid a muddle, we are ensuring that our Sitrep to the War Office agrees with your report to the Prime Minister.

2. I sent a telegram this afternoon to ask if you could give us a line as to the communiques. So far I have put very little in the communiques, but something more lengthy would, no doubt, be appreciated by the public as soon as possible. Walter Monckton[116] comes in to see me morning and evening, and is having a special meeting with the accredited press representatives, which seems to be a success. He tells them nothing but keeps them sweet. One or two items in the local press lately have rather annoyed me, and I have told the people responsible to take them up, and have mentioned them to Walter Monckton.

3. I enclose a statement showing the tank situation, which I hope may be of use.

4. The question arose as to whether the 7th Armoured Bde should be stopped sailing for the Far East. They are due to start tomorrow. General Blamey has decided they shall sail as arranged, and I am sure you will agree that he is right.

5. I have given written instructions to Frank Theron[117] to take with him to South Africa. He leaves tomorrow. I have had a final talk with him, and hope and believe he really understands the problem. He takes with him a personal letter from me to van Ryneveld,[118] stressing the more important points, and I have told van Ryneveld that this letter is a substitute for one which you undoubtedly would

---

116 Walter Monckton, Head of propaganda and information services in Cairo and member of the Middle East war council.

117 Major General Frank Theron, the senior South African liaison officer to GHQ, Middle East.

118 General Sir Hesperus Andrias van Ryneveld, CGS, Union Defence Forces, South Africa.

have written to Field Marshal Smuts had you been able to. I will show you a copy when you return to Cairo.

6.   I did not repeat your telegram to the Minister of State,[119] because his office did not know where he was, and there is a temporary break in communications with BAGHDAD. Tomorrow morning, if security permits, I shall send him a brief resume of what has taken place if I can trace him.

7.   You probably heard that Hutch and Sandy Galloway are not able to reach Rear 8th Army HQ today, owning to weather conditions. They were going up in connection with the vehicle census. Perhaps now is not a particularly opportune moment for their visit.

P.S   As I see it, the chap who sticks it longest and has the best guts is going to win this battle.

JRL, AUC 655

142

Letter from Auchinleck to Lieutenant General Arthur Smith, CGS, Middle East, 27 January 1942

The aircraft could not leave yesterday owing to the weather, which was foul – high wind and much dust – so my yesterday's letter will go with this one. Thank you for sending on the Prime Minister's SUSAN 161 of Jan. 25th, and for getting Blamey to send an answer, which I think suited the circumstances. Please send on any other wires from the same source and send an interim answer if it seems imperative to do so, otherwise better not I think, as the situation here changes so rapidly. Yesterday was a quiet day apparently, and Neil flew over to MECHILI in the afternoon, where he met Godwin Austen, who is now established 13th Corps HQ some five miles East of MECHILI. The Poles are at and round MECHILI, while the 150th Inf Bde should move today to a point South of TENGEDER to block any attempt on the part of the enemy to send fast moving columns by that route against our L of C.

---

119 Oliver Lyttleton, Minister of State and Member of the War Cabinet, resident in Cairo.

The crux of the whole matter is the condition of the 1st Armd Div, which G-A told Neil can no longer be counted on as a fighting force. Its losses are said to be 40 guns and I suppose about 100 or more tanks, and there is much doubt as to whether it was able to inflict any appreciable loss on the enemy. G-A is apparently very pessimistic about it, and says it can not possibly be counted on to cover the flank of 4 Ind Div if the latter remains in BENGASI. However, Neil told G-A that he was to issue orders to it to do this, and to remain at CHARRUBA and take the offensive against the enemy at once. These orders were issued yesterday afternoon.

Meanwhile, Tuker[120] has been ordered to take the offensive with his division against the enemy western flank from MSUS to ANTELAT: If, however, the 1st Armd Div is not capable of protecting the Southern flank of the L of C to BENGASI, we may have to come out, though this is the last thing I want to do. Neil has told G-A to give him an immediate report on the fighting condition of 1 Armd Div, but this has not arrived yet.

Meanwhile, the latest report is that 1 Armd Div with the Guards Bde is organising a defence round CHARRUBA with Armd car patrols on a wide arc, 35 to 40 miles out, from WEST through SOUTH to EAST. There is apparently a detachment of Royals with some A/TK guns on the TRIGH EL ABD watching that line. Orders have been issued to 1 Armd Div again to form offensive columns and move against the enemy. 4 Ind Div were active yesterday, and their fighting patrols were almost in ANTELAT and thence WEST to the coast about RAS BEN HAGEN through BEDA FOMM, and found no enemy. ANTELAT is said to be empty. 4 Ind Div hold SCLEIDIMA and SIDI BRAMM on the escarpment to the North of it, or did yesterday afternoon. They are also in SOLUCH.

Neil is just off with "Mary" Conningham[121] to see Tuker at BENGASI. It was lovely early this morning, but this damned wind has started again, and the dust is getting up.

The Navy were most precipitate in starting their destructive work at BENGASI, and the man in charge anticipated his orders apparently. So far as I can make out no other demolitions were carried out, except of a few enemy stores, and the R.A.F. burnt some petrol unfortunately.

It is early to say yet what may happen, as so much depends on the state of 1 Armd Div. However, the situation seems better than it has been

---

120 Major General Francis Tuker, GOC 4th Indian Division.
121 Air Vice Marshal Arthur 'Mary' Conningham, commanding Desert Air Force.

for some days, and to be coming to hand. The Poles and 150 Inf Bde are being told to be as aggressive as possible with mixed columns, and I hope Tuker will be able really to worry the enemy. He has the offensive spirit all right, and the right ideas. I have great hopes of being able to hold BENGASI and restore the situation, perhaps to the enemy's ultimate detriment. However, as I say, things are delicately balanced still.

As I think I told you, this HQ is in process of establishing itself at SIDI REZEIZ, but the transfer is being effected deliberately and carefully to give no impression of undue haste. There was a possibility of our moving back today but this has been postponed.

I enclose a telegram for the Prime Minister, also a draft communique.

The R.A.F. yesterday gave the enemy hell all along the road MSUS – ANTELAT. The fighters have got their blood up, and reports are still coming in of burning lorries and vehicles all over the place. More power to them!

Please concoct a telegram to C.I.G.S. and Dominions etc. from me, and me a copy. Please send me back copies of all my telegrams and letters if you can. No liaison officer arrived this morning, though a Lockhead came in. Please show copy of my enclosed telegram to Prime Minister to Admiral,[122] as it mentions the Navy.

JRL, AUC 656

143

Letter from Auchinleck to Lieutenant General Arthur Smith, CGS, Middle East, 28 January 1942

The Liaison aircraft isn't in yet, but I hope it will be here soon with John Shearer on board.

2. I enclose my telegram for the Prime Minister which I hope will give you a clear picture of the situation as it is known here. While on this subject, I wonder whether it would not really be better and more informative to the recipients if we worked our own Cositreps more in this style – that is, in narrative form instead of in the very jerky, disjointed, "G[eneral].S[taff]." style we use at present. They are very difficult to read, and, instead of giving form at a glance as they

---

122 Admiral Sir Andrew Cunningham, C in C, Mediterranean.

should, they nearly always entail much meticulous map-reading and intricate calculations of time and space on the part of the reader. In fact, they contain much too much unimportant and ephemeral detail in my opinion. Think it over!

3. Yesterday started quietly, and Neil and "Mary" Conningham flew over to BENGASI to see "Gertie" Tuker, with whom they had a satisfactory interview apparently. Neil says he is in cracking form and full of fight and, what is much more important, of original ideas for beating the enemy. This is most refreshing and again emphasises, if emphasis were needed, the importance of not leaving commanders too long in the same place or the same job! I feel the wanderlust myself!!!

4. The enemy started moving again before lunch yesterday as you know, and true to form has taken the bold stroke of dividing his forces in diametrically opposite directions from a base which can not hold any real reserve of supplies. At least, that is how it looks. Without being too optimistic, it seems as if he may have once again underestimated our capacity to recover and hit back after a reverse – for we have had a reverse – there is no getting away from it. However, I feel that Neil has situation very well in hand. In fact, it looks as if the enemy is doing the very thing Neil was hoping he would do, except that he did not anticipate his splitting his force as he has done. This again, may give us an even better opportunity of hitting him. It looks as if the majority of the enemy armour is in his eastern thrust, though he has apparently got some tanks in the force moving on EL ABIAR.

Neil has just heard from Godwin Austen that Messervy says that 1 Armd Div is reorganised and ready for offensive action. It has been ordered by Godwin in anticipation of orders from Neil to strike south-eastwards against the enemy moving on MECHILI. Tuker and the 4 Div are to hold EL ABIAR and strike East, and South against the flank and rear of the enemy moving on EL ABIAR, which would seem to offer good chance of success, though a report just in indicating movement of small columns of enemy tanks and M.T. Northwards from AGEDABIA West of the escarpment may hamper this move. There is no doubt that today may be critical, and much will depend on the skill and boldness with which the 1st Armd Div is handled, and the ability of 4 Ind Div to hold off the threat from the South while striking East. Both sides are taking big risks, and I hope we can play that game as well as Rommel. He is running absolutely true to form, and putting everything in the shop window. So are we I hope. The difference is, I think, that our supply situation ought to be better than his, and our air is, for the moment, having everything its own way.

As I told you, this H.Q. is moving slowly and by sections to SIDI AZEIZ, and it is possible we may go there today, but that is not yet certain.

5. I send you back Jennings' paper on future organisation and distribution with my pencilled comments in the margin.

I suppose S.D. [?] has been consulted regarding the proposals. It looks as if we shall have to defer the relief of CYPRUS for a bit, but I want the problem kept constantly before the Navy, as it will have to be faced some time.

6. You will have had my telegram about the reformation of 4 Armd Bde.

It should get up here as soon as it possibly can. Will you try and form an armoured car unit – regt or squadron – for inclusion in the group as soon as you can, as I feel this will strengthen it considerably. I absolutely agree that the Bde should be reformed on the new organisation, which is, I am certain, an urgent necessity. I should not be at all surprised to learn that the apparent failure of 1 Armd Div to deal with the enemy in the present operations was due largely to the divorcement of the armour from the infantry. Anyway, go right ahead with it as fast as you can. You will have to find another commander instead of Gatehouse, I think. Don't hesitate to suggest anyone, however junior he may be, and irrespective of his arm of the service. What about Jock Campbell? But let me know as soon as you, M[ilitary].S[ecretary]., Lloyd and anyone else you are to consult, have come to any conclusion.

8th Army will tell you about the transport for 4 Armd Bde.

7. Please send up the 25 armoured cars now available at once to 8 Army, as some of their units are pretty weak. Try and keep enough to form at least a squadron for 4 Armd Bde, but needs of 8 Army must come first, and they would like all the Marmon-Harringtons[123] you can send them as well as the 25 mentioned above. I am anticipating that

---

123 Armoured cars manufactured in South Africa and based on Ford 3 ton lorries.

if things go well, the armoured car may become a most important weapon.

8.   [X] I shall stay on here for a bit, I think, and I fancy A.O.C.-in-C. will stay too. The R.A.F. have been grand – morale sky high and full of hate.

9.   Lloyd's BM/AFV/2/10 of 26 Jan 42 about the tank situation mentions "Stepsister". I am afraid I don't know what this is! Should I?!

10.   Free French are on the move again now. Larminat[124] has just been in.

No more now. I may put in a postscript if John brings anything up with him.

JRL, AUC 663

144

Letter from Lieutenant General Arthur Smith, CGS, Middle East, to Auchinleck, 28 January 1942

With regard to the reinforcement of the 4th Armd Bde Group, I have wired to you today on the subject. I have discussed all this with Strafer,[125] and the dates given in the telegram are in fact the earliest to which we can work if the units are to give any satisfaction on arrival at the front. Being equipped with Grants and M 3s is, of course, new, and a certain amount of training is quite essential if satisfactory results are to be achieved at all.

2.   As regards command, I attach pencilled note by Strafer [see document 145 below] on the subject of Gatehouse.[126] If Gatehouse is unacceptable for command, the following are recommended in the order given:

---

124 General Edgard Larminat, commanding 1st Free French Brigade.
125 Major General W. H. E. Gott.
126 Brigadier Alexander Gatehouse, then commanding 4th Armoured Brigade.

Carr[127]
Davy[128]
Richards.[129]

Of these three, Carr is the least experience[d] but the fittest, probably the least excitable, and in Strafer's opinion likely to produce the best results.

3.   With regard to the question of A.F.V. Directorate, Sandy[130] considers that it will be quite safe to have Gatehouse serve in that capacity with himself and John Harding as D.C.G.S. and D.M.T. respectively. Now that the D.M.T. is settled, what is required in the A.F.V. Directorate is technical knowledge and experience provided particularly, if possible, by a Royal Tanks Corps man. Gatehouse fills this requirement exactly, and there is nobody else in this country with the same qualifications. If you decide against having him as Commander 4th Armd Bde when that formation goes up to the desert, I suggest that he should get on with the training of it now, as he is doing, and that when it leaves under its new commander he could then go to the A.F.V. Directorate and take over. I think that is the best solution, and is the fairest to all concerned, and will produce the best results.

JRL, AUC 664

145

Testimonial concerning Brigadier Alexander Gatehouse[131] written by Major General W. H. E. Gott, commanding 7th Armoured Division, 27 January 1942

Brigadier Gatehouse trained the 4 Armd Bde Group with the American Light Tank in October 1941 & evolved a very sound system of support & co-operation between all arms in the Bde. Gp. & especially between the

---

127 Brigadier W. G. Carr.
128 Brigadier G. M. O. Davy.
129 Brigadier G. W. Richards.
130 Brigadier Alexander Galloway, BGS, 8th Army, 1941–42.
131 This was to no avail, Auchinleck was to note, 'Am afraid GATEHOUSE will not do as Bg. A.F.V. He should go home as arranged with MARTEL'. JRL, AUC

guns of 2 RHA & the Armd Regts. His methods were almost identical with those described in the recent VIII Army directive for A.F.V. training. In my opinion his Bde was most successful. He fought it for over 30 days without any appreciable pause during which time the enemy were driven back from position to position always with heavy loss & frequently as a direct result of the action of his Bde. On the other hand the losses of the 4 A.B. though heavy were not such as to immobilise the Bde. This was because of his skillful handling & sound administration but instead of receiving credit for this the Bde was often accused of being slow and over-cautious. This unjust opinion was never supported by me & is without foundation. To judge by results he was the most successful of the Armd Bde Commanders in either 1st or 7th Armd Div. There are two things against him

(a)　I consider he becomes tired sooner than some commanders & that he then definitely loses fighting efficiency. In these circumstances I have found him a difficult subordinate in a long battle.

(b)　He is believed to have kept alive the feeling between Cavalry & R. Tank Regt. I think there are some grounds for this view but I know that he realises that such an attitude can only do harm to the war effort & to himself. I do not think it will recur.

　　Finally I consider him to be personally brave & loyal & to possess the best all round knowledge of AFVs & their technical & tactical handling of any officer in the Middle East.

For the reason given in (a) I do not recommend him for command of a Division.

I recommend him to continue in command of a Brigade, to command a School or to be Director A.F.V.s.

JRL, AUC 659

667, Letter from Auchinleck to Lieutenant General Arthur Smith, CGS, Middle East, 29 January 1942. Demonstrating the limits of Auchinleck's authority, Gatehouse was to be promoted Major General serving as GOC of the 1st and 10th Armoured Divisions.

146

Cipher message from Auchinleck to Winston Churchill, 30 January 1942

<u>Adv HQ 8 Army 0830 hrs GMT 30 Jan (.)</u>

1 (.) Thank you for your telegram of 28 Jan received yesterday afternoon (.) Very sorry we had to let BENGHASI go but hope loss is temporary only (.)

2 (.) Regarding action 1 Armd Div (.) Am NOT (R[epeat]) NOT certain that enemy tanks were appreciably less in number than ours actually in running order on any one day though it is likely our strength in tanks in the battle area was superior to theirs (.) I have given you in my SUSAN 1712 of 27 Jan some reasons for defeat of our Armd force and I think these still hold good (.) Other and at present irremediable causes which I have already mentioned in a letter to you are short range and inferior performance our two pounder guns compared with German guns and mechanical unreliability our cruiser tanks compared to German tanks (.) In addition I am NOT (R) NOT satisfied that tactical leadership our armoured units is of sufficiently high standard to offset German material advantages (.) This is in hand but can NOT (R[epeat]) NOT be improved in a day unfortunately.

3 (.) I am reluctantly compelled to conclusion that to meet German armoured forces with any reasonable hope of decisive success our armoured forces as at present equipped organised and led must have at least two to one superiority (.) Even then they must rely for success on working in the very closest cooperation with infantry and artillery which except perhaps for their weakness in anti tank guns are fully competent to take on their German opposite numbers (.) These principles are being worked to here as closely as circumstances will permit but I am afraid there are signs that personnel of Royal Armoured Corps are in some instances losing confidence in their equipment (.) Everything possible will be done to rectify this (.)

4 (.) General RITCHIE and I are fully alive to ROMMELS probable intentions but whatever these may be he will certainly try to exploit success by use of even smallest columns until he meets resistance (.) Plans are in train to counter such action (.)

5 (.) It seems possible that some at least of 7 Ind[ian] Inf[antry] Bde Gp may have broken through to EAST of BENGHASI and are now on way to CHARRUBA and MECHILI (.) No details available but fear that their losses must have been severe (.)

6 (.) 4 Ind Div are holding line BARCE MARAUA to join up with CHARRUBA which is held still by 1 Armd Div (.) Yesterday columns from 1 Armd Div operated SOUTH and SOUTHWEST from CHARRUBA and engaged small columns of enemy NORTH of MSUS (.) Only slight enemy movement observed yesterday he is probably reorganising and recuperating (.) Our air force failed to find favourable targets but fighters were most active in support of our forward troops over whole battle area (.)

7 (.) Polish and Free French Bde Gps round MECHILI temporarily under command General DE LARMINAT directly under control 13 Corps which also controls 50 (50) Inf Bde Gp round TENGEDER (.)

8 (.) Our mobile columns are operating vigorously to WEST and SOUTHWEST from MECHILI and TENGEDER (.) 4 Ind Div is being reinforced by Force E (JALO FORCE) from CHARRUBA and by other units (.) South African Div less one Bde is moving to MECHILI (.) Intention is to reform 1 Armd Div behind MECHILI and to include it in striking force to be built up under command 30 Corps HQ.

JRL, AUC 670

147

Letter from Auchinleck to Lieutenant General Arthur Smith, CGS, Middle East, 30 January 1942

We moved here yesterday afternoon, a much more suitable, and incidentally a more pleasant spot, than TMIMI. 13th Corps H.Q. arrived at TMIMI before Neil [Ritchie] and I left, and I had a few minutes with Godwin Austen, who looks very fit and was in good form, very unperturbed, I thought, which is all to the good. They did make a very stupid mistake at 13 Corps H.Q. before they left MECHILI, in that the B.G.S. apparently told the fighters to clear out their landing grounds as they could not guarantee their safety against being raided by small columns. This was, I am sure, quite unnecessary, and made me, and Neil [Ritchie] too, very angry indeed. They were ordered back at once, but will, I am afraid, have lost two whole days of operating from forward landing grounds. A.O.C.-in-C. is naturally very upset, and so was "Mary" Conningham, who, by the way, is really magnificent. He goes from strength to strength, I think!

2. I flew from TMIMI to GAZALA 3, which is now our nearest bus stop; it took only ten minutes in a Blenheim. Neil and I then drove on to MRASSAS, where we found H.Q. 30 Corps and saw Willoughby Norrie, Davy,[132] Lysaght Griffin,[133] Steward the signaller, Aikenhead the gunner, and others. They were all in good form, and very cheered at the prospect of being more actively employed in the near future, in spite of having selected one of the most God-forsaken spots I have ever seen in Africa or Asia as their present headquarters.

3. You know Neil has decided to give 13th Corps the whole front from JEBEL to TENGEDER, both inclusive to 13th Corps, who take over today. This is quite right I think. Army should only control front line troops direct in dire emergency, of which BENGHASI was an instance.

4. Behind 13th Corps he intends to build up his striking force for a renewed offensive. The base of this force will be a reconstituted 1 Armd Div of one Armd Bde Gp and a motorised Bde Gp (G[uar]ds Bde Gp) which might have four battalions in it, i.e. an extra one from Support Gp of 1 Armd Div, the other battalion of the Gp being put in the Armd Bde Gp. I hope to add to this another Armd Bde Gp (4th) and possibly the reconstituted 7th Armd Div of 4th Armd Bde Gp and one motorised brigade group. I would also add 150th Inf Bde Gp and, if maintenance resources permit, perhaps the Free French Bde Gp too. I am afraid that our tank situation vis-à-vis that of the enemy has seriously deteriorated as a result of the fighting in which 22nd and 2nd Armd Bdes have suffered so severely. I have not yet had figures of our total tank losses, but they

---

132 Brigadier G. M. O. Davy.
133 Brigadier E. H. Lysaght-Griffin.

must be large, and all I fear have been abandoned to the enemy, who will certainly put some into running order, thus augmenting his own strength.

5.   We have got to face the fact that, unless we can achieve superiority on the battlefield by better co-operation between the arms and more original leadership of our armoured forces than is apparently being exercised at present, we may have to forego any idea of mounting a strategical offensive, because our armoured forces are tactically incapable of meeting the enemy in the open, even when superior to him in number. Another very serious aspect which is obtruding itself more and more is the growth of an inferiority complex amongst our armoured forces, owing to their failure to compete with the enemy tanks which they consider (and rightly so) superior to their own in certain aspects. This is very dangerous, and will be most difficult to eradicate once it takes root, as I am afraid it is doing now. It becomes, therefore, all the more important to weld the three arms together as closely as possible.

As you will see from the draft telegram enclosed with this letter, I have put this matter very plainly to the Prime Minister, as the military authorities at Home, including Martel, must realise what they are up against, and that it is no good just counting tanks or regiments and pretending that ours are individually as good as the Germans, because they are not. Before we can really do anything against the Germans on land, they have got to be made as good and better both in equipment, organisation and training.

As you know, I am not inclined to pessimism, but I view our present situation with some misgiving, so far as our power to take the offensive on a large scale is concerned. However, we must go all out now to get things right. If you like, get Gott in and Lumsden too, and thrash the matter out with them as frankly and as brutally as you like. No time now for politeness!

6.   I am afraid that 7 Ind Inf Bde must have lost very heavily at BENGHASI, and it is unfortunate that the majority of the artillery of 4th Indian Division was with this brigade. Its loss would be really serious. There are signs this morning that at least part of the Bde Gp may have broken out to the east and south east, as several columns of unknown composition and strength are reported to be nearing CHARRUBA and MECHILI. If they have managed to get away anything substantial in this way, it is a creditable performance.

The rest of the 4th Ind Div has withdrawn, according to orders, to the BARCE – MARAUA line, leaving, I hope, rearguards covering the TOCRA defile, which was blown yesterday, and other delaying positions. Force E is to leave CHARRUBA today, and join 4 Ind Div at MARAUA.

The division is now very weak, as 5th and 11th Bdes have only two bns each. Neil [Ritchie] has sent up 3/1 Punjab to rejoin it, and 1/6 Rajputana Rifles, having collected 2 ½ coys who are going up from TMIMI to join their Bde. (They were taken away by 13 Corps to guard aerodromes and H.Q. at ANTELAT apparently, and were not fully mobile when the Bosche bundled 13 Corps out of the place). I want you to do all you can to equip Worcesters and the other battalion (3/7 Baluch?) of the 29th Inf Bde and send them up as quick as you can to rejoin their H.Q. I am speaking to Sandy[134] about it today if he turns up. Also I want to know if any Indian mountain batteries can be made available for the 4th Ind Div in the JEBEL and, if so, how many and how soon? I believe one of them has been mechanised or partially mechanised and I would like this up at once. I do not think it is much good sending up mule batteries as they are too expensive to maintain, but I am going to discuss this with Neil and Sandy.

I would like the possibility of mechanising these batteries also gone into at once, in case we need them up here.

7. You will have seen from my draft telegram of yesterday to the C.I.G.S what Neil Ritchie's general intentions are, so I will not repeat them here.

8. I am sorry Lyttelton had to interrupt his tour, but I am glad it was for political not military reasons. I did not hear what really happened in the crisis between the King and the Cabinet, though I know how it started.

The liaison officer is not in yet, so I will end. I enclose draft telegram to Prime Minister, and draft communique which John has had some difficulty in writing.

JRL, AUC 671

---

134 Brigadier Alexander Galloway, BGS, 8th Army, 1941–42.

148

Telegram from Auchinleck to General Sir Alan Brooke, 4 February 1942

FIRST (.) GODWIN-AUSTEN has asked to be relieved of command 13 (13) Corps because he finds it difficult to work under RITCHIE (.) Have made enquiries and am sure he can NOT (NOT) be left where he is (.) Have accordingly appointed GOTT to replace him as temporary measure with rank local Lieutenant-General (.) RITCHIE wants him and good commander is essential at once (.)

SECOND (.) Have ordered GODWIN-AUSTEN return CAIRO at once and will then demand his reasons in writing as am NOT (NOT) satisfied regarding his request for relief during critical operations (.) Will let you know result (.)

THIRD (.) Am putting J.C. CAMPBELL from 7 (7) Support Gp temporarily in command 7 (7) Armd Div now reforming in DELTA with the local rank Major-General (.)

FOURTH (.) Hope you will approve these arrangements and request authority for acting ranks [.]

JRL, AUC 681

149

Letter from Lieutenant General N. M. Ritchie to Auchinleck, 6 February 1942

I am sending you herewith three sketches[135] which show in outline the dispositions of EIGHTH ARMY:-

(a) Present conditions.
(b) Intermediate conditions.
(c) Final dispositions.

This will give you an idea of what the aim is at the moment, and I feel that the final dispositions, while being sound for a defensive if

---

135 These do not survive in the Auchinleck papers in the JRL.

we have to fight a main battle against the enemy on the GAZALA – HACHEIM, also lend themselves to preparations for the offensive. The 30th Corps can be built up as a striking force for further operations in CYRENAICA. I would, however, like to make it quite clear that the dispositions envisaged are in fact merely 'back bone' for the fighting of a defensive battle, but that I have no intention of remaining on my heels on the GAZALA – BIR HACHEIM line, but on the contrary to carry out minor offensive operations to drive the enemy as far North and West of this as possible, to re-establish our columns on the general line DERNA – CHARRUBA and deny the enemy the use of the landing grounds at DERNA, MARTUBA and MECHILI.

2. I cannot but help feeling that the enemy must be very weak in front of us now and all the information I have points to the possibility of his having jammed into the Eastern end of the JEBEL a force which I estimate consists approximately of two German Bn Gps with arty and possibly some tanks and a proportion of the TRIESTE Div in rear of this. This "block" of enemy is concentrated roughly in the triangle DERNA – TMIMI – CARMUSA, and from air reconnaissance it seems very doubtful if he has anything within supporting distance of it. I doubt whether in fact he has anything in the JEBEL East of about BARCE. If this is correct I feel that the enemy is starting already to stick out his neck and I have, therefore, told STRAFER to investigate immediately the possibilities of undertaking a minor offensive into the JEBEL directed towards CARMUSA, with the object of cutting off as much as possible of the enemy's elements South of DERNA, where they appear to me to be strung out in a narrow line more or less astride the main road to GAZALA. He is getting down to this at once. This would be the first step towards re-establishing our control in the JEBEL as far as DERNA exclusive. The enemy's maintenance difficulties must be of extreme difficulty so long as he is unable to use BENGHAZI. Comparable, I think, to our operating ourselves in the SIRTE neighbourhood based on TOBRUK, and I know what these difficulties present.

3. I can only say that I am extremely worried about the withdrawal of the 4th Indian Division through the JEBEL. I am making full investigations now but have the impression that they have lost nothing, and that the main concern in the mind of their Commander was to

get away as quickly as possible, leaving no thought to the value of delay, of striking the enemy, or of holding him as far North and West as possible. I must not prejudice the case until I am in possession of all the facts, but I feel that I should let you know that I have every grave doubts as to TUKER's capacity as a commander in a tight situation. I have put STRAFER[136] fully into the picture. As you know, I asked GODWIN AUSTEN whether he was satisfied, and he told me that he was. If my fears prove well-founded, there will be no alternative I think than to remove TUKER from the command. I think he gets terribly tired and in these conditions is inclined to view things in the most depressing light.

4. I cannot tell you what a relief it has been to feel that I have got GOTT with me now. GODWIN AUSTEN proceeds by road to ALEXANDRIA to pick up his kit before going to CAIRO. I do not imagine that he will reach CAIRO for two or three days yet.

JRL, AUC 683

150

Letter from Auchinleck to Lieutenant General N. M. Ritchie, 6 February 1942

Sent by Sandy Galloway. Please return it by Sandy as copies are limited

I enclose a copy of a note DC (42) 20 I put up to the Defence Committee on 4 Feb. They approved of it generally and a telegram based on it is about to go home to the Chiefs of Staff. I thought it would interest you. I do not think it differs in any way from what we have agreed upon already.

2. I hope to send you a comprehensive instruction containing all those points we have recently decided together. I am sending up the draft of this by Sandy for you to read and criticise if you wish before it is finally issued. So analyse it carefully and say what you like about it.

---

136 Major General W. H. E. Gott.

3.   I am so glad Gott is in the saddle, and I hope he will be able to set about any enemy advanced detachments who may put themselves within his reach. A success now, even a minor one, would be invaluable. I won't labour the point as I know you are just as anxious to do this as I am.

4.   The plans for reinforcing you are going ahead well I think. Sandy will explain them to you, and also tell you what I would <u>like</u> to happen about the return of troops to the Delta. But my wishes in this matter come second to your tactical needs. Nothing must happen which might endanger our hold on the present line or the security of TOBRUK.

5.   I note you have split 1st. South African Division and have put some of them on to work on the frontier defences. This is, I suppose, because in the last resort this division might have to hold that particular locality? I agree this is highly desirable. I know, however, you will watch closely the inevitable tendency in operations of this sort for formations to split up and disintegrate. You will remember the trouble we had last Summer trying to get the bits and pieces together!

6.   As Sandy will tell you, I am very willing to leave you the 4th Indian Division to be in reserve and to work on the frontier defences. They know the game very well – better than anyone probably, and are good workers, as you know. I do not want them split up if it can possible be avoided, as after their recent experience, it is very necessary that they should retain their divisional and brigade entities. So far as is possible, too, their divisional troops (gunners, sappers and ancillary troops) should be left with them, though I realise you may want some of their artillery forward, and also that you may have to immobilise them to a great extent to find transport for the New Zealanders.

     I am very anxious to have your views on the withdrawal from BENGHASI and particularly on Tuker's handling of it, also on the present condition of the 4th division as a whole.

7.   I have had a very good wire from the C.I.G.S. about the 13th Corps, approving of all the action taken, so that is all right! What a life!!

8.   If you have time, tell Sandy your final proposals for GIARABUB. Some day I hope to reconstitute the 38th Ind Inf Bde, as I have uses for it. You will bear this in mind, I know.

9. I know you are frightfully busy, but I would like when you can give it to me a brief official account of the recent operations, as I feel I am likely to be asked for one myself before long. I would like you to add your opinion on the conduct of them without any reservations.

10. Your letter HQ/DO/70/6/G(O) (what a portentous number! Are all these really needed?!!) just received. I have just had time to look at your three layout sketches. We had a discussion yesterday on what we could leave with you and what we wanted out if we could get them, without weakening you too much.

The results of this discussion Sandy is taking up to you. They differ to some extent from your picture, but I am sure we can adjust this. I do not feel that 3 Ind Motor Gp is altogether suited to a <u>defensive</u> role in GIARABUB, but perhaps you intend to use it offensively?

I won't say any more now, as Sandy has the whole picture. Good luck to you.

JRL, AUC 686

151

Letter from Auchinleck to General Sir Alan Brooke, CIGS, 6 February 1942

Thank you very much for your letter of the 21st January, which reached me two or three days ago. I have just heard that there is a fast air bag going today, so I have not time to write you a long letter, but I hope to send you one at the weekend.

You will be getting in a day or two a long telegram from the Defence Committee out here, giving my views, as accepted by them, on the possibility of our resuming the offensive at an early date. I hope this telegram will be quite clear, and speak for itself, but in it I purposely refrained from giving the detailed calculations of our prospective tank strength on which we have reached our conclusions, as set out in the telegram. I have done this because I have learnt from previous experience the impossibility of reconciling such figures with those arrived at by calculations carried out at home, and particularly by the Defence Minister. I have, however, sent you under separate cover a note I wrote for the Defence Committee on which the telegram was based. In this note our calculations are given in full, as I thought you would like to have them for your own personal information, and that of your advisers.

I have had your telegram about the change of command in 13th Corps, and I am most grateful to you for your generous and very ready support. As soon as I have got some more information on the subject I will let you know the situation at once.

Thank you very much for your comments about the command of the 9th Army;[137] I am giving them the most careful consideration, and hope to write to you again on the subject very shortly.

JRL, AUC 687

152

Letter from General Sir Alan Brooke, CIGS to Auchinleck, 6 February 1942

My dear Auk,

Very many thanks for a series of long and interesting letters of yours.

I have been through all the points you raised carefully and propose to answer some of them now.

But first and foremost I should like to offer my deep sympathy at the setback that your forces have suffered. I can so well imagine what a deep disappointment this must be to you, and am so very sorry for you.

Looking at Rommel's counter-stroke from the more detached point of view, I cannot help feeling that Shearer's over optimistic intelligence played a large part in accounting for your troubles. You may remember that we doubted his figures here and queried them, and also that in a previous letter I had referred to the danger of his over optimistic reports, which were consistently being proved as under-estimates of the enemy's power of recuperation, resistance, or evasion. I am afraid that it is in his nature to always under-estimate his opponent's strength, a dangerous failing. He suffered, from all accounts, from the same failing when working for Wavell. It is now my own impression but one that I have gathered from all quarters and I do hope you will consider seriously the danger of retaining him as your D.M.I.

---

137 This references discussions as to whether General Sir Maitland Wilson, GOC
9th Army, should be posted to another command. It was to be 21 August 1942
before he was replaced by Lieutenant General William Holmes.

I have read through your proposals for your reorganization with the greatest interest and see that they conform closely to the views you expressed to the Chatfield Committee. I am having your proposals carefully examined with a view to deciding to what extend they are applicable to all theatres of war.

I see all the advantages of such an organization when using small forces as in Libya or in the North-West Frontier of India, and when circumstances necessitate supplying small columns. When operating in European theatres with large forces, large-scale attacks still remain necessary, and the power of delivering such attacks must be retained. In the recent large-scale exercise we carried out last Autumn with some nine divisions and three armoured divisions, one of the outstanding defects was the inability of commanders to stage even a divisional attack, owing to the universal custom of operating by brigade groups.

Meanwhile, I fully appreciate that for the conditions of warfare in which you are engaged, small columns in a brigade group are desirable. I have therefore wired approving your proposed reorganization within your theatre of operations with the stipulation that any transfer of formations from your theatre to another must be on a War Establishment basis.

As soon as we have had our discussion on your organization I shall let you know the results.

I am afraid that Hobart's[138] tour in the Middle East left such an unpleasant taste behind that all the Armoured Corps are still looked upon with suspicion! I can assure you that they have moved a long way since Hobo preached his doctrine. The close co-operation of Infantry, Artillery and tanks in armoured divisions has been an accepted fact at home for the last year and a half.

I am in full agreement with you that all Corps Commanders must be capable of commanding either motorised or armoured divisions, but the commander must be trained for this role, must have a good knowledge of the characteristics of all these arms. Furthermore, and the most important factor of all, the communication must be developed to the highest standard of wireless efficiency to admit of full advantage being taken.

I have approved the promotion of your D.M.T. to Major-General, since you considered it necessary. I do, however, still consider that your organization is wrong as it fails to provide you with the necessary A.F.V. advice on operational, organization and equipment matters in addition to those connected with training. The distribution and general state of

---

138 Major General Percy Hobart, a controversial exponent of armoured warfare.

readiness of your armoured forces at the time of Rommel's counter-stroke is, I feel, an example of the lack of advice on important matters connected with the handling of armoured forces. I do hope you will re-consider the advisability of appointing an A.F.V. Major-General on similar lines to your Chief Gunner and Sapper. There is no reason why such an appointment should lead to a tendency to the formation of a separate "armoured army" such as Hobo was always seeking for.

There are a multitude of important technical points connected with equipment, wireless, armament, etc., which require control from some central head. I do not consider that Rosy Lloyd is the calibre for such a task. If you felt you wanted someone from home for such a job, I should be prepared to pick you the very best we could find.

One of the fundamental defects that requires remedying is the lack of gun power of our tanks. We are doing all we can to get the 6-pr. in as quickly as possible in some form or another. Meanwhile, we have just despatched 150 of the 6-pr. A/T guns; these should assist in replacing 2-prs. and rendering the latter available for arming infantry as you suggest. I can promise you we shall do all we can to press on with the 6-prs.

Turning to Syria, Iraq and Persia, I fully realise the result of the withdrawal of Australian Divisions and of intercepting 18th British Division and 17th and 14th Indian Divisions. It was inevitable to meet Far East threats. Luckily, Russian situation has decreased danger. Recent J.I.C. survey points to the fact that German thrust through Caucasus or Turkey could not materialise much before middle or end of July. But even by that time we shall be lucky if we succeed in getting more than two divisions out to you, plus all reinforcements, A.A. guns, Air, etc.

Shipping is the complete bottle-neck. W.S. convoys[139] won't take more than one division per month at the maximum, and the March convoy, at your request, takes reinforcements etc. so that first division can only start by April convoy (arriving June), and the next May (arriving July)!

We are examining every possible way of improving on this, but prospects are poor. I am still counting on getting some divisions out of India to the Middle East, provided Burma and Far East don't deteriorate further.

I quite agree as regards necessity for better Air Service to the Middle East, we are at present taking this up, but are up against shortage of aircraft.

---

139 'Winston Special' convoys consisted of fast ships which transported troops to Egypt via the Cape of Good Hope.

As regards officers – I am glad you have given Gott a Corps and Campbell[140] an Armoured Division. They ought to do well.

I agree that Freyberg is not really fit for a Corps. I can provide you with an extra Corps H.Q. liberated by U.S.A. relief of Ireland. It is commanded by Anderson[141] and I would sooner that he went with his Corps H.Q. He is not much to look at, but there are few sounder than him.

As regards Blamey, I presume that he will vanish with the bulk of the Australians and shall press for him to do so.

Lavarack,[142] of course, goes with his Corps. Holmes[143] and Stone[144] you have now got fixed up as you wanted.

Jumbo Wilson – I shall await your final verdict.

What about Arthur Smith, ought he to remain on much longer as C.G.S.?

I hear rumours that he is getting rather weary. Have you got anyone in your eye to replace him? Would Neil Ritchie do, or would you want anyone from home if you do think of replacing him.

I still feel that a series of exchanges between Middle East and home would be good value from both sides and am quite ready to fall in with any suggestions you may make.

I am afraid that I have inflicted a long letter on you. I really wish I could have a chance of a talk with you.

JRL, AUC 688

---

140 When Gott was promoted to command 13 Corps, Brigadier John 'Jock' Campbell was promoted Major General to take over 7th Armoured Division. However, Campbell was killed in a road accident on 26 February 1942.

141 Lieutenant General Desmond Anderson commanding 3 Corps.

142 Lieutenant General J. D. Lavarack, commanding 1st Australian Corps.

143 Lieutenant General William Holmes, who had recently been posted to command Ninth Army.

144 Lieutenant General Robert Stone, who had recently replaced Holmes as GOC British Troops, Egypt.

153

Letter from Lieutenant General N. M. Ritchie to Auchinleck, 11 February 1942

Yesterday after many troubles in getting there by air, I spent a long time with the 13th Corps, where I saw TUKER, BRINK,[145] DE LARMINAT[146] and KOPANSKI.[147] The first thing that struck me was the tremendously high morale that exists and the complete confidence amongst them all that they are ready for the enemy should he deign to attack, and that they will give him a thorough thrashing. I must say that it was most refreshing. The POLES are a little bit down on account of the high sick rate and their strengths are a good deal below establishments. I will do all I can, and STRAFER[148] has this in hand, to get them out of the most forward positions as soon as this is feasible.

2. <u>COLUMNS.</u>

We are all very disappointed with the results of the Columns so far and STRAFER left me to go and see CURRIE[149] to discuss how the tactics are to be altered, and the composition of Columns varied, so that they have more punch and can hit harder than in the past. The answer here comes I think in the use of tanks with columns. We had a squadron of Honeys[150] out with CURRIE, but no opportunity for using them occurred. This I attribute to the fact that they were not directed wide enough and were sent into country which was not altogether suitable for their use. This appreciation of suitable country for tanks is, I feel quite convinced, a most important factor in the directions that are issued to commanders of Columns before they commence operations; this will be done. There are more encouraging reports on columns yesterday in the MECHILI area. They gave the enemy a bit of a knock there.

---

145 Major General G. L. Brink, GOC 1st South African Division.
146 General Edgard Larminat, commanding 1st Free French Brigade.
147 General Stanislaw Kopański, commanding Independent Polish Brigade in the Middle East.
148 Lieutenant General W. H. E. Gott, then commanding 13th Corps.
149 Probably Lieutenant Colonel John Currie, then commanding 4th Regiment RHA and soon to take command of 9th Armoured Brigade.
150 The M3 Stuart Light Tank.

3. ## THE SITUATION GENERALLY.

On my return last night I found JOHN SHEARER's appreciation that he had submitted to you and passed on to me for information. Personally I agree that the enemy's moves indicate only one thing and that is to resume offensive operations at the earliest possible moment when he anticipates that we will not be strong and will not be ready for him. I admit that we will not be particular flush in Armour but, nevertheless, I think we can take him on quite well. I would, of course, prefer that he should attack us in about a month's time because then I feel that we would not only give him a knock but might well be able completely to defeat all the forces he employs against us. Due to our lack of armour I doubt whether anything so complete as this will be possible within the next week.

4. ## INFANTRY BRIGADE GROUPS. REQUIRED FOR FWD POSNS.

I have discussed this at great length with STRAFER now that he has had a chance of really appreciating the ground, the enemy's strength and the dispositions that they have taken up. As a result I am quite satisfied that for security we require the equivalent of eight Inf Bde Gps for the defence of the position GAZALA – HACHEIM, and I attach at Appendix "A" a statement showing how these should be disposed. I am quite sure that TOBRUK, which after all is the main supply centre for any dispositions we may assume on this position, must be adequately safe-guarded against long-ranging enemy columns. The way to ensure this is to have the entrances to TOBRUK via ACROMA and the West and EL ADEM and the South adequately secured. This will require an Inf Bde Gp at each of these places.

5. ## AIR SITUATION.

The enemy is becoming a great deal more active in the air and this situation will, I understand, continue for at least the next ten days until the re-equipping of additional squadrons is completed. The troops do not mind this particularly as the enemy efforts so far have been extraordinarily feeble. On the other hand, I think it is important that we should speed up the re-establishment of our air superiority as early as this can be reasonably done, and I know that

"Mary"[151] has raised this matter with the A.O.C.-in-C during his visit to CAIRO. The South Africans shot down two dive-bombers yesterday, which has put up their tails a lot. At the moment the Poles, in the centre of the GAZALA Position, seem to be viewing the greatest [?] in from enemy dive bombers, and they have lost a few in casualties.

6. <u>TUKER.</u>

I had a good talk with TUKER today and as a result I do not consider that his removal from command of the 4th In Div is necessary. There were two occasions during the withdrawal when his attitude worried me a good deal and when I felt he had, to some extent, lost control of the situation. Actually I think that on these two occasions he had to some extent lost his grip but I am satisfied after talking to him, that the reasons for this are his lack of experience of War up to the present and letting himself be worried when information about what is happening ahead does not reach him. He has bought his experience now. He is a deep thinker and has many theories and this last operation through the GEBEL will, I am sure, have brought his theories more into the line with what practice makes possible. In the circumstances I am satisfied to leave him in command. I had a good talk with him about his health, as I wondered whether the sinus[152] trouble he had suffered from before was causing him trouble once more. He assures me however that this is not the case.

7. <u>RELIEFS.</u>

I am sending you at Appendix "B" a statement showing how I think reliefs may go up to about the end of this month. It is of course frightfully hard to forecast but as you have always told me, the tactical situation must dictate primarily what can be released. I think the critical period may be up to the end of this month. As already explained, I feel that eight Inf Bde Gps are necessary for the securing of this position and it is on this basis that I have calculated what formations can be released and when this release can take place.

---

151 Air Vice Marshal Arthur 'Mary' Coningham, commanding Desert Air Force.
152 'sinus'.

8. BATTLE HQ.

Today I am quite satisfied that I am too far back, as I had two mishaps getting to 13 Corps by air, finally having to make a forced landing at GAMBUT. So I am immediately establishing a Battle HQ Centre, forward, which I can occupy at short notice. A reconnaissance for it is being carried out today and I think that it will be somewhere in the GAMBUT neighbourhood. I have no intention of moving the whole of the ordinary Adv Army HQ with me. All I want, and all I need, is a small HQ like the one we had at SIDI DAUD. If I am in that area at any rate I can reach both the Corps in reasonable time by car.

9. FRONTIER DEFENCES.

I am visiting 30 Corps today and going round the SOLLUM defended area. If possible we will get down to MADDELENA as well and see the nature of the proposals for that part of the world.

P.S.   I think it may be difficult to withdraw the 5 N.Z. Bde as kept in Corps reserve, but I hope that this can be arranged.

JRL, AUC 699

154

Letter from Auchinleck to Lieutenant General N. M. Ritchie, 11 February 1942

1.   You will have various appreciations and ideas put forward by John Shearer as to possible future enemy action. I have also seen an excellent appreciation put up by Bob Priest, a copy of which was sent here. This appreciation was written before the enemy's recent moves forward to GIOVANNI BERTA and MECHILI but is none the less valuable for that.

2.   You have, I know, thought out all the possibilities. In fact, I imagine you think of little else! It is, therefore, perhaps wasting your time to task you to read my ideas on the subject. We, too, are thinking hard, and, being in less intimate association with the battle, may perhaps sometimes get a different angle on things. This is my excuse for inflicting these thoughts on you!

3. The enemy has been saying loudly and often in the last few days that he has got us on the run and implying that he is about to stage a major offensive. This may be bluff, or he may really think that we were so heavily defeated in Western Cyrenaica as to make us incapable of offering any real resistance to a further enemy offensive. I don't know which is right, but John Shearer inclines strongly to the second alternative.

4. It seems to me that the enemy has three courses open to him:-

    (i)   To hold his main forces back in Western Cyrenaica, keeping only light forces forward in touch with our troops.
    (ii) To gradually build up his forces in Eastern Cyrenaica until he has sufficient troops and an adequate supply organization to justify him in trying to mount a deliberate offensive against EGYPT.
    (iii) To mount a "blitz" attack with limited forces as soon as he can against out forward forces in the hope of throwing them into confusion and getting TOBRUK. His recent move seems to show that he is not thinking of (i), unless the forces involved are much weaker than would appear from the information at present available to us. It might, however, be equally a prelude to (ii) or (iii).

    The next two or three weeks are critical for us, as during them we shall be building up our strength in the forward area, both in tanks and infantry, to an extent which should make it risky for him to attempt a "blitz" attack on us. Course (iii) is, therefore, the most dangerous and all our immediate effort should be directed to meeting this threat.

5. It looks to me as if the enemy has formed two groups, one consisting of his German tanks and lorried infantry at present in the JEBEL AIDAR, and the other now at MECHILI comprising his Italian tanks and motorised troops. His tanks may be in full strength in these areas but he would seem to be weak in infantry. This look as if he had decided on a "blitz" attack if he has decided to attack at all, as if he were preparing for a deliberate attack he would probably build up his consolidating troops, that is his infantry, before concentrating all his tank force so far forward.

    It is just possible of course that his forward move was due to the fear that we might be thinking of trying to regain the line DERNA

– MECHILI, but this is unlikely I think. We will assume then that he intends to make a "blitz" attack.

6. In a "blitz" attack the enemy tanks must play the major part so it is essential to consider intensively how he is likely to use them.

At the moment they seem to be split, but, by using the road LAMLUDA – MECHILI, he can concentrate them either in the JEBEL or in the Desert. That is he can mount a strong tank attack from TMIMI or from MECHILI. In addition he can, if he wishes, side step his forces, tanks and infantry from DERNA through MECHILI to TENGEDER and attack from there, while containing us on the rest of the front.

7. The direction of his attack may be governed by his immediate objective. If, as seems likely, his object is to disorganise our system of command and supply by a sudden attack on a narrow front, his best objective would be TOBRUK, and he is likely, therefore, to aim at ACROMA – EL ADEM in the first instance. To succeed, his advance must be swift and continuous. Any wide outflanking movement is likely to give us time to change our dispositions to meet it and must complicate his always difficult supply problem.

8. Assuming that he is aiming at ACROMA, how can he best get to it? An attack along the escarpment from TMIMI would have the advantage of giving him the use of the main road for supply purposes and of cutting off our forces to the SOUTH from their main axis of supply. It would, however, open his flank and communications to attack by us from the SOUTH should his attack not go according to plan. It would also be directed against that part of our position which he must assume to be strongly defended and heavily mined in comparison with sectors further to the SOUTH.

9. If he decides against attack on our NORTHERN flank, he may try to envelop or crush our SOUTHERN flank with the object of reaching the area TOBRUK – EL ADEM – ACROMA and cutting off our forces in the GAZALA area. This would entail probably a preliminary concentration at TENGEDER, the building up of at least some reserves of fuel and water in that area, and then a march of 70 odd miles to BIR HACHEIM, which is not weakly held, or if he wishes to avoid attacking it, a still longer detour to the SOUTH, during which time his line of supply will be open to attack by us from the NORTH EAST and NORTH. This movement would

undoubtedly be combined with feint attacks, carried out with vigour and supported probably be some tanks, against our NORTHERN sector to induce us to concentrate our armoured forces in that area. Though the possibility of his adopting this course can not be altogether discounted, it seems unlikely that he will adopt it.

10. The third and last course open to him seems to be to go straight for his presumed objective – the area TOBRUK – EL ADEM – ACROMA. If he believes us to be weak and disorganised, as seems probable, he may think that he can afford to penetrate instead of relying on envelopment. His thrust to the Frontier during the battle of last November will provide him with a precedent, though on that occasion penetration tactics failed.

Should he decide to adopt this course, which I think is most likely, he will undoubtedly try to conceal his real object from us. Deception is likely to take the form of trying to make us believe –

(a) that the centre of gravity of his attack will be along the coast road, or

(b) that he is going to envelop our SOUTHERN flank and move NORTH EAST on TOBRUK.

Of the two the second is possibly the more likely as it should draw our armour away from the decisive point and put it in a position where it may be cut off from its supplies by the enemy thrust.

It is, of course, possible that a diversion by our SOUTHERN flank would, if unopposed, be developed by the enemy into a subsidiary attack so as to give the whole movement a pincer effect so far as the forces on our SOUTHERN flank are concerned.

If he adopts this course, it seems possible that he will side step his German tanks from the JEBEL to MECHILI, sending some of the Italian tanks with motorized units to the TENGEDER area, while everything possible is done to give us the idea that the main weight is on the SOUTH with only holding forces in the NORTH and centre. He will make his NORTHERN sector as strong as he can by field works, etc., in order to prevent us trying to disorganize his preparations and hamper his movements by taking offensive action in this area. In fact this process has already begun. He would then make a very rapid and concentrated advance in the greatest possible strength from the MECHILI area straight on ACROMA, hoping to over run any of our infantry who may be in the way and trusting that they will be unsupported by tanks. He may not even think it necessary or possible to draw off our 2nd Armoured Brigade to the SOUTH by the diversionary movement suggested, but judging by recent experience, may be satisfied that he can overcome any resistance it can offer should it be in his path.

There is a possibility that this operation might be aided by a parachute attack on TOBRUK itself or EL ADEM or on formation H.Q., with a view to causing disorganisation and confusion in our rear. The possibility of small diversionary sea-borne attacks against our communications or aerodromes can not be disregarded. The move of enemy naval personnel to DERNA might conceivably be connected with some such project.

11. These are signs that Rommel, running true on form, may be seriously underestimating our strength and capacity to resist further attacks by him. If this is so it should be possible to turn it to our advantage. To do this we must be able to mislead and surprise him and, if he attacks us, to counterattack him when he gives us the opening. This all needs intense and continuous planning which I am sure is going on all the time.

12. At the risk of being thought to be interfering, I would offer the following remarks which are probably of no value whatever, as you will have thought of them all long ago!

If the enemy attacks in the centre, as I think likely,

(a) We must guard against being led into sending our mobile hitting force – our tanks – away from the centre of gravity; that is we must keep them concentrated behind the centre.

(b) We must make the best possible use of our "infantry" tanks which have been proved to be most valuable in defence. The best use for these might be to strengthen key localities, the loss of which might hamper the mobility and counter-offensive power of our striking force.

(c) We should have a "stop" in the shape of minefields and entrenched positions held by reserve troops behind our centre, preferably WEST and SOUTH WEST of ACROMA, to check any enemy who may break through and force them to diverge to the SOUTH towards EL ADEM which should also be defended if troops are available.

13. We must be ready to strike in flank any enemy force attempting to pass through the twenty mile gap between the flank of the position

held by the infantry of the 1st Armoured Division and the 150th Infantry Brigade Group at BIR HACHEIM.

14. We must hold on at all costs to BIR HACHEIM which should be made as strong as possible, and perhaps be reinforced by some infantry tanks if they can be spared, but I doubt the possibility of this, so long as 1st Army Tank Brigade remains under strength. The stretch of excellent going which lies in this gap might tempt the enemy to use it as a supplementary line of advance, though it is perhaps too far to the SOUTH for his main axis of attack.

15. We must do everything possible to ensure that forward divisional and corps Headquarters are not over-run early in the battle as we cannot afford to have our command and intelligence information disorganized.

16. To sum up. If we are to take advantage of the enemy's apparent underestimation of our strength, and his possible consequent decision to attack us with inadequate forces, we must achieve surprise.

　　Surprise can only be achieved first by hiding from him our strength in tanks, and secondly by stationing them where they can be used to best effect, which implies keeping them concentrated.

　　To give of their best, our tanks must have the maximum support of our artillery and infantry firmly established in positions from which the enemy cannot shift them without risking heavy casualties, which he cannot afford if our information is correct.

　　We must not be led away by feints and movements designed to mislead us at which the enemy is very good. If we are to avoid this, we must have continuous and intensive ground and air reconnaissances of the most offensive kind. Above all we must try and keep track of his main tank concentrations.

P.S.　I signed the Operation Instruction this morning and sent it up to you. Hope it is all right. I am afraid you may be disappointed at the availability dates of reinforcements but I think these are on the safe side, at least I hope so. If you want the regiments of 4th Armoured Brigade sent up independently before the whole Brigade is ready, let me know at once and I'll do what I can. We will do all we can to hasten everyone. Meanwhile, don't send back <u>any</u> troops if you think you need them.

JRL, AUC 700

155

Letter from Auchinleck to Lieutenant General N. M. Ritchie, 12 February 1942

Many thanks for yours of the 11th, which reached me the same evening.

2. I am very glad to hear that morale is so high, and the credit must go to you and your Commanders. I am sorry that the Poles are a little hipped.

3. You are right about the work of the columns. Much depends on their ability to chase the enemy about and prevent him settling down. I was very glad to hear of the good show put up by one of them at MECHILI on the 10th.

   That is what is wanted. Don't hesitate to put in any column leader who brings off a good show for an award, if you think he is worth one. While on this subject, I wonder if you thought of BRIGGS[153] of 7 IND INF BDE in this connection?

4. I entirely agree with you that the next three weeks are critical, and that we must strain every nerve to strengthen ourselves forward. I am sending you up all I can. I have heard some talk, not from you, of "tired troops". Well we have no time to be tired I am afraid – any more than the Bosche has, and he has been through worse times in LIBYA than we have!!

   What do you think?! Withdrawal for ease of re-equipment is a different matter.

5. Your estimate of forces needed is most interesting, and I agree with it. It fits in pretty closely with a somewhat half-baked appreciation I had the temerity to send you to-day. I hope you do not think I am trying to butt in!

   I hope the 5 N.Z. BDE GP will be with you by the 13th, and that this will give you a reasonable margin of strength. As I told you before, you are to keep them as long as you need them, but when the 50 DIVISION begins to arrive, try if you can to keep the New Zealanders in Corps Reserve, but if this can't be done, it doesn't

---

153 Brigadier Harold Briggs.

matter. I wonder if you will be able to get all three Brigades of 50 DIVISION together? Probably not, as this would seem to entail relieving HAYDON'S Brigade[154] at HACHEIM?

I entirely agree with you about ACROMA and EL ADEM being necessary as "back stops" against a "blitz" raid.

6. JOCK spoke to me this evening about WILLOUGHBY NORRIE'S ideas of the areas to be held in the SALUM – MADDALENA sector. He has always disliked the idea of a defended area "in the blue" to the SOUTH, and always wanted to close up the whole system to the NORTH. I do not think he has grasped the idea underlying my conception of the defence, and I am quite certain he is wrong. I believe you agree with me, and I am not going to alter my decision. I hope they are pushing on with the work. I am sure they are. It has the makings of a tremendously strong position, I think.

7. I am very intrigued by what you say about TUKER, and I am glad you have decided as you have about him.

All the same, I should watch him very closely. He is, as you say, a great thinker and theorist, and as such, most valuable. These qualities do not, however, necessarily make a good commander in the field.

8. I am sure you are right to have a Battle H.Q. further forward, but if you go to GAMBUT have it properly dug in, preferably on the escarpment. No sense in running needless risks!

9. I shall be very interested to hear of your visit to the Frontier defences. Where would you put your mobile striking force in this position?

I think the "Playground" minefield can be made to play a very important part in the battle with reference to the use of our reserves.

10. I am sending JOCK up to you tomorrow with conundrums from all Branches. With your agreement, I propose to systematize these visits by senior Staff Officers of all Branches every few days.

The Junior Liaison Officers are not really of much value – no fault of theirs, but they are not big enough!

JRL, AUC 703

---

154 Brigadier C. W. Haydon, commanding 150th Infantry Brigade.

156

Letter from L. S. Amery, Secretary of State for India, to Auchinleck, 13 February 1942

I am very much concerned about the inadequacy, both in numbers and still more in quality, of the officers whom we are sending out for the expansion of the Indian Army. Latterly the War Office has been simply drafting them, with the result that a considerable proportion of them have been found really not in the least the type that could effectively command Indian troops. Then there are all the difficulties of shipping – I need say nothing about the tiresome question of pay, which I hope to get settled in the immediate future.

2. What I cannot help feeling is that the army in the Middle East must contain any number of men in the ranks who have shown the qualities that would fit them for a commission, but for all of whom commissions obviously cannot be found within the cadres of the Middle East. Surely these would make admirable officers in India, bringing real war experience, with the authority that confers, as well as their personal qualities, to the task. In other cases it might be possible to spare men who have already got their commissions to go to India, letting them be replaced in your units by promotion from the ranks. I understand that the War Office some time ago lifted the ban on more than 30 commissions a year being given from the Middle East to India, but I wonder very much whether the business of exchange between Middle East and India has yet been taken up on anything like an adequate scale for the kind of danger that is going to confront India in the next six months. It may well be that we may find ourselves actually fighting a Japanese army of invasion with half-trained and hopelessly under-equipped troops. But even with these, great things can be done if they have the right men to lead them.

3. I know it is hard to suggest to you, with the tremendous tasks immediately before you, to spare anything from your own forces. All I can say is that treating the war as a whole these men will pull far more weight training and leading 50 times their number in India than they would in the ranks of the Middle East, striving gallantly for the next opportunity of earning a commission. Incidentally, from the point of view of shipping – the most serious of all our

bottlenecks – sending them from the Middle East would also be a help.

4. I am afraid you have had to give up a good deal lately anyhow, on the larger scale, to meet the immediate danger in the Far East, and some of it, like the troops sent to Singapore, without saving the situation. I don't know whether the Japanese mean to turn to Burma next, or whether as would be in line with their general strategy of depriving us of the naval approaches – they may send an expedition to seize Ceylon. That would be a very serious thing, for your reinforcements as well as for India.

5. As for your own front, we live from day to day in hopes that, having got Rommel to advance far enough, and having repaired your tanks, you may give him a real knock and send what is left of him flying all the way to Tripoli. But we don't know your difficulties here, and may well be hoping for the impossible. But we badly need a victory somewhere at this hour.

JRL, AUC 705

157

Letter from Auchinleck to General Sir Alan Brooke, CIGS, 14 February 1942

Thank you very much for your letter of the 21st January and the 6th February which reached me on the 11th, and for your manuscript letter of the 21st January which came the same day.

2. I have sent you a telegram about the Major General A.F.V., and I think you will see that we do not really disagree on the subject. I think it must be quite clear, however, that so far as general training is concerned, the D.M.T. must be responsible to me and that the Major General A.F.V. is his advisor in this matter as well as mine. This is on all fours with the position of the Major General R.A. and E.-in-C. Moreover the Major General A.F.V. must not think that he "owns" the R.A.C. any more than the Major General R.A. "owns" the Gunners! All appointments, promotions, etc., must go through the M.S. to me in the same way as for the other arms. M.S. and I and the Selection Boards will, of course, freely consult

the Major General A.F.V. I feel that there should be no difficulty about this.

We have, I think, been a little at cross purposes over the whole affair due to this cursed necessity for having to argue at the end of a telegraph wire or wireless mast! As you know, we have been trying for months, almost years, to get Major Generals for our R.A., A.A., Ordnance and S. & T. heads and I am afraid I did not think there was any hope of getting two more Major Generals – one for D.M.T. and the other for A.F.V. Thinking I was likely to get one only, if I got any, I plumped for the D.M.T. as being the most needed in my opinion! I am sorry if we have worried you and wasted your time over this. I know you have got many more and much bigger things to think about.

If you can spare us a Major General A.F.V. please send him along.

3. I have had Godwin-Austen's report and have sent it to Neil Ritchie for his remarks, which have not yet reached me. I feel the whole affair may have been rather unnecessary but all concerned were under strain and at high pressure. I will let you know more when I next write.

4. As you know, my original intention was to reinforce 8th Army with the New Zealand Division, and orders were issued for this. I did not want to use it again so soon, particularly as it was training for amphibious operations on the Canal, but on the information then available, it seemed that it could be on the spot in LIBYA much sooner than the 50th Division, which was still on its way from IRAQ to SYRIA. However, owing to the difficulties of finding transport with which to re-equip it, it became evident that the 50th Division (of which as you know one brigade group is already with the 8th Army) could be there just as soon, if not sooner, than the New Zealanders. At the time Bernard Freyberg produced a cable from his Government deploring the need for putting the New Zealand Division into the line again so soon after its recent heavy casualties. They did not refuse their consent but were obviously very reluctant to agree. As I myself was also reluctant to use it, I was glad to be able to make the change even at the risk of some confusion occurring. This is not an easy Army to arrange! I am very far from being able to apply to all my soldiers "Do this and he doeth it". They generally do it in the end (not always) but it all takes time and diverts energy from the real business! The New

Zealand Government has been so wonderfully good all through that I was glad to be able to meet their wishes. I am now going to send the New Zealanders to SYRIA which will be a welcome change for them and also, I hope, give them a quiet month or two, though they will have to dig like moles!

5. About John Shearer. If there is any blame it is mine! I really think, if you don't mind my saying so, that you are not quite fair to him. I agree that at the outset of the present campaign some of our early communiques were too rosy, but then so were my own situation reviews to the Prime Minister and the C.I.G.S., and these I write myself and not at Shearer's dictation! We were misled by optimistic reports from the battle front of enemy tanks destroyed and driven off. I think these reports were genuine enough and that their inaccuracy was due to inexperience. I do not think you can say that the great majority of our communiques or reports have been over-optimistic. I "vet" the communiques myself, and Arthur Smith does it for me if I am away. The Press and B.B.C. reports at home <u>were</u> exaggerated and highly coloured but we are not responsible for these nor for high hopes expressed in public by members of the Government. I was optimistic and I am optimistic and I hope I shall stay so! When all is said and done, Rommel suffered a major defeat and I hope he will suffer another before we have done with him! I am sure you share my wishes!

I have found John Shearer's estimates of the enemy strength and intentions consistently good and with a high degree of accuracy. His figures and forecasts have been verified time and again by captured documents and prisoners' estimates.

Your own Intelligence people have challenged his opinions frequently and generally have had to own that he was right and they were wrong. The same applies to the R.N. and R.A.F. here.

I criticize and heckle him mercilessly myself and his optimism does not get past me I think. He is certainly optimistic rather than pessimistic, but a <u>really</u> pessimistic D.M.I. would not be welcome to me I'm afraid. He certainly makes mistakes, but fewer than any other Intelligence officer I have known. His organization is absolutely first-class and his originality, energy and drive are outstanding.

His advice as to cover plans and deception generally have been most valuable – in fact, invaluable.

He has made many enemies here and, I fancy, at home and it is largely his own fault that he is a controversial figure. If your people at the War Office can produce concrete proof of his dangerous over-optimism, I would be very grateful to have it. I do not want to part with him on any account at present, as his knowledge of this theatre and of the enemy is unique in my opinion. I feel that Middle East and the War Office too owe him a lot.

6.   I am writing to you separately on the subject of reorganization which is as you say a very big one, but it must be tackled and urgently in my opinion. We have now got our light armoured divisions forming. Composition –

        one armoured car regiment
        one armoured brigade group
        one motor brigade group.

The armoured brigade group has three tank regiments, one artillery regiment of three eight gun 25-pdr batteries and one sixteen gun anti-tank battery as an integral part of it, and one motor battalion which includes one anti-tank company of sixteen 2-pdrs and three motor companies instead of four as previously.

Have got the Army Commanders here (less Neil) for our monthly conference. Latest news seems to show that the enemy is on the move as expected.

JRL, AUC 706

158

Letter from Lieutenant General N. M. Ritchie to Auchinleck, 15 February 1942

I have just received your DO/ADC/11 dated 14th February. The situation is boiling up here. As you know, it started doing so yesterday, and the enemy is definitely closing up on to us today. I will be sending you an appreciation of how I see the situation, by signal later this evening, as I did this morning, and will not enlarge on the situation in this letter, for it will doubtless completely have changed by the time this reaches you.

    The arrival of the Valentines will certainly help a great deal but it is a thousand pities that we have not a few more days in which to prepare for this.

2. JOCK told me that it was your intention, in future, to place "I" tanks more or less permanently under command of Infantry Divisions. I think this an excellent idea. For one reason, if for no other, it will teach our people how to handle them, and this is one of the things they sadly lack at the moment.

There is only one difficulty that I foresee in this proposal and this is that the "I" tanks cannot keep up with the speed with which motorised or lorry-borne troops move. They would certainly have to be transporter-borne for any long moves, and this is a slow and laboursome process. On the other hand, I am quite sure that "I" tanks within the division will strengthen the offensive powers of divisions tremendously.

3. About SIWA and GIARABUB. Since writing you I have discussed the matter at considerable length with REID who, of course, knows the country well. He advises me most strongly against dividing the forces and feels convinced that GIARABUB only need be held. I am taking up the matter with WILLOUGHBY NORRIE.

GRAHAM, who runs the MIDDLE EAST COMMANDO now has written me suggesting that GIARABUB might be a very suitable centre from which he might operate the COMMANDOS offensively against the enemy's L of C in WESTERN CYRENAICA. I am going to go into this matter further because I think there are great possibilities in it.

4. I replied to your wire of yesterday about the possibility of a change in the situation. I was not sure when I got your message what was the information on which you based your appreciation. Personally, I can see no indications of the Axis Forces withdrawing at the moment and I think that possibly the way in which his covering forces gave way before us on the 12th and 13th was an effort on his part, as you too think possible, to draw us out from our prepared defensive positions. If that was his idea he has, at any rate, failed to that extent. As I wired to you yesterday, I have no hesitation in saying that I am convinced the way to follow him up is with strong columns, and in this STRAFER agrees. I am also equally certain that we must hold the GAZALA position as a secure base from which to operate.

5. I had not meant that the 1st Armoured Division should be taken right out, but only feel that should the situation remain as it is now it would be preferable if the 7th Armoured Division took over the

forward role from the 1st Armoured Division, thus enabling the latter to shake down a bit while still remaining close up.

6. I am delighted to hear that the General Grant Tanks[155] are creating a good impression and I feel sure that they are going to be of inestimable value here.

JRL, AUC 711

159

Notes of an interview between Auchinleck and Major General I. P. de Villiers[156] (with the CGS[157] present) to discuss the future organization of the South African forces in the Middle East, 16 February 1942

1. Agreed that manpower limits total fighting troops to equivalent of four brigade groups, plus sufficient personnel for two or three additional units.

2. Agreed that 20% reinforcements is the figure on which calculations must be based.

3. Agreed that future organization of S.A. Forces could be either –

    (a) One Division of three Brigade Groups plus one Independent Brigade group,
       or
    (b) Two Divisions each of two Brigade Groups.

    Decision as to (a) or (b) to be left to the Field Marshal.[158] (Note: (a) is more economical in manpower, and is strongly preferred

---

155 The Grant Tank was designed and manufactured in the USA and served in the US Army as the Lee Tank. Its armour was up to 57 mm thick and it had a cross country speed of 10 mph. It had a 75 mm gun in sponson and a 37 mm gun in turret and was therefore able to equal the firepower of the heaviest German tanks then serving in the Middle East.

156 Major General Isaac de Villiers, GOC 2nd South African Division.

157 Lieutenant General Arthur Smith, CGS, Middle East.

158 Field Marshal J. C. Smuts.

by Commanders 1 and 2 S.A. Divisions and is acceptable to the Commander-in-Chief.)

4. Agreed that any surplus personnel should be used to form units in the following order:-

    (a) Additional Field Artillery Regiment for the Division (or per Division).

    (b) M.G. Battalion for the Division (or per Div.)

         or

         Reconnaissance Battalion for the Division (or per Div.) organized on an A.C. basis.

5. No change to be made in present organization until the tactical situation stabilizes. Re-organization then to be carried out on a "permanent long term" basis. Possibility of forming a Tank formation to be borne in mind but NOT to prejudice general principles of re-organization outlined above.

JRL, AUC 714

160

Cipher message from Auchinleck to H. D. R. Margesson,[159] Secretary of State for War, 17 February 1942

Understand from A.O.C.-in-C. that Press campaign in full blast at Home attributes our recent reverse in CYRENAICA and fact that we have NOT repeat NOT already reached TRIPOLI to lack of air support and failure to exploit the air superiority gained by R.A.F. after strenuous effort and most skilful handling (.) As you know nothing could be further from the truth (.) Our recent reverse I put down to our having tried to bluff enemy with weak forces in forward area while we strained every nerve to build up reverses in BENGHASI to enable us to bring stronger forces forward (.) Enemy called our bluff and gained tactical success which is always possible contingency in fairly equally matched forces which he

---

159 Margesson was to resign as Secretary of State for War in February 1942. He is generally portrayed as a scapegoat, being held responsible for the fall of Singapore on 15 February.

then exploited with undoubted skill (.) Once he gained command of the Desert by virtue his superior strength in tanks resulting from our relatively heavy losses it became strategically impossible for us to stay in BENGHASI or anywhere in the CYRENAICAN bulge owing to certainty of communications being cut (.) Hence choice of GAZALA position for stabilization this being most WESTERLY line on which stand can be made without grave risk of being easily outflanked or cut off from base in TOBRUK (.) Throughout recent fighting as from beginning of campaign R.A.F. have been magnificent in their aid to the Army which has nothing but praise for them and their commanders (.) I view with greatest anxiety any attempt to revive the controversy between Army and Air Force which has been successfully buried at any rate in the Middle East (.) Revival must cause bad feeling between the Services and might have disastrous results.

JRL, AUC 717

161

Cipher message from Auchinleck to Winston Churchill, 27 February 1942

Review of situation.

First.   We now have strong defensive position thirty six miles square well mined and organised in depth in area GAZALA TOBRUK EL GUBI BIR HACHEIM and designed to meet enemy break through to rear areas with Armd forces in attempt disorganise our system command and supply. Am satisfied that enemy attack on this position should be repulsed with loss and it is too extensive to be enveloped or ignored. Real value of this position is that it provides security for TOBRUK and therefore forms admirable base for future offensive.

Second.   General GOTT Comd 13 Corps holds this position with 1 S A Div (two Bde Gps) 50 Div complete, Polish Bde Gp (three bns, arty etc), Free French Bde Gp (four bns, arty etc.), 29 Ind Inf Bde Gp (four bns), one bn heavy tanks (MATILDAS) and 1 Armd Div comprising 2 Armd Bde (90 Crusaders and 70 Stuarts), 200 Gds Bde Gp and one bn 1 Army Tank Bde with 50 Valentines under command. In addition 5 N Z Inf Bde is at EL ADEM under comd 13 Corps, but is due to go to SYRIA help fill gap left by 70 Div soon as 8 Army can spare it. General GOTT has also following Armd C Regts ROYALS and 4 S A Armd Car Regt.

Third. 30 Corps General NORRIE has 2 S A Div (three Bdes) in SALUM CAPUZZO are and 4 Ind Div (less 7 Ind Inf Bde returning to DELTA to refit) in EL HAMRA area NORTH EAST of MADDALENA, both working on defensive localities. These two localities with extensive minefields and entrenched positions made last autumn and lying to East of them make very strong coordinated position on which to fall back should things go really wrong (.) I look on it as a wise insurance but my intention is to hold firmly the GAZALA TOBRUK position (.) JARABUB already largely prepared for defence before November offensive held by detachment to prevent enemy using it and SIWA as base for raids against our communications and also to keep enemy guessing as to our future intentions (.)

Fourth (.) Enemy dispositions as deduced by me (.) German AFRIKA CORPS of 15 (15) and 21 (21) Armd Divs and all or part of 90 (90) Lt Div Area DERNA TMIMI MARTUBA with possibly 160 (160) medium tanks and 20 (20) light personnel estimated about 15000 (15000) with 110 (110) fd and med guns and 3000 (3000) vehicles (.) BURCKHARDT attachment of parachute and commando troops strength about 800 (800) may also be in this area (.) Italian mobile Corps of ARIETE Armd Div and TRIESTE (,) reinforced by some personnel of TRENTO Div (,) Motor Div round MECHILI with possibly 100 (100) medium and 25 (25) light tanks (.) Personnel estimated about 9000 (9000) with 72 (72) fd and med guns and 600 (600) vehicles (.) Remainder Italian forces comprising SABRATA (,) PAVIA (,) BRESI [?] (,) BOLOGNA and TRENTO divs echeloned along coast from BELAS to EL AGHEILA and beyond strength estimated at 13000 (13000) with 54 (54) guns and very few vehicles (.) Italian LITTORIO Armd Div believed arrived TRIPOLI with possibly 138 (138) medium tanks but almost complete lack of confirmatory evidence (.) All above estimates of personnel (,) guns and tanks may have to be revised when we know something of contents of convoy which reached TRIPOLI on 23 (23) Feb (.) Enemy believed to have weak det in JALO and to be forming long range desert patrols on our pattern (.)

Fifth (.) Enemy recent movements on GAZALA front appear to have been either demonstration to cover some other movement or impress us with their strength or reconnaissances in force (.) As recces they were practically complete failure as they did not draw our fire or approach closely our main position (.) As demonstration they certainly gave us valuable information of enemy strength but had NO other effect (.) Our patrols and mobile columns control NO MANS LAND at the moment and enemy patrols generally withdraw on contact (.) One possibility is that the enemy hoped to entice us to attack Italians in MECHILI and then strike SOUTH with his tanks against our flank and communications but there are signs on other hand that he is NOT anxious to be attacked at present (.) Convoy seven ships reached TRIPOLI 23 (23) Feb and almost certainly brought considerable number tanks (.) Most secret sources show that one ship reaching TRIPOLI on 23 Feb carried 71 (71) tanks which if German would bring tank strength of 15 and 21 Armd Divs up to an estimated total strength of about 233 (233) without reserves (.) This is our present worst case estimate but we do not know if other ships into TRIPOLI on 23 Feb also carried tanks (.) Reinforcements of personnel German and Italian must also be expected to have reached TRIPOLI (.) Some small ships have reached BENGHASI so that henceforward enemys supply problem will be eased somewhat though it must remain difficult owing to his relative shortage of MT (.)

Sixth (.)   Enemy action against our shipping in out of TOBRUK is causing us some anxiety but generally our maintenance situation is strong now that railway has reached SALUM and will grow stronger as railway extends further East towards EL ADEM which is next objective (.) Shortening of our communication has naturally eased transport situation (.) Roads to SIWA and JARABUB being improved and water pipeline being laid to EL HAMRA defended locality.

SEVENTH (.)   Critical nature MALTA maintenance situation thoroughly understood here (.) I fully realise need for recovering landing grounds in CYRENAICA soon as possible irrespective of desirability resumption offensive on wider grounds (.)

EIGHTH (.)   Situation as I see it is that if enemy can keep his main German tank force round DERNA MARTUBA and also maintain Italian mobile corps comprising possibly ARIETE and LITTORIO with strength up to 270 (270) medium tanks round MECHILI we can NOT afford to try to oust him from these positions unless we have enough medium tanks both to defeat Italians round MECHILI and hold off German armour from the NORTH (.) Inferiority of our tanks to German and possibly new Italian tanks in mechanical reliability and gunpower is being slowly rectified but must still be reckoned as decisive factor when computing relative strengths (.) Undoubted excellence German training and leadership compared with ours is also potent factor in this connection (.) Possible by 1 (1) Mar that enemy may have in LIBYA 475 (475) medium tanks and by 1 (1) Apr 630 (630) (.) He MAY not be able to maintain all these in forward area but we must NOT count on this (.)

NINTH (.)   By 1 (1) Apr we on other hand should have ready for battle in forward area two Armd Bdes with total 330 (330) medium tanks and 100 (100) Valentines in addition (.) By 1 (1) May we should have three armoured Bdes with 500 (500) medium also 150 (150) Valentines (.) By 1 (1) June our strength should be four armoured Bdes with 650 (650) medium and maximum 150 (150) Valentines PROVIDED we have NOT had to begin to hold armoured units in readiness for operations on our NORTHERN Front (.) These figures allow for no reserves but balance of tanks in MIDEAST will be largely accounted for by those under repair which will be earmarked for (a) reserves (b) replacement of battle wastage (c) replacement of tanks due for major overhaul (d) issues to units reforming (.) A factor needing consideration is that MAY is worst month for operations owing intense heat causing great expenditure water for radiators all water cooled engines which though it does NOT affect American tanks DOES affect all transport vehicles (.)

TENTH (.)   Assuming possibility of enemy building up tank strength as estimated above and maintaining all these tanks in forward area it is clear that we can NOT have reasonable numerical superiority before 1 (1) June and that to launch major offensive before then would be to risk defeat in detail and possibly endanger safety of EGYPT (.)

ELEVENTH (.)   In infantry a maximum of four divisions should suffice for a major offensive aimed at retaking CYRENAICA (.) Assuming that owing to diversions to INDIA etc my infantry divisions are reduced to eight, it should be just possible to produce these four divisions accepting a considerable reduction in the present garrison of CYPRUS which I am prepared to risk for time being (.) Any threat to NORTHERN Front would probably entail immediate reduction Eighth Army to three infantry divisions plus odd brigade group or two (.) Requisite infantry should therefore be forthcoming (.)

TWELTH (.)   By 1 (1) June railway should reach EL ADEM which would further ease supply of striking force (.) Heat of summer is handicap but enemy would probably feel it more (.)

THIRTEENTH (.)   These are facts affecting possibility major offensive assuming everything favourable to enemy (.) On the other hand enemy may NOT get all tanks credited to him NOR may he be able to keep them forward area (.) I have therefore made plans with General RITCHIE to seize any reasonable chance to make limited offensive with object of regaining general line DERNA MECHILI and consolidating it in preparation for further offensive (.) But even this advance entails our being able to fortify MECHILI strongly and hold it against enemy forces operating from MSUS and possibly BENGHASI (.) This would entail our having enough tanks to defeat in the open any enemy armoured forces which might try to over run garrison of MECHILI or cut its communications (.) It is NOT possible to forecast a date for this operation as its feasibility depends almost entirely on strength and dispositions of enemy tanks (.)

FOURTEENTH (.)   To sum up my intentions for WESTERN Front are:

> ONE (.)   To continue to build up armoured striking force in EIGHTH ARMY forward areas as rapidly as possible
>
> TWO (.)   Meanwhile to make GAZALA – TOBRUK and SALUM – MADDALENA positions strong as possible and push railway forward towards EL ADEM
>
> Three (.)   To build up in forward area reserves of supplies for renewal of offensive
>
> FOUR (.)   To seize first chance of staging limited offensive to regain landing grounds in area DERNA – MECHILI provided this can be done without prejudicing chances of launching major offensive to recapture CYRENAICA or safety of TOBRUK base area (.)

FIFTEENTH (.)   NORTHERN Front intentions already given in telegram CS/747 (CS/747) of 20/2 (20/2) from M.E. Defence Committee to Defence Minister (.)

SIXTEENTH (.)   Am exploring all possibilities of releasing troops of all categories for duty in forward areas (.) Hope secure services brigade Sudanese troops and am pushing on with formation garrison companies for guards and duties from labour units (.) Every use too will be made of local levies in NINTH and TENTH ARMY areas.

MOST IMMEDIATE – CLEAR THE LINE

JRL, AUC 729

162

Cipher message from the Chiefs of Staff to Auchinleck, 27 February 1942

<u>MOST IMMEDIATE – CLEAR THE LINE.</u>

Reference DOBBIES[160] telegrams No. AOA/0762 to War Office and No. 80 to Colonial Office both rep[ea]t[e]d to C in C Mediterranean only.

<u>One.</u> Our view is that MALTA is of such importance both as air staging point and as impediment to enemy reinforcement route that the most drastic steps are justifiable to sustain it. Even if Axis maintain their present scale of attack on MALTA thus reducing value it will continue to be of great importance to war as a whole by containing important enemy air forces during critical months.

<u>Two.</u> We are unable to supply MALTA from the West. Your chances of doing so from the East depend on an advance in CYRENAICA. The situation in MALTA will be dangerous by early MAY if no convoys have got through.

<u>Three.</u> We agree with your CS/747 of 20th. February that prevention of enemy reinforcements for LIBYA and probably also ultimate fate of MALTA depends on recapture of air bases in WESTERN CYRENAICA. We appreciate that the timing of another offensive will depend on building up adequate tank superiority and that its launching may necessitate taking considerable risks in other parts of MIDEAST Command. Nevertheless we feel that we must aim to be so placed in CYRENAICA by April dark period that we can pass substantial convoy to MALTA. It will then be essential not rpt not only to send maintenance necessities but to build up stocks well above present critical level. Please let us have your views on above.

<u>Four</u> Meanwhile every effort must be made to keep stocks at least at present level. We suggest the foll[owing]. methods

(A) A further attempt to pass a convoy in March dark period. No consideration of risk to ships themselves need deter you from this. During the progress of this operation it should be regarded as your primary military commitment.

---

160 Lieutenant General Sir William Dobbie, Governor of Malta.

(B)   Assembling substantial convoy ready to despatch immediately favourable opportunity arises.

(C)   Using Cruiser in connection with complete air reconnaissance of Eastern and Central Mediterranean for fast regular service to MALTA with its own stores and fuel cut down to bare necessities for each trip to make room for reasonable loads.

<u>Five.</u>   ADMIRALTY are considering certain unorthodox methods.

<u>Six.</u>   In view of difficult supply situation we consider that reinforcement of MALTA with Army Units should be discontinued. Details urgently required by C in C MALTA should be sent as opportunity offers.

Please pass to A O C in C as from Air Ministry.

JRL, AUC 730

163

Letter from Auchinleck to Sir James Grigg, Secretary of State for War, 2 March 1942

Everyone here got a good jerk when your appointment as Secretary of State was announced. A real good jerk is an excellent tonic, and I think this was the general effect produced in this burg. Much interest and much speculation on all sides, as you can well imagine, knowing as you do what your reputation is!!

    For myself, I am very glad, and only hope that you will be able to do all that I feel you want to do.

2.   I hope I may write to you now and then, but not to bother you with small things.

3.   There are, however, three things I would like to bring to your notice before you get too caught up in the whirlpool.

4.   First is this matter of I.A. Officers coming into appointments in so-called "British" formations and dropping pay by doing so, or if they do not drop pay, failing to benefit financially by being advanced professionally. I know that this should not weigh with individuals, whose sole thought should be to win the war, even if their families starve, but human nature being what it is, it does weigh with them, and therefore must affect their efficiency.

In the Middle East today I have about 190,000 Indians against about 270,000 British from the U.K., so that, in any event, I must dilute all my staffs from G.H.Q. downwards with Indian Army staff officers, and this is now going on. It is essential to do this. This means that these officers may have a substantial grievance, or think they have, and efficiency without a reasonable degree of contentment is hard to attain. We have, I feel, enough external threats to contend with without adding to them internal discord. One of my main tasks here, if not the main one, is to study the psychology of this very mixed array we call an Army, and I spend most of my time doing this in the hope that it will not disintegrate altogether!

5.   Secondly, there is the matter of giving adequate rank to officers bearing certain responsibilities. I fully realise the objections to inflated staffs and hordes of generals, but you can not get away from the fact that in any Army rank does count, and will always count, however much people may say that it is only the man who should count, and that the rank does not matter. It does matter, and I feel that if a C-in-C. says that he honestly thinks a Major-General is needed instead of a Brigadier, his wishes should be met. I assure you that I do not ask for such things unless I have convinced myself they are needed.

A case in point is a Major-General General Staff on the staff of an "Army", instead of a Brigadier as at present. I am sure this is needed, and that failure to provide it is dangerous and likely to lead to inefficiency and disaster. I won't go into all the reasons, but they are most cogent.

6.   Thirdly, I feel that your Military Secretary either fails to realise the meaning of psychology, or that if he does, he lacks the courage of his convictions. He refuses to allow me to publish in the local press lists of immediate awards until the King has approved them for publication at Home. I am allowed to announce them to the individuals concerned, and put them in orders, but this is not nearly enough. The whole value of these awards is psychological, and this depends entirely on immediate and widespread publication. I am sure you realise this, and I feel that His Majesty would realise it too if it were put to him properly.

It may not be in accordance with "usual practice", but this is an "unusual" war, and it will have an "unusual" end if we do not get a move on and sweep aside cobwebs and precedents and "usual practices". I feel that if anyone can do the sweeping, you will.

7. Finally, I feel that we must move with the times, and move ahead of the Bosche. It is folly to think that we can end this war and the Bosche with an army organised as it was in 1939. We have moved far from the days of rigid organisations which are supposed to be suitable for every part of the world. We must get flexibility and the power to improvise quickly and without disorganisation right down to the smallest formations. The German does it every day.

I feel this is supremely important, and I am trying to do it here, but I feel I am a voice crying in the wilderness, though the great majority here are with me.

This is for your eye alone.

JRL, AUC 732

164

Cipher telegram from Auchinleck to General Sir Alan Brooke, 4 March 1942

1 (.) Draft reply from Cs in C to COS 240 (24) [27 February] covering whole subject already prepared and will be finally approved today at Cs in Cs Conference (.) Conclusions reached unlikely to differ greatly from those in my telegram of Feb 29 to Prime Minister this for your private information (.)

2 (.) I find it hard to believe in view of your telegram of 17/2 that COS 241 (241) had your approval as it seems to fail so signally either to appreciate FACTS as presented from here or to realise that we are fully aware of the situation as regards MALTA in particular to the MIDDLE EAST in general (.) We here are trying to face realities and to present to you situation as it appears to us NOT as we or you would LIKE it to be (.) Para two is particular uncalled for and implies that I and my officers are incompetent (.) For your information FACTS are as follows (.)

3 (.) Tanks received in January GRANTS 48 (48) STUARTS 76 (76) MATILDAS nil CRUSADERS 2 (2) VALENTINES nil total 126 (126) (.) Of these issued to units and schools GRANTS

43 (43) STUARTS 75 (75) CRUSADERS 2 (2) VALENTINES nil MATILDAS nil total 120 (120) Not issued GRANTS 5 (5) STUARTS 1 (1) (.) Reasons undergoing preparation for issue (.) Facts ref tanks now in this Command (.) Repairable in 8 Army area and awaiting transfer to Base Workshops 220 (220) (.) Awaiting repair at base 35 (35) (.) Under repair 273 (273) (.) Total repairable or under repair 528 (528) (.)

Total tanks received from UK or USA under preparation for issue 148 (148) (.) Total with units 591 (591) (.) Serviceable in reserve with RAOC 48 (48) (.) Grand total 1315 (1315) (.)

4 (.) You know that many other factors besides the mere ISSUE of tanks to units govern the readiness of formations for battle and I will be grateful if you will explain this to the Chiefs of Staff and the Defence Minister (.) This applies particular when new types of tanks are received such as GENERAL GRANTS with more powerful weapons necessitating change in tactical procedure (.) We must have time to think how to get full value out of our material (.)

JRL, AUC 734

165

Cipher message from General Sir Alan Brooke to Auchinleck, 6 March 1942

Your appreciation had met with considerable disapproval on part of Defence Minister and resulted in a draft of a telegram which he wished sent to you.

The CHIEFS OF STAFF succeeded in getting his approval to the despatch of C.O.S. 241 (241) in substitution for his. I am quite sure that your feeling would have been much more hurt had the Defence Minister's telegram been despatched instead of ours. You may be sure that I have always made a special point of representing the factors mentioned in first sentence of your para 4 (4).

2. The situation has changed considerably since my telegram of 17/2 was sent. At that time the full gravity of the situation in MALTA was not rpt not apparent, also decision not rpt not to withdraw further forces from the MIDDLE EAST and to leave the Indian

Division which it was previously the intention to withdraw had not rpt not then been taken.

3. The greatest difficulty I had here was in reconciling your figures of tank strengths. In your statement dated 23/2 (23/2) you showed (660) serviceable tanks, yet in your appreciation CS 773 (CS 773) of Feb 27th you have allowed only for 430 (430) tanks on 1/4 (1/4) which seemed to represent the strength of but two brigades and two Army Tank Battalions in the forward area.

JRL, AUC 739

166

Letter from Auchinleck to General Sir Alan Brooke, CIGS, 6 March 1942

I have sent you a telegram (No. SD/67939) giving you details of the reorganisation I propose to effect to make the Army in this theatre fit for its task.

2. The main changes affect the armoured formations, and are meant to bring the three arms much closer together on the battlefield and off it than they have been hitherto. I know that in theory this close association exists, but my experience is that in practice it does not. Moreover, the present organisation is, in the opinion of those out here who have seen the machines working in battle, unbalanced in that there is too much armour and too little infantry. We have, therefore, introduced the armoured brigade group, which contains, besides the three armoured regiments, a motor battalion and a field artillery regiment as permanent components.

The armoured division will include as a permanent part of its organisation a motor brigade group of three battalions and a field regiment. Both groups have their signals, sappers and self-contained transport units, and can if necessary be transferred complete to another formation at any moment.

One feature of this re-organisation – an outcome of our recent experiences – is that each Corps H.Q. must be so organised as to be capable of commanding Armoured and/or Infantry formations. This is now being examined to see what is required in the way of alterations to a standard H.Q. It is also a matter of training, and affects commanders. The same principle applies to Divisional Headquarters. These must also be capable of controlling a varying number of subordinate formations of differing types. This is also being provided for.

The other changes which affect the units of the armoured division are that each of the four motor battalions will contain an anti-tank company of 16 two-pounder (six-pounder in the future, I hope) guns, and each of the two field regiments will include a fourth battery of 16 anti-tank guns.

We shall have also a pool of three "independent" armoured brigade groups organised similarly to those included in the armoured divisions and capable of attachment to any division as circumstances may dictate. In fact, it will be usual for these "independent" brigade groups to be attached to a division for training, administration and battle, but they are equally available for detached duty away from a division. An instance of the way in which they might be used is afforded by the despatch of the 7th Armoured Brigade Group to Burma. In our new organisation, the despatch of such a group can be easily effected without disturbing the basic divisional organisation.

As to the inclusion of the anti-tank weapon in the Motor battalion and the artillery regiment, this is the unanimous recommendation of commanders of all grades and services. The need for this change is not to be challenged, in my opinion.

3.   As regards the infantry division, the basic composition remains the same. The formation of permanent brigade groups only recognises what is already a universal practice and does not in any way preclude the massing of the divisional artillery or the collection under one direction for a particular operations of the divisional engineers. The divisional reconnaissance battalions (of which I have one only now remaining) or, in the case of the Indian Divisions (now 50% of my available infantry) the divisional Cavalry (motorised) regiments will be formed into Motor brigade groups for work with the armoured divisions, thus supplying the very much needed additional infantry element. There is no other way of providing this that I can see, and the role of these reconnaissance units will be performed by the armoured car regiments which, except for those incorporated in the armoured divisions, will be "Army" or "Corps" Troops as they are now.

4. The incorporation of anti-tank guns in the ordinary (as opposed to motor) infantry battalions is also a necessity in modern war. I am convinced of this, and opinion here is practically unanimous about it also. It may be uneconomical in theory but it is essential in practice.

  The attached diagram shows, in outline, a method of incorporating eight Anti-Tank guns – all we can afford for the present – in each Infantry Battalion without upsetting the four Rifle Company organisation. This has been done without loss of fire power or increasing the establishment, and we want fewer men these days and more fire power. This establishment is still under detailed examination.

5. The artillery regiments of the infantry division will also have an anti-tank battery incorporated permanently in them. The handling over of anti-tanks to the infantry will go some way to providing artillerymen, which we so sorely need to fill the gaps in our existing units, due to failure to keep us us to strength. The anti-tank gun was never really an artillery weapon.

6. I think this covers all the main points. As you will see, the changes proposed are not very drastic, but they are, in my opinion, essential if we are to achieve the flexibility and co-operation of all arms demanded by modern war conditions.

JRL, AUC 740

167

Cipher message from Auchinleck to General Sir Alan Brooke, CIGS, 7 March 1942

1 (.) Result my experience so far this war and especially of last three months have reached conclusion that standard of leadership in war our brigade and divisional leaders not nearly high enough (.) This due almost complete absence systematic and continuous instruction in simple principles in peace time (.) Staff College training did not fill and is not filling this gap (.) Am convinced that we must act at once to remedy this want if we are to get best results from excellent material in our armies and to have chance of meeting enemy equal terms (.)

2 (.) INDIA has recognised this some months ago and has a higher war course (.) Consider MIDEAST should start same immediately (.) Need amply borne out of recent LIBYAN operations and present difficulty finding scientifically trained leaders for formations and higher planning appointments (.) GERMANS seem to have good supply competent leaders probably owing systematic pre war training and adherence to simple well tried principles which our Army seems to have mostly forgotten (.)

3 (.) Propose therefore with your approval constitution higher war course as follows (.) Staff one Major General four first grade instructors one operations one maintenance one organisation one air and in addition if available Naval adviser (.) Instructional staff must have highest qualifications (.) Students between fifteen and twenty including if available and willing three or four RAF (.) Course four weeks followed by four weeks tour by syndicates of the fronts of my three armies to study practical application principles learned (.) Four or five courses in the year allowing necessary breaks (.)

4 (.) This theatre offers great variety of terrain and it might well be desirable send students from UK INDIA and elsewhere (.) Am convinced of need for this training on systematic and scientific lines to enable us to make full use our resources now often wasted through uninstructed leadership (.)

5 (.) Seems possible that best location might well be in the Union where facilities ground and climate all excellent and work could be done away from parochial influences (.) Have little doubt that SMUTS would agree (.)

6 (.) Consider essential to start this instruction very earliest possible and not later than April (.) If established in Union course might develop on Empire basis which would immensely increase value (.) Hope you will give this project your blessing [.]

JRL, AUC 742

168

Letter from Auchinleck to
General Sir Alan Brooke, CIGS, 7 March 1942

In the stress of other matters, I never answered your letter of the 30th January. Thank you very much for it, and for suggesting possible successors to Jumbo Wilson. As to Jumbo himself, he is carrying on well at present, and what with all these changes I think he had better stay where he is for a bit until things have settled down if they ever do! You see, he is well in on all this Free French political racket, and believe me it is a racket!

He also knows all about the internal security problems in Syria, and the Lebanon, and is of course well up in the strategical problems affecting that front. While I would be happier with a younger man, I think it would be better to mark time for the present, unless you feel that he ought to go on principle. If you do, then I would not feel justified in protesting.

As to his successor, I know Franklyn[161] – you will remember perhaps that he had 8th Corps under me in Southern Command. I like him and I think he is sound enough, but I should be inclined to agree with you when you wonder if he is not going off. I rather thought the same when I last knew him – over a year ago now. Kenneth Anderson[162] or Irwin[163] would, I am sure, be first class and I would welcome either, but not James Gammel[164] please! I know him too well and I do not believe in him I am afraid I would not have made him a Corps Commander myself – opinions differ however!!

I would much like to know what your intentions are in regard to Holmes. Opinions differ greatly about him. I have found him always sound and forceful; at the same time I always have a small doubt at the back of my mind! Some people say he is a mountebank! I am sure he has

---

161 Lieutenant General Harold Franklyn, GOC Northern Ireland 1941–43.

162 Major General Kenneth Anderson, who commanded 1st Division, 8 Corps and 2 Corps in 1942.

163 Lieutenant General Sir Noel Irwin.

164 Lieutenant General Sir James Gammel commanded 3rd Infantry Division, 1940–41 and Eastern Command, 1942–43. Auchinleck knew him as he had been BGS of 4 Corps in 1940. Gammel was not sent to the Middle East but his career prospered despite Auchinleck's misgivings. He was appointed Chief of Staff to the Supreme Allied Commander, Mediterranean in 1944 and was head of the British Military Mission in Moscow in 1945.

ability but I am doubtful of his stability – a little. Point is that he is very senior as you know, and if you put juniors over his head, he is bound to get disgruntled and therefore less efficient. Personally, I would not mind trying him out as an Army Commander. He certainly gets a move on.

I am grateful to you for your advice about Arthur Smith[165] and John Shearer. I am sure it is right that he should have a change, as has been here a long time. Thank you very much for taking so much trouble to get him suitably placed. He has served me so well and done so much for this headquarters, that I should hate to think that he was leaving with a bad taste in his mouth. Corbett is settling in well and here again I owe you thanks for letting me have him. He will do well here I am sure, and blow away a lot of cobwebs. De Guingand is, I think, going to make a first-class DMI and he will have Shearer's organisation at his disposal.

Blamey went off this morning. We parted great friends. He is a tough old boy with plenty of commonsense.

I hope to leave for a tour of 10th Army area tomorrow by air at 7.30 a.m. I am not quite happy about Quinan yet. He seems to have separatist tendencies, but I think he will be all right!!

I hope you are very well. P.J.'s[166] appointment certainly gave us something to talk about.

JRL, AUC 745

169

Letter from Auchinleck to Lieutenant General N. M. Ritchie, 7 March 1942

I am sorry I have not written before, but things have been rather hectic as you know from Arthur Smith. Tom Corbett hopes to go up to you on Monday, and I hope you will discuss everything very freely with him. I know you will. I am sure he is going to be of great assistance to us all.

2. As you know, we are under much pressure from the usual quarter to do the usual thing. You realise the urgency behind this pressure

---

165 Lieutenant General Arthur Smith, CGS, Middle East. He was to be posted as
    GOC London District and Major General Commanding the Brigade of Guards.
166 P. J. Grigg, appointed Secretary of State for War in March 1942.

as well as I do, but I am determined not to be forced into action which would, in my opinion, be most dangerous at present. All the same, we must be thinking hard all day and every day how we can attack again and how soon. I think of little else, and I am sure you are doing the same.

3. I gather you are getting on with the mobile base organisation for brigade groups. This is very urgent. The whole thing should be worked out scientifically on an area basis. What area will the group require to cover? How many mines and how much wire will it want for this? What tools of all sorts will be wanted? How much water and what supplies? etc. etc. You know it all. As I see it, speed is the essence of the affair, and the whole thing must be a drill, and brigades must be drilled in it, using all the stuff (dummy mines) they would have to use. The ground will vary, of course, in each case, but generally a stereotyped lay out should be capable of being fitted in on most types of ground met with on your front. Do you agree? I look on these mobile base organisations as the foundation of any future offensive operation. I will be very grateful for your views on the subject, and for any conclusions you have reached.

4. We here have been trying to think out various courses of action which we might be able to take, and I will let you have our conclusions shortly. You know I am not trying to intrude, but only to help, and the more brains we bring to bear on the problem the better. I know you agree with this. You will find Tom Corbett very alert and suggestive when it comes to plans.

5. I have been thinking for some days now that it might help you if you had a more experienced Chief of Staff, and one perhaps a little better qualified by personality and knowledge to deal with the Commanders and staffs of your subordinate formations. I like little Redman,[167] and I think he is an able soldier with a good quick brain, but I am not sure that he is yet fitted for his present job, which is really in the nature of a 2nd-in-Command to you. Please don't think I am getting at him, because I'm not, but I do think you want a heavier gun to take some of the work off your shoulders. I hope you will not think that I am in any way dissatisfied with you! Far from it! You know this.

167 Brigadier Harold Redman, BGS, Eighth Army.

Anyway, I'd like to send you Jock Whiteley. He would love to go, I know, and he knows the big picture which is always a help. I hope you would welcome him. I have applied very strongly for the appointment of a M.G.G.S. on the staff of Armies and I hope I will get it. If I do, then Jock would be well worth promoting. Let me know what you think.

6. As you know, I will never press you to disgorge troops if you say you can't. But I do very much want to get the Poles and New Zealanders out of Libya and back to Egypt and Syria respectively. So they must have precedence over 29th and 38th Indian Infantry Brigades. I am bringing a brigade group out of Cyprus at once, and hope to get 5th Div H.Q. out as well before long. I then propose to give you 5 Ind Div, of which 29th Ind Inf Bde forms part. Must 29 Bde come back to Egypt? Can not they stay where they are?

It looks as if 38 Bde would have to be broken up and the H.Q. used to form a motor Bde Gp H.Q.

7. I am most encouraged by the performance of the Grants, and also by the excellent shooting of the 4th Armd Bde. The moral effect of having these fine tanks on the troops is very great.

We must make quite sure that their first appearance in battle comes as a first-class tactical surprise to the enemy, therefore they must not be used in small packets, but in as great strength as we can muster, and the greatest care and trouble must be taken to conceal their presence in the forward area prior to their being engaged. The same applies to the new six-pdr anti-tank gun. Its performance and presence must not be given away to the enemy before it can be given a chance of really doing damage. Everyone must realise the supreme importance of secrecy in this matter, and that any slackness or stupidity will be severely dealt with. I know you will agree with me in this, and that you will see that there is no nonsense about it.

8. Frank Messervy should be back with 7th Armd Div by the 13th of the month. I am glad Herbert Lumsden is doing well. How is Gertie Tuker getting on? I inspected 7th Ind Inf Bde this morning, and was most struck with their appearance, turn out and spirit.

9. I shall soon be asking you for Angus to come back, I am afraid, but I don't want to leave you in the lurch.

10. I am due to leave for Baghdad tomorrow, and to come back on the 14th. I hope you will be able to get in for Army Commanders' Conference on 15th, and that you will stay with us.

JRL, AUC 746

170

Cipher message from Auchinleck to Winston Churchill, 9 March 1942

Am certain that I cannot repeat NOT leave MIDEAST in present circumstances (.) Situation is entirely different to that obtaining last July and I am NOT repeat NOT prepared to delegate authority to anyone while strategical situation is so fluid and liable to rapid change (.) I can give no more information regarding tank situation than I have already given nor would my coming home make it more possible to stage an earlier offensive (.) I earnestly ask you therefore to reconsider your request (.) If you desire it I will gladly send Senior Staff Officer who can explain Tank situation in more detail [.]

JRL, AUC 748

171

Cipher message from General Sir Alan Brooke, CIGS to Auchinleck, 9 March 1942

I put your Private No Camp 2 8.3. before C.O.S. this morning for their consideration. Many important factors bearing on present situation are now being actively considered here such as MALTA LEVANT – CASPIAN Front Far Eastern situation, allotment of forces as between you and WAVELL relative armoured strengths in CYRENAICA etc. Other C.O.S. are in full agreement with me that it is most desirable that you should if possible come home for consultation these matters. We wish therefore to impress on you the urgency for such a visit provided you are not (repeat not) expecting to be engaged in active operations within the next week or so. Since I discussed your first message with C.O.S.

the Prime Minister has received your reply and has instructed me to impress on you the importance of your coming home for consultation. Could not (repeat not) WILSON answer for you during the few days you would be away?

JRL, AUC 749

172

Cipher message from Auchinleck to General Sir Alan Brooke, CIGS, 12 March 1942

1 (.) Reorganisation, redistribution and possibility of active operations in this COMMAND make it impossible to leave even for short time while retaining responsibility. Could not ask WILSON to answer for me in circumstances even for fortnight.

2 (.) Suggest that great value would result from visit by you and if possible C.A.S. to CAIRO or BAGHDAD. WAVELL and PEIRSE could probably come for conference at which all questions mentioned in your cable 75223 could be discussed.

3 (.) Am most anxious to give all help to you and Defence Minister at present time. Have explained my situation as fully and frankly as I can. Fear have not made it clear owing to limitations of cable communication. Feel sure that explanation on the spot is best solution.

JRL, AUC 750

173

Cipher message from Winston Churchill to Auchinleck, 15 March 1942

1. Your appreciation of February 27th contained in your 1723 continues causing deepest anxiety here, both to the Chiefs of Staff and Defence Committee. I therefore regret extremely your inability to come home for consultation. The delay you have in mind will endanger safety of Malta. Moreover there is no certainty that the enemy

cannot reinforce faster than you, so that after all your waiting you will find yourself in relatively the same or even a worse position. Your losses have been far less than the enemy nevertheless chance fighting. For instance the 7th Armoured Div was withdrawn to the Delta to rest although its losses were far less than those of the 15th and 21st German Armd Divs who came back at you with so much vigour. A very heavy German counterstroke upon the Russians must be expected soon, and it will be thought intolerable that the 655,000 men ex Malta on your ration strength should remain unengaged preparing for another set-piece battle in July.

2.   A limited offensive to Derna of which you hold out some prospect would have the advantage at any rate of coming to grips with the enemy and forcing him to consume lives, munitions, tanks and aircraft. In that case if he beats your armour you would have to retire to your defensive zone. But if you beat his armour no one here understands why you should not press your advantage and go farther.

3.   In your 1723 SUSAN [cipher message] Paragraph 8 you estimate possible by March 1st that enemy may have in Libya 475 medium tanks and by April 1st 630. We now know from special sources CS/MSS/793/T.4 that on 11th Panzer Army Africa had in forward area 159 tanks serviceable and Italians 87, total 246, or barely half the number you credited them with by March 1st. Moreover this including the German type of light tanks. Against this War Office report that on March 2nd you had serviceable in Western Desert: Cruisers British Crusader, American M 3 Medium and American M 3 Light 174, serviceable in the Delta 197, new arrivals not yet issued 167, total 538. And I tanks additional, including 6 being unloaded, 252. Total serviceable 790. On your own estimate SUSAN 1723 para 9 by April 1st you will have ready for battle in forward area 330 Medium tanks and 110 Valentines, total 430. This takes no account of the large number of serviceable but repairable.

4.   I greatly admired your action in throwing out Cunningham and I was very glad you got rid of Godwin-Austin.[168] I have done everything in my power to give you continuous support at heavy cost to the whole war. It would give me the greatest pain to feel

---

168 Lieutenant General A. R. Godwin-Austen who was removed from command of 13 Corps.

that mutual understanding has ceased. In order to avoid this I have asked Sir Stafford Cripps to stay for a day in Cairo about 19th or 20th on his way to India and put before you view of the War Cabinet. He will be joined by General Nye,[169] who is proceeding separately and is fully possessed of the Chiefs of Staff's opinions. It is impossible for C.I.G.S. to leave the centre at this moment.

5.   See also Chiefs of Staff No. 73968 of March 3rd.

JRL, AUC 753

174

Letter from Auchinleck to General Sir Alan Brooke, 15 March 1942

As a result of recent experience in the Western Desert, I am not satisfied with the standard of leadership of the unit commanders of the Royal Armoured Corps, nor with that of some of the brigade commanders. It is not the first time that this subject has been raised, but it has come to a head again. Meanwhile many Cavalry officers of the Royal Armoured Corps are coming before the Junior Selection Board for appointment to command armoured regiments, who, in some cases, are clearly not fitted mentally or by training to take command in modern war. The command of an armoured regiment in the field to-day is an intricate process requiring first-rate ability and quite a reasonable degree of mechanical knowledge, in addition to a high general knowledge of soldiering including that of other arms' capabilities and limitations. It is, of course, quite possible for suitable officers of armoured car regiments to be given command of armoured regiments; and it is also quite sound in my opinion – although it is not at present the practice – for selected officers in the R.T.R. Branch of the Royal Armoured Corps to be given command of Cavalry or Yeomanry Tank Regiments. But even this is not sufficient, and since it is now quite apparent that the right type of commander for an armoured regiment, medium or heavy, can only be an officer who has a complete understanding of all the arms which he will have to co-operate in battle, it follows that any

---

169 Lieutenant General Sir Archibald Nye, VCIGS.

highly recommended officer should be eligible for appointment to command an armoured regiment, whether he is R.A.C. (Cavalry) or R.A.C. (R.T.R.) or Infantry.

2. The same principle applies in the case of brigade commanders, and any thoroughly competent officer should be eligible for command of a brigade irrespective of whether he be R.A.C., R.A. or Infantry, or whether the brigade is an armoured brigade, a motorized brigade or an infantry brigade.

3. I will be grateful if you will let me know whether you agree with these suggestions.

JRL, AUC 756

175

Report signed by Auchinleck entitled 'Libya, March 1942', 21 March 1942

THE OBJECT.

1. Our permanent and over-riding object is to secure our bases in EGYPT and IRAQ against enemy attack.

FACTORS AFFECTING THE ACHIEVEMENT OF THE OBJECT.

2. Our policy on the Western Front in NORTH AFRICA has been hitherto: first, to protect our main base area in the DELTA, secondly, to drive the enemy out of NORTH AFRICA so as to increase the security of the DELTA base, to open the Mediterranean sea route, and to provide a base for operations against SICILY and ITALY.

3. So long as the enemy is able to send convoys freely to TRIPOLI and BENGHASI, he is in a better position to build up his forces on this front than we are, because the route is much shorter than our reinforcement route round the Cape and from INDIA. The most effective way, therefore, to secure EGYPT from attack from the West is to control the Central Mediterranean.

4. To gain control of the Central Mediterranean, we require:-

    (i) To operate strong air forces and light naval forces from MALTA. This will not be possible unless we can keep MALTA adequately supplied, and provide it with reasonable protection against air attack.

(ii) To operate strong air forces from basis in WESTERN CYRENAICA.

(iii) To provide air protection for our fleet operating from ALEXANDRIA.

5. If we could establish a high degree of control over the Central Mediterranean, the enemy's strength in NORTH AFRICA must gradually decline. Both the capture of TRIPOLITANIA and, alternatively, the defence of CYRENAICA would then be easier, thus enabling us to release forces for the Northern Front, if required.

It is obvious that the advantages of capturing TRIPOLITANIA would be largely discounted if the enemy could establish himself in TUNISIA. The only certain way of preventing this is to occupy that country ourselves.

6. The carrying out of our policy falls, therefore, into three phases:

(i) The securing of CYRENAICA.

(ii) The building up of our striking forces in CYRENAICA and MALTA, with a view to gaining control of the Central Mediterranean.

(iii) The occupation of TRIPOLITANIA and, if necessary, of TUNISIA.

7. Viewing the war as a whole, we must concede that the enemy will have the initiative during the summer of 1942, and that some reserves are to be expected. This will influence our operations in NORTH AFRICA in the following ways:-

(a) We must not become involved in operations in LIBYA which can not be broken off at short notice. To be in a position to release forces to meet the enemy elsewhere, we must aim at being able to pass quickly to the defensive, and to consolidate our gains without delay.

(b) The morale of the public will require sustaining. A successful offensive would be beneficial, but another failure would have a harmful effect.

8. From the foregoing considerations, the phases of the offensive operations in LIBYA can be defined:

(i) To secure CYRENAICA.

(ii)　To gain control of the sea communications in the Central Mediterranean.

(iii)　To capture or secure TRIPOLITANIA, which may depend on whether operations to secure TUNISIA can also be undertaken, either from the EAST or from the WEST.

FACTORS AFFECTING OFFENSIVE OPERATIONS IN CYRENAICA.

9.　Experience has shown that it is more difficult to hold than to capture CYRENAICA. Therefore, an essential element in the plan to capture CYRENAICA is the destruction of the enemy forces, and particularly the most effective part of them, the German armoured and infantry formations.

10.　The configuration of the coast of the GULF of SIRTE and the defensive possibilities of EL AGHEILA area are the governing considerations in any plan for the defence of CYRENAICA. A much smaller force is needed to defend CYRENAICA in the AGHEILA position, than in any other, and since we must be ready to secure CYRENAICA with the minimum force, the capture and consolidation of the AGHEILA position is essential. This fixes our maintenance needs.

11.　The supply situation in MALTA is bad and will become worse after May. Moreover, MALTA's effort is waning, so that enemy convoys are passing more easily to NORTH AFRICA, and his situation there is improving accordingly. We should, therefore, strike as soon as we can with a reasonable prospect of success, that is, as soon as we have the needed relative superiority over the enemy, and the resources to enable us to sustain the momentum of our attack.

12.　The relative numerical strength of our and the enemy's armoured forces is shown in the Annexure to this paper. In comparing the strength of these forces, the following factors must be borne in mind:-

(a)　The enemy's cruiser tanks are better than ours. The leadership and training of his armoured formations is probably still better than ours. To give a reasonable chance of our offensive succeeding, we should have about 50% numerical superiority over the German armoured forces, though we can accept equality with the Italians.

(b)   Our Valentine tank is too slow to be employed with our Cruiser tanks, as it is, for this reason, at grave disadvantage when operating against enemy cruiser tanks. It is, however, a most valuable asset for counter attack within defensive positions held by our infantry, or to support our infantry in attacks on enemy defensive positions.

(c)   Our infantry formations, supported by Valentine tanks, are superior in quality, and at present in quantity also, to enemy infantry formations.

13.   An examination of the figures in the Annexure shows that we are severely handicapped by the lack of reliable information, which may result in lost opportunities, or in our attempting the impossible. It is clear, however, that we can not pass to the offensive now, but that we might be able to attack about 15th May, though 1st June is a more likely date.

DERNA – MARTUBA.

14.   The maintenance of MALTA would be easier if we could operate air forces from landing grounds in the DERNA and MARTUBA area, and the possibility of a limited operation to secure these aerodromes is being carefully and continuously examined.

    To secure these landing grounds we must secure DERNA and MECHILI. The enemy has prepared positions on this line, and we would be playing into his hands if we attacked him on this ground of his own choosing. We would require the same superiority of forces to capture this line as we would to capture CYRENAICA, because the enemy's strength is all deployed forward. There is no reason for limiting the objective of our offensive to the capture of the line DERNA – MECHILI unless for administrative reasons it is impossible to advance with adequate forces beyond it. Our losses in this limited operation would almost certainly exceed those of the enemy, and the launching of the main offensive would be likely to be correspondingly delayed. Apart from any considerations of supply, should we attempt this operation with inferior armoured forces we would jeopardise the security of EGYPT, because the integrity of our own defensive positions in the GAZALA – TOBRUK – EL HACHEIM and SALUM – MADDALENA areas, strongly entrenched and mined as they are, depends entirely on the availability of a reasonably strong mobile reserve of armoured force with which to counter-attack the enemy armoured troops, should they succeed in breaking through or passing round the infantry positions. The fronts held in these positions are perforce very extended, and the troops available to hold them are relatively few. Consequently, the various defended localities comprised in them are situated at some distance apart, and there is in no sense a continuous line of defence, though the whole may be covered by a more or less continuous minefield. Moreover, if forced to halt on the DERNA – MECHILI position and then to adopt a strategically defensive attitude on our Western Front, we should be much less favourably placed tactically in the GAZALA or SALUM positions, because of the longer frontage to be held, and the far greater vulnerability of our communications, consequent on the configuration of the coast.

CONCLUSIONS.

15. It is evident, therefore:

(i) That our first objective is to secure CYRENAICA.

(ii) That in securing CYRENAICA, we must destroy as much as possible of the enemy's army.

(iii) That to secure CYRENAICA we must be able to maintain sufficient forces in the EL AGHEILA neighbourhood to hold it against heavy enemy attack.

(iv) That the sooner we can launch an offensive the better.

(v) That to give our offensive a reasonable chance of success we should have a numerical superiority in tanks of 50% over the Germans, and an equality with the Italians.

(vi) That a limited offensive to secure the landing grounds in the DERNA – MARTUBA area is likely to need the same relative superiority in tanks as an offensive to recover CYRENAICA, and has nothing to recommend it except that it may be possible, from the maintenance point of view, before the latter.

ANNEXURE "A"

COMPARATIVE ARMOURED STRENGTHS

NOTE:

(i) The enemy figures are based on no new formations being sent other than LITTORIO.

(ii) It has been assumed that enemy tanks are available for shipment.

(iii) Shipping will not be a limiting factor.

| | OURS | ENEMY | | |
		German	Italian	TOTAL
1 APRIL 1942				
Best case for us	300 (a)	260	90	350
Worst case for us	300 (a)	360	140	500
15 May 1942	450 (b)	350	300	650 (c)
1 June 1942	600 (b)	350	300	650 (c)

(a)   Infantry tanks numbering 150 have been omitted. These 300 are cruiser tanks with approximately 40% Grants.

(b)   Infantry tanks numbering 150 have been omitted.

(c)   This represents "worst case" for us. It is not possible at this date to state a "best case".

JRL, AUC 764

176

Letter from Auchinleck to Lieutenant General N. M. Ritchie, 22 March 1942

Many thanks for your letter 70/6/G of 10 March. I was very glad to have you here – I always am, as you know.

2.   I am glad the 13 Corps exercise went off all right. I hope the need to put it into practice will never arise, but it and other similar exercises will be useful in connection with another matter about which I am writing to you separately.

3.   I agree with you that we might make more of our armoured cars than we do. I feel we do not always use them in sufficiently large numbers for specific operations, and that their action when thus used might be better co-ordinated, perhaps. For example, two or three armoured car regiments, backed up by and under command of a motor brigade group, might be capable of doing great execution wide to a flank or far in advance. What do you think?

4. I entirely agree with your views about flanks and looking over one's shoulder. The German does not mind pushing on into the middle of his enemy, and we should not either.

5. I am interested in your distribution of troops, and glad to hear that you think your positions are now so much stronger. They should be ready to withstand bombardment by medium artillery, and I am sure they are.

   I agree that the armoured formations must not be tied in any way to a holding role, and that they must be placed so as to be able to fill their part in the defensive plan which is counter-attack, and if successful in this, pursuit beyond the limits of our positions if the chance offers. Their location is a matter for you to decide, and if El Adem is not too far back it should do well as it will also give them a chance to train meanwhile.

6. Your proposed new dispositions for the infantry of 13th Corps seem sound enough, though they entail putting all the infantry at present available in the front window. I take it, however, that each of the 2nd S.A. and 50th Divs would have one brigade in reserve in depth behind the forward area? With the increased strength of your position this would seem to be feasible and desirable, and I expect you mean to do it.

7. I note you mean to put the Free French into Tobruk. This should be all right, but please be careful not to allow this Bde to become a "guards and duty" formation. They are a temperamental lot, and need plenty of exercise and action if they are not to get into mischief. I am sure you will bear this in mind. There are of course strong political reasons for now allowing them to think they are being treated as being other than first-class troops. A propos of this, I have had to agree to send a battalion of Senegalese troops from Syria to Matruh in an effort to keep them from shooting their officers, as happened in another battalion of the same people last week in Damascus! However, they should be useful in Matruh. Catroux also wants to carry out some reliefs of units in de Larminat's brigade, and I have agreed to this.

8. I am glad you have been able to release the Poles. Many thanks.

9. We have just heard that the Russians refuse to feed the Poles in Russian Turkestan any more, and want us to remove about 70,000 en bloc!! A week ago nothing would induce them to give us any!!!

They are a queer crowd with no thought of anything but their own convenience and gain. However, I am very glad to have the Poles, <u>if</u> we can get the equipment for them. We hope to keep about 40,000, which will be a great reinforcement in these hard times.

10. You say you want to be sure that "we are really secure in Tobruk and at El Adem" before carrying out the moves you have in mind. What scale of attack do you want to be secure against? I thought that Acroma, El Adem and the entrances to Tobruk had already been put in a state of defence? I should have though that with the armour round El Adem and a Bde Gp in Acroma and Tobruk, you ought to feel pretty comfortable, but let me know what is in your mind. Things may move quicker than we thought at one time, and it might be advisable to expedite the readjustments you have in mind; this is, however, a matter for you to decide.

I agree that the allotment of an Armd car regt to each inf div has advantages so long as "no man's land" remains relatively narrow as it is now. Any really wide flung recces must I think be directed and controlled by Army or Corps.

11. I am getting 5 Ind Div out of Cyprus as quickly as I can, and will send advance parties up to you to learn the ropes early. The re-equipment of this div may be a difficulty.

12. Please show Nye everything and tell him everything. The more he learns of conditions as they are now, and likely to be in the future, the better.

13. Hope Jock[170] is settling down. Am sending you my own new map lorry for <u>your</u> personal planning use, and I hope you will like it.

14. Many thanks for releasing Angus.

Good luck,

JRL, AUC 765

---

170 Brigadier John Whiteley, BGS Eighth Army.

Letter from Lieutenant General N. M. Ritchie to Auchinleck, 26 March 1942

I am afraid that this letter will probably not reach you until after your return from Palestine, though possibly it may be sent on to you whilst you are away. There has been something of a lag in our air communication here these last few days due to the weather, but things are better now. I have your two letters, one of the 22nd and the other of the 24th to answer.

2. JOCK has arrived and I sent him up for three days to see the Commanders forward and get an idea of our dispositions, and he is now back here finally taking over. REDMAN will be leaving the day after tomorrow.

3. ARMOURED CAR REGIMENTS.

I believe that there are great possibilities of using armoured cars in numbers with a motor brigade. I can see this happening during an advance when one wants rapidly to get a motor brigade forward to hold some vital ground, especially in circumstances where the situation permits of them holding the ground in rear of a retreating enemy. I am sure this is one of the right ways to use armoured cars, and in such circumstances I think it would often be right to add some punch to the armoured cars by giving them guns. Further, just now when we have no suitable anti-tank guns in our armoured cars, one might well add some anti-tank weapons to them and so add to their strength. Personally, I do not think that, even in the wide frontages of this desert, one would ever employ more than two armoured car regiments working together under a Motor Brigade. With two squadrons up out of the three each armoured car regiment can quite easily cover a frontage of some 30 to 40 miles, which I think is as large as any single motor brigade could adequately control. I foresee that many chances for the use of a force like this may occur and that they will not be confined by any means to occasions when one may be following up a retreating enemy.

4. RE-ARRANGEMENT OF DISPOSITIONS 13 CORPS.

Though possibly it may appear that we would have a large number of our goods in the shop window, I feel that a re-arrangement of our resources on the lines suggested still gives us the requisite depth by the positioning of our armoured formations. The changes would involve putting up two infantry brigade groups and drawing back one motor brigade and the Free French Brigade Groups. I am going into the question of possibly getting greater depth on the front now that our positions are somewhat strengthened. In the case of the 50th Division, this is already to some extent achieved by the fact that the 69th Brigade Group is echeloned back behind the left flank, with one inf bn Gp and a squadron of "Matildas" in divisional reserve further back still. The problem on the frontage of the present 1st S.A. Div is somewhat more difficult because of the extra commitment here of watching the right flank and the possible landing places between GAZALA and the TOBRUK defences. There is, however, quite a considerable depth in the position now on top of the escarpments, especially in the anti-tank defences provided by the siting of the field arty in depth, the location of the "Matildas", and the reserve squadron of the divisional reconnaissance battalion. In regard to TOBRUK and its security, I possibly used the wrong word, for I am quite satisfied in my own mind about its safety against a scale of attack, which in my estimation is unlikely to exceed an armoured raiding force of all arms based on a strength of about one battalion of tanks. What I really was somewhat exercised about is the decisions which might have to be made by the Commander in TOBRUK in regard to the evacuation of personnel in certain conditions, and particularly the ordering of demolitions. But this can be got over, I think, by leaving the responsibility for this in the hands of the sub-area commander at TOBRUK. I have seen too many demolition schemes in the hands of the French ever to feel satisfied again in my own mind that they can really be trusted.

I am anxious to fit in, if possible, the dates for this general reshuffle with other operations about which you have already written to me. To some extent this will hinge on the date by which the 7th Armoured Division has completed its training, and this should be about mid-April or a little before then.

5.   <u>FREE FRENCH.</u>

I am getting a lot of very good reports about the Free French operations with their columns and I gather that they are doing a great deal better than any of us had anticipated would be the case. I quite understand the difficulties about the Free French going into a place like TOBRUK, but I think I can overcome this by ensuring that they still continue to find columns in various parts of the front and are kept fully employed fighting the enemy instead of themselves! No final information has reached me about the Senegalese battalion for MATRUH, nor about reliefs by Free French units from SYRIA with units now serving here. No doubt information about this will reach me shortly.

6.   DECEPTION.

I will make quite certain that the deception staff is used to the best advantage. GOFF, who is my new G.1 here, is shaping very well and has already worked out in outline the general deception plan that is to be followed. He was recently a teacher at the Staff College and is I think going to be very good. He has been in on my plans from the beginning and has been working in conjunction with the Operations and Planning side of my staff here. I will see that a similar procedure is followed in my subordinate formations.

7.   "FULLSIZE".

(a)   The reports received on this operation were, I consider, most inaccurate to begin with and I have already issued a strong letter on this subject to the Corps, because, if our information from the battlefield is to be so inaccurate as this it must inevitably endanger the employment of reserves whose task will largely be decided as a result of the information reaching us from the forward commander. I purposefully avoided giving you any appreciation of mine regarding the situation on D.2 day because I felt that the reports were not sufficiently accurate. Even the next day they still were often exaggerated.

(b)   The gun captures have now been reported. They were as follows:-

4 – 7.62 guns.
1 – 4.7 anti-tank gun.
1 – small anti-tank gun.

(c)   Our losses were more than I thought. Full reports are on the way to me now but I attach a summary of such information as I have got. Without seeing the full reports one hesitates to judge yet as to the causes, but I feel that there were two main ones:-

First, there was the considerable scale of air attack launched against "B" column in the MARTUBA area on D2 afternoon. Communications with this column broke down, I understand, on account of the fact that the W/T vehicles were knocked out and as a result we did not know about air attacks until it was too late to provide air counter measures.

Secondly, I think that "C" column was left out too late on the morning of D3. This again was caused through breakdown in communications. As a result part of their rear party was over-run by enemy tanks.

(d) We have had losses in this show, but nevertheless, I think the results have been good. The whole operation has done the 50th Div a power of good and has shown them that they can take on the Bosche and win on level terms. I think that it caused the enemy to shift the majority of his armour and that he has shown us his reactions, which are now being summarised and will be passed on to G.H.Q. It appears too, that it has caused him to shift his aircraft off MARTUBA to DERNA, which is again a good business, for DERNA is very prone to weather conditions and is nothing like so good as the landing grounds in the MARTUBA area. Finally, I think that there is little doubt this operation definitely prevented the enemy taking any serious air action against the convoy on D2.

8.   <u>LOSSES of 25-prs BY 11 R.H.A.</u>

The full report is on the way now. I have already inquired into the matter, both with the Corps and Divisional Commanders, and it appears that the Free French are not to blame. From all the reports it seems that the loss is due to rash action on the part of the Troop Commander who was determined to get his own back on the Bosche for having captured two of his guns near AGEDABIA. The individual is missing.

9.   It was very nice having ARCHIE NYE up here. I think he enjoyed his visit and perhaps realises better than before some of the difficulties that face us out here. He saw a lot, including a great deal of dust, I am afraid, for his second day here was a particularly bad one.

10. Thank you ever so much for saying you are sending me up your new map lorry, which will be of the greatest use to me. I was just about to pitch a tent for the purpose as I find my present map lorry a difficult place in which to work and plan. The arrival of your lorry will be very welcome.

11. I saw 102 A.Tk Regt (Northumberland Hussars) who are being broken up. I said a few words to the older soldiers. They all fully realise the need, but are naturally sad at the thought of losing their identity as a regt.

12. JUGO-SLAVS are shaping well under "Gertie's"[171] instruction. Haven't seen them yet myself will do so next Wednesday.

JRL, AUC 769

178

Cipher message from General Sir Alan Brooke to Auchinleck, 31 March 1942

I am sure you will realise the importance of starting your offensive as near to the accepted date as possible always provided that circumstances when the time comes indicates reasonable chance of success. It has not rpt not been easy to convince the Prime Minister and Defence Committee as to the necessity for delay and I am certain that any further delays will be unacceptable unless you produce overwhelming reasons. But everything is now clear as a result of our voluminous exchange of cables which I am afraid was unavoidable. I often feel how valuable a talk with you would be but we are both so tied in these critical days that it is impossible at the moment. I hope that NYEs visit has been of assistance to you and am looking forward to hearing account of his visit when he returns. All good wishes and hoping to be able to come for a visit before long.

JRL, AUC 771

---

171 Major General Francis Tuker.

179

Letter from General Sir Alan Brooke
to Auchinleck, 31 March 1942

My dear Auk,

I have just been told that there is a chance of sending you a letter tomorrow so am rushing off a few lines.

I am sorry that you should have had the difficult times that you have been through lately, and I can assure you that it was not owing to lack of efforts to save you from it.

Some of the telegrams which you did not like were the results of saving you from more unpleasant ones.

We have now got the P.M. to accept your dates and arguments, but not in a very pleasant manner. He is accepting the delays only under protest, and with little grace!

It was a pity that you could not come home as I believe it would have assisted matters.

I do hope that circumstances will work out now so that you can live up to your forecasts, otherwise I foresee difficult times ahead of us.

I do not think you realize how difficult he is to handle at times. In that aspect Oliver Lyttelton should be a great help in the future as he knows your difficulties and troubles and can give first hand evidence and advice.

What crushing bad luck about that Malta convoy; I hope they succeed in salvaging some of the stuff.

I hope that your new C.G.S. is now settling down and that he will be a great success.

I am having a little difficulty with the King over Arthur Smith[172] as he wishes to keep on Sergison-Brooke,[173] but I think we can get over the trouble.

I have noted that you propose to keep Jumbo Wilson on for a bit longer. He is getting on in age, but if you want to keep him on a little longer, I can fix it up.

---

172 Lieutenant General Arthur Smith, CGS, Middle East, 1940–42, who Brooke wanted to appoint as GOC London District.

173 Lieutenant General Sir Bertram Sergison-Brooke, GOC London District, 1940–42. Sergison-Brooke's active army career ended with this appointment.

Kenneth Anderson is taking over Eastern Command here so would no longer be available, and Irwin[174] has gone to India. I have made a note that in any case you don't want Gammell.[175] As regards Holmes,[176] I think he has reached his zenith as Corps Commander and should not go any further unless you have a very high opinion of him. I do not trust him over far, and I think he is lazy and unstable. If we put juniors over his head and he gets disgruntled, he must go: there is no room for him if he is going to put his personal feelings above getting on with the job.

I shall do all I can to make up some of your deficiencies in troops and shall try to fill up some of your gaps. The difficulty is ensuring for the adequate safety of India at the same time.

Let me know if at any time I can help you in any way, and remember that I am doing all I can to assist at this end.

Thank you very much for your Review of the situation in Libya (dated 26th February, 1942. It has been most useful.

With best of luck

JRL, AUC 772

180

Letter from Auchinleck to Sir Walter Monckton,[177] Office of Minister of State, Cairo, 7 April 1942

Many thanks for your letter of the 6th April, returning General Wilson's letter to me of the 4th April. I shall be very glad to discuss the whole question of Spears'[178] relations with the Army whenever you like.

---

174 Lieutenant General Sir Noel Irwin.
175 Lieutenant General Sir James Gammell.
176 Lieutenant General William Holmes. Holmes was to be promoted to be given command of Ninth Army in 1942 and promoted to full general before his retirement in 1945 which is an interesting comment on the limit of Alan Brooke's powers.
177 Sir Walter Monckton was, effectively, the acting Minister of State in the Middle East from March to May 1942. Oliver Lyttelton left in February to become Minister of Production and his successor, Richard Casey, the former Australian Minister in Washington did not arrive in Cairo until 5 May.
178 Major General Edward Spears, MP.

I would like, however, to correct any impression that my visit to Catroux[179] at Damascus was in the nature of an "official conversation", as Spears seems to think. Catroux asked me to stay with him, and I accepted with pleasure, as I would in the event of a similar invitation being extended to me by any other commander serving under me. I am afraid I shall do the same again should he be kind enough to give me the opportunity, and I really can not accept the implication that I can not talk to Catroux unless Spears is present. I have always made it quite clear to Spears that in matters affecting operational and military plans, I am free to see Catroux or any other French commander when and how I like, and I am afraid I have no intention of receding from this position.

Also, I am afraid I really can not consult Spears every time I wish to invite Catroux or de Larminat or any French officer to my house for a meal or to sleep, nor do I propose to consult him before accepting similar invitations extended to me.

I do not wish to be difficult, but, to be quite frank, I think Spears' attitude is illogical and absurd. I can not admit that the occurrences were in any way "unfortunate", or at all out of order. I reserve the right to visit French troops and commanders whenever I consider it advisable to do so. They are under my operational command, and it is my duty to visit them, so that I can assure myself of their state of efficiency. I think you will have no difficulty in seeing that to attempt thus to restrict my functions would be ridiculous.

For instance, when next I visit Tobruk, am I to refrain from my acquainting myself of the conditions under which de Larminat's troops are serving, until such time as Spears is pleased to grant me his permission?

I must ask that Spears be disabused of these ideas as soon as possible.

You will note that Spears does not go out of his way to keep responsible authorities informed of his own movements.

JRL, AUC 781

---

179 General Georges Catroux, the Free French High Commissioner to the Levant.

181

Letter from Lieutenant General N. M. Ritchie to Auchinleck, 13 April 1942

1. (a) There are signs, I think, of some re-grouping possibly of the enemy forces opposite the GAZALA position. Personally, I appreciate from the positions of the various H.Q. so far as we know them, that the enemy's ultimate intention is offensive. There is no doubt of this I think. At the same time, his reconnaissance and ground actions indicate, in my estimation, some nervousness on his part about his own right flank and the possibility of our undertaking some operation through TENGEDER. At any rate, this was I feel in his mind a day or two ago. In the last few days he has withdrawn a detachment at GARET EL-ASIDA, U42, from which place it moved, we believe to SEGNALI. In the SEGNALI area itself during the last 24 hours there has been much less ground activity, though air and ground reconnaissance by us indicated up to last night that there was still there a concentration of M.T. On the other hand, he has allowed the 12th Lancers patrols a great deal of freedom of action and yesterday afternoon some of these were able to bypass SEGNALI to the WEST and were up to last light on to the line of the TRIGH ENVER BEI in square U.46. In the centre of his position in the area TEMRAD – BREGHISC, it seems to me that he has been less active and we have identified one or two Italians there. This may indicate the possibility of him bringing up Italian troops to hold this line. In the Coastal Sector there was more activity yesterday and from our patrol reports there appear to be Germans in this area and that there are concealed in the nullas, south of the main road, considerable numbers of them. There have not been any signs so far reported to me of any large numbers of enemy A.F.V's in this area.

There are, I think, some indications that the enemy might attempt his main thrust astride the main road to TOBRUK from TMIMI. His air reconnaissance, including photography, has been very active here over the last few days above the escarpment, apparently locating our forward defences there. The other most prominent place for air reconnaissance has been BIR HACHEIM.

(b)   We have received watchers from the JEBEL back yesterday or the day before who have been on the lookout and in touch with the Arabs since the beginning of March until four days ago. They were not themselves able throughout this whole period to keep continuous watch on all the roads leading to the East through the JEBEL, and into MECHILI from the WEST, but the Arabs say that during this period there has been no major movement of tanks into the JEBEL from the WEST or through MECHILI. Personally,

I do not believe this, for I feel that the enemy reinforcements in A.F.V's that we have observed passing MARBLE ARCH towards the EAST have not been held back in that area. I believe it to be quite possible that these reinforcements in their onward journey to join the enemy's main forces may have moved via MSUS and MECHILI or possibly by a more Northerly route via BENGHASI – EL ABIAR – CHARRUBA – MECHILI, and that this movement may have taken place at night in small parties and so got through our watchers. So I am of the opinion that the reinforcements spotted moving Eastwards past MARBLE ARCH have probably joined the enemy's main forces.

(c)   Three days ago the enemy carried out two air reconnaissances over the 7th Armoured Division area, just WEST of CAPUZZO, and I think that he has possibly discovered them there. Meanwhile, they moved last night and are now between EL ADEM and GUBI.

2.   <u>SEGNALI OPERATION.</u>

The approach march started last night and I do not think was spotted before darkness. We have no news of how it is progressing yet because wireless silence is being strictly maintained until it is apparent to the Commander that the enemy have picked them up. This operation starts with a definite threat towards TENGEDER and the WEST. Dummy tanks are being used to stimulate movement in this direction and we are taking every possible step to watch the enemy's reactions to this.

3.   <u>PLANNING.</u>

We are getting on hard with this. The note that you said would be sent has not yet reached me, but as I am well into your mind in regard to this operation we are getting on with our detailed planning at once. I hope the note may arrive shortly.

4. <u>IMMEDIATE ACTION.</u>

Our front, as I see it, is now divided into two halves, the circumstances in each being different:-

(a) Between the sea and TEMRAD, NO MAN'S LAND is too narrow for the proper use of JOCK Columns. [Annotation: no matter about this.] Here we have to operate with large fighting patrols covering O.P's and sniping guns well forward, and behind this in each brigade a force of all arms ready to take offensive action such as that carried out by the NATAL CARBINERS, when opportunity presents itself. [Annotation: Certainly.]

(b) The other half of the front is difficult because here NO MAN'S LAND is a considerable width. [Annotation: Certainly!] But here also, the JOCK COLUMN, as we know it, is not really suitable because it has not sufficient hitting power. Here I hope to hand over the area to a complete brigade, organised to suit the conditions, whose task it will be to find and strike enemy concentrations. I see this being organised in three echelons:-

(i) <u>Armd Cars for reconnaissance.</u>

(ii) A small support group for the Armd cars to provide a hitting power in the form of guns, to provide the necessary strength to permit the Armd cars to get in against light opposition.

(iii) Columns, including at least a squadron of tanks with each to do the hitting.

This last to remain concentrated under the brigade and to operate in combination under the Commander's direction against any suitable enemy concentrations discovered. A system of this sort will ensure that the actions of these forces are co-ordinated and will, I consider be better than the present system whereby each formation runs its own column or columns on its own front. Finally, in regard to this matter, speed is absolutely essential and, therefore, we must decentralise.

5. <u>GRANT TANKS.</u>

Sixteen of the GRANT tanks have already developed a very high consumption of oil and a loss of power. Of these, three are unserviceable and out of action, while the remaining thirteen are "lamish ducks". As far as we can see the trouble is engines, and with a change of engine all will be well. We have wired in details to G.H.Q., and asked for an expert American Engineer to come up and have also sent back one of the three off the road immediately to the DELTA for examination. This defect has appeared at an average of 500 mile runs. Norrie has written details to MCCREERY.

6. <u>M.T.</u>

I know that you are very worried about the situation and it seems to me, from the forecast I have been given, that by about mid-May we will be about 2,000 vehicles short in the Army. The wear and tear on M.T. is considerable in these mobile operations that have recently been undertaken in front of opposition and these will continue. At an estimate I should say our wastage will be at least 150 to 200 vehicles a week.

6. <u>MAP CARAVAN.</u>

I have now got this running and am trying it out for a few days to see if I can discover all the defects. There are certain of these already apparent, the worst of which is ventilation.

7. <u>ARMY COMMANDERS' MEETING.</u>

I hope you will forgive me for not attending this as the situation here, I think, demands that I should be present for the moment. I am moving my Command Post up to 13 Corps H.Q. this afternoon so as to be there in case any major decision has to be made by me in respect of the use of the 7th Armoured Division, resulting from the enemy's reactions to our operations at SEGNALI.

<u>P.S.</u>   The situation regarding A.P. for 75's in the "Grants" is <u>bad.</u> We have only sufficient to fill the echelons of 7 Armd Div and parts only of 1 Armd Div. I understand there is nothing behind this. I believe there is no shortage of S.A.P. in M.E., but its performance, as you know is much below A.P. Can anything be done? I expect you already know about this and that the matter is currently in hand.

JRL, AUC 802

182

Letter from Lieutenant General N. M. Ritchie to Auchinleck, 22 April 1942

I had a preliminary conference with Strafer and Willoughby yesterday to start them off on their planning for "BUCKSHOT".[180] The directive for PLANNING was got out before I came to Cairo and has since been amended as a result of the decisions reached there. A copy of it, and the amendments, has gone to CORBETT and an Outline PLAN, putting the intended action briefly, follows to you.

A great deal was cleared up yesterday at the conference, which is, I am convinced, the only method of settling uncertainties which almost invariably result from the written word.

2. There was, I gather, a mistake made about Charles' aircraft yesterday, with the result that he will not have got to Cairo till the early afternoon. However, I hope he was there soon enough to see Riddell and clear up certain matters with him in regard to the administrative aspect.

3. I feel that in our planning we should resist relying on BENGHAZI being of any use to us as a port until we have put the enemy out of Cyrenaica.

The Navy has sufficient difficulty already in delivery to TOBRUK, and I do not believe we can rely on them to get much into BENGHAZI.

Therefore I feel ever more convinced that we should apply every administrative resource we have to one thing – establishing ourselves in the desert. We should avoid dispersing our administrative effort, which would certainly be the result if we are to put A.A., Air forces, and even coast defences into BENGHAZI before we have cleared the enemy from CYRENAICA.

4. Though these remarks have not yet been substantiated, I am just starting to hear stories which give me the impression that the

---

180 An operation designed to recapture Benghazi; it was overtaken by events in the face of the renewed Axis offensive.

Commando personnel are neither hard nor even fit, and that their discipline is very indifferent.

These stories reach me through G(R) officers who have been leading small parties of the Commando into the GEBEL in order that I might have a nucleus of their personnel who know the country there.

I have wired WILSON of your Bn[181] to give me his private estimation of their value and GRAHAM should be here to-day or tomorrow and I will have it out with him.

If these stories are true I feel that a further Commando "purge" is needed to get rid of useless people, and I feel that a new squadron commander will be needed to put the matter right.

Jock[182] has written to AIREY about it.

I will put up concrete suggestions later but at the moment I feel that there are two alternatives so far as this front is concerned:-

(a)   to leave them as they are, purge and introduce new blood,
(b)   to purge and then take what is left and form it into a Commando element for the L.R.D.G.

Looking at it from my restricted point of view, I prefer the latter, but I know it will run across the bigger M.E. organisation of Commandos for the whole theatre.

Here in the Western Desert the L.R.D.G. and saboteurs work hand in glove. Actions by the latter may seriously interfere with the former, so very careful co-ordination is essential. So I would like to have both operating under one head, and the best person is PRENDERGAST.

Further, the L.R.D.G. has a great reputation and tradition. If we added a commando element they would quickly pick this up.

I need hardly say that I would like STIRLING[183] to take over this commando element if formed but I anticipate this may not fit in with your need to have him in connection with parachutist training. As a leader of saboteurs and at irregular operations he is a master, and I wonder whether his value to our cause might not be greater in this line of country than with the parachutists.

---

181 Presumably the Black Watch.
182 Brigadier John Whiteley.
183 Major David Stirling.

I will of course be writing officially and this letter is only to give you a line on what is in my mind for the moment.

I am so sure that a saboteur and irregular operations will play a great part that I feel we should leave no stone unturned to get our commando work on a sound basis.

P.S.   I am sending back the Map Lorry to the Delta for alterations. Particulars of what I consider [may go to] Angus.

JRL, AUC 816

183

Cipher message from Auchinleck to Winston Churchill, 27 April 1942

One (.)   The special information dated 21 (21) April reached us in following form (.) Quote 161 (161) Axis tanks were reported serviceable 21 (21) April (.) Comment by M.I.14. This appears to be number of serviceable German tanks in forward area unquote (.) We have asked War Office to elucidate their comment for following reason (.) Every German tank strength return so far received by us from whatever source has given the number of tanks by types (.) The special information of 21 (21) April does NOT do so and we suggest the figure quote 161 (161) unquote to be Italian tanks or else the reply to a specific question (,) such as quote what progress has been made with fitting additional amour plate to tanks unquote (.) A very likely question seems to us to be quote how many serviceable mark III tanks are there now in CYRENAICA unquote (,) since the figure 161 (161) is only about twenty less than we believe the total number of Mark III to be and twenty is a reasonable number unserviceable (.) Figure 161 (161) might alternatively be strength of one German armoured division but this explanation is open to same objection that strength is NOT given by types as invariably heretofore (.)

Two (.)   Even if 161 (161) be strength in forward area (,) and we have asked War Office what they mean by quote forward area unquote (,) strength East of JEDABYA certainly and East of BENGHASI probably must be higher (.) We know from special information that number of serviceable in CYRENAICA as far back as 11 (11) March was 159 (159) German and 87 (87) Italian and L R D G have since visually observed moving into CYRENAICA at least 112 (112) German (,) 46 (46) Italian and 27 (27) unidentified tanks (.)

Three (.)   Fact that special information can NOT be repeated to us verbatim is realised but this must and does reduce its value to us owing to inevitable difficulty of separating original information from comment and of knowing the source of comment (.) This entails very careful weighing and cautious application of this information at this end though we do NOT question its great value (.)

Hope to be able discuss whole question of handling this information with General DAVIDSON[184] who is due here this week.

JRL, AUC 826

184

Memorandum entitled, 'Policy governing the employment of our armour' by Lieutenant General N. M. Ritchie, 1 May 1942, with annotation by Auchinleck

1.   GENERAL.

It appears to me that for the present we are on the defensive, an attitude we must continue to adopt until we feel ourselves strong enough to turn to the offensive. There may, however, be an interim period during the course of which we may well undertake limited offensive action when conditions are such that we see the chance to inflict serious loss on the enemy, especially to his armour or at all events isolated portions of it.

2.   FACTORS GOVERNING OUR ATTITUDE.

In the Western Desert, all other things – such as leadership – being equal, there is no doubt that the stronger armoured force dominates the battlefield. [Annotation: but leadership and good tactics must be our real standby.]

---

184 Major General Francis Davidson, Director of Military Intelligence.

Our object is, therefore, to build up an armoured force superior in strength, fighting qualities and leadership to that of the enemy and to use it concentrated.

At the moment we are the weaker. We are approaching equality in numbers and should, assuming the enemy does not receive any substantial reinforcements, shortly exceed the estimated number of tanks possessed by him.

For adequate superiority to resume the offensive we estimate we should have 3:2 against the German Mk III and IV, and 1:1 against the German Mk II and all types of Italian M.13's. On our estimated present enemy strength we need some 600 tanks of the cruiser types to give us this needed superiority, but for the purposes of these calculations we can reasonably include 100 Valentines which, even if they do nothing else, can at all events be counted upon to contain a portion of the enemy armour.

Apart from equality in numbers there is too the question of training to be considered. 22 Armd Bde has only just arrived and is in some respects backward in training. 2 Armd Bde is only just now commencing to convert to the new organisation which includes GRANT tanks.

Taking all factors into account I feel that our armour cannot be considered to have achieved adequate superiority before 20th May at the earliest, and this assumes no material reinforcement to the enemy.

The provision of the requisite "B" vehicles is also a factor which bears a direct relation to the date when offensive operations should start. It does not appear likely that this will be satisfactory until the last week in May.

3. CONSIDERATIONS GOVERNING OUR POLICY IF ENEMY IS FURTHER REINFORCED.

This note is based on the assumption that the enemy is NOT reinforced in armour. If he is a major problem arises. [Annotation: Quite so.]

Are we ever going to achieve the superiority we estimate that we need? At any rate we are now probably possessed of more troops experienced in the conditions of fighting in the Western Desert than he is. Time will give him the chance to get level with us. We are certainly superior in infantry. In these circumstances it might pay us to adopt a more offensive policy in an attempt to wear the enemy's armour down and to this end use a proportion of our tanks. This situation however has not yet arisen.

4. <u>CONSIDERATIONS GOVERNING OUR PRESENT POLICY.</u>

For the present, while the enemy is superior in armour, it behoves us to husband our resources in armour with the aim always of building up a force that is ultimately to take the offensive. Moreover, we are debarred from using the Grant tank and the 6 pdr gun on minor enterprises.

We cannot therefore afford to fritter our tanks away in countering the enemy's present tactics of covering the establishment of defended localities with armour unless he offers us a real chance of inflicting serious loss on him while we ourselves lose little. In such circumstances we would be justified in using Valentines assisted perhaps by Stuarts. [Annotation: Yes.]

The following policy will therefore govern our action:

(a) We must conserve our armour to build up for the resumption of the offensive.

(b) We must accept the fact that, as the enemy uses portions of his armour to cover the establishment of defended posts, we cannot prevent this without ourselves using armour.
Our armour will therefore NOT be used to prevent the establishment by the enemy of defended localities unless his action in doing so definitely endangers the security of the GAZALA – HACHEIM position, or offers us a really good opportunity of inflicting on him serious loss with little loss to ourselves.

As an interim measure when the Grant tank and the 6 pdr gun have been absorbed into formations the bar on their use may be removed. In this case we may be able to act more offensively even though we may not be strong enough to pass to the offensive.

JRL, AUC 832

185

Letter from Auchinleck to
General Sir Alan Brooke, CIGS, 3 May 1942

I must apologise for not having written you a proper letter for so long, but, as usual, I find I am kept pretty hard at it. Also, I hope Nye took the place of many letters and was able to give you a real picture of what we are doing and how we stand.

2. The matter most in my mind at the moment is the threat to India. The Chiefs of Staff signal of April 23rd giving your views on the situation alarmed me considerably. In fact, for the first time since this war started, I began to have serious misgivings as to the outcome of it. I brought the matter to the notice of the Defence Committee here and they agreed this morning to send a signal to the Chiefs of Staff giving our views.

3. I hope you will not think we are being "busy" by meddling in matters about which the Chiefs of Staff must know much more than we do. As I have said, I am seriously perturbed and can not help wondering whether the dependence of the Middle East on India, strategically and materially, is fully realised at Home. I feel it must be, but, all the same, there are elements in the present situation, which do not seem to fit with a logical view of it. For instance India is still sending fighting troops to the Middle East, which is very nice for us but hardly in keeping with her own apparently very urgent need for all the trained soldiers she can muster.

4. There are now 82,000 odd Indian soldiers in formations in this country and 133,929 others not in formations – a total of 216,270 or about a quarter of the whole. Of the 14 divisions now under my command, 6 are Indian. There is the equivalent of 8 ½ divisions of Indian fighting troops in the Middle East. We are still dependent on India for great quantities of munitions of all kinds. For instance, we drew from her in March about 90,000 tons, including 49,000 tons of R.E. stores and 10,000 tons of Ordnance stores. We are particularly dependent on India for steel.

How it is proposed to replace India as a source of men and munitions should she be invaded by the Japanese, I do not know. Moreover, what the attitude of the Indian troops will be if this situation arises is doubtful, to say the least of it. Magnificently as they have fought till now, often under great handicaps, they may not stand the strain of so hard a test on their loyalty, which is, as you know, not to England but largely to their officers. I feel that these considerations may not have been presented correctly to the Chiefs of Staff or the Defence Minister.

I believe myself that there is no shadow of doubt that we cannot afford to lose India nor even to contemplate its loss. This I believe quite apart from the great uncertainty of our being able to hold on to the Middle East if India goes, because of the threat to our communications.

5. Our life line here runs through the Indian Ocean from South Africa to Suez and from India to Basra and Suez. With the Japanese at Colombo and Bombay I wonder how long we should be able to supply ourselves and how long it would be before our oil supplies from the Persian Gulf were cut off? I quite realise the value of the Middle East as a base for a future offensive designed to reopen the Mediterranean and to carry the war against Germany into Europe. We put this project clearly to the Chiefs of Staff some months ago – before Japan had gained her very startling successes against us on the sea, on the land and in the air. The situation now has completely changed.

6. I feel very strongly that the time has come when we must decide what is vital to our continued existence and what is not. We lost Singapore and then Burma chiefly, I feel, because we did not or could not decide to concentrate our resources on holding what really mattered, while letting less important places go. I am not presuming to criticise and I know I am being wise after the event, but I do hold very strongly that we can no longer afford to dissipate our meagre resources in trying to hold everything irrespective of its permanent, as opposed to its temporary, value.

7. I may be wrong, but I feel that India is vital to our existence and that, once it goes, our hopes of recovery within a reasonable period of years are small indeed.

If I had to choose now between losing India and giving up the Middle East, I would not hesitate. I believe that we can still hold India without the Middle East, but that we can not for long hold the Middle East without India.

8. Do not mistake me. I am not advocating a withdrawal from the Middle East. Far from it, and I see no immediate reason for any such drastic step, even if you do decide to weaken us to strengthen India. Even if we had to leave Egypt after having thoroughly blocked the canal, we might well hold on to Iraq and the oil supplies until the tide turned.

   I assure you I am not in the least defeatist, but I can not help trying to see the situation in its true perspective and that is how it looks to me.

9. As to our projected offensive in Libya, I fully realise its desirability from the political and strategical point of view, but it must be admitted that the material value to be had from it, so far as it may affect the course of the war, is small at present. Had Japan not entered the war, its affect might have been much greater and, ultimately, possibly decisive.

   As I have tried to make clear several times before, the success of our offensive in Libya depends on our being able to collect sufficient tanks to have a reasonable superiority over the enemy, and on our being able to keep sufficient air forces on this front to give us a reasonable measure of air superiority.

   If these two conditions are not fulfilled, the launching of an offensive will be an extremely hazardous operation of war. It is even more hazardous because of the possibility, which is almost a probability, of our having to call a halt to it while still unfinished, owing to the materialisation of the threat to our Northern Front.

   I do not think myself that we can reasonably expect our advance through Cyrenaica to El Agheila to take less than three months. If we do not get to El Agheila we can not be sure of holding Cyrenaica, this requires no further proof.

   If we have to stop our advance while still short of El Agheila, we are almost certain to have no choice but to withdraw to Gazala or to the positions I have prepared on the frontier about Salum and Maddalena. The moral affect of this could hardly be good.

10. We have now got reliable information that by the end of May the enemy is likely to have effective for battle, with formations 350 German tanks and 160 Italian.

    So far we have said that, for an offensive, we need a 2:1 superiority over the Germans and equality with the Italians. Now because of the Grant tank and the six pounder gun which is just coming into service, we are prepared to accept a 3:2 superiority only over the Germans. I must stress that there is a considerable risk in this, as we shall be attacking and can not guarantee always to induce the enemy to fight us on ground of our choosing.

We shall also have I hope about 250 infantry tanks "Valentines" and "Matildas" which, though not suitable to join in the armoured battle should be of considerable value, if properly used, in making the enemy detach some of his fast tanks to watch them and prevent them overrunning his infantry.

This should offset the reduced superiority over the German tank strength, which we are proposing to accept.

11. There are many other factors of course besides mere numbers of tanks – such as the relative strength in anti-tank guns, the efficiency of the field artillery and the handling of the supporting infantry, but it is almost impossible to assess these and I do not propose to try.

12. Let it suffice to say that to offset 360 German and 160 Italian tanks we should have about 700 Cruiser tanks, in addition to our infantry tanks.

We have now in the forward area three armoured brigades, one of which, the 22nd, will not be fit for battle before the middle of the month, as it is still doing its collective training. This gives us roughly 450 tanks.

The next formation to be ready is the 1st Armoured Brigade, just equipped with tanks, but still very short of transport of all kinds, which is extremely scarce.

I do not see how this brigade can be ready for battle before the 15th June.

This would give us about 600[185] Cruiser tanks on that date, and although this is 30 short of the total required, I would be prepared to accept the added risk and launch an offensive with them, particularly as we hope to have good reserves of tanks while the enemy is not likely to be so well off.

13. We have as yet no news as to the state of the Italian Littorio armoured division. Units of it and its headquarters are in Libya we know,

---

185 The figure of 670 was originally given but crossed out and 600 substituted.

but whether it has any tanks or not we do not know. We hope it is merely feeding the Ariete armoured division.

If it does materialise, another 150 or so tanks must be added to the enemy strength and this would completely do away with any superiority on our part.

14. In my opinion, it would be extremely risky to launch an offensive without the requisite superiority in Cruiser tanks. I feel that such an attempt might easily result in a stalemate or even in a definite reverse, the effect of either would I think be disastrous.

15. I do not wish you to think that I am trying to avoid attacking the enemy. Nothing could be further from my desire. I and, so far as I know, all the troops, are desperately anxious to get back at him. Nevertheless I feel that with so much at stake elsewhere, it is my duty to give you the facts as I see them, and I have little doubt that you will wish to put them before the Defence Minister.

JRL, AUC 834

186

Letter from Auchinleck to General Sir Alan Brooke, 3 May 1942

Thank you very much for your approval to the higher war course. I am sure it is badly needed and that it will give good value for the effort and time which will be expended on it. I am sorry we have lost so much time already and I hope there will be no more delay in getting it going. I feel every week counts now, and it is desperately important to ensure that for the future we shall have leaders and senior planning staff officers who have been scientifically trained. There are previous few of them now so far as I can see.

2. I regret deeply your decision about not locating the course in the Union instead of Palestine, and if I may say so with due respect, I think the reasons you give about the aircraft are not really relevant. I tried to tell you in my telegram that there are four services a week to South Africa from here, two B O A C and two run by the Union, which are at their disposal and can not be touched or reduced by us, however much we may wish to do so.

I do not really think that the transport once a month or so of the relatively small number of officers affected would have greatly strained these services. Had I thought so I would not have suggested it. I do feel that Palestine is not a really good location for a course of this kind, first because there it is liable to disturbance any day or night by air attack, and this whole area may very well become a zone of active land operations before the Autumn, and secondly because the atmosphere is bound to be a bit parochial and narrow I think. However you have considered this objection and given your decision and I am carrying it out at once. The course will be located at Sarafand in buildings recently vacated by the Weapon Training School, which are quite suitable. The climate is good too.

3. As to Dorman Smith, I am sorry about this too as I feel that he has the brains, imagination, originality, and energy to give the course a good start. He has it all in his head already. As to experience in command I am afraid I do not place such a great premium on it as you do, and I dare say I am wrong. All the same it is not too easy to find commanders of experience in our Army who have the other qualities which I consider essential as well. As I told you in my signal I would have liked to have put in Messervy,[186] who has had unique experience in command and also in teaching at the Staff College. I felt however I could not take him at this time from his division and so had to ask you for a substitute. John Harding would have done it I think but I can't spare him from D.M.T. which he is doing splendidly. I have hopes of great results from him. I hope you will be able to give me a first rate man and one of those I have suggested. A mediocrity would be worse than useless.

4. The problem of higher command on our Northern front is making me think a lot. The Air Force have decided to put in an A.O.C. over the two local commanders, A.O.C. Levant and A.O.C. Iraq, to coordinate the action of aircraft over the whole front. This is right I am sure but it at once raises the question of cooperation with the Army. This A.O.C. can not be in two places at once and therefore can only concert plans in person with one Army Commander (9th or 10th) at a time.

It is, of course, supremely important that the two heads, Army and Air Force, should live together and have a combined headquarters.

---

186 Major General Frank Messervy, then commanding 7th Armoured Division.

There seem to be three possible solutions –

(a)   To create an Army Group
(b)   To put one Army under the other
(c)   To amalgamate the two Armies and have one Army.

An Army Group in addition to the two Armies is out of the question at present as we have neither the staff or signals.

To put one Army Commander under the other is a compromise and would not, I am afraid, work well in practice.

I believe the solution is to fuse the two Armies into one and have their Corps H.Q. one in Syria and one in Northern Iraq, while turning lower Iraq into an L of C area under G.H.Q. The L.G.A. (Riddell-Webster) is strongly opposed to this on administration grounds, but I am not sure that his arguments are altogether sound. Anyhow I am examining them. If I feel we must amalgamate the two Armies, I would suggest keeping Jumbo Wilson as the Army Commander. He knows the whole problem and has a good grasp of it. He is keeping fit and his brain is working well. If this should happen, Quinan would be out of a job, as I have nothing to offer him here. I dare say India could use him.[187]

I will let you know the results of my further examination of this problem.

5.   I am sorry you could not agree to my suggestion about Freyberg and Morshead[188] being raised to Lieutenant Generals.

I want to make it quite clear to you that the suggestion came from me and not from either of them.

I made it because I think it highly desirable for political reasons to give them the higher rank to bring them more on a level with Army and Corps Commanders. They hold an independent position here, communicate direct with their own Governments and can say "Boo" to me whenever they like!

---

187 Lieutenant General Edward Quinan, GOC Tenth Army. Quinan was, indeed, to see service in India, as Commander North Western Army, before his retirement in 1943.

188 Leslie Morshead was an acting Lieutenant General as of March 1942, when Lieutenant General Thomas Blamey left the Middle East and Morshead took command of all AIF units in the theatre, while remaining GOC 9th Australian Division. Morshead was promoted to the substantive rank of lieutenant general in September 1942.

It is to their credit that they rarely do this! They have much greater responsibility than the ordinary divisional commander as they have large base establishments and training schools to look after.

Moreover their promotion would help us considerably I think in our deception plans. There is the point too, that I do not think either of them are really competent to command Corps, though both are excellent divisional commanders.

If they are not to have Corps, the promotion would be some recompense.

Could you reconsider your decision. I believe it would be worth it in the interests of the general war effort.

There is no ramp of any sort about my proposal.

6. Scobie,[189] my D.A.G. is off Home tomorrow on a liaison visit. I hope you can spare him a few minutes, as I believe it would be of value to you.

7. I wish most earnestly you could come back here and see things for yourself.

Please do if you possibly can and come soon. I hope you are very well.

JRL, AUC 835

187

Letter from Lieutenant General N. M. Ritchie to Auchinleck, 5 May 1942

Thank you so much for your letter of the 2nd which I got on my return here on the night of the 3rd. You sound terribly busy, and I can well realise how difficult it is for you to escape from Cairo.

2. PLANNING.

I held a conference with both Corps Commanders yesterday to go further into details of future action and would like to come down to Cairo to visit you as early as you can see me. There are certain matters I wish very much to discuss if you can spare the time, so

---

189 Major General Ronald Scobie.

I sent a signal to ask if you can see me on the 6th. (I have now got your reply and will come 7th)

The enemy's frontage is getting very extended and I believe this is due in no small measure to anxiety on his part concerning our threats on his right flank. I believe we can play on this even more, and possibly induce him to push further out into the desert in the TENGEDER direction.

I am inclined to believe that he is already starting to offer us the chance of cutting off, and with luck crushing, his right wing from inclusive SEGNALI Southwards. Anyhow there is a good chance of this; if not the whole at any rate that portion of his troops – at present not much I believe – from ASIDA to TENGEDER. Such a situation might give us a first class opening gambit for "BUCKSHOT".

3. <u>GOBI.</u>

Reconnaisances of this area were carried out before with the object of establishing a Bde Gp defensive pivot there, and actually I had further ones done last week.

I have told Willoughby Norrie that he is to prepare a position there, and this can take the form of a training exercise with a Bde Gp of 5 Ind Div including an approach and rapid establishment of a defensive position.

All will work in well with training, our defence and our cover plan.

4. <u>TOBRUK – ACROMA – EL ADEM – BIRGUBI LINE.</u>

Personally I have always considered the GAZALA – TOBRUK – EL ADEM area as one position, and the above line as the most rearward defences within it.

As I see the defensive battle we may well find ourselves in a situation where the enemy has succeeded in penetrating with an armoured force through a portion of our forward defences, and we will then be faced with fighting an armoured battle, possibly the major one, within our defensive system. In such circumstances the garrisons of our forward systems – GAZALA – ALEM HAMZA – HACHEIM – will still be holding out, though doubtless a few localities may have been overrun.

Provided we win the armoured battle, and about this I feel pretty confident, all will be well; and we can turn to the counter offensive or, at worst, re-establish ourselves in the GAZALA Position.

On the other hand, if we are unsuccessful in the armoured battle and assuming the enemy is left with a substantial superiority in armour, I doubt whether we could reasonably hold the line TOBRUK – ACROMA – EL ADEM – GUBI, unless the division from the Frontier is brought up, and even then I doubt the outcome. I repeat that such conditions envisage the enemy possessing considerable superiority in armour, which to my mind implies that we will be in danger of getting ourselves invested in TOBRUK.

To summarise:-

(a) Provided we win the armoured battle we can at the worst continue to hold the GAZALA – HACHEIM POSITION. At best we turn to the offensive. So the problem of the TOBRUK – ACROMA – EL ADEM – GUBI line will not arise.

(b) If we lose the armoured battle and, assuming the enemy to be materially superior in armour, I believe it would be dangerous to stand on this line.

(c) There may be an intermediate set of circumstances. Both we and the enemy may lose heavily in armour and a "stalemate" situation results. In this case we could certainly hold the TOBRUK – GUBI line, but I hope this would not be necessary and that we would be able to continue holding GAZALA – HACHEIM.

5. STATIC OUTPOSTS.

I believe that your solution about the enemy's outposts is the right one. The situation is, I feel, very similar to the way he held the Frontier last year. But I believe he will do all he can to fight his main battle quite close up behind these forward elements of his; certainly well in advance of the vital ground.

6. 22 Armd Bde.

No. There is really no reason at all why 22 Armd Bde, if I do move it up, should not remain under 30 Corps and its own division.

7. DIAMOND "T" TRANSPORTERS.

Yes. The trouble is that the eight-wheeled axles of the power unit dig themselves in. I hope to have more details soon.

At the moment it looks as though the answer might be to add a great deal more weight over the driving wheels – somewhere about 3 to 4 tons.

These transporters will get tanks across the desert, but very slowly and suffering from constant "boggings". Too slow for tactical movement. But we will get over this yet.

8.   GUNS FOR ARMD Cs.

The 75 type is the thing, and should fire portée. Always direct, I think. No gunner nonsense!

Both Corps Commanders agree to the desirability of this, and I believe we can accept a reduction of one troop of Armd Cs per sqn to find the requisite personnel. Scale of guns I suggest is one per Armd C troop, which will work out at four guns per sqn.

Best organisation probably:-

[Diagram omitted]

I am putting this up officially when I have got detailed comments from Corps.

JRL, AUC 838

188

Letter from Auchinleck to General Sir Alan Brooke, CIGS, 7 May 1942

My dear C.I.G.S.

I am afraid I have never answered your letter of the 31st March. Thank you very much for it, and for your effort on our behalf. I know how difficult it is for you at that end, and you, I think, realise how hard it is for us here, and I am most grateful to you for your support and help.

I must say again, however, how difficult it is for me to do my job, when the plainest statements are removed from their context and made to mean the exact opposite of what was intended. Once more, at the risk of being a frightful bore, I do ask you try and ensure that the facts are faced, and that the unpalatable as well as the palatable bits are considered!

You will know by this time that we can not live up to our "forecasts" as you term them. I think that if you will spare a few minutes to read the telegrams in which these "forecasts" are mentioned, you will see that we did all in our power to prevent you or anyone else seizing on these as firm dates. We have rubbed this in several times since, but without much effect apparently. As I say, this sort of thing gets very wearing after a time, and is not exactly encouraging or conducive to full efficiency!

However, I know how it is with you too. I _fully_ realise how difficult a job you have. I learned my lesson when I was Home last July. I hope Oliver Lyttelton really is helping; I have a feeling he may be too absorbed in his new job to be able to help much. Nye ought to be able to help, as I think he does realise conditions out here. Not many others at Home do, I am afraid – through no fault of theirs perhaps.

Corbett is doing very well indeed, and has a realistic and up-to-date outlook.

I note what you say about Holmes. He has not grumbled, and is doing very well. I have not found him lazy.

As for Jumbo, I think he had better stay where he is a bit longer. I have thought this over carefully, and I think this is the right course. He knows the problem thoroughly and has a wise head. Also, he is very good with the French and understands Spears.

The new Minister of State[190] arrived yesterday, and has started in to work straight away. He has a great deal to learn, but I like him very much.

I wish you could come out here; you would soon see then how things are for yourself. Please do not try to make me go Home, as I really can not leave this place for long now, and I can add nothing more to what I have said already. There is a tremendous amount to be thought over and done here, and I find it hard to get time to do it all, even though I try to avoid tackling anything but the big jobs.

I hope you are very well.

JRL, AUC 839

---

190 Richard Casey, who had been Australian Minister to Washington immediately prior to taking up the post of Minister of State, resident in Cairo.

189

Letter from Lieutenant General N. M. Ritchie to Auchinleck, 11 May 1942

I have, since getting back here, been continuing deeply to consider the plan for "BUCKSHOT", and I must confess that there is one particular aspect about it which troubles me. I know it will be difficult for you to spare the time, but it would help me a very great deal if you could give me a short period to discuss this matter when I am down for the Army Commanders' Conference on the 15th or 16th.

2. Personally I have no doubt whatever that the ultimate course the plan is to follow, i.e. to cut across CYRENAICA avoiding the JEBEL, is the correct one. Also that we must avoid precipitating the armoured battle on ground prepared by the enemy and of his choice. All will be well, of course, if the enemy reacts rapidly and does this <u>before</u> we have to establish our fourth defended locality. Once we have to establish the fourth and subsequent localities, I have to start weakening the GAZALA – TOBRUK – HACHEIM position; before this juncture I can provide garrisons for the localities without reducing our strength there.

   One point, therefore, about which I am unhappy is that in my opinion the GAZALA Position is at rock bottom now and cannot be reduced without a grave risk of it not being possible to stop, or seriously delay, a determined enemy attack upon it. If the enemy attacks in strength, for which we must cater, an appreciable number of his tanks will get through. The situation has altered a lot since this plan was first mooted. The enemy is much closer up to us now, and can therefore put on a "blitz" attack with much less warning than before. If we weaken the GAZALA Position there is a risk that the enemy's armour might penetrate to our vitals at TOBRUK and No. 4 Fwd Base before our main armoured force could engage.

3. The strength of the GAZALA Position now, and even at the stage of establishing defended localities, is the presence of our main armoured force ready to crush the enemy's armour. One may hope to position our armour so that it can, while still being able to support the most Westerly of the new defended localities, still be able to support the GAZALA Position.

But I believe that there is one very serious weakness in this. The enemy will hold the tactical initiative and I consider it will be a most dreadfully difficult thing for me to avoid being led up the garden path by the enemy if he divides his armour. He will have time on his side, and speed of armour too.

A possible picture I see is us, in progress of establishing a defended locality at GANIA, while the enemy up to this point has not re-acted at all. Then he starts something that gives me the impression that he is moving an armoured force S.W. via MECHILI and West of the bad-going area on our GANIA post. In desert conditions of visibility our Armd Cs in touch with this force will be unable to see more than the leading elements. From this I certainly will not discover if it is his main force or not. Air reconnaissances may give us some indication, but with the dust and often poor visibility, one cannot be confident of this. So I feel I may well find my self uncertain of what the enemy is doing for [some?] 12 hours, possibly as much as 24 hours. He will have got that start. On top of this the introduction of the GRANTS inevitably materially slows down the moves of our armour.

What I feel is that, if I do find myself in this predicament, I am offering the enemy a chance of drawing off my armour to the West because I have a hostage to fortune there in the form of a defended locality which cannot hold out for more than a limited time without support of armour. In this event, my armour would be out of supporting distances of the GAZALA Position. Admittedly the enemy will have divided his armour but he may well still have sufficient to attack the GAZALA Position and beat us to it at a time when my armour is unable to intervene.

This I fully realise may never arise. It certainly won't if the enemy re-acts before a fourth defended position has to be established. Personally I believe he will re-act because such is his nature, but I cannot see that we are <u>forcing</u> him to do so. This we won't do until we are in a position to threaten his main L. of C. in Western CYRENAICA. This cannot happen for some time, i.e. until we have established a defended post at GANIA.

I must be prepared with a plan in case he does not re-act early, and I do NOT want to go on extending our commitment into the desert, weakening GAZALA and presenting our armour with a task beyond their capabilities, which I believe this to be.

So I definitely do not want to establish a fourth defended locality unless the enemy has re-acted either by:-

    (a)   having attacked us and suffered a serious defeat to his armour;

or (b)   without having first seriously fought, has moved the main portion of his armour West of a North and South line through MECHILI.

4.   I am convinced that we must do all we can to provoke the armoured battle early in the proceedings and as far East as possible. While I realise that we cannot in the estimated balance of tank strengths advance and attack him in his own prepared ground, I feel equally convinced that in this desert the attacker has a tremendous advantage over the defender. I would therefore prefer not to be rigidly committed at this stage to the establishment of further localities.

5.   To conclude, what I ask is that, should the enemy NOT re-act early and fight, I may be left a free hand after the establishment of "A", "B" and "C" localities to take such action as I calculate will cause him to do so, while still maintaining the principle of establishing further localities at a suitable time.

You will have got my signal about alterations in our dispositions. There have been no grand indications today to confirm his anticipated action, but there has been over these last few days a considerable lack of air activity on his part. He is holding up his serviceability, I think.

JRL, AUC 843

190

Letter from Auchinleck to Lieutenant General N. M. Ritchie, 12 May 1942

1.   You will have read by now the J.I.C. paper on IMMEDIATE ENEMY INTENTIONS, which was sent up to you this morning. I think the evidence is sufficiently strong to support the conclusion that the enemy intends to carry out offensive operations in the near future.

2.   I feel that the move forward of Battle Headquarters Panzer Army and Africa Corps and the artillery shoots close to the South African front are other significant factors.

3.   As regards the timing for an attack, there are indications that he would still like another week or two, but I know you agree with me that one cannot take any chances in this respect. Even though he may have planned zero day early in June, moves on our part might well force him to start sooner.

4.   We have been giving a lot of thought to what plan the enemy may adopt. I realise you will have been doing the same, but feel you may like to hear the conclusions we have reached.

I feel that the enemy may carry out one of the following two plans:-

(a)   Make his main attack against 1st South African Bde and then go for TOBRUK, but moving <u>first</u> against HACHEIM as a diversion, in the hope of drawing off our main armoured forces to the Southward.

(b)   To feint and exert pressure on the Northern portion of your front, and make the first stage of his main attack the capture of the HACHEIM area, after which he will use this as a base to assist his attack on TOBRUK.

For either of the above plans he will also do all he can to disrupt our communications and our system of command and supply by making the most ruthless and determined attacks by highly specialised troops on headquarters, aerodromes and vital points on our lines of communication.

5.   The following precautions strike me as being important in meeting such an attack:-

(a)   Strictest orders to be issued that troops in position stay and fight in their positions, even though they may be cut off for a day or two.

(b)   Adequate reserves of ammunition, food and water to be made available in the weapon pits and alongside the guns.

(c)   A good alarm system to be established in rear areas.

(d)   Our main armour to be positioned so that it can compete with either plan of attack.

I have no doubt you have already dealt with all these points, and many others which I am not competent to consider.

6. I am disturbed at the lack of information we get from the air of the enemy's strength and disposition behind his forward positions. I know any Tac R is immediately pounced upon by enemy aircraft, but I am wondering whether it is not worth while laying on a really big show with the maximum fighter cover. I look on this as very important indeed. We must know what he is doing with the mass of his armour.

7. I have ordered the 3rd Indian Motor Bde to move to MATRUH, and 10 Motor Bde to EL ACROMA, so as to strengthen the defence of your L of C.

8. We are trying a new way of getting information out of P.W. RUDOLF. I feel sure he knows something about the enemy's future plans.

9. There is one other matter which I feel may need attention, though I daresay you have already dealt with it thoroughly, as is your habit.

It is the behaviour of troops and transport in rear areas when they hear that the enemy is supposed to have "Broken through". I remember the tendency to panic and dash wildly to the rear when the Germans went for SOLLUM last November. True, it was mostly transport and so-called non-combatants who were affected, but the general result was pretty bad, I think. The exact opposite should be the case. Anyone who has a weapon should go to meet the enemy, not run away from him, while transport carrying much-needed supplies for the troops in front must also go forward, using due caution, and join the units dependent on it. I hope you will agree with the general principle underlying this, and see that it is enforced. Battle discipline must be enforced, and enforced ruthlessly. The German relies on causing panic, and we must prevent it.

10. I need not stress the need for the most thorough defence of all headquarters, and particularly, of course, your own, even at the risk of some increased discomfort. If necessary headquarters must be moved into areas where they are automatically protected by the presence of fighting troops unlikely to be moved. You will of course see that protective troops turn out frequently for practice alarms.

I am sorry to stress these obvious precautions, but I feel that some of our commanders may be too happy-go-lucky in these matters, and apt to regard the hunting about of headquarters by the enemy as rather a joke! It is not the actual commanders I am worried about so much (though I should hate to lose any of them!!) as the absolute necessity for maintaining the system of command in running order. Naturally the closer you can be to the command of your striking force the better, and I understand you have arranged for this.

11. One other matter, and that is the need for hitting back at once with whatever may be available, as soon as the enemy's main line of attack is known. There should be lots of chances of getting in on his tail, and subordinate commanders on the spot must take the initiative and go in on their own with the object of causing the utmost destruction behind the main thrust, and thus delaying it and eventually bringing it to a halt for want of nourishment. This, too, I am sure you have rubbed in to all concerned.

12. Finally, the need for being ready down to the last button for the counterstroke we have discussed before. The more this can be considered, discussed and gone over on the ground the better, I feel.

13. On reading this over I feel you may think I am not trusting you, and trying to teach you your job. You know me well enough, I hope, to know that this isn't so! If you do feel this way however – you must say so!!

I have told the C.I.G.S. that if the enemy attacks us, we would welcome it, as he would be playing our game, so you must excuse any apparent over-anxiety on my part to see that we take full advantage of his temerity. I am sure you will.

JRL, AUC 844

191

Letter from Auchinleck to Lieutenant General N. M. Ritchie, 12 May 1942

Very many thanks for your letter of the 11th (DO/70/6) just received.

Have written you a long and grandmotherly (I am sorry to say!) epistle about possible enemy action. Hope you won't mind my having done so. I am only out to help in any way I can!

2.   Of course I will give you all the time you want to discuss BUCKSHOT. You and I and Tom Corbett will go into secret session – no one else – so we can talk as freely as we like and no record!

3.   I see your difficulty very clearly. I have always seen it, and it is of course the weak spot in the plan. But few plans are without one weak spot, and we must hope for the best when the time comes.

4.   I can assure you that I will not tie you down to any premature action in establishing a fourth locality. We must be guided by the situation at the time. This came out quite clearly in the small war game we played here.

JRL, AUC 845

192

Letter from Lieutenant General N. M. Ritchie to Auchinleck, 13 May 1942

I had hoped that I should be able to send you by Liaison Officer today my full appreciation of what I consider to be the enemy's likely intentions and actions in my area, and the course that I recommend should be adopted to counter these. But I feel that I would like to get all the facts marshalled before sending this, and it would not be completed in detail until tonight. I will therefore bring it down myself tomorrow, or, if I am unable to come myself, by hand of another officer who will be in possession of the necessary facts to discuss this with you if you can see him.

2. MAIN FEATURE OF THE APPRECIATION.

In the existing comparative strength of our own and enemy tanks I feel that we are in a position now, and this position will improve daily, of being able thoroughly to defeat the enemy's armour forward, i.e. forward of the frontier position. But the achievement of this will, I appreciate, be a long drawn out struggle, and it is, in my opinion, dependent on three things:-

(a) Water. We must secure for our own use all water points from inclusive GAZALA to exclusive BARDIA. Equally we must prevent the enemy capturing for his use any of these water points plus the BARDIA water source, the water in storage in the Frontier boxes and the source at BUQ BUQ.

(b) Aerodromes. It is essential that we secure our aerodromes in the area between GAMBUT and exclusive BARDIA, thus preventing the enemy from neutralising our air effort.

(c) TOBRUK. We must ensure that this is absolutely secure and that the reserves of water and supplies there and in No. 4 Fwd Base are not in danger. To do this we must be quite certain that no seaborne or airborne attack on TOBRUK itself succeeds, and we must equally be sure that we can hold the enemy on the line ACROMA – EL ADEM to give depth to our defensive system.

My maintenance situation is such that I have sufficient reserves in TOBRUK and No. 4 Fwd Base to enable me to fight an intensive battle forward for a period of not less than three weeks. These reserves exist there now and their quantity will increase daily as time goes on.

I do not consider that at present, particularly in view of the likelihood of air and seaborne attack, that I am really secure in TOBRUK, and this I can only be if I can produce another two Bde Gps for this purpose. These additional troops I can only find from 5 Ind Div, whose task is, as you know, to secure the Frontier positions in the event of serious attack upon us.

I do not feel that there is any real danger of my getting bottled up in TOBRUK because I am quite convinced that we can break our way out without difficulty provided we do not get into TOBRUK itself with our main forces and keep the enemy at a distance from the South and S.E. faces of it.

3. <u>POLICY.</u>

I am of course not quite completely in the picture of your calls elsewhere, calls which may make this plan of mine too risky. I feel that if we can defeat the enemy forward, and this I believe to be quite possible, it does not matter if my L. of C. is cut for a time; it will not seriously prejudice the main battle if the enemy gets a large raiding force into the CAPUZZO R.H. area, it will not be disastrous if he interferes with our communications at MATRUH. I therefore feel that the best employment for the 5 Ind Div is [Annotation: I never told him to do this did I.] to strengthen our defences of the aerodrome areas, TOBRUK and EL ADEM. This will, of course, mean a major change of policy, involving your releasing me from the obligation to secure the Frontier positions while fighting the battle forward. I.e. keeping one division there.

4. I am of course taking no action in regard to these points, other than to have my reconnaissances carried out so that they may be effected quickly, until I hear whether you approve. The above is naturally only a very brief outline in which I have attempted to explain briefly the main issue.

5. I was very glad to get your special wire concerning the dispositions of the 1 Armd Div, because it showed me that I was thinking on the same lines as you. Their concentration forward will be completed by the evening of the 16th.

JRL, AUC 849

193

Letter from Auchinleck to Lieutenant General N. M. Ritchie, 16 May 1942

Our conversations and discussions yesterday and the day before have assured me that you have a grip on the situation, and know how to deal with it, whether the enemy attacks us or we carry our offensive against him.

2. I feel that you have our offensive plan firmly in your mind, and that you will be able to exploit the opportunities it is likely to offer

you to the fullest possible extent. It is a thoroughly flexible plan, and this is its strongest point.

3. By establishing yourself round the enemy's SOUTHERN flank you at once begin the encircling process, which the German seems to dislike so much. When and how far you can continue this envelopment after the first phase must depend on how the enemy reacts to it. I do not think this is really a weakness of the plan, although at first sight it may seem to be. Having got your forward pivot of manoeuvre you are at liberty to threaten SEGNALI, MECHILI or even BENGHASI from it.

4. In order to turn your initial move to the best advantage, it is essential that you should have the best possible information of the enemy, and you must insist on the R.A.F. making the maximum effort to give you this. I realise the difficulties as pointed out by Coningham last night, and I am sure he will do everything he can to surmount them.

   In addition you must, and I am sure you will, make the boldest use of ground reconnaissance of all kinds, and particularly of officer patrols, to find out the position and movements of the enemy armoured forces. It is not too much to say that the fate of your battle will depend on the receipt by you of early, accurate and continuous news of the enemy, and this is worth running any risks to obtain. I know you are in full agreement with me on this point.

5. I feel myself, and I feel it even more strongly after hearing your views, that the enemy's extreme NORTHERN flank may well prove to be a weak joint in his defence, and that the most careful and thorough plans should be made to take advantage of this should opportunity offer.

6. Although our action after you have established your initial group of defended localities may depend partly on the enemy's reaction to this move, this need not prevent you, I think, from thinking ahead and keeping always in view the main aim of the offensive action, which is to threaten BENGHASI. Every effort should, I feel, be made to effect this aim, consistent of course with the principle of concentrating your striking force in the area where it is likely to be most needed, and whence it can strike at the enemy should he attempt to disrupt our plans by a counter offensive directed against our rear areas. I believe that a lot can be done with light forces,

which can evade the enemy if heavily attacked and yet keep him on tenterhooks and so force him to attack our main concentration.

7.   We are both pretty sure now that the enemy intends to forestall our offensive by launching an attack of his own, and that this is likely to happen with the next ten days or so. From what we know of his plans and preparations, it seems as if his attack, if it does materialise, will be determined and heavy, with the object of inflicting a severe reverse on us and capturing TOBRUK, as a prelude to a further advance against EGYPT. I feel content that your dispositions and plans, as explained to me yesterday by you, are adequate to meet this attack, and I have no doubt that you will defeat the enemy heavily.

As you will realise, it is of the utmost importance that you should be able to turn from the defensive to the offensive, immediately the opportunity offers, and it is absolutely essential that you should be able to carry your counter-offensive to the maximum depth into the enemy's position, and then turn it into a pursuit.

Plans for this counter-offensive and pursuit must be prepared with the greatest care, and be capable of translation into immediate action. Any delay or hesitation may rob us of a decisive victory. I know you are well aware of this, and I am sure you will see that all your commanders realise it too, and at once.

All commanders must be impressed with the supreme need for speed and vigour in following up the enemy, and giving him no respite. A large proportion of his force is Italian, and once he starts to go back, the greatest risks are justified to keep him on the run. We know ourselves how difficult it is to stop a pursuing enemy who holds the initiative and exploits it with boldness.

8.   One last word in connection with a possible counter-offensive.

I think myself that any advance by us in pursuit of the enemy should be on a two corps front and not placed under one commander. The second course is, I feel, likely to result in lack of flexibility and to undue centralisation of control at headquarters of the Army. I wonder if you agree with me.

JRL, AUC 854

194

Cipher message from Auchinleck to Winston Churchill, 19 May 1942

One (.) My intention is to carry out the instructions in paragraph two of your message of May 10/2 (.)

Two (.) I am assuming that your telegram is NOT meant to imply that all that is required is an operation designed solely to provide a distraction to help the MALTA convoy but that the primary object of an offensive in LIBYA is still to be the destruction of the enemy forces and the occupation of CYRENAICA as a step towards the eventual expulsion of the enemy from LIBYA (.) If I am wrong in this assumption then I should be so informed at once as plans for a major offensive differ entirely from those designed merely to produce a distraction (.) I am proceeding as if my assumption is RIGHT (.)

Three (.) Assuming that a major offensive is to be carried out but that its inception must be so timed as to provide distraction to help the MALTA convoy the actual moment of the launching of the offensive will be governed by three consideration (:) first the sailing date of the convoy (,) second enemy action between now and then (,) third the relative air strength of the enemy and ourselves (.) All these are under close and continuous examination here (.)

Four (.) There are strong signs that the enemy intends to attack us in the immediate future (.) If he does attack our future action must be governed by the results of the battle and can not be forecast now (.)

Five (.) Assuming that the enemy does not attack us first it is my intention that General RITCHIE shall launch his offensive in LIBYA on the date which will best fit with the object of providing the maximum distraction for the MALTA convoy (,) and at the same time (,) ensure the fullest degree of readiness in the forces carrying out the offensive (.) These considerations are mutually conflicting as you will realise and entail a certain degree of compromise which it will be my responsibility in consultation with the other Commanders-in-Chief to determine (.) The importance of avoiding an abortive attack has already been fully set out in No. CC/36 of 6 May from Commanders-in-Chief to Chiefs of Staff and does NOT need further explanation from me (.)

<u>Six (.)</u>   In conclusion may I ask your consideration of the fact that owing to the narrowness of our margin of superiority over the enemy both on the land and in the air (,) the success of a major offensive can NOT be regarded as in any way certain (,) though everything will be done to make it as certain as possible (.) In any event success is NOT likely to be rapid or spectacular as progress will probably have to be methodical owing to the special nature of this problem (.)

<u>Seven (.)</u>   I feel therefore that it is of the greatest importance that in the first instance NO publicity at all should be given to our intention to carry out a major offensive even after it has been launched (.) Still less should the public be led to hope for a speedy and striking success (.)

<u>Eight (.)</u>   This telegram has been seen by the Minister of State, Commander-in-Chief Mediterranean and Air Officer Commanding-in-Chief who agree with it (.)

JRL, AUC 857

195

Letter from Lieutenant General N. M. Ritchie to Auchinleck, 19 May 1942

Thank you so much for your letter DO/PSC/11 of 16 May, which I was delighted to receive.

2.   <u>RECONNAISSANCE.</u>

Photographic air recce is at last beginning to bear fruit and good results last night from careful interpretation show 150 Tanks, with over 800 M.T., in the area GABR EL ALMEIMA U.79 – BIR ES SFERI U.67. There is probably more M.T. and the whole concentration represents, I appreciate, the equivalent of one division. There may be more outside the area covered by the photographs. We have already got the country to the East or this covered, but interpretation is not yet complete.

I arranged yesterday for special officers' patrols to go in behind the enemy positions to get information. This will be done either by parties in to lie up, and/or to send up a couple of individuals into the enemy's position in daylight in a captured German vehicle. The latter is the better, and I believe they could drive about picking up all sorts of information and get away with it. Anyhow, it is worth trying.

3.   PLANNING.

Directly after getting back I had a Conference with Corps Commanders and gave them the policy which is:-

(a)   The Battle of the GAZALA – HACHEIM Position.
(b)   Turning to the offensive during (a).
(c)   "BUCKSHOT".

This is the order in which the planning must go and in this priority. (b) and (c) go more or less together.

4.   TURNING TO THE OFFENSIVE.

This either starts with "BUCKSHOT" or, if the enemy attacks first, at some time during the course of the battle of the GAZALA – HACHEIM Position. In the former case – "BUCKSHOT" – we have to create the situation which causes the enemy to sally forth and attack us on ground of our choosing. In the latter case the enemy will have done this for us.

In both sets of circumstances, once the enemy has attacked, our action either to resume or to turn to the offensive, has much in common.

All the possibilities are being investigated, including driving through towards TMIMI, and possibly MECHILI too, with the object of severing the enemy's communications with his main supply bases on the JEBEL and forcing him into the desert. These plans must include a large scale raiding force – basis a motor Bde Gp – to be directed either on to Western CYRENAICA or possibly as a first step to threaten MECHILI from the West. I would, however, make it clear that whatever the course adopted we must stick to the plan of developing the Desert Route and the railway must be constructed across it.

As I told the Corps Commanders, our whole attitude, and this attitude is to permeate through the Army, is that if the enemy should attack this is indeed the chance for which we have been praying and preparing; the chance to thrash him on our own ground and then turn to the offensive.

I believe there will be no lack of speed in getting ourselves on the move forward once the chance occurs.

5. ENEMY INTENTIONS.

Most secret sources reaching me last night give the impression that he is pressing on all he can with his preparations. Almost indecently speedy, I think! This implies some fixed target date which cannot be altered. This may be to coincide with operations in Russia, but that date might be changed. What cannot be changed is the moon, so I believe his attack will come between the 25th May and 1st June.

There is no doubt that his plans involve land, sea and airborne operations in conjunction with one another, but it is mighty difficult to come to any very concrete decision respecting the scale of attack of the last two – sea and airborne.

Also, I feel, there are stronger and stronger indications that TOBRUK is to be the main objective. Further, I think there are indications – demands for more assault boats and the like – which show a greater possibility of an attack on GAZALA and a thrust on TOBRUK by the Coast. Not that this need be of necessity his main effort; I think he would go along the top of the escarpment too if he could. Anyhow, I had a real good look at that part of the area yesterday, and feel quite happy about it. The key of course is the top of the escarpment above GAZALA and this the South Africans fully appreciate.

6. TWO CORPS FRONT FOR COUNTER OFFENSIVE.

You raise this in the last paragraph of your letter. I would prefer not to be committed. If I am to strike deeply into enemy territory I must eliminate every useless mouth. For this reason it might well pay me to have one L. of C. only. Two Corps would tend to get in each other's way on one L. of C. and two corps mean more overheads. These are reasons in favour of following up with one Corps whilst using the other to make good in rear.

You mention "lack of flexibility" and "undue centralisation". I think these can be overcome if one gives the Corps Commander a directive on policy and leaves him to run it. These were the lines on which Jumbo Wilson worked with Dick O'Connor so successfully.

However, I am keeping an open mind and having the various possibilities examined.

I have just had BRIGGS[191] into see me and it is good to have him back again. He knows just what is needed here. The enemy seems to be getting very large tonnage through BENGHASI. I will discuss this with D.M.I.

McCreery told me that you were anxious about the armoured disposition as given. So was I. At the Corps Com[ma]nd[e]rs Conference I asked Norrie to explain them. I am glad to say he prefaced his remarks by saying that he'd ordered repositioning to take place which fitted in exactly with what I wanted. The whole show is far more in hand now.

JRL, AUC 859

196

Cipher message from Winston Churchill to Auchinleck, 20 May 1942

One.   Your paragraph 2. Your interpretation of the instructions contained in my OZ/192 of May 10 is absolutely correct. We feel that the time has come for a trial of strength in CYRENAICA and that the survival of MALTA is involved.

Two.   The greatest care will be taken to prevent newspaper speculation here about attacks either way in CYRENAICA. If and when a battle begins public will merely be informed heavy fighting is in progress. You must impose the same restriction at your end and we can consult together about any definite pronouncement.

Three.   Of course we realise that success cannot be guaranteed. There are no safe battles. But whether this one arises from an enemy attack and your forestalling or manoeuvring counter stroke, or whether it has to be undertaken by you on its own, we have full confidence in you and your glorious Army, and whatever happens we will sustain you by every means in our power.

Four.   I should personally feel even greater confidence if you took direct command yourself as in fact you had to do at SIDI REZEGH. On this however I do not press you in any way.

191 Brigadier Raymond Briggs, commanding 2nd Armoured Brigade.

Five.   Ought not the New Zealand Division to be nearer the battle front? If you want any help in dealing with the New Zealand Government pray refer to me.

JRL, AUC 860

197

Letter from Auchinleck to Lieutenant General N. M. Ritchie, 20 May 1942

I am sending you this by Corbett, as I feel that you should know how I think the enemy may attack you. I have had my ideas put on the enclosed maps in order to make them clearer.

Corbett is thoroughly in my mind, and can explain any doubtful point to you.

Do not think I am trying to dictate to you in any way, but this coming struggle is going to be so vital that I feel that you must have the benefit of our combined consideration here, though I realise we can not be so conversant with the details of the problem as are you and your staff.

2.   As you already know, I feel that there are two main courses open to the enemy:-

(i)   To envelop our SOUTHERN flank, seizing or masking BIR HACHEIM en route and then driving on TOBRUK. This would probably be accompanied by a strong diversion with plenty of artillery, dive bombers and smoke against your NORTHERN flank, aided possibly by landings from small craft in rear of the GAZALA inlet, with a view eventually to clearing the coast road to TOBRUK.

(ii)   To put a very heavy attack on a narrow front with tanks, artillery, dive bombers, smoke and lorried infantry against the centre of the main position, with the object of driving straight on TOBRUK. This would probably be helped by a feint against BIR HACHEIM in which the Italian tanks might well be used with the aim of drawing off the main body of your armour to the SOUTH, and so leaving the way open for the main thrust.

This course would also almost certainly include an attack from the sea round about GAZALA for the same object as before.

3. I feel that the second course is the one he will adopt, and that it is certainly the most dangerous to us, as if it succeeds it will cut our forces in half and probably result in the destruction of the NORTHERN part of them.[192] We must of course be ready to deal with the enemy should he adopt the first course, and in either event, you must of course be most careful not to commit your armoured striking force until you know beyond reasonable doubt where the main body of his armour is thrusting.

4. Now, as to the method I think he is likely to adopt, to put the second course into effect.

I believe he will try to put the main body of his armour through our front on both sides of the GADD EL AHMAR ridge, which, as you know, runs more or less EAST and WEST along the boundary between the 1st S.A. and 50th Divs. This attack will be supported by every kind of weapon, including especially dive bombers and anti-tank artillery. It will be pushed relentlessly on a narrow front.

As we agreed the other day, it is likely that such an attack will break through in spite of our mine fields. Let us assume that it does break through on a comparatively narrow front.

I think that then he will immediately put out defensive flanks, taking full advantage of the main coastal escarpment to the NORTH, and of the escarpment which runs along the TRIGH CAPUZZO to the SOUTH. If he can get his anti-tank and other artillery protected by infantry established on these escarpments, he will have established a corridor which may be difficult to cut, especially for your armour if it is positioned as at present, somewhat far to the SOUTH.

Having secured his flank, he will drive in on TOBRUK, assisted almost certainly by parachute attacks on the place itself and the troops guarding the entrances, and, possibly, also by landings from the sea which may be supported by naval bombardment.

At the same time he may try to open the GAZALA defile for the passage of M.T. and troops by landings from assault boats EAST of it.

---

192 Rommel's offensive, commencing on 26 May, developed more in line with the scenario Auchinleck outlined in 2(i).

As I have already said, this main attack will almost certainly be accompanied by a strong and resolute feint against BIR HACHEIM, which will develop into a real attack if it has any initial success.

5. I know that you have taken and are taking numerous measures to meet an eventuality such as I have described, but I must tell you that, speaking from an office chair at a great distance from the battlefield, I wonder whether you should not put your armoured reserve a good deal further to the NORTH where it can hit the enemy immediately he emerges from his break through, and before he can establish a defensive flank, which all our experience teaches us he will certainly try to do. I suggest that both your armoured divisions complete should be positioned astride the TRIGH CAPUZZO. It does not look from the map as is this would be too far NORTH to meet the main attack should it come round the SOUTHERN flank, instead of against the centre as I anticipate. Your covering troops should give you good warning of any main enveloping movement on your left, even if you do not hear of it before it starts.

As always, the difficulty will be to decide which is the real attack, and which the feint.

6. I feel that your reaction to my suggestion that you should put your armour more behind the centre of your position will be that your SOUTHERN flank will be left bare of any mobile troops to delay and harass the enemy, and also of any armoured units to give immediate support to the Free French. I propose to send you at once the 3rd Indian Motor Bde, which, though not absolutely fully equipped, is fit for battle. I suggest you might like to keep this on your SOUTHERN flank, and that they will obviate any need to leave either of the motor Bdes of the two armoured divisions in this area. I consider it to be of the highest importance that you should not break up the organisation of either of the armoured divisions. They have been trained to fight as divisions, I hope, and fight as divisions they should. Willoughby Norrie must handle them as a Corps Commander, and thus be able to take advantage of the flexibility which the fact of having two formations gives him.

Moreover, you will be getting the 1st Armoured Brigade before long, and it should join the 7 Armd Div, I feel, thus making both divisions similar.

As regards armoured support for the French, I suggest that if you move your armoured divisions further NORTH you might spare some infantry tanks for them. I am sending you up as soon as possible the 7th R Tanks, with one Valentine squadron of the 4th R Tanks and two Matilda squadrons of its own, to increase your force of infantry tanks.

As to the rest of the infantry tanks, I suggest that if possible they should be placed so as to support the infantry in that part of the position which is likely to bear the brunt of the enemy attack. I admit that this may be uneconomical, as tending to immobilise them, but I feel that it is essential to give this infantry all possible support in order to encourage them to hang on. It is of the highest importance that they should hold on whatever happens. I will be glad if you will consider this also.

7. If you can stop the enemy short of TOBRUK and then get at him in flank with your armour and in rear with infantry and guns, I feel you may have the chance of scoring a decisive success.

I think, therefore, that you should at once lay minefields across the corridor between the two escarpments to the WEST of ACROMA, and cover these with guns. You will see from the sketch what I mean.

I suggest also that you should consider mining the coastal corridor also in more depth, so as to stop any breakthrough by that route, which, though it might not be serious, would be a serious nuisance and divert effort from the main task of destroying once and for all the enemy's armour.

8. Finally, I suggest that you should fortify EL GUBI and protect it with mines. I am sure you will feel much more comfortable when you have something there threatening any wide turning movement from the SOUTH against TOBRUK or from the EAST against SALUM, unlikely as this may seem to be. I know you want to keep 5th Indian Div as compact and uncommitted as possible for use as in a mobile role, should opportunity offer, either under Gott or under yourself. I am absolutely certain that this is right. I am sending you, therefore, at once the 11th Inf. Bde of 4th Indian Div to replace 29th Inf Bde in CAPUZZO, in case you still feel you need another Bde there as well as the 2nd Free French Bde. If you don't so much the better, as you might then relieve the 9th Inf Bde of the 5th Indian Div in TOBRUK, and so increase your mobile reserve. You could then use a brigade of the 5th Indian Div for EL GUBI if you feel so inclined.

The 11th Inf Bde is NOT mobile, and I do not want it committed forward of SALUM unless it is absolutely necessary to do so. I am bringing the whole of 10th Indian Div from IRAQ, and the leading brigade will be sent up to you as soon as it arrives in relieve of 11th Inf Bde, which I shall then hope to get back here, as it is part of the garrison allotted to CYPRUS.

9. I am also bringing from SYRIA the Guides Cavalry (armoured cars and wheeled carriers) which I will give you if you want them to replace a battle-worn unit, or for the pursuit which I hope to see you carrying out.

10. I suggest that you must reorganise your system of command for this battle. For a defensive battle I feel you must have your mobile reserve, that is, your armoured force, freed from all static commitments and responsibilities. Your Army falls, as I see it, into two parts, one whose task it to hold the fort, which is the GAZALA – TOBRUK – EL GUBI – EL HACHEIM quadrilateral, and the other whose task it is to hit the enemy wherever he may thrust and destroy him. I think GOTT should be solely responsible for the first, and NORRIE for the second. I would relieve the latter of all responsibility for BIR HACHEIM at once.

I hope you will agree to this, as I think it is of first importance.

11. I am sorry to have inflicted such a long letter on you, but as I said before, so much hangs on this battle that I feel nothing must be left undone by anyone to help win it.

As you know, I have absolute confidence in you and your troops, and I am sure that if the enemy attacks, you will deal him a blow which he may find it difficult, if not impossible, to recover.

That is the object.

JRL, AUC 861

198

Auchinleck to Winston Churchill, 22 May 1942

ONE. Thank you very much for your telegram of May 21st and for confirmation of your instructions contained in your message of May 10th. I am now absolutely clear as to my task and I will do my utmost to accomplish it to your satisfaction.

TWO.   Thank you too for your arrangements regarding publicity which will be scrupulously followed by me here.

THREE.   Am most grateful for your most generous expression of confidence in the army I command and in myself and for the assurance of your support, the measure of which has been proved to us so often and so amply in the past.

FOUR.   Much as I would like to take command personally in LIBYA I feel that it would NOT be the right course to pursue. I have considered the possibility most carefully and have concluded that it would be most difficult for me to keep a right sense of proportion if I became immersed in tactical problems in LIBYA. I feel that a situation may arise almost at any time when I shall have to decide whether I can continue to reinforce and sustain the 8th Army without serious hindrance, or whether I must hold back and consider the building up of our NORTHERN front, which I am now weakening in order to give General RITCHIE all the help possible. On the balance I think my place is here but you can rely on me I hope to adapt myself to the situation and to take hold if need arises. I am in very close touch with General RITCHIE and he is fully in my mind. I hope all will be well.

FIVE.   I have considered fully the desirability of bringing the New Zealand division out of SYRIA into EGYPT. Apart from the political aspect, which I am sure you could settle as you so kindly offer to do, there are other considerations. I am loath to denude SYRIA of troops just now, partly because of the uneasy political situation in the country itself, and partly because of the possible effect on the TURKS, of whose attitude I am NOT too sure. I feel they mean well, but circumstances may be too strong for them, and it is most important that they should NOT get the idea that we are weakening or becoming unable to support them. I am already bringing 10th Indian Division, a well-trained formation, from IRAQ to reinforce 8th Army should need arise, and have meanwhile sent up a brigade of 4th Indian Division as an interim reinforcement. With these reinforcements the 8th Army will about reach saturation point so far as power to provide the army with food and WATER is concerned. WATER especially is a very serious problem. Moreover the N Z division has been severely denuded by the government of senior officers who are needed to command newly-raised troops in NEW ZEALAND, and it is now training officers to replace these. I am watching the whole situation very closely, and IF I have to put the rest of 4th Indian Division into CYPRUS to provide against a possible threat to the island, I should probably have to bring the N Z Division down to EGYPT, but I would rather NOT move it at present.

SIX.   Once more I thank you for your most sustaining message. There will be hard fighting, as there was before. I have great confidence in our troops and in our dispositions. I have a firm hope of victory and pray that it may lead to greater things.

JRL, AUC 865

199

Letter from Lieutenant General N. M. Ritchie to Auchinleck, 23 May 1942

I hope that CORBETT'S visit here has eased your mind in regard to the positioning of the armour and the roles that have been allotted to them. I am extremely sorry that you should have been exercised in your mind about this on account of the fact that the exact positioning had not been accurately given. You have so many things other than this to worry about. The mistake was, I feel, due to McCREERY being given some wrong information from the map board here.

2.   APPRECIATION.

All the indications are I think that we may expect him to attack very shortly. Ground observation, confirmed by air photography yesterday, shows that three "F" lighters were in BOMBA. They would not be there for supply purposes; they would not be sent there for practising seaborne operations; they would not be sent there long before they were needed to be used. All these pointers to seaborne operations starting fairly soon. On the other hand they were not loaded, which is strange were they going to carry tanks, for these I think they would probably load at DERNA and only move them forward to BOMBA at the last possible moment. They may of course be a "plant"!

There is more activity on the German "Y" this morning though little ground activity yet reported, and I think this may possibly portend a movement forward of the 21 Panzer Div which I myself feel is probably still somewhere South of TMIMI. It is difficult to forecast where his main thrust will come, it will certainly be combined with one or more diversionary efforts and undoubtedly with a distracting and disrupting operation by sea and air.

His recent very considerable increase in transport, and the fact that the rate of discharge at BENGHAZI port will have enabled him materially to economize in road transport between TRIPOLI and that place, will give him a greater circuit of action for his striking force. I still feel that if his maintenance makes this possible he will try to go round our Southern flank. In any case there will be a diversion there and this will probably be the Italian Mobile Corps. There are certainly indications of an interest on his part in the BREGHISC – ALEM HAMZA ridge and the main thrust may, of course, come here. But it will be a difficult and costly operation for him as our minefields are strong and our positions there well sited, well supported with artillery and well dug-in. Anyhow, whatever course he may adopt, our main strength is the counter with our armour to destroy him. We are ready for this, TEWTS have been held, the ground carefully studied, and I feel confidence that our armd forces are prepared to operate either to the South or to the North-West.

The sea landing side has been buttoned up. Any landing, other than on a major scale starting from Europe, must, I think, be limited to the portion of the coastline between TOBRUK inclusive and GAZALA. There may be small disruptive parties elsewhere as far to the East as my rear boundary. We have an adequate watching system with suitable communications and this has been interwoven with the existing R.A.F. and A.A. warning systems. The difficulty of course is that we cannot cover with fire permanently every possible beach at which he might land, but I think our system will give us the earliest possible warning of where a landing takes place. I have arranged with "Mary" Coningham that his job will be to put down the highest possible scale of air attack on any landing to delay and disrupt it while I move up the troops to deal with the situation. My calculations at present are that the scale of attack is unlikely to be greater than a large sized Bn Gp with full supporting arms, accompanied by up to 50 tanks. No doubt sea bomb and mines as a side issue.

3. THE "ARENA".

I spent a long day yesterday with Willoughby studying the ground and the positioning of troops for the battle there after a conference with Strafer to co-ordinate the action of his various armd columns going into this battle. I was to have done this the day before, but had to postpone it on account of CORBETT'S visit. I feel quite satisfied that an enemy armd force that gets into this "arena" area opens itself to fighting at a great disadvantage and should offer us every chance of destroying it utterly. The minefield connecting ACROMA escarpment and the sea was reconnoitred yesterday, and mines are on the way up now. The other minefield running from ACROMA Southwards will go as far as approximately B.674 in Square 3842 leaving a gap from that spot Southwards as far as B.653 in square 3841. The escarpment running Eastwards from the latter point as far as about B.651 in square 3941 is a very good obstacle except at certain places which can be easily defended from the top. This will give us a tank obstacle from ACROMA Southwards and then turning East along the escarpment with gaps astride the EL ADEM – ACROMA road and between the escarpment at B.653 in 3841 and B.674. Both these gaps will be filled by dummy minefields and covered by our guns and their use thus denied to the enemy. Work on this minefield is starting at once.

Our strength for our "arena" battle will, I have come to the conclusion, be greatly strengthened if we have a post at point 209 in 3743, and I have ordered one to be established there, and I am arranging to give it some 75 mm post guns and one 88 mm. From this point one can see the whole of the Northern part of the "arena" and also interfere with any effort by the enemy to use the escarpment passage just to the West of B.111 in square 3743. This point dominates EL UET ET–TAMAR in 3742.

4. 2 ARMD BDE.

I am most anxious to keep the GRANTS in this BDE and the 6 pdrs just about to be issued somewhere near where they can fire, but I have told Willoughby NORRIE to go into the question of making the necessary arrangements for moving everything else up now; all details to move Grants etc at the greatest speed in case of need. Everyday of added training there enormously improves the fighting value of the Bde. They are coming on well, their equipment is improving and their training with the GRANTS is getting better daily.

5.   COMMAND.

I wish I had an additional Divisional H.Q. to run the Southern flank, including the command of the Free French, 3 Ind Motor Bde and the 29 Inf Bde at GUBI, but none is available. I cannot spare the 5 Ind Div H.Q. Willoughby[193] is letting me know today how this is being organised and I am proposing to send him over my BRA and extra staff and Signals to co-ordinate this for him or he will run it himself with his own R.A. staff. I will of course provide the additional Signals.

P.S.   I am anxious about the preparation for the "PALMERSTON"[194] party. This is a show to which I attach the very greatest importance. If things look not too good I can lay it on quickly and I believe it might well turn the scale of the battle. This is, of course, quite apart from the possibility of its use for this counterstrike after the enemy's armour has been broken. So naturally I am most anxious that there should be no delay and that all preparations be finished ahead with least possible delay. This includes moving the T.L.C.'s up here and the sailing up of the tanks.

JRL, AUC 867

200

Letter from Auchinleck to Lieutenant General N. M. Ritchie, 23 May 1942

Very many thanks for you DO/70/6 of the 21st May, which reached me last night. Tom Corbett also got back yesterday evening, so I feel now that I am pretty well in your mind for the time being.

2.   I am now quite happy about the positioning of the armoured divisions, and I am glad we were thinking on the same lines; this is always comforting!

---

193 Lieutenant General Willoughby Norrie, commanding 30 Corps.
194 A British special forces operation designed to dislocate the Axis headquarters in the Cyrenaica region.

I hope 3rd Indian Motor Brigade will prove adequate for the job you are giving them. They ought to be good.

3. I am glad you hope to be able to establish a pivot at GUBI, even if you do not find it necessary to occupy it permanently. I feel it rounds off the position and gives it the depth on the SOUTHERN flank, which I think was needed.

4. I quite understand about the infantry tanks, and the dispositions as explained by you seem excellent to me. I had a mistaken idea that before you moved up the armoured divisions, the 1st Army Tank Bde column behind the 150th Infantry Bde area has a sort of roving commission. I agree that you have got them where you want them, including those in the ACROMA column, which should be most useful. I am glad you hope to be able to give some tanks to the Free French at BIR HACHEIM. I am sending up H.Q. 32 Army Tank Bde to join you at once.

5. I agree with all you say about new minefields, and that these should be most valuable as giving more depth to the position as a whole.

6. I hope you will not have to denude the reserves of mines for the frontier positions to too great an extent. Let me know about this, and whether you want more. I feel too that any troops stationed in the frontier positions should go on working on them to the best of their ability. One never knows what may happen in this kind of war!!

My latest information, which is up to the end of April, shows the minefields 60% to 70% completed in HALFAYA/SALUM and only 20% in EL HAMRA; while infantry positions are shown as 50% complete in both areas. What about the water supply at HAMRA? Someone said the pipeline has been taken up again? I suppose this was necessary, but I feel rather uneasy about it, and would like to know how you view the situation.

7. I note what you say about the division of responsibility between the two Corps H.Q., and I agree that it would be difficult to adopt my suggestion, and that you are right to keep things as they are. My only reason for making the suggestion was that I did not like the possibility of Willoughby Norrie being bothered about a feint attack, or even a real attack, on BIR HACHEIM while he was fighting a decisive action to the NORTH! I quite see that BIR HACHEIM as well as EL GUBI and the New Guards Bde defensive locality

may each all be pivots of manoeuvre for the amour, and therefore of great interest to 30th Corps.

8.   I am glad you hope to be able to maintain the organisation of the armoured divisions, though I fully realise that you or Norrie may very well have to change brigades from one division to the other, once the battle is joined. This doesn't matter, and the organisation is, as you know, designed to permit of it being done.

9.   I note what you say about the armoured car units. I must warn you that it <u>may</u> be necessary, in the first instance, to keep back the Guides at BAGUSH to give better protection to the important installations and landing grounds in that area, now left rather bare by the forward move of the 3rd Indian Motor Bde. I will, however, release them for you as soon as I can. I feel that even if they reach you a bit late they may form a very valuable replacement for a battle-worn unit, and it is just as well to have something up one's sleeve! This applies also to the 10th Indian Div.

10.   There are two further suggestions I would like you to think over.

(i)   I feel it might be most valuable if you could possibly mount some kind of diversionary operation before the enemy launches his attack. The object would be to throw him off his balance and delay him. As you know, every day gained just now is worth a lot to us, particularly in connection with the availability of 1st Armoured Bde. I wonder if you could put in an attack to throw forward the northern part of your line, pivoting, say, on the point of junction of the 3rd and 2nd South African Bdes, and aiming at pinching out the enemy localities near the coast in the area between Kilos 90 and 95.

This would avoid offering an exposed flank to an armoured counter-attack, and might make the enemy nervous about TMIMI and MARTUBA again, both of which are very sensitive parts of his anatomy, I feel! I realise that you would probably not wish to disturb the troops already holding the line, and so possibly weaken their chances of resisting attack, and it is not easy to see where you are to get fresh troops from. All the same, I feel that you might get a lot of help from some such operation if it came off at the right time, and that is why I suggest it for your consideration.

(ii) If I am right in thinking that the enemy main thrust is likely to come in against the 1st South African Bde salient, I feel that he must already be collecting a considerable quantity of heavy and medium artillery in the TEMRAD – BREGHISC area. Would it be possible to raid this area with a fairly strong force by night, and do all the damage you can to anything you find? The troops used would have to go "all out" of course, and be prepared to suffer relatively heavy loss, and to stop at nothing to gain their object.

I feel there is something in this idea. I believe that jolts of this kind might go a long way to lowering the morale of his troops, and especially of the Italians. Remember how he reacted to your Martuba raid. Will you consider the possibility?

JRL, AUC 868

201

Letter from Lieutenant General N. M. Ritchie to Auchinleck, 25 May 1942

Your DO/PSC/11 of 23rd May has just reached me and I am delighted to have got it. I am so pleased to feel that you are happy about the positioning of the armour. I was sure that you would be once you were in possession of the correct facts. Since I last wrote we have moved our Headquarters some 6 or 7 miles further East to a position about a mile North of the main road.

2. The advance party of the 3 Indian Motor Brigade has arrived up and gone forward to report to 30 Corps. I am not quite sure how soon they will be able to take over completely to relieve 7 Motor Brigade on the Southern portion of the front as they are deficient of certain items, the chief amongst which are wireless sets. However, we will get on with this matter as soon as this is possible.

3. 29 Infantry Brigade moved off morning 24th from the CAPUZZO neighbourhood to GUBI for the establishment of the defended locality there. Reconnaissances were carried out previously, and this affair is being carried out as an operation to practise them in the speedy establishment of a Brigade defended locality. I wired to

you last night asking whether you would allow me to use one Bn. of 11 Indian Motor Brigade for a position which I feel necessary in the BEL HAMED/EL DUDA area, which will ensure that no small parties of the enemy who may penetrate can sit on the axis road and deny its use to us. Furthermore, a small locality here will be able to cover No. 4 Forward Base should the enemy succeed in getting any parties through there. Thank you for agreeing.

4.   Thank you for sending up the Headquarters of 32 Army Tank Brigade which will be of inestimable value to us for the co-ordination of the action of "I" tanks behind 1 S.A. Div.

I have just had C.G.S's message about an Operational H.Q. of 4 Ind Div being made available to control the left flank. This is splendid and I have replied accordingly.

5.   We are having to use mines previously earmarked for the defences in the Frontier area to enable us quickly to provide the additional anti-tank mines needed to strengthen up the GAZALA – HACHEIM position, and this is undoubtedly a weakening of the Frontier line. Full details of the situation have already been sent to you, and the summary in round figures is as follows:

Mines – frontier area. [Annotation: What about some more?]

Laid on Frontier	25,000
Stacked on Frontier	135,000
Total on Frontier	160,000
Issued from Frontier's stock	90,000
Original demand for Frontier	250,000.

The pipeline at HAMRA was taken up because it was needed to provide the necessary piping for the pushing on of our pipehead to BIR HACHEIM. The situation regarding water in the Frontier defences is as follows:-

(a)   There is a pipeline from HABATHA to HAMRA which enables water carried by train to HABATHA to be pumped to HAMRA. The storage at HAMRA is satisfactory.

(b)   In the SALUM – HALFAYA area there are 2,000 tons stored. BIRS for another 500 tons have now been prepared and a search for BIRS for another 500 tons is now being made. [Annotation: Does it evaporate much?]

There has not been much work done on the Frontier defences this month as you will have realised. The South African L.O.B. [Labour Battalion?] have been going on steadily and the French have done a bit. We have done some tidying up on the stores and equipment side.

Personally I am satisfied that we can fight in this position now. I do not for one moment suggest that it could not be improved, for this it certainly can be and strengthened too, but I would say that it is fightable as it stands today. But I would like more mines to replace those used forward.

6. While I quite agree that it would be an excellent thing for us to carry out a limited offensive operation with the object of throwing the enemy off his balance before he attacks, I myself do not feel that, as at present situated, and especially having regard to the relative strengths of ourselves and the enemy, I can afford to do so. May I take the two suggestions contained in your letter in turn.

7. <u>PIVOTING FORWARD THE RIGHT FLANK.</u>

In order adequately to threaten TMIMI and MARTUBA, we would have to stay there and this would involve a very considerable lengthening of our present position. It would, in fact, I estimate, increase the length of the line by 5 to 6 miles, and I do not feel that, having regard to the number of guns available, we can well afford to undertake this extra commitment. As you say, the difficulty will be to find fresh troops for this operation, and in my own estimation it would be necessary for us to use tanks for the purpose. Furthermore, I feel that in doing this we would be undertaking an operation that is not on ground of our own choosing and has been prepared by the enemy, and this enemy would be unshaken by any previous operations and, as far as I can see, unweakened there. I am not quite clear about an operation of this sort not offering an exposed flank to an armoured counter attack unless it is your intention that this action should be carried out entirely North of the escarpment except for infantry infiltrating along the top of the escarpment itself? For the above reasons I am not keen on this plan.

8. <u>RAID ON TEMRAD – BREGHISC.</u>

This plan might, I feel, offer a better chance of achieving the object, but at the moment I think it is extremely hard to say that the enemy is, in fact, concentrating heavy and medium artillery in that neighbourhood. So much depends on whether it is his intention to attack in the ALEM HAMZA area as his main effort. The difficulty I would find in laying on this operation now is that of discovering a real objective for the raid. The area is some 8 to 10 miles from the nearest point of our minefield and would, therefore, entail a deep penetration. I do not think that it can be undertaken without VALENTINE tanks and, if this is the case, it means re-positioning these tanks within our defended system and I would definitely prefer that this is not undertaken at the moment. I will, however, go further into this matter today.

9. While I do feel very much that a limited offensive on the lines suggested might well be a tremendous help I feel myself to be tied by the legs somewhat because, as I have said before, I cannot lay my hands on fresh troops for the operation. Furthermore, an operation in the Northern part of the front, if it is really to achieve the object of unbalancing the enemy before his attack, depends so very greatly on whether the enemy does really intend to attack for his main effort in that part of the world. Personally I am doubtful if this will be the case. I only pray it may be. After going over the ground, seeing to our plans, and with the additional minefields there, I feel that no place could suit us better for his attack than here.

10. There is not much to report from the front this last 24 hours. We took a prisoner from ASIDA belonging to H.Q. of the 90 L[igh]t Div. He is lying a lot I believe. But yet there are some indications that something more has been moved down there, though no signs yet of large numbers of tanks. These, I believe are still mostly behind the BREGHISC – SEGNALI gap.

It seems to me that, broadly speaking, the armour is in two groups, but it is so far impossible to say whether these groups are made up of:

   (a)   (i)   Italians in the South,
         (ii) Germans in the North.
or (b)   (i)   Italians and about 100 (one Bn.) Germans in the South,
         (ii) Rest of the Germans in the North.

I believe it is either one or other of these combinations, probably (b) I should deduce from photographs.

JRL, AUC 872

Letter from Auchinleck to
Lieutenant General N. M. Ritchie, 26 May 1942

Many thanks for your letter of the 23rd, which reached me yesterday.

I am most grateful to you for the information about your defences and dispositions in what you call the "Arena". It is a great help to have these accurately shown on my map in the War Room, as I can then follow your plans, and also the battle should it ever take place in this area.

2.   I quite see your point about the 2nd Armoured Brigade being able to go on with its training as long as possible in the SOUTHERN area, and I am sure you are right. When it moves is entirely a matter for you to decide. I am glad to hear they are getting on well, and I hope they will get a chance before long of getting their own back on the Bosche. I am certain they will take it.

3.   I am glad we have been able to give you Tuker and an operational headquarters from 4th Divisional H.Q. I take it he will be under 30th Corps H.Q. He is staying the night with me.

4.   I have never discarded the possibility of the enemy making his main thrust round the SOUTHERN flank, and it would be most dangerous to make up one's mind that he must attack in one place only. Nevertheless, my opinion, for what it is worth, is that the great majority of the indications point to a very heavy attack on a narrow front on the NORTHERN sector of your front, probably against the front of the 1st South African Bde. If this attack does materialise, it will, I feel certain, be supported by the largest possible concentration of artillery and dive bombers, and the effect of this bombardment may be such as to crush the defence, temporarily at any rate.

This was Rommel's plan for attacking TOBRUK, as you may remember. A narrow thrust, and then a fanning out along a natural obstacle to form a defensive flank, while the spearhead continued to go on. I hope that in the break through he may lose heavily in tanks and men, and thus offer a weakened force for your armoured divisions to hit and destroy. It is possible, however, that the weight of the supporting fire may be so great as to prevent the defending infantry and artillery from taking any serious toll of his tanks.

Have you considered the desirability of altering the infantry and artillery dispositions in this sector I wonder? I expect they have the usual alternative positions, but I was thinking of a more drastic alteration than that, even amounting to an increase of depth in the position by withdrawing troops from the forward areas, and so reducing the effect of his initial bombardment. I feel this merits close examination, which of course I am not competent to give it at this distance.

5. Once again, at the risk of being tiresome, I would like to stress the absolute necessity for preventing him establishing defensive flanks if he does try to attack in the way I have suggested. Don't think I am becoming a mono-maniac on this subject! I do feel, however, that if he does try this method, he will put all his resources into it, as it depends for success on speed, which can only be made possible by brute force. Do not forget that he does not know that we know as much as we do, nor can he yet have found out how much the measures taken recently by you have strengthened your position generally. He may yet deliver himself into your hands by attacking where we are stronger than he thinks. I hope he does!

6. If he comes by the SOUTH, time should be on your side, and you ought to get ample warning from your motorised troops, armoured cars and the air. An offensive on this flank will very soon expose his supply lines to your attack, and should give you the chance of having at his weak infantry, once he has committed his armour beyond BIR HACHEIM. Do you agree with this?

7. We are agreed, I know, that the most difficult thing to decide will be when to change from the defensive to the offensive. I feel the time will surely come when this decision has to be made, and when it is made everyone must spring forward to the attack, and seek out the enemy wherever he is, and give him no peace till he is destroyed. I know you have impressed this on all commanders, but it can not be said too often, so please keep saying it! We are apt to be slow in the uptake, and may lose precious chances thereby, unless everyone is imbued with the idea of swift and daring action when you give the word.

8. One other matter, which I expect you have already planned and arranged.

If the enemy does break through on a narrow front, I am sure he will do his best to neutralise our armoured forces by attacking them heavily from the air with low-flying aircraft armed with anti-tank guns, which we know he has. As the issue of the whole battle is likely to rest on your ability or failure to bring his "Blitz" to a standstill on ground of your choosing, and then to destroy his tanks before they can get back to the protection of his guns and infantry, I feel it is essential that our air should be used to the limit to keep our own tanks in being, and to prevent them being neutralised or destroyed by the enemy's air. I am convinced that this must be their primary task in the circumstances I have envisaged. How they do it is not for me to attempt to say, but it seems pretty obvious that heavy direct support will be needed over the battlefield itself, whatever more distant help may be given by attacking enemy aerodromes. How do you feel about this?

9. I have just got your letter of the 25th, signed by Jock Whiteley.

I am glad you are happy. So am I generally, though I feel I may not have made myself clear about the possibilities of a heavy raid on the enemy forward areas with the object of destroying guns and tanks if found.

I was thinking of a fast-moving bold affair at night, certainly not using tanks. I had no idea of using tanks, and I agree that this would be a mistake at present. I know you may feel it difficult to find troops, but you have now got quite a lot of them, certainly many more infantry than the enemy has, as his divisions are still pretty weak, if our information is correct, and I have no reason to suppose it is not.

I would like you to consider this proposition again and have it examined if you can. I feel myself that anything you can do to upset the enemy at this juncture may be tremendously valuable. I feel, too, that plans for offensives all along the front must be made ready to put into effect immediately opportunity offers. I gather you have done this?

10. In your para 10 you say that the bulk of his tanks appear to be behind the BREGHISC – SEGNALI gap. Our latest information goes to show, I think, that his big German tank concentration is behind TEMRAD and to the NORTH. We can't both be right! I have asked D.M.I. to check up on this. We agree that the Ariete Division and some German infantry are in the SOUTH.

11. I hope to get this off by TUKER in the morning.

JRL, AUC 877

203

Letter from Auchinleck to Lieutenant General N. M. Ritchie, 28 May 1942, with annotations by Auchinleck

We have been thinking hard over the possibility of your changing over to the offensive immediately you have cracked the enemy armour, which you now seem to have got where you always wanted it. Well done you!

I enclose the result of our thinking, for what it may be worth.

I have specified certain formations for certain tasks, but only in order to prove to myself that the troops needed would be available, and not with the slightest intention of laying down the law about them.

I feel we must be ready to move at once, whichever way the cat jumps. Have just sent you a long telegram so will say no more.

Good luck,

LIBYA 1942.

III. COUNTER-OFFENSIVE

SITUATION

1.   ENEMY RESOURCES.

As a result ACROMA battle, enemy original armoured attacking force practically wiped out.

Enemy left with, say:-

> 100 ITALIAN tanks – in arena, & some escaped
> 50 – 60 GERMAN tanks – TEMRAD area
> Four ITALIAN divisions of about 4 – 5000 men (strength 27 May) and 20 f[iel]d guns and 15 A.T. guns each.
> Part of 90 GERMAN Light Division, say 3 Bns and 12 f[iel]d guns.

2.   OUR RESOURCES.

1 ARMD BDE GP complete	-	150 tanks
Residue 1 and 7 ARMD DIVS	-	100 tanks
Residue 1 ARMY TK BDE	-	50 tanks
32 ARMY TANK BDE	-	75 tanks
TOTAL:	250 medium and 125 heavy tanks.	

375 BRITISH tanks against 250 GERMAN and ITALIAN tanks

Three Infantry Divisions of about 52,000 men and 216 fd guns holding our positions GAZALA – TOBRUK – BIR HACHEIM.

5 and 10 IND DIVS mobile and available for offensive, plus possibly greater part 3 IND MOTOR BDE GP as well as two Motor Brigade Groups of 1 and 7 Armd Divs.

If necessary, two infantry Brigade Groups (not fully mobile) of 4 IND DIV can also be made available to hold defensive positions and so release mobile infantry for the offensive.

3. <u>OBJECT</u>

Object is to destroy the enemy army as soon as possible, so as to prevent it slipping to the WEST.

4. <u>METHOD</u>

Enemy's SOUTH flank is always in this theatre, his vital point. Therefore, assuming that we can now count on reasonable superiority in tanks and great superiority in infantry, we should go straight for it. Our immediate objective should be, therefore, SEGNALI.

To pin the enemy further to the NORTH, we should put in a secondary attack, preferably with 50 DIV. and heavy tanks against TEMRAD, while 1 S.A. DIV demonstrates against enemy extreme LEFT but does NOT push home attack as we <u>want</u> enemy to stay in this area.

Further to encircle the enemy, all available light mobile forces should strike hard at MECHILI and even BENGHASI, while LRDG and "COMMANDOS" must harass enemy L of C everywhere possible.

The main air target should be enemy communications forward of, and including BENGHASI, and his aerodromes in the same area.

5. <u>ALLOTMENT OF TROOPS</u>

(i) <u>MAIN ATTACK ON SEGNALI</u>

All medium tanks and half heavy tanks.
Armd Car Regts and Motor Bde Gps of 1 and 7 ARMD DIVS.
5 IND DIV.
10 IND DIV.
Two Regts Medium Artillery.

(ii)   SECONDARY ATTACK ON TEMRAD

50 DIV
Half heavy tanks
One Regt Medium Artillery

(iii)   MOVEMENT ON MECHILI AND BENGHASI

3 IND MOTOR BDE GP [Annotation: ? Report of stragglers?
How effective will 3 Ind Motor Bde be?]
Three or four Armd Car Regts.

(iv)   GAZALA POSITION

1 S.A. DIV
2 S.A. DIV
1 FREE FRENCH BDE GP

(v)   TOBRUK AND EL ADEM etc

5 and 11 IND Inf Bde Gps. [Annotation: How effective will
3 Ind Motor Bde be?]

SITUATION B.

1.   Two possibilities:-

Enemy Armoured Force in ACROMA area after severe losses
attempt to escape:-

(i)   SOUTH Both alternatives with help of attack directed EAST
from TEMRAD.

(ii)   WEST

2.   If enemy Armoured Forces attempt to escape SOUTH:

OUR ACTION:

(a)   Our Armoured divisions pursue and all available mobile
columns from 50 DIV, 1 FREE FRENCH BDE GP and 3
IND MOTOR BDE shepherd enemy SOUTH and harass
his flanks and rear.

(b)   Attack by 50 DIV to secure SIDI BREGHISC area 5 IND
DIV to take over 50 DIV front and be prepared to pass
through 50 DIV after they have captured and consolidated
BREGHISC, 10 IND DIV to TOBRUK – EL ADEM.

3. If enemy Armoured Forces attempt to escape WEST:

OUR ACTION:

(a) Enemy passage of our defences opposed and harassed by heavy tanks and garrisons of our defences.

(b) Our Armoured Divisions and all mobile troops together with 5 INDIAN DIVISION move via HACHEIM on SEGNALI with eventual objective enemy's rear, area EZZRIAT – TMIMI.

(c) 50 DIVISION holding attack directed on BREGHISC

(d) 10 INDIAN DIVISION to relieve 50 DIVISION.

4. Other action against MECHILI and BENGHASI as in SITUATION A.

JRL, AUC 881

204

Letter from Auchinleck to Lieutenant General N. M. Ritchie, 3 June 1942

1. You will have had my signal in answer to your U.1205 of today.

2. I am glad you think the situation is still favourable to us and that it is improving daily. All the same I view the destruction of 150th Brigade and the consolidation by the enemy of a broad and deep wedge in the middle of your position with some misgiving. I am sure, however, there are factors known to you which I do not know.

3. I feel myself,

(a) that if the enemy is allowed to consolidate himself in his present positions in the area SIDRA – HARMAT – MTEIFEL, our GAZALA position including BIR HACHEIM will become untenable eventually even if he does not renew his offensive.

(b) that situated as he is, he is rapidly becoming able to regain the initiative which you have wrested from him in the last week's fighting. This can not be allowed to happen.

4. I agree with you entirely that you can not let your armour be destroyed in detail and that you can not risk it against his now

strongly defended front NORTH and SOUTH of EL HARMAT. Therefore he must be shifted by other means and quickly before he can begin to act against the exposed SOUTHERN flank of 50th Division or against BIR HACHEIM, or in an attempt to cut your supply line EAST of EL ADEM, all of which seem possible courses for him to adopt.

5. I feel that the quickest and easiest way to shift him is by an offensive directed towards TEMRAD so as to threaten his bases, coupled with threats from SEGNALI and the SOUTH against his lines of supply.

His tanks can not be in two places at once and you still have some infantry tanks with which to support your infantry and protect your artillery of which you should have a good deal now. It is I think, highly important that you should keep at least one infantry division concentrated and complete in mobile reserve, so that you have at your disposal a really strong weapon with which to strike. I am a little perturbed by the apparent dispersion of 5th Indian Division, but I daresay it is more apparent than real.

6. I repeat that in my opinion you must strike hard and at once if we are to avoid a stalemate, that is unless the enemy is foolish enough to fling himself against your armour. I wish he would but I don't think you can count on this at present. [Annotation: de Guingand knows what is in my mind.]

JRL, AUC 896

205

Letter from Lieutenant General N. M. Ritchie to Auchinleck, 3 June 1942

Your special message reached me in the middle of last night. Thank you so much for it. I agree almost entirely with all its contents, but there are one or two points I would like to make.

The two alternatives appear to me to be:

(a) to resume the offensive as early as possible directed on the line TMIMI – AFRAG;
(b) to deal first with the "cauldron".

Of these two alternatives it had been my intention to resume the offensive and leave the armour to mask the "cauldron" and I left this H.Q. at 5.a.m. this morning for a conference with the Corps Commanders to get this fixed up. For various reason, with which I am dealing, replacements in armour are not coming through as quickly as they should. This is due to the crews not being collected together quickly enough; that is most serious. It will be righted today, [Annotation: Yes! I hope so.] but the net result is that I now feel that our armour may not be able to contain the enemy while the offensive is in progress and the enemy's armour may therefore be a real danger to me being able to continue supplies forward and against the rear of the GAZALA – ALEM HAMZA position.

2. I was, as you are, most keen to carry out the offensive with the right shoulder forward, but the enemy in his present position makes it extremely difficult to form up a Division behind our present frontage between the GAZALA and ALEM HAMZA without fear of its preparations being interrupted. For this reason I had to discard that plan.

3. My next idea was to make a very wide turning movement with the 5 Ind Div South of HACHEIM directed on AFRAG, but after the information I have had from the Corps Commanders today respecting the strength of our armour I cannot risk this.

4. It is absolutely essential that we should wrest from the enemy the initiative which he is now starting to exercise and this must be done at the soonest possible moment. In the circumstances I have decided that I must crush him in the "cauldron" and the plan for doing this will be a pincer movement, one arm coming from the North with 69 Inf Bde supported by "I" tanks, the other from the East to be carried out by 5 Ind Div supported by 4 RTR and 22 Armd Bde for exploitation. This latter will, of course, be the main thrust, the one from the North I would not bring further South than SIDRA 3641. Much of the preparatory reconnaissance and work for the main thrust has already been covered by the operations of 10 Inf Bde and I am re-assured in my belief of the feasibility of this operation being carried out by night by the fact that Frank MESSERVY is of opinion that it is quite feasible. I hope by this means to drive a wedge through the enemy's anti-tank defences under cover of darkness and seize the ground in the vicinity of GOT EL SCERAB, and this will enable me to exploit the armour

through this corridor into the rear of the enemy and close the gaps behind him. Once it is completed we will return to the offensive generally on the lines of the right shoulder forward.

5. I am going at once into the question of a raiding force to threaten the MARTUBA and DERNA landing grounds, and I am sorry that I had not understood your intention in regard to this matter.

6. The operation I have decided to undertake is the one which can be put into action quickest and will therefore wrest the initiative from the enemy in the shortest possible time.

7. Freddie de GUINGAND takes this letter and can give you more details of my plan.

JRL, AUC 897

206

Letter from Auchinleck to Lieutenant General N. M. Ritchie, 3 June 1942

You asked me yesterday about the date of the convoy which you said you urgently required to know. I hope De Guingand has given you the information today. I must admit that I feel that this date will not now have nearly as much influence on any offensive movement you have in mind as must the tactical situation which will result from the present fighting.

2. You would not, I imagine, think of holding back your offensive solely to synchronise with the sailing of the convoy. I feel that your offensive must be made immediately the tactical situation on your front permits. The primary effect of a successful offensive will be to deny the landing grounds in the area MARTUBA – DERNA to the enemy. The second and even more important result would be to allow us the use of these landing grounds for our own aircraft, thus greatly increasing the cover for the convoy.

The sooner we can produce these effects the better, and the longer we have to consolidate ground gained before the convoy sails, the easier it will be to produce the second result, which is supremely desirable.

3. Of course if things should go really well, and we can get on even still further, so much the better, as the power of the enemy air to interfere with the convoy decreases as he is driven further back. This again is another reason for getting forward as soon as it is humanly possible to do so. But I know you realise all this just as well as I do, and I have no doubts at all that if you can get on, you will.

4. You will, I am sure, have made all arrangements for suitable forces to defend the landing grounds, should we get them, from enemy counter-attacks, which must be expected. It will mean getting a good lot of anti-aircraft artillery forward pretty quickly I imagine.

5. I saw Stirling this morning, and I think he has a good show laid on.[195]

6. The news this morning did not surprise me. I expected the enemy to renew his efforts to carry out his original plan as soon as he felt he had a secure base inside our position. He should, however, be nothing like as strong as he was before. In particular, your relative superiority in tanks should be much greater, and I feel you may have a good chance of cracking him now. I hope you will keep him out of BIR HACHEIM, as if that goes I feel our mobility will be greatly restricted, and his ability to worry our flanks and rear correspondingly increased.

7. I feel a little anxious lest he should now turn against 50 Div from the SOUTH, using his anti-tank guns to form a protective flank to the EAST and so keep off our tanks. I expect you are ready for this.

8. It may be that he intends to try his double attack against our NORTHERN front once more, that is tanks from the East and tanks, artillery and infantry (90 Lt Div) from the WEST. I know you are ready for this too.

9. I am puzzled whether the attack on HACHEIM was a feint to draw off attention from a real attack in the NORTH, or whether the reverse is the case. He has sent apparently an equal number of tanks in each direction – towards TAMAR and also BIR HACHEIM.

---

195 Presumably the SAS jeep raids on Italian airfields in the vicinity of Fuka on 7 July, led by Major David Stirling.

It looks as if the HACHEIM attack was meant to succeed. I hope it hasn't!

No more now. Good luck to you and your men. I think of nothing else.

JRL, AUC 898

207

Directive defining the duties of the Minister of State, Middle East, 4 June 1942

The directive of the Minister of State approved by the Prime Minister now stands as follows:-

1. The Minister of State in the Middle East will represent the War Cabinet in that area and will act in its name.

2. The principal task of the Minister of State will be to ensure a successful conduct of the operations in the Middle East by:-

    (a) relieving the Commanders-in-Chief as far as possible of extraneous responsibilities;
    (b) giving the Commanders in-Chief political guidance;
    (c) settling promptly matters within the policy of His Majesty's Government, more particularly where several local authorities or Departments are concerned;
    (d) Keeping the War Cabinet and Ministers generally informed of what is happening in his sphere.

3. Examples of (a) above are:-

    (i) Relations with the Free French.
    (ii) The administration of occupied enemy territory (subject to paragraph 4 below).
    (iii) Propaganda, and subversive and economic warfare.
    (iv) Financial questions of an emergency character.
    (v) Civil supply questions, including the Middle East Supply Centre.

4. As regards the administration of occupied territory, the Commander-in-Chief, Middle East, and the General Officer Commanding-in-Chief, East Africa, have delegated their powers to the Chief Political

Officers at Cairo and Nairobi respective. These two Officers will keep the Minister of State generally informed. With the concurrence of their respective Commander-in-Chief, they have discretion to refer matters to him and take his instructions when reference to London is unnecessary or would entail unacceptable delay. The Minister of State for his part will be entitled to give directions to the Chief Political Officers, with the agreement of the Commanders-in-Chief, on matters which seem to him to require such directions.

5. The Minister of State will be fully informed of the approved policy of His Majesty's Government on all major issues. If any question should arise on which he requires special guidance, he will, provided that there is time, refer the matter home. He will, in any case, report constantly to His Majesty's Government and will receive from time to time their directions. His normal channel of communications will be through the medium of His Majesty's Embassy in Cairo and the Foreign Office, but he may also make use of any other available and convenient channel. He will also address personal telegrams directly to the Prime Minister and Minister of Defence whenever convenient. On Departmental matters he will communicate with Departments direct. In general, except where an immediate decision is required, he will consult the Minister concerned on any proposed action before it is taken if it is not clearly in accordance with approved policy. When on grounds of urgency the Minister acts on any important matter without prior consultation with London, he will report the circumstances as soon as possible to the appropriate department.

6. The Minister of State will preside over meetings of the Middle East War Council and Defence Committee.

7. On the diplomatic and political side, the Minister of State will co-ordinate so far as is necessary the activities and recommendations of His Majesty's representatives:-

(i) acting in Egypt, the Sudan, Palestine and Trans-Jordan, Iraq, Saudi Arabia (subject to certain reservations), Aden the Aden Protectorate, Persia, Abyssinia, British Somaliland, occupied territories (Eritrea and Italian Somaliland), Syria, the Lebanon, Cyprus and Malta, and

(ii) concerned with the Yemen and French Somaliland.

This instruction in no way detracts from the existing individual respon-sibilities of His Majesty's representatives in the above territories of their official relationships with their respective departments at home.

JRL, AUC 899

208

Cipher message from Winston Churchill to Auchinleck, 9 June 1942

ONE.   I have been continually thinking about your great battle and how we can best sustain your Army, so that it may be fought out to a victorious end. Here is some good news.

TWO.   The 8th Armoured Division is now at the CAPE and the 44th Division is nearing FREETOWN. We have deliberately kept an option on the ultimate destination of these Divisions until we could see our way more clearly.

THREE.   Some time ago I promised the Australian Government that if AUSTRALIA were seriously invaded we should immediately divert both these Divisions to their assistance. AUSTRALIA up to date has not repeat not been seriously invaded, and in view of Naval losses which JAPANESE have sustained in the battles of the CORAL Sea and off MIDWAY Island, we regard a serious invasion in the near future as extremely improbable.

FOUR.   We are also prepared, though we have never promised WAVELL to send both these Divisions to INDIA if it looked as though the JAPANESE had an invasion of INDIA in mind. This also seems extremely improbable at the moment and INDIA have already got the 2nd, 5th and 90th BRITISH Divisions.

FIVE.   We have therefore decided with the full agreement of the Chiefs of Staff, that the 8th Armoured Division and the 44th Division should be sent to you unless AUSTRALIA is threatened with serious invasion within the next few days. You may therefore make your plans for the battle on the assumption that the 8th Armoured Division will reach SUEZ at the end of June and the 44th Division by mid-July.

SIX. Thereafter, depending on the general situation then prevailing, you should be prepared to send to INDIA one of your INDIAN Divisions and the 252nd INDIAN Armoured Brigade. Pray let us have your proposals so that we may tell General WAVELL.

SEVEN. A detailed account of the exact state of the 8th Armoured Division and of the technical preparedness of its tanks, together with the exact loading on the various ships and their dates of arrival, is being sent you separately. You can thus make the best possible plans for disembarking, organizing and bringing it into action in the most effective manner with the least delay. We feel that with this rapidly approaching reserve behind you, you will be able to act with greater freedom in using your existing resources. All good wishes. Message ends.

JRL, AUC 910

209

Cipher message from Auchinleck to Winston Churchill, 10 June 1942

1 (.) Thank you for your telegram OZ/240 (24) of 9/6 (9/6) for which I am most grateful (.) I feel much encouraged by your good wishes and hope I will be able to show you some results for all the hard and bitter fighting of the past two weeks (.)

2 (.) The prospect of our getting the 8 Armoured and 44th Divisions in this theatre is most welcome and encouraging (.) I realise that the decision may be changed but am proceeding at once with plans to make best use of these formations (.) The commander 8th Armoured Division is now in CAIRO (.)

3 (.) I note that I may be required to send an Indian armoured brigade and an Indian infantry division to INDIA later (.) As you know we have nothing like enough troops to defend PERSIA or to meet a German attack through ANATOLIA (.) I realise these threats may NOT materialise but nevertheless I must plan to meet them (.) I realise that the threat to INDIA may materialise quicker and in more serious form than a threat to my NORTHERN and NORTH EASTERN fronts (,) and that the allotment of troops to meet these eventualities can be made by you alone as the largest strategical

issues will be involved (.) I mention the matter of our commitments in PERSIA IRAQ and SYRIA only to remind you that the chances of a successful defence in these theatres with our existing resources are small (,) unless we receive <u>substantial</u> reinforcements before the enemy have penetrated too deeply (.)

4 (.) The knowledge that these two fresh and powerful divisions are on the way will as you say greatly increase my freedom of action in respect of the forces I already have (.) As you probably know I have already brought considerable forces from IRAQ to LIBYA to str[e]ngthen 8th Army (.)

5 (.) We are most grateful to you [.]

<u>CLEAR THE LINE</u>

JRL, AUC 912

210

Letter from Brigadier Jock Whiteley, BGS Eighth Army to Auchinleck, enclosing some notes dictated by Lieutenant General N. M. Ritchie, entitled 'Appreciation of Situation by Comd. Eighth Army, 0900 hrs, 11 June 1942', with annotations by Auchinleck noted in italics.

Your signal of 11/6 arrived just before breakfast this morning. General Neil had arranged to go forward to see the Corps Comds, leaving here at 9 o'clock. He dictated some notes to me before he went and in the short time available I have tried to put them in the best form that I can. I thought it would be better to give you the material in a somewhat disjointed form by today's L[iaison]. O[fficer]. rather than to delay an answer.

General Neil thinks that you are not in touch quite with our picture and suggests that you send up a Senior Staff officer tomorrow if you can manage to do so.

I have not even had time to check it.

ENEMY AND OWN TROOPS.

ARMOUR.

1. I consider that our armour and the enemy armour is very evenly balanced. It is probable that our armour reinforcements are likely to be slightly in excess of those of the enemy. *Your U 1339 10/6 ours 330 tanks. 270 with ? 10/6. Enemy 200250?? Enemy G = 220? I = 60? = 280*

INFANTRY.

2. I estimate that the enemy has the equivalent of 10 ½ Bde Gps. He has suffered some casualties but he has not been forced to withdraw any formations.

3. We have the equivalent of ten Bde Gps made up as follows:-

50 Div	2	
5 Ind Div	1	*– 9 & 10 Bdes?*
10 Ind Div	1	*– 3 Bdes*
1 S.A. Div	2	
2 S.A. Div	3	
11 Ind Bde Gp	1	
Total	10.	

    If the Free French Bde Gp succeeds in withdrawing without heavy casualties it should be possible to put them into the line again in the course of a few days.

4. We have the following Bde Gps re-forming:

    3 Motor Bde Gp on a reduced scale.
    21 Bde Gp.   *– 25 Bde Gp ? ? ?*
    9 Bde Gp.   *– where is the other?*

    Moreover 5 Ind Inf Bde Gp will be arriving shortly.

5. Numerically, therefore, our relative strengths in infantry are evenly balanced. The morale of our infantry is infinitely superior, but the lack of training of some formations prevents us from taking advantage of this moral superiority. *1 SA Div, 2 SA Div, which?*

ARTILLERY.

6. The enemy is definitely stronger than we are in A.Tk guns. He has perhaps been able to recoup some of his losses by captures from us. On the other hand we have more ROBERTS guns deployed today than at any previous period of the operation because in the initial stages we had the greatest difficulty in issuing ROBERTS guns to troops engaged in operations.

   Deduction: Our forces are very evenly balanced with those of the enemy and we must place our reliance more upon moral factors than on material.

   Tanks??

AIR.

7. At the moment we are not seriously troubled by enemy air action and we have received the greatest help from our own Air Force. Provided we can continue to operate our Air Force from the GAMBUT group of landing grounds we expect to continue to enjoy this superiority.

MAINTENANCE.

8. Our maintenance arrangements are elastic. We have

   (a) approximately seven days dumped at every locality;
   (b) considerable holdings of all types (with minor exceptions) at TOBRUK, No. 4 Forward Base and CAPUZZO. The over-running of one of these bases would not cripple our position.
   (c) We can maintain our force from TOBRUK or from No. 4 Forward Base or via a Southerly desert route direct from CAPUZZO.

   We have therefore considerable advantage in dispersed reserves and in dispersed lines of supply.

PROBABLE ENEMY ACTION.

9. I consider that the enemy is aiming at strengthening his position in the Cauldron with a view to passing to the offensive as soon as possible. In the meantime he hopes that we will attack him in what is a strong position. If we do not do this I consider that he will either:

   (a) strike North with a view to isolating the two Divisions of 13 Corps on the GAZALA posn, or

454

(b)   strike East against our communications.

(c)   go away   (d)   stay put

There are local indications that his intention is to strike East and, in my opinion, this is the most probable course. *What are they?*

10.   As a preliminary to striking East the enemy may occupy GUBI as a pivot of manoeuvre. This will be an isolated position for him and we must take full advantage of it. *Yes how?* In the meanwhile we must lift the minefield.

11.   The enemy's L. of C. is precarious. Since we have started harassing them East of the minefield he has been forced to conform to the extent of air action and withdrawing troops and anti-tank guns. *Confirmed? To what extent?*

COURSES OPEN TO US.

12.   My aim is to destroy the enemy armoured forces. The more we can succeed in doing this the easier will our subsequent task be. The two main courses open to me are:-

(a)   To attack him in the Cauldron.

(b)   To attack his weakest spot along the L. of C.

The essential condition which I must fulfil is to leave a force around the Cauldron area sufficient to give me security. My infantry resources do not enable me to occupy any more positions. I must therefore pin my main reliance upon armour to stem any enemy advance from the Cauldron. *Or artillery & anti-tank pos[itio]ns? Enemy does not stop us with his armour.*

13   (a)   I have examined the possibilities of attacking the Cauldron from the South. Our old minefield would delay this attack and surprise would be difficult to achieve. I reject this.

(b)   I have considered repeating the attack from the North and from the East to gain the observation over the Cauldron. This has failed once and I do not consider that I have the resources to attempt it again. I have therefore rejected this.

(c)   An attack on the Cauldron from the West through the enemy gaps would be hazardous because we would have to make a final approach through the defiles in the minefields which the enemy must be assumed to hold. There would be no surprise and therefore I reject this.

14. <u>Harass the vulnerable enemy L. of C. with all the resources that I can spare from the "Arena" area.</u>

   This is a very vulnerable point to the enemy; although the fall of HACHEIM will release considerable forces I consider that these will not be enough to afford protection to his L. of C. from the North and from the South between the minefield and CHERIMA and ROTONDA AFRAG. If necessary I am prepared to go wide to the West to get my target. *What is the target?*

   If, in the meanwhile, the enemy attacks me I should hope to inflict greater loss upon him than he will on me. In this way we may be able to pave the way to destroy his armour but I am <u>not</u> relying on this.

<u>PLAN.</u>

15. My plan is therefore to attack his L. of C. which I regard as his main vulnerable point:

   (a)   From the North on 50 Div front. Valentine tanks will be used to support these attacks.
   (b)   From the South with a Motor Bde Gp and with such armour as I can spare from the "Arena" area without endangering security.

   At the moment I estimate this to be approx. 30 Stuart type tanks. I am keeping the closest watch on the tank situation because on this depends whether I can increase or decrease this detached tank force. In this way I hope to force the enemy to conform either by attacking me or by withdrawing troops from the Cauldron area to protect his L. of C. *A Piddle? Knightsbridge? What decision does this lead to?*

16. To take advantage of the situation which may result from this action I must be able to pass an armd div quickly from the "Arena" area to the West of the minefield. I intend to do this through the gap on 50 Div front. I am straining every nerve to ensure that this will be possible when I require it.

17. In the meantime I am taking all possible precautions to safeguard the GAMBUT aerodrome area and my L. of C.

JRL, AUC 916

211

Letter from Auchinleck to General Sir Alan Brooke, CIGS, 13 June 1942

My dear C.I.G.S.

Thank you very much for your long letter of the 16th May which reached me on the 3rd June.

2. Charles Gairdner[196] has arrived and is hard at work preparing his course, he hopes to get it going in early July. It is not so easy to find students but I think I have got together a good lot. I had hoped to include Hayden[197] of the 150th Infantry Brigade but I hear he is a prisoner unfortunately.

Please do not bother about the location of the course. It will do very well in Palestine, I am sure, unless it has to remove itself to avoid the enemy! I hope this won't happen! I am sure you are right about the aircraft and I gather the Union have cut down their services. The location of the course is very suitable I think and Gairdner is pleased with it. I hope D.M.T. or his deputy will be able to pay us a visit and have a look at it, and also at our Training Centre, in which all tactical and weapon training schools are now concentrated.

3. I am still trying to get the right solution for the organisation of command on our northern and north-eastern fronts. As you know I am planning to keep the Germans out of the good air base area around Teheran and to do this, I hope to be able to move into Persia at least four divisions and one or two armoured divisions from the rest of the command. This will entail switching 10th Army into Persia and relieving it of responsibility for Iraq. The two together would be too much for one commander I feel.

4. This would fit in all right with my original idea of making 9th Army take over Northern Iraq as well as Syria with a Corps H.Q. in each. I can only find the troops for Persia by stripping Iraq and

---

196 Major General Charles Gairdner who was sent to establish a Staff College in Palestine, having commanded the 6th Armoured Division in the UK. In August 1942 he was to take command of 8th Armoured Division in the Middle East.
197 Brigadier C. W. Haydon.

Syria, and this can be done only if there is no threat to Anatolia. On present calculations the decision to move troops into Persia from Syria (one New Zealand and one Australian division) and Northern Iraq (one Indian division) must be taken about the 15th July. You will realise that it will be a very difficult decision to take, and that it must, in any event, be a tremendous gamble. By that time, possibly, the policy of reinforcing this command may be more defined, and I might perhaps expect to get troops to fill some of the large gaps in Syria and Iraq, but I do not feel I can count on this until the situation in India becomes more settled. In any event with such small resources and such large commitments, I feel that the whole business is a terrible gamble and I believe you are of the same opinion.

5. Well there it is, and I am making all preparation to meet the worst case, which is pressure in Libya, a threat to Syria and Iraq through Anatolia and a drive from the Caucasus towards the Persian Gulf. As I have said before as plainly as I can, we can not expect to do more than delay a really determined advance by the enemy with our present resources in these circumstances. You I am sure realise this and I hope the Defence Minister does too.

6. If the Germans delay the launching of their new offensive much longer, they may not arrive on the northern frontier of Persia until mid-autumn, in which event the climate may prevent a further large scale exploitation.

   I do not think it would be wise to rely on this, as we are too apt to rely on the weather and the terrain to stop our enemy for us.

7. If there is a threat to Anatolia and we can not send troops from Syria and Iraq to fight the enemy in northern Persia, then I feel it is only a question of time before he can reach the head of the Gulf and the oil supplies.

   He will naturally begin bombing them as soon as he is established in Teheran.

8. We can not organise the defence of northern Persia unless we have full facilities now for reconnaissance and preparation in the Russian sphere as well as our own, and that is why I have been so insistent on obtaining the Russian consent to this. There is no way out of it. We must have these facilities, otherwise we can not hope to be ready. Time is short enough as it is.

9. This brings me back to the organisation of command. With 9th Army responsible for Syria and northern Iraq and 10th Army for Persia, we must I think have a base and line of communications commander whose responsibilities will include the Iraq and Persian bases and the two lines of communication up to and including Baghdad in the west and up the Persia railway in the east, possibly as far as Teheran itself. This commander should I feel combine in himself as well the functions of a Deputy Adjutant and Quarter-Master General responsible directly to the L.G.A and G.H.Q. and through him, of course, to me.

I think we must do this as the responsibility for maintenance in this huge area can not be placed upon the shoulders of an army commander, whose chief business should be to fight the enemy. There will, in effect, be a detached echelon of G.H.Q. at Baghdad or Basra, thus ensuring the maximum of decentralisation so far as local detailed administration is concerned, and also the essential minimum of co-ordination by G.H.Q. This eastern base, as opposed to the western base in Egypt and Palestine, will serve the right wing of the 9th Army and the whole of the 10th Army. General control over big movements must continue to be exercised by the Director of Movements at G.H.Q. over the whole command. This responsibility can not be divided in my opinion.

I enclose a note giving my proposals. Riddell-Webster does not like it but I do not think his objections can be sustained and I do not agree with his proposed solution. So for the only time, I think, since we have worked here together, I am going to overrule him!

10. If the project of defending northern Persia fails to materialise we shall have to think again but I still feel that northern Iraq will have to come under the 9th Army in order to ensure proper co-operation on this front, especially with the Air Force.

11. Quinan is all right but he is, I think, a better administrator and organiser than strategist. However, I have no serious complaint to make, though I do feel that for the command in Persia we might do better. He has lots of energy and drive and is getting on well with the planning and preparation. We hope to have a war game on the north-eastern front problem next week, and I will see how he comes out of that.

12. You will have seen that the Australian Government on their own have made Morshead a Lieutenant-General and that the New Zealand Government are following suit with Freyberg!

So that settles that little problem!

13. I am glad to hear that you think Japan does not intend to invade India or Australia. I was much perturbed by the original appreciation sent us by the Chiefs of Staff, which seemed to envisage an immediate attack on Ceylon coupled with an invasion of India. I hope you are right, and it certainly seems as if you are, for Japan seems to be turning on China. I wish we could help the latter. With China out of the war I feel Japan will be in a very strong position, which it may take us years to upset.

14. I am not personally so anxious about fifth column activities in India. Although there is a lot of political froth on the surface, I believe the great majority of the solid mass of the people are behind us. So far there has been no sign of any dangerous tendencies in the Indian Army in this theatre at any rate. They are fighting magnificently and are an example to all.

15. As to the Libyan front, I knew you would not like our arguments based on mathematical calculation of tank strengths. As I told you we have been into the whole problem most exhaustively, and have prepared very full appreciations which when all was said and done led us to exactly the same conclusions as the mathematical calculations! Moreover I know from past experience that the mathematical argument is the only one which gives a safe basis for discussion with the Defence Minister. In fact this mathematical calculation holds the field at this very moment. Ritchie is counting his tanks until he has enough to hold the enemy in front while he strikes him in the rear with the rest. I am afraid you can not get away from it in the Desert, where movement is practically free everywhere. It sounds terrible, I know, but its true all the same. I think Sandy Galloway will bear me out. You mention that some of my arguments made it difficult for you to support my case. I am sorry that this was so and I'd very much like to know what these were. I used the same arguments with Cripps and Nye and they seem to have accepted them, but I am only too anxious to do all I can to help you, as I know how greatly you have helped me and are helping me. Believe me, I am most grateful to you.

I imagine that you are glad now that we did not adhere to the 15th May target in view of the strength the enemy has since disclosed. I know I am!

16. I am sorry I could not agree to come home. I wonder whether the vastness and complexity of this command is even yet realised at home. It does not seem to us out here that it is. I really do not feel that I can lightly lay down my responsibilities for what may easily be a month's absence, judging by the irregularity of the air service, if anything at all is brewing on any of my fronts. In any event I think it is a good principle that the higher commander should go forward to see the lower, if he can manage it, and not vice versa! I know you agree with this!!

As for taking cover behind the Defence Committee, that you know is not true. The whole mechanism of the joint direction of the war in this theatre is very delicately balanced as I think you realise, and any attempt by one of the three commanders to take action on his own, or even to receive and answer instructions addresses solely to him is liable at once to throw it out of gear. I am scrupulously careful therefore never to act on any privately received signal even from the Prime Minister without consulting Tedder and the Admiral.[198] I think you will admit the results have been satisfactory.

17. I think we really have done a good deal about the exchanging of officers to which you refer. I will send you a list of recent changes. It includes Arthur Smith, Galloway, Lloyd George Clark, Aizelwood, Collingwood Barker (Signals) and others. I will certainly let you know at once of any others who should have a change. Marriott[199] is one.

18. We all like Casey very much. He lacks Lyttelton's knowledge and experience, and is a little inclined perhaps to bother over details, particularly of strategy, but he is very good indeed and is going to be a success I feel.

19. We shall be very glad to see the A.G. whenever he can come. I wish you would come with him!

---

198 Admiral Sir Henry Harwood, C in C, Mediterranean.
199 Brigadier J. C. O. Marriott commanding 22nd Guards Brigade.

THE MILITARY PAPERS OF FIELD MARSHAL SIR CLAUDE AUCHINLECK

20.   I won't say anything about the battle in Libya. I have given you the
      fullest accounts I can and I hope they have been what you want. It
      has been and still is a most anxious time for all of us. We have had
      heavy losses but so has he I hope. I have just got back from 8th
      Army HQ. The battle did not go well yesterday but Neil & I have
      decided to hang on & fight it out.

JRL, AUC 922

212

Cipher message from Auchinleck to
Field Marshal J. C. Smuts, 14 June 1942

General THERON[200] has shown me your signal G/20037 (20037) of
12/6 (.) A strong counterattack was put in against enemy centre on
5/6 June and had initial success but was counter attacked in its turn by
strong enemy forces and driven back with heavy loss (.) HACHEIM
had in my opinion largely fulfilled its purpose and I think RITCHIE
was right to evacuate it when he did although it may have released some
though not many enemy troops to move against us in NORTH (.) Chief
enemy attacks against HACHEIM seem to have been by bombing and
shell fire (.) FREE FRENCH losses were not heavy apparently and
they are now reorganising (.) After discussion with THERON who fully
understands am communicating your message to FREE FRENCH
through General CATROUX and not to General KOENIG as former
commands all FREE FRENCH forces (.) Considerations explained to
THERON who will inform you later (.) Have just got back from 8 Army
H.Q. (.) Situation is serious but by no means irretrievable and I am
confident that RITCHIE will retrieve it (.) Enemy is not (R) not in an
enviable position and is being attacked and harassed on all side (.) Quite
understand that there is feeling of concern in UNION and realise this
makes things difficult (.) For this reason I am also concerned but I am
doing my best to right the situation and pray that I may be successful (.)
There is no doubt that superior enemy antitank gun gives him very great

---

200 Major General Frank Theron, Smut's senior liaison officer to GHQ, Middle
    East.

advantage which he is very ably exploiting to the full and our tank losses are serious although every effort is being made to recover damaged tanks and replace losses [.]

JRL, AUC 924

213

Cipher message from Auchinleck to Winston Churchill, 15 June 1942

1 (.) Have ordered General RITCHIE to deny to the enemy general line ACROMA – EL ADEM – EL GUBI (.) This does NOT mean that this can or should be held as a continuous fortified line but that the enemy is NOT to be allowed to establish himself EAST of it (.) The two Divisions from GAZALA position will be available to help in this (.) ALTHOUGH I do <u>NOT</u> intend that EIGHTH ARMY should be besieged in TOBRUK I have NO intention whatever of giving up TOBRUK (.) My orders to General RITCHIE (vide my signal CS/1256 14/6 to CIGS) are

(A) To deny general line ACROMA – EL ADEM – EL GUBI to the enemy (.)
(B) NOT to allow his forces to be invested in TOBRUK (.)
(C) To attack and harass the enemy whenever occasion offers (.)

Meanwhile I propose to build up strong as possible reserve in SALUM – MADDALENA area with the object of launching counter offensive soon as possible (.)

2 (.) N.Z. DIVISION already moving should be fully concentrated in about ten or twelve days but leading elements will naturally be available earlier if required (.)

3 (.) Trust information you are getting in my signals to C.I.G.S. is adequate [.]

JRL, AUC 925

214

Cipher message from Auchinleck to Winston Churchill, 16 June 1942

War Cabinet interpretation is correct (.) General RITCHIE is putting into TOBRUK what he considers an adequate force to hold it even should it become temporarily isolated by the enemy (.) Basis of garrison is four bde gps with adequate stocks of ammunition (,) food (,) fuel and water (.) Basis of immediate future action by 8 Army is to hold EL ADEM fortified area as pivot of manoeuvre and to use all available mobile forces to prevent enemy establishing himself EAST of EL ADEM or TOBRUK (.) Very definite orders to this effect have been issued to General RITCHIE and I trust he will be able to give effect to them (.) Position is quite different from last year as WE and NOT enemy now hold fortified positions on frontier and can operate fighter aircraft over TOBRUK even if use GAMBUT landing grounds should be temporarily denied to us (.) It seems to me that to invest TOBRUK AND to mask our forces in the frontier positions the enemy would need more troops than our information shows him to have (.) This being so we should be able to prevent the area between the frontier and TOBRUK passing under enemy control (,) I have discussed matter with Minister of State and other Commanders in Chief who agree with the policy proposed.

JRL, AUC 929

215

Cipher message from Winston Churchill to Auchinleck, 16 June 1942

One.   I am thankful you have succeeded in regrouping the 8(8)th ARMY on the new front in close contact with your reinforcements, and the Cabinet was very glad to know that you intend to hold TOBRUK at all costs. Let us know whether much stores fell into enemy's hands.

Two.   We cannot of course judge at the present time battle tactics from here. Certainly it would seem however that advantages would be gained if the whole of our Forces were engaged together at one time if the initiative could be recovered. It may be the new situation will give you this opportunity, especially if the enemy, who is evidently himself hard-pressed, is given no breathing space.

Armoured Warfare seems to favour the offensive because it allows a design to be unfolded step by step, whereas the defensive, which was so powerful in the last War, has to yield itself continually to the plans of the attacker.

All good wishes.

JRL, AUC 932

216

Letter from Auchinleck to Lieutenant General N. M. Ritchie, 17 June 1942

I enclose an extract from a telegram I have just had from the Prime Minister. As it seems so exactly to coincide with your views and mine on the subject, I want to be able to tell him that we are acting on it at once. Hence my insistence, which I hope you will forgive, on the prime need for not waiting to reorganise 1 S.A. Div and 50 Div, which presumably came out as formed units, and for getting their artillery and mobile infantry into action again at once under Gott, who is now I understand, in command of all the forward area.

2. The enemy must be kept under the heaviest pressure, and the action of the Tobruk troops yesterday sets an excellent example. I want to see your troops working wide to the West, well beyond El Adem, and biting at the enemy wherever met, especially by the Italians who are now having to come into the open.

3. You must not tolerate Trieste [Division] messing round Gott's southern flank.

4. I think "Mary" Coningham's effort is perfectly magnificent, and an inspiration to all of us, including myself.

5. The return I have of food, water, ammunition and fuel in TOBRUK seems satisfactory, and I am assuming that you are taking the most urgent action to make up deficiencies such as 25 pdr and S.A. ammunition by road convoy.

Are you happy about the water situation? All available storage should be filled to capacity if this has not already been done.

6. I presume the troops in the SOLLUM – HAMRA defences are pressing on with their completion and finishing up minefields and wire etc. It is as well to have this base as secure as possible before we go forward in force again.

7. If you are going to keep the 201st Motor Bde in the TOBRUK sector, I trust they will be used to the full in their mobile capacity to attack the enemy. I am sure this is your intention.

8. Your present tactical H.Q. seems somewhat inaccessible from the air. Are you staying there, or can you find a more convenient place?

9. I have said it so often before that I am afraid you must be sick of it, but I say it again! The task of the 8th Army now is not to receive blows but to give them, and to give them on an ever increasing scale until we can go forward again in a general offensive.

10. I am sure the enemy is exhausted and weakened, and would give anything for a period of rest and reorganisation now. Also he has great anxiety over his fuel situation.

11. We must keep him under pressure, and this calls for the greatest personal energy on that part of all concerned, commanders and staff, officers alike from the highest to the lowest.

12. I rely on you personally to see that the necessary drive and ruthlessness is forthcoming.

13. If any of your commanders are tired, send them back to rest. You have a surplus at the moment I think.

Good luck and go to it.

JRL, AUC 934

217

Cipher message from Auchinleck to Field Marshal J. C. Smuts, 19 June 1942

Many thanks your G/20460 18/6 (.) Have NO intention of giving up TOBRUK which I hope is only temporarily isolated (.) RITCHIE will defend TOBRUK and the strong SALUM HAMRA MADDALENA position prepared long ago against such a contingency as has now arisen and will do all he can to keep situation fluid in the space between SALUM and TOBRUK by using maximum number mobile troops available (.) These will also I hope harry enemy communications (.) Meanwhile I am planning as always to destroy enemy (.)

KLOPPER[201] commands in TOBRUK and has full confidence RITCHIE and myself (.) He will make himself as offensive as possible and has I think an adequate force under him which is well supplied with necessities [.]

JRL, AUC 937

218

Letter from Auchinleck to Lieutenant General N. M. Ritchie, 20 June 1942

I have been thinking over the position as regards your Corps Commanders and have come to the following decisions.

I propose that GOTT should take over the 30th Corps from NORRIE and train and command the striking force now being built up.

NORRIE is in need of a rest, and there is no other employment available for him here, so I shall send him home and recommend him for further employment there.

My proposal for the 13th Corps is RAMSDEN.[202] The fact that he knows the conditions and is apparently offensively minded is strongly in his favour.

As the matter is so very urgent, I have embodied most of the above in a signal I have just sent you about the reorganisation of your Army.

JRL, AUC 939

---

201 Major General H. B. Klopper, who had commanded 2nd South African Division and, on 15 June had taken command of all troops in the Tobruk garrison.
202 Major General William Ramsden, GOC 50th Division, 1940–42. Commanded 30 Corps, July to September 1942 as Acting Lieutenant General.

219

Cipher message from Winston Churchill
(in Washington) to Auchinleck, 22 June 1942

Begins.   Your telegrams of 20th and 21st instant and MINISTER OF STATE's No. MS/20 of 21st received, also CABINET's telegram No. OZ.544 in reply to your NO.CC/68.

C.I.G.S., DILL and I earnestly hope stern resistance will be made on the SOLLUM frontier line special Intelligence has shown stresses which Enemy has undergone. Very important reinforcements are on their way. A week gained may be decisive. We do not know exact days of deployment NEW ZEALAND Division but had expected it would be by the end of the month. Eighth Armoured and Forty fourth are approaching and near. We agree with General SMUTS that you may draw freely upon Ninth and Tenth Armies as the danger from North is more remote. Thus you can effect drastic roulement with the Three Divisions now East of the Canal.

TWO.   I was naturally disconcerted by your news which may well put us back to where we were eighteen months ago and leave all the work of that period to be done over again. However I do not repeat not feel that the defence of the DELTA cannot be effectively maintained and I hope no-one will be unduly impressed by the spectacular blows which the Enemy has struck at us.

(My 06353/22 Part Two follows)

PART TWO FINAL

I am sure that with your perseverance and resolution and continued readiness to run risks, the situation can be restored, especially in view of the large reinforcements approaching.

THREE.   Here in WASHINGTON the PRESIDENT is deeply moved by what has occurred and he and other High UNITED STATES authorities show themselves disposed to lend the utmost help. They authorize me to inform you that the Second UNITED STATES Armoured Division, specially trained in Desert warfare in CALIFORNIA, will leave for SUEZ ABOUT July 5th and should be with you in August. You need not send the INDIAN Division and 288 INDIAN Armoured Brigade back to INDIA as proposed. Measures are also being taken, in addition to those described in the Chiefs of Staff telegram No. C.O.S.(M.E.) 275 to divert INDIA-bound aircraft to the LIBYAN theatre. The HALPRO force is remaining and will be brought up to full strength. I have told C.A.S. to give you his schedules of deliveries, including the four HALIFAX Squadrons, unless he has already done so.

FOUR.   The main thing now is for you to inspire all your forces with an intense will to resist and strive and not to accept the freak decisions produced by ROMMEL's handful of heavy armour. Make sure that all your manpower plays a full part in these critical days. His MAJESTY's Government is quite ready to share your responsibilities in making the most active and daring defence.

JRL, AUC 946

220

Cipher message from Auchinleck to Field Marshal J. C. Smuts, 22 June 1942

Since my latest report to you I have had further news from RITCHIE (.) The enemy assault on TOBRUK on June 20 developed with great speed and by 2200 hrs enemy had gained possession of the portion of TOBRUK occupied EAST of TOBRUK – EL ADEM road (.) KLOPPER reported that all his tanks were out of action and half his guns lost (.) Under the circumstances he asked RITCHIE for permission to fight his way out (.) RITCHIE immediately authorised him to do so (.) But later KLOPPER reported that almost all his M.T. had been captured by the enemy and consequently only a small proportion of the garrison could attempt to fight their way out (.) Before communication was finally closed with EIGHTH ARMY KLOPPER reported that organised resistance was breaking down and he was doing the worst (,) which RITCHIE concluded was capitulation (,) and considered to be the only possible course (.) Report from EIGHTH ARMY received 1930 (1930) hrs 21 June stated that yesterday morning there were indications that some posts are still holding out (.) It is too early yet to say whether any parts of garrison have broken out but in view of the capture of so much of their M.T. by the enemy I do not except that much will have come away.

JRL, AUC 948

221

Cipher message from Auchinleck to General Sir Alan Brooke, CIGS, 23 June 1942

The unfavourable course of the recent battle in CYRENAICA culminating in the disastrous fall of TOBRUK impels me to ask you seriously to consider the advisability of retaining me in my command (.) No doubt you are already considering this and quite rightly but I want you to know that I also realise the probable effect of the past months fighting (.) Personally I feel fit to carry on and reasonably confident of being able to turn the tables on the enemy in time (.) All the same there is no doubt that in a situation like the present (,) fresh blood and new ideas at the top may make all the difference between success and stalemate (.) I acted on this idea myself last summer when I replaced BERESFORD-PEIRSE[203] and CREAGH[204] by new men (.) After steeping oneself for months in the same subject all day and every day one is apt to get into a groove and to lose originality (.) For this theatre originality is essential and a change is quite probably desirable on this account alone apart from all other considerations such as loss of influence due to lack of success (,) absence of luck and all the other things which affect the morale of an army (.) It occurred to me that you might want to use ALEXANDER who is due here in a day or two (.) Personally I do NOT think WILSON could do it now but he might (.) I have thought over this a lot and feel I must tell you what I think [.]

JRL, AUC 950

222

Cipher message from Auchinleck to Winston Churchill, 24 June 1942

1 (.) I deeply regret that you should have received this severe blow at so critical a time as a result of the heavy defeat suffered by the forces

---

203 Lieutenant General Noel Beresford-Peirse, who Auchinleck had removed from command of the Western Desert Force in September 1941.
204 Major General Sir Michael O'Moore Creagh who was removed from command of 7th Armoured Division in September 1941.

under my command (.) I fear that the position is now much what it was a year ago when I took over command except that the enemy now has TOBRUK which may be of considerable advantage to him not only from the supply point of view but because he has no need to detach troops to contain it as was the case last year (.)

2 (.) The considerations governing continued resistance in the Frontier position at SOLLUM and SOUTH of it are set out (,) clearly I hope (,) in signal CC/69 of 23/6 to Deputy Prime Minister from Middle East Defence Committee which was repeated to you (.) In the circumstances this position is untenable against determined enemy attack because of our weakness in armour and any attempt to hold other than with mobile forces which can evade encirclement must in my opinion result in further defeat of our forces in detail (.) I have therefore agreed to its evacuation by all except mobile forces whose task it is to maintain themselves in and about the Frontier positions for as long as they can (,) and if forced to withdraw (,) to continue to keep the enemy as far to the WESTWARD as possible (.) Meanwhile the bulk of our infantry is occupying and organising the MATRUH position where a new armoured reserve is also being built up as fast as possible so as to be ready to meet the enemy armour should he try to attack this position (.) The forces holding this position will comprise 50 DIV (two Bdes only) (,) 50 and 10 IND DIVS (three Bdes each) and N.Z. DIV (complete) also one or more of 1 (,) 7 and 10 ARMD DIVS according to the availability of tanks (.) 8 ARMD DIV will be added to this force when it arrives and after the necessary training to fit it to fight in the Desert (.) We have learned by experience that troops fresh from the U.K. are a liability rather than an asset in Desert fighting until they have had the requisite training (.) It is my firm intention to resume the offensive immediately our armoured forces are strong enough to give a reasonable chance of success and far reaching plans for reorganisation to make our formations more suitable for the task they have to do are well advanced (.)

3 (.) I have already drawn two and a third infantry Div from 9 and 10 Armies besides one Corps HQ and signals (,) two Armoured Car Regts (,) one medium artillery regiment (,) two field artillery regiments and one A.Tk Regt (.) Not counting Polish (,) Greek (,) Free French and Trans-Jordan contingents which are not yet trained or equipped for battle there remain in this vast area one and two

third Indian infantry divisions (,) one Indian Armoured Brigade Group just being issued with its tanks (,) One Indian Armoured Car Regt and the 9 Australian Division (.) I am prepared to take great risks but must remind you of what occurred in SYRIA and IRAQ and very nearly in PERSIA early in 1941 when the enemy began infiltrating by air into these countries (.) NOT ONE of these countries is stable or yet sure of our ultimate victory (.) Quite apart from any question of resisting enemy attack there is always present a grave risk of internal trouble which might well lead to incalculable damage to our bases and oil supplies unless we have troops at hand to deal with it (.) I do NOT feel at the moment that I can draw any more troops from this area nor do I think that the tactical situation in the WEST demands more INFANTRY (,) what is required is more ARMOUR and this is NOT available from 9 or 10 Army Fronts (.) End of First part.

PART TWO final (.)

4 (.) We are deeply grateful to you and the President of the United States for the generous measure of help which you propose to give us and for the speed with which you are arranging to send it (.) The Second United States Armoured Division will indeed be a welcome reinforcement as will the Grant and Lee tanks diverted from INDIA (.) Your assurance that the Indian infantry division and the Indian Armoured Brigade need NOT now be sent back to INDIA will greatly ease my difficulties in regard to the internal security problem in IRAQ and PERSIA (,) especially in the oilfield areas (.) Air Marshal TEDDER informs me that the diversion of aircraft to this theatre and the permission to retain the HALPRO force here will strengthen our hands immensely while the HALIFAX Squadrons will greatly increase our offensive power in the air (.)

5 (.) With regard to your para four (.) I believe that practically without exception the troops in the 8th Army are as determined to beat the enemy as ever they were which is saying much and that their spirit is unimpaired (.) As to accepting decisions brought about by enemy action we will do all we can by improving our tactics and leadership to prevent their recurrence but as you know we are trying to train an army and use it on the battlefield at the same time (.) We are catching up but have NOT caught up yet (.) As to using all my manpower I hope I am doing this BUT infantry can NOT win battles in the desert so long as the enemy has superiority

in armour and nothing can be said or done to change this fact (.) Guns and armour and just enough infantry to give them and their supply organisation local protection are what is needed (.) Masses of infantry are NO use without guns and armour (.) We can NOT have too many guns or too many tanks and the tanks must be American medium tanks which can stand up to German tanks and NOT Crusaders with only two pounder guns in them (,) though Crusaders with six pounder guns should be all right (.)

I thank you personally most sincerely for all your help and support during the past year and deeply regret the failures and setbacks of the past month for which I accept the fullest responsibility.

JRL, AUC 953

223

Cipher message from Winston Churchill (in Washington) to Auchinleck, 24 June 1942

1. Do not have the slightest anxiety about course of affairs at home. Whatever views I may have about how the battle was fought or whether it should have been fought a good deal earlier you have my entire confidence and I share your responsibilities to the full.

2. I have just shown your message to the President who was strongly moved and means to come to our aid. The difficulties about shipping the American Armoured Division which are considerable are in process of being flattened out. The Americans are also trying to send a large number of a new kind of anti-tank rocket gun, of which they have great hopes.

   Meanwhile you have heard of the American air reinforcements which are already being directed to the Middle East. Plans are being formed to send another large wave perhaps 100 long-range bombers as fast as possible, also to hurry out to you further improved Grant tanks. Shall propose to President tomorrow placing an American General under your command, with a seat on the Middle East Council, observing that he would speak both for American air and Army units.

3.   Please tell Harwood that I am rather worried about reports of undue despondency and alarm in Alexandria, and of the Navy hastening to evacuate to the Red Sea although various precautionary moves may be taken and "Queen Elizabeth" should be got out at earliest. I trust a firm confident attitude will be maintained.

PART 2.

The President's information from Rome is that Rommel expects to be delayed three or four weeks before he can mount a heavy attack on the Mersa Matruh position. I should think the delay might be greater.

4.   I hope the crisis will lead to all uniformed personnel in the Delta and all available loyal manpower being raised to the highest fighting condition. You have over 700,000 men on your ration strength in the Middle East. Every fit male should be made to fight and die for victory. There is no reason why units defending the Mersa Matruh position should not be reinforced by several thousands of officers and administrative personnel ordered to swell the battalions or working parties. You are in the same kind of situation as we should be if England were invaded and the same intense drastic spirit should reign.

JRL, AUC 954

224

Cipher message from Auchinleck to General Sir Alan Brooke, CIGS, 25 June 1942

Am taking over command 8 Army from RITCHIE this afternoon (.) Propose send him on leave temporarily to PALESTINE but consider he should go home soon as possible and be given command of a corps or a General Staff appointment (.) I feel that though sound and resolute he is apt to be slow and I fear Army has to some extent lost confidence in him (.) Shall use DORMAN SMITH as my Chief of Staff leaving CORBETT to represent me at G.H.Q.

JRL, AUC 957

225

Cipher message from Auchinleck to General Sir Alan Brooke, CIGS, 28 June 1942

Appreciation situation regarding defence of EGYPT (.)

One (.) Enemy in WESTERN DESERT is still markedly superior to Eighth Army in Tanks (.) Owing absence natural obstacles to mechanised movement and ease which given superior tank force desert flank of all positions (,) except EL ALAMEIN – QATTARA Depression line can be turned (,) armour still remain dominant factor governing retention of initiative (.)

Two (.) ENEMY (.) Has gained all recent successes with his three German divisions (.) ITALIANS have played minor part (.) His tactics have been excellent while his adherence to first principles (,) speed of movement and ability to keep forward troops supplied have been most remarkable (.) His leaders are well trained and know how to re-act to situations usually to be expected in battle (.) Success will have greatly heightened German morale locally (,) but nationally his morale is steadily deteriorating so that with an end of success he is likely to go to other extreme (.) Italian morale will also be higher but their reaction will be even greater should the tide turn (.) So far as we know enemy is unlikely to get much more in reinforcements of material and MEN but hope of gaining EGYPT might lead to diversion of forces EVEN from RUSSIA (.) Against this his sea communications with LIBYA are again becoming precarious and he is always experiencing scarcity one commodity or another (.) Occupation of EGYPT would greatly ease his supply problem (.) His ability to keep his forces supplied should he try to advance against the DELTA can NOT (R) NOT be accurately forecast BUT he has done great things already and has captured much of our transport so we must be prepared for this (.)

Three (.) OBJECT (.) Our object must be at all costs to prevent the enemy stopping our supply of men and material through the RED SEA ports BEFORE we have rebuilt an adequate armoured force to regain initiative and resume offensive (.) Also essential to prevent him increasing his armoured forces in LIBYA and this entails maximum interference with his sea communications (.)

Four (.)   SEA COMMUNICATIONS (.) Retention of MALTA and ALEXANDRIA and of aerodromes as far WEST as possible in EGYPT is essential if we are seriously to interrupt enemy sea communications with LIBYA (.)

Five (.)   AIR STRENGTH (.) We cannot (R) not resume the offensive on land until we have rebuilt our armoured forces to the required strength (.) Meanwhile our only offensive weapon is our air striking force which it is essential to maintain at the maximum possible strength as it alone enables us to retain any semblance of the initiative (.)

Six (.)   INTENTION (.) My intention with which A.O.C. in C. is in full agreement is to keep Eighth Army in being as a mobile field force and resist by every possible means any further attempt by the enemy to advance EASTWARDS (.)

Seven (.)   METHOD (.) First (.) Utmost delay possible without entailing encirclement or destruction Eighth Army will be imposed on enemy on FUKA line and then on EL ALAMEIN position (.) Second (.) Should withdrawal from EL ALAMEIN position be forced on us (.) Eighth Army (less 1 S.A. Div) will withdraw along the "BARREL TRACK" leading from DEIR EL QATTARA to CAIRO and continue to oppose enemy should he try to advance on CAIRO direct (.) 1 S.A. Div now holding EL ALAMEIN defended area will withdraw on ALEXANDRIA (.) Third (.) 1 S.A. Div, 9 Aus Div and improvised forces and columns now forming in DELTA will constitute DELTA FORCE under Lieut. Gen. STONE and be responsible for defence WESTERN edge DELTA (,) for fighting enemy step by step if he penetrates DELTA and for defending ALEXANDRIA (.) Fourth (.) If enemy moves along coast on ALEXANDRIA Eighth Army will attack his SOUTHERN flank and rear (.) If he moves direct on CAIRO (,) DELTA FORCE will attack his NORTHERN flank and rear (.) Fifth (.) Meanwhile striking force will be built up ready to assume offensive by BARREL TRACK or coast road or both according to situation (.) Sixth (.) If driven from EL ALAMEIN position I shall assume direct control of both Eighth Army and DELTA FORCE with an improved operational H.Q. outside CAIRO (.) Lieutenant-General CORBETT will take over Eighth Army (.)

Eight (.)   Instructions to give effect to these plans have been issued and preparations are in hand.

JRL, AUC 961

226

Cipher message from Winston Churchill to Auchinleck, 3 July 1942

On the First of July we told you our special information that enemy after feinting at your Southern flank would attack centre of your position about where 18 (18) Brigade lay and thereafter turn Northwards to cut off EL ALAMEIN strong point.

This is exactly what he appears to be trying to do. Are you getting these priceless messages (which have never errored) in good time. Every such telegram ought to be in your hands without a moment's delay.

Two.   How is the 8 (8) Armoured Division getting on and when can it come wholly or partly into action. What is the state and position of 9 (9) AUSTRALIAN Division. Have they got all their guns.

Three.   Should be glad to have your opinion at leisure about how ROMMEL's tanks would get on among Canals and irrigation of DELTA.

Four.   GERMANS are enquiring whether inundations have been made. This was all planned two years ago with WAVELL. Presume it has been carried out. Whole idea is that EGYPT should be defended just as drastically as if it were KENT or SUSSEX without regard to any other consideration than destruction of the enemy.

Five.   Everyone here greatly heartened by your splendid fight. Overwhelming Vote House of Commons confidence in Government and your Army.

JRL, AUC 967

227

Cipher message from Lieutenant General T. W. Corbett to Winston Churchill, 3 July 1942

Am answering for Commander in Chief to avoid delay (.) Your message being passed to him with this reply (.)

ONE (.)   Every special source message goes direct EIGHTH ARMY and received there as early as at G.H.Q. (.) These messages of great value (.) Some arrive in time to be operationally of use others not so (.) Things can be checked your end (.)

TWO (.)   8 ARMOURED DIVISION (.) two squadrons Valentines already gone forward to reinforce EIGHTH ARMY manned by personnel 1 ARMY TANK BRIGADE (.) Personnel of this Division start landing 4 (4) July (.) Dependent on physical condition of men possible move forward one armoured brigade group complete about middle July (.) Not yet possible forecast readiness second brigade owing necessity replacement tanks already sent EIGHTH ARMY and provision artillery support (.) 9 AUSTRALIAN DIVISION less one brigade group arrived in ALEXANDRIA defences from which one battle group moving today join EIGHTH ARMY (.) This battle group composed of twentyfour 25 prs with proportionate escort anti-tank and infantry (.) Third brigade group completes arrival ALEXANDRIA area 4 (4) July (.) Steps taken put whole Division on mobile basis (.) Divisional artillery has seventytwo 25 prs and fiftyfive anti-tank guns of which fifteen are 6 prs (.)

THREE (.)   Tank movement among waterways and irrigation channels much restricted (.) No reason suppose ROMMEL could do any more with his tanks in this area than ourselves (.) Large numbers tank hunting commandos formed from schools and depots for operations in enclosed DELTA area (,)

FOUR (.)   ALEXANDRIA area (.) Complete inundations not possible yet as essential retain use of aerodromes which would be affected (.) Remaining inundations now being put into effect (.) CAIRO area (,) partial inundation carried out (.) Completion of scheme still under negotiation with EGYPTIAN Government (.) Water in West branch of NILE which is normally fordable in many places at this time of year being increased (.) Arrangements have been made to defend the DELTA with every available man and all resources.

MOST IMMEDIATE CLEAR THE LINE.

JRL, AUC 968

228

Cipher message from
Lieutenant General Sir Archibald Nye, VCIGS,
to Lieutenant General T. W. Corbett, 6 July 1942

The fall of TOBRUK after such a very short resistance involving the capture of so many prisoners and the loss of so much material seems from this distance quite inexplicable. AXIS reports state that the General surrendered and in any case it is evident that the greatest capital can be made by enemy from the whole incident which has caused considerable criticism in this country of the fighting spirit of our Commanders. Cabinet wish Deputy Adjutant General to enquire and report as soon as possible on the circumstances in which the capitulation took place and in particular on the conduct of the General in command.

JRL, AUC 971

229

Cipher message from Auchinleck to
General Sir Alan Brooke, CIGS, 8 July 1942

Please see personal 99606 (VCIGS) 6/7 from VCIGS to CORBETT (.) I can NOT believe that Cabinet has ordered my D.A.G. to report independently on an operation carried out under MY command and I shall be grateful for an early explanation of this request which seems to be extraordinary (.) If the Cabinet intend to send out a Committee of Enquiry from home well and good but to depute a staff officer of mine without my sanction is not tolerable to me and I am sure was NOT intended (.) I would greatly appreciate direct instructions from you on matters of such personal importance (.) As CORBETT has told VCIGS I have already instituted an enquiry into the fall of TOBRUK under WILSON who is a very competent judge (.) I do not propose to take any other action [.]

JRL, AUC 973

230

Letter from Field Marshal Sir John Dill, British Joint Staff Mission, Washington to Auchinleck, 9 July 1942

Many thanks for your letter of the 24th June which has just reached me.

I realised at the time what terrible anguish you were suffering in those days when Rommel was driving forward & you were losing so heavily. I was hoping that you might be able not to attempt to hold Tobruk because of the difficulty of giving it a sufficient garrison and the still greater difficulty of keeping it supplied with such a reduced Mediterranean Fleet. But of course I was in no position to judge such matters at this distance and when you decided to hold it no one could have anticipated that it would not hold out – at any rate much longer.

But I happened to be somewhat mixed up on a fairly high level with our defeats in March 1918. At that time things could not have looked worse & we certainly had nothing left with which to hold Amiens. And yet the tide turned & as so often happens when the enemy was at the top of his [best?] he made mistakes. It took us a long time to find out that the Bosche had really shot his bolt.

In these days the army did not lose faith in Douglas Haig & yet he had unquestionably suffered a great defeat. And I am quite sure that your Army has not lost faith in you. They know as everyone else knows that you took over command of the 8th Army at a very critical period and what you have achieved & are achieving in the El Alamein area must have created great confidence.

The Americans – that is what they call the top Americans have been splendid. In no way critical – at any rate to our faces – and all out to help in any way they could.

Brooke was here when your telegram about which you speak in your letter reached him. So of course was the P.M. There was, I may say, great relief when they knew that you had taken command of the 8th Army yourself. There may have been some bewilderment at the turn of events but there was no criticism – unless perhaps "it's a pity he didn't do it sooner" if you can call that a criticism.

The war is still young and you have already played an important part in it & you have I am sure a still greater part to play. So keep fit & keep the confidence in yourself that others have – I in particular. And do all you can to keep under the sensitiveness which I have always known you have & will never entirely eliminate. However sore & bumped you may feel after your desperate battles, you must remember that you are filling a historic & even an heroic part and it is the last battle that counts. When Americans came to me when things were looking very bad I told them that we had had a bad beating but that one of our national characteristics was that we never knew when we were beaten. And even if the Army is beaten as long as its Commander is not beaten it will come again. Good luck to you & give my love to your Lady when you write. She certainly won't think you have let her down any more than I do.

JRL, AUC 974

231

Letter from Lieutenant General N. M. Ritchie to Auchinleck, 12 July 1942

I am due to leave to-morrow for home and am sorry that I have not seen you again before my departure.

Thank you for your letter of the 26th June[205] which I prize having received. It has been a great help. I have not replied before as I well realise that you have little time for reading in these days.

This is just to bid you au revoir, for I hope I may serve you again some day. It will still be a long drawn out struggle, But I know you will win however hard the battle may prove to be.

Perhaps I can be of some use at home even if all I can do is to do something towards getting those who matter there to understand the equipment aspect – guns and A.F.V.s

The last fortnight has been the greatest hell, this feeling that one was doing nothing to help in shouldering some little part of the burden that rests on you.

I know the Eighth Army will win.

JRL, AUC 975

---

205 This must have been a private letter, telling Ritchie that he was being removed as GOC in C of the Eighth Army. No copy survives in the Auchinleck papers.

232

Cipher message from Auchinleck to Winston Churchill, 14 July 1942

1 (.) Of Valentines received with 8th Armoured Div. first 67 (67) inspected revealed that approx. 500 (500) items required workshop attention (.) Time spent on each tank varied from 140 (140) to 200 (200) hours (.)

2 (.) General conditions of these tanks was better than those received earlier this year but the performance of the engines was below standard (.) Some higher gears could not be engaged (.) In a number of cases the cylinder head gaskets were blowing (.) All engines required tuning and adjustments to steering gear had to be carried out (.) In most cases clutch withdrawal levers required adjustment (.) All 2 (2) pdr guns required buffer piston clearances checked (.) This is an M.E. modification which must be done in U.K. (.) They are not marked so checking had to be done (.)

3 (.) Approx. 160 (160) items of tank fittings were deficient of which 120 (120) were important such as towing shackles (.) Armament components ( ) Periscope components (.) Power traverse control boxes (.) Some of these items may have been pilfered in transit (.)

4 (.) There was no (R) NO evidence of bad stowage or of serious damage in transit (.)

5 (.) The general condition of the majority of the tanks is that to be expected after a long voyage which involves movement by Road (,) Rail and Sea under varying climatic conditions (.) Tanks cannot (R) NOT be battle worthy after such a voyage without considerable attention [.]

JRL, AUC 980

233

Letter from General Sir Alan Brooke, CIGS to Auchinleck, 17 July 1942

My dear Auk

Very many thanks for your letters, I am so sorry not to have answered them sooner.

1. You have constantly been in my thoughts since Rommel started his attacks, and I have so well realized the difficult and anxious times that you have been through. I only wish that it was possible to do more to help you from this distance.

2. It is such a joy to see you gradually regaining the mastery over the enemy. I do hope that this heavier equipment in the shape of 6 pr. tanks, and latest American tanks, will arrive soon enough to provide the additional striking power you require. Neil Ritchie has just arrived, I had a long talk with him yesterday and am having another long one tonight. I shall see that he also has talks with all the D.C.I.G.S. department so that we may gather from him all we possibly can as to required improvements in equipment, etc.

3. I did not answer your very kind wire of June 23rd more fully as I had seen the Prime Minister's wire to you expressing full confidence in you. It is his confidence that is the important factor. You know how temperamental he is apt to be at times, so I hope you do not attach too much importance if occasionally his telegrams are not quite as friendly as they might be. I can assure you that I do all that is within my power to guard you against unnecessary repercussions from outside, and to let you carry on with the least possible interference. But even with the best will in the world, results often fall short of what I should wish! I should however like you to realize how much I feel for you in the difficult times you have been through, and to know that you can rely on me to do all I can to help you from this end.

4. I have now got your organization for your Northern front and am getting it pushed through. It seems a little top-heavy at present with the reduced forces that are in Syria, Iraq and Persia, but it provides a sound basis to build on if we can find forces for you. That is the main difficulty at present! Archie Wavell at a pinch can

spare two Divisions, and we are preparing to send two more after the 51st Division. This might assist in delaying the initial German penetration into Persia if Russia cracks, but will not go far. The whole matter is only of time and space. If we could succeed in checking the Germans in Northern Persia during the Winter there might be an opportunity of building up some force before the Spring, but even this would be dependent on diverting shipping from all other proposed enterprises of Americans and ourselves! We are at present hard at it working out all the various alternatives and should soon be able to let you have some sort of plan to meet a crack on the Russian front. But as you say with our limited resources both in forces and in shipping we are compelled to gamble whether we like it or not!

You are quite right and we must not rely on weather and terrain exercising an undue delaying effect on the enemy. I have just returned the latest J.I.C. estimate to them on that account. Their estimate of rate of German advance through Caucasus and through Persia is far too optimistic as to the slow rate of advance.

5. I have had particular difficulties both with the Foreign Office and the Cabinet with reference to the reconnaissance facilities which you have been asking for in Northern Persia. They refuse to realize how essential this reconnaissance is to our future defence. I am hoping that with our rather better relations with the Russians we should now succeed in getting something done.

6. From what you have told me of Quinan I do not feel very happy about his power of command in the event of Persia becoming an active front. Have you any idea of replacing him under such conditions?

7. I am glad the Australian and New Zealand Governments solved your problem of Freyberg's rank. That should now keep him happy and quiet!

8. I am so glad that you like Casey, I thought you would from what I saw of him here.

9. Our visit to America was useful in many ways, and at any rate secured additional equipment for you. But the problem of running a co-ordinated war with them is not going to be an easy one! There are many interests and many ideas that conflict, and it will take superhuman efforts to direct all the power that is being created into the best channel for an early conclusion of the war!

10.   I have every hope of being able to escape to pay you a visit before long, and am preparing plans. Shall let you know results as soon as I can fix something definite. Am looking forward to it tremendously.

With very best of luck to you in your trying and difficult task.

JRL, AUC 984

234

Special Order of the Day, to all ranks of the 8th Army from Auchinleck, 25 July 1942

You have done well. You have turned a retreat into a firm stand and stopped the enemy on the threshold of Egypt. You have done more. You have wrenched the initiative from him by sheer guts and hard fighting and put HIM on the defensive in these last weeks.

He has lost heavily and is short of men, ammunition, petrol and other things. He is trying desperately to bring these over to Africa but the Navy and the Air Force are after his ships.

You have borne much but I ask you for more. We must not slacken. If we can stick it we will break him.

STICK TO IT.

JRL, AUC 987

235

Letter from Auchinleck to General Sir Alan Brooke, CIGS, 25 July 1942

My dear Alan

Thank you very much indeed for your letter of the 17th July which arrived on the 22nd and so reached me very quickly.

I would like you to know how greatly I appreciate what you said in it and, still more, the way in which you said it! Your confidence and encouragement mean very much to me.

2. We have succeeded, though only just I am afraid, in regaining some measure of local initiative, and I think that it was due to our first effort in this direction, the threatening of his Southern flank, which stopped the enemy continuing with his designs to attack El Alamein from the South-West.

Our subsequent efforts in the North against Tel El Eisa and the Ruweisat Ridge in the centre kept the ball rolling and made the Germans move their troops about to stiffen the Italians.

We also inflicted considerable loss on the Italian part of his Army in these operations. I was disappointed when our big effort of the 21st/22nd July came to nothing as I had great hopes of it. I still do not know the full story of the battle in the centre, but it does seem as if the 23rd Armoured Brigade, though gallant enough, lost control and missed direction. The Infantry, too, seem to have made some avoidable mistakes. Perhaps I asked too much of them, but one can only plan on the information available. Well, there it is, we undoubtedly gave the enemy a rude shock, judging from the many intercepted messages from the various enemy units, but we failed to get our object, which was to break through. The Australians had some success in the North and gained more depth to their position West of El Alamein. In the South the efforts of the 7th Armoured Division were most disappointing, especially as they had been reinforced by the 69th Infantry Brigade. The grain of the country is against them and the enemy is strongly posted though he can not be strong in numbers, I feel.

We are going on trying to find a way round or through in the South, but I am not too hopeful about it at the moment.

3. The enemy has now got his German infantry, irrespective of what formation or unit they belong to, sandwiched in between the remnants of his Italian divisions along the whole front, so that we can no longer fall on Italians and put them in the bag as easily as we did at first. However, we are watching for a weak spot and will, I hope, find one soon. I feel that owing to the great length of front he is holding the enemy can not have much depth to his position, except in the centre, where he holds his German armour in reserve. His Italian armour is behind his Southern sector. The trouble is that I have really no reserve with which to stage new attacks or to keep up the momentum of an attack once started.

I have to transfer troops from one part of the front to another, and this takes time as the distances are great and the going often atrocious. Moreover, there is no cover from the air and large movements must be made at night if secrecy is to be obtained.

4. This lack of flexibility due to the absence of a real reserve is aggravated of course by the impossibility of detaching subordinate Dominion formations, such as a brigade group, or a divisional artillery, from its parent division, whether it is New Zealand, South African, or Australian. All commanders of these formations are only too anxious to help but they are all adamant on the principles that their troops shall fight under their own direct command only. In the light of past events, and of political conditions, this is understandable, but it does make it most damnably difficult to get any real flexibility, particularly as the brigade or brigade group is really the fighting unit in this theatre and not the division, whatever the theorists may say. You will I am sure understand that I make no reflections on the qualities of these troops who are magnificent fighters, taken all round, though they vary in degree. They are, moreover, none of them really trained for highly mobile fighting such as this. You will ask why aren't they trained after their stay in Syria and Palestine? Well, there are several reasons.

First, they were working hard on the various defensive positions which had to be prepared as an insurance to set off our deficiencies in numbers. Secondly, it has never been possible, and never will be possible I am afraid, to give divisions in quiet areas, anything more than a training scale of transport, and without a full scale of transport, you can not really train units to be fully mobile in mechanised war, where everyone moves in a motor vehicle of one sort or another. Thirdly, these Dominion forces, magnificent material as they contain, are very hard to teach. They are apt to think that once they have been in battle, they have little to learn and are on the whole deeply suspicious of any attempts by us to teach them. Some of them say quite openly that we are incompetent ourselves and so unfit to teach them or anyone else. They are not alone in their opinion of course! Fourthly, there is no doubt that their intensely democratic feelings make it most difficult for their officers to insist on real hard work being done, when they are out of the battle zone. They simply do not understand the meaning of continuous and intensive training. Freyberg is an exception of course and does insist on hard training, but he has very few trained or experienced officers to back him up and he has had to send the best of his leaders back to New Zealand.

You will think, perhaps, that I am complaining of my tools, but I am not. I only want you to realise that commanding an army of this composition is not a straightforward business to be conducted on the simple lines advocated in F.S.R. and the textbooks! I am sure you do realise this, but I doubt if others do. However, the enemy has his "Wops"[206] to contend with, so the difficulties are not all on our side!

5. I agree that our Northern front organisation looks ridiculously heavy now that there are only about four brigade groups in the whole area, but we must plan against the possibility of our having to deploy large forces in Persia and Northern Iraq. I quite realise the problem continually before me, and our planning staff are always working at it. As it is we are just taking a hundred per cent. risk on the Germans not being able to get through the Caucasus, and, unless we are definitely prepared to abandon Egypt, I do not see what else we can do. I said as much in my telegram to the Prime Minister the other day. As regard the command there, I think it is all right for the present and preparations and planning are going well.

Quinan has as you know managed to get into some sort of touch with the Russians, but their attitude is that they will defend the Caucasus and Persia, and that, if they fail, it is no use our thinking we can do anything! I have Corbett in mind as a successor to Quinan when the time comes. He has lots of energy and foresight and has made a special study of all that part of the world and has thought deeply about the use of armour in these wide desert countries. In fact his ideas are in my opinion considerably ahead of teaching at Home, or even here, in spite of all the experience gained in the Western Desert. I should then want a new C.G.S. and will be very grateful if you can produce one for me. As you know I think already, Gammel[207] and I do not make a good pair so please leave him out of it.

6. The Eighth Army will need a commander of its own again someday, I suppose, though I propose to stay here until the present battle ends one way or another. I think I must see it through and I certainly want to, though it is not too easy filling a dual role. However, Corbett is

---

206 Derogatory term applied to Italians.
207 Lieutenant General Sir James Gammell.

doing excellently in Cairo, and I deal only with the biggest points of policy, though there are quite a lot of these, as you can imagine.

I believe Gott might command Eighth Army well and so far as I can see he shows no signs of weariness and is learning how to handle big formations every day. He has, however, been a long time in the Desert and he might go to Ninth Army in Syria, that is if you consider he is ripe for an Army command. He impresses me most favourably in every way.

I think that when Wilson has finished these enquiries he might go, though he is admirable in his handling of his problems in Syria and has shown no recent signs of tiredness. We should then want a commander for Eight Army from Home or India. (Beresford-Pierse[208] would not be suitable, in my opinion). He must be a man of vigour and personality and have a most flexible and receptive mind. He must also be young, at any rate in mind and body, and be prepared to take advice and learn unless he has had previous Western Desert experience.

7. I am sending Harding home to give you all we know of the recent fighting and my views for the future. I hope he will supply all the information you need. I think he is wholly admirable and I would like him back please as soon as you can send him, as I want him for my second D.C.G.S., which appointment will, I hope, be sanctioned by you soon. I feel it necessary and it will not mean an increase as I will reduce the D.M.T. to a Brigadier again.

8. I have decided to relieve Whitely as B.G.S. Eighth Army by de Guingand. He badly needs a complete change and I hope you will be able to find him a niche in the planning organisation for which he is eminently suitable. I do not think he is cut out for high staff appointments in a field formation, though he is first class in high G.H.Q. appointments. He is, worth promoting to Major-General in my opinion and I hope you will consider him for this. He certainly deserves it on his record of the last two years. I have sent in a special report on him.

---

208 Lieutenant General Sir Noel Beresford-Peirse who was then Commander 15 Indian Corps.

9. Ramsden[209] is doing well in command of 30th Corps and he and Gott and I are working well and very closely together. I have Dorman-Smith[210] helping me here and have found him most valuable. Messervy[211] has been deputising for him as D.C.G.S. but is now off to India to raise and train a new armoured division.

10. I can not tell how much I appreciate the way in which the Prime Minister and yourself have given me your confidence or how grateful I am for all the help you have given and are giving us. I will do my utmost to repay you by sparing no effort to defeat the enemy and remove the imminence of the threat to Egypt, but I do not want to hold out hopes of an early decision. I feel that we have been near it once or twice during the last month, but the scales are very evenly balanced, and on the 1st July I would not myself have gambled on our being able to stay on this position for more than a few days. The troops have recovered themselves wonderfully, I think, and have acquired a new tactical technique, based really on the proper use of artillery and the retention of mobility, remarkably quickly. They have still a great deal to learn of course, but the gunners have been very good indeed, and the Bosche does not like our shell fire at all, now that it is centrally controlled and directed. We are using a terrible lot of 25 pounder ammunition, but that can not be helped.

We may yet have to face a withdrawal from our present positions, but I hope this will not be necessary. Should it be unavoidable we have now got a strong defensive position, organised in depth for thirty miles and more, based on strong points, within supporting field artillery range of each other and sited to command all the intervening ground and to deny this essential observation to the enemy. These strong points are to be held by the minimum number of infantry with some artillery, while the great mass of the artillery escorted by sufficient infantry, who will be fully mobile, is to remain

---

209 Major General William Ramsden who had commanded 50th Division, 1940–42 was placed in command of 30 Corps as a Temporary Lieutenant General in July to September 1942.

210 As Acting Major General, Eric Dorman-Smith was acting in an unorthodox role as, effectively, Auchinleck's Chief of Staff in the field.

211 Major General Frank Messervy, who having commanded 7th Armoured Division was to take command of the 43rd Indian Armoured Division.

mobile and operate in the intervening spaces, moving to attack the enemy, wherever he may try to penetrate.

Behind this system again is a similar but smaller system based on the Wadi Natrun obstacle which fits in with the Western defences of Alexandria, the defences along the water line of the Delta and the Mena defences, which include the barrage, covering Cairo. Whatever happens I intend to keep the Eighth Army or the greater part of it as a mobile field force. I feel the enemy will need great strength to battle his way through this defence, and that if he tries, this theatre will become even more of a "second front" than it is now, and become a serious drain on his air and land resources, thus aiding Russia.

Apropos of this demand for a "second front", we feel that you have already a "second front" of no mean importance here! As to its being necessary to establish a "second front" in Europe, Northern Africa and the whole of the Mediterranean basin, is, I suggest, really "Europe" for strategical purposes, and inseparable from it. Would it not be a good thing to try and make the public understand this?

I still hold very strongly that the way to beat the enemy is from the South, through Italy into Austria and thence into Southern Germany. I feel convinced that an attempt to battle a way into Germany from Northern France through the strongest part of his defensive system and into the stronghold of Prussianism, is likely to land you in a war of position which may last as long as the last one did!

JRL, AUC 988

236

Cipher message from Winston Churchill to Auchinleck, 27 July 1942

ONE. I have not troubled you with messages while you have been so fearfully engaged but you and your Army have never been out of our thoughts for an hour.

TWO. It seems to me you have the advantage of ROMMEL in the air, communications and above all in the reinforcements which luckily we sent in good time.

THREE.   I should be glad if you would let me know when the 44th DIVISION will be able to go into action and I hope you will find it possible to let it fight as a Unit and not be forced to melt it down like so much else for the exigencies of battle.

FOUR.   Could you also reassure me about the SIWA OASIS on which I asked C.I.G.S. to send you a telegram. I have no doubt you have thought it all out.

FIVE.   C.I.G.S. is coming out to you early next week. He will be able to tell you about our plans which are considerable. See my immediately following telegram which should be deciphered by your personal staff.

JRL, AUC 989

237

Letter from Winston Churchill, writing from Cairo, to Auchinleck, 8 August 1942

Dear General Auchinleck,

On June 23 you raised in your telegram to the C.I.G.S. (telegram CS/1316) the question of your being relieved in this Command, and you mentioned the name of General Alexander as a possible successor. At the time of crisis to the Army His Majesty's Government did not wish to avail themselves of your high-minded offer. At the same time you had taken over the effective Command of the battle, as I had long desired and had suggested to you in my telegram OZ.261 of May 20. You stemmed the adverse tide and at the present time the front is stabilized.

2.   The War Cabinet have now decided, for the reasons which you yourself had used, that the moment has come for a change. It is proposed to detach Iraq and Persia from the present Middle Eastern theatre. Alexander will be appointed to Command the Middle East, Montgomery to command the Eighth Army, and I offer you the Command of Iraq and Persia including the Tenth Army, with Headquarters at Basra or Baghdad. It is true that this sphere is to-day smaller than the Middle East, but it may in a few months become the scene of decisive operations and reinforcements to the Tenth Army are already on the way. In this theatre, of which you

have special experience, you will preserve your associations with India. I hope therefore that you will comply with my wish and directions with the same disinterested public spirit that you have shown on all occasions. Alexander will arrive almost immediately, and I hope that early next week, subject of course to the movements of the enemy, it may be possible to effect the transfer of responsibility on the Western battlefront with the utmost smoothness and efficiency.

3.　　I shall be very glad to see you at any convenient time if you should so desire.

Believe me.

P.S.　Colonel Jacob who bears this letter is who charged by me to offer my sympathy in the sudden loss of General Gott.[212]

JRL, AUC 990

238

Letter from Lieutenant General T. W. Corbett to Auchinleck, 14 August 1942

My dear Chief,
　I feel I should be unable to say these things, and so I am writing them to you.
　I want you to know that I am exceedingly proud of having had the privilege of serving you in war as your principal Staff Officer. The short time I have been with you has been full of constructive work, the fruits of which are yet to be seen.
　You have been laying foundations which one day will prove their soundness. I know that you retain the implicit confidence of the troops you have been commanding. When the story of the battle that started on 25th May is told, it will, I know, enhance both your prestige and your reputation as a soldier.
　Your achievement in stopping the rot in a beaten army, in restoring its morale so speedily, in wresting the initiative from a triumphant enemy,

---

212 Lieutenant General William Gott had been selected to command Eighth Army but he was killed when his transport aircraft was attacked on 7 August 1942.

and inflicting on him crippling losses, will one day be recognised. I shall make it my business to see that it is.

I am convinced that by depriving you of your Command, the Higher Direction of the war is making a grievous mistake for which I very much fear the Allied Nations will yet have to pay a terrible price. I pray I may be wrong.

I am most grateful to you personally for all your help and consideration always, and for the trust you have placed in me. Although I have done my best I feel that it has not been enough.

May the day soon come when you are back in an important Command, and allowed to play the part that people of your experience alone can play to ensure victory. As I said to you, there is no successful British Commander in this war so far. There could not be one yet, considering the disabilities from which any Commander, however good, must suffer in the Armies of the Empire which have had to serve their apprenticeship in war, and learn what total war really means.

You of all the Commanders-in-Chief who have so far led our Armies are the only one who has defeated the Germans in the field.

So much for our official relationships. I would like to tell you that my friendship for you and my regard are firmer than ever. You have all my sympathy, and all my very best wishes.

JRL, AUC 994

Biographical Notes

Alexander, Field Marshal Harold Rupert Leofric George (Earl Alexander) (1891–1969). Commanded 1st Infantry Division and 1 Corps, 1939–40. C in C Burma, 1942. C in C Middle East, 1942–43. Eisenhower's Deputy Land Force Commander, Mediterranean, 1943–44 (18th Army Group and 15th Army Group). Supreme Allied Commander, Mediterranean, 1944–45.

Amery, Leopold Stennett (1873–1955). Conservative MP for South (later Sparkbrook) Division of Birmingham, 1911–45. Secretary of State for India, 1940–45.

Anderson, Lieutenant General Desmond (1885–1967). GOC 45th Division, 1940; Assistant Chief of the Imperial General Staff, 1940 and GOC 46th Division, 1940. Commanded 3 Corps, 1940–43 and 2 Corps, 1943–44.

Beresford-Peirse, Lieutenant General Sir Noel (1887–1953). Commanded 4th Indian Division, 1940–41 and Western Desert Force, April–Sept. 1941. GOC Sudan, 1941–42; Commander 15 Indian Corps 1942 and GOC in C Southern Army, India, 1942–45. Welfare General in India, 1945–47.

Blamey, Field Marshal Sir Thomas (1884–1951). GOC 6th Australian Division, 1939–40, Commander 1 Australian Corps, 1940–41 and Deputy C in C Middle East and GOC Australian Imperial Force, 1941–42. C in C Allied Land Forces, South West Pacific Area, 1942–45.

Boyle, Admiral William Henry Dudley (12th Earl of Cork and Orrery) (1873–1967). C in C Home Fleet, 1933–35 and C in C Portsmouth, 1937–39. C in C RN forces, Norway, 1940.

Brooke, Field Marshal Alan (Viscount Alanbrooke) (1883–1963). Commanded 2 Corps, BEF, 1939–40 and Home Forces, 1940–41. Chief of the Imperial General Staff, 1941–46.

Casey, Richard (Baron Casey) (1890–1976). Member of Australian House of Representatives for Corio, 1931–40 and Minister for Supply and Development, Australia, 1939–40. Australian Minister to the USA, 1940–42. Minister of State Resident in the Middle East and Member of the War Cabinet of the UK, 1942–43. Governor of Bengal, 1944–46. Re-elected to Australian House of Representatives for La Trobe, 1949 and Minister for External Affairs, 1951–60. Governor General of Australia, 1965–69.

Cassels, General Sir Robert Archibald (1876–1959). Adjutant General, India, 1928–30; GOC in C, Northern Command, India, 1930–34 and C in C, India, 1935–41.

Coningham, Air Marshal Sir Arthur (1895–1948). Commanded 4 Group, Bomber Command, 1939–41. Commanded 204 Group, 1941 and Desert Air Force 1941–43. Formed 1st Tactical Air Force in French North Africa, 1943 and was AOC in C Second Tactical Air Force, 1944–45. Known as 'Mary', a play on 'Maori' due to his upbringing in New Zealand.

Corbett, Lieutenant General Thomas (1888–1981). Commanded 4 Indian Corps, Middle East, 1942. Chief of the General Staff, Middle Eastern Command, March to August 1942. GOC 7th Indian Division, 1942–43.

Creagh, Major General Sir Michael O'Moore (1892–1970). Commanded 7th Armoured Division, 1939–41 and 3 Armoured Group, 1941–42. Commanded Hampshire and Dorset District, 1942–44.

Cunningham, General Sir Alan (1887–1983). Commanded 5th Anti-Aircraft Division, followed by 66th, 9th and 51st TA Divisions, 1938–40. GOC East Africa, 1940–41. Commanded Eighth Army, 10 September to 26 November 1941. Commandant, Army Staff College, 1941–42. GOC Northern Ireland, 1943–44 and GOC in C Eastern Command 1944–45. High Commissioner and C in C Palestine, 1945–48.

Cunningham, Admiral Sir Andrew (Viscount) (1883–1963). Deputy Chief of Naval Staff, 1938–39. C in C Mediterranean, 1939–42 and 1943. Head of British Admiralty Delegation to Washington, 1942. First Sea Lord, 1943–46.

De Guingand, Major General Sir Francis (1900–79). Director of Military Intelligence, Middle East, 1942. BGS, Eighth Army, 1942. Field Marshal B. L. Montgomery's Chief of Staff, 1942–45.

Dill, Field Marshal Sir John Greer (1881–1944). Chief of the Imperial General Staff, 1940–41, Head of British Joint Staff Mission to Washington, 1941–44.

Dobbie, Lieutenant General Sir William (1879–1964). GOC Malaya, 1935–39; Colonel Commandant RE, 1940 and Governor and Commander in Chief, Malta, 1940–42.

Dorman-Smith, Brigadier Eric (1895–1969). Deputy Chief of the General Staff, Middle East, 1942. Commanded 160th Infantry Brigade in the UK 1942–43 and 3rd Infantry Brigade in Italy, 1944. Known as 'Chink'. After retiring from the British Army he changed his surname to Dorman-O'Gowan.

Freyberg, Lieutenant General Bernard (1889–1963). GOC New Zealand Division and Commanded New Zealand forces in the Mediterranean for the campaigns in Greece, Crete, North Africa and Italy, 1941–45.

Galloway, Lieutenant General Sir Alexander (1895–1977). BGS, Eighth Army, 1941–42. Director of Staff Duties, War Office, 1942–43. Commanded 1st Armoured Division, 1943–44 and 3rd Infantry Division, 1945.

Gatehouse, Major General Alexander (1895–1964). Commanded 4th Armoured Brigade, 1941–42 and 1st and 10th Armoured Divisions, 1942.

Godwin-Austen, Lieutenant General Sir Alfred (1889–1963). Commanded 13 Corps in Eighth Army, 1941–42. Director of Research, War Office, 1943. Vice-Quartermaster-General, War Office, 1943–45. Quartermaster General, India, 1945–47.

Gott, Lieutenant General William (1897–1942). Commanded 7th Armoured Division and 13 Corps in Eighth Army. Chosen to command Eighth Army, but killed when his transport aircraft was attacked, 7 August 1942. Known as 'Strafer'.

Grigg, Sir (Percy) James (1890–1964). Permanent Under-Secretary of State for War, 1939–42. Member of Parliament for East Cardiff and Secretary of State for War, 1942–45.

Gubbins, Major General Sir Colin McVean (1896–1976). Commissioned into RFA, 1914. Served in north Russia, 1919 and Ireland 1920–22. As Lieutenant Colonel served in G (R) (later MI (R)) preparing manuals on irregular warfare, 1938–39. August 1939 Chief of Staff to British military mission to Poland. October 1939 liaison officer with Czech and Polish forces in France. March 1940 recalled to UK to form 'independent companies' and commanded them in Norway. Formed auxiliary units in England, Summer 1940. November 1940 transferred to SOE as Acting Brigadier; Major General and Head of SOE September 1943. Retired 1946.

Haining, General Sir Robert (1882–1959). GOC Palestine and Trans-Jordan, 1939–40; Vice Chief Imperial General Staff, 1940–41 and Intendant General, Middle East, 1941–42. Retired 1942.

Harding, Field Marshal Sir John (1896–1989). BGS, Western Desert Force and 13 Corps 1940–42. Director of Military Training, Middle East 1942. Commander 7th Armoured Division, 1942–43. Chief of Staff to Field Marshal Sir Harold Alexander, 1944–45. Commander 13 Corps, 1945.

Holmes, Lieutenant General Sir William (1892–1969). Commanded 42nd Division, 1938–1940 and 10 Corps, 1940–41. GOC British Troops, Egypt, 1941–42; GOC Ninth Army, 1942–45.

Hope, Victor Alexander John (2nd Marquess of Linlithgow) (1887–1952). Civil Lord of the Admiralty, 1922–24 and Viceroy and Governor-General of India, 1936–43.

Hutchinson, Lieutenant General Sir Balfour (1889–1967). Deputy QMG, Middle East, 1940–42; GOC Sudan and Eritrea, 1942–43 and QMG, India, 1944–45.

Hutton, Lieutenant General Sir Thomas (1890–1981). GOC Western Independent District, India, 1938–40; Deputy Chief of General Staff, India, 1940–41; Chief of the General Staff, India, 1941; GOC Burma 1942 and Secretary War Resources and Reconstruction Committees of Council (India), 1942–44.

Ismay, General Hastings (1887–1965). Secretary, Committee of Imperial Defence, 1938–40 and Chief of Staff to Minister of Defence, 1940–45. Known as 'Pug'.

Kennedy, Major General Sir John (1893–1970). Director of Military Operations and Intelligence, War Office, 1940–43. Assistant Chief of the Imperial General Staff (Operations and Intelligence), 1943–45.

Lumsden, Major General Herbert (1897–1945). Commanded 1st Armoured Division and 10 Corps, 1942. Winston Churchill's special representative to General Douglas MacArthur in the Pacific, 1943–45. Killed when a Japanese aircraft hit the bridge of the USS *New Mexico*, 6 January 1945.

Lyttleton, Oliver (Viscount Chandos) (1893–1972). Controller of Non-Ferrous Metals, 1939–40; Conservative MP for Aldershot, 1940–54; President Board of Trade, 1940–41; Minister of State and Member of the War Cabinet, resident in Cairo, June 1941 to February 1942; Minister of Production 1942–45.

McCreery, General Sir Richard (1898–1967). Commanded 2nd Armoured Brigade, BEF, 1940. Major General AFV Middle East, 1942. Chief of Staff to Field Marshal Sir Harold Alexander, 1942–43. Commanded 10 Corps, 1943–44 and Eighth Army, 1944–45.

Mackesy, Major General Pierse Joseph (1883–1956). Commanded 3rd Infantry Brigade in Bordon and Palestine, 1935–38 and 49th (West Riding) Division, 1938–40. Initial C in C Land Forces, Narvik, 1940. Retired from the Army, August 1940. Employed in offices of the War Cabinet, 1941. Military Correspondent of the *Daily Telegraph*, 1941–47.

Martel, Lieutenant General Sir Giffard Le Quesne (1889–1958). Commanded 50th (Northumbrian) Division, 1939–40. Commander Royal Armoured Corps, 1940–43. Head of Military Mission at Moscow, 1943–44.

Messervy, Lieutenant General Frank (1893–1974). GSO1 5th Indian Division, 1939–40; commanded Gazelle Force, Sudan and Eritrea, 1940–41 and 9th Indian Infantry Brigade, 1941. Commanded 4th Indian Division, 1941–42; 1st Armoured Division and 7th Armoured Division, 1942. DCGS, Middle East Command, 1942. Commanded 43rd Indian Armoured Division, 1942–43; 7th Indian Division 1944 and 4 Corps, Burma, 1944–45.

Monckton, Walter (1st Viscount Monckton) (1891–1965). Director-General of the press and censorship bureau in the Ministry of Information Office 1939–40 and Director-General Ministry of Information 1940–41. Head of propaganda and information services in Cairo and member of the Middle East war council 1941–42. Acting Minister of State resident in Cairo, February–May 1942.

Montgomery, Field Marshal Bernard Law (Viscount Montgomery) (1887–1976). GOC 3rd Division, 1939–40, 5 Corps 1940, 12 Corps 1941 and South-Eastern Army 1942. Commanded Eighth Army 1942–43 and

British Group of Armies and Allied Armies 1944. Commanded 21st Army Group 1944–45. CIGS, 1946–48. Chairman of the Commanders in Chief Committee of the Western Union 1948–51 and Deputy Supreme Commander Europe, NATO, 1951–58.

Morshead, Lieutenant General Sir Leslie (1889–1959). Commanded 18th Infantry Brigade, Australian Imperial Force, 1940–41 and 9th Australian Division, 1941–43, along with all AIF personnel in the Middle East from March 1942. On returning to Australia with 9th Australian Division in 1943, he commanded II Australian Corps 1943–44, Second Australian Army 1944 and I Australian Corps, 1944–45.

Norrie, Lieutenant General Sir (Charles) Willoughby (Moke) (1893–1977). Commanded 1st Armoured Brigade, 1938–40 and Inspector RAC, 1940. GOC 1st Armoured Division 1940–41 and 30 Corps, 1941–42. Major General, Royal Armoured Corps, 1942–43.

Nye, Lieutenant General Sir Archibald (1895–1967). Commander Nowshera Brigade, 1939. Director of Staff Duties, War Office, 1940–41. Vice Chief of the Imperial General Staff, 1941–46.

Pope, Major General Vyvyan (1891–1941). Commander 3rd Armoured Brigade, 1939–40. Director of AFV at the War Office, 1940. GOC 30 Corps September 1941. Killed in an air accident on 5 October 1941.

Portal, Marshal of the RAF, Sir Charles (1st Baron) (1893–1971). Air Member for Personnel on the Air Council, 1939–40; AOC in C, Bomber Command, 1940 and Chief of the Air Staff, 1940–45.

Pownall, Lieutenant General Sir Henry (1887–1961). CGS, BEF, France 1940. Inspector General Local Defence Volunteers/Home Guard 1940. GOC Northern Ireland 1940–41. Vice Chief Imperial General Staff, 1941. C in C Far East 1941–42 but Japan entered the war before he could take up command. Chief of Staff, South West Pacific, 1942. C in C Ceylon, 1942–43 and Persia and Iraq, 1943. Chief of Staff, South East Asia Command, 1943–44.

Quinan, General Sir Edward (1885–1960). District Commander, Waziristan, 1938–41. GOC Iran and Iraq, 1941–42; GOC Tenth Army, 1942–43 and Commander North Western Army in India, 1943.

Ramsden, Major General William (1888–1969). Commanded 25th Infantry Brigade, 1939–40; 50th Infantry Division, 1940–42; 30 Corps,

July to September 1942 and 3rd Infantry Division, 1942–43. Commander Sudan Defence Force and British Troops, Sudan and Eritrea, 1944–45.

Richardson, General Sir Charles (1908–94). Instructor, Middle East Staff College, 1940–42; GSO1 (Plans), Eighth Army, 1942 and BGS, Eighth Army, 1943. Deputy Chief of Staff, US Fifth Army, 1943. BGS (Plans), 21st Army Group, 1944–46.

Riddell-Webster, General Sir Thomas (1886–1974). Director of Movements and Quartering, War Office, 1938–9; Deputy Quarter Master General, 1939–40 and GOC in C, Southern India, 1941. Lieutenant General i/c Administration, Middle East, 1941–42 and Quarter Master General to the Forces, 1942–46.

Ritchie, General Sir Neil (1897–1983). BGS, 1939 and commanded 51st (Highland) Division, 1940–41. Deputy Chief of Staff, Middle East 1941 and GOC Eighth Army (with acting rank of Lieutenant General), 26 November 1941 to 25 June 1942. Commanded 52nd (Lowland) Division in UK, 1942–43 and 12 Corps in North-West Europe, 1944–45. GOC in C, Scottish Command, 1945–47; C in C South East Asia Land Forces, 1947–49 and Commander British Army Staff, Washington, 1949–51.

Scobie, Lieutenant General Sir Ronald (1893–1969). AAG, War Office, 1938–39 and Deputy Director of Mobilisation, 1939–40. BGS, Sudan, 1940–41 and commanded 6th (renamed 70th Division), 1941. GOC Tobruk Garrison October to December 1941. Deputy Adjutant General, Middle East, 1942 and GOC Malta, 1942–43. Chief of Staff, Middle East, 1943 and commanded British troops in Greece, 1944–46.

Shearer, Brigadier Eric James ('John') (1892–1980). Career army officer 1911–29. Retired from the army to join Fortnum & Mason Ltd. of which he was joint managing director, 1933–38. Returned to the army on the outbreak of war and was Commandant of the Intelligence School in Britain 1939 and Director of Military Intelligence, Middle East, 1940–42.

Slim, Field Marshal William 'Bill' (1891–1970). Commanded 10th Brigade, 5th Indian Division, 1939–41; 10th Indian Division, 1941–42 and 4 Indian Corps, 1942. Moved to Burma he commanded 1 Burma Corps (Burcorps) 1942; 15 Corps in India 1942–43 and C in C Eastern Army (renamed Fourteenth Army) 1943–45.

Smith, Lieutenant General Sir Arthur (1890–1977). BGS, British Troops in Egypt, 1938–39 and CGS, Middle East 1940–42. GOC London District and Major General commanding Brigade of Guards, 1942–44. GOC in C, Persia and Iraq Command, 1944–45; GOC in C Eastern Command, India, 1945–46; CGS, India, 1946; Deputy C in C, India, 1947 and commander, British troops in India and Pakistan, 1947.

Smuts, Field Marshal Jan Christian (1870–1950). Prime Minister and Minister of Native Affairs, South Africa, 1919–24 and Prime Minister and Minister of External Affairs and Defence, South Africa, 1939–48. Officer Commanding Union of South Africa Defence Forces 1940–48 and appointed a British Field Marshal in 1941.

Tedder, Air Chief Marshal Sir Arthur (1st Baron) (1890–1967). Director General of Research and Development, Air Ministry, 1938–40; Deputy AOC in C, Middle East, 1940–41 and AOC in C, Middle East, 1941–43. Commander Mediterranean Air Command, 1943 and Deputy Supreme Commander, SHAEF, 1943–45. Chief of Air Staff, 1946–50 and Chairman of British Joint Services Mission, Washington, 1950.

Tuker, Lieutenant General Sir Francis (1894–1967). Director of Military Training, GHQ, India, 1940–41; commanded 34th Indian Division, 1941–42 and 4th Indian Division 1942–44. GOC Ceylon, 1945 and commanded 4 Indian Corps, Netherlands East Indies 1945. Commanded Lucknow District, India 1945–46 and GOC in C, Eastern Command, India, 1946–47. Known as 'Gertie'.

Wavell, Field Marshal Archibald (Viscount) (1883–1950). C in C Middle East, 1939–41 and C in C India, 1941–43. Supreme Commander, South West Pacific, 1942. Viceroy of India, 1943–47.

Whiteley, General Sir John (1896–1970). BGS (Operations) Middle East, 1940–42 and BGS Eighth Army, 1942. Deputy Chief of Staff at Eisenhower's Allied Force Headquarters, 1942–43. Head of Intelligence, then Deputy Head of the Operations Section, SHAEF, 1944–45. Army Instructor, IDC, 1945–47 and Commandant of Royal Military College of Canada, 1947–49. DCIGS 1949–53; Chairman of the British Joint Services Mission, Washington and UK Representative on the NATO Standing Group, 1953–56. Known as 'Jock'.

Wilson, Field Marshal Sir Henry Maitland (Baron) (1881–1964). Lieutenant General commanding British troops in Egypt, 1939, Commander of expeditionary force to Greece, February 1941, GOC

British troops in Palestine and Trans-Jordan, May 1941, GOC Ninth Army in Syria and Palestine, Dec. 1941, C in C Persia–Iraq 1942–43 and C in C Middle East, 1943. Supreme Allied Commander, Mediterranean, 1944. Head of British Joint Staff Mission in Washington, and British member of the Combined Chiefs of Staff, 1944–47.

Bibliography

Manuscript Sources

John Rylands Library, University of Manchester
Papers of Field Marshal Sir Claude Auchinleck.
Papers of Major General Eric Dorman-Smith.

The National Archives, Kew
War diaries of 62nd Punjabis, 1915–18, WO95/5178/1 and 2.

Parliamentary Papers

Official publications

Army List.

Auchinleck, Claude, 'Operations in the Middle East from 1st November 1941 to 15th August 1942', *Supplement to the London Gazette*, 13 January 1948, 309–400.

Collier, Basil, *The Defence of the United Kingdom* (London, 1957).

Derry, T. K., *The Campaign in Norway* (London, 1952).

The London Gazette.

Playfair, I. S. O., ed., *The Mediterranean and Middle East: Vol. I: The early successes against Italy* (London, 1954).

Playfair, I. S. O., ed., *The Mediterranean and Middle East: Vol. II: 'The Germans come to the Help of their Ally'* (London, 1956).

Playfair, I. S. O., ed., *The Mediterranean and Middle East: Vol. III: British Fortunes reach their Lowest Ebb* (London, 1960).

Playfair, I. S. O., ed., *The Mediterranean and Middle East: Vol. IV: The Destruction of the Axis Forces in Africa* (London, 1966).

Prasad, Bisheshwar, *Official History of the Indian Armed Forces in the Second World War 1939–45: Defence of India: Policy and plans* (New Delhi, 1963).

Prasad, S. N., *Official History of the Indian Armed Forces in the Second World War 1939–45: Expansion of the armed forces and defence organisation 1939–45* (Calcutta, 1956).

Contemporary works, memoirs and biographies

Belchem, David, *All in the day's march* (London, 1978).

Bond, Brian, ed., *Chief of Staff: The Diaries of Lieutenant-General Sir Henry Pownall: Volume Two 1940–1944* (London, 1974).

Brooks, Stephen, ed., *Montgomery and the Eighth Army* (London, 1991).

Connell, John, *Auchinleck: A Biography of Field Marshal Sir Claude Auchinleck* (London, 1959).

Danchev, Alex and Todman, Dan, eds, *Field Marshal Lord Alanbrooke: War Diaries, 1939–1945* (London, 2001).

De Guingand, Francis, *Operation Victory* (London, 1947).

Egremont, Max, *Under Two Flags: The Life of Major General Sir Edward Spears* (London, 1997).

Greacen, Lavinia, *Chink: A Biography* (London, 1989).

Greenwood, Alexander, *Field Marshal Auchinleck* (Brockerscliffe, 1990).

Hamid, Shahid, *Disastrous Twilight: A personal record of the partition of India* (London, 1986).

Hamilton, Nigel, *Monty: The Making of a General, 1887–1942* (London, 1981).

Hart-Davis, Duff, ed., *King's Counsellor: Abdication and War: The diaries of Sir Alan Lascelles* (London, 2006).

Ismay, Hastings, *The Memoirs of General the Lord Ismay* (London, 1960).

Lewin, Ronald, *Slim: The Standardbearer* (Ware, 1999).

McGilvray, Evan, *Field Marshal Claude Auchinleck* (Barnsley, 2020).

Parkinson, Roger, *The Auk: Auchinleck, Victor at Alamein* (London, 1977).

Richardson, Charles, *Flashback: A Soldier's Story* (London, 1985).

Slim, Field Marshal Sir William, *Defeat into Victory* (London, 1956).

Syk, Andrew, ed., *The military papers of Lieutenant General Frederick Stanley Maude, 1914–17* (Stroud, 2012).

Tedder, Lord, *With Prejudice: The War Memoirs of Marshal of the Royal Air Force Lord Tedder* (London, 1966).

Warner, Philip, *Auchinleck: The Lonely Soldier* (London, 1981).

Wavell, Field Marshal Sir Archibald, *Generally Speaking* (London, 1946).

Wingate, Ronald, *Lord Ismay: A biography* (London, 1970).

Wright, Margaret M., 'The Military Papers, 1940–48, of Field-Marshal Sir Claude Auchinleck: A Calendar and Index', *Bulletin of the John Rylands University Library of Manchester*, 70: 2 (1988), 146–393.

Secondary sources

Barkawi, Tarak, 'Culture and Combat in the colonies: The Indian Army in the Second World War', *Journal of Contemporary History*, 14: 2 (2006), 325–55.

Barkawi, Tarak, *Soldiers of Empire: Indian and British Armies in World War II* (Cambridge, 2017).

Barnett, Correlli, *Britain and Her Army, 1509–1970: A Military, Political and Social Survey* (London, 1970).

Barnett, Correlli, *The Desert Generals* (London, 2nd edition, 1983).

Barr, Niall, *Pendulum of War: The Three Battles of El Alamein* (London, 2004).

Barua, Pradeep, 'Strategies and doctrines of imperial defence: Britain and India, 1919–45', *Journal of Imperial and Commonwealth History*, 25: 2 (1997), 240–66.

Barua, P. P., *Gentlemen of the Raj: The Indian Army Officer Corps, 1817–1949* (Westport, 2003).

Best, Geoffrey, *Churchill and War* (London, 2005).

Bond, Brian, *British Military Policy between the Two World Wars* (Oxford, 1980).

Bowman, Timothy and Connelly, Mark, *The Edwardian Army: Recruiting, training and deploying the British Army, 1902–1914* (Oxford, 2012).

Buckley, John, *Monty's Men: The British Army and the Liberation of Europe* (London, 2013).

Callahan, Raymond, *Churchill and his Generals* (Lawrence, Kansas, 2007).

Carver, Michael, *El Alamein* (London, 1962).

Carver, Michael, *Dilemmas of the Desert War: The Libyan Campaign 1940–1942* (Staplehurst, 2002).

Ceva, Lucio, 'The North African campaign 1940–43: A reconsideration', *Journal of Strategic Studies*, 13: 1 (1990), 84–104.

Cohen, Stephen, *The Indian Army* (New Delhi, 1991).

Coombs, Benjamin, *British Tank Production and the War Economy, 1934–1945* (London, 2013).

D'Este, Carlo, *Warlord: A Life of Churchill at War, 1874–1945* (London, 2008).

Deshpande, Anirudh, *British military policy in India, 1900–1945* (New Delhi, 2005).

Doherty, Richard, *Irish generals in the British Army in the Second World War* (Belfast, 1993).

Edwards, Jill, ed., *El Alamein and the struggle for North Africa: International perspectives from the Twenty-first century* (Cairo, 2012).

Farrell, B. P., *The Defence and Fall of Singapore 1940–1942* (Stroud, 2005).

Fennell, Jonathan, *Combat and Morale in the North African Campaign: The Eighth Army and the Path to El Alamein* (Cambridge, 2011).

Fennell, Jonathan, 'Courage and cowardice in the North African campaign: The Eighth Army and defeat in the Summer of 1942', *War in History*, 20: 1 (2013), 99–122.

Fennell, Jonathan, *Fighting the People's War: The British and Commonwealth Armies and the Second World War* (Cambridge, 2019).

Fox, Frank, *The Royal Inniskilling Fusiliers in the Second World War, 1939–45* (Aldershot, 1951).

French, David, 'Colonel Blimp and the British Army: British divisional commanders in the war against Germany, 1939–1945', *English Historical Review*, CXI: 444 (1996), 1182–1201.

French, David, *Raising Churchill's Army: The British Army and the War against Germany 1919–1945* (Oxford, 2000).

Gladman, W. G., *Intelligence and Anglo American Air Support in World War Two: The Western Desert and Tunisia, 1940–43* (Basingstoke, 2009).

Gooch, John, *Mussolini's War: Fascist Italy from Triumph to Collapse 1935–1943* (London, 2020).

Gupta, P. S. and Deshpande, Anirudh, eds, *The British Raj and its Indian Armed Forces 1857–1939* (New Delhi, 2002).

Hanham, H. J., 'Religion and Nationality in the Mid-Victorian Army', in *War and Society: Historical essays in honour and memory of J. R. Western 1928–1971*, ed. M. R. D. Foot (London, 1973), pp. 159–81.

Hargreaves, Andrew, Rose, Patrick and Ford, Matthew, eds, *Allied Fighting Effectiveness in North Africa and Italy, 1942–1945* (Leiden, 2014).

Hastings, Max, *Finest Years: Churchill as Warlord 1940–45* (London, 2009).

Imy, Kate, *Faithful Fighters: Identity and Power in the British Indian Army* (Stanford, 2019).

Jackson, Ashley, *Persian Gulf Command: A History of the Second World War in Iran and Iraq* (London, 2018).

Jeffreys, Alan, *Approach to Battle: Training the Indian Army during the Second World War* (Solihull, 2017).

Jeffreys, Alan and Rose, Patrick, eds, *The Indian Army, 1939–47: Experience and Development* (Farnham, 2012).

Johnson, Rob, ed., *The British Indian Army: Virtue and Necessity* (Newcastle, 2014).

Khan, Yasmin, *The Raj at War: A People's History of India's Second World War* (London, 2015).

Kiszely, John, *Anatomy of a campaign: The British Fiasco in Norway, 1940* (Cambridge, 2017).

Kitchen, Martin, *Rommel's Desert War: Waging World War II in North Africa, 1941–1943* (Cambridge, 2009).

Kudaisya, Gyanesh, '"In Aid of Civil Power": The Colonial Army in Northern India, c. 1919–42', *Journal of Imperial and Commonwealth History*, 32: 1 (2004), 41–68.

Kundu, Apurba, *Militarism in India: The Army and Civil Society in Consensus* (London, 1998).

Mackenzie, S. P., *The Home Guard* (Oxford, 1995).

Majdalany, Fred, *The Battle of El Alamein* (London, 1965).

Marston, Daniel, *Phoenix from the Ashes: The Indian Army in the Burma Campaign* (London, 2003).

Marston, Daniel, *The Indian Army and the End of the Raj* (Cambridge, 2014).

Marston, Daniel and Sundaram, Chandar eds, *A Military History of India and South Asia* (Westport, 2007).

Mason, Philip, *A Matter of Honour* (London, 1974).

Menezes, Lieutenant General S. L., *Fidelity and Honour: The Indian Army from the Seventeenth to the Twenty-first Century* (New Delhi, 1999).

Moreman, Tim, *The Army in India and the development of frontier warfare, 1849–1947* (Basingstoke, 1998).

Moreman, Tim, *The Jungle, the Japanese and the British Commonwealth armies at war, 1941–45* (London, 2005).

Newsome, David, *A History of Wellington College, 1859–1959* (London, 1959).

Omissi, David, *The Sepoy and the Raj: The Indian Army, 1860–1940* (London, 1994).

Perry, F. W., *The Commonwealth Armies: Manpower and organisation in Two World Wars* (Manchester, 1988).

Perry, Nicholas, 'The Irish Landed Class and the British Army, 1850–1950', *War in History*, 18: 3 (2011), 304–32.

Pitt, Barrie, *The Crucible of War 2: Auchinleck's Command* (London, 1980).

Porch, Douglas, *Hitler's Mediterranean gamble: The North African and Mediterranean campaigns in World War II* (London, 2004).

Raghavan, Srinath 'Building the sinews of power: India in the Second World War', *Journal of Strategic Studies*, 42: 5 (2019), 577–99.

Raghavan, Srinath, *India's War: The making of South Asia, 1939–1945* (London, 2016).

Raghavan, Srinath, 'Protecting the Raj: The Army in India and internal security c. 1919–1939', *Small Wars and Insurgencies*, 21: 2 (2010), 253–79.

Rand, Gavin and Wagner, K. A., 'Recruiting the "martial races": identities and military service in colonial India', Patterns of Prejudice, 46: 3–4 (2012), 232–54.

Roy, Kaushik, *The Army in British India: From colonial warfare to total war, 1857–1947* (London, 2013).

Roy, Kaushik, *Brown Warriors of the Raj: Recruitment & the Mechanics of Command in the Sepoy Army, 1859–1913* (New Delhi, 2008).

Roy, Kaushik, *India and World War II: War, armed forces and society, 1939–45* (New Delhi, 2016).

Roy, Kaushik, ed., *The Indian Army in Two World Wars* (Leiden, 2012).

Roy, Kaushik, 'Military loyalty in the colonial context: A case study of the Indian Army during World War II', *Journal of Military History*, 73: 2 (2009), 497–529.

Roy, Kaushik, *Sepoys against the Rising Sun: The Indian Army in the Far East and South-East Asia, 1941–45* (Leiden, 2016).

Roy, Kaushik, ed., *War and society in Colonial India, 1807–1945* (New Delhi, 2006).

Sharma, Gautam, *Nationalisation of the Indian Army* (New Delhi, 1996).

Sinha, B. P. N. and Chandra, Sunil, *Valour and Wisdom: Genesis and growth of the Indian Military Academy* (New Delhi, 1992).

Stewart, Andrew, *The First Victory: The Second World War and the East African campaign* (New Haven, 2016).

Streets, Heather, *Martial races: The military, race and masculinity in British imperial culture, 1857–1914* (Manchester, 2004).

Townshend, Charles, *When God made hell: the British invasion of Mesopotamia and the creation of Iraq, 1914–1921* (London, 2010).

Wilson, Catherine, 'Responsible History? Churchill's portrayal of the Indian Army in the Second World War', *Ex Historica*, 4 (2012), 96–124.

Unpublished Thesis

Jacobsen, M. H., 'The modernisation of the Indian Army, 1925–39' (University of California PhD thesis, 1979).

Rose, Patrick, 'British Army command culture 1939–45: A comparative study of British Eighth and Fourteenth Armies' (University of London (KCL): PhD thesis, 2008).

Index